Paris

timeout.com/paris

Time Out Guides Ltd
Universal House
251 Tottenham Court Road
London W1T 7AB
United Kingdom
Tel: +44 (0)20 7813 3000
Fax: +44 (0)20 7813 6001
Email: guides@timeout.com
www.timeout.com

Published by Time Out Guides Ltd, a wholly owned subsidiary of Time Out Group Ltd.
Time Out and the Time Out logo are trademarks of Time Out Group Ltd.

© **Time Out Group Ltd 2009**
Previous editions 1989, 1990, 1992, 1995, 1997, 1998, 1999, 2000, 2001, 2002, 2003, 2004, 2005, 2006, 2007, 2008.

10 9 8 7 6 5 4 3 2 1

This edition first published in Great Britain in 2009 by Ebury Publishing.
A Random House Group Company
20 Vauxhall Bridge Road, London SW1V 2SA

Random House Australia Pty Ltd 20 Alfred Street, Milsons Point, Sydney, New South Wales 2061, Australia

Random House New Zealand Ltd 18 Poland Road, Glenfield, Auckland 10, New Zealand

Random House South Africa (Pty) Ltd Isle of Houghton, Corner Boundary Road & Carse O'Gowrie, Houghton 2198, South Africa

Random House UK Limited Reg. No. 954009

For further distribution details, see www.timeout.com.

ISBN: 978-1-84670-073-6

A CIP catalogue record for this book is available from the British Library.

Printed and bound by Firmengruppe APPL, aprinta druck, Wemding, Germany.

The Random House Group Limited supports The Forest Stewardship Council (FSC), the leading international forest certification organisation. All our titles that are printed on Greenpeace approved FSC certified paper carry the FSC logo. Our paper procurement policy can be found at http://www.rbooks.co.uk/environment.

Time Out carbon-offsets its flights with Trees for Cities (www.treesforcities.org).

Contents

Introduction

No city in the world has the same weight of fable and history as Paris, much less the same wealth and complexity of association and influence. Royal and republican, religious and secular, French and foreign, artistic and monumental – Paris has lived up to all these contradictions. Although it's older than Christianity, it's a city with a forward-thinking administration that crafts 21st-century urban refinements, which are subsequently copied across Europe and beyond. And it's the capital of a country that regards it with jealousy and disdain, whose residents are supposed to be standoffish with outsiders – especially those who don't speak the lingo.

You only have to look at any panoramic view of the city painted in the 17th century to realise, with a pleasurable shock, that Paris is a city of no fixed abode. Three centuries ago, nearly all its roofs were terracotta, as though it were in Provence. And you need only explore the multi-ethnic north-eastern quarters to see that its population is as changeable as its fabric. Paris is fascinating not because it's so reassuringly itself. Rather, Paris is dizzyingly exciting because it's a city you can never really know. For the visitor, there's no greater gift: however many times you see the place, you'll never get to the bottom of it.

The aim of this introduction is not to trot out reasons to visit the city, but to suggest how to go about things once you're here. The best way to approach Paris is with a blend of open-mindedness and scepticism; a blend that, as it happens, is one of the many admirable characteristics of Parisians themselves. The periphery is not necessarily more 'authentic' than the main attractions, and there's much of interest hidden in plain view – above second-storey level, say, where hundreds of stone faces watch passers-by with rarely an answering gaze.

When you visit the famous sights and museums, more numerous and better all the time, try to do so early in the morning – or, if they open late, at the end of the day. Get out of the centre. Explore on foot as much as you can. Go out after midnight, or set the alarm clock and depart at dawn. And finally, speak to the locals in their own language, even if it's just a couple of words. Not the least unfamiliar thing about Paris is how easily defrosted most Parisians are. *Dominic Earle, Editor*

Paris in Brief

PARIS IN CONTEXT

Over a series of essays, our In Context section details the fabled history that helps make Paris such a fascinating town. However, it also throws the spotlight on the 21st-century city, currently undergoing substantial changes under mayor Bertrand Delanoë. Redevelopment is rife and racial problems remain, although a new breed of performers are helping to bridge the divide.
► *For more, see pp15-50*.

SIGHTS

Tourists touting the I-Spy Book of Paris Sights head straight for the Louvre and the Eiffel Tower, and with good reason – you can't go wrong with either. But these two honeypot attractions aren't the sum total of the city's attractions: you'll also find everything from cute cafés to breathtakingly beautiful cemeteries, dazzling modern architecture to centuries-old cathedrals. They're all featured here.
► *For more, see pp51-151*.

CONSUME

Few cities retain such a towering culinary reputation as Paris, but you're by no means on safe ground with every restaurant and café here: the town's great restaurants, listed here, are supplemented by a great many ordinary eateries. Also in this section, you'll find a full guide to shopping in the city and our picks for Paris's best hotels, with more than 100 properties detailed in full.
► *For more, see pp153-272*.

ARTS & ENTERTAINMENT

You don't have to speak French to enjoy Paris's cultural scene, but it helps: much of the theatre scene is off-limits to non-French speakers, and the nuances of chanson may get lost in translation even to listeners fluent in the native tongue. However, all is not lost: there's also an exceptional classical music scene, a thriving collection of galleries, and nightlife that's envied around Europe.
► *For more, see pp273-346*.

ESCAPES & EXCURSIONS

For all the city's wealth of charms, it's worth considering an escape from the hubbub. You certainly won't need to travel far to find one: the grand, handsome Fontainebleau is only around an hour away, with historic Chantilly, bucolic Giverny (Monet's inspiration) and the genuinely astonishing palace of Versailles even closer. Got more time to explore? Park the car and sample champagne country.
► *For more, see pp348-362*.

Paris in 48 Hours

Day 1 From a Marais Morning to an After-Hours Bistro

9AM Start the day in the Marais with an awesome croissant from **Au Levain du Marais** (32 rue de Turenne, 3rd), an easy stroll from beautiful 17th-century place des Vosges. The Marais is abuzz with culture, shops, bars and, in its imposing *hôtels particuliers*, important cultural institutions: take your pick from the **Musée Carnavalet** (*see p101*), the **Musée National Picasso** (*see p101*) and the **Maison Européenne de la Photographie** (*see p103*). Shoppers, meanwhile, will find rich pickings in the streets leading off the main shopping thoroughfare of rue des Francs-Bourgeois.

NOON From the Marais, head across the Seine via the Pont de Sully to the **Institut du Monde Arabe** (*see p121*), which holds a fine collection of Middle Eastern art and a rooftop café with fabulous views down the Seine. (Other wonderful panoramas in Paris include the summit of the **Parc des Buttes-Chaumont** (*see p113*) and the **Sacré-Coeur** (*see p93*), although the latter is worth saving for dusk.) After a wander along the Left Bank to lunch in the back room at **La Palette** (*see p236*), a classic café, meander along the stone quays that border the Seine and leaf through old revues and tatty paperbacks at the riverside *bouquiniste* stalls (*see p242*).

4PM From the quays, either hop on a boat or explore the islands. On the Ile de la Cité, visit the **Mémorial des Martyrs de la Déportation** (*see p57*). On the Ile St-Louis, snag an ice-cream from **Berthillon** (*see p58*) before popping into **Notre-Dame** (*see p56*).

9PM Evenings start with aperitifs. Join the sociable crowd on the terrace seats at **Le Bar du Marché** (*see p235*) and watch the Left Bank people-traffic pass by over a kir and a light supper. Then cross the river to the **Rex** (*see p330*), the city's leading club. Post-dancefloor hunger pangs can be satiated at welcoming Les Halles bistro **La Poule au Pot** (9 rue Vauvilliers, 1st, 01.42.36.32.96), open until 6am.

NAVIGATING THE CITY

Neatly contained within the Périphérique and divided by the Seine into left and right banks, Paris is a compact city. The city's 20 arrondissements (districts) spiral out, clockwise and in ascending order, from the Louvre. Each piece of this jigsaw has its own character.

The Paris métro is reliable, and local buses are frequent and cheap. However, the city is best seen from ground level, whether on foot or, courtesy of the Vélib'

free bike-hire scheme, on two wheels. For full details of transport, *see p364*.

SEEING THE SIGHTS

To avoid queues, try to avoid visiting major attractions at the weekend. Major museums are less busy during the week, especially if you take advantage of the late-night opening offered by many of the big museums. Pre-booking is essential before 1pm at the Grand Palais, and it's also possible to pre-book at the Louvre.

Day 2 Culture, Coffee and a Room with a View

9AM If you'd like to see the **Louvre** (see p59), now's the time: early, before the crowds have descended (and preferably not on a weekend). Otherwise, cross the **Pont des Arts** and head south through the narrow Left Bank streets to **St-Sulpice** church (see p129), followed by a restorative coffee at **Le Rostand** (see p236). Then stroll across the road to the **Jardin du Luxembourg** (see p129), pull up two green chairs (using one as a footrest) and size up the park life. The adjacent **Musée National du Luxembourg** (see p131) hosts world-class art exhibitions.

1PM From here, hop on the métro to Jacques Bonsergent. Amble along the tree-lined **Canal St-Martin**, crossing over its romantic bridges to explore little shops and waterside cafés and maybe stopping at *cave à vins* **Le Verre Volé** (see p234) for a plate of charcuterie and cheese. On Sundays, traffic is outlawed from the quai de Valmy and the bar-lined quai de Jemmapes. There are plenty of boutiques in the area, alongside by kitsch merchants **Antoine et Lili** (see p254). For a swift demi near the water, head to friendly **Chez Prune** (see p231), before catching the métro to Alma Marceau.

5PM Modern art lovers should make a point of visiting the wonderful collection at the **Musée d'Art Moderne de la Ville de Paris** (see p86); it's a neighbour to the **Palais de Tokyo** (see p87), dynamic contemporary art space. From here, you can walk to the **Champs-Elysées** and take a nighttime hike up the **Arc de Triomphe** to see the lights of the avenue stretching into the city.

8PM Head back to the Palais de Tokyo and relax with an expertly shaken cocktail at the hip bar with its terrace overlooking the Seine (see p225). Then, credit card in hand, go for a blowout treat at **Jules Verne** (see p218), Alain Ducasse's haute cuisine eyrie 123 metres up the **Eiffel Tower**. Still got energy? Our Nightlife chapter (see p326) awaits…

Note that most national museums are closed on Tuesdays, but all are free on the first Sunday of the month. Many municipal museums close on Mondays.

PACKAGE DEALS
The most economical way to visit a large number of museums is with a **Paris Museum Pass** (www.parismuseumpass.fr), which offers access to more than 60 museums and attractions. Participating attractions, which include the Louvre and the Musée d'Orsay, are denoted in our listings with **PMP**. Covering two days (€30), four days (€45) or six days (€60), passes are available from participating locations and tourist offices.

The Galeries Nationales du Grand Palais also now operate an annual pass. The **Sesame** (www.rmn.fr) grants free entry (with queue-jumping rights), shop discounts and various other privileges. The card costs €45 for an individual, €75 for a couple and €22 for 13-25s.

Paris in Profile

THE SEINE & ISLANDS

Ile de la Cité is the bullseye of the capital, where its history begins – home to the law courts, Notre-Dame and a dinky flower market. East from here, **Ile St-Louis** is one of the smartest addresses in the capital, but it costs nothing to explore its charming streets and characterful shops.
▶ *For more, see pp53-58.*

THE LOUVRE

The world's largest museum, the Louvre is home to some 35,000 works of art, from ancient Egypt to the 19th century. Crowds can be oppressive, especially around the *Mona Lisa*, but there's also plenty of space for contemplation.
▶ *For more, see pp59-65.*

OPERA TO LES HALLES

At the western end of this stretch, it's all large-scale consumerism and high-end culture; to the east are sleaze, buzz and Les Halles, home to the grim Forum des Halles mall. Heading south, the Tuileries gardens provide respite.
▶ *For more, see 66-81.*

CHAMPS-ELYSEES & WESTERN PARIS

The city's most famous thoroughfare, the **Champs-Elysées** has been transformed of late. At its western end, the Arc de Triomphe is also gleaming after a refurb. **Western Paris** is a civilised mix of important museums and grand residences.
▶ *For more, see pp82-90.*

MONTMARTRE & PIGALLE

Montmartre has one of the city's densest concentrations of tourists. After the views and the Sacré-Coeur, explore the romantic sidestreets. The popular image of the **Pigalle** covers sex shops and neon, but the area is cleaning up its act.
▶ *For more, see pp91-96.*

BEAUBOURG & THE MARAIS

Beaubourg is home to the Centre Pompidou, which holds Europe's largest collection of modern art. The **Marais**, with ancient buildings and a street plan largely unmolested by Haussmann, is the heartland of Jewish and gay Paris.
▶ *For more, see pp97-103.*

BASTILLE & EASTERN PARIS

Bastille is not so much revolutionary as creative these days; the area around iconic place de la Bastille is stocked with record shops, music venues and bars. Further east is Paris's biggest park, the Bois de Vincennes.
▶ *For more, see pp104-107.*

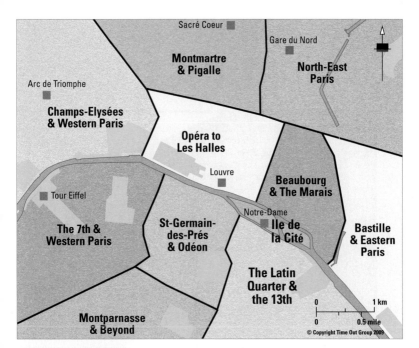

Sacré Coeur

Gare du Nord

Montmartre & Pigalle

North-East Paris

Arc de Triomphe

Champs-Elysées & Western Paris

Opéra to Les Halles

Louvre

Tour Eiffel

Beaubourg & The Marais

Notre-Dame

The 7th & Western Paris

St-Germain-des-Prés & Odéon

Ile de la Cité

Bastille & Eastern Paris

The Latin Quarter & the 13th

Montparnasse & Beyond

0   1 km
0   0.5 mile
© Copyright Time Out Group 2009

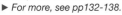

NORTH-EAST PARIS

The drab Gare du Nord is many visitors' first taste of Paris. But west is Belleville, one of the city's most multicultural areas. North-east Paris is home to Père-Lachaise cemetery.
▶ For more, see pp108-113.

THE LATIN QUARTER & THE 13TH

Academic tradition persists in the **Latin Quarter**, home to the Panthéon and the Sorbonne. Further east, the vast ZAC Rive Gauche development project means the **13th** is on the up.
▶ For more, see pp114-124.

ST-GERMAIN-DES-PRES & ODEON

Intellectual heritage and some of the most expensive coffee in the city are to be found in St-Germain-des-Prés & Odéon, now best known for its fashion houses and luxury brands.
▶ For more, see pp125-131.

MONTPARNASSE & BEYOND

There's just enough of a good-time feel in Montparnasse at night to recall the area's artistic heyday in the '20s and '30s. South, Parc Montsouris offers relief from the urban sprawl.
▶ For more, see pp132-138.

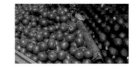

THE 7TH & WESTERN PARIS

The 7th is home to many of Paris's finest museums and the Eiffel Tower, its most celebrated monument. Elsewhere, this is a rarefied area of smart shops and posh homes.
▶ For more, see pp139-146.

Institut Français is one of the oldest established of the 150 Instituts Français which exist throughout the world. Founded in 1910, it has an unrivalled reputation for its cultural programme and the quality of its classes, which explore both language and culture. The fact that the Institut Français is part of the French Ministry of Foreign Affairs' cultural network is a guarantee of the highest degree of professionalism and skill and it is also an accredited examination centre. All the tutors at the Institut Français are native French speakers who are trained in the latest methods for teaching French as a foreign language.

What's on offer

The Institut Français offers a wide range of classes and timetables to suit even the most hectic of diaries, it can cater for all those wishing to discover France through the medium of its language. Courses range from General French (once or several times a week) to specialised French in language, culture and business. Moreover its comprehensive exam preparation classes will get your French up to speed. Whether you're working towards a qualification in general, business or legal French, its experienced teaching staff will provide the support students need to help them pass their exams. Also on offer are one-to-one courses providing flexible, effective, and tailor-made solutions to your specific French language needs. Whatever the level, and whether on an individual or group basis the Institut Français can fine-tune a programme of study and arrange the most appropriate time, place and frequency of classes to meet your requirements. Corporate tuition is also available on a one-to-one basis or small groups, at the Institut Français or at your desk.

Location

The Institut Français, Language Centre is housed in charming listed buildings in the very heart of South Kensington and is a stone's throw from its Cultural Centre which houses the Ciné Lumière (UK's leading showcase for French cinema, screening a mix of new releases and classic films. All films are shown with English subtitles) and the largest French multi-media library in the UK.

Facilities

The Language Centre offers a language laboratory, video and audio visual equipment, the latest teaching aids and a direct satellite link to French TV enabling students to feast on French programmes with their coffee in the cafeteria. Moreover the multi-media library offers a wide variety of documentation for Francophiles and French language-learners of all levels. Everyone studying at the Language Centre is entitled to one year's free membership of the Institut Français Cultural Centre.

STUDENT PROFILE - Samuel Rippon, Macfarlanes, Corporate Training student
"I find that each lesson is carefully structured and it is clear that there is a long term teaching plan in place to ensure thorough recapitulation and revision of new grammar and vocabulary we have learnt. However, our tutor is always able to be flexible with the materials and the structure of the lessons to allow us to work on particular areas of weakness, or particular areas of interest. Enormous effort has gone in to gearing the topics covered to our particular profession, and this has been done to great effect. I have never attended language lessons as enjoyable as these.

 Paris

Editorial
Editor Dominic Earle
Copy Editors Edoardo Albert, Emma Howarth, Ros Sales, Charlotte Thomas
Listings Editor Julien Sauvalle
Proofreader Simon Cropper
Indexer Ismay Atkins

Managing Director Peter Fiennes
Editorial Director Ruth Jarvis
Series Editor Will Fulford-Jones
Business Manager Dan Allen
Editorial Manager Holly Pick
Assistant Management Accountant Ija Krasnikova

Design
Art Director Scott Moore
Art Editor Pinelope Kourmouzoglou
Senior Designer Henry Elphick
Graphic Designers Kei Ishimaru, Nicola Wilson
Advertising Designer Jodi Sher

Picture Desk
Picture Editor Jael Marschner
Deputy Picture Editor Lynn Chambers
Picture Researcher Gemma Walters
Picture Desk Assistant Marzena Zoladz
Picture Librarian Christina Theisen

Advertising
Commercial Director Mark Phillips
International Advertising Manager Kasimir Berger
International Sales Executive Charlie Sokol

Marketing
Marketing Manager Yvonne Poon
Sales & Marketing Director, North America & Latin America Lisa Levinson
Senior Publishing Brand Manager Luthfa Begum
Marketing Designers Anthony Huggins

Production
Group Production Director Mark Lamond
Production Manager Brendan McKeown
Production Controller Damian Bennett
Production Coordinator Julie Pallot

Time Out Group
Chairman Tony Elliott
Group General Manager/Director Nichola Coulthard
Time Out Communications Ltd MD David Pepper
Time Out International Ltd MD Cathy Runciman
Group IT Director Simon Chappell
Head of Marketing Catherine Demajo

Contributors

Introduction Simon Cropper. **History** Simon Cropper (*Sarkozy's Suburban Nightmare* Rich Woodruff). **Paris Today** Rich Woodruff. **Architecture** Natasha Edwards. **Crossing the Divide** Natasha Edwards. **Sightseeing** Simon Cropper, Rich Woodruff (*Bone Diggers*, *Dead Famous* Jonathan Derbyshire; *Lessons in Love* Anna Brooke; *Arty Parties* Alison Culliford). **Hotels** Anna Brooke. **Restaurants** Rosa Jackson. **Cafés & Bars** Anna Brooke. **Shops & Services** Alison Culliford. **Festivals & Events** Charlotte Thomas. **Cabaret, Circus & Comedy** Anna Brooke. **Children** Anna Brooke. **Dance** Estelle Ricoux. **Film** Simon Cropper. **Galleries** Natasha Edwards. **Gay & Lesbian** Robert Vallier. **Music** *Classical & Opera* Stephen Mudge; *Rock, Roots & Jazz* David McKenna. **Nightlife** Anna Brooke. **Sport & Fitness** Rich Woodruff. **Theatre** Anna Brooke. **Escapes & Excursions** Anna Brooke. **Directory** Julien Sauvalle.

Maps john@jsgraphics.co.uk, except: pages 415-416.

Photography Olivia Rutherford, except: pages 5 (Eiffel Tower), 8 (Louvre), 9 (Le Pantheon), 53, 56, 119, 144, 274, 279, 334, 337 Heloise Bergman; page 6, 7, 183, 194, 264, 265 Jean-Christophe Godet; pages 9 (Café Deux Magots), 10 (vegetables), 59, 60 (bottom), 61 (left), 84, 151, 184, 185, 197, 203, 204, 215, 217, 341, 348, 356, 357, 358 Karl Blackwell; pages 16, 29, 299 Getty Images; pages 24, 26 Bridgeman Art Library; page 31 ABACA; page 36 Lucas Dolega/epa/Corbis; page 46 Tony Barson/WireImage; page 48 © D.R.; page 50 AFP/Getty Images; page 188 Gerard Bedeau; pages 208, 209 Ed Marshall; page 218 Eric Laignel; page 267 Elan Fleisher; page 276 © Musée National d'Art Moderne; page 288 Jean-Claude Coutausse; page 291 Pascale Simard; page 301 © Centre Pompidou, Georges Meguerditchian, Paris, 2008; pages 313, 319 © Jean-Baptiste Pellerin, libre de droits; page 323 Thomas Bouet; page 335 Michael Steele/ Getty Images; page 345 Roger Viollet/Getty Images; page 351 Jean-Pol Stercq http://poloster.free.fr; page 360 courtesy of Moët & Chandon. The following pictures were provided by the featured establishments/artists: pages 49, 140, 159, 244, 249, 354.

The Editor would like to thank all contributors to previous editions of *Time Out Paris*, whose work forms the basis for parts of this book.

The Editor travelled to Paris with Eurostar (08705 186 186, www.eurostar.com).

About the Guide

GETTING AROUND
The back of the book contains street maps of Paris, as well as overview maps of the city and its surroundings. The maps start on page 395; on them are marked the locations of hotels (**❶**), restaurants (**❶**), and cafés and bars (**❶**). The majority of businesses listed in this guide are located in the areas we've mapped; the grid-square references in the listings refer to these maps.

THE ESSENTIALS
For practical information, including visas, disabled access, emergency numbers, useful websites and local transport, please see the Directory. It begins on page 363.

THE LISTINGS
Addresses, phone numbers, websites, transport information, hours and prices are all included in our listings, as are selected other facilities. All were checked and correct at press time. However, business owners can alter their arrangements at any time, and fluctuating economic conditions can cause prices to change rapidly.

The very best venues in the city, the must-sees and must-dos in every category, have been marked with a red star (★). In the Sights chapters, we've also marked venues with free admission with a FREE symbol.

THE LANGUAGE
Many Parisians speak a little English, but a few basic French phrases go a long way. You'll find a primer on page 382, along with some help with restaurants on page 208.

PHONE NUMBERS
The area code for Paris is 01. Even if you're calling from within Paris, you'll always need to use the code. From outside France, dial your country's international access code (00 from the UK, 011 from the US) or a plus symbol, followed by the French country code (33), 1 for Paris (dropping the initial zero) and the eight-digit number. So, to reach the Louvre, dial +33.1.40.20.50.50. For more on phones, *see p379.*

FEEDBACK
We welcome feedback on this guide, both on the venues we've included and on any other locations that you'd like to see featured in future editions. Please email us at guides@timeout.com.

Time Out Guides

Founded in 1968, Time Out has grown from humble beginnings into the leading resource for anyone wanting to know what's happening in the world's greatest cities. Alongside our influential weeklies in London, New York and Chicago, we publish more than 20 magazines in cities as varied as Beijing and Beirut; a range of travel books, with the City Guides now joined by the newer Shortlist series; and an information-packed website. The company remains proudly independent, still owned by Tony Elliott four decades after he launched *Time Out London*.

Written by local experts and illustrated with original photography, our books also retain their independence. No business has been featured because it has advertised, and all restaurants and bars are visited and reviewed anonymously.

ABOUT THE EDITOR
Dominic Earle is a freelance travel writer. In addition to editing Time Out City Guides to Paris, Copenhagen and Stockholm, he has also contributed to publications including *The Guardian* and *The Independent*.

A full list of the book's contributors can be found opposite. However, we've also included details of our writers in selected chapters throughout the guide.

In Context

History

Heads will roll.

TEXT: SIMON CROPPER

Simon Cropper has lived in Paris for several years and writes about the city, food and cinema for Time Out.

The earliest settlers seem to have arrived in Paris around 120,000 years ago. One of them lost a flint spear-tip on the hill now called Montmartre, and the dangerous-looking weapon is to be seen today in the Stone Age collection at the Musée des Antiquités Nationales. There was a Stone Age weapons factory under present-day Châtelet, and the redevelopment of Bercy in the 1990s unearthed ten Neolithic canoes, five of which are now high and dry in the Musée Carnavalet.

By 250 BC, a Celtic tribe known as the Parisii had put the place on the map. The Parisii were river traders, wealthy enough to mint gold coins; the Musée de la Monnaie de Paris has an extensive collection of their small change. Their most important *oppidum*, a primitive fortified town, was located on an island in the Seine, which is generally thought to have been what is today's Ile de la Cité.

'Legend has it that when Denis of Athens was decapitated on Montmartre, he picked up his head and walked to St-Denis, to be buried there.'

ROMAN PARIS

A superb strategic location and the capacity to generate hard cash were guaranteed to attract the attention of the Romans. Julius Caesar arrived in southern Gaul as proconsul in 58 BC, and soon used the pretext of dealing with invading barbarians to stick his Roman nose into the affairs of northern Gaul. Caesar had a battle on his hands, but eventually the Paris region and the rest of Gaul were in Roman hands. Roman Lutetia (as Paris was known) was a prosperous town of around 8,000 inhabitants. Apart from centrally heated villas and a temple to Jupiter on the main island (the remains of both are visible in the Crypte Archéologique), there were the sumptuous baths (now the Musée National du Moyen Age) and the 15,000-seater Arènes de Lutèce.

CHRISTIANITY

Christianity arrived in around 250 AD in the shape of Denis of Athens, who became the first bishop of Paris. Legend has it that when he was decapitated by Valerian on Mons Martis, the mount of the martyrs (today better known as Montmartre), Denis picked up his head and walked with it to what is now St-Denis, to be buried there. The event is depicted in Henri Bellechose's *Retable de Saint-Denis*, now exhibited in the Louvre.

Gaul was still a tempting prize. Waves of barbarian invaders began crossing the Rhine from 275 onwards. They sacked more than 60 cities in Gaul, including Lutetia, where the population was massacred and the buildings on the Montagne Ste-Geneviève were pillaged and burned. The bedraggled survivors used the rubble to build a rampart around the Ile de la Cité and to fortify the forum.

It was at this time that the city was renamed Paris. Protected by the Seine and the new fortifications, its main role now was as a rear base for the Roman armies defending Gaul, and it was here in 360 that Julian was proclaimed emperor by his troops. Around 450, with the arrival of the Huns in the region, the people of Paris prepared once again to flee. They were dissuaded by a feisty woman named Geneviève, famed for her piety. Seeing the walls of the city defended against him, no less a pillager than Attila the Hun turned back and was defeated soon afterwards.

CLOVIS

In 464, Paris managed to resist another siege, this time by the Francs under Childeric. However, by 486, after a further blockade lasting ten years, Geneviève had no option but to surrender the city to Childeric's successor, Clovis, who went on to conquer most of Gaul and founded the Merovingian dynasty. He chose Paris as capital of his new kingdom, and it stayed that way until the seventh century, in spite of conflicts among his successors. Under the influence of his wife, Clotilde, Clovis converted to Christianity. He founded, and was buried in, the basilica of the Saints-Apôtres, later rededicated to St Geneviève when the saviour and future patron saint of Paris was interred there in 512. All that remains of the basilica today is a pillar in the grounds of the Lycée Henri IV; but there's a shrine dedicated to St Geneviève and some relics in the fine Gothic church of St-Etienne-du-Mont next door. Geneviève and Clovis had set a trend. The Ile de la Cité was still the heart of the city, but, under the Merovingians, the Left Bank was the up-and-coming area for fashion-conscious Christians, with 11 churches built here in the period (whereas there were only four on the Right Bank and one on the Ile de la Cité). Not everyone was sold on the joys of city living, though. From 614 onwards, the Merovingian kings preferred the

IN CONTEXT

YOU KNOW WHO YOU ARE.

PARIS • 14 BOULEVARD MONTMARTRE
0033 1 53 24 60 00 • HARDROCK.COM

The martyrdom of **Saint-Denis**.

banlieue at Clichy, or wandered the kingdom trying to keep rebellious nobles in check. By the time one of the rebels, Pippin 'the Short', decided to do away with the last Merovingian in 751, Paris was starting to look passé.

Pippin's son, Charlemagne, built his capital at Aix-la-Chapelle, and his successors, the Carolingian dynasty, moved from palace to palace, consuming the local produce. Paris, meanwhile, was doing nicely as a centre for Christian learning, and had grown to a population of 20,000 by the beginning of the ninth century. This was the high point in the political power of the great abbeys like St-Germain-des-Prés, where transcription of the Latin classics was helping to preserve much of Europe's Roman cultural heritage. Power in the Paris area was exercised by the counts of Paris.

PARIS FINDS ITS FEET

From 845, Paris had to fight off another threat – the Vikings. But after various sackings and seiges, the Carolingians were finally able to secure the city. The dynasty gave way to the Capetian dynasty in 987, when Hugues Capet was elected king of France. Under the Capetians, although Paris was now at the heart of the royal domains, the city did not yet dominate the kingdom. Robert 'the Pious', king from 996 to 1031, stayed more often in Paris than his father had done, restoring the royal palace on the Ile de la Cité, and Henri I (1031-60) issued more of his charters in Paris than in Orléans. In 1112, the abbey of St-Denis replaced St-Benoît-sur-Loire as principal monastery.

Paris itself still consisted of little more than the Ile de la Cité and small settlements under the protection of the abbeys on each bank. On the Left Bank, royal largesse helped to rebuild the abbeys of St-Germain-des-Prés, St-Marcel and Ste-Geneviève, although it took more than 150 years for the destruction wrought there by the Vikings to be repaired. The Right Bank, where mooring was easier, prospered from river commerce, and three boroughs grew up around the abbeys of St-Germain-l'Auxerrois, St-Martin-des-Champs and St-Gervais. Bishop Sully of Paris began building the cathedral of Notre-Dame in 1163.

The reign of Philippe-Auguste (1180-1223) was a turning point in the history of Paris. Before, the city was a confused patchwork of royal, ecclesiastical and feudal authorities. Keen to raise revenues, Philippe favoured the growth of the guilds, especially the butchers, drapers, furriers, haberdashers and merchants; so began the rise of the bourgeoisie.

He also ordered the building of the first permanent market buildings at Les Halles, and a new city wall, first on the Right Bank to protect the commercial heart of Paris, and later on the Left Bank. At the western end of the wall, Philippe built a castle, the Louvre, to defend the road from the ever-menacing Normandy, whose duke was also King of England.

A GOLDEN AGE

Paris was now the principal residence of the king and the uncontested capital of France. To accommodate the growing royal administration, the Palais de la Cité, site and symbol of power for the previous thousand years, was remodelled and enlarged. Work was begun by Louis IX (later St Louis) in the 1240s, and continued under Philippe IV ('le Bel'). This architectural complex, of which the Ste-Chapelle and the nearby Conciergerie can still be seen, was inaugurated with great pomp at Pentecost 1313.

The palace was quickly filled with functionaries, so the king spent as much of his time as he could outside Paris at the royal castles of Fontainebleau and, especially, Vincennes. The needs of the plenipotentiaries left behind to run the kingdom were met by a rapidly growing city population, piled into rather less chic buildings.

Paris was also reinforcing its identity as a major religious centre: as well as the local clergy and dozens of religious orders, the city was home to the masters and students of the university of the Sorbonne (established in 1253), who were already gaining a reputation for rowdiness. An influx of scholars from all over Europe gave the city a cultural and intellectual cachet it was never to lose.

By 1328, Paris was home to 200,000 inhabitants, making it the most populous city in Europe. However, that year was also notable for being the last of the medieval golden age: the dynasty of Capetian kings spluttered to an inglorious halt when Charles IV died without an heir. The English quickly claimed the throne for Edward III, the son of Philippe IV's daughter. Refusing to recognise his descent through the female line, the late king's cousin, Philippe de Valois, claimed the French crown as Philippe VI. So began the Hundred Years War between France and England – a war that in fact would go on for 116 years.

TROUBLES AND STRIFE

To make matters worse, the Black Death (bubonic plague) ravaged Europe from the 1340s onwards. Citizens not finished by the plague had to contend with food shortages, ever-increasing taxes, riots, repression, currency devaluations and marauding mercenaries. Meanwhile, in Paris, the honeymoon period for the king and the bourgeoisie was coming to an end. Rich and populous, Paris was expected to bear the brunt of the war burden; and as defeat followed defeat (notably the disaster at Crécy in August 1346), the bourgeoisie and people of the city were increasingly exasperated by the futility of the sacrifices they were making for the hideously expensive war. To fund the conflict, King Jean II tried to introduce new tax laws – without success. When the king was captured by the English at Poitiers in 1356, his problems passed to his 18-year-old son, Charles.

The Etats Généraux, consultant body to the throne, was summoned to the royal palace on the Ile de la Cité to discuss the country's woes. The teenage king was besieged with angry demands for reform from the bourgeoisie, particularly from Etienne Marcel, then provost of the local merchants. Marcel seized control of Paris and began a bitter power struggle with the crown; in 1357, fearing widespread revolt, Charles fled to Compiègne. But as he ran, he had Paris blockaded. Marcel called on the peasants, who were also raging against taxes, but they were quickly crushed. He then called on Charles 'the Bad' of Navarre, ally to the English, but his arrival in Paris made many of Marcel's supporters nervous. On 31 July 1358, Marcel was murdered, and the revolution was over. As a safeguard, the returning Charles built a new stronghold to protect Paris: the Bastille.

By 1420, following the French defeat at Agincourt, Paris was in English hands; in 1431, Henry VI of England was crowned King of France in Notre-Dame. He didn't last. Five years later, Henry and his army were driven back to Calais by the Valois king, Charles VII. Charles owed his power to Jeanne d'Arc, who led the victorious French in the Battle of Orléans, only to be betrayed by her compatriots, who decided she was getting too big for her boots. She was captured and sold to the English, who had her burned as a witch.

By 1436, Paris was once again the capital of France. But the nation had been nearly bled dry by war and was still divided politically, with powerful regional rulers across France continuing to threaten the monarchy. Outside the French borders, the ambitions of the

Austrian Habsburg dynasty represented a serious threat. In this general atmosphere of instability, disputes over trade, religion and taxation were all simmering dangerously in the political background.

RENAISSANCE AND REFORMATION

In the closing decades of the 15th century, the restored Valois monarchs sought to reassert their position. A wave of building projects was the public sign of this effort, producing such masterpieces as St-Etienne-du-Mont, St-Eustache and private homes like the Hôtel de Cluny (which today houses the Musée National du Moyen Age) and the Hôtel de Sens, which now accommodates the Bibliothèque de Forney. The Renaissance in France had its peak under François I. As well as being involved in the construction of the magnificent châteaux at Fontainebleau, Blois and Chambord, François was also responsible for transforming the Louvre from a fortress into a royal palace.

Despite burning heretics by the dozen, François was unable to stop the spread of Protestantism, launched in Germany by Martin Luther in 1517. Resolutely Catholic, Paris was the scene of some horrific violence against the Huguenots, as supporters of the new faith were called. By the 1560s, the situation had degenerated into open warfare.

Aiming for the Top

French politics can be a deadly business.

Paris is notorious for its revolutions; much less familiar is this blood-soaked city's equally distinguished record of assassination. Its annals of political violence tell of the day in 1610 when Catholic fanatic François Ravaillac ran into a traffic jam near Les Halles to stab Henri IV, and of the rifle bullets fired at Jacques Chirac by a lone far-right supporter on Bastille Day in 2002. One of the city's most famous killings produced one of its most famous paintings, David's portrait of Marat, knifed in his bath in 1793; other political murders have been largely forgotten, including the shooting of President Paul Doumer by a Russian émigré in 1932.

The victim of the most resonant Paris assassination was neither king nor president, but the charismatic leader of the Socialist party, Jean Jaurès. At 9.40pm on 31 July 1914, the aptly named Raoul Villain leaned in through an open window of the Café du Croissant, on the corner of rue du Croissant and rue Montmartre, and aimed his revolver at the bearded Jaurès, sitting with friends on the other side of the room. One shot went wide, but the other hit Jaurès in the head, and he died within minutes.

The shooting was remarkable in several ways, not least for an almost unparalleled stroke of reporter's luck. A correspondent for the *Manchester Guardian* happened to be dining in the café that evening, and witnessed the whole event. The following day, he described the immediate aftermath as 'heartrending – men and women were in tears'. Public shock was heightened by the tense mood across Europe; the loss of Jaurès, a prominent anti-war campaigner, deepened the gloom as the great powers geared up for World War I.

Villain was locked up for the duration of the conflict, only to be acquitted at a new trial in 1919 on the ludicrous grounds that he had done France a patriotic favour; more ludicrous still, Jaurès' widow was ordered to pay costs. Villain moved to Spain, but met a sticky end of his own in 1936, when he was executed as a spy by opponents of Franco. Seven decades later, nearly every town and city in France has a thoroughfare named after Jaurès – and the Café du Croissant is still in business, a pleasant spot whose awning and a commemorative plaque remind passers-by of that bloody night in 1914.

IN CONTEXT

'On his way to the disaster of Moscow, Napoleon gave France the lycée system, the Legion of Honour, the Banque de France and La Bourse.'

Catherine de Médicis, the scheming Italian widow of Henri II, was the real force in court politics. It was she who connived to murder prominent Protestants gathered in Paris for the marriage of the king's sister on St Bartholomew's Day (23 August 1572). Catherine's main aim was to dispose of her powerful rival, Gaspard de Coligny, but the situation got out of hand, and as many as 3,000 people were butchered. Henri III attempted to reconcile the religious factions and eradicate the powerful families directing the conflict, but the people of Paris turned against him and he was forced to flee. His assassination in 1589 brought the Valois line to an end.

THE BOURBONS
The throne of France being up for grabs, Henri of Navarre declared himself King Henri IV, launching the Bourbon dynasty. Paris was not impressed. The city closed its gates against the Huguenot king, and the inhabitants endured a four-year siege by supporters of the new ruler. Henri managed to break the impasse by having himself converted to Catholicism (and is supposed to have said, *'Paris vaut bien une messe'* – Paris is well worth a mass).

Henri set about rebuilding his ravaged capital. He completed the Pont Neuf, the first bridge to span the whole Seine. He commissioned place Dauphine and the city's first enclosed residential square – the place Royale – now place des Vosges.

Henri also tried to reconcile his Catholic and Protestant subjects, issuing the Edict of Nantes in 1598, effectively giving each religion equal status. The Catholics hated the deal, and the Huguenots were suspicious. Henri was the subject of at least 23 attempted assassinations by fanatics of both persuasions. Finally, in 1610, a Catholic by the name of François Ravaillac fatally stabbed the king while he was in traffic on rue de la Ferronnerie.

TWO CARDINALS
Since Henri's son, Louis XIII, was only eight at the time of his father's death, his mother, Marie de Médicis, took up the reins of power. We can thank her for the Palais du Luxembourg and the 24 paintings she commissioned from Rubens, now part of the Louvre collection. Louis took up his royal duties in 1617, but Cardinal Richelieu, chief minister from 1624, was the man who ran France. Something of a schemer, he outwitted the king's mother, his wife (Anne of Austria) and a host of others. Richelieu helped to strengthen the power of the monarch, and he did much to limit the independence of the aristocracy.

The Counter-Reformation was at its height, and lavish churches such as the Baroque Val-de-Grâce were an important reassertion of Catholic supremacy. The 17th century was 'le Grand Siècle', a time of patronage of art and artists, even if censorship forced the brilliant mathematician and philosopher René Descartes into exile. The first national newspaper, *La Gazette*, hit the streets in 1631; Richelieu used it as a propaganda tool. The cardinal founded the Académie Française, which is still working, slowly, on the dictionary of the French language that Richelieu commissioned from them in 1634. Richelieu died in 1642; Louis XIII followed suit a few months later. The new king, Louis XIV, was five years old. Anne of Austria became regent, with the Italian Cardinal Mazarin, a Richelieu protégé, as chief minister. Rumour has it that Anne and Mazarin may have been married. Mazarin's townhouse is now home to the Bibliothèque Nationale de France – Richelieu.

Endless wars against Austria and Spain had depleted the royal coffers and left the nation drained by exorbitant taxation. In 1648, the royal family was chased out of Paris by a popular uprising, 'la Fronde', named after the catapults used by some of the rioters.

Parisians soon tired of the anarchy that followed. When Mazarin's army retook the city in 1653, the boy-king was warmly welcomed. Mazarin died in 1661 and Louis XIV, now 24 years old, decided he would rule France without the assistance of any chief minister.

SHINE ON, SUN KING

The 'Roi Soleil', or Sun King, was an absolute monarch. 'L'état, c'est moi' (I am the State) was his vision of power. To prove his grandeur, the king embarked on wars against England, Holland and Austria. He also refurbished and extended the Louvre, commissioned place Vendôme and place des Victoires, constructed the Observatory and laid out the *grands boulevards* along the line of the old city walls. The triumphal arches at Porte St-Denis and Porte St-Martin date from this time too. His major project was the palace at Versailles. Louis moved his court there in 1682.

Louis XIV owed much of his brilliant success to the work of Jean-Baptiste Colbert, nominally in charge of state finances, but eventually taking control of all the important levers of the state machine. Colbert was the force behind the Sun King's redevelopment of Paris. The Hôtel des Invalides was built to accommodate the crippled survivors of Louis' wars, the Salpêtrière to shelter fallen women. In 1702 Paris was divided into 20 *quartiers* (not until the Revolution was it re-mapped into arrondissements). Colbert died in 1683, and Louis' luck on the battlefield ran out. Hopelessly embroiled in the War of the Spanish Succession, the country was devastated by famine in 1692. The Sun King died in 1715, leaving no direct heir. His five-year-old great-grandson, Louis XV, was named king, with Philippe d'Orléans as regent. The court moved back to Paris. Installed in the Palais-Royal, the regent set about enjoying his few years of power, hosting lavish dinners that degenerated into orgies. The state, meanwhile, remained chronically in debt.

THE ENLIGHTENMENT

Some of the city's more sober residents were making Paris the intellectual capital of Europe. Enlightenment thinkers such as Diderot, Montesquieu, Voltaire and Rousseau were all active during the reign of Louis XV. Literacy rates were increasing – 50 per cent of French men could read, 25 per cent of women – and the publishing industry was booming.

The king's mistress, Madame de Pompadour, encouraged him to finance the building of the Ecole Militaire and the laying out of place Louis XV, known to us as place de la Concorde. The massive church of St-Sulpice was completed in 1776. Many of the great houses in the area bounded by rue de Lille, rue de Varenne and rue de Grenelle date from the first half of the 18th century. The private homes of aristocrats and wealthy bourgeois, these would become the venues for numerous salons, the informal discussion sessions often devoted to topics raised by Enlightenment questioning.

The Enlightenment spirit of rational humanism finally took the venom out of the Catholic–Protestant power struggle, and the increase in public debate helped to change views about the nature of the state and the place and authority of the monarchy. As Jacques Necker, Louis XVI's finance minister on the eve of the Revolution, put it, popular opinion was 'an invisible power that, without treasury, guard or army, gives its laws to the city, the court and even the palaces of kings'. Thanks to the Enlightenment, and an ever-growing burden of taxation on the poorest strata of society to prop up the wealthiest, that power would eventually overturn the status quo.

THE FRENCH REVOLUTION

The great beneficiary of the French Revolution, Napoleon Bonaparte, once remarked that lucky generals were to be preferred over good generals. The same applies to kings, and the gods of fortune certainly deserted Louis XVI in 1789, when bad weather and worse debts brought France to its knees. But few would have predicted that the next five years would see the execution of the king and most of the royal family, terror stalking the streets in the name of revolution, and the steady rise of a young Corsican soldier. For an account of the Revolution, *see p26* **The French Revolution**.

The Battle of Waterloo by
Robert Alexander Hillingford.

NAPOLEON

Amid the post-Revolutionary chaos, power was divided between a two-housed Assembly and a Directory of five men. The French public reacted badly to hearing of England's attempts to promote more popular rebellion; when a royalist rising in Paris needed to be put down, a young officer from Corsica was the man to do it – Napoleon Bonaparte.

Napoleon quickly became the Directory's right-hand man. When they needed someone to lead a campaign against Austria, he was the man. Victory saw France – and Napoleon – glorified. After a further, aborted, campaign to Egypt in 1799, Napoleon returned home to put down another royalist plot, made himself the chief of the newly governing three-man Consul – and by 1804 was emperor.

After failing to squeeze out the English by setting up the Continental System to block trade across the Channel, Napoleon waged massive wars against Britain, Russia and Austria. On his way to the disaster of Moscow, Napoleon gave France the *lycée* educational system, the Napoleonic Code of civil law, the Legion of Honour, the Banque de France, the Pont des Arts, the Arc de Triomphe, the Madeleine church (he re-established Catholicism as the state religion), La Bourse and rue de Rivoli. He was also responsible for the centralised bureaucracy that still drives the French mad.

As Russian troops – who had chased Napoleon's once-mighty army all the way from Moscow and Leipzig – invaded France, Paris itself came under threat. Montmartre, then named Montnapoléon, had a telegraph machine at its summit, one that had given so many of the emperor's orders and transmitted news of so many victories. The hill fell to Russian troops. Napoleon gave the order to blow up the city's main powder stores, and thus Paris itself. His officer refused. Paris accommodated carousing Russian, Prussian and English soldiers while Napoleon was sent to exile in Elba. A hundred days later, he was back, leading an army against Wellington and Blücher's troops in the mud of Waterloo, near Brussels. A further defeat saw the end of him. Paris survived further foreign occupation. The diminutive Corsican died on the South Atlantic prison island of St Helena in 1821.

ANOTHER ROUND OF BOURBONS

Having sampled revolution and military dictatorship, the French were now ready to give monarchy a second chance. The Bourbons got back in business in 1815, in the person of Louis XVIII, Louis XVI's elderly brother. Several efforts were made to adapt the monarchy to the new political realities, though the new king's Charter of Liberties was not a wholly sincere expression of how he meant to rule.

When another brother of Louis XVI, Charles X, became king in 1824, he decided that enough royal energy had been wasted trying to reconcile the nation's myriad factions. It was time for a spot of old-fashioned absolutism. But the forces unleashed during the Revolution, and the social divisions that had opened as a result, were not to be ignored – and the people were happy to respond with some old-fashioned rebellion.

In the 1830 elections, the liberals won a hefty majority in the Chamber of Deputies, the legislative body. Charles's unpopular minister Prince Polignac, a returned émigré, promptly dissolved the Chamber, announced a date for new elections and curtailed the number of voters. Polishing off this collection of bad decisions was the 26 July decree abolishing the freedom of the press. The day after its issue, 5,000 print workers and journalists filled the streets and three newspapers went to press. When police tried to confiscate copies, they sparked a three-day riot, 'les Trois Glorieuses', with members of the disbanded National Guard manning the barricades. On 30 July, Charles dismissed Polignac, but it was too late. He had little choice but to abdicate, and fled to England. As French revolutions go, it was a neat, brief affair.

Another leftover from the *ancien régime* was now winched on to the throne – Louis-Philippe, Duc d'Orléans, who had some Bourbon blood in his veins. A father of eight who never went out without his umbrella, he was eminently acceptable to the newly powerful bourgeoisie. But the poor, who had risked their lives in two attempts to change French society, were unimpressed by the new king's promise to embrace a moderate and liberal version of the Revolutionary heritage.

THE NINETEENTH CENTURY

Philosopher Walter Benjamin declared Paris 'the capital of the 19th century', and he had a point. Though it was smaller than its global rival, London, in intellectual and cultural spheres it reigned supreme. On the demographic front, its population doubled to one million between 1800 and 1850. Most of the new arrivals were rural labourers, who had come to find work on the city's ever-expanding building sites. Meanwhile, the middle classes were doing well, thanks to the relatively late arrival of the industrial revolution in France, and the solid administrative structures inherited from Napoleon. The poor were as badly off as ever, only now there were more of them. The back-breaking hours worked in the factories would not be curbed by legislation: 'Whatever the lot of the workers is, it is not the manufacturer's responsibility to improve it,' said one trade minister. In Left Bank cafés, a new bohemian tribe of students derided the materialistic government. Workers' pamphlets and newspapers, such as *La Ruche Populaire*, gave voice to the starving, crippled poor. A wave of ill feeling was gradually building up against Louis-Philippe.

On 23 February 1848, hundreds of Parisians – men, women and students – moved along the boulevards towards a public banquet at La Madeleine. The king's minister, François Guizot, had forbidden any direct campaigning by opposition parties in the forthcoming election, so the parties held banquets instead of meetings.

One diarist of the time noted that some of the crowd had stuffed swords and daggers underneath their shirts, but the demonstration was largely peaceful – until the troops stationed on the boulevard des Capucines opened fire, igniting a riot.

As barricades sprang up all over the city, a trembling Louis-Philippe abdicated and a liberal provisional government declared a republic. The virtual epidemic of poverty and unemployment was stemmed by creating national *ateliers*, but such 'radical' reforms made the right extremely nervous. A conservative government took power in May 1848, and shut down the *ateliers*. A month later, the poor were back in the streets. Some 50,000 took part in the 'June Days' protests, which were quite comprehensively crushed by General Cavaignac's troops. In total, about 1,500 Parisians died and some 5,000 were deported.

As the pamphleteer Alphonse Karr said of the revolution's aftermath, 'plus ça change, plus c'est la même chose' (the more things change, the more they stay the same). In December 1848, Louis Bonaparte – nephew of Napoleon – was elected president. By 1852, he had moved into the Tuileries palace and declared himself Emperor Napoleon III.

IN CONTEXT

The French Revolution

1789 and all that.

IN CONTEXT

As the bitter winter of 1788 turned into 1789, Louis XVI was losing his grip on his country's problems. Wars had left the state practically bankrupt; harvests had failed and food prices soared. Distress and discontent reigned, and with it came demands for an end to absolute monarchy and pressure for wider participation in government, particularly from the nation's bourgeoisie.

Under pressure, Louis allowed the formation of an Assemblée Nationale, a body with representatives from the nobility and clergy, but dominated by the bourgeoisie, which began work on a national constitution. Louis, however, was not prepared to tolerate this threat to his authority. Behind the scenes, he began gathering troops to force it to disband; and on 12 July he dismissed the commoner's ally, finance minister Jacques Necker, prompting a violent counter-coup. On 14 July a crowd stormed the Bastille prison. Only seven prisoners were inside, but the symbolic victory was immense. An emasculated Louis came to Paris on 17 July to acknowledge the crowds at Hôtel de Ville.

The establishment of the constitution forged ahead. Tax breaks for the nobility and clergy were abolished; Church property was seized. But one of Louis'

original problems, the price of bread, had not budged. In October, a mob of starving women marched the 12 miles to Versailles and demanded that the king come to Paris. He promised to send the women grain, an offer they rejected by decapitating some of his guards.

Louis transferred to the Tuileries. In the months that followed, the Jacobins – the more radical of the revolutionary elements – roused powerful Republican feeling. The king and his family attempted to flee Paris on 20 June 1791, with Louis disguised as a valet. But the family were apprehended and brought back to Paris in disgrace.

On 14 September, Louis accepted the new constitution, and the revolution seemed to be over. But other monarchies were plotting to reinstate the king. In 1792, Austrian and Prussian troops invaded France. The Republicans, rightly, suspected Louis of conspiring with the enemy, and scrabbled together their own army to capture him. After two days of fighting in the Tuileries, the royal family was incarcerated in the Temple prison by the radical Commune de Paris, headed by Danton, Marat and Robespierre.

Then came a massacre. Revolutionaries invaded the prisons and murdered 2,000 so-called traitors. The monarchy was abolished on 22 September; the king was executed on 21 January 1793. Headed by Robespierre, the Jacobins vowed to wage terror against all dissidents. The Great Terror of 1794 saw the guillotine slice through 1,300 necks in six weeks.

Eventually, with foes domestic and foreign defeated, there was no more stomach for the killing. Robespierre and his cohorts attempted some democratic reform, but most people wanted them gone. On 28 July 1794, he was executed and the Reign of Terror collapsed. The biggest and bloodiest of revolutions was over.

THE SECOND EMPIRE

The emperor appointed a lawyer as *préfet* to mastermind the reconstruction of Paris. In less than two decades, prefect Georges-Eugène Haussmann had created the most magnificent city in Europe. His goals included better access to railway stations, better water supplies, and a long list of new hospitals, barracks, theatres and *mairies*. It was a colossal project, and it transformed the capital with a network of wide, arrow-straight avenues that were more hygienic than the narrow streets they replaced.

Not everyone was happy. Haussmann's works destroyed thousands of buildings, including beautiful Middle Ages monuments; on the whole of Ile de la Cité only Notre-Dame and a handful of houses survived. Entire residential areas were wiped off the map, and only the owners of the buildings themselves were compensated; tenants were merely booted out. Writers and artists lamented the loss of the more quirky Paris they used to know, and criticised the unfriendly grandeur of the new city. But there was no going back.

At home, the city's rapid industrialisation saw the rise of Socialism and Communism among the disgruntled working classes, and Napoleon III gave limited rights to trade unions. Abroad, though, the now constitutional monarch was a disaster. After the relatively successful Crimean War of the mid 1850s, he tried in vain to impose the Catholic Maximilian as ruler of Mexico. The Franco-Prussian war was his next misadventure. France was soon defeated. At Sedan, in September 1870, 100,000 French troops were forced to surrender to Bismarck's Prussians; Napoleon III himself was captured, never to return.

The war continued, and back in Paris, a provisional government hastily took power. Elections gave conservative monarchists the majority, though the Paris vote was firmly Republican. Former prime minister Adolphe Thiers assumed executive power. Meanwhile, Prussian forces marched on Paris and laid siege to the city. Paris held out, starving, for four brave months, its citizens picking rats from the gutter for food. Léon Gambetta, a young politician, escaped in style (by hot-air balloon) but failed to raise an army in the south. In January 1871, the provisional government signed a bitter armistice that relinquished the industrial heartlands of Alsace and Lorraine and agreed to pay a five-million-franc indemnity. German troops would stay on French soil until the bill was paid.

But with occupying army camps stationed around their city, Parisians considered the treaty a dishonour and remained defiant. Thiers ordered his soldiers to enter the city and strip it of its cannons, but the insurgents cut them short. The new government scuttled off to the haven of Versailles, and on 26 March Paris elected its own municipal body, the Commune, so called in memory of the spirit of 1792. The 92 members of the Commune hailed from the left and working classes; their agenda was liberal (schools would be secularised, debts suspended) but war-like (Germany must be defeated). Paris itself was given a little makeover: the column extolling Napoleonic glory on place Vendôme was pulled down, and statues of the great emperor were smashed all over town.

Thiers would not stand by and watch. Artillery fire picked at the Communards' sandbag barricades on the edges of Paris, and the suburbs fell by 11 April. In the sixth week of fighting, troops broke in through the Porte de St-Cloud and covered the springtime city in blood. The ill-equipped Communards faced a massacre: some 25,000 were killed in a matter of days. In revenge, around 50 hostages were taken and shot, including the Archbishop of Paris. The infamous *pétroleuses*, women wielding petrol bombs, burned off their anger, torching the Tuileries and the Hôtel de Ville. On the last day of *la semaine sanglante*, 28 May, 147 Communards were trapped and shot in Père-Lachaise cemetery, against the 'Mur des Fédérés', still an icon of the Commune struggle. The dead were buried in the streets, the prisons crammed with 40,000 Communards; thousands were deported, many to penal colonies in New Caledonia.

THE THIRD REPUBLIC

Thanks mainly to the huge economic boost provided by colonial expansion in Africa and Indo-China, the horrors of the Commune were soon forgotten in the self-indulgent materialism of the turn of the century and the Third Republic. The Eiffel Tower was built as the centrepiece of the 1889 Exposition Universelle. For the next Exposition Universelle, in 1900, the Grand Palais and Petit Palais, the Pont Alexandre III and the Gare d'Orsay (now the Musée d'Orsay) were built to affirm France's position as a world power, and the first line of the métro opened. The first film screening had been held (1895), and clubs like the Moulin Rouge were buzzing. The lurid life of Montmartre, depicted by Toulouse-Lautrec – and its cheap rents – would attract the world's artistic community.

THE GREAT WAR

On 3 August 1914, Germany declared war on France. Although the Germans never made it to Paris in World War I – German troops were stopped 20 kilometres (12 miles) short of the city thanks to the French victory in the Battle of the Marne – the artillery was audible. Paris, and French society as a whole, suffered terribly, despite ultimate victory.

The nations gathered at Versailles to make the peace, and established new European states. The League of Nations was formed. Artists responded to the horrors and absurdity of the conflict with Surrealism, a movement founded in Paris by André Breton, a doctor who treated troops in the trenches and embraced Freud's theories of the unconscious. In 1924, Surrealism had a manifesto, a year later its first exhibition. Again, artists (and photographers) flocked to Paris. Montmartre was now too expensive, and Montparnasse became the hub of artistic life. The interwar years were a whirl of activity in artistic and political circles. Paris became the avant-garde capital of the world, recorded by Hemingway, F Scott Fitzgerald and Gertrude Stein, who had made the city their home.

Meanwhile, the Depression unleashed a wave of political violence, Fascists fighting Socialists and Communists for control. At the same time, many writers were leaving Paris for Spain to cover – and, indeed, to take part in – the Civil War. Across the German border, the contentious territories of Alsace-Lorraine – and the burden of the World War I peace agreements signed in Paris – became one of many bugbears held by the new chancellor, Adolf Hitler. As war broke out, France believed that its Maginot line would hold strong against the German threat. When the Nazis attacked France in May 1940, they simply bypassed the fortifications and came through the Ardennes.

WORLD WAR II

Paris was in German hands by June. The city fell without a fight. A pro-German government was set up in Vichy, headed by Marshall Pétain, and a young army officer, Charles de Gaulle, went to London to organise the Free French opposition. For Frenchmen happy to get along with the German army, the period of the Occupation presented few hardships and, indeed, some good business opportunities. Food was rationed, and tobacco and coffee went out of circulation, but the black market thrived. For people who resisted, there were the Gestapo torture chambers at avenue Foch or rue Lauriston. The Germans further discouraged uncooperative behaviour with executions: one victim, whose name now adorns a métro station, was Jacques Bonsergent, a student caught fly-posting and shot because he refused to reveal the names of his friends who escaped.

The Vichy government was so eager to please the Germans, it organised anti-Semitic measures without prompting. As of the spring of 1941, the French authorities deported Jews to the death camps, frequently via the internment camp at Drancy. Prime Minister Pierre Laval argued that it was a necessary concession to his Third Reich masters. In July 1942, 12,000 Jewish French citizens were rounded up in the Vélodrome d'Hiver, a sports complex on quai de Grenelle, and then dispatched to Auschwitz.

THE LIBERATION

Paris survived the war practically unscathed, ultimately thanks to the bravery of one of its captors. On 23 August 1944, as the Allied armies of liberation approached the city, Hitler ordered his commander, Dietrich von Choltitz, to detonate the explosives that had been set all over town in anticipation of a retreat. Von Choltitz refused. On 25 August, French troops, tactfully placed at the head of the US forces, entered the city, and General de

Riots, May 1968.

Gaulle led the parade down the Champs-Elysées. Writers and artists swept back into Paris to celebrate. Hemingway held court at the Ritz and Scribe hotels with the great journalists of the day, clinking glasses with veterans of the Spanish Civil War such as photographer Robert Capa and George Orwell. Picasso's studio was besieged by well-wishers.

However, the Liberation was by no means the end of France's troubles. De Gaulle was the hero of the hour, but relations between the interim government he commanded and the Resistance – largely Communist – were still tricky. Orders issued to *maquis* leaders in the provinces were often ignored. The Communists wanted a revolution, and de Gaulle suspected them of hatching plans to seize Paris prior to August 1944. Meanwhile, de Gaulle knew that he had to commit every available French soldier to the march on Germany, or risk being sidelined by the other Allies after the war. He had to leave homeland security to the very people – the 'patriotic militias' – who were most likely to be at least sympathetic to the Communist cause; or, even more dubiously, gendarmes who had previously worked with the occupying power.

Recovery was slow. There were shortages of everything; indeed, many complained they had been better off under the Germans. Even in the ministries, paper was so scarce that correspondence had to be sent out on Vichy letterhead with the sender crossing out 'Etat Français' at the top and writing 'République Française' instead.

THE FOURTH REPUBLIC

On 8 May 1945, de Gaulle made a broadcast to the nation to announce Germany's surrender. Paris went wild, but the euphoria didn't last. There were strikes. And more strikes. Liberation had proved to be a restoration, not the revolution the Communists, now the most powerful political force in the land, had hoped for. The Communist Party was, in at least one respect, as pragmatic as everyone else: it did its utmost to turn parliamentary democracy to its advantage, to wit, getting as many of the top jobs as it could.

A general election was held on 21 October 1945. The Communists secured 159 seats, the Socialists got 146 and the Catholic Mouvement Républicain Populaire got 152. A fortnight later, at the Assemblée Nationale's first session, a unanimous vote was passed maintaining de Gaulle in his position as head of state – but he remained an antagonistic leader. His reluctance to take a firm grip on the disastrous economic situation alienated many intellectuals and industrialists who had once been loyal to him, and his characteristic aloofness only made the misgivings of the general populace worse. He, on the other hand, was disgusted by all the political chicanery. On 20 January 1946, de Gaulle resigned.

France, meanwhile, looked to swift industrial modernisation under an ambitious plan put forward by internationalist politician Jean Monnet. Although the economy and daily life remained grim, brash new fashion designer Christian Dior put together a stunning collection of strikingly simple clothes: the New Look. Such extravagance horrified many locals, but the fashion industry boomed. Meanwhile, the divisions in Paris between its fashionable and its run-down working-class areas became more pronounced. The northern and eastern edges – areas revived only in the late 20th century by a taste for retro, industrial decor and cheap rent – were forgotten about.

Félix Gouin, the new Socialist premier, quickly nationalised the bigger banks and the coal industry. But the right wing was growing, and there was even a rise of royalist hopes. A referendum was held in May 1946 to determine the crucial tenet of the Fourth Republic's constitution: should the Assemblée Nationale have absolute or restricted power? The results were a narrow victory for people who, like de Gaulle, had insisted the Assemblée's power should be qualified. De Gaulle's prestige increased, but it was to be another 12 years, and a whole new constitution – the Fifth Republic – before he got his hands back on the levers of power. He spent much of his '*passage du désert*' writing his memoirs.

THE ALGERIAN WAR AND MAY 1968

The post-war years were marked by the rapid disintegration of France's overseas interests and her rapprochement with Germany to create what would become the European Community. When revolt broke out in Algeria in 1956, almost 500,000 troops were sent in to protect national interests. A protest by Algerians in Paris on 17 October 1961 led to the deaths of hundreds of people at the hands of the city's police. The extent of the violence was officially concealed for decades, as was the use of torture against Algerians by French troops. Algeria became independent in 1962.

Meanwhile, the slow, painful discoveries of collaboration in World War II, often overlooked in the rush to put the country back on its feet, were also being faced. The younger generation began to question the motives of the older one. De Gaulle's Fifth Republic was felt by many to be grimly authoritarian. In the spring of 1968, students unhappy with overcrowded university conditions took to the streets of Paris at the same time as striking Renault workers. These *soixante-huitards* sprang the greatest public revolt in French living memory. Many students were crammed into universities that had been cheaply expanded to accommodate them. Political discourse grew across the campuses, turning against the government's stranglehold on the media and President de Gaulle's poor grasp of the economy. Ministers did indeed at the time have a sinister habit of leaning on the leading newspaper editors of the day, and television was dubbed 'the government in your dining room'. Inflation was high, and the gap between the working classes and the bourgeoisie was becoming a chasm. Still, de Gaulle echoed many when he said the events of May 1968 were '*incompréhensible*'. The touchpaper was lit at overcrowded Nanterre university, on the outskirts of Paris, where students had been protesting against the war in Vietnam and the tatty state of the campus.

On 2 May, exhausted by the protests, the authorities closed the university down and threatened to expel some of the students. The next day, a sit-in was held in sympathy at the Sorbonne. Police were called to intervene, but made things worse, charging into the crowd with truncheons and tear gas. The city's streets were soon flooded with thousands of student demonstrators, now officially on strike. The trade unions followed, as did the *lycées*. By mid May nine million people were on strike. On 24 May, de Gaulle intervened. His speech warned of civil war and pleaded for people's support. It didn't go down well: riots broke out, with students storming the Bourse, only to be thwarted by police tear gas.

Five days later, as the street violence peaked, de Gaulle fled briefly to Germany and Prime Minister Pompidou sent tanks to the edges of Paris. But the crisis didn't materialise. Pompidou conceded pay rises of between seven and ten per cent and increased the minimum wage; the country went back to work. A general election was called for 23 June, by which time the right had gathered enough momentum to gain a safe majority.

Sarkozy's Suburban Nightmare

Anger and resentment turn to violence in the banlieue riots.

In November 2005, violent suburban riots in Paris sent shockwaves throughout the country. The rundown housing estates around the capital became the scene for explosive confrontations with the police, as warehouses, restaurants and cars were set ablaze. Before long, the violence had spread to other French cities, making these riots the country's most serious since 1968. President Chirac's government responded by calling a state of emergency, imposing curfews and banning public meetings at the weekends. Nevertheless, it was almost three weeks before the worst of the rioting was over.

The trigger for this unprecedented outbreak of violence was the accidental death on 27 October of two North African teenagers, in the north-east Paris suburb of Clichy-sous-Bois. According to locals, Bouna Traore, 15, and Zyed Benna, 17, panicked when they saw other black youths being chased by the police, and sought shelter in an electrical sub-station. As they entered the site, they were electrocuted. To make matters worse, the incident came just two days after then Interior Minister Nicolas Sarkozy had made some inflammatory remarks about the need to rid the banlieue of the 'racaille', a perjorative term that can be translated as 'rabble'.

If this chain of events formed an explosive catalyst for the riots, the root cause went much deeper. In the post-World War II revival period, an influx of immigrants led the government to develop high-rise housing estates (called *cités*) in the vicinity of suburban factories. When the economy plummeted in the 1970s, the populations of these estates found themselves struggling with factory closures and unemployment. While the wealthier moved to more desirable areas, the remaining residents – mainly North African families – were effectively left stranded in a suburban desert.

Over the three weeks of violence, nearly 3,000 arrests were made, more than 10,000 cars were set ablaze, and 300 buildings were firebombed. Initially, the government seemed to take a more liberal view of its immigrant population, voting in a number of equal opportunities measures that aimed to promote youth employment in high-risk urban areas and combat discrimination. Yet just two months later, Sarkozy's uncompromising immigration bill reintroduced a hard line, laying down much stricter terms for immigrants seeking residency.

IN CONTEXT

MITTERRAND

Following the presidencies of right-wingers Georges Pompidou and Valéry Giscard d'Estaing, the Socialist François Mitterrand took up the task in 1981. His grands projets had a big impact on Paris. Mitterrand commissioned IM Pei's Louvre pyramid, the Grande Arche de la Défense, the Opéra Bastille and the more recent Bibliothèque Nationale de France – François Mitterrand.

CHIRAC, BUSH AND IRAQ

France may still boast the world's fourth-largest economy, the nuclear deterrent and a permanent seat on the UN Security Council, but her influence on the world stage had been waning for years until President Chirac, flushed from re-election and well aware he was on to a PR winner, stood up in early 2003 to oppose the US-led invasion of Iraq. France's official disapproval of George Bush culminated in the threat to use her Security Council veto against any resolution authorising the use of force without UN say-so. Chirac's stance brought him popularity at home and abroad. But his domestic popularity couldn't last. His prime minister, Jean-Pierre Raffarin, and the centre-right government began attacking some of France's more prized national institutions with a programme of reforms, starting with the state pension system. This led to some of the largest nationwide protests France has seen since 1995, with striking métro staff, hospital workers, postmen, teachers and rubbish collectors creating havoc and bringing the capital to a virtual standstill. Planned restrictions on the uniquely Gallic, exceptionally generous system of unemployment benefit for out-of-work performing-arts professionals led to a further round of protests, as well as the cancellation of France's equivalents of Edinburgh and Glyndebourne, the Avignon and Aix summer cultural festivals. Then came the official mismanagement and aloofness that characterised the two-week heatwave of August 2003, during which as many as 14,000 elderly people died. The national mood stayed gloomy through 2004, and the clouds darkened further in 2005, as Paris surprisingly lost its Olympic bid.

Then, in October 2005, the accidental deaths of two North African teenagers in Clichy-sous-Bois sparked riots that spread through the *banlieue* like wildfire (*see p31* **Sarkozy's Suburban Nightmare**). Eventually Chirac declared an official state of emergency that was only lifted in January 2006. Then, in March, trouble flared once again, this time provoked by an unpopular new employment bill, the CPE – which, after three months of strikes and street protests, the government was forced to withdraw.

PRESIDENT BLING-BLING

Despite his provocations during the riots, Sarkozy was elected president in May 2007, beating the Socialist candidate Segolène Royal. Aside from a few desultory Molotov cocktails hurled in place de la Bastille on the night of the election, the response on the Left to Sarkozy's victory was characterised more by bemusement than anger. For a few months, bemusement held sway in the population at large, especially when Sarkozy embarked on a very public whirlwind romance with *chanteuse* and ex-model Carla Bruni. But voters soon sickened of the unprecedented (and unpresidential) spectacle, and of Sarkozy's parallel courtship of several tycoons; by the time 'Président Bling-Bling' married Bruni in February 2008, his popularity had plummeted to less than 35 per cent; a televised skirmish at the Salon de l'Agriculture a few weeks later, in which he hissed 'pauvre con' ('stupid twat') at a man in the crowd, was a further dent in his image.

Sarko's ratings picked up slightly during 2008, but he remains a powerfully divisive head of state. Not least contentious is his ambition to shake up the relations between Paris and its suburbs, and to launch new building projects on a scale not seen since the Second Empire. If his Grand Paris scheme goes ahead, the city's administrative footprint will balloon to an area similar to Greater London; large swathes of the urban fabric, especially near the Périphérique, could be entirely redesigned; and a new canal could be built to strengthen links between Paris and the north of the country. For France's capital, these are indeed interesting times.

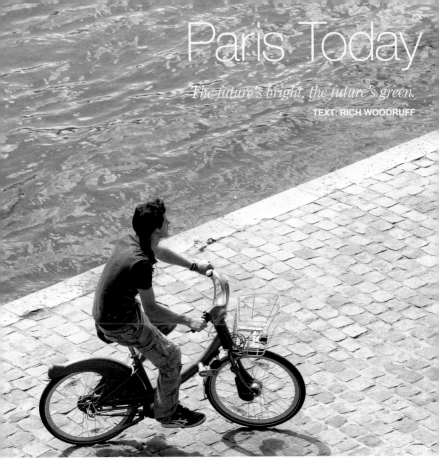

Paris Today

The future's bright, the future's green.

TEXT: RICH WOODRUFF

Rich Woodruff is a Paris-based journalist and video producer, specialising in cinema, culture, sport and travel.

When Socialist incumbent Bertrand Delanoë was re-elected as mayor of Paris in March 2008, it was as much a vote of confidence in his fun-loving, progressive policies as it was a show of discontent towards right-wing President Sarkozy. Since coming to power in 2001, Delanoë has reshaped Paris with green projects, cultural innovations and forward-thinking strategies. Sarkozy, meanwhile, has made more headlines for his social life and political gaffes.

Although Sarkozy's romance with Carla Bruni intrigued the international media, it exasperated Parisians. The consensus was that the President would be better off investing his energy in the faltering economy. By February 2008, Sarkozy's popularity had reached a record low, with 58 per cent of people polled saying they had an 'unfavourable opinion' of the President. Compare that to the 57.7 per cent of votes won by Delanoë, the city's first openly gay mayor, in the second round of the 2008 mayoral elections.

Discover the Show of the Moulin Rouge !

1000 costumes of feathers, rhinestones and sequins,
sumptuous settings, original music, the giant Aquarium,
the world famous French Cancan and … the 60 Doriss Girls !

Dinner & Show at 7pm from €150 • Show at 9pm : €102, 11pm : €92

Montmartre - 82, boulevard de Clichy - 75018 Paris
Reservations : 33 (0)1 53 09 82 82 • www.moulin-rouge.com

'The trend to move out of the city centre represents a significant turning point in the historic Paris/banlieue divide.'

A CITY ON THE RISE

Although Delanoë's eco-friendly policy-making has sometimes met with controversy, Paris has undoubtedly become a more liveable city since his arrival, thanks to improved public transport (including the highly successful Vélib bike hire initiative), anti-car measures and more green spaces (*see p37* **Bertrand's Big Clean-up**). The mayor has also invested in modern technology: public parks, libraries and a smattering of big-name tourist locations are now equipped with free Wi-Fi, and a project has been launched to equip 80 per cent of Paris buildings with an ultra-high-speed internet connection by 2010.

Emboldened by these successes, Delanoë has set in motion a controversial plan to erect high-rise buildings in Paris. For years, the subject has been taboo, thanks to a 1977 by-law that fixes maximum heights for Paris buildings at 37 metres (120 feet) or ten storeys. Despite public and political opposition (including dissent from his close partners, the Green party), Delanoë has held firm with the plan, determined to revitalise a city so often accused of '*muséification*'. The mayor believes tower blocks represent the most efficient way to resolve the city's accommodation shortage and to deliver on his promise of creating more social housing. At present, six sites have been identified on the city limits just inside the Périphérique (ring road) to house 15-storey tower blocks, as well as 200-metre (650-foot) skyscrapers that would provide office space, shops and childcare centres.

IN CONTEXT

Paris Tourism Day

Enforcing the entente cordiale.

Paris may be the most visited city in the world, but at times relations between tourists and locals can be fraught: grumpy waiters, rude cab drivers and unhelpful shop assistants are as much a part of the city's reputation as its pavement cafés. In fact, so strong is the foreign perception of unfriendliness that the Japanese report an average of 12 cases of 'Paris Syndrome' a year, a state of shock brought on when the city fails to meet expectations.

But now Mayor Delanoë has called for an end to hostilities with the establishment of the Journée du Tourisme à Paris (Paris Tourism Day). The plan? To encourage Parisians to adopt a more sympathetic view of tourists, and remember that an estimated

two million jobs in the city are linked to tourism. Launched in 2007, the project is set to become a regular fixture.

Improving relations started with the Charter for the Parisian and Visitor, an attempt to show each party how to avoid misunderstandings. Commitments included 'I will take time to give information to visitors' and 'I will take advantage of my stay to try French products'. This lesson in etiquette was administered by 'welcome ambassadors' who had set up outposts in and around Paris's major monuments.

However, considering that an estimated 97 per cent of visitors intend to return to Paris, it makes you wonder how bad the entente cordiale was in the first place.

BUILDING ON SUCCESS

The Périphérique project comes on the heels of a number of major urban developments: notably in the up-and-coming area around the Bibliothèque Nationale de France, now home to a major university campus, multiple international business headquarters and a floating open-air swimming pool on the Seine. The area will be further boosted by the opening of the ultra-ambitious Cité de la Mode et du Design, which promises to bring trendy designers and nocturnal thrill-seekers to a previously lifeless Seine-side area. The complex will house the Institut Français de la Mode (French Fashion Institute), along with shops, restaurants and a riverside walkway. Other major projects in the pipeline include a facelift for the much-maligned Les Halles gardens and subterranean shopping centre.

Another area destined for regeneration is La Défense, the business district to the west of Paris. Announced in 2008, Jean Nouvel's 300-metre (980-foot) Signal tower is set to form the centrepiece of a development plan dubbed La Défense 2015. As well as providing for the renovation of the existing site and the creation of more business space, the project aims to attract inhabitants by including 1,400 flats in the showcase towers scheduled for construction. Not known for its liveliness outside working hours, the area will be rendered more liveable by new green spaces and improved transport links. Like Delanoë's high-rise towers, the project is partly a response to an accommodation crisis in the capital that has been exacerbated by escalating property prices. Although the rate of increase has slowed down, the five-year price rise for flats in Paris still stood at 74.4 per cent in the first quarter of 2008. In their search for affordable property, families have turned to the suburbs.

This trend for Parisians to move out of the centre represents a significant turning point in the historic Paris/*banlieue* divide. Traditionally, Parisians regard the suburbs with a certain disdain, and the cultural, geographical and administrative divisions between Paris and its suburbs are only exaggerated by the physical barrier formed by the Périphérique.

Bertrand Delanoë.

Bertrand's Big Clean-up

Delanoë's drive for a pollution-free Paris.

Since his election as mayor in 2001, Bertrand Delanoë has worked hard to make Paris a more eco-friendly city. Working with deputy mayor Denis Baupin of the Green party, the charismatic Delanoë has created multiple bus lanes, laid down an extra 200 kilometres (125 miles) of cycle tracks, slashed residential parking fees by 80 per cent, reduced speed limits and widened pavements. Between 2002 and 2007, private car use in the city dropped by 15 per cent, and traffic-related pollution fell by 32 per cent. Even dog mess, that age-old Paris pollutant, has been targeted, with owners now eligible for a €183 fine if they don't clean up after their pet.

The main thrust of the mayor's green-focused initiatives has been transport, with the tram making a triumphant return in 2006. Bordered by lawns and trees, the initial eight-kilometre (five-mile) stretch runs along the southern edge of the city, and work has already begun on an extension as far as Porte de la Chapelle for 2012. In 2008, Delanoë turned to the water. Voguéo currently offers a six-station commuter boat service along a south-eastern stretch of the Seine. The indisputable transport success story, however, has been the Vélib bike-hire system, launched in July 2007. After just one year, the Vélib fleet had increased to some 16,000 bikes that could be picked up from and returned to any of 1,200 stations around the city. With 110,000 journeys registered daily, Vélib has been a major factor in bolstering city bike use by 94 per cent since 2001. Plans are underway to add more bikes and create more stations – including some 300 in the suburbs.

Spurred on by this success, Delanoë has launched another initiative based on the Vélib model. Dubbed Autolib, the latest project aims to introduce 4,000 self-service hybrid cars spread out over 700 stations, many of which will be underground and/or in the inner suburbs. Expected to launch at the end of 2009, Autolib could be included in a single ticket that would give access to public transport, taxis, Vélib and car parks.

By offering such attractive transport options, Delanoë hopes to encourage Parisians to abandon their cars. Just in case they need an extra push, however, the mayor has put forward a number of more aggressive proposals, including closing the central four arrondissements to all non-residential private vehicles and reserving one lane of the Périphérique exclusively for taxis and buses. Both plans are awaiting approval.

Transport has not been the only focus for a greener city. When he was re-elected in 2008, Delanoë promised to create an additional 75 acres of green space. Other eco-friendly initiatives include a project to reduce greenhouse gas emissions by 75 per cent for 2050. To prove its commitment to alternative energy, the Mairie has even launched a new generation of public bench. Equipped with a table, the bench also has a solar-charged power point, perfect for a spot of al fresco surfing. For Parisians, it seems, there is now no excuse not to go green.

IN CONTEXT

'The loss of the 2012 Olympics to London still has a bitter taste for Parisians.'

Closing this gap is one of the avowed objectives of both mayor Delanoë and President Sarkozy. Public transport development has been based on this objective, with several métro lines being expanded outside the city limits, and a new circular line planned to link together the various suburbs. Accessibility to the neighbouring *banlieue* has also been improved by an initiative that consists of covering sections of the frequently congested Périphérique with landscaped gardens and sports fields. Furthermore, Parisians are starting to take an interest in cultural life outside their 20 arrondissements, as exemplified by the cutting-edge MAC/VAL art gallery and restaurant in the suburb of Vitry-sur-Seine.

THE CULTURE CLUB

Central Paris, meanwhile, has recently enjoyed a number of cultural developments and innovations, and several new sites have also given a significant lift to the city's cultural scene. In 2008, the Maison des Métallos, a former trade union centre, reopened as a cutting-edge showcase for up-and-coming artists, and an old funeral parlour was transformed into 104, a centre for contemporary art. The Théâtre de la Gaîté Lyrique, meanwhile, is set to reopen as a hub for digital arts and contemporary music in 2010.

Construction has also begun on the Cité Européenne du Cinéma in the northern suburb of St-Denis. Due for completion in 2010, the complex will house nine studios sand promises to give the national film industry a massive boost. Even so, the French film industry remains in extremely good health. In 2008, the home-grown comedy *Bienvenue Chez les Ch'tis*, about a southerner who is relocated to the north of France, became the country's second biggest grossing film of all time, and actress Marion Cotillard took home an Oscar for her interpretation of iconic *chanteuse* Edith Piaf in *La Vie en Rose*.

Perhaps the most unexpected cultural export, though, took the form of a dance. Involving flailing arms and vigorous body movements somewhere between hip hop and techno, Tecktonik came out of Paris's clubs and went mainstream. Thanks to videos on the internet and exposure at the city's annual Techno Parade, the craze took to the streets and spread across France and beyond. The mohawk-mullet cut became the movement's trademark hairstyle and the name Tecktonik was even registered as an official brand.

If Paris's cultural scene is booming, the sporting scene has been less dynamic. A plan to create a basketball superteam by merging the area's two biggest clubs got off to an abysmal start when the newly born Paris-Levallois Basket was relegated to the national second division in its first season. The city's football team, Paris St-Germain, narrowly escaped the same fate, but its poor performances are not the only source of concern. In a match against Lens in 2008, fans unfurled a large racist banner directed at their northern opponents. The incident provoked an outcry in the media, and resulted in the dissolution of the Boulogne Boys, the supporters' club with a reputation for right-wing activities.

The passage of the Olympic flame through Paris, prior to the 2008 Games in Beijing, also proved far from successful, as pro-Tibet demonstrators held up the parade, forcing flame carriers to jump aboard a bus on several occasions. The Olympics, it seems, do not sit well with Paris. The loss of the 2012 Games to London still has a bitter taste for many Parisians, and it remains the most glaring failure of Delanoë's time in office.

Still, the Olympics setback represents a mere blip in the otherwise steadily ascending career of the city's mayor. Many believe Delanoë will follow a now well-established career strategy and use his popularity as Paris mayor as a springboard to make a challenge at the presidency in 2012 – where he could come up against Nicolas Sarkozy. If the polls in 2008 are anything to go by, that would give Delanoë a good chance of becoming France's first left-wing President since François Mitterrand stepped down in 1995.

IN CONTEXT

Architecture

*From Gothic gargoyles
to grands projets.*

TEXT: NATASHA EDWARDS

*Natasha
Edwards
writes on French
contemporary art,
design, food and
travel for* Condé
Nast Traveller,
the Daily
Telegraph, Elle
Decoration *and
the* Independent.

Few cities boast such instantly recognisable icons as Paris,
legacy of building policies that have always reflected
the ambitions of its rulers. Long before Haussmann's
boulevards, François I began turning the Louvre fortress
into a modern palace, Henri IV created the first planned
squares, while Louis XIV's minister Colbert boosted the
royal image with triumphal arches. When Paris expanded,
it did so in organised leaps, absorbing rural villages lying
outside the city walls in roughly concentric circles. Yet
despite its apparent uniformity, the city's architecture
has often been marked by radical experimentation.

ROMANESQUE TO GOTHIC

Medieval Paris congregated on the Ile de la Cité and the Latin Quarter, following the broad lines of the Roman city. Although the clusters of medieval housing built around Notre-Dame were razed by Haussmann in the 19th century, much of the medieval street plan remains. A few churches survive as examples of simple Romanesque architecture, including **St-Germain-des-Prés** (*see p126*) and the well-preserved interior of **St-Julien-le-Pauvre** (*see p115*) – a pilgrim pit stop in the late 12th century.

The Gothic trademarks of pointed arches, ogival vaulting and flying buttresses – allowing the multiplication of windows and spanning of large areas by stone – had their beginning at the **Basilique St-Denis** (*see p148*), started in the 12th century and completed in the 13th by master mason Pierre de Montreuil. **Notre-Dame** (*see p57*) continued the style with its rich, delicate rose windows and fine, tendon-like buttresses (not to mention its characterful menagerie of gargoyles). Montreuil's **Sainte-Chapelle** (*see p57*), built 1246-48, represents the peak of Gothic design, reducing stonework to a minimum between the expanses of stained glass. The Flamboyant Gothic style that followed unleashed an orgy of decoration. **Eglise St-Séverin** (*see p115*), with its twisting spiral column, is particularly original. Civil architecture can be seen in the impressive vaulted halls of the **Conciergerie** (*see p57*). The **Tour Jean Sans Peur** (*see p81*) is a rare fragment of an early 15th-century mansion, and the city's two finest medieval mansions are the Hôtel de Cluny (now the **Musée National du Moyen-Age**; *see p116*) and the **Hôtel de Sens** (*see p103*) in the Marais. Although still distinctly Gothic in form and decoration, they set the pattern for Paris's later *hôtels particuliers*, with the main building set back behind a courtyard.

RENAISSANCE

Italianate town planning, with its ordered avenues, neat squares and public spaces, came late to Paris. It was instigated by François I towards the end of his reign, when he realised the beneficial effects that a well-organised urban landscape could have on trade. He installed Leonardo da Vinci at Amboise, brought over Primaticcio and Rosso to work on his palace at **Fontainebleau** (*see p353*), and began transforming the **Louvre** (*see p59*) with the Cour Carrée. The **Eglise St-Etienne du Mont** (*see p118*) and the massive **Eglise St-Eustache** (*see p81*) display a transitional style, adding the classical motifs of the Renaissance over an essentially Gothic structure. Aristocratic quarters were established in St-Germain-des-Prés and the newly developing Marais; the latter has the **Hôtel Carnavalet** (*see p101*) and the **Hôtel de Lamoignon** (24 rue Pavée, 4th), the finest examples of Renaissance mansions to be found in Paris, reflecting a new, comfortable lifestyle with their large windows and grand first-floor salons.

THE ANCIEN REGIME

Henri IV took control of Paris after a long siege. He found a city knee-deep in bodies and broken buildings, and promptly organised public building projects. Timber was banned, to be replaced by brick and stone, and bridges over the Seine were cleared of the houses and shops that dangerously cluttered their paths. The Pont Neuf's construction was sped up with a new levy on wine imports. **Place Dauphine** (1st) and **place des Vosges** (*see p102*) reflected Henri's taste for Italian classicism, the latter irresistibly elegant, with its symmetrical design, red brick vaulted galleries and pitched roofs.

The nouveaux riches flocked to build mansions in the Marais and on the Ile St-Louis. Those in the Marais follow a symmetrical U-shaped plan, with a secluded courtyard; look through the archways to the *cour d'honneur* of the **Hôtel de Sully** (*see p100*) or the **Hôtel Salé** (*see p101*), where façades are richly decorated, in contrast with the face they present to the street.

The **Palais du Luxembourg** (*see p129*), built in the 1620s by Salomon de Brosse in Italianate style for Marie de Médicis, combines classic French château design with elements of the Pitti Palace in Marie's native Florence. The 17th century was a high point in French power, and the monarchy desired buildings that reflected its grandeur.

IN CONTEXT

'Napoleon confiscated land from the aristocracy and the Church for development, and went on a massive building spree.'

Great architects emerged under court patronage: de Brosse, François Mansart, Libéral Bruand and landscape architect André le Nôtre, who redesigned the Tuileries gardens and planned the Champs-Elysées. The **Eglise du Val-de-Grâce** (see p119), designed by Mansart and finished by Jacques Lemercier, is a grand baroque statement, with its painted dome and barley sugar columns. Hospitals got the royal treatment: Libéral Bruand created the grand classical façades and polygonal chapel at the **Salpêtrière** (13th) and **Les Invalides** (see p141), with its grandiose galleried courtyard and domed double church. But even at **Versailles** (see p355), however, ultimate architectural symbol of royal absolutism in the mammoth scale and glittery reflections of the Hall of Mirrors, baroque never reached the decorative excesses of Italy or Austria, as French architects followed Cartesian principles of harmony and balance, with an emphasis on space and volume.

Under Colbert, Louis XIV's chief minister, the creation of stage sets to magnify the Sun King's power proceeded apace. The Louvre grew as Claude Perrault created the sweeping west wing, while Hardouin-Mansart's sweeping, circular **place des Victoires** (see p74) and **place Vendôme** (see p72), an elegant octagon, were both designed to show off equestrian statues of the king.

ROCOCO AND NEO-CLASSICISM

In the early 18th century, the Faubourg St-Germain overtook the Marais as the city's most fashionable quarter, as the nobility built smart mansions with tall windows and elegant wrought ironwork, such as the **Hôtel Matignon**, today home of the French prime minister. The finest example of frivolous rococo decoration is the **Hôtel de Soubise** (60 rue des Francs-Bourgeois, 3rd), with panelling, plasterwork and paintings by celebrated decorators of the day, including Boucher, Restout and van Loo. In furniture-makers' **Faubourg St-Antoine**, a different sort of accommodation grew up, with workshops around long, narrow courtyards and lodgings up above.

Under Louis XV, a number of sumptuous buildings were commissioned, among them **La Monnaie** (now the **Musée de la Monnaie de Paris**; see p127), the **Panthéon** (see p119), the **Ecole de Droit** (place du Panthéon, 5th) and many new theatres. Soufflot's Panthéon, like Jacques-Ange Gabriel's neo-classical **place de la Concorde** (see p72), was inspired by the majestic monuments of ancient Rome, as were the toll gates put up in 1785 by Nicolas Ledoux, famed for his almost minimalist geometrical style (still visible at Nation, Denfert-Rochereau and Parc Monceau) for the Mur des Fermiers Généraux.

THE 19TH CENTURY

The street fighting of the revolution left Paris in a dilapidated state. Napoleon redressed this situation with a suitably grandiose vision to make Paris the most beautiful city in the world. He confiscated land from the aristocracy and the Church for development, and ordered a massive building spree. As well as five new bridges and 56 ornamental fountains, he built the **Eglise de la Madeleine** (see p74), a mock Greek temple in honour of the Grande Armée, plus a rash of self-aggrandising statues and arches, most notably the **Arc de Triomphe** (see p83) and the shamelessly gaudy **Arc du Carrousel** (see p67).

Bonaparte's nephew Louis Napoleon, envious of London's energy and the glory of ancient Rome, decided that Paris once again needed a makeover. In 1853 he appointed Baron Haussmann as the *préfet* of Paris. A fearsome administrator rather than a

Build It with Feeling

Size isn't everything for Paris's 21st-century architects.

The most exciting projects going up in the capital just now are more organic than phallic. Inspired by nature and flowing forms, these low-rise buildings make their mark with irregular silhouettes and their use of glass and colour.

Frank Gehry's **Fondation Louis Vuitton** contemporary art centre is set to alight on the edge of the Bois de Boulogne like a glass cloud. Cascading panes of glass will encase a series of white cubes and an interior garden, like a giant greenhouse for art, which plays with volumes, spirals and transparency.

Along the Seine, the striking bright green **Cité de la Mode et du Design** (*pictured*), designed by Jakob + MacFarlane, is due to open in early 2009, containing restaurants and cafés, a concert and club venue, shops, the Institut Français de la Mode fashion and management school, and a riverside promenade. The most radical element is what the Franco-New Zealand duo have called their 'plug over' system – a framework of green steel tubing and screenprinted glass that clips on to the 1907 reinforced concrete warehouse complex beneath to create a new fluid public space. The colour was chosen 'to echo the turgid green of the Seine,' says Jakob, who is refreshingly down-to-earth when she talks about the building, which has been variously described as a wave and a crocodile.

Jean Nouvel's design for the **Philharmonie** concert hall at La Villette is due to open in 2012. Unlike the totally rectilinear vertical boxes of his forthcoming Tour Signal at La Défense, the Philharmonie appears to have a succession of colliding plates, or perhaps scrumpled record sleeves, an impression also felt inside the auditorium, with its flowing, floating balconies.

In the 16th arrondissement, the prize-winning design for the **Stade Jean Bouin** rugby stadium, by Bandol-based architect Rudy Ricciotti, uses a lacy web of reinforced concrete. The stadium is a squat, asymmetrical structure that suggests movement and the body. As Ricciotti puts it: 'The form is not inspired but revealed, just as Man Ray's famous photograph of a nude body enveloped in a transparent drape reveals a true eroticism.'

A sexy rugby stadium? Proof, if it were needed, that big is not always beautiful in the world of urban planning.

professional architect, Haussmann faced problems of sanitation, sewage and traffic-clogged streets. Bestowing upon himself the honorific 'demolition artist' (others preferred the less flattering 'Alsatian Attila'), he set about bringing order to the city's chaotic street plan, cutting broad, long boulevards through the urban fabric. An estimated 27,000 houses were razed in the process, including many of the patrician Left Bank *grands hôtels*, which made way for the boulevard St-Germain. The Haussmannian apartment block has endured, setting a format that endured well into the 20th century, its utilitarian lines set off by rows of wrought-iron balconies.

Haussmann also introduced English-style public parks, such as the **Buttes-Chaumont** (*see p113*), along with prisons, hospitals, train stations and sewers. Amid the upheaval, one building epitomised the grand style of the Second Empire: Charles Garnier's sumptuous **Palais Garnier** opera house (1862-75; *see p317*).

Haussmann could also be an innovator, persuading Baltard to build the new market pavilions at Les Halles in lacy iron rather than stone. Iron frames had already been used by Henri Labrouste in his lovely reading room at the **Bibliothèque Ste-Geneviève** (1844-50; 10 place du Panthéon, 5th), and they became increasingly common: stations such as Hittorf's **Gare du Nord** (1861-65; *see p109*) and Laloux's Gare d'Orsay (now **Musée d'Orsay**; *see p143*) are simply shells around an iron frame, producing spacious, light-filled interiors. The most daring iron construction of them all was, of course, the **Eiffel Tower** (*see p145*). When it was built in 1889, it was the tallest structure in the world. Stylistically, eclecticism ruled, from the neo-Renaissance **Hôtel de Ville** (*see p99*) to neo-Byzantine **Sacré-Coeur** (*see p93*).

EARLY 20TH CENTURY

An outburst of extravagance for the 1900 Exposition Universelle marked the beginning of the 20th century, notably the **Grand Palais**, with its massive glass and steel nave. The **Train Bleu** brasserie in the Gare de Lyon (*see p203*) is an ornate example of the heavy, florid Beaux Arts style of this period. Art nouveau at its most fluid and flamboyant can be seen in Hector Guimard's instantly recognisable métro stations and his 1901 **Castel Béranger**.

All of this was a long way from the roughly contemporary work of Henri Sauvage, who created a large social housing project in **rue des Amiraux** (18th), tiled artists' studio flats in **rue La Fontaine** (16th), and the more overtly art deco 1920s extension of **La Samaritaine** (19 rue de la Monnaie, 1st). Funded by philanthropists, social housing began to be put up across the city, such as the Rothschilds' estate in **rue de Prague** in the 12th arrondissement.

THE MODERN MOVEMENT

After World War I, two names stand out by virtue of their innovation and influence: Auguste Perret, architect of the **Théâtre des Champs-Elysées** (*see p318*), and Le Corbusier. A third architect, Robert Mallet-Stevens, is unrivalled for his elegance. Paris is one of the best cities in the world for Modern Movement houses and studios (many in the 16th and Montparnasse, and in western suburbs like Boulogne and Garches), but also in a more diluted form for town halls and schools built in the socially minded 1930s.

Perret stayed largely within a classical aesthetic, but was a pioneer in the use of reinforced concrete. Le Corbusier tried out his ideas in private houses, such as the **Villa Savoy** in Poissy and **Villa La Roche** in the 16th (now **Fondation le Corbusier**). His **Pavillon Suisse** at the **Cité Universitaire** (*see p138*) and **Armée du Salut** hostel (12 rue Cantagrel) in the 13th can be seen as an intermediary point between these villas and his Villes Radieuses mass housing schemes, which became so influential and so debased in projects across Europe after 1945.

Meanwhile, the new love of chrome, steel and glass found its way into art deco cafés and brasseries such as **La Coupole** (*see p214*). As in the 19th century, world fairs provided an excuse for grandiose state architecture, with a return to monumental classicism in the Palais de la Porte Dorée, built for the 1931 Exposition Coloniale, and the Palais de Chaillot and Palais de Tokyo, built for the 1937 Exposition Internationale.

'After the construction of the controversial Tour Montparnasse, Giscard d'Estaing prevented the Paris horizon from rising any higher.'

POST-WAR PARIS

The aerodynamic aesthetic of the post-war era yielded the 1958 **UNESCO building** (see p145) by Bernard Zehrfuss, Pier Luigi Nervi and Marcel Breuer, and the beginnings of **La Défense** (see p147) with the same architects' **CNIT** building, then the largest concrete span in the world. In the 1960s and '70s, tower blocks sprouted in the suburbs and new towns to replace the dismal *bidonvilles* (shanty towns) that had served as immigrant housing. Inside the city, redevelopment was limited, although new regulations allowed taller buildings, notably in the 13th and 19th; and the raised *dalle* style of architecture of Les Olympiades (13th) and Centre Beaugrenelle (15th) did away with the conventional idea of a street plan.

President Georges Pompidou embraced modernity too, disastrously in the case of the expressways along the Seine, and more benignly in the form of Piano and Rogers' high-tech **Centre Pompidou** (see p98), which opened in 1977 and was the first of the daring prestige projects that subsequently became a trademark of modern Paris. But after the construction of the controversial **Tour Montparnasse** (see p137), Pompidou's successor, Valéry Giscard d'Estaing, prevented the Paris horizon from rising any higher.

THE 1980S AND '90S

President François Mitterrand's *grands projets* dominated the 1980s and '90s, with Jean Nouvel's **Institut du Monde Arabe** (see p121), IM Pei's **Louvre Pyramid** (see p59) and Johan Otto Von Sprecklesen's **Grande Arche de la Défense** (see p148), as well as Carlos Ott's more dubious **Opéra Bastille** (see p317), Dominique Perrault's **Bibliothèque Nationale** (see p124) and Chemetov & Huidobro's **Bercy** finance ministry. Stylistically, the buzzword was 'transparency', from Pei's pyramid to Nouvel's **Fondation Cartier** (see p134), with its clever slices of glass. Christian de Portzamparc pursued a more eclectic postmodern style with his **Cité de la Musique** (see p112), a series of geometrical blocks set around a colourful internal street. The city also invested in public housing; of note are the developments around **Parc de la Villette** (see p112) and **Parc André-Citroën** (see p146), Piano's red tile and glass ensemble in **rue de Meaux** (19th).

THE 21ST CENTURY

The age of the *grands projets* is over, although Jacques Chirac managed to squeeze one last legacy project into his reign with the completion of Nouvel's **Musée du Quai Branly** (see p146) in 2006, a highly colourful baroque structure. Younger architects are making their mark too: Manuelle Gautrand's **Citroën** showcase on the Champs-Elysées, for instance, cleverly plays on the chevrons logo in a fine example of architecture as branding.

The vast **Seine Rive Gauche** (see p124) development in the 13th arrondissement has at last taken shape, with a mixture of new-build and rehabilitated industrial buildings around the Bibliothèque Nationale for office, residential and university use, designed by an army of French and international architects, along with Jakob and MacFarlane's **Cité de la Mode et du Design** (see p124) and Dietmer Feichtinger's exciting Simone de Beauvoir footbridge.

Other areas are also coming up for a makeover: the 1970s **Forum des Halles** (see p81) is set for a new green canopy and re-landscaped gardens; skyscrapers by Morphosis, Valode et Pistre, Nouvel, Arquitectonica et al soar at La Défense; a spaceship-like hotel and commercial complex by Rotterdam architects Neutelings Riedijk is due to land at Porte de la Villette; and in the 20th, the new Philippe Starck-designed **Mama Shelter** hotel (see p173) forms part of a housing and library complex designed by Roland Castro.

Crossing the Divide

Meet France's new black-blanc-beur.

TEXT: NATASHA EDWARDS

In recent years, it's become increasingly common for the international press to home in on Paris's race problems, especially the sporadic episodes of rioting and car burning in the *banlieue*. But this is only part of the picture: it overlooks the enormous cultural shift that has occurred over the past decade, during which a new, dynamic and multi-ethnic generation has made its mark on the city's politics, business and creative industries.

The worlds of contemporary art, cinema, literature, theatre, dance and comedy are all seeing the rise of a new elite of North African descent – whether born in or outside France – that has been dubbed the '*beurgeoisie*' by some (*beur* being slang for Arab immigrants). As one blogger on website beurgeoisie.fr puts it: 'Today one can be *beur* and succeed.'

'The common denominator of these black-blanc-beur comedians is that they are young, funny and wickedly un-PC.'

SCREEN STARS

In France's dynamic film industry (the largest in Europe), a growing band of actors and directors of African descent are providing a welcome injection of new blood. Although most of them grew up in the *banlieue*, their films encompass many genres, from mass-market comedies to arthouse movies in the French tradition of *cinéma d'auteur*; exponents of the latter include writer-directors such as Rachid Bouchareb and Abdellatif Kechiche, who directed *La Graine et le Mulet* (*Couscous*; *see p48* **A Feast for the Senses**). Although these films often touch on topics of identity, nationality and yearnings for the homeland, most of the images portrayed are far removed from the stereotypes of the *banlieue*.

Emblematic of the new generation of film stars and France's willingness, finally, to acknowledge the less savoury aspects of its colonial past is Rachid Bouchareb's 2006 film *Indigènes* (*Days of Glory*). It focuses on the plight of the 110,000 North African soldiers who enlisted in the French army of liberation in 1943. 'I've always been caught up in the history of immigration,' says Bouchareb. 'It's my family's past. One of my uncles fought in the Indochina war, we lived through the Algerian war, and I even have a grandfather who fought in World War I.' Telling the stories of four men as they march across Italy and France towards their last stand in defence of an Alsatian village, the film earned a joint Best Male Actor award at Cannes for its five leads: Roschdy Zem, Jamel Debbouze, Samy Naceri and Sami Bouajila as the four volunteers, and Bernard Blancan as their white sergeant.

For Samy Naceri, star of the Luc Besson-produced *Taxi* series, the award marked a departure from his image as the bad boy of French cinema, as renowned for his off-screen antics as for his acting. Roschdy Zem also came from humble beginnings, selling clothes on a stall at the Puces de Clignancourt before being spotted by veteran arthouse director André Téchiné. He has since appeared alongside the likes of Juliette Binoche and Daniel Auteuil in Téchiné's *J'Embrasse Pas*, *Ma Saison Préferée* and *Alice et Martin*, and has worked with film-makers Laeticia Masson and Xavier Beauvois. Recently, he made his directorial debut with *Mauvaise Foi*, the tale of a mixed marriage between a Jewish girl and Muslim man, and starred with Fabrice Luchini in Anne Fontaine's romantic comedy *La Fille de Monaco*.

Fans of *Amélie* will recognise Jamel Debbouze as the Montmartre grocer's assistant she befriends. He has continued to make waves in other screen appearances, which range from *Indigènes* to the recent *Astérix aux Jeux Olympiques* (the most expensive film ever made in France) and even a role in Spike Lee's *She Hate Me*. Prior to his career in film, he made his name on the comedy circuit, where his mastery of streetwise *tchatche* was revealed in off-the-cuff sketches and improvisation on cult Canal+ chat show *Nulle Part Ailleurs*.

TAKING THE STAGE

Debbouze has recently returned to his comedy roots, reinvigorating France's stand-up scene by hosting the Jamel Comedy Club as a springboard for new talent. The principle is simple: a mic, an empty stage and seven minutes to make an impression. In contrast to the vulgarity and slapstick that pervaded the previous generation of French comedy, these black-blanc-beur comedians are young, funny and wickedly un-PC. After the show toured France in 2006 and 2007, Debbouze worked his magic in the capital, opening the new 120-seat Comedy Club (*see p283*) in a former cinema on boulevard Bonne-Nouvelle in April 2008. Other breakthrough roles came for Dany Boon and Ked Merad, who both emerged from the *café-théâtre* circuit to star in Boon's *Bienvenue chez les Ch'tis*, a brilliantly funny romp through northern French clichés, and France's most successful film ever.

IN CONTEXT

A Feast for the Senses

Couscous conquers all at the Césars.

While UK and US audiences went wild for Marion Cotillard's rose-tinted Piaf in *La Vie en Rose*, a much lower budget art-house flick, set in the small Languedoc fishing port of Sète, was attracting serious acclaim. *La Graine et le Mulet* (*Couscous*) went on to win Best Film, Best Director and Best Screenplay for Abdellatif Kechiche, plus Best Newcomer for 21-year-old lead actress Hafsia Herzi at the César awards. Telling the story of Slimane, an elderly Tunisian made redundant after 30 years in the shipyards, who uses his redundancy pay to realise his dream of opening a couscous restaurant with the help of his mistress's daughter Rym, Kechiche has spun a memorable film that goes far beyond the usual immigrant family stereotypes.

Kechiche draws an affectionate portrait of Slimane's complicated extended family, with its mixed marriages, cheating eldest son and Slimane's own moped journeys between the housing estate home of his ex-wife, and his mistress, owner of the shabby bar-hotel where he lives. The film's title – *La Graine* (couscous) *et le Mulet* (grey mullet, an extremely stubborn species of fish, according to Kechiche in an interview) – refers to the restaurant's principle dish,

but is also a metaphor for seeds, growth and the generation gap between Rym and Slimane. Their relationship forms the central axis of the film, as they team up to convert a rusty ship into a restaurant, encountering the subtle racism of bankers and bureaucrats along the way.

As in Kechiche's two earlier films, *La Faute à Voltaire* and *L'Esquive*, most of the cast are newcomers; Slimane is played by Habib Boufares, a 60-year-old former labourer. The style, which alternates between lyrical sequences and fly-on-the-wall realism, has led some observers to compare Kechiche to Maurice Pialat, and the rawness of the dialogue is reminiscent of Ken Loach.

The symbolism of food as a sensual expression of relationships and love permeates the film, from Slimane eating alone in his hotel room to the gargantuan family lunch prepared communally by the women. It also underpins the story's climax: the restaurant's inaugural feast, to which the town's dignitaries are invited. Suspense is drawn out as the action cuts between Slimane chasing vainly after his stolen moped and the expectant diners in the restaurant, where, to traditional Arabic music, Herzi performs an astonishing belly dance. Delicious.

The Seine & Islands

The river that helps define the city.

Paris owes its very existence to the Seine, and dutifully acknowledges the importance of its river with waves and a sailboat on the city's coat of arms. The value of the Seine as a transport route was one of the things that brought settlers here in the first place, and the stream that rises near a tiny village in Burgundy has been a vital force shaping the capital throughout its history.

The Seine's role has been as much cultural as economic, not least as the psychosocial frontier between intellectual Paris on the Left Bank and mercantile Paris on the Right. It has featured in

| Map p406 | Restaurants p184 |
| Hotels p155 | |

paintings, novels, films and songs, and has its own ghostly folklore – the largely vanished traditions of the bargemen whose way of life Jean Vigo romanticised in *L'Atalante*. But it also continues to help shape the city today.

ALONG THE SEINE

It's perhaps surprising that it took so long for the Seine to become a tourist magnet. For much of the 19th and 20th centuries, it was barely given a second thought by anyone who wasn't working on it or driving along its quayside roads. But in 1994, UNESCO added 12 kilometres of Paris riverbank to its World Heritage register. Floating venues such as **Batofar** (*see p329*) became super-trendy; and in the last ten years, it's been one new Seine-side attraction after another.

It's at its best in summer. Port de Javel and Jardin Tino-Rossi become open-air dancehalls; and there's the summer jamboree of Paris-Plage, Mayor Delanoë's inspired civic beach that brings sand, palm trees, loungers and free entertainment to both sides of the Seine. After a few teething problems, the new **Piscine Joséphine-Baker** (*see p341*), has revived the floating swimming pool concept that was so popular in the 19th and early 20th centuries. Come on Sundays, and stretches of riverside roads will be closed for the benefit of cyclists and rollerskaters. And, of course, there's a wealth of boat tours (*see p55* **Inside Track**).

What's more, the river itself is cleaning up its act. The recent crackdown on pollution had

a big symbolic payoff in August 2008, when, for the first time since records began, a sea trout was caught in the Seine on the western outskirts of the city. The catch was significant because the sea trout is particularly fussy about the quality of the water in which it swims.

The bridges

From the honeyed arches of the oldest, the **Pont Neuf**, to the handsome, swooping lines of the newest, the **Passerelle Simone-de-Beauvoir**, the city's 37 bridges are among the best-known landmarks in the city, and enjoy some of its best views.

There was already a bridge on the site of today's **Petit Pont** in the first century BC, when the Parisii Celts ran their river trade and toll-bridge operations. The Romans put up a cross-island thoroughfare in the form of a reinforced bridge to the south of Ile de la Cité, and another one north of it (where the **Pont Notre-Dame** now stands), thus creating a straight route all the way from Orléans through to Belgium.

Since then, the city's *ponts* have been bombed, bashed by buses and boats, weather-beaten and even trampled to destruction: in 1634, the Pont St-Louis collapsed under the

SIGHTS

La Conciergerie. *See p57.*

SIGHTS

weight of a religious procession. In the Middle Ages, the handful of bridges linking the islands to the riverbanks were lined with shops and houses, but the flimsy wooden constructions regularly caught fire or got washed away. The Petit Pont sank 11 times before councillors decided to ban building on top of bridges.

The Pont Neuf was inaugurated in 1607 and has been standing sturdy, gargoyles a-goggle, ever since. This was the first bridge to be built with no houses to obstruct the view of the river. It had a raised stretch of road at the edge to protect walkers from traffic and horse dung (the new-fangled 'pavement' soon caught on); the semicircular alcoves that now make handy pit stops for lovers were once filled with tooth-pullers, peddlers and *bouquinistes*.

The 19th century was boom time for bridge-building: 21 were built in all, including the city's first steel, iron and suspension bridges. The **Pont de la Concorde** used up what was left of the Bastille after the storming of 1789; the romantic **Pont des Arts** was the capital's first solely pedestrian crossing (built in 1803 and rebuilt in the 1980s). The most glitteringly exuberant bridge is the **Pont Alexandre III**, with its bronze and glass, garlanding and gilded embellishments. More practical is the **Pont de l'Alma**, with its Zouave statue that has long been a flood monitor: when the statue's

toes get wet, the state raises the flood alert and starts to close the quayside roads; when he's up to his ankles in Seine, it's no longer possible to navigate the river by boat. This offers some indication of how devastating the great 1910 flood was, when the plucky Zouave disappeared up to his neck – as did large parts of central Paris.

The 20th century brought some spectacular additions. **Pont Charles-de-Gaulle**, for example, stretches resplendent like the wing of a huge aeroplane, and iron **Viaduc d'Austerlitz** (1905) is striking yet elegant as it cradles métro line 5. The city's newest crossing, the Passerelle Simone-de-Beauvoir, is a walkway linking the Bibliothèque Nationale to the Parc de Bercy in the 12th arrondissement.

ILE DE LA CITE

In the 1st & 4th arrondissements.

The Ile de la Cité is where Paris was born around 250 BC, when the Parisii, a tribe of Celtic Gauls, founded a settlement on this convenient bridging point of the Seine. Romans, Merovingians and Capetians followed, in what became a centre of political and religious power right into the Middle Ages: royal authority at one end, around the Capetian palace; the Church at the other, by Notre-Dame.

When Victor Hugo wrote *Notre-Dame de Paris* in 1831, the Ile de la Cité was still a bustling quarter of narrow medieval streets and tall houses: 'the head, heart and very marrow of Paris'. Baron Haussmann performed a marrow extraction when he supervised the expulsion of 25,000 people from the island, razing tenements and some 20 churches, and leaving behind large, official buildings – the law courts, the **Conciergerie**, Hôtel-Dieu hospital, the police headquarters and the cathedral. The lines of the old streets are traced into the parvis in front of **Notre-Dame**.

Perhaps the most charming spot on the island is the western tip, where Pont Neuf spans the Seine. Despite its name, it is in fact the oldest bridge in Paris, begun under the reign of Henri III and Catherine de Médicis in 1578 and taking 30 years to complete. Its arches are lined with grimacing faces, said to be modelled on some of the courtiers of Henri III. In 1991, the bridge (or, rather, a full-size facsimile of it) starred in Leos Carax's budget-busting film *Les Amants du Pont Neuf*.

Down the steps is a leafy triangular garden, square du Vert-Galant. You can take to the water here on the Vedettes du Pont Neuf. In the centre of the bridge is an equestrian statue of Henri IV; the original went up in 1635, was melted down to make cannons during the Revolution, and replaced in 1818. On the bridge's eastern side, place Dauphine, home to restaurants, wine bars and the ramshackle Hôtel Henri IV, was built in 1607, on what was then a sandy bar that flooded every winter. It was commissioned by Henri IV, who named it in honour of his son, the future King Louis XIII. The brick and stone houses, similar to those in place des Vosges (though subsequently much altered to accommodate sun terraces), look out over the quays and square. The third, eastern side was demolished in the 1860s, when the new Préfecture de Police was built. Known by its address, quai des Orfèvres, it was immortalised by Clouzot's film and Simenon's Maigret novels.

The towers of the Conciergerie dominate the island's north bank. Along with the Palais de Justice, it was originally part of the Palais de la Cité, residential and administration complex of the Capetian kings. It occupies the site of an earlier Merovingian fortress and, before that, the Roman governor's house. Etienne Marcel's uprising prompted Charles V to move the royal retinue to the Louvre in 1358, and the Conciergerie was assigned a more sinister role as a prison for people awaiting execution. The interior is worth a visit for its prison cells and the vaulted Gothic halls. On the corner of boulevard du Palais, the Tour de l'Horloge, built in 1370, was the first public clock in Paris.

Sainte-Chapelle, Pierre de Montreuil's masterpiece of stained glass and slender Gothic columns, stands among the nearby law courts. Enveloping the chapel, the Palais de Justice was built alongside the Conciergerie. Behind elaborate wrought-iron railings, most of the present buildings around the fine neo-classical entrance courtyard date from the 1780s reconstruction by Desmaisons and Antoine. After passing through security, you can visit the **Salle des Pas Perdus**, busy with plaintiffs and barristers, and sit in on cases in the civil and criminal courts. The Palais is still the centre of the French legal system, though it's rumoured that the law courts will one day be moved to the 13th or 15th arrondissement.

Across boulevard du Palais, behind the Tribunal du Commerce, place Louis-Lépine is occupied by the Marché aux Fleurs, where horticultural suppliers sell flowers, cacti and exotic trees. On Sundays, they are joined by caged birds and small animals in the Marché aux Oiseaux. The Hôtel-Dieu, east of the market place, was founded in the seventh century. During the Middle Ages your chances of survival here were, at best, slim; today the odds are much improved. The hospital originally stood on the other side of the island facing the Latin Quarter, but after a series of fires in the 18th century it was rebuilt here in the 1860s.

Notre-Dame cathedral dominates the eastern half of the island. On the parvis in front of the cathedral is the bronze 'Kilomètre Zéro' marker, the point from which distances between Paris and the rest of France are measured. The **Crypte Archéologique** hidden under the parvis gives a sense of the island's multi-layered past, when it was a tangle of alleys, houses, churches and cabarets. Notre-Dame is still a place of worship, and holds its Assumption Day procession, Christmas Mass and Nativity scene on the parvis.

Walk through the garden by the cathedral to appreciate its flying buttresses. To the north-east, a medieval feel persists in the few streets untouched by Haussmann, such as rue

SIGHTS

SIGHTS

Profile Cathédrale Notre-Dame de Paris

Paris's Gothic masterpiece.

Notre-Dame was commissioned in 1160 by Bishop Maurice de Sully, who wanted to rival the smart new abbey that had just gone up in St-Denis. It replaced the earlier St-Etienne basilica, built in the sixth century by Childebert I on the site of a Gallo-Roman temple to Jupiter. Notre-Dame was constructed between 1163 and 1334, and the amount of time and money spent on it reflected the city's growing prestige. Pope Alexander III may have laid the foundation stone; the choir was completed in 1182, the nave in 1208; the west front and twin towers went up between 1225 and 1250. Chapels were added to the nave between 1235 and 1250, and to the apse between 1296 and 1330. The cathedral was plundered during the French Revolution, and then rededicated to the cult of Reason. The original statues of the Kings of Judah from the west front were torn down by the mob (who believed them to represent the kings of France) and rediscovered only during the construction of a car park in 1977 (they're now in the Musée National du Moyen-Age).

By the 19th century, the cathedral was looking pretty shabby. Victor Hugo, whose novel *Notre-Dame de Paris* had been a great success, led the campaign for its restoration. Gothic revivalist Viollet-le-Duc restored Notre-Dame to her former glory in the mid 19th century, although work has been going on ever since.

The west front remains a high point of Gothic art for the balanced proportions of its twin towers and rose window, and the three doorways with their rows of saints and sculpted tympanums: the *Last Judgement* (centre), *Life of the Virgin* (left) and *Life of St Anne*

(right). Inside, take a moment to admire the long nave with its solid foliate capitals and high altar with a marble Pietà by Coustou; the choir was rebuilt in the 18th century by Robert le Cotte, but is surrounded by medieval painted stone reliefs depicting the Resurrection (south) and Nativity (north).

To truly appreciate the masonry, climb up the towers. The route runs up the north tower and down the south. Between the two you get a close-up view of the gallery of chimeras – the fantastic birds and leering hybrid beasts designed by Viollet-le-Duc along the balustrade. After a detour to see the Bourdon (the massive bell), a staircase leads to the top of the south tower.

NOTRE-DAME'S BIG DATES

1430
Henry VI of England crowned

1804
Napoleon crowns himself Emperor

1909
Joan of Arc beatified

Chanoinesse, rue de la Colombe and rue des Ursins, though the crenellated medieval remnant on the corner of rue des Ursins and rue des Chantres was redone in the 1950s for the Aga Khan. The capital's oldest love story unfolded in the 12th century at 9 quai aux Fleurs, where Héloïse lived with her uncle Canon Fulbert, who had her tutor and lover, the scholar Abélard, castrated. Héloïse was sent to a nunnery. Behind the cathedral, in a garden at the eastern end of the island, is the **Mémorial des Martyrs de la Déportation**, remembering people sent to Nazi concentration camps.

★ FREE Cathédrale Notre-Dame de Paris

Pl du Parvis-Notre-Dame, 4th (01.42.34.56.10/ www.cathedraledeparis.com). M° Cité/RER St-Michel. **Open** 8am-6.45pm Mon-Fri; 8am-7.15pm Sat, Sun. *Towers* Apr-Sept 10am-6.30pm daily *(June, Aug* until 11pm Sat, Sun). Oct-Mar 10am-5.30pm daily. **Admission** free. *Towers* €7.50; €4.80 reductions; free under-18s. PMP. **Credit** MC, V. **Map** p406 J7.
See p56 **Profile**.

★ La Conciergerie

2 bd du Palais, 1st (01.53.40.60.80). M° Cité/ RER St-Michel Notre-Dame. **Open** *Mar-Oct* 9.30am-6pm daily. *Nov-Feb* 9am-5pm daily. **Admission** €6.50; €4.50 reductions; free under-18s (accompanied by an adult). *With Sainte-Chapelle* €10; €8 reductions. PMP. **Credit** MC, V. **Map** p408 J6.
The Conciergerie looks every inch the forbidding medieval fortress. However, much of the façade was added in the 1850s, long after Marie-Antoinette, Danton and Robespierre had been imprisoned here. The 13th-century Bonbec tower, built during the reign of St Louis, the 14th-century twin towers, César and Argent, and the Tour de l'Horloge all survive from the Capetian palace. The visit takes you through the Salle des Gardes, the medieval kitchens with their four huge chimneys, and the Salle des Gens d'Armes, an impressive vaulted Gothic hall built between 1301 and 1315 for Philippe 'le Bel'. After the royals moved to the Louvre, the fortress became a prison under the watch of the Concierge. The wealthy had private cells with their own furniture, which they paid for; others crowded on beds of straw. A list of Revolutionary prisoners, including a hairdresser, shows that not all victims were nobles. In Marie-Antoinette's cell, the Chapelle des Girondins, are her crucifix, some portraits and a guillotine blade. *Photo p54.*

La Crypte Archéologique

Pl Jean-Paul II, 4th (01.55.42.50.10). M° Cité/RER St-Michel Notre-Dame. **Open** 10am-6pm Tue-Sun. **Admission** €3.30; €1.60-€2.20

reductions; free under-14s. PMP. **Credit** (€15 minimum) MC, V. **Map** p406 J7.
Hidden under the forecourt in front of the cathedral is a large void that contains bits and pieces of Roman quaysides, ramparts and hypocausts, medieval cellars, shops and pavements, the foundations of the Eglise Ste-Geneviève-des-Ardens (the church where Geneviève's remains were stored during the Norman invasions), an 18th-century foundling hospital and a 19th-century sewer, all excavated since the 1960s. It's not always easy to work out exactly which wall, column or staircase is which – but you do get a vivid sense of the layers of history piled one atop another during 16 centuries.

FREE Mémorial des Martyrs de la Déportation

Sq de l'Ile de France, 4th (01.46.33.87.56). M° Cité/RER St-Michel Notre-Dame. **Open** *Oct-Mar* 10am-noon, 2-5pm daily. *Apr-Sept* 10am-noon, 2-7pm daily. **Admission** free. **Map** p406 J7.
This sober tribute to the 200,000 Jews, Communists, homosexuals and *résistants* deported to concentration camps from France in World War II stands on the eastern tip of the island. A blind staircase descends to river level, where simple chambers are lined with tiny lights and the walls are inscribed with verse. A barred window looks out at the Seine.

Sainte-Chapelle

6 bd du Palais, 1st (01.53.40.60.97). M° Cité/RER St-Michel Notre-Dame. **Open** *Mar-Oct* 9.30am-6pm daily. *Nov-Feb* 9am-5pm daily. **Admission** €7.50; €4.80 reductions; free under-18s (accompanied by an adult). PMP. *With Conciergerie* €10; €8 reductions. **Credit** MC, V. **Map** p408 J6.
Devout King Louis IX (St Louis, 1226-70) had a hobby of accumulating holy relics (and children: he fathered 11). In the 1240s he bought what was advertised as the Crown of Thorns, and ordered Pierre de Montreuil to design a suitable shrine. The result was the exquisite Flamboyant Gothic Sainte-Chapelle. With 15m (49ft) windows, the upper level, intended for the royal family and the canons, appears to consist almost entirely of stained glass. The windows depict hundreds of scenes from the Old and New Testaments, culminating with the Apocalypse in the rose window.

ILE ST-LOUIS

In the 4th arrondissement.

The Ile St-Louis is one of the most exclusive residential addresses in the city. Delightfully unspoiled, it has fine architecture, narrow streets and pretty views from the tree-lined quays, and still retains the air of a tranquil backwater, curiously removed from city life.

SIGHTS

For hundreds of years, the island was a swampy pasture belonging to Notre-Dame, known as Ile Notre-Dame and used as a retreat for fishermen, swimmers and courting couples. In the 14th century Charles V built a fortified canal through the middle, thus creating the Ile aux Vaches ('Island of Cows'). Its real-estate potential wasn't realised until 1614, though,when speculator Christophe Marie persuaded Louis XIII to fill in the canal (present-day rue Poulletier) and plan streets, bridges and houses. The island was renamed in honour of the king's pious predecessor, and the venture proved a huge success, thanks to architect Louis Le Vau, who from the 1630s built fashionable new residences along the quai d'Anjou, quai de Bourbon and quai de Béthune, as well as the **Eglise St-Louis-en-l'Ile**. By the 1660s the island was full up; its smart reception rooms were set at the front of courtyards to give residents riverside views.

Rue St-Louis-en-l'Ile – lined with fine historic buildings that now house quirky gift shops and gourmet food stores (many open on Sunday), quaint tearooms, stone-walled bars, restaurants and hotels – runs the length of the island. The grandiose **Hôtel Lambert** at no.2 was built by Le Vau in 1641 for Louis XIII's secretary, and has sumptuous interiors by Le Sueur, Perrier and Le Brun. At no.51 – **Hôtel Chenizot** – look out for the bearded faun adorning the rocaille doorway, which is flanked by stern dragons supporting the balcony. There's more sculpture on the courtyard façade, while a second courtyard hides craft workshops and an art gallery. Across the street, the **Hôtel du Jeu de Paume** at no.54 was once a tennis court; at no.31, famous ice-cream maker **Berthillon** still draws a crowd. At the western end there are great views of the flying buttresses of Notre-Dame from the terraces of the **Brasserie de l'Ile St-Louis** and the **Flore en l'Ile** café.

Baudelaire wrote part of *Les Fleurs du Mal* while living at the Hôtel de Lauzun at 17 quai d'Anjou; he and fellow poet Théophile Gautier also organised meetings of their dope-smokers' club here. A couple of centuries earlier, Racine, Molière and La Fontaine resided as guests of La Grande Mademoiselle, cousin of Louis XIV. At 6 quai d'Orléans, the **Adam Mickiewicz library-museum** (01.43.54.35.61, open 2-6pm Thur) is dedicated to the Romantic poet, journalist and campaigner for Polish freedom.

🆓 Eglise St-Louis-en-l'Ile

19bis rue St-Louis-en-l'Ile, 4th (01.46.34.11.60/ www.saintlouisenlile.com). M° Pont Marie. **Open** 9am-noon, 3-7pm Tue-Sun. **Admission** free. **Map** p409 L7.
The island's church was built between 1664 and 1765, following plans by Louis Le Vau and later completed by Gabriel Le Duc. The baroque interior boasts Corinthian columns and a sunburst over the altar, and sometimes hosts classical music concerts.

Vedettes de Paris. *See p55.*

The Louvre

Museum city.

As in large swathes of the rest of Paris, there are changes afoot at the Louvre. Work continues on the new Islamic Arts department, which should open in 2010; when it does, it will probably be the final major expansion project at what was already the biggest museum in the world. But the Louvre's ambitions can't be so easily constrained: 'Louvre' is becoming a sort of franchise, with outposts going up in Lens (www.louvrelens.fr) and Abu Dhabi. It's an interesting reversal of the process whereby art from all over the world was brought to a single Paris address.

ABOUT THE LOUVRE

Much like the building itself, the Louvre's collections were built up over the centuries. They encompass a rich visual history of the western world, from Ancient Egypt and Mesopotamia to the 19th century. Indeed, one of the most impressive things about the Louvre is the way it juxtaposes architecture and content. Look up from a case of Greek or Roman antiquities and you might see an 18th-century painted ceiling, or two doves by Braque. In the Egyptian department you'll find Louis XIV's bedchamber, complete with gilded bed, while Renaissance art is housed in the Grande Galerie, where the Sun King performed the 'scrofula ceremony', blessing the sick. In between exhibits, the Louvre's long windows afford stunning views of the building's façades, formal gardens and beautiful interior courtyards.

Some 35,000 works of art and artefacts are on show, split into eight departments and housed in three wings: **Denon**, **Sully** and **Richelieu**. Under the atrium of the glass pyramid, each wing has its own entrance, though you can pass from one to another. Treasures from the Egyptians, Etruscans, Greeks and Romans each have their own galleries in the Denon and Sully wings, as do Middle Eastern and Islamic works of art. The first floor of Richelieu is taken up with European decorative arts from the Middle Ages up to the 19th century, including room after room of Napoleon III's lavish apartments.

The main draw, though, is the painting and sculpture. Two glass-roofed sculpture courts contain the famous Marly horses on the ground floor of Richelieu, with French sculpture below

and Italian Renaissance pieces in the Denon wing. The Grand Galerie and Salle de la Joconde (home to the *Mona Lisa*), like a mini Uffizi, run the length of Denon's first floor with French Romantic painting alongside. Dutch and French painting occupies the second floor of Richelieu and Sully. Jean-Pierre Wilmotte's minimalist galleries in the Denon wing were designed as a taster for the Musée du Quai Branly, with art from Africa, the Americas and Oceania.

Mitterrand's Grand Louvre project expanded the museum two-fold by throwing out the Ministry of Finance and other government offices that once inhabited the Cour Napoléon. But the organisation and restoration of the Louvre is still a work in progress: check the website or lists in the Carrousel du Louvre to see which galleries are closed on certain days to avoid missing out on what you want to see.

The museum is also subtly moving with the times and trying to strike a healthy balance between highbrow culture and accessibility. Photography was banned in 2005 at the request of mainly French visitors, who complained that it interfered with their enjoyment; meanwhile, the link with Dan Brown's *Da Vinci Code* has been embraced with a dedicated audio guide.

SIGHTS

INSIDE TRACK
SOUVENIR TIME

Save your shopping for the end. The RMN bookshop and separate souvenir shops are open an hour after closing, except when the museum stays open late.

Laminated panels found throughout provide a surprisingly lively commentary, and the superb website is a technological feat unsurpassed by that of any of the world's major museums.

ADVANCE TICKETS AND ENTRY

IM Pei's glass pyramid is a wonderful piece of architecture, but it's not the only entrance to the museum – there are three others from which to choose. Buying a ticket in advance means you can go in directly via the passage Richelieu off rue de Rivoli, or via the Carrousel du Louvre shopping mall (there are steps down either side of the Arc de Triomphe du Carrousel, at 99 rue de Rivoli or from the métro).

Advance tickets are valid for any day, and are available from the Louvre website or from branches of **Fnac** and **Virgin Megastore** (for both, *see p271*). You can buy one at the Virgin in the Carrousel du Louvre and use it immediately. Another option is to buy a ticket at the Cour des Lions entrance (closed Fridays) in the south-west corner of the complex, convenient for the Italian collections. The Louvre is also accessible with the all-in **Paris Museum Pass**. Finally, don't forget that the Louvre is closed on Tuesdays.

OTHER TIPS
● The Louvre's website, much of which is in English, is an unbeatable resource for planning your visit. Every single work on display is photographed, and you can search the website's Atlas database by room, artist or theme.
● Laminated cards in each room provide useful background information. Audioguides

(€5; ID must be left) are available at the main entrances in the Carrousel du Louvre.

● Don't attempt to see more than two collections in one day. Your ticket is valid all day and you can leave and re-enter as you wish.

● Evening visits can be made on Wednesdays and Fridays till 9.45pm. On Fridays after 6pm entry is free for the under-26s, but if you plan to make several visits, the Carte Louvre Jeunes, at €15 for the year, is worth getting.

● Some rooms are closed on a weekly basis – check on 01.40.20.51.51 or at www.louvre.fr.

LISTINGS INFORMATION

Louvre, Rue de Rivoli, 1st (01.40.20.50.50/ recorded information 01.40.20.51.51/disabled access 01.40.20.59.90/www.louvre.fr). Mº Palais Royal Musée du Louvre. **Open** 9am-6pm Mon, Thur, Sat, Sun; 9am-10pm Wed, Fri. **Admission** *Permanent collections* €9 (incl entry to the Musée Delacroix but not shows at the Salle Napoléon); €6 6-9.45pm Wed, Fri; free under-18s at all times, under-26s 6-9.45pm Fri, all 1st Sun of mth. PMP. *Exhibitions* €9.50. *Combined ticket* €13; €11 6-9.45pm Wed, Fri. **Credit** AmEx, MC, V. **Map** p403 G5.

REFRESHMENTS

Take your pick from **Richelieu**, **Denon** or **Mollien** cafés; the latter is just off the Mollien staircase and has a terrace. Under the pyramid, there's a sandwich bar and the smart, sophisticated **Grand Louvre** restaurant. The **Restorama**, in the Carrousel du Louvre, has self-service outlets. The terrace of **Café Marly** serves pricey brasserie fare and cocktails.

The collections

History of the Louvre

Sully: lower ground floor. Shown as dark brown on Louvre maps.

Here you can explore the medieval foundations of the Louvre, dating back to Philippe-Auguste's reign. Uncovered in 1985 during excavations for the Grand Louvre project, they include the remains of the moat that once surrounded the fort and the pillars of two drawbridges; the La Taillerie tower, with heart symbols cut into the stone by masons; and the outside of the dungeons. A well and a portion of ground have been left undisturbed, showing artefacts just as they were found, and a scale model shows the fortress at the time of Charles V. An exhibition in the Saint-Louis room – a guard room from the era of Philippe-Auguste, discovered in 1882 – recounts the history of the Louvre through rare archaeological finds, as well as an unfinished staircase and carved pillars.

Ancient Egypt

Denon: lower ground floor; Sully: lower ground, ground & 1st floors. Green on Louvre maps.

Announced by the pink granite Giant Sphinx (1898-1866 BC), the Egyptian department divides into two routes. The Thematic Circuit on the ground floor presents Nile culture (fishing, agriculture, hunting, daily and cultural life, religion and death). One of the big draws is the Mastaba of Akhethetep, a decorated burial chamber from Sakkara dating back to 2400 BC. Six small sphinxes, apes from Luxor and the lion-headed goddess Sekhmet recreate elements of temple complexes, while stone sarcophagi, mummies, amulets, jewellery and entrails form a vivid display on funeral rites. A display of Egyptian furniture (room 8, ground floor) dating from 1550-1069 BC contains pieces that look almost contemporary in design.

On the first floor the Pharoah Circuit is laid out chronologically, from the Seated Scribe and other stone figures of the Ancient Empire, via the painted figures of the Middle Empire, to the New Empire, with its animal-headed statues of gods and goddesses, hieroglyphic tablets and papyrus scrolls. Look for the statue of the god Amun protecting Tutankhamun, and the black diorite 'cube statues' of priests and attendants. The collection, one of the largest hoards of Egyptian antiquities in the world, has its origins in Napoleon's Egyptian campaign of 1798 and 1799, as well as the work of Egyptologist Jean-François Champollion, who deciphered hieroglyphics in 1824. The Coptic gallery, on the lower ground floor, houses textiles and manuscripts.

Oriental antiquities

Richelieu: lower ground & ground floors; Sully: ground floor. Yellow on Louvre maps.

This section deals with Mesopotamia, Persia and the Levant from the fifth millennium BC to the first century AD. The huge Mesopotamian rooms contain glistening diorite sculptures from the Akkad dynasty and Gudea from the third millennium BC; in some cases, only the feet have survived intact. Make sure you don't miss the serene alabaster sculpture of Ebih-II, the superintendent of Mari (room 1b), and the earliest evidence of writing, in the form of fourth-century BC Sumerian tablets (room 1a). The Hammurabi Code, an essential document

Picking Up the Pieces

The treasures of the whole world, assembled in Paris.

How did the Louvre manage to come by all these fabulous works of art? It's popularly supposed that the majority of the pieces held here are merely loot – but although the spoils of Napoleon's campaigns do indeed make up a significant part, other legitimate methods of acquisition were also involved.

Much of the royal collection, for instance, was presented as offerings to the ruling monarchs and acted as diplomatic sweeteners. The talent of Leonardo da Vinci was fought over as a commodity and sign of prestige during the reign of Louis XII, who petitioned for a portrait in Lombardy even as Milan

was being sacked by his troops. It was François I who brought an entire Italian court to France, resulting in a rich collection of then contemporary art and antiquities that included the *Mona Lisa*.

And then there are the treasures that were bequeathed to the state in lieu of death duties; still others are acquired in an ongoing process by the Réunion des Musées Nationaux.

The Louvre itself became a museum in 1793, its revolutionary opening to the people a true expression of the art-for-all ethic still in force every first Sunday of the month, when entrance to the museum is free.

of Babylonian civilisation, is a black basalt stele recording 282 laws beneath reliefs of the king and the sun god; it's one of the oldest collections of laws in the history of mankind (room 3).

Next come two breathtaking palace reconstructions: the great court, c713 BC, from the palace of Sargon II at Khorsabad (in present-day Iraq), with its giant bearded and winged bulls and friezes of warriors and servants (room 4); and the palace of Darius I at Susa (now Iran), c510 BC, with its glazed-brick reliefs of archers, lions and griffins (room 12). The double-bull-headed column was one of 36 such gigantic supports at the palace. Entering the Iranian section, you find 5,000-year-old statues from Susa housed in the circular room 8, and a fine view of the Cour Napoléon. The Levantine section includes Cypriot animalistic vases and carved reliefs from Byblos.

Islamic arts

Richelieu: lower ground floor. Turquoise on Louvre maps.
The Islamic decorative arts on show include early glassware, tenth- to 12th-century dishes decorated with birds and calligraphy, traditional Iranian blue-and-white wares, Iznik ceramics, intricate inlaid metalwork from Syria, tiles, screens, weapons and funerary steles. The highlight is three magnificent 16th-century kelims. In 2005 a Saudi prince, Prince Walid bin Talal, gave over €17 million – one of the largest donations in French cultural history – for a new Islamic wing to be built as an extension to the southern wing. It's expected to open in the cour Visconti by 2010.

Greek, Roman & Etruscan antiquities

Denon: lower ground & ground floors; Sully: ground & 1st floors. Blue on Louvre maps.
The *Winged Victory of Samothrace*, a headless Greek statue dating from the second century BC, stands sentinel at the top of the grand staircase, giving an idea of its original dramatic impact on a promontory overlooking the Aegean sea. This huge department is made up of pieces amassed by François I and Cardinal Richelieu, plus the Borghese collection (acquired in 1808), and the Campana collection of thousands of painted Greek vases and small terracottas. Endless dark rooms on the first floor harbour small bronze, silver and terracotta objects, but the really exciting stuff is on the ground floor. The grandiose, vaulted marble rooms are a fitting location for masterpieces such as the 2.3m (7.5ft) *Athena Peacemaker* and the *Venus de Milo* (room 12), and overflow with gods and goddesses, swords and monsters.

Also on the ground floor are artefacts from the Etruscan civilisation of south-central Italy,

spanning the seventh century BC until submission to the Romans in the first century AD. The highlight is the painted terracotta Sarcophagus of the Cenestien Couple (c530-510 BC), which illustrates a smiling couple reclining at a banquet. Key Roman antiquities include a vivid relief of sacrificial animals, intricately carved sarcophagi, mosaic floors and the Boscoreale Treasure: magnificent silverwork excavated at a villa near Pompeii. Pre-classical Greek art on the lower ground floor includes a large Cycladic head and Mycenean triad.

French painting

Denon: 1st floor; Richelieu: 2nd floor; Sully: 2nd floor. Red on Louvre maps.
There are around 6,000 of the most famous paintings in the world on show here, the most impressive being the huge 18th- to 19th-century canvases hanging in the Daru and Mollien rooms in the Denon wing, serving Classicism and Romanticism respectively. Here, art meets politics with David's enormous *Sacre de Napoléon*, Gros's propagandising *Napoléon Visitant le Champ de Bataille d'Eylau* and Delacroix's flag-flying *La Liberté Guidant le Peuple*. Géricault's beautiful but disturbing *Le Radeau de la Méduse* illustrates the grisly true story of the abandoned men who resorted to cannibalism and murder after a famous shipwreck in 1816, while his generals on flame-eyed horses fuel the myth of the dashing French officer. Biblical and historical scenes rub shoulders with aristocracy and grand depictions of great moments in mythology. Ingres' *Grande Odalisque* is also found here, along with a new Ingres acquisition, a portrait of the Duc d'Orléans.

In the Richelieu wing you can find the earliest known non-religious French portrait, an anonymous depiction of French king Jean Le Bon (c1350); the *Pietà de Villeneuve-les-Avignon*, later attributed to Enguerrand Quarton; Jean Clouet's *Portrait of François I* (marking the influence of the Italian Renaissance on portraiture); and various works from the Ecole de Fontainebleau, including the anonymous *Diana the Huntress*, an elegant nude who strangely resembles Diane de Poitiers, the mistress of Henri II. Poussin's religious and mythological subjects epitomise 17th-century French classicism, and are full of erudite references for an audience of cognoscenti. His works spill over into the Sully wing, where you'll also find Charles Le Brun's wonderfully pompous *Chancellier Séguier* and his four grandiose battle scenes, in which Alexander the Great is a suitable stand-in for Louis XIV.

The 18th century begins with Watteau's *Gilles* and the *Embarkation for Cythera*. Works by Chardin include sober still lifes, but also fine

SIGHTS

figure paintings. If you're used to the sugary images of Fragonard, don't miss the *Fantaisies*, which forgo sentimentality for fluent, broadly painted fantasy portraits, intended to capture moods rather than likenesses. Also in the Sully wing are sublime neo-classical portraits by David, Ingres' *La Baigneuse* and *Le Bain Turc*, portraits and Orientalist scenes by Chassériau, and landscapes by Corot.

French sculpture
Richelieu: lower ground & ground floors.
Light brown on Louvre maps.
French sculpture is displayed in and around the two covered courts created by the Grand Louvre scheme. A tour of the medieval regional schools takes in the *Virgins* from Alsace, 14th-century figures of Charles V and Jeanne de Bourbon that once adorned the exterior of the Louvre, and the late 15th-century tomb of Philippe Pot, an effigy of a Burgundian knight carried by eight mourners. Fine Renaissance memorials, fountains and portals include Jean Goujon's friezes from the Fontaine des Innocents.

In the Cour Marly, pride of place goes to Coustou's *Chevaux de Marly*, rearing horses being restrained by their grooms, plus two earlier equestrian pieces by Coysevox. Hewn from single blocks of marble, they were sculpted for the royal château at Marly-le-Roi before being moved to the Tuileries gardens, where copies now stand. In Cour Puget are the four bronze captives by Martin Desjardins, Clodion's rococo frieze and Pierre Puget's twisting, baroque *Milo of Croton*. Amid the 18th-century heroes and allegorical subjects, look out for Pigalle's *Mercury* and *Voltaire*.

Italian & Spanish painting
Denon: 1st floor. Red on Louvre maps.
Starting from the Sully end of the Denon wing, three rooms of fragile frescoes by Botticelli, Fra Angelico and Luini, and 13th- to 15th-century Florentine paintings on wood by Cimabue, Giotto, Fra Angelico and Lippi, open the Italian department, before you move into the long, skylit Grande Galerie. To the right, the Salle des Sept Mètres has highlights of the Sienese school, including Simone Martini's *Christ Carrying the Cross* and Piero della Francesca's *Portrait of Sigismondo Malatesta*. Now that the *Mona Lisa* has moved, there is no need to bowl along the Grande Galerie at speed in your haste to see her, missing the wonders on either side.

Most notably, about a quarter of the way along on the left are Leonardo's *Virgin of the Rocks*, *Virgin and Child with Saint Anne* and *Saint-Jean Baptiste*, which form part of the Northern Italian section, along with Bellini's *Calvary* and *Portrait of a Man* and Raphael's *Portrait of Dona Isabel de Requesens*. The first

turning on the right after the da Vincis leads into the Salle de La Joconde, whose toffee-coloured brushed concrete walls provide a suitably golden setting for Veronese's lavish *Wedding at Cana*, his *Crucifixion* and *Sainte Famille* and other Venetian masterpieces such as Lotto's *Adulterous Woman* and red-robed *Christ Carrying the Cross*, Tintoretto's *Suzanne Bathing* and Bassano's earthy canvases. Don't miss the exquisite Titians hidden behind the *Mona Lisa* on her stand-alone wall.

A trip back down the Passage de Mollien, containing 16th-century cartoons, frames Giorgio Vasari's *Annunciation*, revealing how much better it is to stand back and look at these paintings. In between the two in the Grande Galerie are Arcimboldo's famous *Four Seasons*, various Bronzinos and Caravaggios, plus 17th-century works by Albani, Carracci and Reni. A small Spanish section takes in *Christ on the Cross Adored by Two Donors* by El Greco and his contemporary Jusepe de Ribera's *Club Foot*.

Graphic arts
Denon: 1st floor; Sully: 2nd floor.
Pink on Louvre maps.
The Louvre's huge collection of drawings includes works by Raphael, Michelangelo, Dürer, Holbein and Rembrandt. However, owing to their fragility, drawings are not shown as permanent exhibits. Four galleries (French and Northern schools on the 2nd floor; Italian and the latest acquisitions on the 1st) feature changing exhibitions. Other works can be viewed in the Salle de Consultation only upon written application to the management (01.40.20.51.94, fax 01.40.20.53.51).

Italian, Spanish & Northern sculpture
Denon: lower ground & ground floors.
Light brown on Louvre maps.
Michelangelo's *Dying Slave* and *Captive Slave* (sculptures planned for the tomb of Pope Julius II in Rome) are the real showstoppers here, but other Renaissance treasures include a painted marble relief by Donatello, Adrien de Vriesse's bronze *Mercury and Psyche*, Giambologna's *Mercury* and the ethereal *Psyche Revived by Cupid's Kiss* by Antonio Canova. Benvenuto Cellini's *Nymph of Fontainebleau* relief is on the Mollien staircase.

Napoleon III's former stables were reopened in 2004 to house princely collections of statuary acquired by Richelieu and the Borghese and Albani families in the 17th and 18th centuries. The statues, either copies of classical works or restored originals, demonstrate the relationship between antique and modern sculpture. The height of the room also allows oversized works such as *Jupiter* and *Albani Alexander* to be displayed. Northern sculpture, on the lower ground floor, ranges from Erhart's Gothic *Mary Magdalene* to the neo-classical work of Thorvaldsen; pre-Renaissance Italian pieces include Donatello's clay relief *Virgin and Child*.

Northern schools

Richelieu: 2nd floor; Sully: 1st floor.
Red on Louvre maps.
Northern Renaissance works include Flemish altarpieces by Memling and van der Weyden, Bosch's fantastical, proto-surrealist *Ship of Fools*, Metsys' *The Moneylender and his Wife*, and the northern mannerism of Cornelius van Haarlem. The Galerie Médicis houses Rubens' Médicis cycle; Marie de Médicis, the widow of Henri IV, commissioned the 24 canvases for the Palais de Luxembourg in the 1620s. They blend historic events and classical mythology for the glorification of the queen, never afraid to put her best features on public display. Look out for Rubens' more personal portrait of his second wife, *Hélène Fourment and her Children*, plus van Dyck's *Charles I and his Groom* and David Teniers the Younger's peasant-filled townscapes.

Dutch paintings in this wing include early and late self-portraits by Rembrandt, his *Flayed Ox* and the warmly glowing nude *Bathsheba at her Bath*. There are Vermeer's *Astronomer* and *Lacemaker* amid interiors by De Hooch and Metsu, and the meticulously finished portraits and framing devices of Dou, plus works from the Haarlem school. German paintings in side galleries include portraits by Cranach, Dürer's *Self-Portrait* and Holbein's *Anne of Cleves*.

The rooms of Northern European and Scandinavian paintings include Caspar David Friedrich's *Trees with Crows*, the sober, classical portraits of Christian Købke, and pared-back views by Peder Balke. A fairly modest but high-quality British collection located on the first floor of the Sully includes landscapes by Wright of Derby, Constable and Turner, and portraits by Gainsborough, Reynolds and Lawrence.

INSIDE TRACK
FINDING YOUR WAY

Pick up a map at the information desk. The eight collections are colour-coded on it, and signs point the way to the most popular exhibits. Leaflets suggesting various thematic trails are also available. *Destination Louvre* (€7.50), from the Réunion des Musées Nationaux shop in the Carrousel du Louvre, is a good English-language guide.

Decorative arts

Richelieu: 1st floor; Sully: 1st floor.
Magenta on Louvre maps.
The decorative arts collection runs from the Middle Ages to the mid-19th century, often with royal connections, and includes entire rooms decorated in the fashion of the day. Many of the finest medieval items came from the treasury of St-Denis, amassed by the powerful Abbot Suger, counsellor to Louis VI and VII, among them Suger's 'Eagle' (a porphyry vase), a serpentine plate surrounded by precious stones, and the sacred sword of the kings of France, dubbed 'Charlemagne's Sword' by the Capetian monarchs as they sought to legitimise their line.

The Renaissance galleries take in ornate carved chests, German silver tankards and the *Hunts of Maximilien*, a dozen 16th-century tapestries depicting the months, zodiac and hunting scenes. Seventeenth- and 18th-century French decorative arts are displayed in superb panelled rooms, and include characteristic brass and tortoiseshell pieces by Boulle. Displays then move on to French porcelain, silverware, watches and scientific instruments. Napoleon III's opulent apartments, used until the 1980s by the Ministry of Finance, have been preserved, with chandeliers and upholstery intact.

Next to the Denon wing, the Galerie d'Apollon reopened in 2004 after four years of restoration. A precursor to the Hall of Mirrors at Versailles, it was built for Louis XIV and is a showcase of talents from this golden age: architecture by Louis Le Vau, painted ceilings by Charles Le Brun and sculpture by François Girardon, the Marsy brothers and Thomas Regnaudin. Napoleon III then commissioned Delacroix to paint the central medallion, *Apollo Vanquishing the Python*, and now it houses the crown jewels and Louis XIV vases. Merry-Joseph Blondel's *Chute d'Icare* graces the ceiling of an anteroom of the adjacent Rotonde d'Apollon.

African, Asian, Oceanic & American arts

Denon: ground floor. White on Louvre maps.
A new approach to '*arts premiers*' is seen in these eight rooms in the Pavillon des Sessions, prefiguring the Musée du Quai Branly. The spare, modern design of Jean-Michel Wilmotte allows each of the 100 key works to stand alone in something midway between an art gallery and a museum. The pure aesthetics of such objects as a svelte Zulu spoon with the breasts and buttocks of a woman, a sixth-century BC Sokoto terracotta head, a recycled iron sculpture of the god Gou that anticipates Picasso, and a pot-bellied, terracotta Chupicaro from Mexico can be appreciated in their own right. Computer terminals with mahogany benches offer visitors multimedia resources.

SIGHTS

Opéra to Les Halles

Of monarchs and money men.

The swathe of the Right Bank between the Grands Boulevards and the Seine is, and has been for centuries, a commercial powerhouse. The two stock exchanges and the Banque de France are here, and so was the city's wholesale food market – until 1969, when it moved from Les Halles to the suburbs. For many observers, French and foreign, the demise of the market was an injury from which Paris could never recover; and there's no denying that the soulless shopping centre that took its place was no compensation for the loss of local colour and tradition that the market sellers had built up over centuries. But life and money-making march onwards: 40 years later, the area as a whole can match any other part of the city for shopping opportunities, and outdo most of them for art and history.

Champs-Elysées & Western Paris	Montmartre & Pigalle	North-East Paris
Opéra to Les Halles		
	Louvre	Beaubourg & The Marais
Tour Eiffel		**Notre-Dame**
The 7th & Western Paris	St-Germain-des-Prés & Odéon	Bastille & Eastern Paris
Montparnasse & Beyond		The Latin Quarter & the 13th

| **Map** p401 & p402 | **Restaurants** p187 |
| **Hotels** p158 | **Cafés & bars** p221 |

TUILERIES & PALAIS-ROYAL

In the 1st arrondissement.

Once the monarchs had moved from the Ile de la Cité to spacious new quarters on the Right Bank, the Louvre and, later, the palaces of the **Tuileries** and **Palais-Royal** became the centres of royal power. **The Louvre** (*see pp59-65*) still exerts considerable influence today: first as a grandiose architectural ensemble, a palace within the city; and, second, as a symbol of the capital's cultural pre-eminence. What had been simply a fortress along Philippe-Auguste's city wall in 1190 was transformed into a royal residence with all the latest Gothic comforts by Charles V; François I turned it into a sumptuous Renaissance palace. For centuries it was a work in progress: everyone wanted to make their mark – including the most monarchical of presidents, François Mitterrand, who added IM Pei's glass pyramid, doubled the exhibition space and added the Carrousel du Louvre shopping mall, auditorium and food halls.

The palace has always attracted crowds: first courtiers and ministers; then artists; and, since 1793, when it was first turned into a museum, art lovers – though the last department of the Finance Ministry moved out as late as 1991.

Around the Louvre, other subsidiary palaces grew up: Catherine de Médicis commissioned Philibert Delorme to begin work on one in the Tuileries; and Richelieu built the Palais Cardinal, which later became the Palais-Royal.

On place du Louvre, opposite Claude Perrault's grandiose western façade of the Louvre, is **Eglise St-Germain-l'Auxerrois**, once the French kings' parish church and home to the only original Flamboyant Gothic porch in Paris, built in 1435. Mirroring it to the left of the belfry is the 19th-century 1st arrondissement *mairie*, with its fanciful rose window and classical porch. Next door is the stylish **Le Fumoir** (*see p220*), with a Mona Lisa of its own: amaretto, orange juice and champagne.

Across rue de Rivoli from the Louvre, past the **Louvre des Antiquaires** antiques emporium (*see p268*), stands the understatedly elegant **Palais-Royal**, once Cardinal Richelieu's private mansion and now the Conseil d'Etat and ministry of culture. After a stroll in its quiet gardens, it's hard to believe that this was once the most debauched corner of Paris and the seedbed of the French Revolution.

In the 1780s, the Palais was a boisterous centre of Paris life, where aristocrats and the financially challenged inhabitants of the *faubourgs* rubbed shoulders. The coffee-houses in its arcades generated radical debate: here Camille Desmoulins called the city to arms on the eve of the storming of the Bastille; and after the Napoleonic Wars, Wellington and Field Marshal von Blücher lost so much money in the gambling dens that Parisians claimed they had won back their entire dues for war reparations. Only haute cuisine restaurant **Le Grand Véfour** (*see p187*), founded as Café de Chartres in the 1780s, survives from this era, albeit with decoration from a little later.

The **Comédie Française** theatre ('La Maison de Molière'; *see p344*) stands on the south-west corner. The company, created by Louis XIV in 1680, moved here in 1799. Molière himself is honoured with a fountain on the corner of rue Molière and rue de Richelieu. Brass-fronted **Café Nemours** on place Colette – Colette used to buy cigars from old-fashioned **A la Civette** nearby (157 rue St-Honoré, 1st, 01.42.96.04.99) – is another thespian favourite. In front of it, the métro entrance by artist Jean-Michel Othoniel, all glass baubles and aluminium struts, is a kitsch take on Guimard's celebrated art nouveau métro entrances.

Today, the stately arcades of the Palais-Royal house an eclectic succession of antiques dealers, philatelists, specialists in tin soldiers and musical boxes – and fashion showcases. Here you'll find the recently opened European flagship of renowned New York designer **Marc Jacobs** (*see p248*), chic vintage clothes specialist **Didier Ludot** (*see p256*), and the elegant perfumery **Salons du Palais-Royal**

Shiseido (*see p267*). Passing through the arcades to rue de Montpensier, the neo-rococo Théâtre du Palais-Royal and the centuries-old café **Entr'acte** (*see p220*), you'll find narrow, stepped passages that run between here and rue de Richelieu. On the other side of the palace towards Les Halles is galerie Véro-Dodat. Built by rich *charcutiers* during the Restoration period, it features wonderfully preserved neo-classical wooden shopfronts.

At the western end of the Louvre, by rue de Rivoli, are the **Musée des Arts Décoratifs**, the **Musée de la Mode et du Textile** and the **Musée de la Publicité**. All of these are administered independently of the Musée du Louvre, but were refreshed as part of the Grand Louvre scheme. Across place du Carrousel from the Louvre pyramid, the **Arc du Carrousel**, a mini-Arc de Triomphe, was built in polychrome marble for Napoleon from 1806 to 1809. The chariot on the top was originally drawn by the antique horses from San Marco in Venice, snapped up by Napoleon but returned in 1815. From the arch, the extraordinary axis along the **Jardin des Tuileries**, the Champs-Elysées up to the Arc de Triomphe and on to the Grande Arche de la Défense is plain to see.

The Jardin des Tuileries stretched as far as the Tuileries palace, until that was destroyed in the 1871 Paris Commune. The garden was laid out in the 17th century by André Le Nôtre and remains a pleasure area, with a funfair in summer; it also serves as an open-air gallery for modern art sculptures. Overlooking focal

SIGHTS

Food for Thought

Art meets science at the Laboratoire.

Viruses, pollution, food and the activity of the brain are all potential subjects fermenting in **Le Laboratoire** (4 rue du Boulot, 1st, 01.78.09.49.50, www.le laboratoire.org), Paris's latest public art space. In fact, art is just one aspect of this initiative dedicated to the brave new world of 'artscience'. But what does this mean in practice?

For its opening shows, on a broad theme of intelligence, artist Fabrice Hyber developed a series of paintings entitled 'Food for Thought' from his meeting with MIT biotechnology professor Robert Langer. The works showed the artist's visualisation of stem cell transformations.

The collaboration between David Edwards and hot young designer Mathias Lehanneur showed more concrete

potential with Lehanneur's striking Bel-Air project, a prototype living air filter system. Adapting Nasa research on air pollution in space capsules to household pollution from everyday furniture and carpets, Lehanneur has designed a ventilation system by which air is wafted through glass globes containing pollution-absorbing plants to clean the air in domestic interiors.

Other recent projects have included chef Thierry Marx exploring the future of food with physicist Jérôme Bibette of the ESPCI (Ecole Supérieure de Physique et de Chimie Industrielles), and Indian artist Shilpa Gupta in dialogue with neuroscientist Dean Mobbs on the effect of media indoctrination on the brain: brainstorming guaranteed.

Jardin des Tuileries. See p77.

place de la Concorde is the **Musée de l'Orangerie**, reopened in May 2006 after a complete renovation; and the **Jeu de Paume**, built as a court for real tennis, now a centre for photographic exhibitions.

The stretch of rue de Rivoli running beside the Louvre towards Concorde was laid out by Napoleon's architects Percier and Fontaine from 1802 to 1811, and is notable for its arcaded façades. It runs in a straight line between place de la Concorde and rue St-Antoine, in the Marais; at the western end it's filled with tacky souvenir shops – though old-fashioned hotels remain, and there are also gentlemen's outfitters, bookshop **WH Smith** (*see p243*) and tearoom **Angelina** (*see p219*). The area was inhabited by English aristocrats, writers and artists in the 1830s and '40s after the Napoleonic Wars, sleeping at **Le Meurice** (*see p157*) and dining in the fancy restaurants of the Palais-Royal.

Place des Pyramides, at the junction of rue de Rivoli and rue des Pyramides, contains a gleaming gilt equestrian statue of Joan of Arc.

One of four statues of her in the city, it's fêted as a proud symbol of French nationalism every May Day by supporters of the Front National.

Ancient rue St-Honoré, running parallel to rue de Rivoli, is one of those streets that changes style as it goes along: smart shops line it near place Vendôme, small cafés and inexpensive bistros predominate towards Les Halles. The baroque **Eglise St-Roch** is still pitted with bullet holes made by Napoleon's troops when they crushed a royalist revolt in 1795. With its old houses, adjoining rue St-Roch still feels wonderfully authentic; a couple of shops are built into the side of the church. Further up stands **Chapelle Notre- Dame de l'Assomption** (1670-76), now used by the city's Polish community, its dome so disproportionately large that locals have dubbed it *sot dôme* ('stupid dome'; a pun on 'Sodom').

Concept store **Colette** (*see p251*) brought some glamour to what was once a staid shopping area, drawing a swarm of similar stores along in its wake. All are ideally placed

for the fashionistas and film stars who touch down at **Hôtel Costes** (*see p157*). Opposite Colette is rue du Marché-St-Honoré, which once led to the covered Marché St-Honoré, since replaced by offices, in a square lined with trendy restaurants; to the north, rue Danielle-Casanova boasts 18th-century houses.

Further west along rue St-Honoré lies the wonderful, eight-sided **place Vendôme** and a perspective stretching from rue de Rivoli up to Opéra. At the end of the Tuileries, place de la Concorde, originally laid out for the glorification of Louis XV, is a masterclass in the use of open space, and spectacular when lit up at night. The winged Marly horses (only copies, the originals are in the Louvre) frame the entrance to the Champs-Elysées.

Smart rue Royale has tearoom **Ladurée** (*see p225*) and the famed restaurant **Maxim's** (3 rue Royale, 1st, 01.42.65.27.94), with a fabulous art nouveau interior. Rue Boissy d'Anglas proffers stylish shops and the trendy **Buddha Bar** (no.8, 1st, 01.53.05.90.00); and sporting luxuries at **Hermès** (*see p247*) on rue du Fbg-

St-Honoré (a westward extension of rue St-Honoré), and high-end designs at **Yves Saint Laurent** (*see p250*), **Gucci** (no.2, 1st, 01.44. 94.14.70), **Chloé** (no.54, 1st, 01.44.94.33.00) and others set the plush tone.

FREE Eglise St-Germain-l'Auxerrois

2 pl du Louvre, 1st (01.42.60.13.96). M° Louvre Rivoli or Pont Neuf. **Open** 9am-7pm Mon-Sat; 9am-8.30pm Sun. **Admission** free. **Map** p406 H6. The architecture of this former royal church spans several eras: most striking is the elaborate Flamboyant Gothic porch. Inside, there's the 13th-century Lady Chapel and a canopied, carved bench by Le Brun made for the royal family in 1682. The church achieved notoriety on 24 August 1572, when its bell rang to signal the St Bartholomew's Day massacre.

★ FREE Eglise St-Roch

296 rue St-Honoré, 1st (01.42.44.13.20). M° Pyramides or Tuileries. **Open** 9am-7pm daily. **Admission** free. **Map** p401 G5.

River-boat shuttle service

B TOBUS

P A R I S

Tour Eiffel

Musée d'Orsay

St-Germain-des-Prés

Notre-Dame

Jardin des Plantes

Hôtel-de-Ville

Louvre

Champs-Élysées

1 Pass
8 Stops
To discover Paris

Information : ▶ N° Indigo **0 825 05 01 01** **www.batobus.com**
0,15 € TTC / MN

Begun in the 1650s in what was then the heart of Paris, this long church was designed chiefly by Jacques Lemercier; work took so long, the church was consecrated only in 1740. Famed parishioners and patrons are remembered in funerary monuments: Le Nôtre, Mignard, Corneille and Diderot are all here, as are busts by Coysevox and Coustou, Falconet's statue *Christ on the Mount of Olives* and Anguier's superb *Nativity*. Bullet marks from a 1795 shoot-out between royalists and conventionists still pit the façade.

★ FREE Jardin des Tuileries

Rue de Rivoli, 1st. M° Concorde or Tuileries.
Open 7.30am-7pm daily. **Admission** free.
Map p401 G5.
Between the Louvre and place de la Concorde, the gravelled alleyways of these gardens have been a chic promenade ever since they opened to the public in the 16th century; and the popular mood persists with the funfair that sets up along the rue de Rivoli side in summer. André Le Nôtre created the prototypical French garden with terraces and central vista running down the *Grand Axe* through circular and hexagonal ponds. When the Tuileries palace was burned down during the Paris Commune in 1871, the park was expanded. As part of Mitterrand's Grand Louvre project, fragile sculptures such as Coysevox's winged horses were transferred to the Louvre and replaced by copies, and the Maillol sculptures were returned to the Jardins du Carrousel; a handful of modern sculptures has been added, including bronzes by Laurens, Moore, Ernst, Giacometti, and Dubuffet's *Le Bel Costumé*. Replanting has restored parts of Le Nôtre's design and replaced damaged trees, and there's a specialist gardeners' bookshop by place de la Concorde. *Photo p68.*

Jeu de Paume

1 pl de la Concorde, 8th (01.47.03.12.50/www. jeudepaume.org). M° Concorde. **Open** noon-9pm Tue; noon-7pm Wed-Fri; 10am-7pm Sat, Sun (last entry 30mins before closing). **Admission** €6; €3 reductions. **Credit** MC, V. **Map** p401 F5.
The Centre National de la Photographie moved into this site in 2005. The building, which once served as a tennis court, has been divided into two white, almost hangar-like galleries. It is not an intimate space, but it works well for showcase retrospectives. A video art and cinema suite in the basement shows new digital installation work, as well as feature-length films made by artists. There's also a sleek café and a decent bookshop.
▶ *The Jeu de Paume's smaller site is the former Patrimoine Photographique at the Hôtel de Sully; see p100.*

★ Musée des Arts Décoratifs

107 rue de Rivoli, 1st (01.44.55.57.50/www. lesartsdecoratifs.fr). M° Palais Royal Musée du Louvre or Pyramides. **Open** 11am-6pm Tue,

Wed, Fri; 10am-6pm Sat, Sun. Closed some hols.
Admission (with Musée de la Mode & Musée de la Publicité) €8; €6.50 reductions; free under-18s.
PMP. **Credit** MC, V. **Map** p402 H5.
Taken as a whole along with the Musée de la Mode et du Textile and Musée de la Publicité (for both, *see below*), this is one of the world's major collections of design and the decorative arts. Located in the west wing of the Louvre since its opening a century ago, the venue reopened in 2006 after a decade-long, €35-million restoration of the building and of 6,000 of the 150,000 items donated mainly by private collectors.
The major focus here is French furniture and tableware. From extravagant carpets to delicate crystal and porcelain, there is much to admire. Clever spotlighting and black settings show the exquisite treasures – including *châtelaines* made for medieval royalty and Maison Falize enamel work – to their best advantage. Other galleries are categorised by theme: glass, wallpaper, drawings and toys. There are cases devoted to Chinese head jewellery and the Japanese art of seduction with combs. Of most immediate attraction to the layman are the reconstructed period rooms, ten in all, showing how the other (French) half lived from the late 1400s to the early 20th century.

Musée de la Mode et du Textile

107 rue de Rivoli, 1st (01.44.55.57.50/www. lesartsdecoratifs.fr). M° Palais Royal Musée du Louvre or Pyramides. **Open** *Exhibitions* 11am-6pm Tue-Fri; 10am-6pm Sat, Sun. **Admission** €8; €6.50 reductions; free under-18s. PMP.
Credit MC, V. **Map** p402 H5.
This municipal fashion museum holds Elsa Schiaparelli's entire archive and hosts exciting themed exhibitions. Dramatic black-walled rooms make a fine background to the clothes, and video screens and a small cinema space show how the clothes move, as well as interviews with the creators.

★ Musée de l'Orangerie

Jardin des Tuileries, 1st (01.44.77.80.07/ www.musee-orangerie.fr). M° Concorde. **Open** 12.30-7pm Mon, Wed, Thur, Sat, Sun; 12.30-9pm Fri. **Admission** €6.50; €4.50 reductions; free under-18s. PMP. **Credit** MC, V. **Map** p401 F5.
The long-delayed reopening of this Monet showcase finally took place in 2006, and the Orangerie is now firmly back on the tourist radar: expect long queues. Stylistically, the new look is utilitarian and fuss-free, with the museum's eight, tapestry-sized *Nymphéas* (water lilies) paintings housed in two plain oval rooms. They provide a simple backdrop for the astonishing, ethereal romanticism of Monet's works, painted late in his life. Depicting Monet's 'jardin d'eau' at his house in Giverny, the *tableaux* have an intense, dreamy quality – partly reflecting the artist's absorption in the private world of his garden. Downstairs, the Jean Walter and Paul Guillaume collection of Impressionism and the Ecole

SIGHTS

Art Attack

Daniel Buren's columns remain as controversial as ever.

The black-and-white striped columns in the courtyard of the **Palais-Royal** have never been far from controversy. More than 20 years ago, the state's commission of the Daniel Buren installation sparked criticism on an unprecedented scale – and the work is once again the cause of contention, following the decision to renovate it at considerable cost.

Today, Buren's columns (officially titled 'Les Deux Plateaux') have become a favourite photo stop for visiting tourists, but for a long time they were best known for attracting protestors. When minister for culture Jack Lang announced the project back in 1985, there was uproar at the idea of erecting a contemporary artwork in the classical surroundings of the Palais-Royal. Furthermore, Buren had a reputation as an anti-authoritarian, hardly a suitable image for a place that had long been associated with state authority and power.

Almost immediately, journalists launched press campaigns to stop the installation. Demonstrations were organised, graffiti appeared decrying Lang as 'Jack the Ripper', and the Mairie even started legal proceedings to halt the construction. For months, the whole controversy was a regular focus for television and radio shows, as well as a favourite topic for debate in parliament.

Despite these setbacks, Buren's work was finally unveiled to the public on 30 July 1986. Seeing the columns for the first time, most observers were astonished at the success of the project, and had to admit they had judged too hastily. Once the tourists began arriving, local shop and restaurant owners were more than happy, and the hysteria died down. The work was even made a national monument in 1994.

Over the years, though, Buren's columns have fallen into disrepair – to such an extent that the ever-controversial artist threatened in 2007 to destroy his own work if it were not renovated. Although the state had at least paid to polish the 260 marble columns, Buren bemoaned the lack of care accorded to the other elements of his work, the electric lighting and water fountains, which had not been functioning for several years. For Buren, the installation was conceived as a play on positive and negative space, and an essential part of the work is the visibility of lighting and the sounds of water coming from beneath the visitors' feet. 'Would you only show half a painting in a museum?' Buren asked.

The artist's tactics worked. Renovation began on the installation in September 2008, and the €3.2 million project includes restoration of the whole courtyard. The decision itself attracted its fair share of protestors; art critic Pierre Souchaud, who said the renovation was a waste of taxpayers' money. Almost 25 years after their construction, Buren's columns are still roundly dividing opinion.

SIGHTS

de Paris is a mixed bag of sweet-toothed Cézanne and Renoir portraits, along with works by Modigliani, Rousseau, Matisse, Picasso and Derain.

Musée de la Publicité
107 rue de Rivoli, 1st (01.44.55.57.50/www. lesartsdecoratifs.fr). M° Palais Royal Musée du Louvre or Pyramides. **Open** 11am-6pm Tue, Wed, Fri; 11am-9pm Thur; 10am-6pm Sat, Sun. **Admission** (with Musée des Arts Décoratifs & Musée de la Mode) €8; €6.50 reductions; free under-18s. PMP. **Credit** MC, V. **Map** p402 H5.
The upstairs element of the trio of museums in the Louvre west wing, the advertising museum has a distressed interior by Jean Nouvel. Only a fraction of the vast collection of posters, promotional objects and packaging can be seen at one time; vintage posters are accessed in the multimedia space.

★ FREE Palais-Royal
Pl du Palais-Royal, 1st. M° Palais Royal Musée du Louvre. **Open** Gardens 7.30am-8.30pm daily. **Admission** free. **Map** p402 H5.
Built for Cardinal Richelieu by Jacques Lemercier, the building was once known as the Palais Cardinal. Richelieu left it to Louis XIII, whose widow Anne d'Autriche preferred it to the chilly Louvre and rechristened it when she moved in with her son, the young Louis XIV. In the 1780s the Duc d'Orléans, Louis XVI's fun-loving brother, enclosed the gardens in a three-storey peristyle and filled it with cafés, shops, theatres, sideshows and accommodation to raise money for rebuilding the burned-down opera. In contrast to Versailles, the Palais-Royal was a place for people of all classes to mingle in, and its arcades were a trysting venue. Daniel Buren's

modern installation of black-and-white striped columns (*see p72* **Art Attack**) graces the main courtyard; the stately buildings around it house the Conseil d'Etat and ministry of culture.

FREE Place de la Concorde
1st/8th. M° Concorde. **Map** p401 F5.
This is the city's largest square, its grand east-west perspectives stretching from the Louvre to the Arc de Triomphe, and north-south from the Madeleine to the Assemblée Nationale across the Seine. Royal architect Gabriel designed it in the 1750s, along with the two colonnaded mansions astride rue Royale; the west one houses the chic Hôtel de Crillon (*see p157*) and the Automobile Club de France, the other is the Naval Ministry. In 1792 the centre statue of Louis XV was replaced with the guillotine for Louis XVI, Marie-Antoinette and many more. The square was embellished in the 19th century with sturdy lampposts, the Luxor obelisk (from the Viceroy of Egypt), and ornate tiered fountains that represent navigation by water. *Photo p77.*

FREE Place Vendôme
1st. M° Opéra or Tuileries. **Map** p401 G4.
Elegant place Vendôme got its name from a *hôtel particulier* built by the Duc de Vendôme that stood on the site. Opened in 1699, the eight-sided square was conceived by Hardouin-Mansart to show off an equestrian statue of the Sun King, torn down in 1792 and replaced in 1806 by the Colonne de la Grande Armée. Modelled on Trajan's Column in Rome and featuring a spiral comic strip illustrating Napoleon's military exploits, it was made from 1,250 Russian and Austrian cannons captured at the Battle of Austerlitz. During the 1871 Commune this symbol

SIGHTS

of 'brute force and false glory' was pulled down; the present column is a replica. Hardouin-Mansart only designed the façades, with their ground-floor arcade and giant Corinthian pilasters; the buildings behind were put up by nobles and speculators. Today the square houses sparkling jewellers, top fashion houses and the justice ministry. At no.12, you can visit the Grand Salon where Chopin died in 1849; its fabulous allegorical decoration dates from 1777 and has been restored as part of the new museum above the jewellers Chaumet (01.44.77.26.26).

THE BOURSE

In the 1st & 2nd arrondissements.

Far less frenzied than Wall Street, the city's traditional business district is squeezed between the elegant calm of the Palais-Royal and shopping hub the Grands Boulevards. Along rue du Quatre-Septembre, **La Bourse** (the stock exchange) is where financiers and stockbrokers beaver away in grandiose buildings. The Banque de France, France's national central bank, has occupied the 17th-century **Hôtel de Toulouse** since 1811, its long gallery still hung with Old Masters. Nearby, fashion and finance meet at stylish **place des Victoires**, designed by Hardouin-Mansart, forming an intimate circle of buildings today dedicated to fashion.

West of the square is shop-lined galerie Vivienne, the smartest of the covered passages in Paris, adjoining galerie Colbert. Also look out for temporary exhibitions at the **Bibliothèque Nationale de France – Richelieu**. You can linger at the luxury food and wine merchant **Legrand** (*see p263*), or head along passage des Petits-Pères to admire the 17th- to 18th-century **Eglise Notre-Dame-des-Victoires**, the remains of an Augustine convent with a cycle of paintings around the choir by Carle van Loo.

Rue de la Banque leads to the Bourse, behind a commanding neo-classical colonnade. The area has a relaxed feel – it's dead at weekends – but animated pockets exist at places such as **Le Vaudeville** (29 rue Vivienne, 2nd, 01.40.20.04.62) and **Gallopin** (40 rue Notre-Dame-des-Victoires, 2nd, 01.42.36.45.38), busy brasseries

frequented by stockbrokers and journalists. Rue des Colonnes is a quiet street lined with graceful porticos and acanthus motifs dating from the 1790s; its design nemesis, the 1970s concrete-and-glass HQ of Agence France-Presse, the nation's biggest news agency, stands on the other side of busy rue du Quatre-Septembre. Although most newspaper offices have moved elsewhere, *Le Figaro* is still based in rue du Louvre. On the corner of rue Montmartre and rue du Croissant, take a look at the Café du Croissant, where Socialist politician Jean Jaurès was assassinated in 1914 (*see p21* **Aiming for the Top**).

★ Bibliothèque Nationale de France – Richelieu & Musée du Cabinet des Médailles

58 rue de Richelieu, 2nd (01.53.79.59.59/ www.bnf.fr). M° Bourse. **Open** *Galeries Mansart/Mazarine, exhibitions only* 10am-7pm Tue-Sat; noon-7pm Sun. *Cabinet des Médailles* 1-5.45pm Mon-Fri; 1-4.45pm Sat; noon-6pm Sun. **Admission** *Galeries* €5-€7. *Cabinet des Médailles* free. **Credit** AmEx, MC, V. **Map** p402 H4.

The history of the French National Library began in the 1660s, when Louis XIV moved manuscripts that couldn't be housed in the Louvre to this lavish Louis XIII townhouse, formerly the private residence of Cardinal Mazarin. The library was first opened to the public in 1692, and by 1724 it had received so many new acquisitions that the adjoining Hôtel de Nevers had to be added.

Some of the original painted decoration by Romanelli and Grimaldi can still be seen in Galeries Mansart and Mazarine, now used for temporary exhibitions (and closed otherwise). The highlights, however, are the two circular reading rooms: the Salle Ovale, which is full of researchers, note-takers and readers, and the magnificent Salle de Travail, a temple to learning, with its arrangement of nine domes supported on slender columns clearly influenced by the Ottoman architecture of the Levant. The latter is now hauntingly empty, as most of its books have been moved to the Bibliothèque Nationale de France – François Mitterrand (*see p124*).

On the first floor is the Musée du Cabinet des Médailles, a modest two-room collection of coins and medals, including Greek, Roman and medieval examples. There is also a miscellany of other items, including Merovingian king Dagobert's throne, Charlemagne's chess set and small artefacts from the Classical world and ancient Egypt.

La Bourse

Palais Brongniart, pl de la Bourse, 2nd (01.49.27.14.70/http://palaisbourse.euronext. com). M° Bourse. **Open** Guided tours only; call 1 wk in advance. **Admission** €8.50; €5.50 reductions. **No credit cards. Map** p402 H4.

After a century at the Louvre, the Palais-Royal and rue Vivienne, in 1826 the Stock Exchange was transferred to the Bourse, a dignified testament to First Empire classicism designed at Napoleon's behest by Alexandre Brongniart. It was enlarged in 1906 to create a cruciform interior, where brokers buzzed around a central enclosure known as the *corbeille* ('basket' or 'trading floor'). Computers have made the design obsolete, but the pace remains frenetic.

FREE **Place des Victoires**

1st, 2nd. M° Bourse. **Map** p402 H5.
This circular square, the first of its kind, was designed by Hardouin-Mansart in 1685 to show off a statue of Louis XIV that marked victories against Holland. The original statue was destroyed after the Revolution (although the massive slaves from its base are now in the Louvre), and replaced in 1822 with an equestrian statue by Bosio. Among the occupants of the grand buildings that encircle the 'square' are fashion boutiques Kenzo and Victoire.

OPERA & GRANDS BOULEVARDS

In the 2nd, 8th, 9th & 10th arrondissements.

Opéra & Madeleine

Charles Garnier's wedding-cake **Palais Garnier** is all gilt and grandeur, as an opera house built for the ritzy **Café de la Paix** (*see p221*) and the **InterContinental Paris Le Grand** (*see p161*) overlooking place de l'Opéra. Behind, in the basement of what is now the Hôtel Scribe, the Lumière brothers held the world's first public cinema screening in 1895. Outfitter **Old England** (no.12, 9th, 01.47.42.81.99), just opposite on boulevard des Capucines, with its wooden counters, Jacobean-style ceilings and old-style goods and service, could have served as their costume consultants. The **Olympia** concert hall (*see p322*), the celebrated host of the Beatles, Piaf and anyone in *chanson*, was knocked down, but rose again nearby. Over the road at no.35, pioneering portrait photographer Nadar opened a studio in the 1860s, frequented by the likes of Dumas père, Offenbach and Doré. In 1874, it hosted the first Impressionists' exhibition. Pedestrianised rue Edouard VII, laid out in 1911, leads to the octagonal square of the same name with Landowski's equestrian statue of the English monarch. Through an arch, another square contains the belle époque **Théâtre de l'Athénée-Louis Jouvet**.

The **Madeleine**, a monument to Napoleon's army, guards the end of the boulevard. At the head of rue Royale, its classical portico mirrors the Assemblée Nationale on the other side of place de la Concorde over the river, and the interior is a riot of marble and altars. Well worth a browse is extravagant delicatessen **Fauchon** (*see p265*) and other luxury food shops; here, too, is haute cuisine restaurant **Senderens** (*see p193*).

Landmark department stores **Printemps** (*see p240*) and the **Galeries Lafayette** (*see p239*), which opened just behind the Palais Garnier in the late 19th century, also merit

SIGHTS

Gilt Trip

Operatic opulence at the Palais Garnier.

The **Palais Garnier** (*see p77*) is a monument to Second Empire high society. The opera company had been founded by Louis XIV in 1669, moving home after fires and assassination attempts. In 1860, a tender for a grander and safer opera house was launched.

The award was won by then-unknown 35-year-old Charles Garnier, who described opera as 'a temple with art for divinity' and designed his building with the auditorium as a sanctuary and the foyer as a nave. Delayed by money, fire, the Paris Commune and the Franco-Prussian War, it wasn't inaugurated until 1875.

The comfortably upholstered auditorium seats more than 2,000 people – and the exterior is just as opulent, with sculptures of music and dance on the façade, Apollo topping the copper dome, and nymphs bearing torches. Carpeaux's sculpture *La Danse* shocked Parisians with its frank sensuality: in 1869, someone threw a bottle of ink over its marble thighs. The original is now safe in the Musée d'Orsay (*see p144*), where there's also a massive scale model of the building.

The Grand Foyer, with its mirrors and parquet, coloured marble, moulded stucco, sculptures and paintings by Baudry, have all been magnificently restored. You can also visit the Grand Escalier, the auditorium with a false ceiling painted by Chagall in 1964, red satin and velvet boxes, and the library and museum – it was once the emperor's private salons, where he could arrive directly by carriage on the ramp at the rear of the building.

investigation. Behind the latter stands the Lycée Caumartin, designed as a convent in the 1780s by Bourse architect Brongniart, and later one of the city's most prestigious schools. West along boulevard Haussmann is a small square containing the **Chapelle Expiatoire** dedicated to Louis XVI and Marie-Antoinette.

★ Chapelle Expiatoire

29 rue Pasquier, 8th (01.44.32.18.00). M° St-Augustin. **Open** 1-5pm Thur-Sat. **Admission** €5; €3.50 reductions; free under-18s. PMP. **Map** p401 F3.

The chapel was commissioned by Louis XVIII in memory of his executed predecessors, his brother Louis XVI and Marie-Antoinette. Their remains, along with those of 3,000 victims of the Revolution, including Camille Desmoulins, Danton, Malesherbes and Lavoisier, were found in 1814 on the spot where the altar stands. The year after, the bodies of Louis XVI and Marie-Antoinette were transferred to the Basilique St-Denis; the pair are now represented by marble statues, kneeling at the feet of Religion. Every January ardent (albeit unfulfilled) royalists gather here for a memorial service.

FREE Eglise de la Madeleine

Pl de la Madeleine, 8th (01.44.51.69.00/ www.eglise-lamadeleine.com). M° Concorde or Madeleine. **Open** 9am-7pm daily. **Admission** free. **Map** p401 G4.

The building of a church on this site began in 1764, and in 1806 Napoleon sent instructions from Poland for Barthélémy Vignon to design a 'Temple of Glory' dedicated to his Grand Army. After the emperor's fall, construction slowed and the building, by now a church again, was finally consecrated in 1845. The exterior is ringed by huge, fluted Corinthian columns, with a double row at the front, and a frieze of the Last Judgement just above the portico. Inside are giant domes, an organ and pseudo-Grecian side altars in a sea of multicoloured marble. The painting by Ziegler in the chancel depicts the history of Christianity, with Napoleon prominent in the foreground. It's a favourite venue for society weddings.

FREE Eglise St-Augustin

46 bd Malesherbes, 8th (01.45.22.23.12). M° St-Augustin. **Open** Sept-June 10am-6pm Mon-Fri; 10am-7.30pm Sat, Sun. *July, Aug* 10am-12.45pm, 3.30-6pm Tue-Fri; 10am-noon, 4-7.30pm Sat; 10am-noon, 4.30-6pm Sun. **Admission** free. **Map** p401 F3.

St-Augustin, designed between 1860 and 1871 by Victor Baltard, architect of the defunct Les Halles pavilions, is not what it seems. The domed, neo-Renaissance stone exterior is merely a shell: inside is an iron vault structure; even the decorative angels are cast in metal. Impressive paintings by Adolphe William Bouguereau hang in the transept.

Musée de la Franc-Maçonnerie

16 rue Cadet, 9th (01.45.23.43.97). M° Cadet. **Open** 2-6pm Tue-Fri; 1-5pm Sat. Closed 2wks July, Aug, 1wk Sept. **Admission** €2; free under-12s. **No credit cards. Map** p402 H3.

Tucked away at the back of the French Masonic Great Lodge, this museum opened in 1973. It traces the history of French freemasonry, from stonemasons' guilds to prints of masons General Lafayette and 1848 revolutionary leaders Blanc and Barbès. Note that the museum is closed until mid 2009.

Musée de l'Opéra

Palais Garnier, 1 pl de l'Opéra, 9th (01.53.79.37.47/www.bnf.fr). M° Opéra. **Open** *Oct-June* 10am-5pm daily. *July-Sept* 10am-6pm Mon-Fri, Sun; 10am-5pm Sat. **Admission** €7; €5 reductions; free under-10s. **No credit cards. Map** p401 G4.

The Palais Garnier houses temporary exhibitions relating to current opera or ballet productions, and a permanent collection of paintings, scores and bijou opera sets housed in period cases. Entrance includes a visit to the auditorium, if rehearsals permit.

FREE Musées des Parfumeries-Fragonard

9 rue Scribe, 9th (01.47.42.04.56) & 39 bd des Capucines, 2nd (01.42.60.37.14). M° Opéra. **Open** 9am-6pm Mon-Sat; 9am-5pm Sun. **Admission** free. **Map** p401 G4.

Two museums showcase the collection of perfume house Fragonard: five rooms at rue Scribe range

SIGHTS

Place de la Concorde. *See p73.*

from Ancient Egyptian ointment flasks to Meissen porcelain scent bottles; the second museum has bottles by Lalique and Schiaparelli.

★ Palais Garnier

1 pl de l'Opéra, 9th (08.92.89.90.90/www. operade paris.fr). M° Opéra. **Open** 10am-5pm daily. *Guided tours in English (01.40.01.22.63)* July, Aug 11.30am & 2.30pm daily. Sept-June Wed, Sat & Sun. **Admission** €8; €4 reductions. *Guided tours* €12; €6-€10 reductions. **Credit** AmEx, MC, V. **Map** p401 G4.
See p75 **Gilt Trip**.

Quartier de l'Europe

Its streets named after European cities, the area from Gare St-Lazare towards place de Clichy was the Impressionists' quarter. In those days it epitomised modernity, with the station, which opened in 1837, serving the line from Paris to St-Germain-en-Laye (it was rebuilt in the 1880s). The long shabby commuter hub has had a revamp; a glass dome now disgorges travellers from the métro interchange. The adjoining **Hôtel Concorde St-Lazare** (*see p161*) was the city's first great station hotel, with a grandiose hallway built by Eiffel in 1889 for visitors to the Exposition Universelle as he was putting up his Tower. Monet, who lived nearby in rue d'Edimbourg, depicted the steam age in *La Gare St-Lazare* and *Pont de l'Europe*; Pissarro and Caillebotte painted views of the new boulevards, and Manet had a studio on rue de St-Petersbourg. Rue de Budapest remains a red-light district; rue de Rome has long been home to stringed-instrument makers. East of St-Lazare stands the **Eglise de la Trinité**.

FREE Eglise de la Trinité

Pl Estienne-d'Orves, 9th (01.48.74.12.77). M° Trinité. **Open** 11am-8pm Mon-Sat; 10.30am-8pm Sun. **Admission** free. **Map** p401 G3.
Noted for its tiered bell tower, this neo-Renaissance church was constructed between 1861 and 1867.
▶ *Composer Olivier Messiaen (1908-92) was organist at the church for over 30 years.*

The Grands Boulevards

Contrary to popular belief, the string of Grands Boulevards between Madeleine and République (des Italiens, Montmartre, Poissonnière, Bonne-Nouvelle, St-Denis, St-Martin) was not built by Baron Haussmann, but by Louis XIV in 1670, replacing the fortifications of King Philippe-Auguste's city wall. Their ramparts have left their traces in the strange changes of levels, with stairways climbing up to side streets at the eastern end. The boulevards burgeoned after the French Revolution, as residences, theatres and covered passages were put up on land taken from aristocrats and monasteries. To this day they offer a glimpse of the city's divergent personalities – a stroll from Opéra to République runs from luxury shops via

SIGHTS

St-Denis prostitutes – and the phrase *théâtre des boulevards* is still used for lowbrow theatre. Between boulevard des Italiens and rue de Richelieu is place Boïeldieu and the **Opéra Comique** (*see p318*), where Bizet's *Carmen* had its première in 1875.

The 18th-century Hôtel d'Angny, now the town hall of the ninth arrondissement, was once home to the infamous *bals des victimes*, where every guest had to have a relative who had lost his or her head to the guillotine. The **Hôtel Drouot** auction house is ringed by antiques shops, coin- and stamp-dealers and wine bar Les Caves Drouot, where auction-goers and valuers congregate.

There are several grand *hôtels particuliers* on rue de la Grange-Batelière, which leads on one side down the curious passage Verdeau, occupied by antiques dealers, and on the other back to the boulevards via passage Jouffroy. With its grand, barrel-vaulted glass-and-iron roof, this is home to the lovely **Hôtel Chopin** (*see p163*), shop windows of doll's houses, antique walking sticks, art books and film posters, and the colourful entrance of the **Grévin** waxworks (*see p287*).

Over the boulevard, passage des Panoramas is the oldest remaining covered arcade in Paris. When it opened in 1800, panoramas – vast illuminated circular paintings – of Rome,

Jerusalem, London and other cities drew large crowds. Today it contains tearoom **L'Arbre à Cannelle** (no.57, 2nd, 01.45.08.55.87), coin- and stamp-sellers, furniture-makers and old-fashioned printer **Stern** (no.47), established in 1840. The passage leads into a tangle of other little passages and the stage door of the **Théâtre des Variétés** (7 bd Montmartre, 2nd, 01.42.33.09.92), a pretty neo-classical theatre where Offenbach premièred *La Belle Hélène*.

Rue du Fbg-Montmartre is home to celebrated belle époque *bouillon* **Chartier** (no.7, 9th, 01.47.70.86.29), which serves up hundreds of meals a day to the budget-minded. The street is also part of a significant Jewish quarter, less well known than the Marais, that grew up in the 19th century. There are several kosher bakers, restaurants and France's largest synagogue at 44 rue de la Victoire (01.45.26.95.36), an opulent Second Empire affair completed in 1876. Cobbled Cité Bergère, constructed in 1825 with desirable residences, now houses budget hotels, though the pretty iron-and-glass *portes-cochères* remain. On rue Richer stands the art deco **Folies-Bergère** (no.32, 9th, 08.92.68.16.50), only sporadically used for cabaret revues. To the south of boulevard Bonne-Nouvelle lies **Sentier**, and to the north rue du Fbg-Poissonnière is a mixture of rag-trade outlets and *hôtels particuliers*.

Forum des Halles. *See p81.*

SIGHTS

Back on the boulevard is evidence of a move north of the Marais by trendsetting hubs, including **Rex** (*see p330*) and chic **De la Ville Café** (*see p223*). East of here are Louis XIV's twin triumphal arches, the **Porte St-Martin** and **Porte St-Denis**, which were erected to commemorate his military victories.

★ Le Grand Rex
1 bd Poissonnière, 2nd (01.45.08.93.58/ reservations 08.92.68.05.96/www.legrandrex. com). Mº Bonne Nouvelle. **Tour** *Les Etoiles du Rex every 5mins 10am-7pm Wed-Sun; daily during school hols.* **Admission** €8; €7 under-16s. *Tour & film* €12. **Credit** AmEx, MC, V. **Map** p402 J4.
Opened in 1932, this huge art deco cinema was designed by Auguste Bluysen with fantasy Hispanic interiors by US designer John Eberson. Go behind the scenes in the crazy 50-minute guided tour (*see p287*), which includes a presentation about the construction of the auditorium and a visit to the production room, complete with nerve-jolting Sensurround effects.

Hôtel Drouot
9 rue Drouot, 9th (01.48.00.20.20/www. drouot.fr). Mº Richelieu Drouot. **Open** 11am-6pm Mon-Sat. **Auctions** 2pm Mon-Sat. **Map** p402 H3.

A spiky aluminium-and-marble concoction is the unlikely location for France's second largest art market – though it's now rivalled by Sotheby's and Christie's. Inside, escalators take you up to a number of small salerooms, where everything from medieval manuscripts and antique furniture to oriental arts, modern paintings, posters, jewellery and fine wines might be up for sale. Details of forthcoming auctions are published in the weekly *Gazette de l'Hôtel Drouot,* sold at various newsstands around the city.
Other locations Drouot-Montaigne, 15 av Montaigne, 8th (01.48.00.20.80); Drouot Nord, 64 rue Doudeauville, 18th (01.48.00.20.99).

FREE Porte St-Denis & Porte St-Martin
Rue St-Denis/bd St-Denis, 2nd/10th; 33 bd St-Martin, 3rd/10th. Mº Strasbourg St-Denis. **Map** p402 K4.
These twin triumphal gates were erected in 1672 and 1674 at important entry points to the city as part of Colbert's strategy to glorify Paris and celebrate Louis XIV's victories on the Rhine. They are modelled on the triumphal arches of Ancient Rome. The Porte St-Denis is based on a perfect square with a single arch, bearing Latin inscriptions and decorated with military trophies and battle scenes. Porte St-Martin bears allegorical reliefs of Louis XIV's campaigns.

LES HALLES & SENTIER

In the 1st & 2nd arrondissements.

Les Halles is an ugly nexus of commerce and entertainment, with a massive RER-métro interchange as its centrepiece. The area is due for a makeover in the next few years, however.

For centuries, Les Halles was the city's wholesale food market. Covered markets were set up here in 1181 by King Philippe-Auguste; in the 1850s Baltard's spectacular cast-iron and glass pavilions were erected. In 1969 the market was relocated to the southern suburb of Rungis. Baltard's ten pavilions were knocked down (one was saved and now stands at Nogent-sur-Marne), leaving a giant hole. After a long political dispute, it was filled in the early 1980s by the miserably designed **Forum des Halles** underground shopping and transport hub, and the unloved Jardin des Halles.

East of the Forum, in the middle of place Joachim-du-Bellay, stands the **Renaissance Fontaine des Innocents**. The canopied fountain has swirling stone reliefs of water nymphs and titans by Jean Goujon (the ones you see today are copies; the originals are in the Louvre). It was inaugurated for Henri II's arrival in Paris in 1549 on the traditional royal route along rue St-Denis. It was moved and reconstructed here when the nearby Cimetière des Innocents, the city's main burial ground, was demolished in 1786, after flesh-eating rats started gnawing into people's living rooms; the bones were transferred to the catacombs.

Pedestrianised rue des Lombards is a beacon of live jazz, with **Sunset/Sunside**, **Baiser Salé** and **Au Duc des Lombards** (for all, *see p325*) from which to choose. In 1610, King Henri IV was assassinated by a Catholic fanatic named François Ravaillac on nearby rue de la Ferronnerie. Today, the street has become an extension of the Marais gay circuit.

The ancient, easternmost stretch of rue St-Honoré runs into the southern edge of Les Halles. The Fontaine du Trahoir stands at the corner with rue de l'Arbre-Sec. Opposite, the **Hôtel de Truden** (52 rue de l'Arbre-Sec) was built in 1717 for a rich wine merchant; in the courtyard on rue des Prouvaires, the market-traders' favourite **La Tour de Montlhéry** (*see p190*) serves up meaty fare through the night. Fashion chains line the commercial stretch of the rue de Rivoli south of Les Halles. Running towards the Seine, ancient little streets such as rue des Lavandiers-Ste-Opportune and rue Jean-Lantier show a different side of Les Halles. Between rue de Rivoli and the Pont Neuf is department store La Samaritaine, currently closed for safety reasons. Next door, a former section of it contains the chic **Kenzo** flagship,

spa and the **Kong** restaurant and bar (*see p220*), offering more great views. From here, quai de la Mégisserie, lined with horticultural suppliers and pet shops, leads towards Châtelet.

Looming over the northern edge of the Jardin des Halles is the massive **Eglise St-Eustache**, with Renaissance motifs inside and chunky flying buttresses outside. At the western end of the gardens is the circular, domed **Bourse de Commerce**. In front of it, an astrological column is all that remains from a grand palace belonging to Marie de Médicis that stood here.

The empire of French designer **Agnès b** (*see p253*) stretches along most of rue du Jour, with streetwise outlets such as **Kiliwatch** (*see p256*) clustered along the buzzing rue Tiquetonne. On rue Etienne-Marcel, the restored **Tour Jean Sans Peur** is a weird Gothic relic of the fortified medieval townhouse of Jean Sans Peur, duke of Burgundy.

Busy, pedestrianised rue Montorgueil is lined with grocers, delicatessens and pavement cafés. Some historic façades remain from when this was an area in which the well-heeled and the working class mingled: **Pâtisserie Stohrer** (no.51, 2nd, 01.42.33.38.20), founded in 1730 and credited with the invention of the sugary *puits d'amour*; **Le Rocher de Cancale** (no.78, 01.42.33.50.29); and, back towards Les Halles, the golden snail sign hanging in front of **L'Escargot Montorgueil** (no.38, 01.42.36.83.51), a restaurant established in 1832.

Stretching north, bordered by boulevard de Bonne-Nouvelle to the north and boulevard Sébastopol to the east, lies Sentier, the historic garment district, and cocky rue St-Denis, which has long relied on strumpets and strip joints. The grime is unremitting along its northern continuation, rue du Fbg-St-Denis.

Rue Réaumur is lined with striking art nouveau buildings, constructed as industrial premises in the early 1900s. Between rue des Petits-Carreaux and rue St-Denis is the site of the medieval Cour des Miracles – a refuge where paupers would 'miraculously' regain use of their eyes or limbs. A disused aristocratic estate, it was a sanctuary for the underworld until it was cleared out in 1667.

Sentier's streets and passages buzz with porters shouldering linen bundles, as sweatshops churn out passable copies of catwalk creations. Streets such as rue du Caire, rue d'Aboukir and rue du Nil reflect the Egyptian craze that followed Napoleon's Egyptian campaign in 1798 and 1799 – look out too for the sphinx heads and mock hieroglyphics at 2 place du Caire.

FREE Bourse de Commerce
2 rue de Viarmes, 1st (01.55.65.55.65).
M° Louvre Rivoli. **Open** *tour groups* 9am-6pm Mon-Fri. **Admission** free. **Map** p402 J5.

SIGHTS

Housing the Paris chamber of commerce, this trade centre for coffee and sugar was built as a grain market in 1767. The circular building was then covered by a wooden dome, replaced by an avant-garde iron structure in 1809. It is sadly underused.

FREE Eglise St-Eustache

Rue du Jour, 1st (01.42.36.31.05/www.saint-eustache.org). M° Les Halles. **Open** 9am-7.30pm daily. **Admission** free. **Map** p402 J5.
This massive, barn-like church, built between 1532 and 1640, has a Gothic structure but Renaissance decoration in its façade and Corinthian capitals. Among the paintings in the side chapels are a *Descent from the Cross* by Luca Giordano; contemporary pieces by John Armleder were added in 2000. Murals by Thomas Couture adorn the 19th-century Lady chapel. There is a magnificent 8,000-pipe organ, and free recitals are held at 5.30pm on Sundays.

FREE Forum des Halles

1st. M° Les Halles/RER Châtelet Les Halles. **Admission** free. **Map** p402 J5.
The labyrinthine mall and transport interchange extends three levels underground and includes the Ciné Cité multiplex cinema and the Forum des Images, as well as clothing chains, a branch of Fnac and the Forum des Créateurs, a section for young designers. Despite an open central courtyard, a sense of gloom prevails. All should change by 2012, with a new landscaping of the whole area. *Photo p78.*

Pavillon des Arts

Les Halles, 101 rue Rambuteau, 1st (01.42.33. 82.50). M° Châtelet. **Open** 11.30am-6.30pm Tue-Sun. **Admission** €5.50; €2.50-€4 reductions; free under-14s. **No credit cards. Map** p402 K5.
This gallery in Les Halles hosts exhibitions on anything from photography to local history.

★ Tour Jean Sans Peur

20 rue Etienne-Marcel, 2nd (01.40.26.20.28/ www.tourjeansanspeur.com). M° Etienne Marcel. **Open** *Nov-Mar* 1.30-6pm Wed, Sat, Sun. *Apr-Oct* 1.30-6pm Wed-Sun. **Tour** 3pm. **Admission** €5; €3 reductions; free under-7s. *Tour* €8. **No credit cards. Map** p402 J5.
This Gothic turret (1409-11) is the remnant of the townhouse of Jean Sans Peur, duke of Burgundy. He was responsible for the assassination of his rival Louis d'Orléans, which sparked the Hundred Years' War and saw Burgundy become allied to the English crown. Jean had this show-off tower added to his mansion to protect him from vengeance by the aggrieved widow and her husband's followers, known as the 'Armagnacs'. In 1419 he was assassinated by a partisan of the dauphin, the future Charles VII. You can climb the tower, which has rooms leading off the stairway. Carved vaulting halfway up depicts naturalistic branches of oak, hawthorn and hops, symbols of Jean Sans Peur and Burgundian power. The huge mansion originally spanned Philippe-Auguste's city wall.

SIGHTS

Tour Jean Sans Peur.

Champs-Elysées & Western Paris

Culture and couture combine on the Elysian Fields.

The eighth arrondissement is all wealth and grandeur, and those qualities spill over into much of the 16th and the nearer parts of the 17th. Through the heart of this district runs the Champs-Elysées, the city's most iconic thoroughfare and one of Europe's most famous streets.

For all its historic associations, the 'Elysian Fields' underperformed for years, offering little other than fast-food joints and drab shops. But the area is now jumping again with new hotels and restaurants, luxury and concept stores, and renovations of old landmarks –

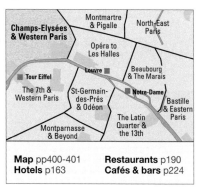

| Map pp400-401 | Restaurants p190 |
| Hotels p163 | Cafés & bars p224 |

including the Grand Palais and the Arc de Triomphe. And it's not all conspicuous consumption: the western end of town is also museum turf, with topics ranging from the history of building to forgery, human evolution to the naval past.

CHAMPS-ELYSEES

In the 8th & 16th arrondissements.

The Champs-Elysées is, and has long been, a symbolic gathering place. Sports victories, New Year's Eve, displays of military might on 14 July – all are celebrated here. Over the past decade, the avenue has undergone a renaissance, thanks initially to a facelift instigated by Jacques Chirac.

Chi-chi shops and chic hotels have set up in the 'golden triangle' (avenues George V, Montaigne and the Champs): **Louis Vuitton** (*see p248*), **Chanel** (*see p247*) and **Jean-Paul Gaultier** (*see p247*), the **Marriott** (70 av des Champs-Elysées, 8th, 01.53.93.55.00) and **Pershing Hall** (*see p166*). The **Four Seasons George V** (*see p163*) has undergone a revamp, and fashionable restaurants such as **Spoon, Food & Wine** (12 rue de Marignan, 8th, 01.40.76.34.44) draw affluent and screamingly fashionable crowds. Crowds line up for the glitzy **Le Lido** cabaret (*see p280*), the now commercialised **Queen** nightclub (*see p333*)

and numerous cinemas, or stroll down the avenue to floodlit **place de la Concorde** (*see p73*). The famous **Drugstore Publicis** (*see p240*) is where locals head to stock up on late-night wines and groceries. Founded by an advertising agency back in the 1960s, it was recently given a rather tacky cladding of swirly metal bars by American architect Michele Saee.

This great spine of western Paris started life as an extension to the Tuileries, laid out by Le Nôtre in the 17th century. By the Revolution, the avenue had reached its full extent, but it was during the Second Empire that it became a focus for fashionable society, military parades and royal processions. Bismarck was so impressed when he arrived with the conquering Prussian army in 1871 that he had a replica, the Ku'damm, built in Berlin, and Hitler's troops made a point of marching down it in 1940, as did their Allied counterparts four years later.

The lower, landscaped reach of the avenue hides two theatres and elegant restaurants **Laurent** (41 av Gabriel, 8th, 01.42.25.00.39) and **Ledoyen** (1 av Dutuit, 8th, 01.53.05.10.01), housed in fancy Napoleon III pavilions. At the

Rond-Point des Champs-Elysées, no.7 (now the Artcurial gallery bookshop and auction house) and no.9 give visitors some idea of the magnificent mansions that once lined the avenue. From here on, it's platinum cards and lanky women aplenty, as avenue Montaigne rolls out a full deck of fashion houses.

Models and magnates nibble on the terrace at fashionable restaurant **L'Avenue** (no.41, 8th, 01.40.70.14.91). You can admire the lavish **Hôtel Plaza Athénée** (*see p165*) and Auguste Perret's innovative 1911-13 **Théâtre des Champs-Elysées** concert hall (*see p318*), with an auditorium painted by Maurice Denis and lights by Lalique.

South of the avenue, the glass-domed **Grand Palais** and Petit Palais, both built for the 1900 Exposition Universelle and still used for major art exhibitions, create a magnificent vista across the elaborate Pont Alexandre III to Les Invalides. The rear wing of the Grand Palais, opening on to avenue Franklin-D-Roosevelt, contains the **Palais de la Découverte** science museum.

To the north lie more smart shops, antiques dealers and officialdom; on circular place Beauvau, wrought-iron gates herald the Ministry of the Interior. The 18th-century Palais de l'Elysée, the official presidential residence, is at 55-57 rue du Fbg-St-Honoré. Nearby, with gardens extending to avenue Gabriel, are the palatial **British Embassy** and ambassadorial residence, once the Hôtel Borghèse.

The western end of the Champs-Elysées is dominated by the **Arc de Triomphe** towering above place Charles-de-Gaulle, also known as L'Etoile. Built by Napoleon, the arch

was modified to celebrate the Revolutionary armies. From the top, visitors can gaze over the square (commissioned later by Haussmann), with 12 avenues radiating out in all directions.

South of the arch, avenue Kléber leads to the monumental buildings and terraced gardens of the panoramic Trocadéro, now housing the aquarium and cinema, **Cinéaqua**. The vast 1930s **Palais de Chaillot** dominates the hill and houses four museums, plus the **Théâtre National de Chaillot** (*see p344*).

To the west of Chaillot, on avenue du Président-Wilson, are two major museums: the **Musée d'Art Moderne de la Ville de Paris** and the **Palais de Tokyo Site de Création Contemporaine** are both inside the the **Palais de Tokyo** building. Opposite is the **Musée Galliera**, used for fashion exhibitions, and up the hill at place d'Iéna are the Asian and oriental art collections of the **Musée National des Arts Asiatiques – Guimet**.

Towards the Champs-Elysées, the former townhouse of avant-garde patron Marie-Laure de Noailles has been given a cheeky revamp. It now houses the **Galerie-Musée Baccarat**.

SIGHTS

Arc de Triomphe

Meet the Moderns

Amid the grandeur, the 16th houses a wealth of avant-garde architecture.

In the early 1900s, the 16th arrondissement was a hotbed of architectural experimentation. Artists' studios, apartment blocks and luxury villas sprang up regularly, all around a district that had only recently been incorporated into Paris proper.

One such building was the **Castel Béranger** (*see p90*). It's the art nouveau masterpiece of Hector Guimard, who also designed the rampart tendrils sprouting from the wrought-iron fence of the Hôtel Mezzara, at no.60. Guimard's home, where he lived with his American artist wife Adeline Oppenheim, was on nearby avenue Mozart (no.122).

North-west from here is rue du Dr-Blanche, home to the **Fondation Le Corbusier** (8-10 square du Dr-Blanche; *see p90*). Housed in two villas designed by the architect in 1923, the interior reveals his mastery of multiple viewpoints, fluidity of space and surprising use of colour. Just off rue du Dr-Blanche, turning right into rue Mallet-Stevens, stand six exclusive cubist houses by Robert Mallet-Stevens, the glamorous architect and designer who best combined the elegance of art deco with the rigour of modernism.

Further east, at rue Raynouard, nos. 51-55 were designed by Auguste Perret in reinforced concrete, cunningly tinted golden yellow to match Paris stone. The building contained apartments and Perret's architectural offices. There's more Perret at no.25bis rue Benjamin-Franklin: behind the leaf-motif tiles, the 1904 building was one of the first to be constructed around a concrete frame. The revolutionary structure freed up the floor plan from load-bearing walls, creating the light, airy spaces associated with modernism – as well as giving all the occupants a view of the Seine.

A little further on stands the **Palais de Chaillot** (pl du Trocadéro), an example of gigantesque 1930s state classical revival. It was designed by Léon Azéma, Louis-Hippolyte Boileau and Jacques Carlu for the Exposition Universelle of 1937, with two curved wings, giant bronze sculptures by Henri Bouchard and Pommier and quotations by Paul Valéry. The east wing is home to the **Cité de l'Architecture** (*see p85*), complete with a walk-in replica of an apartment from Le Corbusier's Cité Radieuse in Marseille.

Palais de Chaillot.

★ Arc de Triomphe

Pl Charles-de-Gaulle (access via underpass), 8th (01.55.37.73.77). M° Charles de Gaulle Etoile. **Open** *Oct-Mar* 10am-10.30pm daily. *Apr-Sept* 10am-11pm daily. **Admission** €9; €5.50 reductions; free under-18s. PMP. **Credit** AmEx, MC, V. **Map** p400 C3.

Napoleon ordered the Arc de Triomphe's construction in 1809 as a monument to the achievements of his armies, but his empire began to collapse almost immediately; the arch was completed only in 1836. Still, it bears the names of Napoleon's victories, and is decorated on its flanks with a frieze of battle scenes and sculptures, including Rude's famous *Le Départ des Volontaires* (aka *La Marseillaise*). French troops finally got their victory march through it at the end of World War I; the annual Bastille Day military procession now starts here (*see p276*). Climb the stairs for wonderful views, a fully renovated interior and a new museum, which opened in 2008 with interactive displays.

FREE Cimetière de Passy

2 rue du Commandant-Schloesing, 16th (01.53.70.40.80). M° Trocadéro. **Open** *16 Mar-5 Nov* 8am-5.30pm Mon-Fri; 8.30am-5.30pm Sat; 9am-5.30pm Sun. *6 Nov-15 Mar* 8am-6pm Mon-Fri; 8.30am-6pm Sat; 9am-6pm Sun. **Admission** free. **Map** p400 B5.

Since 1874, this has been one of the most desirable Paris locations in which to be laid to rest. Here you'll find composers Debussy and Fauré, painters Manet and his sister-in-law Berthe Morisot, writer Giraudoux, and various generals and politicians.

★ Cinéaqua

2 av des Nations Unies, 16th (01.40.69.23.23/ www.cineaqua.com). M° Trocadéro. **Open** 10am-8pm daily. **Admission** €19.50; €12.50-€15 reductions; free under-3s. **Credit** MC, V. **Map** p400 B5.

Opened in 2006, this aquarium and three-screen cinema is a wonderful attraction and a key element in the renaissance of the once moribund Trocadéro. Many have baulked at the admission price, though.

★ Cité de l'Architecture et du Patrimoine

Palais de Chaillot, 1 pl du Trocadéro, 16th (01.58.51.52.00/www.citechaillot.fr). M° Trocadéro. **Open** 11am-7pm Mon, Wed, Fri-Sun; 11am-9pm Thur. **Admission** €8; €5 reductions; free under-18s. **Credit** MC, V. **Map** p400 B5.

Opened in 2007 in the eastern wing of the Palais de Chaillot, this architecture and heritage museum impresses principally by its scale. The expansive ground floor is filled with life-size mock-ups of cathedral façades and heritage buildings, and interactive screens place the models in context. Upstairs, darkened rooms house full-scale copies of medieval and Renaissance murals and stained-glass windows.

The highlight of the modern architecture section is the walk-in replica of an apartment from Le Corbusier's Cité Radieuse in Marseille. Temporary exhibitions are housed in the large basement area.

FREE Fondation d'Enterprise Paul Ricard

12 rue Boissy d'Anglas, 8th (01.53.30.88.00/ www.fondation-enterprise-ricard.com). M° Concorde. **Open** 10am-7pm Mon-Fri. **Admission** free. **Map** p401 F4.

The Pastis firm promotes modern art with the Prix Paul Ricard, where young French artists are shortlisted by an independent curator for an annual prize. ▶ *The Prix Paul Ricard coincides with FIAC (see p278) each autumn.*

FREE Fondation Mona Bismarck

34 av de New-York, 16th (01.47.23.38.88/ www.monabismarck.org). M° Alma Marceau. **Open** 10.30am-6.30pm Tue-Sat. Closed Aug. **Admission** free. **Map** p400 C5.

The Fondation provides a chic setting for eclectic exhibitions, from Etruscan antiquities to folk art.

Fondation Pierre Bergé Yves Saint Laurent

3 rue Léonce-Reynaud, 16th (01.44.31.64.00/ www.fondation-pb-ysl.net). M° Alma Marceau. **Open** *Exhibitions* 11am-5.30pm Tue-Sun. Closed Aug. **Admission** €5; €3 reductions; free under-10s. **Credit** AmEx, MC, V. **Map** p400 D5.

When Yves Saint Laurent bowed out of designing in 2002, he reopened his fashion house as this foundation, exhibiting Picasso and Warhol paintings with the dresses they closely inspired. Every sketch and every *toile* has been carefully catalogued, and many of Saint Laurent's friends and clients have presented the designer with the dresses he created for them, stored in the upper floors at precisely 18 degrees centigrade and a hygrometric level of 50 per cent.

★ Galerie-Musée Baccarat

11 pl des Etats-Unis, 16th (01.40.22.11.00/ www.baccarat.fr). M° Boissière or Iéna. **Open** 10am-6pm Mon, Wed-Sat. **Admission** €7; €3.50 reductions; free under-18s. **Credit** *Shop* AmEx, DC, MC, V. **Map** p400 C4.

Philippe Starck has created a neo-rococo wonderland in the former mansion of the Vicomtesse de Noailles. From the red carpet entrance with a chandelier in a fish tank to the Alchemy room, which was decorated by Gérard Garouste, there's a play of light and movement that makes Baccarat's work, past and present, sing. See items by great designers Georges Chevalier and Ettore Sottsass, services made for princes and maharajahs, and monumental show-off items made for the great exhibitions of the 1800s. ▶ *If you want to eat at the opulent Le Cristal Room restaurant (01.40.22.11.10), be warned that there's a two-month waiting list.*

Galeries Nationales du Grand Palais

3 av du Général-Eisenhower, 8th (01.44.13.17.
17/reservations 08.92.68.46.94/www.grand
palais.fr). M° Champs-Elysées Clemenceau. **Open**
10am-8pm Mon, Thur-Sun; 10am-10pm Wed; pre-
booking compulsory before 1pm. **Admission**
Before 1pm with reservation €11.10. *After 1pm*
without reservation €10; €8 reductions; free
under-13s. **Credit** MC, V. **Map** p401 E5.
Built for the 1900 Exposition Universelle, the Grand
Palais was the work of three different architects,
each of whom designed a façade. During World War
II it accommodated Nazi tanks. In 1994 the magnificent glass-roofed central hall was closed when bits
of metal started falling off, although exhibitions continued to be held in the other wings. After major
restoration, the Palais reopened in 2005.

Musée d'Art Moderne de la Ville de Paris

11 av du Président-Wilson, 16th (01.53.67.40.
00/www.mam.paris.fr). M° Alma Marceau or
Iéna. **Open** 10am-6pm Tue-Sun. **Admission**
Temporary exhibitions €4.50-€9; €2.50-€4.50
reductions; free under-13s. **No credit cards.**
Map p406 H7.
This monumental 1930s building, housing the city's
modern art collection, reopened in 2006 with a Pierre
Bonnard exhibition. The museum is strong on the
Cubists, Fauves, the Delaunays, Rouault and Ecole
de Paris artists Soutine, Modigliani and van Dongen.

Musée de la Contrefaçon

16 rue de la Faisanderie, 16th (01.56.26.14.00).
M° Porte Dauphine. **Open** 9am-12.30pm, 2-
5.30pm Tue-Sun. **Admission** €4; €3 reductions;
free under-12s. **No credit cards. Map** p400 A4.
This museum was set up by the French anti-coun-
terfeiting association with the aim of deterring forg-
ers – but playing spot-the-fake with brands such as
Reebok, Lacoste and Vuitton is fun for visitors too.

Musée Dapper

35bis rue Paul-Valéry, 16th (01.45.00.91.75/www.
dapper.com.fr). M° Victor Hugo. **Open** 11am-7pm
Mon, Wed-Sun. **Admission** €6; €3 reductions;
free under-16s. **Credit** MC, V. **Map** p400 B4.
Named after the 17th-century Dutch humanist Olfert
Dapper, the Fondation Dapper began as an organi-
sation dedicated to preserving sub-Saharan art.
Reopened in 2000, the venue created by Alain Moatti
houses a performance space, bookshop and café.
Each year it stages two African-themed exhibitions.

Musée Galliera

10 av Pierre-1er-de-Serbie, 16th
(01.56.52.86.00). M° Iéna. **Open** *Exhibitions*
10am-6pm Tue-Sun. **Admission** (incl audio-
guide) €7.50; €3.50 reductions; free under-14s.
Credit MC, V. **Map** p400 D5.

This look at clothes through history takes an
academic approach to its subject. Housed in a *hôtel*
particulier built by Eiffel, the Galliera has a huge costume collection. It has links with the fashion industry, and its initiative with young designers shows
innovative work the moment it hits the shops.

★ Musée de l'Homme

Palais de Chaillot, 17 pl du Trocadéro, 16th
(01.44.05.72.72/www.mnhn.fr). M° Trocadéro.
Open 10am-5pm Mon, Wed-Fri; 10am-6pm Sat,
Sun. **Admission** €7; €5 reductions; free under-
14s. **Credit** *Shop* MC, V. **Map** p400 B5.
This department of the Muséum National d'Histoire
Naturelle (*see p287*) considers human evolution,
genetic diversity and the population explosion. The
prehistoric department covers from 3.7 million years
ago to the Bronze Age. *See right* **Human Nature.**

★ Musée National des Arts Asiatiques – Guimet

6 pl d'Iéna, 16th (01.56.52.53.00/www.musee
guimet. fr). M° Iéna. **Open** 10am-5.45pm Mon,
Wed-Sun (last entry 5.15pm). **Admission** €6; €4
reductions, all Sun; free students, under-18s, all
1st Sun of mth. PMP. **Credit** *Shop* AmEx, DC,
MC, V. **Map** p400 C5.
Founded by industrialist Emile Guimet in 1889 to
house his collection of Chinese and Japanese religious art, and later incorporating oriental collections
from the Louvre, the museum has 45,000 objects
from Neolithic times onwards, in a voyage across
Asian religions and civilisations. Lower galleries
focus on India and South-east Asia, centred on stunning Hindu and Buddhist Khmer sculpture from
Cambodia. Don't miss the Giant's Way, part of the
entrance to a temple complex at Angkor Wat.
Upstairs, Chinese antiquities include mysterious
jade discs. Afghan glassware, Tibetan mandalas
and Moghul jewellery also feature.

Musée National de la Marine

Palais de Chaillot, 17 pl du Trocadéro, 16th
(01.53.06.69.53/www.musee-marine.fr). M°
Trocadéro. **Open** 10am-6pm Mon, Wed-Sun.
Admission *Main collection & temporary*
exhibitions €9; €5-€7 reductions; free under-6s.
Main collection €6.50; €4 reductions; free under-
18s. PMP. **Credit** *Shop* MC, V. **Map** p400 B5.
French naval history is outlined in detailed models
of battleships and Vernet's series of paintings of
French ports (1754-65). There's also an imperial
barge, built when Napoleon's delusions of grandeur
were reaching their zenith in 1810.

FREE Palais de Chaillot

Pl du Trocadéro, 16th. M° Trocadéro.
Admission free. **Map** p400 C5.
This immense pseudo-classical building was constructed by Azéma, Boileau and Carlu for the 1937
international exhibition, with giant sculptures of

Apollo by Henri Bouchard, and inscriptions by Paul Valéry. It stands on the foundations of an earlier complex put up for the 1878 World Fair.

▶ *The Palais houses the Musée National de la Marine and the Musée de l'Homme (for both, see right). In the east wing are the Théâtre National de Chaillot (see p344) and the Cité de l'Architecture et du Patrimoine (see p85).*

★ Palais de la Découverte
Av Franklin-D.-Roosevelt, 8th (01.56.43.20.21/ www.palais-decouverte.fr). M° Champs-Elysées Clemenceau or Franklin D. Roosevelt. **Open** 9.30am-6pm Tue-Sat; 10am-7pm Sun (last entry 30mins before closing). **Admission** €7; €4.50 reductions; free under-5s. *Planetarium* €3.50. **Credit** AmEx, MC, V. **Map** p401 E5.
This science museum houses designs dating from Leonardo da Vinci's time to the present day. Models,

real apparatus and audio-visual material bring the displays to life, and permanent exhibits cover astrophysics, astronomy, biology, chemistry, physics and earth sciences. The pertinent Planète Terre section highlights the latest developments in meteorology, and one room is dedicated to the sun. There are shows at the Planetarium too, and 'live' experiments take place at weekends and during school holidays.

Palais de Tokyo: Site de Création Contemporaine
13 av du Président-Wilson, 16th (01.47.23. 54.01/www.palaisdetokyo.com). M° Alma Marceau or Iéna. **Open** noon-midnight Tue-Sun. **Admission** €6; €4.50 reductions; free under-18s, art students. **Map** p400 B5.
When it opened in 2002, many thought the Palais' stripped-back interior was a design statement. In fact, it was a practical answer to tight finances. The

Human Nature

The Musée de l'Homme gets a long-overdue makeover.

It's been a long time coming, but the **Musée de l'Homme** (*see p86*) is finally getting a facelift. Situated in the west wing of the imposing Palais de Chaillot just opposite the Eiffel Tower, this 70-year-old museum had been left to sad decline, its display cabinets and explanatory texts looking ever more archaic and uninviting. To make matters worse, the museum's entire ethnographic collection was removed in 2000 for inclusion in the new Musée du Quai Branly, the state's showcase for its non-Western art collection.

The renovation project will bring a revamp for the building and a reorientation in the museum's direction. The new-look museum will focus on man's evolution and relationship with his environment. Alongside a stylish and large space for the permanent collection, the revamped building will also include research laboratories, teaching facilities and a well-stocked library. The aim is to redefine the museum not just as a showcase for anthropology, but also as a leader in anthropological research.

As for the presentation and organisation of the collection itself, no clear decision has yet been taken. A report published in 2004 surmised that the new museum should take into account recent breakthroughs in anthropological thinking by presenting man's relationship with his environment in all its diversity. Using

interactive displays and waxwork figures, the exhibition will aim to make visitors think about their origins, history, future and their place in the world today. Despite the loss of its ethnographic works, the Musée de l'Homme still possesses an extremely rich collection, and the vast renovation project should help put it back on the tourist map. Visitors will have to wait until 2012 to appreciate the finished project, but the museum is scheduled to stay open during most of the renovation work.

SIGHTS

Grand Palais.

century, when a stay in Paris was essential to the education of every Russian aristocrat, it is still at the heart of an émigré little Russia.

Famed for its stand during the 1871 Paris Commune, the Quartier des Batignolles to the north-east towards place de Clichy is more working class, housing the rue de Lévis market, tenements lining the deep railway canyon and square des Batignolles park, with the pretty **Eglise Ste-Marie-de-Batignolles** looking on to a semi-circular square. It's fast becoming trendy, with a restaurant scene to match.

★ FREE Alexander Nevsky Cathedral
*12 rue Daru, 17th (01.42.27.37.34). M°
Courcelles.* **Open** times vary. **Admission** free.
Map p400 D3.
All onion domes, icons and incense, this Russian Orthodox church was completed in 1861 in the neo-Byzantine Novgorod-style of the 1600s, by the tsar's architect Kouzmin, responsible for the Fine Arts Academy in St Petersburg. Services, on Sunday mornings and Orthodox saints' days, are in Russian.

FREE Cimetière des Batignolles
*8 rue St-Just, 17th (01.53.06.38.68). M° Porte de
Clichy.* **Open** *16 Mar-6 Nov* 8am-5.45pm Mon-Fri; 8.30am-5.45pm Sat; 9am-5.45pm Sun &
public hols. *7 Nov-15 Mar* 8am-5.15pm Mon-Fri;
8.30am-5.15pm Sat; 9am-5.15pm Sun & public
hols. **Admission** free.
Squeezed inside the Périphérique are the graves of poet Paul Verlaine, Surrealist André Breton, and Léon Bakst, costume designer of the Ballets Russes.

FREE Musée Cernuschi
*7 av Velasquez, 8th (01.53.96.21.50/www.
cernuschi. paris.fr). M° Monceau or Villiers.*
Open 10am-6pm Tue-Sun. **Admission** free.
Temporary exhibitions €7.50; €3.80-€6
reductions; free under-18s. **Map** p401 E2.
Since the banker Henri Cernuschi built a *hôtel particulier* by the Parc Monceau for the treasures he found in the Far East in 1871, this collection of Chinese art has grown steadily. The museum has been expanded to twice its size, and was reopened back in 2005 with a total exhibition area of 3,200sq m (34,500sq ft) and 1,000 exhibits. The fabulous displays range from legions of Han and Wei dynasty funeral statues to refined Tang celadon wares and Sung porcelain.

★ Musée Jacquemart-André
*158 bd Haussmann, 8th (01.45.62.11.59/www.
musee-jacquemart-andre.com). M° Miromesnil
or St-Philippe-du-Roule.* **Open** 10am-6pm daily.
Admission €10; €7.30 reductions; free under-7s.
Credit AmEx, MC, V. **Map** p401 E3.
Long terrace steps and a stern pair of stone lions usher visitors into this grand 19th-century mansion,

1937 building has now come into its own as an open-plan space with a skylit central hall, hosting exhibitions, shows and performances. Extended hours and a funky café have succeeded in drawing a younger audience, and the roll-call of artists is impressive (Pierre Joseph, Wang Du and others). The name dates to the 1937 Exposition Internationale, but is also a reminder of links with a new generation of artists from the Far East.

MONCEAU & BATIGNOLLES

In the 8th & 17th arrondissements.

Parc Monceau, with its neo-antique follies and large lily pond, lies at the far end of avenue Hoche (the main entrance is on boulevard de Courcelles, the circular pavilion by Ledoux). Three museums capture the extravagance of the area when it was newly fashionable in the 19th century: the **Musée Jacquemart-André**, with its Old Masters, the **Musée Nissim de Camondo** (superb 18th-century decorative arts), and the **Musée Cernuschi** (Chinese art). There are some nice exotic touches too, such as the unlikely red lacquer **Galerie Ching Tsai Too** (48 rue de Courcelles, 8th), built in 1926 for a dealer in oriental art near the wrought-iron gates of Parc Monceau, or the onion domes of the Russian Orthodox **Alexander Nevsky Cathedral** on rue Daru. Built in the mid 19th

home to a collection of equally stately *objets d'art* and fine paintings. The collection was built up by Edouard André and his artist wife Nélie Jacquemart, using money inherited from his rich banking family. The mansion was made to order to house their art hoard, which includes Rembrandts, Tiepolo frescoes and various works by Italian masters Uccello, Mantegna and Carpaccio. The visit unfolds in style, from the richly decorated ground floor past a marble winter garden and up a double spiral staircase.
▶ *The adjacent tea room, with its fabulous tottering cakes, is a favourite with the smart lunch set.*

Musée Nissim de Camondo
63 rue de Monceau, 8th (01.53.89.06.40/ www.lesartsdecoratifs.fr). M° Monceau or Villiers. **Open** 10am-5.30pm Wed-Sun. **Admission** €6; €4.50 reductions; free under-18s. PMP. **Credit** AmEx, MC, V. **Map** p401 E3.
Put together by Count Moïse de Camondo, this collection is named after his son Nissim, killed in World War I. Moïse replaced the family's two houses near Parc Monceau with this palatial residence and lived here in a style in keeping with his love of the 18th century. Grand first-floor reception rooms are filled with furniture by craftsmen of the Louis XV and XVI eras, silver services, Sèvres and Meissen porcelain, Savonnerie carpets and Aubusson tapestries.

FREE Parc Monceau
Bd de Courcelles, av Hoche, rue Monceau, 8th. M° Monceau. **Open** *Nov-Mar* 7am-8pm daily. *Apr-Oct* 7am-10pm daily. **Admission** free. **Map** p401 E2.
Surrounded by grand *hôtels particuliers* and elegant Haussmannian apartments, Monceau is a favourite with well-dressed children and their nannies. It was laid out in the 18th century for the Duc de Chartres in the English style, with a lake, lawns and a variety of follies: an Egyptian pyramid, a Corinthian colonnade, Venetian bridge and sarcophagi.

PASSY & AUTEUIL
In the 16th arrondissement.

West of l'Etoile, the extensive 16th arrondissement is the epitome of bourgeois respectability, with grandiose apartments and

---

INSIDE TRACK
THEATRE EATS

At the top of the Théâtre des Champs-Elysées is the sleek, glass-fronted **Maison Blanche** restaurant (01.47.23.55.99), with views across the Seine to the Eiffel Tower.

---

exclusive residences lining the private roads. It's also home to some seminal examples of modernist architecture, plus several of the city's most important museums.

When Balzac lived at no.47 rue Raynouard in the 1840s, Passy was a country village (it was absorbed into the city in 1860) where the rich came to take cures at its mineral springs – a history alluded to by rue des Eaux. The novelist's former abode, **Maison de Balzac**, is open to the public. The **Musée du Vin** is of interest if only for its setting in the cellars of the wine-producing Abbaye de Minimes, destroyed in the Revolution. Rue de Passy, formerly the village high street, and parallel rue de l'Assomption, are the focus of local life, with fashion shops and *traiteurs*, the department store **Franck et Fils** (80 rue de Passy, 16th, 01.44.14.38.00) and a pricey covered market.

The former Passy station is now restaurant **La Gare** (19 chaussée de la Muette, 16th, 01.42.15.15.31). Ladies who shop stop by the lovely art deco **La Rotonde** café (12 chaussée de la Muette, 16th, 01.45.24.45.45) or stock up on cakes at Japanese *pâtisserie* **Yamazaki** (6 chaussée de la Muette, 16th, 01.40.50.19.19).

West of the former high society pleasure gardens of the Jardin du Ranelagh you'll find the **Musée Marmottan**, with its superb collection of Monet's late water-lily canvases, other Impressionists and Empire furniture.

Next to the Pont de Grenelle stands the circular **Maison de Radio-France**, the giant home of state broadcasting. You can attend concerts (*see p317*) or take a tour around its endless corridors; employees nickname the place 'Alphaville', after the Jean-Luc Godard film. From here, in more upmarket Auteuil, you can head up rue Fontaine, the best place to find art nouveau architecture by Hector Guimard, of métro entrance fame. He also designed the less ambitious nos.19 and 21. At no.96 pay homage to Marcel Proust. This is the house where he was born.

Nearby, the **Fondation Le Corbusier** occupies two of the architect's avant-garde houses in square du Dr-Blanche. A little further up rue du Dr-Blanche sculptor Henri Bouchard himself commissioned the studio and house that is now the dusty **Atelier-Musée Henri Bouchard**. Much of the rest of Auteuil is private territory, with exclusive streets of residences off rue Chardon-Lagache; the studio of 19th-century sculptor Jean-Baptiste Carpeaux remains, looking rather lost, at no.39 boulevard Exelmans. The top storey was later added by Guimard.

West of the 16th, across the Périphérique, sprawls the parkland of **Bois de Boulogne**. At porte d'Auteuil are the romantic **Serres d'Auteuil** and sports venues the **Parc des**

SIGHTS

Princes, home of football club Paris St-Germain (for both, *see p334*), and **Roland Garros** (*see p334*), host of the French Tennis Open. Another attraction will open in 2009: the **Fondation Louis-Vuitton**, to be housed in a new Frank Gehry glass construction.

★ FREE Bois de Boulogne

16th. M° Les Sablons or Porte Dauphine. **Admission** free.

Covering 865 hectares, the Bois was once the Forêt de Rouvray hunting grounds. It was landscaped in the 1860s, when artificial grottoes and waterfalls were created around the Lac Inférieur. The Jardin de Bagatelle (route de Sèvres à Neuilly, 16th, 01.40.67.97.00) is famous for its roses, daffodils and water lilies, and contains an orangery that rings to the sound of Chopin in summer. The Jardin d'Acclimatation (*see p290*) is a children's amusement park, complete with a miniature train, farm, rollercoaster and boat rides. The Bois also boasts two racecourses (Longchamp and Auteuil), sports clubs and stables, and restaurants, including Le Pré Catelan (route de Suresnes, 16th, 01.44.14.41.14).

Today, there are plans to reduce the traffic and replant some of the scrubby woodland. The opening of the Fondation Louis-Vuitton in 2009 should also change the character of the area. For the time being, it attracts picnickers and dog walkers, with a boating lake and nearby cycle hire, but by night it's transformed into a parade ground for transsexuals and swingers of every stripe.

Castel Béranger

14 rue La Fontaine, 16th. M° Jasmin. Closed to the public.

Guimard's masterpiece of 1895-98 epitomises art nouveau in Paris. From outside you can see his love of brick and wrought iron, asymmetry and renunciation of harsh angles not found in nature. Green seahorses climb the façade, and the faces on the balconies are thought to be self-portraits, inspired by Japanese figures, to ward off evil spirits.

Fondation Le Corbusier

Villa La Roche, 8-10 square du Dr-Blanche, 16th (01.42.88.41.53/www.fondationlecorbusier.fr). M° Jasmin. **Open** 1.30-6pm Mon; 10am-12.30pm, 1.30-6pm Tue-Thur; 10am-12.30pm, 1.30-5pm Fri; 10am-5pm Sat. Closed Aug. **Admission** €2-€4; free under-14s. **No credit cards.**

Designed by Le Corbusier in 1923 for a Swiss art collector, this house shows the architect's ideas in practice, with its stilts, strip windows, roof terraces and balconies, built-in furniture and an unsuspected use of colour inside: sludge green, blue and pinky beige. A sculptural cylindrical staircase and split volumes create a variety of geometrical vistas; inside, Le Corbusier's own neo-Cubist paintings and furniture sit alongside pieces by Perriand. Adjoining Villa Jeanneret houses the foundation's library.

FREE Le Jardin des Serres d'Auteuil

3 av de la Porte d'Auteuil, 16th (01.40.71.75.23). M° Porte d'Auteuil. **Open** *Winter* 10am-5pm daily. *Summer* 10am-6pm daily. **Admission** free.

These romantic glasshouses were opened in 1895 to cultivate plants for Paris parks and public spaces. Today there are seasonal displays of orchids and begonias. Look out for the steamy tropical pavilion with palms, birds and Japanese ornamental carp.

Maison de Balzac

47 rue Raynouard, 16th (01.55.74.41.80/www. paris.fr/musees). M° Passy. **Open** 10am-6pm Tue-Sun. **Admission** €4; €2-€3 reductions; free under-13s. **Credit** MC, V. **Map** p404 B6.

Honoré de Balzac rented this apartment in 1840 to escape his creditors. Converted into a museum, it has a collection of mementos spread over several floors. Memorabilia includes first editions and letters, plus portraits of friends and the novelist's mistress Mme Hanska, with whom he corresponded for years before they married. Along with a 'family tree' of his characters that extends across several walls, you can see Balzac's desk and the monogrammed coffee pot that fuelled all-night work on *Comédie Humaine*.

★ Musée Marmottan – Claude Monet

2 rue Louis-Boilly, 16th (01.44.96.50.33/www. marmottan.com). M° La Muette. **Open** 10am-6pm Mon, Wed-Sun (last entry 5.30pm); 11am-9pm Tue (last entry 8.30pm). **Admission** €9; €5 reductions; free under-8s. **Credit** MC, V.

Originally a museum of the Empire period left to the state by collector Paul Marmottan, this old hunting pavilion has become a famed holder of Impressionist art thanks to two bequests: the first by the daughter of the doctor of Manet, Monet, Pissarro, Sisley and Renoir; the second by Monet's son Michel. Its Monet collection, the largest in the world, numbers 165 works, plus sketchbooks, palette and photos. A special circular room was created for the breathtaking late water lily canvases; upstairs are works by Renoir, Manet, Gauguin, Caillebotte and Berthe Morisot, 15th-century primitives, a Sèvres clock and a collection of First Empire furniture.

Musée du Vin

Rue des Eaux, 16th (01.45.25.63.26/www.musee duvinparis.com). M° Passy. **Open** 10am-6pm Tue-Sun. **Admission** (with guidebook and glass of wine) €9; €7-€7.50 reductions; free under-14s, diners in the restaurant. **Credit** *Shop, restaurant* AmEx, DC, MC, V. **Map** p404 B6.

Here the Confrères Bacchiques defend French wines from imports and advertising laws. In the cellars of an old wine-producing monastery are displays on the history of viticulture, with waxwork peasants, old tools, bottles and corkscrews. Visits finish with a wine tasting and, a paid extra, a meal.

SIGHTS

Montmartre & Pigalle

Uphill for romance, downhill for sleaze.

For such a young part of Paris – it was only annexed by the city in 1860 – Montmartre has astonishing renown, among foreigners as much as Frenchmen. It doesn't take much exploring before you realise that the fame and affection are deserved: the steep streets and staircases, the ghosts of some of the 19th and 20th centuries' greatest artists, and the present-day buzz of hip cafés and bars all produce a charm that even mass tourism can't obscure. The same can't be said of louche Pigalle at the bottom of the hill, with its sex shops and grime. Still, these days, many of the red lights are attached not to brothels but to hot music venues and nightspots.

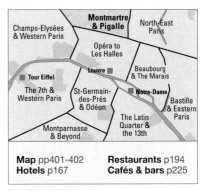

Champs-Elysées & Western Paris	**Montmartre & Pigalle** North-East Paris
	Opéra to Les Halles
Tour Eiffel	Louvre Beaubourg & The Marais
The 7th & Western Paris	St-Germain-des-Prés & Odéon Notre-Dame Bastille & Eastern Paris
Montparnasse & Beyond	The Latin Quarter & the 13th

Map pp401-402	**Restaurants** p194
Hotels p167	**Cafés & bars** p225

MONTMARTRE

In the 18th arrondissement.

Perched on a hill (or *butte*), Montmartre is the highest point in Paris, its tightly packed houses spiralling round the mound below the dome of **Sacré-Coeur**. Despite the many tourists, it's surprisingly easy to fall under the spell of this unabashedly romantic district. Climb quiet stairways, peer down narrow alleys and into ivy-covered houses and quiet squares, and explore streets such as rue des Abbesses, rue des Trois-Frères and rue des Martyrs, with their cafés, boutiques and bohemian residents.

For centuries, Montmartre was a tranquil village. When Haussmann sliced through the city centre in the mid 19th century, working-class families started to move out, and migrants poured into an industrialising Paris from across France. The population of Montmartre swelled. The *butte* was absorbed into the city of Paris in 1860, but remained proudly independent. Its key role in the Commune in 1871, fending off government troops, is marked by a plaque on rue du Chevalier-de-la-Barre.

Artists moved into the area from the 1880s. Renoir found subject matter in the cafés and *guinguettes*, and Toulouse-Lautrec patronised the local bars and immortalised its cabarets in his famous posters. Later, it was frequented by Picasso and artists of the Ecole de Paris.

You can start a wander from Abbesses métro station, one of only two in Paris (along with Porte Dauphine) to retain its original art nouveau metal-and-glass awning designed by Hector Guimard. Across place des Abbesses is art nouveau **St-Jean-de-Montmartre** church, a pioneering reinforced concrete structure with turquoise mosaics around the door. Along rue des Abbesses and adjoining rue Lepic, which winds its way up the hill, are food shops, boutiques, wine merchants and cafés, including the ever-popular **Le Sancerre** (*see p226*).

In the other direction from Abbesses, at 11 rue Yvonne-Le-Tac, is the **Chapelle du Martyr** According to legend, St Denis picked up his head here after his execution in the third century (hence one plausible explanation of the name Montmartre – martyr's mount). Rue Orsel, with a typical local cluster of retro design, ethnic and second-hand clothes shops, leads to place Charles-Dullin, where a cluster of cafés overlook the respected **Théâtre de l'Atelier** (1 pl Charles-Dullin, 18th, 01.46.06.49.24).

Up the hill, the cafés of rue des Trois-Frères are a popular spot for an evening drink. The street leads into sloping place Emile-Goudeau, whose staircases, wrought-iron streetlights and old houses are particularly evocative of days gone by. The Bâteau Lavoir, a piano factory that stood at no.13, witnessed the birth of Cubism. Divided into a warren of studios in the 1890s for impoverished artists of the day, it was here that

Sacré-Coeur.

SIGHTS

Picasso painted *Les Demoiselles d'Avignon* in 1906 and 1907, when he, Braque and Juan Gris were all residents. The building burned down in 1970, but has since been reconstructed.

On rue Lepic, which winds up the hill from rue des Abbesses, are the village's two remaining windmills: the **Moulin du Radet**, which was moved here in the 17th century from its hillock in rue des Moulins near the Palais-Royal; and the **Moulin de la Galette**, site of the celebrated dancehall depicted by Renoir (now in the Musée d'Orsay) and today a smart restaurant. Vincent van Gogh and his beloved brother Theo lived at no.54 from 1886 to 1888.

On tourist-swamped place du Tertre at the top of the hill, painters flog lurid sunset views of Paris or offer (sometimes aggressively) to draw your portrait; nearby **Espace Dalí** (11 rue Poulbot, 18th, 01.42.64.40.10) has rather more illustrious art. Round here, so legend has it, the bistro concept was born in the early 1800s, when Russian soldiers shouted '*Bistro!*' ('Quickly!') to be served. Just off the square is **St-Pierre-de-Montmartre**, the oldest church in the district, with columns that have bent with age. Founded by Louis VI in 1133, it's an example of early Gothic, in contrast to its extravagant neighbour, the Sacré-Coeur basilica.

For all its kitsch and swarms of tourists, **Sacré-Coeur** is well worth the visit for its sheer 19th-century excess. Rather than the main steps, take the staircase down rue Maurice-Utrillo to pause on a café terrace on the small square at the top of rue Muller, or wander down through the adjoining park to the Halle St-Pierre. The old covered market is now used for shows of naïve art, but the surrounding square and streets, known as the **Marché St-Pierre**, are packed with fabric shops.

On the north side of place du Tertre in rue Cortot is the quiet 17th-century manor that houses the **Musée de Montmartre**, dedicated to the neighbourhood and its former famous inhabitants. Dufy, Renoir and Utrillo all used to have studios in the entrance pavilion. Nearby in rue des Saules is the Montmartre vineyard, planted by local artist Poulbot in 1933 in commemoration of the vines that once covered the area. The grape harvest here every autumn is a local highlight (*see p278* **Vintage Paris**), celebrated with great pomp. Further down the hill, among rustic, shuttered houses, is the cabaret **Au Lapin Agile** (*see p281*). This old artists' meeting point got its name from André Gill, who painted the inn sign of a rabbit (the 'lapin à Gill').

A series of squares leads to rue Caulaincourt, crossing the **Cimetière de Montmartre** (enter on avenue Rachel, reached by stairs from rue Caulaincourt or place de Clichy). A stone's throw south of here is the pocket-sized *chanson* venue **Les Trois Baudets** (2 rue Coustou, 18th, 01.42.62.33.33, www.lestroisbaudets.com), which saw the Paris debuts of Brel, Brassens, Vian, Gainsbourg, Gréco and others, and was relaunched under Mairie management in 2008. Winding down the back of the hill, avenue Junot is lined with exclusive residences, such as the avant-garde house built by Adolf Loos for poet Tristan Tzara at no.15, exemplifying his Modernist maxim: 'Ornament is crime.'

★ FREE Cimetière de Montmartre

20 av Rachel, access by staircase from rue Caulaincourt, 18th (01.53.42.36.30). M° *Blanche or Place de Clichy.* **Open** *6 Nov-15 Mar* 8am- 5.30pm Mon-Sat; 9am-5.30pm Sun & public hols. *16 Mar-5 Nov* 8am-6pm Mon-Sat; 9am-6pm Sun & public hols. **Admission** free. **Map** p401 G1.

Truffaut, Nijinsky, Berlioz, Degas, Offenbach and German poet Heine are all buried here. So, too, are La Goulue, the first great cancan star and model for Toulouse-Lautrec, celebrated local beauty Mme Récamier, and the consumptive heroine Alphonsine Plessis, inspiration for Dumas's *La Dame aux Camélias* and Verdi's *La Traviata*. Flowers are still left on the grave of pop diva and gay icon Dalida (*see p93* **The Diva of Montmartre**), who used to live on nearby rue d'Orchampt.

▶ *For a walk around celebrity-filled Père-Lachaise cemetery, see p108.*

Musée d'Art Halle St-Pierre

2 rue Ronsard, 18th (01.42.58.72.89/www.halle saintpierre.org). M° Anvers. **Open** *Jan-July, Sept-Dec* 10am-6pm daily; *Aug* noon-6pm Mon-Fri. **Admission** €7; €5.50 reductions; free under-4s. **Credit** *Shop* MC, V. **Map** p402 J2.

The former covered market in the shadow of Sacré-Coeur specialises in *art brut, art outsider* and *art singulier* from its own and other collections.

Musée de Montmartre

12 rue Cortot, 18th (01.49.25.89.37/www. musee demontmartre.fr). M° Abbesses or Lamarck Caulaincourt. **Open** 11am-6pm Wed-Sun. **Admission** €7; €5.50 reductions; free under-10s. **Credit** *Shop* MC, V. **Map** p402 H1.

At the back of a garden, this 17th-century manor displays the history of the hilltop, with rooms devoted to composer Gustave Charpentier and a tribute to the Lapin Agile cabaret, with original Toulouse-Lautrec posters. There are paintings by Suzanne Valadon, who had a studio above the entrance pavilion, as did Renoir, Raoul Dufy and Valadon's son Maurice Utrillo.

★ FREE Sacré-Coeur

35 rue du Chevalier-de-la-Barre, 18th (01.53.41.89.00/www.sacre-coeur-montmartre. com). M° Abbesses or Anvers. **Open** *Basilica* 6am-10.30pm daily. *Crypt & dome* Winter 10am-5.45pm daily. Summer 9am-6.45pm daily. **Admission** free. *Crypt & dome* €5. **Credit** MC, V. **Map** p402 J1.

Work on this enormous mock Romano-Byzantine edifice began in 1877. It was commissioned after the nation's defeat by Prussia in 1870, voted for by the Assemblée Nationale and built from public subscription. Finally completed in 1914, it was consecrated in 1919 – by which time a jumble of architects had succeeded Paul Abadie, winner of the original competition. The interior boasts lavish mosaics.

La Goutte d'Or

The area north of Barbès Rochechouart métro station was the backdrop for Zola's *L'Assommoir*, his novel set among the district's laundries and absinthe cafés. Today, heroin has replaced absinthe as the means of escape.

The Diva of Montmartre

Dalida's cult following lives on, 20 years after her suicide.

Singers are a revered breed in France, and Egyptian-born Dalida was a bona fide icon. During her 30-year career, she recorded more than 1,000 songs, scoring 45 gold records and two platinum albums. However, her professional success was offset by extreme personal lows. Three of her lovers committed suicide, and Dalida ended her own life in the late 1980s.

Her success in the anglophone world was limited, but in Paris, her adopted town, it feels as if Dalida's every step has been sanctified. Two decades after her death, a cult dedicated to the singer continues to evolve.

Much of the Dalida myth is rooted in Montmartre, where she lived in the 'Castle of Sleeping Beauty', a four-storey house on rue d'Orchampt. Cartographic consecration may be an honour usually reserved for generals, cardinals and artists, but Dalida has had one of the most picturesque squares in the neighbourhood dedicated to her. Place Dalida is graced by a bronze bust of the idol, and her grave in the Montmartre cemetery is another place of pilgrimage.

Paris's latest ode to the singer came in the form of an exhibition at the Hôtel de Ville in September 2007. Everything from mythical dresses to family photographs and personal letters went on display. Dalida's presence lives on as Paris refuses to let the memory of one of its most flamboyant residents fade.

La Goutte d'Or is primarily an African and Arab neighbourhood, and can seem like a colourful slice of the Middle East or a state under perpetual siege due to the frequent police raids. Down rue Doudeauville, you'll find lively ethnic music shops; rue Polonceau contains African grocers and Senegalese restaurants. Mayor Delanöe has tried to attract young designers to the area by designating rue des Gardes 'rue de la mode', and square Léon is the focus for **La Goutte d'Or en Fête** (*see p276*) in June, which brings together local musicians. Some of them, such as Africando and the Orchestre National de Barbès, have become well known across Paris. A market sets up under the métro tracks along boulevard de la Chapelle on Monday, Wednesday and Saturday mornings, with stalls of exotic vegetables and rolls of African fabrics.

Further north, at porte de Clignancourt, is the city's largest flea market, the **Marché aux Puces de Clignancourt** (*see p269*).

PIGALLE

In the 9th arrondissement.

Pigalle is Paris's centre of sleaze. Despite a police crackdown, which sought to eliminate tourist rip-offs and rough-ups, passers-by may still be hassled by barkers and hawkers trying to corral them into some peep show or other.

In the 1890s, Toulouse-Lautrec's posters of Jane Avril at the Divan Japonais, Chat Noir and Moulin Rouge, and of *chanson* star Aristide

Bruant, immortalised the area's cabarets and were landmarks of art and advertising. At the end of the 19th century, 25 of the 58 buildings on rue des Martyrs were cabarets (a few, such as the drag shows Michou and Madame Arthur, remain today); others were *maisons closes*. But it's still a happening street: Le Divan Japonais is now **Le Divan du Monde** (*see p320*), a club and music venue; a hip crowd packs into **La Fourmi** (*see p225*) opposite; and up the hill, there's a cluster of *atelier-boutiques* where designers have set up their sewing machines at the back of the shop.

Along the boulevard, behind its bright red windmill, the **Moulin Rouge** (*see p281*), once the image of naughty 1890s Paris, is now a cheesy tourist draw. Its befeathered dancers still cancan and cavort across the stage, but are no substitute for La Goulue and Joseph Pujol – *le pétomane* who could pass wind melodically. In stark contrast is the **Cité Véron** next door, a cobbled alley with a small theatre and cottagey buildings; writer and jazz musician Boris Vian lived at 6bis between 1953 and 1958. The famous **Elysée Montmartre** music hall (*see p329*) today has an array of concerts and club nights, but the **Folies Pigalle** (*see p329*) nightspot retains undeniable Pigalle flavour with its after-parties and drag queens.

Musée de l'Erotisme

72 bd de Clichy, 18th (01.42.58.28.73/www. musee-erotisme.com). M° Blanche. **Open** 10am-2am daily. **Admission** €8; €6 students. **Credit** MC, V. **Map** p401 H2.

La Goutte d'Or.

SIGHTS

Seven floors of erotic art and artefacts amassed by collectors Alain Plumey and Joseph Khalif. The first three run from first-century Peruvian phallic pottery through Etruscan fertility symbols to Yoni sculptures from Nepal; the fourth gives a history of Paris brothels; and the recently refurbished top floors host exhibitions of modern erotic art.

La Nouvelle Athènes

Just south of Pigalle and east of rue Blanche lies this often overlooked quarter, dubbed the New Athens when it was colonised by a wave of artists, writers and composers in the early 19th century. Long-forgotten actresses and *demi-mondaines* had mansions built here; some are set in tiny rue de la Tour-des-Dames, which refers to one of the many windmills owned by Couvent des Abbesses. To glimpse more of these miniature palaces, wander through the adjoining streets and passageways.

Just off rue Taitbout is square d'Orléans, a remarkable housing estate built in 1829 by the English architect Edward Cresy. These flats and studios attracted the glitterati of the day, including George Sand and her lover Chopin. In the house built for Dutch painter Ary Scheffer in nearby rue Chaptal, the **Musée de la Vie Romantique** displays Sand's mementos.

The **Musée Gustave Moreau** on rue de La Rochefoucauld is reason alone to visit, featuring the artist's apartment and magnificent studio. Fragments of bohemia can still be gleaned in the area, although the Café La Roche, where Moreau would meet Degas for drinks and rows, has been downsized to **La Joconde** (57 rue Notre-Dame-de-Lorette, 9th, 01.48.74.10.38). The area is steeped in history: Degas painted most of his memorable ballet scenes in rue Frochot, and Renoir hired his first proper studio at 35 rue St-Georges. A few streets away in Cité Pigalle, a collection of studios, is van Gogh's last Paris house (no.5), from where he moved to Auvers-sur-Oise. There is a plaque here, but nothing marks the building in rue Pigalle where Toulouse-Lautrec sat and slowly drank himself to an early grave.

The area around the neo-classical **Eglise Notre-Dame-de-Lorette**, built in the form of a Greek temple, was built up in Louis-Philippe's

reign and was famous for its courtesans or *lorettes*, elegant ladies named after their haunt of rue Notre-Dame-de-Lorette. In 1848, Gauguin was born at no.56; from 1844 to 1857, Delacroix had a studio at no.58. The latter then moved to place de Furstemberg in the sixth (now the Musée Delacroix). Rue St-Lazare contains some delightfully old-fashioned shops and bistros.

The lower stretch of rue des Martyrs is packed with tempting food shops, and a little further up the hill you should look out for the prosperous residences of the Cité Malesherbes and avenue Trudaine. The circular place St-Georges was home to the true Empress of Napoleon III's Paris: the Russian-born Madame Païva. She lived in the neo-Renaissance no.28, thought to be outrageous at the time of its construction. La Païva shot herself after a passionate affair with the millionaire cousin of Chancellor Bismarck.

★ Musée Gustave Moreau

14 rue de La Rochefoucauld, 9th (01.48.74.38.50/ www.musee-moreau.fr). M° Trinité. **Open** 10am-12.45pm, 2-5.15pm Mon, Wed-Sun. **Admission** €5; €3 reductions, all Sun; free under-18s. PMP. **Credit** MC, V. **Map** p401 G3.

This wonderful museum combines the small private apartment of Symbolist painter Gustave Moreau (1825-98) with the vast gallery he built to display his work – set out as a museum by the painter himself, and opened in 1903. Downstairs shows his obsessive collector's nature with family portraits, Grand Tour souvenirs and a boudoir devoted to the object of his unrequited love, Alexandrine Durem. Upstairs is Moreau's fantasy realm, which plunders Greek mythology and biblical scenes for canvases filled with writhing maidens, trance-like visages, mystical beasts and strange plants. Don't miss the trippy masterpiece *Jupiter et Sémélé* on the second floor.
► *Printed on boards that you can carry around the museum are the artist's lengthy, rhetorical and mad commentaries.*

FREE Musée de la Vie Romantique

Hôtel Scheffer-Renan, 16 rue Chaptal, 9th (01.55.31.95.67/www.vie-romantique.paris.fr). M° Blanche or St-Georges. **Open** 10am-6pm Tue-Sun. *Tearoom* May-Oct 11.30am-5.30pm Tue-Sun. **Admission** free. *Exhibitions* €7; €3.50 reductions; free under-14s. **Credit** AmEx, DC, MC, V. **Map** p401 G2.

When Dutch artist Ary Scheffer lived in this small villa, the area teemed with composers, writers and artists. Aurore Dupin, Baronne Dudevant (George Sand) was a guest at Scheffer's soirées, and many other great names crossed the threshold, including Chopin and Liszt. The museum is devoted to Sand, although the watercolours, lockets, jewels and plastercast of her right arm that she left behind reveal little of her ideas or affairs.

**INSIDE TRACK
MOVIE MOMENTS**

The famous **Studio 28** cinema (10 rue Tholozé, 18th), opened in 1928 and still going strong, is where Luis Buñuel's Surrealist classic *L'Age d'Or* had its riotous premiere in 1930.

Beaubourg & the Marais

Modern art, medieval architecture and modish magasins.

Beaubourg and its eastern neighbour the Marais are a chunk of town largely untouched by Haussmann, which means lots of small streets in which to get lost and – to a degree – a sense of old Paris. The clean-up operation begun in the Marais in the 1960s by culture minister André Malraux did much to primp and preserve the old buildings. However, although much of the fabric is ancient, the people and the activities are resolutely fashionable and exuberant. This, famously, is the city's gay quarter, but it's just as popular with other inclinations – museums, boutiques, bars and restaurants abound, and the crowds, particularly at the weekends, can be almost oppressive. Come with plenty of time, and money, to spare.

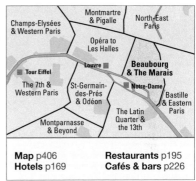

Montmartre & Pigalle | North-East Paris
Champs-Elysées & Western Paris
Opéra to Les Halles
Tour Eiffel | Louvre | **Beaubourg & The Marais**
The 7th & Western Paris | St-Germain-des-Prés & Odéon | Notre-Dame | Bastille & Eastern Paris
The Latin Quarter & the 13th
Montparnasse & Beyond

Map p406   **Restaurants** p195
Hotels p169   **Cafés & bars** p226

BEAUBOURG & HOTEL DE VILLE

In the 4th arrondissement.

Modern architecture in Paris took off with the **Centre Pompidou**, a benchmark of inside-out high-tech designed by Richard Rogers and Renzo Piano that's as much an attraction as the **Musée National de l'Art Moderne** within. The piazza outside attracts street performers and artists; the reconstructed **Atelier Brancusi**, left by the sculptor to the state, was moved here from the 15th arrondissement.

On the other side of the piazza, rue Quincampoix houses galleries, bars and cobbled passage Molière, with its old shopfronts and the **Théâtre Molière** (01.44.54.53.00). Beside the Centre Pompidou is place Igor-Stravinsky and the Fontaine Stravinsky – full of spraying kinetic fountains, and a colourful snake by the late artists Nikki de St-Phalle and Jean Tinguély – and the red-brick **IRCAM** music institute (*see p317*), also designed by Renzo Piano.

South of here stands the spiky Gothic **Tour St-Jacques**. Towards the river, on the site of

the Grand Châtelet (a fortress put up in the 12th century to defend Pont au Change), place du Châtelet's Egyptian-themed fountain is framed by twin theatres designed by Davioud as part of Haussmann's urban improvements in the 1860s. They're now two of the city's main arts venues: the **Théâtre de la Ville** (*see p346*) and the **Théâtre du Châtelet** (*see p325*), an opera and concert hall.

Beyond Châtelet, the **Hôtel de Ville** (city hall) has been the symbol of municipal power since 1260. The equestrian statue out front is of 14th-century merchant leader and rebel Etienne Marcel. Revolutionaries made the Hôtel de Ville their base in the 1871 Commune, but it was set on fire by the Communards themselves and wrecked during savage fighting. It was rebuilt according to the original model, on a larger scale, in fanciful neo-Renaissance style, with knights in armour along the roof and statues of French luminaries dotted all over the walls. The square outside was formerly called place de Grève, after the nearby riverside wharf where goods were unloaded for market. During the 16th-century Wars of Religion, Protestant heretics were burned in the square, and the

Centre Pompidou.

SIGHTS

guillotine stood here during the Terror, when Danton, Marat and Robespierre made the Hôtel de Ville their own seat of government. Today the square hosts an ice rink every December, and screenings of major sports events. Across the road stands the Bazar de l'Hôtel de Ville department store, or **BHV** (*see p239*).

FREE Atelier Brancusi

Piazza Beaubourg, 4th (01.44.78.12.33/ www. centrepompidou.fr). M° Hôtel de Ville or Rambuteau. **Open** 2-6pm Mon, Wed-Sun. **Admission** free. **Credit** AmEx, V. **Map** p406 K6.
When Constantin Brancusi died in 1957, he left his studio and its contents to the state, and it was later moved and rebuilt by the Centre Pompidou. His fragile works in wood and plaster, the endless columns and streamlined bird forms show how Brancusi revolutionised sculpture.

★ Centre Pompidou (Musée National d'Art Moderne)

Rue St-Martin, 4th (01.44.78.12.33/www.centre pompidou.fr). M° Hôtel de Ville or Rambuteau. **Open** 11am-9pm (last entry 8pm) Mon, Wed-Sun (until 11pm some exhibitions); 11am-11pm Thur. **Admission** *Museum & exhibitions* €10 (€12 May-mid Aug); €8 reductions; free under-18s, 1st Sun of mth (museum only). PMP. **Credit** AmEx, DC, MC, V. **Map** p406 K6.
The primary colours, exposed pipes and air ducts make this one of the best-known sights in Paris. The then-unknown Italo-British architectural duo of Renzo Piano and Richard Rogers won the competition with their 'inside-out' boilerhouse approach, which put air-conditioning, pipes, lifts and the escalators on the outside, leaving an adaptable space within. The multi-disciplinary concept of modern art

museum (the most important in Europe), library, exhibition and performance spaces, and repertory cinema was also revolutionary. When the centre opened in 1977, its success exceeded all expectations. After a two-year revamp, the centre reopened in 2000 with an enlarged museum, renewed performance spaces, vista-rich Georges restaurant and a mission to get back to the stimulating interdisciplinary mix of old. Entrance to the forum is free (as is the library, which has a separate entrance), but you now have to pay to go up the escalators.

The Centre Pompidou (or 'Beaubourg') holds the largest collection of modern art in Europe, rivalled only in its breadth and quality by MOMA in New York. Sample the contents of its vaults (50,000 works of art by 5,000 artists) on the website, as only a fraction – about 600 works – can be seen for real at any one time. There is a partial rehang each year. For the main collection, buy tickets on the ground floor and take the escalators to level four for post-1960s art. Level five spans 1905 to 1960. There are four temporary exhibition spaces on each of these two levels (included in the ticket). Main temporary exhibitions take place on the ground floor, in gallery two on level six, in the south gallery, level one and in the new Espace 315, devoted to the under-40s.

On level five, the historic section takes a chronological sweep through the history of modern art, via Primitivism, Fauvism, Cubism, Dadaism and Surrealism up to American Color-Field painting and Abstract Expressionism. Masterful ensembles let you see the span of Matisse's career on canvas and in bronze, the variety of Picasso's invention, and the development of cubic orphism by Sonia and Robert Delaunay. Others on the hits list include Braque, Duchamp, Mondrian, Malevich, Kandinsky, Dali, Giacometti, Ernst, Miró, Calder, Magritte, Rothko and Pollock. Don't miss the reconstruction of a wall of André Breton's studio, combining the tribal art, folk art, flea-market finds and drawings by fellow artists that the Surrealist artist and theorist had amassed. The photography collection also has an impressive roll call, including Brassaï, Kertész, Man Ray, Cartier-Bresson and Doisneau.

Level four houses post-'60s art. Its thematic rooms concentrate on the career of one artist or focus on movements such as Anti-form or *arte povera*. Recent acquisitions line the central corridor, and at the far end you can find architecture and design. Video art and installations by the likes of Mathieu Mercier and Dominique Gonzalez-Foerster are in a room devoted to *nouvelle création*.

FREE Hôtel de Ville

29 rue de Rivoli, 4th (01.42.76.40.40/www. paris.fr). M° Hôtel de Ville. **Open** 10am-7pm Mon-Sat. **Map** p406 K6.
Rebuilt by Ballu after the Commune, the palatial, multi-purpose Hôtel de Ville is the heart of the city administration, and a place in which to entertain visiting dignitaries. Free exhibitions are held in the Salon d'Accueil (open 10am-6pm Mon-Fri). The rest of the building, accessible by weekly guided tours (book in advance), has parquet floors, marble statues, crystal chandeliers and painted ceilings.

Tour St-Jacques

Square de La-Tour-St-Jacques, 4th. M° Châtelet. **Map** p406 J6.
Loved by the Surrealists, this solitary Flamboyant Gothic belltower with its leering gargoyles is all that remains of the St-Jacques-La-Boucherie church, built for the powerful Butchers' Guild in 1508-22. The statue of Blaise Pascal at the base commemorates his experiments on atmospheric pressure, carried out here in the 17th century. A weather station now crowns the 52m (171ft) tower, not open to the public.

THE MARAIS

In the 3rd & 4th arrondissements.

The narrow streets of the Marais contain aristocratic *hôtels particuliers*, art galleries, boutiques and stylish cafés, with beautiful carved doorways and early street signs carved into the stone. The Marais, or 'marsh', started life as a piece of swampy ground inhabited by a few monasteries, sheep and market gardens. This was one of the last parts of central Paris to be built up. In the 16th century, the elegant Hôtel Carnavalet and Hôtel Lamoignon sparked the area's phenomenal rise as an aristocratic residential district; Henri IV began building **place des Vosges** in 1605. Nobles and royal officials followed, building smart townhouses

where literary ladies such as Mme de Sévigné held court. The area fell from fashion a century later; many of the narrow streets remained unchanged as mansions were transformed into workshops, crafts studios, schools, tenements, and even, on rue de Sévigné, a fire station.

Rue des Francs-Bourgeois, crammed with impressive mansions and original boutiques, runs like a backbone right through the Marais, becoming more aristocratic as it leaves the food shops of rue Rambuteau behind. Two of the most refined early 18th-century residences are **Hôtel d'Albret** (no.31), a venue for jazz concerts during the Paris Quartier d'Eté festival (*see p277*), and the palatial **Hôtel de Soubise** (no.60), the national archives. Begun in 1704 for the Prince and Princesse de Soubise, it has interiors by Boucher and Lemoine and currently hosts the **Musée de l'Histoire de France**, along with the neighbouring Hôtel de Rohan. There's also a surprising series of rose gardens.

Facing the Archives Nationaux, the **Crédit Municipal** (no.55) acts as a sort of municipal pawnshop: people exchange goods for cash, and items never reclaimed are sold at auction. On the corner of rue Pavée is the Renaissance Hôtel Lamoignon, with a magisterial courtyard adorned with Corinthian pilasters. Built in 1585, it now contains the **Bibliothèque Historique de la Ville de Paris** (no.24, 01.44.59.29.40). Further up, the **Musée Carnavalet** runs across the Hôtel Carnavalet and the Hôtel le Peletier de St-Fargeau.

At its eastern end, rue des Francs-Bourgeois leads into the beautiful brick-and-stone place des Vosges. At one corner is the **Maison de Victor Hugo**, where the writer lived from 1833 to 1848. An archway in the south-west corner leads to the **Hôtel de Sully**, accommodating the Patrimoine Photographique. Designed in 1624, the building belonged to Henri IV's minister, the Duc de Sully.

Several other important museums are also found in sumptuous *hôtels*. The Hôtel Salé on rue de Thorigny, built in 1656, was nicknamed ('salty') after its owner, Fontenay, who collected the salt tax. Beautifully restored and extended to house the **Musée National Picasso**, it has an elegant courtyard adorned with sphinxes and a baroque stairwell carved with garlands, imperial busts and gambolling cupids. Nearby, the pretty Hôtel Donon, built in 1598, contains the **Musée Cognacq-Jay** and has remarkable 18th-century panelled interiors, and the Hôtel Guénégaud contains the **Musée de la Chasse et de la Nature** hunting museum.

The Marais has also long been a focus for the Jewish community. Today, Jewish businesses are clustered along rue des Rosiers, rue des Ecouffes and rue Pavée, where there's a synagogue designed by Guimard. Originally

SIGHTS

made up mainly of Ashkenazi Jews, who fled the pogroms in Eastern Europe at the end of the 19th century (many were later deported during World War II), the community expanded in the 1950s and '60s with a wave of Sephardic Jewish immigration after French withdrawal from North Africa.

The lower ends of rue des Archives and rue Vieille-du-Temple are the centre of café life and the hub of the gay scene. Bars such as the **Open Café** (*see p307*) draw gay crowds in the early evening. In their midst, the 15th-century **Cloître des Billettes** at 22-26 rue des Archives is the only surviving Gothic cloister in Paris.

Workaday rue du Temple is full of surprises. Near rue de Rivoli, **Le Latina** specialises in Latin American films and holds tango balls in the room above. At no.41, an archway leads into the former Aigle d'Or coaching inn, now the **Café de la Gare** café-théâtre (*see p283*). Further north, at no.71, the grandiose Hôtel de St-Aignan, built in 1650, contains the **Musée d'Art et d'Histoire du Judaïsme**. The top end of rue du Temple and adjoining streets such as rue des Gravilliers are packed with costume jewellery, handbag and rag-trade wholesalers in what is the city's oldest Chinatown.

The north-west corner of the Marais hinges on the **Musée des Arts et Métiers**, a science museum with early flying machines displayed in the 12th-century chapel of the former priory of St-Martin-des-Champs, and the adjoining Conservatoire des Arts et Métiers. Across rue St-Martin on square Emile-Chautemps, the **Théâtre de la Gaîté Lyrique** (*see p102* **Computer Culture**) is currently undergoing renovation, and will reopen in 2010 as a centre for contemporary music and the 'digital arts'.

Despite the Marais' rise to fashion, the less gentrified streets around the northern stretch of rue Vieille-du-Temple towards place de la République are awash with designers on the rise and old craft workshops. Rue Charlot, housing an occasional contemporary art gallery at the passage de Retz at no.9 (01.48.04.37.99), is typical of the trend. At the top, the **Marché des Enfants-Rouges** (once an orphanage whose inhabitants were attired in red uniforms) is one of the city's oldest markets, founded in 1615.

★ FREE Espace Claude Berri

8 rue Rambuteau, 3rd (01.44.54.88.50). Mº Rambuteau. **Open** 11am-1pm, 2-7pm Tue-Sat. Closed Aug. **Admission** free. **Map** p409 K6.
For years, Claude Berri was best known as one of France's most successful film directors and producers, but the 74-year-old is now making a name for himself in another field: the fast-moving world of contemporary art. The aim of this new space is to alternate themed exhibitions of works from Berri's private collection with solo shows organised around

artists, critics or gallery owners. For the opening event, in March 2008, the ground floor was filled with giant installations by Frenchman Gilles Barbier.

Hôtel de Sully

62 rue St-Antoine, 4th (01.42.74.47.75). Mº St-Paul. **Open** noon-6.30pm Tue-Fri; 10am-6.30pm Sat, Sun. **Admission** €5; €2.50 reductions. **Credit** MC, V. **Map** p409 L7.
Along with the Jeu de Paume, the former Patrimoine Photographique forms part of the two-site home for the Centre National de la Photographie.

FREE Maison de Victor Hugo

Hôtel de Rohan-Guéménée, 6 pl des Vosges, 4th (01.42.72.10.16/www.musee-hugo.paris.fr). Mº Bastille or St-Paul. **Open** 10am-6pm Tue-Sun. **Admission** free. *Exhibitions* prices vary. **Credit** MC, V. **Map** p409 L6.
Victor Hugo lived here from 1833 to 1848, and today the house is a museum devoted to the life and work of the great man. On display are his first editions, nearly 500 drawings and, more bizarrely, Hugo's home-made furniture.

★ Musée d'Art et d'Histoire du Judaïsme

Hôtel de St-Aignan, 71 rue du Temple, 3rd (01.53.01.86.60/www.mahj.org). Mº Rambuteau. **Open** 11am-6pm Mon-Fri; 10am-6pm Sun. Closed Jewish hols. **Admission** €6.80; €4.50 reductions; free under-18s. **Credit** *Shop* MC, V. **Map** p409 K6.
It's fitting that a museum of Judaism should be lodged in one of the grandest mansions of the Marais, for centuries the epicentre of local Jewish life. It sprung from the collection of a private association formed in 1948 to safeguard Jewish heritage after the Holocaust. Pick up a free audio-guide in English to help you navigate through displays illustrating ceremonies, rites and learning, and showing how styles were adapted across the globe through examples of Jewish decorative arts. Photographic portraits of modern French Jews, each of whom tells his or her own story on the audio soundtrack, bring a contemporary edge. There are documents and paintings relating to the emancipation of French Jewry after the Revolution and the infamous Dreyfus case, from Zola's *J'Accuse!* to anti-Semitic cartoons. Paintings by the early 20th-century avant-garde include works by El Lissitsky and Chagall. The Holocaust is marked by Boris Taslitzky's stark sketches from Buchenwald and Christian Boltanski's courtyard memorial to the Jews who lived in the building in 1939, 13 of whom died in the camps.

Musée des Arts et Métiers

60 rue Réaumur, 3rd (01.53.01.82.00/www.arts-et-metiers.net). Mº Arts et Métiers. **Open** 10am-6pm Tue, Wed, Fri-Sun; 10am-9.30pm Thur. **Admission** €6.50; €4.50 reductions; free under-18s. PMP. **Credit** V. **Map** p402 K5.

The 'arts and trades' museum is, in fact, Europe's oldest science museum, founded in 1794 by the constitutional bishop Henri Grégoire, initially as a way to educate France's manufacturing industry in useful scientific techniques. Housed in the former Benedictine priory of St-Martin-des-Champs, it became a museum proper in 1819; it's a fascinating, attractively laid out and vast collection of treasures. Here are beautiful astrolabes, celestial spheres, barometers, clocks, weighing devices, some of Pascal's calculating devices, amazing scale models of buildings and machines that must have demanded at least as much engineering skill as the originals, the Lumière brothers' cinematograph, an enormous 1938 TV set, and still larger exhibits like Cugnot's 1770 'Fardier' (the first ever powered vehicle) and Clément Ader's bat-like, steam-powered Avion 3. The visit concludes in the chapel, which now contains old cars, a scale model of the Statue of Liberty, the monoplane in which Blériot crossed the Channel in 1909, and a Foucault pendulum.

▶ *Try to time your visit to coincide with one of the spellbinding demonstrations of the museum's old music boxes in the Théâtre des Automates.*

★ FREE Musée Carnavalet

23 rue de Sévigné, 3rd (01.44.59.58.58/www. carnavalet.paris.fr). M° St-Paul. **Open** 10am-6pm Tue-Sun. **Admission** free. *Exhibitions* €7; €3.50-€5.50 reductions; free under-13s. **Credit** *Shop* AmEx, MC, V. **Map** p409 L6.

Here, 140 chronological rooms depict the history of Paris, from pre-Roman Gaul to the 20th century. Built in 1548 and transformed by Mansart in 1660, this fine house became a museum in 1866, when Haussmann persuaded the city to preserve its beautiful interiors. Original 16th-century rooms house Renaissance collections, with portraits by Clouet and furniture and pictures relating to the Wars of Religion. The first floor covers the period up to 1789, with furniture and paintings displayed in restored, period interiors; neighbouring Hôtel Le Peletier de St-Fargeau covers the period from 1789 onwards. Displays relating to 1789 detail that year's convoluted politics and bloodshed, with prints and memorabilia, including a chunk of the Bastille. There are items belonging to Napoleon, a cradle given by the city to Napoleon III, and a reconstruction of Proust's cork-lined bedroom.

★ Musée de la Chasse et de la Nature

Hôtel Guénégaud, 62 rue des Archives, 3rd (01.53.01.92.40/www.chassenature.org). M° Rambuteau. **Open** 11am-6pm Tue-Sun. **Admission** €6; €4.50 reductions; free under-18s. **Map** p409 K5.

A two-year overhaul turned the three-floor hunting museum from a musty old-timer into something really rather special. When it reopened in 2007, it had kept the basic layout and proportions of the two

adjoining 17th-century mansions it occupies, but many of its new exhibits and settings seem more suited to an art gallery than a museum. The history of hunting and man's larger relationship with the natural world are examined in things like a quirky series of wooden cabinets devoted to the owl, wolf, boar and stag, each equipped with a bleached skull, small drawers you can open to reveal droppings and footprint casts, and a binocular eyepiece you can peer into for footage of the animal in the wild. A cleverly simple mirrored box contains a stuffed hen that is replicated into infinity on every side; and a stuffed fox is set curled up on a Louis XVI chair as though it were a domestic pet. Thought-provoking stuff.

FREE Musée Cognacq-Jay

Hôtel Donon, 8 rue Elzévir, 3rd (01.40.27.07.21/ www.paris.fr/musees). M° St-Paul. **Open** 10am-6pm Tue-Sun. **Admission** free. **Map** p409 L6.

This cosy museum houses a collection put together in the early 1900s by La Samaritaine founder Ernest Cognacq and his wife Marie-Louise Jay. They stuck mainly to 18th-century French works, focusing on rococo artists such as Watteau, Fragonard, Boucher, Greuze and pastellist Quentin de la Tour, though some English artists (Reynolds, Romney, Lawrence) and Dutch and Flemish names (an early Rembrandt, Ruysdael, Rubens), plus Canalettos and Guardis, have managed to slip in. Pictures are displayed in panelled rooms with furniture, porcelain, tapestries and sculpture of the same period.

Musée de l'Histoire de France

Hôtel de Soubise, 60 rue des Francs-Bourgeois, 3rd (01.40.27.60.96/www.archivesnationales. culture.gouv.fr/chan/chan/musee). M° Hôtel de Ville or Rambuteau. **Open** 10am-12.30pm, 2-5.30pm Mon, Wed-Fri; 2-5.30pm Sat, Sun. **Admission** €3; €2.30 reductions; free under-18s. **Credit** V. **Map** p409 K6.

Generally housed in one of the grandest Marais mansions, the Hôtel de Rohan, this museum is currently undergoing renovation. In the meantime, documents and artefacts covering everything from the founding of the Sorbonne to an ordinance about umbrellas are displayed in the neighbouring Hôtel de Soubise. Its rococo interiors feature paintings by Boucher and van Loo.

Musée National Picasso

Hôtel Salé, 5 rue de Thorigny, 3rd (01.42.71.25.21/www.musee-picasso.fr). M° Chemin Vert or St-Paul. **Open** Oct-Mar 9.30am-5.30pm Mon, Wed-Sun. *Apr-Sept* 9.30am-6pm Mon, Wed-Sun. **Admission** €6.50 Mon-Sat; €4.50 Sun; free under-18s, 1st Sun of mth. PMP. *Exhibitions* prices vary. **Credit** *Shop* AmEx, MC, V. **Map** p409 L6.

Picasso's paintings, sculptures, collages, drawings and ceramics are shown off in style in this stately Marais mansion, complete with sweeping staircase.

Computer Culture

Digital art comes to the Gaîté-Lyrique.

What is digital art? The answer is simple enough: it's any work that uses digital technology in the process of creation, and it encompasses everything from reworked photographs and sculptures to computer-generated paintings and installations. And, in common with the contemporary art world, Paris is embracing it, particularly by investing in festivals and centres devoted to the form.

Two of France's biggest digital arts festivals take place in the Paris suburbs. The Cube Festival (www.cubefestival.com), organised by the innovative Le Cube digital arts centre, hosts a six-day programme of multimedia installations, screenings, performances, workshops and electro-visual live shows. The Bains Numériques festival (www.bainsnumeriques.com), meanwhile, invites visitors to discover its digital village and research labs, erected around Enghien-les-Bains' gardens and lakes for one week every summer.

The biggest news on Paris's digital arts scene, however, is the creation of a major centre devoted specifically to this new medium. The **Théâtre de la Gaîté Lyrique** (3bis rue Papin, 3rd) in the heart of Paris is set to reopen in 2010 as a cultural complex for digital arts and contemporary music. Built in 1861-62, the theatre was originally managed by

composer Jacques Offenbach, who performed some of his most famous works here, but it fell into decline and, in the 1980s, was given an ill-advised makeover as an indoor children's amusement park – an episode that lasted just weeks. Long abandoned, the theatre is finally being given new life with a redesign by architect Manuelle Gautrand.

The centrepiece of the new space is an auditorium, with seating for over 300, which will be used for film screenings, concerts and a variety of performances. Other areas open to the public will include a theatre, library, café and two spaces for exhibitions. In a spirit of fostering creativity, the complex will also provide 12 artists with studios and living quarters.

At the head of programming is Jérôme Delormas, who worked as co-director of Nuit Blanche, the city's popular nocturnal cultural festival. For Delormas, the aim is for the theatre to become one of the world leaders in digital arts by entering into partnerships with some of France's biggest contemporary art spaces, such as the Centre Pompidou and the Ferme du Buisson (www.lafermedubuisson.com). To keep its edge on the rapidly changing digital arts scene, the centre also plans to collaborate with leading international organisations, such as the ZKM in Karlsruhe and the V2 in Rotterdam.

The collection, donated to the state by Picasso's family in lieu of inheritance tax, gives a panorama of his career from precocious early sketches to later stylistic whimsies, via delightful oddities like a papier-mâché goat. Many of the 'greatest hits' hang in other state-owned Paris museums, but to get a feeling for Picasso's artistic development this is the best resource in the city. From a haunting, blue-period self-portrait and rough studies for the *Demoiselles d'Avignon,* the collection moves to Picasso's Cubist and classical phases, the surreal *Nude in an Armchair* and assorted portraits of his abundant lovers, in particular Marie-Thérèse and Dora Maar. A small covered sculpture garden displays pieces that sat around Picasso's studio until his death.

FREE **Place des Vosges**
4th. M° St-Paul. **Map** p409 L6.
Paris's first planned square was commissioned in 1605 by Henri IV and inaugurated by his son Louis XIII in 1612. With harmonious red-brick and stone

arcaded façades and steeply pitched slate roofs, it differs from the later pomp of the Bourbons. Laid out symmetrically with carriageways through the taller Pavillon de la Reine on the north side and Pavillon du Roi on the south, the other lots were sold off as concessions to royal officials and nobles (some façades are imitation brick). It was called place Royale prior to the Napoleonic Wars, when the Vosges was the first region of France to pay its war taxes. Mme de Sévigné, salon hostess and letter-writer, was born at no.1bis in 1626. At that time the garden hosted duels and trysts; now it attracts children from the nearby nursery school.

The St-Paul district

In 1559, Henri II was fatally wounded jousting on today's rue St-Antoine, marked by Pilon's marble *La Vierge de Douleur* in the **Eglise St-Paul-St-Louis**. South of rue St-Antoine is the sedate residential area of St-Paul, lined with dignified 17th- and 18th-century façades. The linked courtyards of Village St-Paul house antiques sellers. On rue des Jardins-St-Paul is the largest surviving section of the fortified wall of Philippe-Auguste (www.philippe-auguste.com), complete with towers.

By St-Paul métro station on the corner of rue François-Miron and rue de Fourcy is the Hôtel Hénault de Cantorbe, renovated and given a minimalist modern extension as the **Maison Européenne de la Photographie**. Down rue de Fourcy towards the river, across a medieval formal garden, you can see the rear façade of the Hôtel de Sens, a rare medieval mansion built as the Paris residence of the Archbishops of Sens in the 15th century, with a lovely array of turrets. It houses the **Bibliothèque Forney** (1 rue du Figuier, 01.42.78.14.60, closed Mon & Sun), specialising in exhibitions of applied arts and graphic design.

Near Pont Sully are square Henri-Galli, with a rebuilt piece of the Bastille, and the **Pavillon de l'Arsenal**, built by a rich timber merchant to put on art shows, and home to displays relating to Paris architecture.

Winding rue François-Miron leads you back towards the Hôtel de Ville. At 17 rue Geoffroy-l'Asnier, the Mémorial du Martyr Juif Inconnu is being extended as part of the **Mémorial de la Shoah**, a museum, memorial and study centre devoted to the Holocaust that opened in 2005. As you pass no.26, note the Cité des Arts complex of artists' studios, and the ornate lion's head and giant shell motif on the doorway of the 17th-century Hôtel de Châlon-Luxembourg. Rue du Pont-Louis-Philippe contains jewellers, designer furniture and gift shops, and stepped rue des Barres boasts tearooms overlooking the chevet of the **Eglise St-Gervais-St-Protais**.

FREE Eglise St-Gervais-St-Protais

Pl St-Gervais, 4th (01.48.87.32.02). M° Hôtel de Ville. **Open** times vary. **Admission** free. **Map** p409 K6.
Gothic at the rear and classical at the front, this church also has an impressive Flamboyant Gothic interior, most of which dates from the 16th century. The nave gives an impression of enormous height, with tall columns that soar up to the vault. There are plenty of fine funerary monuments, especially the baroque statue of Chancellor Le Tellier.

FREE Eglise St-Paul-St-Louis

99 rue St-Antoine, 4th (01.42.72.30.32). M° St-Paul. **Open** 8am-8pm daily. **Admission** free. **Map** p409 L7.
This domed baroque Counter-Reformation church is modelled, like all Jesuit churches, on the Chiesa del Gesù in Rome. Completed in 1641, it features a single nave, side chapels and a three-storey hierarchical façade featuring statues of Saints Louis, Anne

and Catherine – all replacements. The provider of confessors to the kings of France, the Eglise St-Paul-St-Louis was richly endowed until Revolutionary iconoclasts pinched its treasures, including the hearts of Louis XIII and XIV. Afterwards, in 1802, it was converted back into a church, and today it houses Delacroix's *Christ in the Garden of Olives*.

Maison Européenne de la Photographie

5-7 rue de Fourcy, 4th (01.44.78.75.00/www.mep-fr.org). M° St-Paul. **Open** 11am-7.30pm Wed-Sun. **Admission** €6; €3 reductions; free under-8s, all 5-8pm Wed. **Credit** MC, V. **Map** p409 L6.
Probably the capital's best photography exhibition space, hosting retrospectives by Larry Clark and Martine Barrat, along with work by emerging photographers. The building, an airy mansion with a modern extension, contains a huge permanent collection.
▶ *The venue organises the biennial Mois de la Photo and the Art Outsiders festival of new media web art in September.*

★ FREE Le Mémorial de la Shoah

17 rue Geoffroy-l'Asnier, 4th (01.42.77.44.72/www.memorialdelashoah.org). M° Pont Marie or St-Paul. **Open** 10am-6pm Mon-Wed, Fri-Sun; 10am-10pm Thur. *Research centre* 10am-5.30pm Mon- Wed, Fri, Sun; 10am-7.30pm Thur. **Admission** free. **Map** p409 K6.
Airport-style security checks mean queues, but don't let that put you off: the Mémorial du Martyr Juif Inconnu is an impressively presented and moving memorial to the Holocaust. Enter via the Wall of Names, where limestone slabs are engraved with the first and last names of each of the 76,000 Jews deported from France from 1942 to 1944 with, as an inscription reminds the visitor, the say-so of the Vichy government. The excoriation continues in the basement-level permanent exhibition, which documents the plight of French and European Jews through photographs, texts, films and individual stories: 'The French,' reads one label (captioning is also given in English), 'were not particularly interested in the fate of French Jews at this point.'

FREE Pavillon de l'Arsenal

21 bd Morland, 4th (01.42.76.33.97/www.pavillon-arsenal.com). M° Sully Morland. **Open** 10.30am-6.30pm Tue-Sat; 11am-7pm Sun. **Admission** free. **Credit** *Shop* MC, V. **Map** p409 L7.
The setting is a fantastic 1880s gallery with an iron frame and glass roof; the subject is the built history of Paris; the result is disappointing. The ground floor houses a permanent exhibition on the city's development, but space and funds are lacking to the extent that exhibits are limited to a few storyboards, maps and photos, and three city models set into the floor (done far more impressively at the Musée d'Orsay).

SIGHTS

Bastille & Eastern Paris

Liberté, Egalité, Fraternité.

French history's biggest event took place in this part of town: the storming of the grim fortress-prison that kicked off the Revolution in 1789. There were only seven prisoners inside the jail when the rebels stormed into it, but the event provided the rebels with arms and gave the insurrection momentum that it never lost. Although the prison has long since disappeared, the traffic-choked place de la Bastille where its ramparts used to stand is still a prime spot for political emonstrations, and also the site of the Bastille Day ball every July. The Colonne de Juillet, topped by a gilded *génie* of Liberty, is a monument to Parisians who fell in the revolutions of July 1830 and 1848.

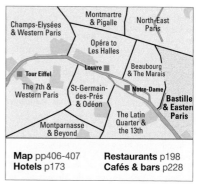

Map pp406-407	**Restaurants** p198
Hotels p173	**Cafés & bars** p228

BASTILLE

In the 11th and 12th arrondissements.

Place de la Bastille has been a potent symbol of popular rebellion ever since 1789. The area was transformed in the 1980s with the arrival of the **Opéra Bastille** (*see p317*), along with fashionable cafés, restaurants and bars. The present-day square occupies the site of the long-vanished prison ramparts, and is dominated by Opéra's curved façade. Opened in 1989 on the bicentenary of Bastille Day, the venue remains controversial, criticised for its poor acoustics and design. South of the square is the Port de l'Arsenal marina, where the Canal St-Martin meets the Seine. The canal continues underground north of the square, running beneath boulevard Richard-Lenoir, site of a lively outdoor market on Sunday mornings.

Rue du Fbg-St-Antoine has been the heart of the furniture-makers' district for centuries. Furniture showrooms still line the street, though they've been joined by clothes shops and bars. Cobbled rue de Lappe typifies the shift, as the last remaining furniture workshops hold out against theme bars overrun at weekends by suburban youths. Pockets of bohemian resistance remain on rue de Charonne, however, with the **Pause Café** (*see p229*) and its busy terrace, bistro **Chez Paul** (no.13, 11th, 01.47.00.34.57) and dealers in colourful 1960s furniture. Rue des Taillandiers and rue Keller are a focus for record stores, streetwear shops and fashion designers.

Narrow street frontages hide cobbled alleys, lined with craftsmen's workshops or quirky bistros dating from the 18th century. Note the cours de l'Ours, du Cheval Blanc, du Bel Air (and hidden garden) and de la Maison Brûlée, the passage du Chantier on rue du Fbg-St-Antoine, the rustic-looking passage de l'Etoile d'Or and the passage de l'Homme, with wooden shopfronts on rue de Charonne. This area was originally located outside the city walls on the lands of the Convent of St-Antoine (parts of which survive as the Hôpital St-Antoine). In the Middle Ages, skilled furnituremakers not belonging to the city's restrictive guilds earned the neighbourhood a reputation for free thinking that was cemented a few hundred years later during the Revolution.

Further down rue du Fbg-St-Antoine is place d'Aligre, home to a rowdy, cheap produce

SIGHTS

market, a more sedate covered food hall and the only flea market within the city walls, where a handful of *brocanteurs* sell junk and old books. The road ends in the major intersection of place de la Nation, another grand square. It was originally called place du Trône, after a throne that was positioned here when Louis XIV and his bride Marie-Thérèse entered the city in 1660. After the Revolution, between 13 June and 28 July 1799, thousands were guillotined on the site, their bodies carted to the nearby Cimetière de Picpus. The square still has two of Ledoux's toll houses and tall Doric columns from the 1787 Mur des Fermiers-Généraux. In the centre stands Jules Dalou's sculpture *Le Triomphe de la République*, erected for the centenary of the Revolution in 1889. East of place de la Nation, broad cours de Vincennes has a market on Wednesday and Saturday mornings and kerb-crawlers by night.

North of place de la Bastille, boulevard Beaumarchais divides Bastille from the Marais. East of place Voltaire, on rue de la Roquette, which heads east towards the Ménilmontant area and Père-Lachaise cemetery, a small park and playground marks the site of the prison de la Roquette, where a plaque remembers the 4,000 Resistance members imprisoned here in World War II.

La Maison Rouge – Fondation Antoine de Galbert

10 bd de la Bastille, 12th (01.40.01.08.81/ www.lamaisonrouge.org). M° Quai de la Rapée. **Open** 11am-7pm Wed, Fri-Sun; 11am-9pm Thur. **Admission** €6.50; €4.50 reductions; free under-13s. **Credit** MC, V. **Map** p406 M7.
Founded by collector Antoine de Galberg, and set in a former printworks, the Red House is an independently run space that alternates monographic shows of contemporary artists' work with pieces from different private art collections.

BERCY & DAUMESNIL

The **Viaduc des Arts** is a former railway viaduct along avenue Daumesnil; its row of glass-fronted arches enclose craft boutiques and workshops. Above sprout the blooms and bamboo of the **Promenade Plantée**, which continues through the Jardin de Reuilly and east to the **Bois de Vincennes**.

Eglise du St-Esprit is a copy of Istanbul's Hagia Sofia; the nearby **Cimetière de Picpus** contains the graves of many of the victims of the Terror, as well as American War of Independence hero General La Fayette.

Just before the Périphérique, the **Palais de la Porte Dorée** was built in 1931 for the Exposition Coloniale. It features striking, albeit politically incorrect, reliefs on the façade and

two beautiful art deco offices. Originally the Musée des Colonies, then the Musée des Arts d'Afrique et d'Océanie (its collections now absorbed by the **Musée du Quai Branly**; *see p146*), it's the new home of the **Cité Nationale de l'Histoire de l'Immigration**. There's also an aquarium in the basement.

As recently as the 1980s, wine was unloaded from barges at Bercy, but after redevelopment this stretch of the Seine is now home to the vast Ministère de l'Economie et du Budget and, to the west, the **Palais Omnisports de Paris-Bercy** (*see p334*). To the east is the Bercy Expo exhibition and trade centre. In between lie the modern **Parc de Bercy** and the former American Center, built in the 1990s by Frank Gehry. It has since reopened as the Cinémathèque Française. At the eastern edge of the park is **Bercy Village**, where warehouses have been restored and opened as shops and cafés. The result is lively, if somewhat antiseptic; typical is mainstream **Club Med World** (*see p332*). Another conversion is the Pavillons de Bercy, with the **Musée des Arts Forains**, a collection of fairground rides and carnival salons.

★ FREE Bois de Vincennes

12th. M° Château de Vincennes or Porte Dorée.
This is Paris's biggest park, created, like the Bois de Boulogne in the west, when the former royal hunting forest was landscaped by Alphand for Baron

Place de la Bastille.

SIGHTS

French Lessons

Diversity comes under the microscope at Paris's new immigration museum.

Immigration in New York is commemorated on Ellis Island, in Québec at the Musée de la Civilisation. So what of the Paris region? Well, there's Parc Astérix – proof that all Frenchmen are descendants of Astérix the Gaul, right? Wrong.

The French ministry of culture has finally chosen to celebrate the ethnological diversity of France's population and render homage to the immigrants that made the mighty Gaul what it is today with a spanking new museum – the **Cité Nationale de l'Histoire de l'Immigration** (*see p107*). Set in the stunning, colonial-themed Palais de la Porte Dorée (built in 1931 for the World Colonial Fair and the former home of many primitive arts exhibits now on show in the **Musée du Quai Branly**), the permanent collections trace over 200 years of history via a series of thought-provoking images (film and photography), everyday objects (suitcases, accordions, sewing machines and so on) and artworks that symbolise the struggles immigrants had to face when integrating into French society. Look out for Bathélémy Toguo's giant bunk-bed installation, *Climbing Down* – a humorous take on the precarious accommodation in which some immigrants are forced to live; and don't miss the permanent exhibition area, *Repères* (bearings), that looks at why many immigrants chose France, the problems they faced upon arrival, and the way sport, work, language, religion and culture can ease integration. One of the most moving areas is the Galerie des Dons – a collection of personal memorabilia donated by individuals whose families came from foreign countries.

At the end, head downstairs to see some real-life immigrants from the animal kingdom. The palace's aquarium has been preserved and still displays a small collection of fish, turtles and crocodiles.

Forthcoming exhibitions include 'A chacun ses étrangers? France-Allemagne de 1871 à nos jours' (until 19 April 2009) and 'Banlieues: photographies de Patrick Zachmann' (28 May-30 September 2009).

Haussmann. There are boating lakes, a Buddhist temple, a racetrack, restaurants, a baseball field (*see p336*) and a small farm. The park also contains the city's main zoo (*see p289*), now largely closed because of lack of maintenance, and the Cartoucherie theatre complex (*see p344*). The Parc Floral is a cross between a botanical garden and an amusement park. Amusements include Paris-themed crazy golf, with water drawn from the Seine, and an adventure playground. Next to the park stands the imposing Château de Vincennes, where England's Henry V died in 1422.

▶ *Jazz concerts take place in the Parc Floral on summer weekends; see p276.*

Cimetière de Picpus
35 rue de Picpus, 12th (01.43.44.18.54). Mº Daumesnil, Nation or Picpus. **Open** *15 Apr-14 Oct* 2-6pm Tue-Sun. *15 Oct-14 Apr* 2-4pm Tue-Sun. **Admission** €3. **No credit cards.** **Map** p407 Q8.

Redolent with revolutionary associations, French and American, this cemetery in a working convent is the resting place for the thousands of victims of the Revolution's aftermath, guillotined at place du Trône (now place de l'Ile-de-la-Réunion) between 14 June and 27 July 1794. At the end of a walled garden is a graveyard of aristocratic French families. In one corner is the tomb of General La Fayette, who fought in the American War of Independence and was married to the aristocratic Marie Adrienne Françoise de Noailles. Clearly marked are the sites of two communal graves, and you can see the doorway where the carts arrived. It was thanks to a maid who had seen the carts that the site was rediscovered, including the cemetery and adjoining convent, founded by descendants of the Noailles family. In the chapel, two tablets list the names and occupations of the executed: 'domestic servant', 'farmer' and 'employee' figure alongside 'lawyer' and 'prince and priest'.

★ Cité Nationale de l'Histoire de l'Immigration – Palais de la Porte Dorée
293 av Daumesnil, 12th (01.58.51.52.00/ www.histoire-immigration.fr). Mº Porte Dorée. **Open** 10am-5.30pm Tue-Fri; 10am-7pm Sat, Sun. **Admission** €5; €3 reductions; free under-18s. *Aquarium* €4.50; €3 reductions. PMP. **No credit cards.**
See p106 **French Lessons.**

FREE Eglise du St-Esprit
186 av Daumesnil, 12th (01.44.75.77.50/www. st-esprit.org). Mº Daumesnil. **Open** 9.30am-noon, 3-7pm Mon-Fri; 9.30am-noon, 3-6pm Sat; from 9am Sun. **Admission** free. **Map** p407 P9.

Behind a red-brick exterior cladding, this unusual 1920s concrete church follows a square plan around a central dome, lit by a scalloped ring of windows. Architect Paul Tournon was directly inspired by the

INSIDE TRACK
PROMENADE PLANTEE

The railway tracks atop the **Viaduc des Arts** (*see below*) were replaced in the late 1980s by a handsome promenade planted with roses, shrubs and rosemary. It continues at ground level through the Jardin de Reuilly and the Jardin Charles Péguy on to the Bois de Vincennes.

Hagia Sofia cathedral in Istanbul, though rather than mosaics, the inside is decorated with frescoes by Maurice Denis and others.

Musée des Arts Forains
53 av des Terroirs-de-France, 12th (01.43.40.16.22/www.pavillons-de-bercy.com). Mº Cour St-Emilion. **Open** groups only, min 15 people, by appointment. **Admission** €12.50; €4 reductions. **No credit cards.** **Map** p407 P10.

Housed in a collection of Eiffel-era, iron-framed wine warehouses is a fantastical collection of 19th- and early 20th-century fairground attractions. The venue is hired out for functions on most evenings, and staff may well be setting the tables when you visit. Of the three halls, the most wonderful is the Salon de la Musique, where a musical sculpture by Jacques Rémus chimes and flashes in time with the 1934 Mortier organ and a modern-day digital grand piano playing *Murder on the Orient Express*. In the Salon de Venise you are twirled round on a gondola carousel; in the Salon des Arts Forains you can play a ball-throwing game that sets off a race of moustachioed waiters or brave the Vélocipède, a nightmarish carousel of penny farthings. The venue is open only to groups of 15 or more, but individuals can visit as part of a guided tour. Call ahead.

FREE Parc de Bercy
Rue de Bercy, 12th. Mº Bercy or Cour St-Emilion. **Open** *Winter* 8am-5.30pm Mon-Fri; 9am-5.30pm Sat, Sun. *Summer* 8am-9pm Mon-Fri; 9am-9pm Sat, Sun. **Map** p407 N9/10.

Created in the 1990s, the Bercy park features a large lawn, a grid with square rose, herb and vegetable plots, an orchard, and gardens laid out to represent the four seasons.

FREE Le Viaduc des Arts
15-121 av Daumesnil, 12th (www.viaduc-des-arts.com). Mº Gare de Lyon or Ledru-Rollin. **Map** p407 M8/N8.

Glass-fronted workshops in the arches beneath the Promenade Plantée provide showrooms for furniture and fashion designers, picture-frame gilders, tapestry restorers, porcelain decorators, and chandelier, violin and flute makers. Design industry body VIA holds exhibitions of work at Nos.29-35.

SIGHTS

North-east Paris

Keeping it real on the streets of Belleville.

Traditionally, the area north and north-east of place de la République was a staunchly proletarian district, shot through by the Canal St-Martin that brought raw goods and rough barges into the city. Many streets around here are still tatty and dingy, but others, especially those near the canal, have been fashionable for at least ten years. Gentrification as such is not much in evidence – unless you take the rise in rents as an index, in which case it's rampant. But to the visitor, unconcerned by property prices, this part of Paris

| Map p403 & p407 | Restaurants p203 |
| Hotels p173 | Cafés & bars p229 |

has much to offer: there's a palpable buzz and strong sense of authenticity on streets such as rue du Fbg-St-Denis – and any number of side streets that take you into a completely different world.

Still further north-east are the manifold delights of La Villette, with its science and music museums, performance venues and unusual landscaped gardens, and a new arts space in the former city undertaker's.

FBG-ST-DENIS TO GARE DU NORD

In the 10th arrondissement.

North of Porte St-Denis and Porte St-Martin, two of the oldest thoroughfares leading out of the city, rue du Fbg-St-Denis and rue du Fbg-St-Martin, traverse an area that was transformed in the 19th century by the railways, when it became the site of the Gare du Nord and Gare de l'Est. The grubby rue du Fbg-St-Denis is almost souk-like with its food shops, narrow passages and sinister courtyards. Garishly lit passage Brady is a surprising piece of India in Paris, full of restaurants, hairdressers and costume shops, whereas the art deco passage du Prado is more a continuation of the Sentier rag trade. The rue du Fbg-St-Martin follows the trace of the Roman road out of the city, and is full of children's clothes wholesalers, atmospheric courtyards and the ornate Mairie for the tenth. Rue des Petites-Ecuries ('Little Stables Street') was once known for saddlers, but now has shops, cafés and jazz venue **New Morning** (*see p325*), and is home to Turkish and Afro-Caribbean communities.

Rue de Paradis is known for its porcelain and glass outlets, and rue d'Hauteville shows traces of the area's grander days (notably the **Petit Hôtel Bourrienne**, at no.58, a Consulaire-style apartment open to the public). Opposite, the Cité Paradis is an alley of early industrial buildings. At the top of the street are the twin towers and terraced gardens of the **Eglise St-Vincent-de-Paul**. Behind, on rue de Belzunce, is Chez Casimir at no.6 (10th, 01.48.78.28.80). On boulevard Magenta, **Marché St-Quentin**, built in the 1860s, is one of the city's last few remaining cast-iron, covered market halls.

Boulevard de Strasbourg was cut through in the 19th century to create a vista up to the Gare de l'Est. At no.2, a neo-Renaissance creation houses the last fan-maker in Paris and the **Musée de l'Eventail**. Towards the station, Eglise St-Laurent (69 bd de Magenta, 119 rue du Fbg-St-Martin, 10th) is one of the city's oldest churches, an eclectic composition with a 12th-century tower, Gothic nave, baroque lady chapel, 19th-century façade and 1930s stained glass. Between the Gare de l'Est and Canal St-Martin are the restored **Couvent des Récollets** and Square Villemin park.

SIGHTS

FREE Couvent des Récollets

148 rue du Fbg-St-Martin, 10th. M° Gare de l'Est. **Admission** free. **Map** p402 L3.
Founded as a monastery in the 17th century when still outside the city walls, this barracks, spinning factory and hospice was a military hospital from 1860 to 1968. Left empty, the convent was squatted by artists, Les Anges des Récollets, in the early 1990s. The buildings were renovated and reopened in 2004. One half, the Maison des Architectes, hosts a garden café and architectural debates. The other is the Centre International d'Accueil et d'Echanges des Récollets: 85 studios and duplexes for foreign 'creators' – artists and researchers (from painters to neurobiologists) – invited to stay here for extended periods. In rehabilitating the building, architect Frédéric Vincendon left traces of its history: the ghostly 17th-century stonework, 20th-century reinforced concrete columns and squatters' graffiti.

★ FREE Eglise St-Vincent-de-Paul

5 rue Belzunce, 10th (01.48.78.47.47). M° Gare du Nord. **Open** 2-7pm Mon; 8am-noon, 2-7pm Tue-Fri; 8am-noon, 2-7.30pm Sat; 9.30am-noon, 4.30-7.30pm Sun. **Admission** free. **Map** p402 K2.
Set at the top of terraced gardens, this church was begun in 1824 by Lepère and completed in 1844 by Hittorff. The twin towers, pedimented Greek temple portico and sculptures of the four evangelists along the parapet are done in high classical mode. The interior has a splendid double-storey arcade of columns, murals by Flandrin and church furniture by Rude.

FREE Gare du Nord

Rue de Dunkerque, 10th (08.91.36.20.20). M° Gare du Nord. **Map** p402 K2.
The grandest of the great 19th-century train stations (and Eurostar terminal since 1994) was designed by Hittorff between 1861 and 1864. A conventional stone façade, with Ionic capitals and statues representing towns served by the station, hides a vast iron-and-glass vault. The airy refurbishment of the suburban section by rue du Fbg-St-Denis makes the Eurostar's glass-topped digs look a little drab.

INSIDE TRACK
LITTLE SPARROW

Legend has it that **Edith Piaf** was born on the pavement outside 72 rue de Belleville, as marked on the plaque: 'On the steps of this house was born on the 19 December 1915, in the greatest poverty, Edith Piaf, whose voice would later move the world.' Devotees run the nearby appointment-only **Musée Edith Piaf** (5 rue Crespin-du-Gast, 11th, 01.43.55.52.72), a modest two-room museum.

Canal St-Martin. See p111.

Musée de l'Eventail

2 bd de Strasbourg, 10th (01.42.08.90.20/www.annehoguet.fr). M° Strasbourg St-Denis. **Open** 2-6pm Mon-Wed (Mon-Fri during school hols). *Children's activities* Wed afternoons. Closed Aug. **Admission** €6; €3-€4 reductions; free under-8s. **No credit cards. Map** p402 K4.
Anne Hoguet keeps the tradition of her ancestors alive in this arcane museum in a 19th-century apartment, a fan-maker's *atelier* since 1805. One room houses the tools of the trade; beside it is Hoguet's studio, where she works on fans for fashion and the stage. The former *salle d'exposition*, lined in blue silk, is where the collection of almost 1,000 historic fans is shown in glass cases and stored in cabinets.

Petit Hôtel Bourrienne

58 rue d'Hauteville, 10th (01.47.70.51.14). M° Bonne Nouvelle or Poissonnière. **Open** *Guided visits 1-15 July, Sept* noon-6pm daily. Rest of year by appointment Sat. **Admission** €7. **No credit cards. Map** p402 K3.
A rare example of the Consulaire style, this small *hôtel particulier* was built in 1789-98. It was occupied by Fortunée Hamelin, born (like her friend the Empress Josephine) in Martinique, and notorious for parading topless down the Champs-Elysées. A bedroom boudoir painted with tropical birds was her only decoration before the site was taken over by Louis Fauvelet de Bourrienne, Napoleon's private secretary. He had it decorated according to the latest fashion, making sure to keep his political options open (the dining room ceiling is painted with motifs favourable to monarchy and empire).

SIGHTS

Walk Dead Famous

Visit Père-Lachaise, home to many of France's most illustrious corpses.

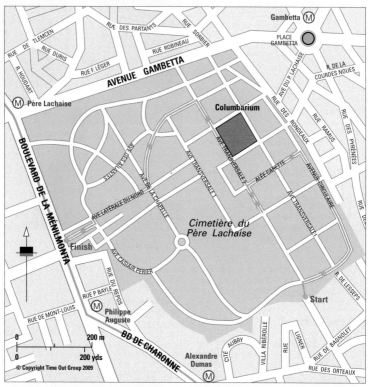

SIGHTS

The Cimetière du Père-Lachaise, Paris's largest cemetery, is probably still best known to foreign visitors as the final resting place of one **James Douglas Morrison**, lead singer of the Doors. But ask a local what this 48-hectare site in the 20th arrondissement means to them, and they're more likely to mention the Mur des Fédérés or **Molière** than the Lizard King. On this walk, therefore, you'll pay tribute to the heroes and victims of French political history, and visit the tombs of some of France's greatest writers.

Rather than entering Père-Lachaise by the main entrance on boulevard Ménilmontant, start at the much more discreet gate set into the southern wall of the cemetery on rue de la Réunion,

just off rue de Bagnolet. You join avenue Circulaire, which hugs the cemetery wall. Turn right and then follow the path until you reach the Mur des Fédérés in the south-east corner.

It was here, in the last week of May 1871, that the few remaining partisans of the **Paris Commune** (known as *fédérés* or communards) were lined up against a wall and summarily executed by troops loyal to the National Assembly at Versailles. A memorial procession to the wall, the Montée au Mur des Fédérés, takes place every year in May.

Across the path, in plot or 'division' 97, stand a number of memorials to the victims of Nazism and Fascism. Next to an urn containing ashes from the crematorium at the Flossenburg concentration camp is a striking ziggurat commemorating people who were 'tortured, gassed, shot or hanged' at Mauthausen. And just behind this loom two enormous manacled hands hewn from stone, a deeply unsettling monument to the women who died at Ravensbruck. A little further along avenue Circulaire, on the same side, is the tomb of people who perished in 1962 at the hands of the police, not far from here at the Charonne métro station, after a demonstration in favour of Algerian independence.

Follow avenue Circulaire along the northern wall until you reach the Jardin du Souvenir. Turn left up avenue Carette, keeping an eye out on your right for the monumental sarcophagus housing the remains of **Oscar Wilde**, who died in Paris in 1900.

When you reach avenue Transversale no.2, turn left and walk down the hill, until you reach a bronze effigy of **Victor Noir**, a journalist who was shot by a cousin of Napoleon III in 1870. You'll notice that the effigy depicts Noir with a distinct enlargement in the region of the groin, and also that the area in question appears to have been rubbed down rather energetically: many *parisiennes* have believed that a little *frottage* with Victor would make them fertile.

Now retrace your steps in the direction of the crematorium and columbarium. On your left, in division 86, is the rough-hewn headstone of **Guillaume Appolinaire**. Across the path, **Marcel Proust** lies in an austere marble tomb with other members of his family.

Continue along avenue Transversale No.2, until you reach avenue des Thuryas. Turn left and walk down the hill into gently curving chemin Casimir Delavigne. About halfway down on the right is a bronze bust of **Honoré de Balzac**. The bust is accompanied by a bronze book and quill, upon which, on our most recent visit, an admirer had left an apple with a heart carved in it.

Walk straight on, down chemin Mont-Louis. Through the trees you'll catch tantalising glimpses of the Paris skyline as you head for avenue Principale, and beyond that the main gate, and the din and traffic of boulevard Ménilmontant.

CANAL ST-MARTIN TO LA VILLETTE

In the 10th & 19th arrondissements

Canal St-Martin, built between 1805 and 1825, begins at the Seine at Pont Morland, disappears underground at Bastille, hides under boulevard Richard-Lenoir, then emerges after crossing rue du Faubourg-du-Temple, east of place de la République. Rue du Faubourg-du-Temple itself is scruffy and cosmopolitan, lined with cheap grocers and discount stores, hidden courtyards and stalwarts of Paris nightlife: **Le Gibus** (*see p329*), bar-restaurant **Favela Chic** (*see p333*) and vintage dancehall **La Java** (*see p333*), as well as the **Palais des Glaces** (no.37, 10th, 01.42.02.27.17, www.palaisdesglaces.com), which programmes seasons of French comics.

The first stretch of the canal, lined with shady trees and crossed by iron footbridges and locks, has the most appeal. The quays are traffic-free on Sundays. Many canalside warehouses have been snapped up by artists and designers or turned into loft apartments. You can take a boat as far as La Villette.

East of here, the Hôpital St-Louis was commissioned in 1607 by Henri IV to house plague victims, and was built as a series of isolated pavilions in the same brick-and-stone style as place des Vosges, far enough from the town to prevent risk of infection. Behind the hospital, the rue de la Grange-aux-Belles housed the Montfaucon gibbet, put up in 1233, where victims were hanged and left to the elements. East of the hospital, the lovely cobbled rue Ste-Marthe and place Ste-Marthe have a provincial air, busy at night with multi-ethnic eateries.

North, on place du Colonel-Fabien, is the headquarters of the **Parti Communiste Français**, a modernist masterpiece built between 1968 and 1971 by Brazilian architect Oscar Niemeyer with Paul Chemetov and Jean Deroche. The canal disappears briefly again under place de Stalingrad, a locale best avoided after dark. The square was landscaped in 1989 to showcase the Rotonde de la Villette, one of Ledoux's grandiose 1780s toll houses that once marked the boundary of Paris; it now displays exhibitions and archaeological finds.

Here the canal widens into the Bassin de la Villette, and the new developments along the quai de Loire and further quai de la Marne, as well as some of the worst 1960s and '70s housing in the colossal blocks that stretch along rue de Flandres. At 104 rue d'Aubervilliers, the old municipal undertaker's has been turned into a multimedia art space, **104**.

At the eastern end of the basin is an unusual 1885 hydraulic lifting bridge, Pont de Crimée. Thursday and Sunday mornings add vitality

SIGHTS

with a market at place de Joinville. East of here, the Canal de l'Ourcq (created in 1813 to provide drinking water, as well as for freight haulage) divides: Canal St-Denis runs north towards the Seine, and Canal de l'Ourcq continues east through La Villette and the suburbs. Long the city's main abattoir district, still reflected in the Grande Halle de la Villette and in some of the old meaty brasseries along boulevard de la Villette, the neighbourhood has been revitalised since the late 1980s by the postmodern **Parc de la Villette** complex, with the **Cité des Sciences et de l'Industrie** science museum and the **Cité de la Musique** concert hall.

★ 104

104 rue d'Aubervilliers, 19th (01.53.35.50.00/ www.104.fr). M° Riquet. **Open** 11am-8pm Mon, Sun; 11am-11pm Tue-Sat. **Admission** free. *Exhibitions* €5; €3 reductions. **Credit** AmEx, MC, V.

It's more than a century since tourist-choked Montmartre was the centre of artistic activity in Paris. But now the north of Paris is again where the action is – albeit a couple of kilometres east of place du Tertre, in a previously neglected area of bleak railway goods yards and dilapidated social housing. 104, described as a 'space for artistic creation', occupies a vast 19th-century building on the rue d'Aubervilliers that used to house Paris's municipal undertakers. The site was saved from developers by Roger Madec, the mayor of the 19th, who's made its renovation the centrepiece of a massive project of cultural and urban renewal. There aren't any constraints on the kind of work the resident artists do – 104 is open to 'all the arts' – but they're expected to show finished pieces in one of four annual 'festivals'. And they're also required to get involved in projects with the public, the fruits of which are shown in a space next door.

★ La Cité des Sciences et de l'Industrie

La Villette, 30 av Corentin-Cariou, 19th (01.40.05.70.00/www.cite-sciences.fr). M° Porte de la Villette. **Open** 10am-6pm Tue-Sat; 10am-7pm Sun. **Admission** €8; €6 reductions; free under-7s. PMP. **Credit** MC, V. **Map** p403 inset.
This ultra-modern science museum pulls in five million visitors a year. Explora, the permanent show, occupies the upper two floors, whisking visitors through 30,000sq m (320,000sq ft) of space, life, matter and communication: scale models of satellites including the Ariane space shuttle, planes and robots, plus the chance to experience weightlessness, make for an exciting journey. In the Espace Images, try the delayed camera and other optical illusions, draw 3D images on a computer or lend your voice to the *Mona Lisa*. The hothouse garden investigates developments in agriculture and bio-technology.
▶ *The Cité des Enfants runs workshops for younger children. See the website for details.*

Musée de la Musique

Cité de la Musique, 221 av Jean-Jaurès, 19th (01.44.84.45.00/www.cite-musique.fr). M° Porte de Pantin. **Open** noon-6pm Tue-Sat; 10am-6pm Sun. **Admission** €8; €6.40 reductions; free under-18s, over-60s. PMP. **Credit** AmEx, MC, V. **Map** p403 (inset).
Alongside the concert hall, this innovative music museum houses a gleamingly restored collection of instruments from the old Conservatoire, interactive computers and scale models of opera houses and concert halls. Visitors are supplied with an audio guide in a choice of languages, and the musical commentary is a joy, playing the appropriate instrument as you approach each exhibit. Alongside the trumpeting brass, curly woodwind instruments and precious strings are more unusual items, such as the Indonesian gamelan orchestra, whose sounds influenced the work of Debussy and Ravel. Concerts in the amphitheatre use instruments from the collection.

★ FREE Parc de la Villette

Av Corentin-Cariou, 19th (01.40.03.75.75/www. villette.com). M° Porte de la Villette. Av Jean-Jaurès, 19th. M° Porte de Pantin. **Map** p403 inset.
Dotted with red pavilions, or *folies*, the park was designed by Swiss architect Bernard Tschumi and is a postmodern feast (guided tours 08.03.30.63.06, 3pm Sun in summer). The *folies* serve as glorious giant climbing frames, as well as a first-aid post, burger bar and children's art centre. Kids shoot down a Chinese dragon slide, and an undulating suspended path follows the Canal de l'Ourcq. As well as the lawns, which are used for an open-air film festival in summer, there are ten themed gardens bearing evocative names such as the Garden of Mirrors, of Mists, of Acrobatics and of Childhood Frights. South of the canal are the Zénith (*see p320*), and the Grande Halle de la Villette – now used for trade fairs, exhibitions and September's jazz festival (*see p277*). It is flanked by the Conservatoire de la Musique and the Cité de la Musique, with rehearsal rooms, concert halls and the Musée de la Musique.

BELLEVILLE, MENILMONTANT & CHARONNE

In the 11th, 19th & 20th arrondissements.

When the city boundaries were expanded in 1860, Ménilmontant, Belleville and Charonne, once villages that provided Paris with fruit, wine and weekend escapes, were all absorbed. They were built up with housing for migrants, first from rural France and later from former colonies in North Africa and South-east Asia. The main tourist attraction is **Père-Lachaise** cemetery, but the area also encompasses one of the city's most beautiful parks, the romantic **Buttes-Chaumont**. Despite attempts to

SIGHTS

North-east Paris

dissipate workers' agitation by splitting the village between the 11th, 19th and 20th administrative districts, Belleville became the centre of opposition to the Second Empire. Cabarets, artisans and workers typified 1890s Belleville; colonised by artists in the 1990s, today Belleville is a trendy hangout.

On boulevard de Belleville, Chinese and Vietnamese shops rub shoulders with Muslim and kosher groceries, couscous and falafel eateries, and a street market takes place on Tuesday and Friday mornings.

North of here, along avenue Simon-Bolivar, is the Parc des Buttes-Chaumont. This is the most desirable part of north-east Paris, with Haussmannian apartments overlooking the park: to the east, near place de Rhin-et-Danube, is a small area of tiny, hilly streets lined with small houses and gardens, known by locals as the Quartier Mouzaïa.

Up on the slopes of the Hauts de Belleville, there are views over the city from rue Piat and rue des Envierges, which lead to the modern but charming **Parc de Belleville** with its Maison des Vents devoted to birds and kites. Below the park, rue Ramponneau mixes new housing and relics of old Belleville. At no.23 an old smithy has been transformed into La Forge, an artists' squat, many of them members of La Bellevilloise association, which is trying to save the area from redevelopment.

'Mesnil-Montant' used to be a few houses on a hill with vines and fruit trees – then came the bistros, bordellos and workers' housing. It became part of Paris in 1860 along with Belleville, and has a similar history. These days it's a thriving centre of alternative Paris, as artists and young professionals have moved in. Boulevard de Ménilmontant divides this trendy nightlife quarter from the cemetery of Père-Lachaise. Although side streets still have male-only North African cafés, rue Oberkampf is home to some of the city's most humming bars, many following the runaway success of the pivotal **Café Charbon** (see p231).

The area mixes 1960s and '70s housing projects with older dwellings, some gentrified, some derelict. Just below rue des Pyrénées, which cuts through the 20th, you can rummage around the rustic Cité Leroy or Villa l'Ermitage, cobbled cul-de-sacs of little houses and gardens, and old craft workshops. Rue de l'Ermitage has a curious neo-Gothic house at no.19 – and a bird's eye view from the junction with rue de Ménilmontant, right down the hill to the Centre Pompidou. On rue Boyer, **La Maroquinerie** (see p321) puts on an eclectic mix of literary events, political debate and live music, and at 88 rue de Ménilmontant, graffiti-covered art squat **La Miroiterie** opens house for art shows and the *magasin gratuit*, a free swap shop.

East of Père-Lachaise on rue de Bagnolet, La Flèche d'Or (see p321), a converted station on the defunct Petite Ceinture railway line, is a landmark music venue. Beyond, the medieval **Eglise St-Germain-de-Charonne** is at the heart of what is left of the village of Charonne. Set at the top of steps next to its presbytery, below a hill once covered with vines, it is the only church in Paris, except St-Pierre-de-Montmartre, still to have its own graveyard. Below here, centred on the old village high street of rue St-Blaise, is a prettified backwater of quiet tearooms and bistros, where old shops have been taken over by art classes.

Towards porte de Bagnolet, where rue de Bagnolet and rue des Balkans meet on the edge of a small park, the **Pavillon de l'Hermitage** is a small aristocratic relic built in the 1720s for Françoise-Marie de Bourbon, the daughter of Louis XIV, when it was in the grounds of the Château de Bagnolet. A little further south at porte de Montreuil, cross the Périphérique for the Puces de Montreuil flea market.

★ FREE Cimetière du Père-Lachaise

Bd de Ménilmontant, 20th (01.55.25.82.10). M° Père-Lachaise. **Open** *6 Nov-15 Mar* 8am-5.30pm Mon-Fri; 8.30am-5.30pm Sat; 9am-5.30pm Sun. *16 Mar-5 Nov* 8am-6pm Mon-Fri; 8.30am-6pm Sat; 9am-6pm Sun & hols. **Admission** free. **Map** p407 P5.

Père-Lachaise is the celebrity cemetery – it has almost anyone French, talented and dead that you care to mention. Not even French, for that matter. Creed and nationality have never prevented entry: you just had to have lived or died in Paris or have an allotted space in a family tomb. *See p110* **Walk**.

FREE Eglise St-Germain-de-Charonne

Pl St-Blaise, 20th (01.43.71.42.04). M° Porte de Bagnolet. **Admission** free. **Open** 9am-7pm.
The old village church of Charonne dates mainly from the 15th century, though one massive column and the bell tower remain from an earlier structure. The interior is almost square, with a triple nave and a simple organ loft. Two side altars have striking modern paintings (a crucifixion and a pietà) by Paul Rambié; a niche contains a wood statue of St Blaise.

★ FREE Parc des Buttes-Chaumont

Rue Botzaris, rue Manin, rue de Crimée, 19th. M° Buttes Chaumont. **Open** *Oct-Apr* 7am-8.15pm daily. *May, mid Aug-Sept* 7am-9.15pm daily. *June-mid Aug* 7am-10.15pm daily. **Map** p407 N2.
With its meandering paths and vertical cliffs, this lovely park was designed by Adolphe Alphand for Haussmann in the 1860s. A bridge (cheerfully named the Pont des Suicides) crosses the lake to an island crowned by a mini-temple.

The Latin Quarter & the 13th

From the scholarly old to the screamingly new.

The Latin Quarter holds a considerable mystique for many foreign visitors, thanks to the historical presence of Hemingway, Orwell and Miller and the seedbed of the 1968 revolt. However, traces of those fabled eras are harder to find: property in the Latin Quarter is now among the dearest in Paris, and every year another relic is renovated out of existence. To cite just one example, the removal of the ancient wooden 'Vieux Chêne' sign from a building in rue Mouffetard in 2005 went almost wholly unnoticed and unlamented.

Map p406	**Restaurants** p205
Hotels p174	**Cafés & bars** p234

The 'Latin' in the area's name probably derives from the fact that it has been the university quarter since medieval times, when Latin was the language of instruction. But while the still-scholarly Latin Quarter is home to the city's most important Roman remains, the corner of the 13th arrondissement known as the ZAC Rive Gauche has seen plenty of development in the last 15 years: a new library, a new bridge, a floating swimming pool, and, in early 2009, the newest big cultural centre, the Cité de la Mode et du Design. And there are more projects on the way.

ST-SEVERIN & ST-JULIEN-LE-PAUVRE

In the 5th arrondissement.

Boulevard St-Michel used to be synonymous with student rebellion; now it's a largely unprepossessing ribbon of fast-food joints and clothing shops, though Gibert Joseph (*see p242*) continues to furnish books and stationery to students. East of here, the semi-pedestrianised patch by the Seine has retained much of its medieval street plan. Rue de la Huchette and rue de la Harpe are now best known for their kebabs and pizzas, though there are 18th-century wrought-iron balconies and carved masks in the latter street. At the tiny **Théâtre de la Huchette** (*see p346*), Ionesco's absurdist drama *La Cantatrice Chauve* (*The Bald Soprano*) has been playing

continuously since 1957. Also of interest are rue du Chat-qui-Pêche, supposedly the city's narrowest street, and rue de la Parcheminerie, named after the parchment sellers and copyists who once lived here. Among the tourist shops stands the city's most charming medieval church, the **Eglise St-Séverin**, with leering gargoyles, spiky gabled side chapels and an exuberantly vaulted Flamboyant Gothic interior.

Across ancient rue St-Jacques is the **Eglise St-Julien-le-Pauvre**, built as a resting place for 12th-century pilgrims. Nearby rue Galande has old houses and the Trois Mailletz cabaret at no.56 (5th, 01.43.54.42.94). The medieval cellars of the **Caveau des Oubliettes** jazz club (*see p324*) were used as a prison after the French Revolution (*oubliette* is the French word for a pit into which prisoners were thrown, then forgotten). At no.42, the arts cinema **Studio Galande** draws goths for late-night

SIGHTS

screenings of the *Rocky Horror Picture Show* every Friday and Saturday. Just outside the church, in place Viviani, stands what is perhaps the city's oldest tree, a false acacia that was planted in 1602; it's now half-swamped by ivy and propped up by concrete buttresses.

The little streets between here and the eastern stretch of boulevard St-Germain are among the city's oldest: streets such as rue de Bièvre (*photo p124*), which follows the course of the Bièvre river that flowed into the Seine in the Middle Ages, rue du Maître-Albert, and rue des Grands-Degrès, with traces of old shop signs painted on its buildings' façades. Remnants of the Collège des Bernardins, built for the Cistercian order, can be seen in rue de Poissy, where the 13th- to 14th-century gothic monks' refectory is being restored after service as firemen's barracks. Nearby are the **Eglise St-Nicolas-de-Chardonnet** (23 rue Bernardins, 5th, 01.44.27.07.90), associated with the schismatic Society of St Pius X and one of a small number of churches where you can hear the Tridentine Mass in Paris, and the art deco **Maison de la Mutualité** (24 rue St-Victor, 5th, 01.40.46.12.00), where you'll find everything from trade unions meetings to rock concerts.

At 47 quai de la Tournelle, the 17th-century Hôtel de Miramion now contains the **Musée de l'Assistance Publique**, devoted to the history of Paris hospitals. You'll find food for all budgets along quai de la Tournelle, starting with Michelin-starred haute-cuisine restaurant La Tour d'Argent (*see p174* **Nautical but Nice**), said to have been founded as an inn in 1582. After 60 years at the helm, owner Claude Terrail died in 2006, passing the restaurant to his son André. Nearby is the Tintin shrine, *café-tabac* **Le Rallye** (no.11, 5th, 01.43.54.29.65). Place Maubert, now a breezy morning marketplace (Tue, Thur, Sat), witnessed the hanging of Protestants during the 16th-century Wars of Religion. Just behind the square, the modern police station is home to an array of grisly criminal evidence in the **Musée de la Préfecture de Police**.

On the corner of boulevard St-Germain and boulevard St-Michel stand the striking ruins of the late second-century **Thermes de Cluny**, the Romans' main baths complex; the adjoining Gothic Hôtel de Cluny provides a suitable setting for the **Musée National du Moyen Age**, the national collection of medieval art. Adjoining boulevard St-Germain, its garden has been replanted with species portrayed in medieval tapestries, paintings and treatises.

FREE Eglise St-Julien-le-Pauvre

Rue St-Julien-le-Pauvre, 5th (01.43.54.52.16/ bookings 01.42.26.00.00). M° Cluny La Sorbonne. **Open** 9.30am-1pm, 3-6.30pm daily. **Admission** free. **Map** p408 J7.
A former sanctuary for pilgrims en route to Compostela, this much-mauled church dates from the late 12th century, on the cusp of Romanesque and Gothic, and has capitals richly decorated with vines, acanthus leaves and winged harpies. Once part of a priory, it became the university church when colleges migrated to the Left Bank, and was the site of riotous university assemblies. Since 1889, it has been used by the Greek Orthodox Church.

★ FREE Eglise St-Séverin

3 rue des Prêtres-St-Séverin, 5th (01.42.34. 93.50). M° Cluny La Sorbonne or St-Michel. **Open** 11am-7.30pm daily. **Admission** free. **Map** p408 J7.
Built on the site of the chapel of the hermit Séverin, itself set on a much earlier Merovingian burial ground, this lovely Flamboyant Gothic edifice was long the parish church of the Left Bank. It was rebuilt on various occasions to repair damage after ransacking by Normans and to meet the needs of the growing population. The church dates from the 15th century, though the doorway, carved with foliage, was added in 1837 from the demolished Eglise St-Pierre-aux-Boeufs on Ile de la Cité. The double ambulatory is famed for its forest of 'palm tree' vaulting, which meets at the end in a unique spiral column that inspired a series of paintings by Robert Delaunay. The bell tower, a survivor from one of the earlier churches on the site, has the oldest bell in Paris (1412). Around the nave are stained-glass windows dating from the 14th and 15th centuries (most of those in the side chapels are by 19th-century Chartres master Emile Hersh), and the choir apse has striking stained glass designed by artist Jean René Bazaine in the 1960s. Next door, around the former cemetery, is the only remaining charnel house in Paris.

Musée de l'Assistance Publique

Hôtel de Miramion, 47 quai de la Tournelle, 5th (01.40.27.50.05/www.aphp.fr). M° Maubert Mutualité. **Open** 10am-6pm Tue-Sun. Closed Aug. **Admission** €4; €2 reductions; free under-13s. PMP. **No credit cards**. **Map** p406 K7.
The history of Paris hospitals, from the days when they were receptacles for abandoned babies to the dawn of modern medicine, is shown through paintings, prints, and a mock ward and pharmacy.

INSIDE TRACK
GO IN SEINE

If you fancy a dip in the river, the floating **Piscine Josephine-Baker** (*see p341*), named after the singer and Resistance fighter, uses filtered water from the Seine to fill its 25-metre (82-foot) pool.

SIGHTS

What Lies Beneath

Medieval treasures and Roman remains at the Musée National du Moyen Age.

The **Musée National du Moyen Age** (*see below*) is best known for the beautiful, allegorical *Lady and the Unicorn* tapestry cycle, but it also has important collections of medieval sculpture and enamels. The building itself, commonly known as Cluny, is also a rare example of 15th-century secular Gothic architecture, with its foliate Gothic doorways, hexagonal staircase jutting out of the façade and vaulted chapel. It was built from 1485 to 1498 – atop a Gallo-Roman baths complex dating from the second and third centuries – to lodge priests, at the request of Jacques d'Amboise, abbot of the powerful Abbey of Cluny in Burgundy. The baths, built in characteristic Roman bands of stone and brick masonry, are the finest Roman remains in Paris. The vaulted *frigidarium* (cold bath), *tepidarium* (warm bath), *caldarium* (hot bath) and part of the hypocaust heating system are all still visible. A themed garden fronts the whole complex.

With its U-shaped residential building set behind an entrance courtyard, Cluny was a precursor of the Marais *hôtels particuliers* of the 16th and 17th centuries. After serving as a printworks and laundry, the *hôtel* was rented in the 1830s by medievalist Alexandre du Sommerand to house his collection, which laid the foundations for this museum created in 1844. Recent acquisitions include the illuminated manuscript *L'Ascension du Christ* from the Abbey of Cluny, dating back to the 12th century, and the 16th-century triptych *Assomption de la Vierge* by Adrien Isenbrant of Bruges. The mesmerising *Lady and the Unicorn*

cycle depicts convoluted allegories of the five senses via six late 15th-century Flemish millefleurs tapestries, beautifully displayed in a special circular room. Other textiles include fragile Coptic embroidery, Edward III's emblazoned saddle cloth and a cycle of the life of St Stephen. The heads of the Kings of Judah from Notre-Dame cathedral, mutilated in the Revolution and rediscovered (minus their noses) in 1979, are considered the highlight of the sculpture collection.

★ Musée National du Moyen Age – Thermes de Cluny

6 pl Paul-Painlevé, 5th (01.53.73.78.00/ www.musee-moyenage.fr). M° Cluny La Sorbonne. **Open** 9.15am-5.45pm Mon, Wed-Sun. **Admission** €7.50; €5.50 reductions, all on Sun; free under-18s, all on 1st Sun of mth. PMP. **Credit** *Shop* MC, V. **Map** p408 J7.
See above **What Lies Beneath**.

FREE Musée de la Préfecture de Police

4 rue de la Montagne-Ste-Geneviève, 5th (01.44.41.52.50/www.prefecture-police-paris.

interieur.gouv.fr). M° Maubert Mutualité. **Open** 9am-5pm Mon-Fri; 10am-5pm Sat. **Admission** free. **No credit cards**. **Map** p406 J7.
The police museum is housed in a working *commissariat*, which makes for a slightly intimidating entry procedure. You need to walk boldly past the police officer standing guard outside and up the steps to the lobby, where you have to ask at the reception booth to be let in – queuing, if necessary, with locals there on other, but usually police-related, errands. The museum is on the second floor; start from the *Accueil* and work your way clockwise.

None of the displays is labelled in English (though there is a bilingual booklet), and a handful are not labelled at all; but if you have basic French and any sort of interest in criminology, this extensive collection is well worth seeing. It starts in the early 17th century and runs to the Occupation, via the founding of the Préfecture de Police by Napoleon in 1800. Exhibits include a prison register open at the entry for Ravaillac, assassin of Henri IV; a section on the Anarchist bombings of the 1890s; the automatic pistol used to assassinate President Doumer in 1932; a blood-chilling collection of murder weapons – hammers, ice picks and knives; sections on serial killers Landru and Petiot; and less dangerous items, such as a gadget used to snag banknotes from the apron pockets of market sellers.

THE SORBONNE, MONTAGNE STE-GENEVIEVE & MOUFFETARD

In the 5th arrondissement.

An influx of well-heeled residents in the 1980s put paid to the days of horn-rims, pipes and turtlenecks: accommodation here is now well beyond the reach of most students. The intellectual tradition persists, however, in the concentration of academic institutions around the Montagne Ste-Geneviève, and students throng the specialist bookstores and art cinemas on rue Champollion and rue des Ecoles.

The district's long association with learning began in about 1100, when a number of renowned scholars, including Pierre Abélard, began to live and teach on the Montagne, independent of the established cathedral school of Notre-Dame. This loose association of scholars came to be referred to as a 'university'. The Paris schools attracted students from all over Europe, and the 'colleges' – in reality student residences dotted round the area (some still survive) – multiplied, until the University of Paris was given official recognition with a charter from Pope Innocent III in 1215.

By the 16th century, the university – named the **Sorbonne**, after the most famous of its colleges – had been co-opted by the Catholic Church. A century later, Cardinal Richelieu rebuilt it. Following the Revolution, when it was forced to close, Napoleon revived the Sorbonne as the cornerstone of his new, centralised education system. The university participated enthusiastically in the uprisings of the 19th century; it was also a seedbed of the 1968 revolt, when it was occupied by protesting students. These days, it's decidedly less turbulent. Also on rue des Ecoles, the independent **Collège de France** was founded in 1530 by a group of humanists led by Guillaume Budé under the patronage of François I. The neighbouring **Brasserie Balzar** (no.49, 5th, 01.43.54.13.67) has been fuelling amateur philosophy for years.

From here, climb rue St-Jacques to rue Soufflot for the most impressive introduction to place du Panthéon. Otherwise, follow rue des Carmes – with its baroque chapel, now used by the Syrian Church – and continue on rue Valette past the brick and stone entrance of the **Collège Ste-Barbe**, where Ignatius Loyola, Montgolfier and Eiffel studied. Alternatively, follow the serpentine rue de la Montagne-Ste-Geneviève; at the junction of rue Descartes, cafés and eccentric wine bistros overlook the sculpted 19th-century entrance to what was once the elite Ecole Polytechnique (since moved to the suburbs) and is now the research ministry. There's a small park here, and popular bistro **L'Ecurie** (2 rue Laplace, 5th, 01.46.33.68.49) – an old stable burrowed into medieval cellars.

Louis XV commissioned the huge, domed **Panthéon** to honour Geneviève, the city's patron saint, but it was converted during the Revolution into a secular temple for France's *grands hommes*. The surrounding place du Panthéon, also conceived by Panthéon architect Jacques-Germain Soufflot, is one of the city's great set pieces: looking on to it are the elegant fifth arrondissement town hall and, opposite, the law faculty. On the north side, the Ste-Geneviève university library (no.10, 5th, 01.44.41.97.97), built by Labrouste with an iron-framed reading room, contains medieval manuscripts. On the other side you'll find the historic **Hôtel des Grands Hommes** (no.17, 5th, 01.46.34.19.60, www.hoteldesgrandshommes.com), where Surrealist mandarin André Breton invented 'automatic writing' in the 1920s.

Pascal, Racine and the remains of Sainte Geneviève are all interred within **Eglise St-Etienne-du-Mont**, on the north-east corner of the square. Just behind it, within the illustrious and elitist Lycée Henri IV, is the Gothic-Romanesque **Tour de Clovis**, part of the former Abbaye Ste-Geneviève. Take a look through the entrance (open during termtime) and you'll also catch glimpses of the cloister and other monastic structures.

Further from place du Panthéon, along rue Clovis, is a chunk of Philippe-Auguste's 12th-century city wall. The exiled monarch James II once resided at 65 rue du Cardinal-Lemoine, in the severe buildings of the former Collège des Ecossais (now a school), founded in 1372 to house Scottish students; the king's brain was preserved here until carried off and lost during the French Revolution. Other well known ex-residents include Hemingway, who lived at 79 rue du Cardinal-Lemoine (note the plaque) and 39 rue Descartes in the 1920s, and James Joyce, the latter completed *Ulysses* while staying at 71 rue du Cardinal-Lemoine. Rimbaud lived in rue Descartes, and Descartes himself lived on nearby rue Rollin.

SIGHTS

SIGHTS

This area is still a mix of tourist picturesque and gentle village, where some of the buildings hide surprising courtyards and gardens. Pretty place as the Contrescarpe has been a famous rendezvous since the 1530s, when writers as renowned as Rabelais, Ronsard and Du Bellay frequented the Cabaret de la Pomme de Pin at no.1; it still has some lively cafés. When George Orwell stayed at 6 rue du Pot-de-Fer in 1928 and 1929 (he described his time here and his work as a dishwasher in *Down and Out in Paris and London*), it was a place of astounding poverty; today, the street is lined with bargain bars and restaurants, and the restored houses along rue Tournefort bear little relation to the garrets of Balzac's *Le Père Goriot*.

Rue Mouffetard, originally the road to Rome and one of the oldest streets in the city, winds southwards as a suite of cheap bistros, Greek and Lebanese tavernas and knick-knack shops thronged with tourists; the vibe described by Hemingway – 'that wonderful narrow crowded market street, beloved of bohemians' – has faded. The street market (Tue-Sat, Sun morning) on the lower half seethes on weekends, when it spills on to the square and around the cafés in front of the **Eglise St-Médard**. There's another busy market, more frequented by locals, at place Monge (Wed, Fri, Sun morning).

Back to the west of the Panthéon, head south beyond rue Soufflot and you'll notice that rue St-Jacques becomes prettier. Here you'll find several ancient buildings, including the elegant *hôtel* at no.151, good food shops, vintage bistro **Perraudin** (no.157, 5th, 01.46.33.15.75) and the **Institut Océanographique** (no.195, 5th, 01.44.32.10.70, www.oceano.org/io), which has well-stocked aquariums much loved by children. Rue d'Ulm contains the elite **Ecole Normale Supérieure** (no.45, 5th, 01.44.32.30.00, www.ens.fr), occupied in protest by the unemployed in January 1998; in an echo of 1968, students also joined in.

Turn off up hilly rue des Fossés-St-Jacques to discover place de l'Estrapade; in the 17th century the *estrapade* was a tall wooden tower from which deserters were dropped repeatedly until they died. Nearby, in rue des Irlandais, the Centre Culturel Irlandais hosts concerts, exhibitions, films, plays and spoken-word events promoting Irish culture. Back to the west of rue St-Jacques, rue Soufflot and broad rue Gay-Lussac (a hotspot of the May 1968 revolt), with their Haussmannian apartment buildings, lead to boulevard St-Michel and the Jardin du Luxembourg (*see p129*).

Further south along rue St-Jacques, in the potters' quarter of Roman Lutetia, is the least altered and most ornate of the city's baroque churches, the landmark **Eglise du Val-de-Grâce**. Round the corner, at 6 rue du

Val-de-Grâce, is the former home of Alfons Maria Mucha, the influential Moravian art nouveau artist, best known for his posters of Sarah Bernhardt.

FREE Collège de France

11 pl Marcelin-Berthelot, 5th (01.44.27.12.11/ 01.44.27.11.47/www.college-de-france.fr). M° *Cluny La Sorbonne or Maubert Mutualité/ RER Luxembourg.* **Open** 9am-5pm Mon-Fri. **Admission** free. **Map** p408 J7.
Founded in 1530 with the patronage of François I, the college is a place of learning and a research institute. The present building dates from the 16th and 17th centuries; there's also a later annexe. All lectures are free and open to the public; some have been given by such eminent figures as anthropologist Claude Lévi-Strauss, philosopher Maurice Merleau-Ponty and mathematician Jacques Tits.

★ FREE Eglise St-Etienne-du-Mont

Pl Ste-Geneviève, 5th (01.43.54.11.79). M° *Cardinal Lemoine/RER Luxembourg.* **Open** 10am-7pm Tue-Sun. **Admission** free. **Map** p408 J8.
Geneviève, patron saint of Paris, is credited with having miraculously saved the city from the ravages of Attila the Hun in 451, and her shrine has been a site of pilgrimage ever since. The present church was built in an amalgam of Gothic and Renaissance styles between 1492 and 1626, and once adjoined the abbey church of Ste-Geneviève. The façade mixes Gothic rose windows with rusticated roman columns and reliefs of classically draped figures. The interior is wonderfully tall and light, with soaring columns and a classical balustrade. The stunning Renaissance rood screen, with its double spiral staircase and ornate stone strapwork, is the only surviving one in Paris, and was possibly designed by Philibert Delorme. The decorative canopied wooden pulpit by Germaine Pillon dates from 1651, and is adorned with figures of the Graces and supported by a muscular Samson sitting on the defeated lion. Sainte Geneviève's elaborate neo-Gothic brass-and-glass shrine (shielding the ancient tombstone) is located to the right of the choir, surrounded by an assorted collection of reliquaries and dozens of marble plaques bearing messages of thanks. At the back of the church (reached through the sacristy), the catechism chapel constructed by Baltard in the 1860s has a cycle of paintings relating the saint's life story.

FREE Eglise St-Médard

141 rue Mouffetard, 5th (01.44.08.87.00). M° *Censier Daubenton.* **Open** 8am-noon, 2.30-7.30pm daily. **Admission** free. **Map** p406 J9.
The original chapel here was a dependency of the Abbaye Ste-Geneviève. The rebuilding towards the end of the 15th century created a somewhat larger, late Gothic structure best known for its elaborate vaulted ambulatory.

Eglise du Val-de-Grâce

Pl Alphonse-Laveran, 5th (01.40.51.47.28).
RER Luxembourg or Port-Royal. **Open** noon-
6pm Tue, Wed, Sat, Sun. **Admission** €5; €2.50
reductions; free under-6s. **No credit cards**.
Map p406 H9.

Anne of Austria, the wife of Louis XIII, vowed to
erect 'a magnificent temple' if God blessed her with
a son. She got two. The resulting church and surrounding Benedictine monastery – these days a military hospital and the Musée du Service de Santé des
Armées – were built by François Mansart and
Jacques Lemercier. This is the most luxuriously
baroque of the city's 17th-century domed churches,
its ornate altar decorated with twisted barley-sugar
columns. The swirling colours of the dome frescoes
painted by Pierre Mignard in 1669 (which Molière
himself once eulogised) are designed to give a
foretaste of heaven. In contrast, the surrounding
monastery offers the perfect example of François
Mansart's classical restraint. Phone in advance if
you're after a guided visit.

Musée du Service de Santé des Armées

*Val de Grâce, pl Alphonse-Laveran, 5th
(01.40.51.51.94). RER Luxembourg or Port
Royal.* **Open** noon-5pm Tue, Wed, Sat, Sun.
Admission €5; €2.50 reductions; free under-6s.
No credit cards. **Map** p406 J9.

Housed in the royal convent designed by Mansart,
next door to a military hospital, this museum traces
the history of military medicine via replicas of field
hospitals and ambulance trains, and antique medical
instruments. The section on World War I demon-
strates how the conflict propelled medical progress.

★ Le Panthéon

*Pl du Panthéon, 5th (01.44.32.18.00). M° Cardinal
Lemoine/RER Luxembourg.* **Open** 10am-6pm
(until 6.30pm summer) daily. **Admission** €7.50;
€4.80 reductions; free under-18s (if accompanied
by an adult). **PMP**. **Credit** MC, V. **Map** p408 J8.

Soufflot's neo-classical megastructure was the architectural *grand projet* of its day, commissioned by a
grateful Louis XV to thank Sainte Geneviève for his
recovery from illness. But by the time it was ready
in 1790, a lot had changed; during the Revolution,
the Panthéon was rededicated as a 'temple of reason'
and the resting place of the nation's great men. The
austere barrel-vaulted crypt now houses Voltaire,
Rousseau, Hugo and Zola. New heroes are installed
but rarely: Pierre and Marie Curie's remains were
transferred here in 1995; Alexandre Dumas in 2002.
Inside are Greek columns and domes, and 19th-
century murals of Geneviève's life by Symbolist
painter Puvis de Chavannes, a formative influence
on Picasso during the latter's blue period.

Mount the steep spiral stairs to the colonnade
encircling the dome for superb views. A replica of
Foucault's Pendulum hangs here; the original proved
that the earth does indeed spin on its axis, via a universal joint that lets the direction of the pendulum's
swing rotate as the earth revolves.

La Sorbonne

*17 rue de la Sorbonne, 5th (01.40.46.22.11/
www.sorbonne.fr). M° Cluny La Sorbonne.*
Open *Tours* by appointment. Closed July
& Aug. **Map** p408 J7.

Founded in 1253, the University of the Sorbonne was
at the centre of the Latin Quarter's intellectual activity from the Middle Ages until 1968, when it was

Le Panthéon.

occupied by students and stormed by the riot police. The authorities then split the University of Paris into safer outposts, but the Sorbonne still houses the Faculté des Lettres. Rebuilt by Richelieu and reorganised by Napoleon, the present buildings date from the late 1800s, and have a labyrinth of classrooms and lecture theatres, as well as an observatory tower. The elegant dome of the 17th-century chapel dominates place de la Sorbonne; Cardinal Richelieu is buried inside. It's only open to the public for exhibitions or concerts.

AROUND THE JARDIN DES PLANTES

In the 5th arrondissement.

The quiet, easternmost part of the fifth arrondissement is home to yet more academic institutions, the Paris mosque and another Roman relic. Old-fashioned bistros on rue des Fossés-St-Bernard contrast with the forbidding 1960s architecture of the massive university campus of Paris VI and VII, the science faculty (known as Jussieu) built on what had been the site of the important Abbaye St-Victor. Between the Seine and Jussieu is the strikingly modern, glass-faced **Institut du Monde Arabe**, which has a programme of concerts and exhibitions and a restaurant with a great view. The **Jardin Tino Rossi**, by the river, contains the slightly dilapidated **Musée de la Sculpture en Plein Air**; in summer this is a spot for dancing and picnicking.

Hidden among the hotels of rue Monge is the entrance to the **Arènes de Lutèce**, a Roman amphitheatre. The remains of a circular arena and its tiers of stone seating were discovered

Jardin Tino Rossi. *See p122.*

SIGHTS

in 1869, when the street was being built. Excavation started in 1883, thanks to lobbying by Victor Hugo. Nearby rise the white minaret and green pan-tiled roof of the **Mosquée de Paris**, built in 1922. Its beautiful Moorish tearoom is a student haunt.

The mosque looks over the **Jardin des Plantes** botanical garden. Opened in 1626 as a garden for medicinal plants, it features an 18th-century maze and a winter garden bristling with rare species. It also houses the Muséum National d'Histoire Naturelle, with its brilliantly renovated **Grande Galerie de l'Evolution**, and a zoo, La Ménagerie, an unlikely by-product of the Revolution, when royal and noble collections of wild animals were impounded. Street names and the lovely animal-themed fountain on the corner of rue Cuvier pay homage to the many naturalists and other scientists who worked here. A short way away, at 11-13bis rue Geoffroy-St-Hilaire, the words 'Chevaux', 'Poneys' and 'Anes' are still visible on the façade of the old horse market.

FREE Arènes de Lutèce

Rue Monge, rue de Navarre or rue des Arènes, 5th. Mº Cardinal Lemoine or Place Monge. **Open** *Summer* 8am-10pm daily. *Winter* 8am-5.30pm daily. **Admission** free. **Map** p406 K8.
This Roman arena, where wild beasts and gladiators fought, could seat 10,000 people. It was still visible during the reign of Philippe-Auguste in the 12th century, then disappeared under rubble. The site was rediscovered in 1869 and now incorporates a romantically planted garden. These days, it attracts skateboarders, footballers and boules players.

★ Grande Galerie de l'Evolution

36 rue Geoffroy-St-Hilaire, 2 rue Bouffon or pl Valhubert, 5th (01.40.79.56.01). Mº Gare d'Austerlitz or Jussieu. **Open** *Grande Galerie* 10am-6pm Mon, Wed-Sun. *Other galleries* 10am-5pm Mon, Wed-Fri; 10am-6pm Sat, Sun. **Admission** *Grande Galerie* €8; €6 reductions; free under-4s. *Other galleries* (each) €7; €5 reductions; free under-4s. **No credit cards**. **Map** p406 K9.
One of the city's most child-friendly attractions, this is guaranteed to bowl adults over too. Located within the Jardin des Plantes (*see right*), this beauty of a 19th-century iron-framed, glass-roofed structure has been modernised with lifts, galleries and false floors, and filled with life-size models of tentacle-waving squids, open-mawed sharks, tigers hanging off elephants and monkeys swarming down from the ceiling. The centrepiece is a procession of African wildlife across the first floor that resembles the procession into Noah's Ark. Glass-sided lifts take you up through suspended birds to the second floor, which deals with man's impact on nature and rewiring of evolution (crocodile into handbag).

The third floor focuses on endangered and extinct species. The separate Galerie d'Anatomie Comparée et de Paléontologie contains over a million skeletons and a world-class fossil collection.

Institut du Monde Arabe

1 rue des Fossés-St-Bernard, 5th (01.40.51.38.38/www.imarabe.org). Mº Jussieu. **Open** *Museum* 10am-6pm Tue-Sun. *Library* 1-8pm Tue-Sat. *Café* noon-6pm Tue-Sun. *Tours* 3pm Tue-Fri; 3pm & 4.30pm Sat, Sun. **Admission** *Roof terrace, library* free. *Museum* €5; €4 reductions; free under-12s. PMP. *Exhibitions* varies. *Tours* €8. **Credit** MC, V. **Map** p406 K7.
A clever blend of high-tech and Arab influences, this Seine-side *grand projet* was constructed between 1980 and 1987 to a design by Jean Nouvel. Shuttered windows, inspired by the screens of Moorish palaces, act as camera apertures, contracting or expanding according to the amount of sunlight. A museum covering the history and archaeology of the Islamic Arab world occupies the upper floors: start at the seventh with Classical-era finds and work down via early Islamic dynasties to the present day. Unfortunately, the layout and arrangement are somewhat uninspired – objects in glass cases without much in the way of context. However, the Institut hosts several major, crowd-pleasing exhibitions throughout the year. What's more, there's an excellent Middle East bookshop on the ground floor and the views from the roof terrace (to which access is free) are fabulous.
▶ *Jean Nouvel's other landmark Paris buildings include the Musée du Quai Branly (see p146) and the Fondation Cartier (see p134).*

★ FREE Jardin des Plantes

36 rue Geoffroy-St-Hilaire, 2 rue Bouffon, pl Valhubert or 57 rue Cuvier, 5th. Mº Gare d'Austerlitz, Jussieu or Place Monge. **Open** *Main garden* Winter 8am-dusk daily. Summer 7.30am-8pm daily. *Alpine garden* Apr-Sept 8am-4.30pm Mon-Fri; 1-5pm Sat, Sun. Closed Oct-Mar. *Ménagerie* Apr-Sept 9am-5pm daily. **Admission** *Alpine Garden* free Mon-Fri; €1 Sat, Sun. *Jardin des Plantes* free. *Ménagerie* €7; €5 reductions; free under-4s. **Credit** AmEx, MC, V. **Map** p406 L8.
Although small and slightly dishevelled, the Paris botanical garden – which contains more than 10,000 species and includes tropical greenhouses and rose, winter and Alpine gardens – is an enchanting place. Begun by Louis XIII's doctor as the royal medicinal plant garden in 1626, it opened to the public in 1640. The formal garden, which runs between two dead-straight avenues of trees parallel to rue Buffon, is like something out of *Alice in Wonderland*. There's also the Ménagerie (a small zoo) and the terrific Grande Galerie de l'Evolution (*see p121*). Ancient trees on view include a false acacia planted in 1636

SIGHTS

Lessons in Love

Sign up at the school of seduction.

They invented the French kiss, speak the language of love and are renowned the world over for their powers of seduction. So you'd be forgiven for thinking that the French would know a thing or two about romance. Think again. According to Véronique J Corniola, founder of **L'Ecole de la Séduction** (01.42.61.84.45, www. ecoledeseduction.com), France's first school in the art of wooing, the French have forgotten how to make contact with each other: 'They live in fear of rejection; men and women no longer know how to seduce and be seduced. They have problems meeting each other, communicating and falling in love.'

And the culprits behind this sad state of affairs? The internet and TV, among others. As in other Western countries, Véronique says, 'French society is becoming increasingly individualist. Many of my male clients have only slept with call girls and don't know how to attract normal women. My female clients can usually meet men easily, but have problems sustaining a relationship. Whatever their gender, age or background, they feel lonely and lost.'

So how does it all work? Véronique (who is also qualifying as a sex therapist) works closely with several life coaches, a psychologist and an image consultant. Over eight months, they delve deeply into their students' personal history, dusting out cobwebs, skeletons or whatever else may be lurking in their innermost closets, boosting self-esteem and, where necessary, offering haircuts, a new wardrobe and even singles holidays and soirées. The best results, it appears, come from practice in situ, so students are encouraged to hit the town over an eight-day module, during which the teachers give training in body language, self-image, and breathing and voice techniques, before following them into bars, restaurants and nightclubs to watch them in action. It's a pricey business: €6,000 minimum (modules and holidays are extra), but it seems to work. Since the school opened in 1995, Véronique boasts a 90 per cent success rate – a success being a 'constructive, amorous relationship with somebody in the year following the lessons'.

So what is the secret to nabbing a partner in France today? According to Véronique, it's pretty much the same across the world: you have to be generous, empathetic and warm.

---

and a cedar from 1734. A plaque on the old laboratory declares that this is where Henri Becquerel discovered radioactivity in 1896.

████ Jardin Tino Rossi (Musée de la Sculpture en Plein Air)
Quai St-Bernard, 5th. Mº Gare d'Austerlitz. **Open** 8am-dusk Mon-Fri; 9am-dusk Sat, Sun. **Admission** free. **Map** p406 L8.
This open-air sculpture museum by the Seine fights a constant battle against graffiti. Still, it's a pleasant enough, if traffic-loud, place for a stroll. Most of the works are second-rate, aside from Etienne Martin's bronze *Demeure I* and the Carrara marble *Fenêtre* by Cuban artist Careras. *Photo p120.*
► *From May to September, the gardens turn into an open-air dance studio, with informal classes in everything from hip hop to salsa; see p293.*

La Mosquée de Paris
2 pl du Puits-de-l'Ermite, 5th (01.45.35.97.33/ tearoom 01.43.31.38.20/baths 01.43.31.18.14/ www.mosquee-de-paris.net). Mº Monge. **Open** *Tours* 9am-noon, 2-6pm Mon-Thur, Sat, Sun

(closed Muslim hols). *Tearoom* 10am-11.30pm daily. *Restaurant* noon-2.30pm, 7.30-10.30pm daily. *Baths* (women) 10am-9pm Mon, Wed, Sat; 2-9pm Fri; (men) 2-9pm Tue, Sun. **Admission** €3; €2 reductions; free under-7s. *Tearoom* free. *Baths* €15-€35. **Credit** MC, V. **Map** p406 K9.
Some distance removed from the Arabic-speaking inner-city enclaves of Barbès and Belleville, this vast Hispano-Moorish construct is nevertheless the spiritual heart of France's Algerian-dominated Muslim population. Built from 1922 to 1926 with elements inspired by the Alhambra and the Bou Inania Medersa in Fès, the Paris mosque is dominated by a stunning green-and-white tiled square minaret. In plan and function it divides into three sections: religious (grand patio, prayer room and minaret, all for worshippers and not curious tourists); scholarly (Islamic school and library); and, via rue Geoffroy-St-Hilaire, commercial (café and domed hammam). La Mosquée café (open 9am-midnight daily) is delightful – a modest courtyard with blue-and-white mosaic-topped tables shaded beneath green foliage and scented with the sweet smell of sheesha smoke

(€6). Charming waiters distribute *thé à la menthe* (€2), along with syrupy, nutty North African pastries, sorbets and fruit salads.

LES GOBELINS
& LA SALPETRIERE

In the 13th arrondissement.

Its defining features might be 1960s tower blocks, but the 13th arrondissement is also historic, especially in the area bordering the fifth. The **Manufacture Nationale des Gobelins**, home to the state weaving companies, continues a tradition founded in the 15th century, when tanneries, dyers and weaving workshops lined the River Bièvre. This putrid waterway became notorious, and the slums that grew up around it were depicted in Victor Hugo's *Les Misérables*.

The area was tidied up in the 1930s, when a small park, square René-Le-Gall, was laid out on the allotments used by tapestry workers. The river was built over, but local enthusiasts have since opened up a small stretch in the park. Nearby, through a gateway at 17 rue des Gobelins, you can spot the turret and first floor of a medieval house, recently renovated as apartments. The so-called Château de la Reine Blanche on rue Gustave-Geffroy is named after Queen Blanche of Provence, who had a château here; it was probably rebuilt in the 1520s for the Gobelin family. Blanche was also associated with a nearby Franciscan monastery, of which a fragmentary couple of arches survive on the corner of rue Pascal and rue de Julienne.

In the northern corner of the 13th, next to Gare d'Austerlitz, sprawls the huge Hôpital de la Pitié-Salpêtrière founded in 1656, with its striking **Chapelle St-Louis**.

The busy intersection of place d'Italie has seen a number of developments in recent years. Opposite the 19th-century town hall stands the Centre Commercial Italie 2, a bizarre high-tech confection. It houses a shopping centre but, sadly, no longer the Gaumont Grand Ecran Italie cinema. You'll also find a food market on boulevard Auguste-Blanqui (Tue, Fri, Sun).

FREE Chapelle St-Louis-de-la-Salpêtrière
47 bd de l'Hôpital, 13th (01.42.16.04.24). M° Gare d'Austerlitz. **Open** 8.30am-6pm Mon-Fri, Sun; 11am-6pm Sat. **Admission** free. **Map** p406 L9.
This austerely beautiful chapel, designed by Libéral Bruand and completed in 1677, features an octagonal dome in the centre and eight naves in which the sick were separated from the insane, the destitute from the debauched. Around the chapel sprawls the vast Hôpital de la Pitié-Salpêtrière, founded on the site of a gunpowder factory (hence the name, derived

from saltpetre) by Louis XIV to house rounded-up vagrant women. It became a centre for research into insanity in the 1790s, when renowned doctor Philippe Pinel began to treat some of the inmates as sick rather than criminal; Charcot later pioneered neuropsychology here, famously receiving a visit from Freud. Salpêtrière is today one of the city's main teaching hospitals, but the chapel is also used for contemporary art installations, notably during the Festival d'Automne (*see p278*), when its striking architecture provides a backdrop for artists such as Bill Viola, Anish Kapoor and Nan Goldin.

Manufacture Nationale des Gobelins
42 av des Gobelins, 13th (tours 01.44.08.53.49). M° Les Gobelins. **Open** *Tours* 2pm, 3pm Tue-Thur. **Admission** €10; €6 reductions; free under-7s. **No credit cards. Map** p406 K10.
The royal tapestry factory was founded by Colbert when he set up the Manufacture Royale des Meubles de la Couronne in 1662; it's named after Jean Gobelin, a dyer who owned the site. It reached the summit of its renown during the *ancien régime*, when Gobelins tapestries were produced for royal residences under artists such as Le Brun and Oudry. Tapestries are still made here (mainly for French embassies around the world), and visitors can watch weavers at work. The tour (in French) through the 1912 factory takes in the 18th-century chapel and the Beauvais workshops. Arrive 30 minutes before the tour starts.

CHINATOWN &
THE BUTTE-AUX-CAILLES

South of rue de Tolbiac, the shop signs suddenly turn Chinese or Vietnamese, and even McDonald's is decked out *à la chinoise*. The city's main Chinatown runs along avenue d'Ivry, avenue de Choisy and into the 1960s tower blocks between. Whereas much of the public housing in and around Paris is pretty bleak, here a distinctly eastern vibe reigns, with restaurants, Vietnamese *pho* noodle bars and Chinese pâtisseries, hairdressers and purveyors of exotic groceries; not to mention the expansive **Tang Frères** supermarket (48 av d'Ivry, 13th, 01.45.70.80.00). There's even a Buddhist temple hidden in a car park beneath the tallest tower (av d'Ivry, opposite rue Frères d'Astier-de-la-Vigerie, 13th). Lion and dragon dances, and martial arts demonstrations, take place on the streets at **Chinese New Year** (*see p279*).

In contrast to Chinatown, the villagey Butte-aux-Cailles, occupying the wedge between boulevard Auguste-Blanqui and rue Bobillot, is a neighbourhood of old houses, winding streets, funky bars and restaurants. This area, home in the 19th century to many small factories, was one of the first to fight during the 1848 Revolution and the Paris Commune.

SIGHTS

The Butte has preserved its rebellious character, with residents standing up to urban planners and commercial developers. This predominantly *soixante-huitard* resistance is concentrated in the cobbled rue de la Butte-aux-Cailles and rue des Cinq-Diamants. Here you'll find relaxed, inexpensive bistros such as **Le Temps des Cérises** (18 rue Butte-aux-Cailles, 13th, 01.45.89.69.48), run as a co-operative; **Chez Gladines** (30 rue des Cinq-Diamants, 13th, 01.45.80.70.10) and more upmarket **Chez Paul** (22 rue Butte-aux-Cailles, 13th, 01.45.89.22.11). The cottages built in 1912 in a mock-Alsatian style around a central green at 10 rue Daviel were among the earliest public-housing schemes in Paris. Just across rue Bobillot, the **Piscine Butte-aux-Cailles** (*see p340*) is a charming Arts and Crafts-style swimming pool.

Further south, you can explore passage Vandrezanne, the little houses and gardens of square des Peupliers, rue des Peupliers and rue Dieulafoy, and the flower-named streets of the Cité Florale. By the Périphérique, the **Stade Charléty** (17 av Pierre-de-Coubertin, 13th, 01.44.16.60.60) is that unlikely thing, a superb piece of stadium architecture.

Further east

The construction in the mid-1990s of the **Bibliothèque Nationale de France** breathed life into the desolate area, now known as the ZAC Rive Gauche, between Gare d'Austerlitz and the Périphérique. The ambitious, long-term ZAC project includes a new university quarter, new housing projects and a tramway providing links to the suburbs. The city's newest bridge, the pedestrian-only **Passerelle Simone-de-Beauvoir**, spans the Seine between the BNF and the Cinémathèque Française; the floating Piscine Josephine-Baker (*see p341*) is now a focus for the extended Paris-Plage entertainments; and Paris's latest big cultural venue, the **Cité de la Mode et du Design (Docks en Seine)**, is due to open in early 2009.

Further south-east, rue Watt is the lowest street in Paris (it runs below river level). At 12 rue Cantagrel is Le Corbusier's Cité de Réfuge de l'Armée de Salut hostel, a reinforced-concrete structure built from 1929 to 1933 to house 1,500 homeless men, and a precursor of the architect's Cité Radieuse in Marseille.

Bibliothèque Nationale de France François Mitterrand

10 quai François-Mauriac, 13th (01.53.79.59.59/www.bnf.fr). M° Bibliothèque François Mitterrand. **Open** 2-7pm Mon; 9am-7pm Tue-Sat; 1-7pm Sun. **Admission** *1 day* €3.30. *2 weeks* €20. *1 year* €35; €18 reductions. **Credit** MC, V. **Map** p407 M10.
Opened in 1996, the new national library was the last and costliest of Mitterrand's *grands projets*. Its architect, Dominique Perrault, was criticised for his curiously dated design, which hides readers underground and stores the books in four L-shaped glass towers. He also forgot to specify blinds to protect books from sunlight; they had to be added afterwards. In the central void is a garden (filled with 140 trees, which were transported from Fontainebleau at enormous expense). The library houses over ten million volumes and can accommodate 3,000 readers. The research section, just below the public reading rooms, opened in 1998. Much of the library is open to the public: books, newspapers and periodicals are accessible to anyone over 18, and you can browse through photographic, film and sound archives in the audiovisual section.
▶ *The library is now accessible by Voguéo (www.vogueo.fr), a new scheduled boat service linking Gare d'Austerlitz and Maisons-Alfort.*

Cité de la Mode et du Design (Docks en Seine)

28-36 quai d'Austerlitz, 13th. M° Chevaleret or Gare d'Austerlitz.
See p43 **Build it with Feeling.**

Rue de Bièvre.
See p115.

St-Germain-des-Prés & Odéon

Literati and glitterati on the Left Bank.

In the first half of the 20th century, St-Germain-des-Prés was prime arts and literature territory. Writers and painters swapped concepts and girlfriends on its café terraces before World War II, and former GIs jammed in its cellars when the fighting was over. The heart of the Paris jazz boom and haunt of Camus, Prévert, Picasso and Giacometti epitomised – and to a large extent coined – a very Parisian amalgam of carefree living and audacious thinking. Some of that intellectual and hedonistic lore still clings to this small part of the Left Bank, but for decades the main concern here has been more sartorial than Sartrian. St-Germain-des-Prés is now serious fashion territory, and has some of the most expensive property – and cafés – in the city.

| **Map** pp405-406 | **Restaurants** p211 |
| **Hotels** p175 | **Cafés & bars** p235 |

FROM THE BOULEVARD TO THE SEINE

In the 6th arrondissement.

Hit by shortages of coal during World War II, Sartre shunned his cold flat on rue Bonaparte. 'The principal interest of the Café de Flore,' he noted at the time, 'was that it had a stove, a nearby métro and no Germans.' Although you can spend more on a few coffees here than on a week's heating these days, the **Café de Flore** (*see p235*) remains an arty favourite, and hosts *café-philo* evenings in English. Its rival, **Les Deux Magots** (*see p235*), facing historic **Eglise St-Germain-des-Prés**, is frequented largely by tourists. Nearby is the celebrity favourite **Brasserie Lipp** (151 bd St-Germain, 6th, 01.45.48.53.91); art nouveau fans prefer **Brasserie Vagenende** (142 bd St-Germain, 6th, 01.43.26.68.18). The swish bookshop **La Hune** (*see p242*) provides sustenance of a more intellectual kind.

St-Germain-des-Prés grew up around the medieval abbey, the oldest church in Paris and site of an annual fair that drew merchants from across Europe. There are traces of its cloister and part of the abbot's palace behind the church on rue de l'Abbaye. Constructed in 1586 in red brick with stone facing, the palace prefigured the architecture of **place des Vosges**. Charming place de Furstemberg (once the palace stables) is home to the house and studio where the elderly Delacroix lived when painting the murals in St-Sulpice; it now houses the **Musée National Delacroix**. Wagner, Ingres and Colette all lived on nearby rue Jacob; its elegant 17th-century *hôtels particuliers* now contain specialist book, design and antiques shops and a few pleasant hotels.

Further east, rue de Buci hosts a street market and upmarket food shops, and is home to cafés **Les Etages** (no.5, 6th, 01.46.34.26.26) and **Bar du Marché** (no.16, 6th, 01.43.26.55.15). **Hôtel La Louisiane** (60 rue de Seine, 6th, 01.44.32.17.17, www.hotellalouisiane.com) has hosted jazz stars Chet Baker and Miles Davis, and Existentialist lovers Sartre and de Beauvoir. Rue de Seine, rue des Beaux-Arts and rue Bonaparte (Manet was born in the latter, at no.5, in 1832) are still packed with art galleries. It was in rue des Beaux-Arts, at the Hôtel

Time Out Paris 125

d'Alsace, that Oscar Wilde complained about the wallpaper and then checked out for good. Now fashionably renovated, it has rechristened itself **L'Hôtel** (*see p175*). **La Palette** (*see p236*) and **Bistro Mazarin** (42 rue Mazarine, 6th, 01.43.29.99.01, www.bistrotmazarin.com) are good pit stops with enviable terraces; rue Mazarine, with shops selling lighting, vintage toys and jewellery, also has Terence Conran's brasserie **L'Alcazar** (no.62, 6th, 01.53.10.19.99, www.alcazar.fr) and hip club **Wagg** (*see p330*).

On quai de Conti stands the neo-classical Hôtel des Monnaies, built at the demand of Louis XV by architect Jacques-Denis Antoine; formerly the mint (1777-1973), it's now the **Musée de la Monnaie**, a coin museum. Next door stands the domed **Institut de France**, cleaned to within an inch of its crisp, classical life. Opposite, the iron Pont des Arts footbridge leads directly to the Louvre. Further along, the city's main fine arts school, the **Ecole Nationale Supérieure des Beaux-Arts**, occupies an old monastery.

In the 18th century, Dr Joseph-Ignace Guillotin first tested out his notorious device – designed, believe it or not, to make executions more humane – in the cellars of what is today the **Pub St-Germain** (17 rue de l'Ancienne-Comédie, 6th, 01.56.81.13.13); the first victim was, reputedly, a sheep. Jacobin regicide Billaud-Varenne was among those who felt the steel of Guillotin's gadget; his former home at 45 rue St-André-des-Arts was the site of the first girls' *lycée* in Paris, the Lycée Fénelon, founded in 1883.

Ecole Nationale Supérieure des Beaux-Arts (Ensb-a)

14 rue Bonaparte, 6th (01.47.03.50.00/ www.ensba.fr). M° St-Germain-des-Prés. **Open** *Courtyard* 9am-5pm Mon-Fri. *Exhibitions* 1-5pm Tue-Sun. **Admission** €4; €2 reductions. *Exhibitions* prices vary. **Credit** V. **Map** p408 H6.

The city's most prestigious fine arts school resides in what remains of the 17th-century Couvent des Petits-Augustins, the 18th-century Hôtel de Chimay, some 19th-century additions and some chunks of assorted French châteaux moved here after the Revolution (when the buildings briefly served as a museum of French monuments, before becoming the art school in 1816). The entrance is on quai Malaquais.

★ FREE Eglise St-Germain-des-Prés

3 pl St-Germain-des-Prés, 6th (01.55.42.81.33/ www.eglise-sgp.org). M° St-Germain-des-Prés. **Open** 8am-7.45pm Mon-Sat; 9am-8pm Sun. **Admission** free. **Map** p408 H7.

The oldest church in Paris. On the advice of Germain (later Bishop of Paris), Childebert, son of Clovis, had a basilica and monastery built here around 543. It was first dedicated to St Vincent, and came to be known as St-Germain-le-Doré ('the gilded') because of its copper roof, then later as St-Germain-des-Prés ('of the fields'). During the Revolution the abbey was burned and a saltpetre refinery installed; the spire was added in a clumsy 19th-century restoration. Still, most of the present structure is 12th century, and ornate carved capitals and the tower remain from the 11th. Tombs include those of Jean-Casimir,

Jardin du Luxembourg. See p129.

the deposed King of Poland who became Abbot of St-Germain in 1669, and of Scots nobleman William Douglas. Under the window in the second chapel is the funeral stone of philosopher-mathematician René Descartes; his remains have been here since 1819.

Institut de France
23 quai de Conti, 6th (01.44.41.44.41/www. institut-de-france.fr). M° Louvre Rivoli or Pont Neuf. **Open** *Guided tours* Sat, Sun (01.44.41.43.32/ www.monum.fr; call for times). **Admission** €8; €6 reductions. **No credit cards. Map** p408 H6.
This elegant domed building with two sweeping curved wings was designed as a school by Louis Le Vau and opened in 1684. The five academies of the Institut (Académie Française, Académie des Inscriptions et Belles-Lettres, Académie des Beaux-Arts, Académie des Sciences, Académie des Sciences Morales et Politiques) moved here in 1805. Inside is Mazarin's ornate tomb by Hardouin-Mansart, and the Bibliothèque Mazarine (open to over-18s with ID and two photos; €15/year). The Académie Française was founded by Cardinal Richelieu in 1635 with the aim of preserving the purity of French from corrupting outside influences (such as English).

Musée de la Monnaie de Paris
11 quai de Conti, 6th (01.40.46.56.66/www. monnaie deparis.fr). M° Odéon or Pont Neuf. **Open** 11am-5.30pm Tue-Fri; noon-5.30pm Sat, Sun. Closed Aug. **Admission** (incl audio guide) €8; free under-16s. **Credit** *Shop* AmEx, MC, V. **Map** p408 H6.
Housed in the handsome neo-classical mint built in the 1770s, this high-tech museum tells the tale of global and local coinage from its pre-Roman origins, using sophisticated displays and audiovisual presentations. The history of the franc, from its wartime debut in 1360, is outlined in detail.

Musée National Delacroix
6 pl de Furstemberg, 6th (01.44.41.86.50/www. musee-delacroix.fr). M° St-Germain-des-Prés. **Open** *Sept-May* 9.30am-5pm Mon, Wed-Sun. *June-Aug* 9.30am-5.30pm Mon, Wed-Sun. **Admission** €5; free under-18s, all on 1st Sun of mth. PMP. **Credit** MC, V. **Map** p408 H7.
Eugène Delacroix moved to this apartment and studio in 1857 in order to be near the Eglise St-Sulpice, where he was painting murals. This collection includes small oil paintings, free pastel studies of skies, sketches and lithographs, as well as his palette.

ST-SULPICE & THE LUXEMBOURG

In the 6th arrondissement.

Crammed with historic buildings and inviting shops, the quarter south of boulevard St-Germain between Odéon and Luxembourg

---

> ## INSIDE TRACK
> ## DRINK IN HISTORY
>
> Coffee was first sold in Paris in 1686 at **Café Procope** (13 rue de l'Ancienne-Comédie, 6th, 01.40.46.79.00, www. procope.com), where the customers have included Voltaire, Rousseau and Verlaine. Look out for Voltaire's desk and a postcard from Marie-Antoinette. The back opens on to the cobbled passage du Commerce-St-André, home to toy shops and jewellers.

epitomises civilised Paris. Just off the boulevard lies the covered market of St-Germain, now the site of a shopping arcade, auditorium, food hall and underground swimming pool. There are bars and bistros along rue Guisarde, nicknamed rue de la Soif ('thirst street') thanks to its carousers; it contains the late-night **Birdland** bar (no.8, 6th, 01.43.26.97.59) and a couple of notable bistros: **Mâchon d'Henri** (no.8, 6th, 01.43.29.08.70) and **Brasserie Fernand** (no.13, 6th, 01.43.54.61.47). Rue Princesse and rue des Canettes are a mix of budget restaurants and nocturnal haunts.

Pass the fashion boutiques, pâtisseries and antiquarian book and print shops and you come to **Eglise St-Sulpice**, a surprising 18th-century exercise in classical form with two unmatching turrets and a colonnaded façade. The square in front was designed in the 19th century by Visconti; it contains his imposing, lion-flanked Fontaine des Quatre Points Cardinaux (a pun on cardinal points and the statues of Bishops Bossuet, Fénelon, Massillon and Flechier, none of whom was actually a cardinal). It's now the centrepiece for the **Foire St-Germain**, a summer arts fair.

Among shops of religious artefacts, the chic boutiques on place and rue St-Sulpice include **Yves Saint Laurent** (*see p250*), **Vanessa Bruno** (*see p254*) and milliner **Marie Mercié** (*see p259*). Prime shopping continues further west: clothes on rue Bonaparte and rue du Four, and accessory and fashion shops on rue du Dragon, rue de Grenelle and rue du Cherche-Midi. If you spot a queue in the latter, it's most likely for the bread at **Poilâne** (*see p262*). Across the street, at the junction of rue de Sèvres and rue du Cherche-Midi, César's bronze *Centaur* is the sculptor's tribute to Picasso.

The early 17th-century chapel of St-Joseph-des-Carmes – once a Carmelite convent, now hidden within the **Institut Catholique** (21 rue d'Assas, 6th, 01.44.39.52.00, www.icp.fr) – was the scene of the murder of 115 priests during

SIGHTS

the Terror in 1792. To the east lies wide rue de Tournon, lined by such grand 18th-century residences as the elegant Hôtel de Brancas (no.6), with figures of Justice and Prudence over the door. This street opens up to the **Palais du Luxembourg**, which now serves as the Senate, and the adjoining **Jardin du Luxembourg**.

Towards boulevard St-Germain is the neoclassical **Odéon, Théâtre de l'Europe** (*see p346*), built in 1779 and recently renovated. A house in the square in front was home to Revolutionary hero Camille Desmoulins, who incited the mob to attack the Bastille in 1789. It's now occupied by **La Méditerranée** (2 pl de l'Odéon, 6th, 01.43.26.02.30); the restaurant's menus and plates were designed by Jean Cocteau. Joyce's *Ulysses* was first published in 1922 by Sylvia Beach at the celebrated **Shakespeare & Co** (*see p244*) at 12 rue de l'Odéon. Next door is the venerable, jukebox-filled **Le Bar Dix** (*see p235*).

Further along the street, at 12 rue de l'Ecole-de-Médecine, is the neo-classical Université René Descartes (Paris V) medical school, and the **Musée d'Histoire de la Médecine**. The Club des Cordeliers, set up by Danton in 1790, devised revolutionary plots across the street at the **Couvent des Cordeliers** (no.15); the 14th-century refectory, all that remains of the monastery founded by St Louis, houses modern art exhibitions. Marat, one of the club's leading lights, was stabbed to death in the bathtub at his home in the same street; David depicted the moment after the crime in his iconic painting, the *Death of Marat*. This was the surgeons' district: observe the sculpted doorway of the neighbouring *hôtel* and the domed building at no.5, once the barbers' and surgeons' guild.

Climb rue André-Dubois to rue Monsieur-le-Prince to reach budget restaurant **Polidor** (no.41, 6th, 01.43.26.95.34), open since 1845.

FREE Eglise St-Sulpice

Pl St-Sulpice, 6th (01.42.34.59.98/www.paroisse-saint-sulpice-paris.org). M° St-Sulpice. **Open** 7.30am-7.30pm daily. **Admission** free. **Map** p408 H7.

It took 120 years (starting in 1646) and six architects to finish the church of St-Sulpice. The grandiose Italianate façade, with its two-tier colonnade, was designed by Jean-Baptiste Servandoni. He died in 1766 before the second tower was finished, leaving one tower a good five metres shorter than the other. The trio of murals by Delacroix in the first chapel – *Jacob's Fight with the Angel, Heliodorus Chased from the Temple* and *St Michael Killing the Dragon* – create a suitably sombre atmosphere.

★ FREE Jardin & Palais du Luxembourg

Pl Auguste-Comte, pl Edmond-Rostand or rue de Vaugirard, 6th (01.44.54.19.49/www.senat.fr/visite). M° Odéon/RER Luxembourg. **Open** *Jardin* summer 7.30am-dusk daily; winter 8am-dusk daily. **Map** p408 H8.

The palace itself was built in the 1620s for Marie de Médicis, widow of Henri IV, by Salomon de Brosse on the site of the former mansion of the Duke of Luxembourg. Its Italianate style, with Mannerist rusticated columns, was intended to remind her of the Pitti Palace in her native Florence. The palace now houses the French parliament's upper house, the Sénat (open only by guided visits).

The mansion next door (Le Petit Luxembourg) is the residence of the Sénat's president. The gardens, though, are the real draw: part formal (terraces and

SIGHTS

Arty Parties

Join in the fun at a vernissage, when the Paris art world comes out to play.

Timing your trip to Paris with a night of *vernissages* (private views) gives a taste not only of the art on offer but of the personalities who frequent the art scene. Providing you look the part – and obvious freeloading is ill-advised – you can turn up at most private views without an invitation.

The journal *L'Officiel Galeries & Musées*, which you can pick up free in most galleries, has a diary of *vernissages*. The second and last Thursdays of the month are the most popular dates, with ten to 15 galleries opening a new exhibition. But the big rendezvous of the year is **Art St-Germain-des-Prés** (www.artsaintgermaindespres.com) at the end of May.

Nicknamed the 'block party', it sees almost 50 galleries get together to showcase their top artists, with red carpets spread outside each gallery.

The galleries are concentrated on rue de Seine, rue des Beaux-Arts, rue Visconti, rue Guénégaud and rue Mazarine, and a whole cross-section of boho locals turn out for a drop of wine and conversation: artists, dealers, ageing musicians, film directors, eccentrics, fur-clad ladies, rich kids and celebrities (Kylie's ex Olivier Martinez likes to bring his friends) – this is most definitely one weekend when *flânerie* will get you everywhere.

Cycle Left Bank Lunch

Pedal your way to a perfect picnic.

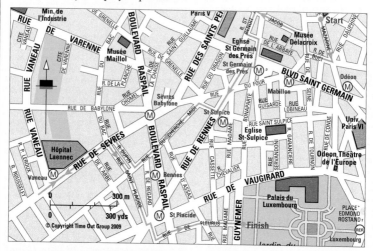

SIGHTS

St-Germain-des-Prés may be more Louis Vuitton than Boris Vian these days, but there are still enough small galleries and bookshops to ensure that it retains a whiff of its bohemian past. Aside from art and books, the sixth arrondissement (and its neighbour the seventh) is also a great place to shop for food, since it has some of the finest artisanal bakeries and *traiteurs* in Paris.

And thanks to Vélib (www.velib.paris.fr), it's easier than ever to get around the *quartier* in order to stock up. What's more, the standard-issue bike is equipped with a basket that should carry all you'll need for a sumptuous picnic. This itinerary will probably take you the best part of two hours. Don't bother searching for a station each time you need to stop; just use the chain provided to lock your bike.

Detach your bike from the *borne* at 1 rue Jacques-Callot, 6th (Mº Mabillon) and cycle down rue Mazarine as far as the carrefour de Buci. Turn left into rue de Buci and carry on until the junction with rue de Seine. The stretch of rue de Seine between here and boulevard St-Germain is lined with butchers and greengrocers. Ignore the smell of roasting chickens (you'll be getting cooked meat elsewhere), and just buy salad leaves and fruit. Then head back down rue de Seine towards the

river. About halfway down, turn left into rue Jacob. Cross rue Bonaparte and take the next left into rue St-Benoît. Pause for a moment to look in the window of **Librairie St-Benoît-des-Prés** (2 rue St-Benoît, 6th, 01.46.33.16.16), which specialises in rare books, manuscripts, letters and autographs.

Continue down rue St-Benoît as far as place St-Germain-des-Prés, where you'll find three venerable St-Germain institutions: **Café de Flore** (*see p235*), **Les Deux Magots** (*see p235*) and **La Hune** bookshop (*see p242*). The Flore and the Deux Magots buzz more with tourists than writers these days, though the former is still a favoured haunt of ageing enfant terrible Bernard-Henri Lévy. If you spot a man with a mane of black hair and a white shirt open to the navel poring over a notebook, it's probably BHL. Next door, **La Hune**, which opened in 1949, is a kind of holy shrine for that nearly extinct species, the Left Bank Intellectual.

But it's not books we're after, it's bread; so pick your way across boulevard St-Germain and follow rue Gozlin round into the rue de Rennes. This is a broad, thunderously busy main road lined with chain stores. There's not a great deal to distract as you bowl south for half a kilometre or so, until you reach rue du

Vieux-Colombier on the right. You'll have to do battle with buses and taxis in this narrow cut-through, which leads to the altogether more charming rue du Cherche-Midi. On the left-hand side of the street, wedged in among the boutiques, jewellers and galleries, stands **Poilâne** (*see p262*), the renowned family bakers. You can expect to have to queue here for the famous Poilâne loaf – but it's worth it: dark, firm and distinctively flavoured. The tarts and the biscuits are wonderful too.

Having loaded the bread into your basket, carry on down rue du Cherche-Midi. Go straight across boulevard Raspail. Take the first right into rue Dupin. You'll eventually reach rue de Sèvres. Lock your bike up against the railings here and cross the road on foot to La Grande Epicérie, the food hall in Paris's oldest department store, **Le Bon Marché** (*see p239*). This is a gastronome's paradise, a super-abundant temple to food. Make your way to the *traiteurs* in the centre of the hall and choose from a staggering array of cooked meats: succulent hams and pungent garlic sausages in dizzying profusion. While you're here, you can also pick up wine dressing for the salad and a bottle of wine (and a corkscrew if you don't already have one).

It just remains to buy some cheese, and for this you'll need to cycle a little further south down rue de Sèvres. You'll pass the wonderful art deco entrance to the Vaneau metro station on the right, with its green iron lattices and globe lanterns. A little further along on the same side of the street, on the corner of rue Pierre-Leroux, stands **Fromagerie Quatrehomme** (*see p262*). Run by Marie Quatrehomme, this place is famous across Paris for its comté fruité, beaufort and oozy st-marcellin.

Your basket will now be near to overflowing. It's time to head for a picnic spot in the Jardin du Luxembourg. Turn round and cycle back up rue de Sèvres, then turn right into rue St-Placide. Shortly after you pass the St-Placide métro station, turn left into rue de Fleurus. The **Jardin du Luxembourg** (*see p129*) is ahead of you, on the far side of rue Guynemer. There's a Vélib station at 26 rue Guynemer. As is usual in Paris, the grass here is not for sitting on. Instead, find a bench in the shade and tuck in.

gravel paths), part 'English garden' (lawns and mature trees), they are the quintessential Paris park. The garden is crowded with sculptures: a looming Cyclops (on the 1624 Fontaine de Médicis), queens of France, a miniature Statue of Liberty, wild animals, busts of Flaubert and Baudelaire, and a monument to Delacroix. There are orchards (300 varieties of apples and pears) and an apiary. The Musée National du Luxembourg (*see below*) hosts prestigious exhibitions, with lesser shows in the former Orangerie. Most interesting, though, are the people: an international mixture of *flâneurs* and *dragueurs*, chess players and martial-arts practitioners, as well as children on ponies, in sandpits, on roundabouts and playing with the sailing boats on the pond. *Photo p126.*

▶ *For more child-friendly Paris parks, see p290.*

Musée d'Histoire de la Médecine
Université René Descartes, 12 rue de l'Ecole-de-Médecine, 6th (01.40.46.16.93/www.bium.univ-paris5.fr/musee). M° Odéon or St-Michel. **Open** *Mid July-Sept* 2-5.30pm Mon-Fri. *Oct-mid July* 2-5.30pm Mon-Wed, Fri, Sat. **Admission** €3.50; €2.50 reductions; free under-8s. **No credit cards. Map** p408 H7.
The history of medicine is the subject of the medical faculty collection. There are ancient Egyptian embalming tools, a 1960s electrocardiograph and a gruesome array of saws used for amputations. You'll also find the instruments of Dr Antommarchi, who performed the autopsy on Napoleon, and the scalpel of Dr Félix, who operated on Louis XIV.

★ Musée des Lettres et Manuscrits
8 rue de Nesle, 6th (01.40.51.02.25/www.musee des lettres.fr). M° Odéon. **Open** 1-8pm Tue-Fri; 10am-6pm Sat-Sun. Closed Nov. **Admission** €6; €4.50 reductions. **Credit** (€16 minimum) MC, V. **Map** p408 H7.
More than 2,000 documents and letters give an insight into the lives of the great and the good, from Magritte to Mozart. Einstein arrives at the theory of relativity on notes scattered in his authentic disorder, Baudelaire complains about his money problems in a letter to his mother, and HMS *Northumberland*'s log-book records the day Napoleon boarded the ship to be taken to St Helena.

Musée National du Luxembourg
19 rue de Vaugirard, 6th (01.42.34.25.95/www. museeduluxembourg.fr). M° Cluny La Sorbonne or Odéon/RER Luxembourg. **Open** 10.30am-10pm Mon, Fri, Sat; 10.30am-7pm Tue-Thur; 9.30am-7pm Sun. **Admission** €11; €9 reductions; free under-8s. **Credit** MC, V. **Map** p408 H7.
When it opened in 1750, this small museum was the first public gallery in France. Its current stewardship by the national museums and the French Senate has brought imaginative touches and some impressive coups. Book ahead to avoid queues.

SIGHTS

Montparnasse & Beyond

The art of falling apart.

'Montparnasse was in full swing. We'd all get together at the Dôme, at the Jockey, at the Rotonde. I felt as though I was at the centre of the world. At the summit.'

So wrote the novelist Nathalie Sarraute, long after Montparnasse's artistic and intellectual glory had faded. Its heyday was short, but for a few years between the two World Wars, it epitomised the 'gay Paree' mix of high-mindedness and high (or, indeed, loose) living. As many of its prominent figures were foreign as French (including its best chronicler, the Hungarian photographer Brassaï) – the late-night bars and artists' studios formed a bubble of excellent international relations that, in hindsight, looks all the more poignant for floating between two periods of such monstrous global conflict.

Map pp404-405
Hotels p179
Restaurants p213
Cafés & bars p237

MONTPARNASSE

In the 6th & 14th arrondissements.

Artists Picasso, Léger and Soutine fled to 'Mount Parnassus' in the early 1900s to escape the rising rents of Montmartre. They were soon joined by Chagall, Zadkine and other refugees from the Russian Revolution, along with Americans such as Man Ray, Henry Miller, Ezra Pound and Gertrude Stein. Between the wars the neighbourhood was the epitome of modernity: studios with large windows were built by avant-garde architects; artists, writers and intellectuals drank and debated in the quarter's showy bars; and naughty pastimes – including the then risqué tango – flourished.

Sadly, the Montparnasse of today has lost much of its former soul, dominated as it is by the lofty **Tour Montparnasse** – the first skyscraper to be built in central Paris. The dismay with which its construction was greeted prompted a change in building regulations in the city. At its foot are a shopping centre,

the **Red Light** (*see p330*) and **Mix Club** (*see p333*) nightclubs and, in winter, an open-air ice rink. There are fabulous panoramic views from the café on the 56th floor.

The old Montparnasse station witnessed two events of historical significance. In 1898, a runaway train burst through its façade; and on 25 August 1944, the German forces surrendered Paris here. The station was rebuilt in the 1970s, a grey affair above which can be found the surprising **Jardin Atlantique** (*see p133* **Inside Track**), the **Mémorial du Maréchal Leclerc** and the **Musée Jean Moulin**.

Rue du Montparnasse, appropriately for a street near the station that sends trains to Brittany, is dotted with crêperies. Nearby, strip joints have replaced most of the theatres on ever-saucy rue de la Gaîté, but boulevard Edgar-Quinet has pleasant cafés and a street market (Wed, Sat), plus the entrance to the **Cimetière du Montparnasse**. Boulevard du Montparnasse still buzzes at night, thanks to its many cinemas and dining spots: giant art deco brasserie **La Coupole** (*see p214*);

SIGHTS

Jardin Atlantique.

SIGHTS

opposite, classic café **Le Select** (*see p237*); **Le Dôme** (no.108, 14th, 01.43.35.25.81), now a top-notch fish restaurant and bar; and restaurant **La Rotonde** (no.105, 6th, 01.43.26.48.26). All were popularised by the literati between the wars, and now use this heritage to their advantage; Le Select seems the most authentic. Nearby, on boulevard Raspail, stands Rodin's statue of Balzac, whose rugged rather than flattering appearance caused such a scandal that it was put in place only after the sculptor's death.

For a whiff of Montparnasse's artistic history, wander down rue de la Grande-Chaumière. Bourdelle and Friesz taught at the venerable **Académie de la Grande-Chaumière** (no.14), frequented by Calder, Giacometti and Pompon among others (it still offers drawing lessons); Modigliani died at no.8 in 1920, ruined by tuberculosis, drugs and alcohol; nearby **Musée Zadkine** occupies the sculptor's old house and studio. Rue Vavin and rue Bréa, leading to the Jardin du Luxembourg, have become an enclave of children's shops. Look out for no.6, the 1912 white-tiled apartment building where art nouveau architect Henri Sauvage lived.

Further east on boulevard du Montparnasse, literary café **La Closerie des Lilas** (no.171, 6th, 01.40.51.34.50) was a pre-war favourite with everyone from Lenin and Trotsky to Picasso and Hemingway; brass plaques on the tables indicate where each historic figure used to sit. Next to it is the lovely **Fontaine de l'Observatoire**, featuring bronze turtles

and thrashing sea horses by Frémiet, and figures of the four continents by Carpeaux.

From here, the Jardins de l'Observatoire form part of the green axis between the Palais du Luxembourg and the royal observatory, the **Observatoire de Paris**. A curiosity next door is the Maison des Fontainiers, built over an expansive (now dry-ish) underground reservoir originally commissioned by Marie de Médicis to supply water to fountains around the city.

A relatively recent addition to boulevard Raspail is the glass and steel **Fondation Cartier pour l'Art Contemporain**. Designed by architect Jean Nouvel, it houses the jewellers' head offices and an exhibition space dedicated to contemporary art and photography.

West of the train station, the redevelopment of Montparnasse is also evident in the circular place de Catalogne, a piece of 1980s postmodern neo-classicism by Mitterrand's favourite architect, Ricardo Bofill, and the housing estates of rue Vercingétorix.

**INSIDE TRACK
PARIS'S SECRET GARDEN**

Perhaps the hardest of all the gardens in Paris to find, the **Jardin Atlantique** is an engineering feat: a modest oasis of granite paths, trees and bamboo spread over a roof, 18 metres (59 feet) above the tracks of Montparnasse train station.

SIGHTS

Fondation Cartier pour l'Art Contemporain.

There are still traces of the old, arty Montparnasse for those willing to look: in impasse Lebouis, an avant-garde studio building has recently been converted into the **Fondation Henri Cartier-Bresson**; at 21 avenue du Maine, an ivy-clad alleyway of old studios contains the artist-run exhibition space Immanence, as well as the **Musée du Montparnasse**, housed in the former academy and canteen of Russian painter Marie Vassilieff; on rue Antoine-Bourdelle, the **Musée Bourdelle** includes another old cluster of studios, where sculptor Bourdelle, Symbolist painter Eugène Carrière and, briefly, Marc Chagall worked. Towards Les Invalides, on rue Mayet, craft and restoration workshops still hide in the old courtyards.

FREE Cimetière du Montparnasse
*3 bd Edgar-Quinet, 14th (01.44.10.86.50). M°
Edgar Quinet or Raspail.* **Open** *16 Mar-5 Nov*
8am-6pm Mon-Fri; 8.30am-6pm Sat; 9am-6pm
Sun. *6 Nov-15 Mar* 8am-5.30pm Mon-Fri;
8.30am-5.30pm Sat; 9.30am-5.30pm Sun.
Admission free. **Map** p405 G9.
This huge cemetery was formed by commandeering three farms (you can still see the ruins of a windmill by rue Froidevaux) in 1824. As with much of the Left Bank, the Montparnasse boneyard has literary clout: Beckett, Baudelaire, Sartre, de Beauvoir, Maupassant, Ionesco and Tristan Tzara all rest here. There are also artists, including Brancusi, Henri Laurens, Frédéric Bartholdi (sculptor of the Statue of Liberty) and Man Ray. The celebrity roll-call continues with Serge Gainsbourg, André Citroën, comedian Coluche and actress Jean Seberg.

★ **Fondation Cartier pour l'Art Contemporain**
*261 bd Raspail, 14th (01.42.18.56.50/recorded
information 01.42.18.56.51/www.fondation.
cartier.fr). M° Denfert-Rochereau or Raspail.*
Open 11am-10pm Tue; 11am-8pm Wed-Sun.
Admission €6.50; €4.50 reductions; free under-
10s & under-18s 2-6pm Tue-Sun. **Credit** AmEx,
MC, V. **Map** p405 G9.
Jean Nouvel's glass and steel building, an exhibition centre with Cartier's offices above, is as much a work of art as the installations inside. Shows by artists and photographers often have wide-ranging themes, such as 'Birds' or 'Desert'. Live events around the shows are called Nuits Nomades.

Fondation Dubuffet
*137 rue de Sèvres, 6th (01.47.34.12.63/www.
dubuffetfondation.com). M° Duroc.* **Open** 2-6pm
Mon-Fri. Closed Aug. **Admission** €4; free under-
10s. **No credit cards. Map** p405 E8.

doors to other disciplines with three annual shows. The convivial feel of the Fondation – and its Le Corbusier armchairs – fosters relaxed discussion with staff and other visitors.

FREE Mémorial du Maréchal Leclerc de Hauteclocque et de la Libération de Paris & Musée Jean Moulin

Jardin Atlantique, 23 allée de la 2e DB (above Gare Montparnasse), 15th (01.40.64.39.44/ www.ml-leclerc-moulin.paris.fr). M° Montparnasse Bienvenüe. **Open** 10am-6pm Tue-Sun. **Admission** free. *Exhibitions* €4; €2-€3 reductions; free under-13s. **Credit** *Shop* MC, V. **Map** p405 F9.

This double museum retraces World War II and the Resistance through the Free French commander General Leclerc and left-wing hero Jean Moulin. Documentary material and film archives complement an impressive 270° slide show, complete with sound effects retelling the Liberation of Paris.

FREE Musée-Atelier Adzak

3 rue Jonquoy, 14th (01.45.43.06.98). M° Plaisance. **Open** usually 3-7pm Sat, Sun (call in advance). **Admission** free.

The eccentric house, studio and garden built by the late Roy Adzak, a British-born painter and sculptor who died in 1987, harbour traces of the conceptual artist's plaster body columns and dehydrations. Now a registered British-run charity, it gives mostly foreign artists a chance to exhibit in Paris.

FREE Musée Bourdelle

16-18 rue Antoine-Bourdelle, 15th (01.49.54.73.73/www.bourdelle.paris.fr). M° Falguière or Montparnasse Bienvenüe. **Open** 10am-6pm Tue-Sun. **Admission** free. *Exhibitions* prices vary. **Credit** MC, V. **Map** p405 F8.

The sculptor Antoine Bourdelle (1861-1929), a pupil of Rodin, produced a number of monumental works including the modernist relief friezes at the Théâtre des Champs-Elysées, inspired by Isadora Duncan and Nijinsky. Set around a small garden, the museum includes the artist's apartment and studios, which were also used by Eugène Carrière, Dalou and Chagall. A 1950s extension tracks the evolution of Bourdelle's equestrian monument to General Alvear in Buenos Aires, and his masterful *Hercules the Archer*. A new wing by Christian de Portzamparc houses bronzes including various studies of Beethoven in different guises.

Musée du Montparnasse

21 av du Maine, 15th (01.42.22.91.96/ www.museedumontparnasse.net). M° Montparnasse Bienvenüe. **Open** 12.30-7pm Tue-Sun. **Admission** €5; €4 reductions; free under-12s. **No credit cards.** **Map** p403 F8.

You walk up a winding garden path to get to this museum, founded by Jean Dubuffet, wine merchant and master of *art brut*, a decade before his death in 1985. The foundation ensures that a fair body of his works is accessible to the public. There's a changing display of Dubuffet's lively drawings, paintings and sculptures, as well as models of the architectural sculptures from the *Hourloupe* cycle.

▶ *The foundation looks after the Closerie Falballa, the 3D masterpiece of the Hourloupe cycle, housed at Périgny-sur-Yerres, east of Paris (viewings by appointment only, €8).*

★ Fondation Henri Cartier-Bresson

2 impasse Lebouis, 14th (01.56.80.27.00/www. henricartierbresson.org). M° Gaîté. **Open** 1-6.30pm Tue-Fri, Sun; 1-8.30pm Wed; 11am-6.45pm Sat. Closed Aug & between exhibitions. **Admission** €6; €3 reductions, all 6.30-8.30pm Wed. **No credit cards.** **Map** p405 F10.

Opened in 2003, this two-floor gallery is dedicated to the work of acclaimed photographer Henri Cartier-Bresson. It consists of a tall, narrow *atelier* in a 1913 building, with a minutely catalogued archive, open to researchers, and a lounge on the fourth floor screening films. In the spirit of Cartier-Bresson, who assisted on three Jean Renoir films and drew and painted all his life (some drawings are also found on the fourth floor), the Fondation opens its

SIGHTS

View from **Tour Montparnasse**.

Set in one of the last surviving alleys of studios, this was home to Marie Vassilieff, whose own academy and cheap canteen welcomed poor artists Picasso, Cocteau and Matisse. Trotsky and Lenin were also guests. Shows focus on present-day artists and the area's creative past.

Musée Pasteur

Institut Pasteur, 25 rue du Dr-Roux, 15th (01.45.68.82.83/www.pasteur.fr). M° Pasteur. **Open** 2-5.30pm Mon-Fri. Closed Aug. **Admission** €3; €1.50 reductions. **Credit** MC, V. **Map** p405 E9.

The flat where the famous chemist and his wife lived at the end of his life (1888-95) has not been touched; you can see their furniture and possessions, photos and instruments. An extravagant mausoleum on the ground floor houses Pasteur's tomb, decorated with mosaics depicting his scientific achievements.

Musée de la Poste

34 bd de Vaugirard, 15th (01.42.79.24.24/ www.museedelaposte.fr). M° Montparnasse Bienvenüe. **Open** 10am-6pm Mon-Sat. **Admission** €5; €3.50 reductions; free under-18s. PMP. *Permanent & temporary exhibitions* €6.50; €5 reductions; free under-18s. **No credit cards. Map** p405 E9.

From among the uniforms, pistols, carriages, official decrees and fumigation tongs emerge snippets of history: during the 1871 Siege of Paris, hot-air

balloons and carrier pigeons were used to get post out of the city, and *boules de Moulins*, balls crammed with hundreds of letters, were floated down the Seine in return, mostly never to arrive. The second section covers French and international philately.

★ FREE Musée Zadkine

100bis rue d'Assas, 6th (01.55.42.77.20/ www.zadkine.paris.fr). M° Notre-Dame-des-Champs/RER Port-Royal. **Open** 10am-6pm Tue-Sun. **Admission** free. *Exhibitions* €4; €2-€3 reductions; free under-13s. **Credit** (€15 minimum) MC, V. **Map** p408 G8.

Works by the Russian-born Cubist sculptor Ossip Zadkine are displayed around this tiny house and garden near the Jardin du Luxembourg. Zadkine's works cover musical, mythological and religious subjects, and his style varies with his materials. There are drawings and poems by Zadkine and paintings by his wife, Valentine Prax.

FREE Observatoire de Paris

61 av de l'Observatoire, 14th (01.40.51.22.21/ www.obspm.fr). M° St-Jacques/RER Port-Royal. **Open** *Tours* 1st Sat of mth (except Aug) by written reservation only to: Service de la Communication (service des visites), Observatoire de Paris, 61 av de l'Observatoire, 75014 Paris. **Admission** free. **Map** p405 H10.

The Paris observatory was founded by Louis XIV's finance minister, Colbert, in 1667; it was designed by Claude Perrault (who also worked on the Louvre), with labs and an observation tower. The French meridian line drawn by François Arago in 1806 (which was used here before the Greenwich meridian was adopted as an international standard) runs north–south through the centre of the building. The dome on the observation tower was added in the 1840s, but what with urban light pollution, most stargazing takes place in Meudon and Provence.

▶ *You'll need to apply for an appointment at the Observatoire by letter, but check the website for openings linked to astronomical happenings – or visit on the Journées du Patrimoine (see p277).*

★ **Tour Montparnasse**
33 av du Maine, 15th (01.45.38.52.56/www. tourmontparnasse56.com). Mº Montparnasse Bienvenüe. **Open** *1 Oct-31 Mar* 9.30am-10.30pm daily. *1 Apr-30 Sept* 9.30am-11.30pm daily. **Admission** €10; €7-€4.50 reductions; free under-7s. **Credit** MC, V. **Map** p405 F9.

Built in 1974 on the site of the old station, this 209m (686ft) steel-and-glass monolith is shorter than the Eiffel Tower, but better placed for fabulous views of the city – including, of course, the Eiffel Tower itself. A lift whisks you up in 38 seconds to the 56th floor, where you'll find a display of aerial scenes of Paris, an upgraded café-lounge, a souvenir shop – and plenty of sky. On a clear day you can see up to 40km (25 miles). Another lift takes you up to the roof. Classical concerts are held on the terrace.

DENFERT-ROCHEREAU & MONTSOURIS

In the 14th & 15th arrondissements.

In the run-up to the 1789 Revolution, the bones of six million Parisians were taken from the handful of overcrowded city cemeteries and wheelbarrowed to the Catacombes (*see below* **Bone Diggers**), a vast network of tunnels that

---

Bone Diggers

Meet some Paris old-timers in the chilling, creepy Catacombes.

By the mid 1780s, Paris's largest cemetery near Les Halles had become so dangerous and insalubrious that it was closed by royal decree. Bones were to be transferred to a disused subterranean quarry beneath what is now avenue René-Coty in the 14th arrondissement. The new *ossuaire municipal*, better known as the **Catacombes** (*see p138*), received its first consignment of mortal remains in 1786; this traffic continued well into the 19th century, as the contents of 16 Paris cemeteries were systematically exhumed, transported and reinterred in the Catatcombes. Today, the ossuary is

the only portion of the network of tunnels spreading beneath the city that is officially open to the public.

In high season, you may have to queue for up to 90 minutes to get into the catacombs, but it's worth the wait. A damp, cramped tunnel takes you through a series of galleries, remnants of the old quarry, before you reach the ossuary itself, the entrance to which is announced by a sign egraved in the stone: 'Stop! This is the empire of death.'

Along each wall stand row upon row of tightly packed bones, interspersed with the occasional row of skulls. Fragments of skull and other unidentifiable bits of corporeal detritus are arranged along the top row. In some places, the bones are so densely stacked that they give the impression of a kind of macabre pebble-dashing. Each set of bones is dated and its cemetery of origin marked. There is a good deal of funerary poetry carved into the walls too, much of it defiantly unconsoling. 'Virtuous or vicious,' runs one line, 'man must expire'.

Suitably chastened, you climb towards the surface up an extremely narrow and steep spiral staircase, before emerging, blinking and somewhat unsettled, on to an anonymous backstreet several hundred metres from where you started on place Denfert-Rochereau.

SIGHTS

SIGHTS

stretches under much of Paris. The sections under the 13th and 14th arrondissements are open to the public; the gloomy Denfert-Rochereau entrance is next to one of the toll gates of the Mur des Fermiers-Généraux, built by Ledoux in the 1780s.

The bronze *Lion de Belfort* dominates the traffic-laden place Denfert-Rochereau, a favourite starting point for the city's countless political demonstrations. The regal beast was sculpted by Bartholdi, of Statue of Liberty fame, and is a scaled-down replica of one in Belfort that commemorates the brave defence by Colonel Denfert-Rochereau of the town in 1870. Nearby, the southern half of rue Daguerre is a sociable, pedestrianised market street (Tuesday to Saturday, Sunday mornings) brimming with cafés and food stores.

One of the big draws here is the **Parc Montsouris**, with lovely lakes, dramatic cascades and an unusual history. Surrounding the western edge of the park are a number of modest, quiet streets – including rue du Parc Montsouris and rue Georges-Braque – that used to be lined in the 1920s and '30s with charming villas and artists' studios by avant-garde architects Le Corbusier and André Lurçat. On the southern edge of the park sprawls the **Cité Universitaire** complex.

★ Les Catacombes

1 av du Colonel-Henri-Rol-Tanguy, 14th (01.43.22.47.63/www.catacombes-de-paris.fr). M°/RER Denfert Rochereau. **Open** 10am-5pm Tue-Sun. **Admission** €7; €3.50-€5.50 reductions; free under-14s. **Credit** (€15 minimum) MC, V. **Map** p407 H10. *See p137* **Bone Diggers**.

FREE Cité Universitaire

17 bd Jourdan, 14th (01.44.16.64.00/ www.ciup.fr). RER Cité Universitaire. The Cité Internationale Universitaire de Paris is an odd mix. Created between the wars in a mood of internationalism and inspired by the model of Oxbridge colleges, its 37 halls of residence across landscaped gardens were designed in a variety of supposedly authentic national styles. Some are by architects of the appropriate nationality (Dutchman Willem Dudok, for instance, designed the De Stijl-style Collège Néerlandais); others, such as the Khmer sculptures and bird-beak roof of the Asie du Sud-Est building, are merely pastiches. The Brits get what looks like a minor public school; the Maison Internationale is based on Fontainebleau; the Swiss and Brazilians get Le Corbusier. You can visit the sculptural white Pavillon Suisse (01.44.16.10.16, www.fondationsuisse.fr), which has a Le Corbusier mural on the ground floor. The spacious landscaped gardens are open to the public, and the newly reno-vated theatre stages drama and modern dance.

FREE Parc Montsouris

Bd Jourdan, 14th. RER Cité Universitaire. **Open** 8am-dusk Mon-Fri; 9am-dusk Sat, Sun. The most colourful of the capital's many parks, Montsouris was laid out for Baron Haussmann by Jean-Charles Adolphe Alphand. It includes a series of sweeping, gently sloping lawns, an artificial lake and cascades. On the opening day in 1878 the lake inexplicably emptied, and the engineer responsible committed suicide.

The 15th arrondissement

The expansive 15th arrondissement has little to offer tourists, though as a largely residential district it has plenty of good restaurants, street markets, and some good small shops, notably on rue du Commerce and rue Lecourbe. It's worth making a detour to visit **La Ruche** ('beehive'), designed by Eiffel as a wine pavilion for the 1900 Exposition Universelle and moved here to serve as artists' studios. Nearby is **Parc Georges Brassens**, opened in 1983, and at the porte de Versailles the sprawling **Paris-Expo** exhibition centre was created in 1923.

FREE Parc Georges Brassens

Rue des Morillons, 15th. M° Porte de Vanves or Porte de Versailles. **Open** 8am-dusk Mon-Fri; 9am-dusk Sat, Sun. **Map** p404 D10. Built on the site of the old Abattoirs de Vaugirard, Parc Georges Brassens prefigured the industrial regeneration of Parc André Citroën and La Villette. The gateways, crowned by bronze bulls, have been kept, as have a series of iron meat-market pavilions, which house a second-hand book market at week-ends. The Jardin des Senteurs is planted with aro-matic species, and a small vineyard yields 200 bottles of Clos des Morillons every year.

Paris-Expo

1 pl de la Porte de Versailles, 15th (01.72.72.17.00/www.paris-expo.fr). M° Porte de Versailles. **Map** p404 B10. This vast exhibition centre, spread over different halls, hosts all manner of trade and art fairs. Many, such as the Foire de Paris (*see p275*) and art fair FIAC (*see p278*), are open to the public.

La Ruche

Passage de Dantzig, 15th (www.la-ruche.fr). M° Convention or Porte de Versailles. **Map** p404 D10. Have a peep through the fence or sneak in behind an unsuspecting resident to see the iron-framed former wine pavilion built by Gustave Eiffel for the 1900 Exposition Universelle, and later rebuilt by philan-thropic sculptor Alfred Boucher to be let as studios for struggling artists. Chagall, Soutine, Brancusi, Modigliani, Lipchitz and Archipenko all spent peri-ods here, and the 140 studios are still sought after by today's artists and designers.

The 7th &
Western Paris

Home to the city's greatest landmark and its most illustrious corpse.

The seventh arrondissement is the Paris of the establishment: home to the French parliament, the Assemblée Nationale, to several French ministries and several foreign embassies, to the army's famous training establishment, the Ecole Militaire, and to the headquarters of UNESCO. Much of it is rather formal and lacking in soul, with few visitor-friendly cultural and historic attractions. However, the attractions that do occupy this lofty district are appropriately big hitters: the Musée d'Orsay, Les Invalides and the Eiffel Tower.

Map pp404-405	**Restaurants** p214
Hotels p179	**Cafés & bars** p237

Near to St-Germain-des-Prés is the cosy Faubourg St-Germain, with its historic mansions and upmarket shops. Further west is the 15th arrondissement, with its predominantly residential buildings done in a suprisingly broad array of architectural styles.

THE FAUBOURG ST-GERMAIN

In the 7th arrondissement.

In the early 18th century, when the Marais went out of fashion, aristocrats built palatial new residences on the Faubourg St-Germain, the district developing around the site of the former city wall. It is still a well-bred part of the city, government ministries and foreign embassies colouring the area with flags and diplomatic plates. Many fine *hôtels particuliers* survive; glimpse their elegant entrance courtyards on rue de Grenelle, rue St-Dominique, rue de l'Université and rue de Varenne.

Just west of St-Germain, the 'Carré Rive Gauche' or 'Carré des Antiquaires' – the quadrangle enclosed by quai Voltaire, rue des Sts-Pères, rue du Bac and rue de l'Université – is filled with antiques shops. On rue des Sts-Pères, *chocolatier* **Debauve & Gallais** (no.30, 7th, 01.45.48.54.67), with its period interior, has been making chocolates since 1800. Rue du

Pré-aux-Clercs, named after a field where students used to sort out their differences by duelling, is now a favourite with fashion insiders. There are still students to be found on adjoining rue St-Guillaume, home of the prestigious **Fondation Nationale des Sciences-Politiques** (no.27, 7th, 01.45.49. 50.50), more commonly known as 'Sciences-Po'.

Rue de Montalembert is home to two of the Left Bank's most fashionable hotels: the **Hôtel Montalembert** (*see p181*) and the Hôtel du Pont-Royal, a gastronomic magnet ever since the addition of the trendy **Atelier de Joël Robuchon** (*see p188*). By the river, a Beaux-Arts train station – the towns once served still listed on the façade – houses the unmissable art collections of the **Musée d'Orsay**; outside on the esplanade are 19th-century bronze animal sculptures. Next door is the lovely 1780s Hôtel de Salm, a mansion built for a German count, once the Swedish embassy and now the **Musée National de la Légion d'Honneur et des Ordres de Chevalerie** (2 rue de Bellechasse, 7th, 01.40.62.84.25), devoted to France's honours

SIGHTS

system since Louis XI. The Legion of Honour was established by Napoleon in 1802. Across the street, a modern footbridge, the Passerelle Solférino, crosses the Seine to the Tuileries. The fancy Hôtel Bouchardon today houses the **Musée Maillol**. Right beside its curved entrance, the Fontaine des Quatre Saisons by Edmé Bouchardon features statues of the seasons surrounding allegorical figures of Paris above the rivers Seine and Marne.

You'll have to wait for the open-house **Journées du Patrimoine** (*see p277*) to see the decorative interiors and private gardens of other *hôtels*, such as the **Hôtel de Villeroy** (Ministry of Agriculture; 78 rue de Varenne, 7th), **Hôtel Boisgelin** (Italian Embassy; 47 rue de Varenne, 7th), **Hôtel d'Avaray** (Dutch ambassador's residence; 85 rue de Grenelle, 7th), **Hôtel d'Estrées** (Russian ambassador's residence; 79 rue de Grenelle, 7th) or **Hôtel de Monaco** (Polish Embassy;

57 rue St-Dominique, 7th). Among the most beautiful is the **Hôtel Matignon** (57 rue de Varenne, 7th), residence of the prime minister. Once used by French statesman Talleyrand for lavish receptions, it contains the biggest private garden in Paris. The Cité Varenne at no.51 is a lane of exclusive houses with private gardens.

Rue du Bac is home to the city's oldest and most elegant department store, **Le Bon Marché** ('the good bargain'), and to an unlikely pilgrimage spot, the **Chapelle de la Médaille Miraculeuse**. On nearby rue de Babylone, handy budget bistro **Au Babylone** (no.13, 7th, 01.45.48.72.13) has been serving up cheap lunches for decades, but the Théâtre de Babylone, where Beckett's *Waiting for Godot* was premiered in 1953, is long gone.

At the foot of boulevard St-Germain, facing place de la Concorde across the Seine, is the **Assemblée Nationale**, the lower house of the French parliament. Behind, elegant place

History Maker

Where would Gaul be without de Gaulle?

Charles André Joseph Pierre-Marie de Gaulle's list of notable achievements is almost as long as his name: he headed the Resistance in World War II, granted women the right to vote in 1944, founded the Fifth Republic in 1958, gave independence back to Algeria in 1962, and contributed to French history in a way that few politicians could ever hope to achieve.

With such sparkling credentials but nowhere to show them off, the Musée de l'Armée at the Hôtel des Invalides (*see p141*) and the Charles de Gaulle Foundation got together to create the **Historial Charles de Gaulle**, a state-of-the-art audiovisual monument that deals with the whole of de Gaulle's life, particularly his role in World War II, the war in the Pacific and in Algeria.

Sunk several metres below the Invalides' Cour de Valeur wing, it is split into three sections: a 200-seater cinema showing a 25-minute film on de Gaulle (in five languages); a circular walkway of eight light, sound and video installations covering French history from the belle époque to man's first walk on the moon; and a series of interactive alcoves that allow you to pick out as many snippets of de Gaulle's history as you can digest (mostly in Fench and untranslated).

The building itself is a feat of modern technology: it lies below the water table

and is designed to withstand flooding from the Seine. Construction had to be carried out by hand so as not to endanger the Invalides' surrounding buildings, which were erected without foundations (although ironically, builders discovered a World War II bunker that had to be destroyed).

du Palais-Bourbon leads into rue de Bourgogne, a rare commercial thoroughfare amid the official buildings, with some delectable pâtisseries and designer-furniture showrooms.

Nearby, the mid 19th-century E**glise Ste-Clotilde** (12 rue Martignac, 7th, 01.44.18.62.60), with its skeletal twin spires, is an early example of Gothic Revival. Beside the Assemblée is the Foreign Ministry, often referred to by its address, 'quai d'Orsay'. Beyond it, a long, grassy esplanade leads up to golden-domed Les Invalides. The vast military hospital complex, with its Eglise du Dôme and St-Louis-des-Invalides churches, all built by Louis XIV, epitomises the official grandeur of the Sun King as expression of royal and military power. It now houses the **Musée de l'Armée**, as well as Napoleon's tomb inside the Eglise du Dôme. Stand with your back to the dome to survey the cherubim-laden Pont Alexandre III and the **Grand** and **Petit Palais** over the river, all put up for the 1900 Exposition Universelle.

Just beside Les Invalides is the **Musée National Rodin**, occupying the charming 18th-century Hôtel Biron and its romantic gardens. Many of his great sculptures, including the *Thinker*, the *Burghers of Calais* and the swarming *Gates of Hell*, are displayed in the building and around the gardens – as are those of his mistress, Camille Claudel.

FREE Assemblée Nationale

33 quai d'Orsay, 7th (01.40.63.60.00/www.assemblee-nationale.fr). Mº Assemblée Nationale. **Map** p405 F5.
Like the Sénat, the Assemblée Nationale (also known as the Palais Bourbon) is a royal building adapted for republicanism. It was built between 1722 and 1728 for the Duchesse de Bourbon, daughter of Louis XIV and Madame de Montespan, who also put up the neighbouring Hôtel de Lassay for her lover, the Marquis de Lassay. The *palais* was modelled on the Grand Trianon at Versailles, with a colonnaded *cour d'honneur* opening on to rue de l'Université and gardens running down to the Seine. The Prince de Condé extended the palace, linked the two *hôtels* and laid out place du Palais-Bourbon. The Greek temple-style façade facing Pont de la Concorde (the rear of the building) was added in 1806 to mirror the Madeleine.

Flanking this riverside façade are statues of four great statesmen: L'Hôpital, Sully, Colbert and Aguesseau. The Napoleonic frieze on the pediment was replaced by a monarchist one after the restoration: between 1838 and 1841, Cortot sculpted the figures of France, Power and Justice. After the Revolution, the palace became the meeting place for the Conseil des Cinq-Cents. It was the forerunner of the parliament's lower house, which set up here for good in 1827. Visits are by arrangement through a serving *député* (if you're French) – or, after long queuing, during the Journées du Patrimoine (*see p277*).

★ FREE Chapelle de la Médaille Miraculeuse

Couvent des Soeurs de St-Vincent-de-Paul, 140 rue du Bac, 7th (01.49.54.78.88). Mº Sèvres Babylone. **Open** 7.45am-1pm, 2.30-7pm daily. **Admission** free. **Map** p405 F7.
In 1830, saintly Catherine Labouré was said to have been visited by the Virgin, who gave her a medal that performed miracles. This kitsch chapel – murals, mosaics, statues and the embalmed bodies of Catherine and her mother superior – is one of France's most visited sites, attracting two million pilgrims every year. Reliefs in the courtyard tell the nun's story – and slot machines sell medals.

FREE Espace Fondation EDF

6 rue Récamier, 7th (01.53.63.23.45/www.edf.fr). Mº Sèvres Babylone. **Open** noon-7pm Tue-Sun. **Admission** free. **Map** p405 G7.
This former electricity substation, converted by Electricité de France for PR purposes, is now used for varied, well-presented exhibitions examining the likes of garden designer Gilles Clément.

★ Les Invalides & Musée de l'Armée

Esplanade des Invalides, 7th (01.44.42.38.77/ museum 08.10.11.33.99/www.invalides.org). Mº La Tour Maubourg or Les Invalides. **Open** Apr-Sept 10am-6pm daily. Oct-Mar 10am-5pm daily. Closed 1st Mon of mth. **Admission** *Courtyard* free. *Musée de l'Armée & Eglise du Dôme* €8; €6 reductions; free under-18s. PMP. **Credit** MC, V. **Map** p405 E6.
Topped by its gilded dome – a glorious sight when illuminated after dusk – the Hôtel des Invalides was (and in part still is) a hospital. Commissioned by Louis XIV for wounded soldiers, it once housed as many as 6,000 invalids. Designed by Libéral Bruand (the foundations were laid in 1671) and completed by Jules Hardouin-Mansart, it's a magnificent monument to Louis XIV and Napoleon. Behind lines of cannons and bullet-shaped yews, the main (northern) façade has a relief of Louis XIV (Ludovicus Magnus) and the Sun King's sunburst. Wander through the main courtyard and you'll see grandiose two-storey arcades and a statue of Napoleon glaring down from the end; the dormer windows around the courtyards are sculpted to look like suits of armour.

The complex contains two churches – or, rather, a sort of double church: the Eglise St-Louis for the soldiers, the Eglise du Dôme for the king. An opening behind the altar connects the two. The long, barrel-vaulted nave of the church of St-Louis is hung with flags captured from enemy troops. Since 1840 the baroque Eglise du Dôme has been dedicated to the worship of Napoleon, whose body was brought here from St Helena. On the ground floor, under a dome painted by de la Fosse, Jouvenet and Coypel, are chapels featuring monuments to Vauban, Foch and Joseph Napoleon (Napoleon's older brother and

SIGHTS

VEDETTES DE PARIS

The sightseeing cruise of Paris: Get the best in 1 hour

www.vedettesdeparis.com

Port de Suffren, 7th district + 00 33 (0)1 44 18 19 50
Mᵒ Bir-hakeim & Trocadero RER Champs de Mars

Departures:
From October to February
2 departures per hour from 11.00am to 6.45pm & week end
to 10.00pm on Saturday & 7.30 on Sunday
May, June & September
1 departure every 30 minutes from 11.30am to 10.00pm
July and August
1 departure every 30 min from 10.30am to 10.00pm

Rates €11; €5 4-12's; free under 4's

The Parisian sightseeing cruise has to be at the top
of your list of things to do when in the French
capital. Ideally located right by the Eiffel Tower,
its charming boats enhance the pleasure of a guided
cruise on the River Seine. Listed by the UNESCO
World Heritage, the river banks offer you some of
the most appreciated and well-known monuments
such as the Eiffel Tower, the Louvre and Notre
Dame Cathedral amongst others. The tour includes
a recorded multilingual commentary.

Another **taste of Paris**

vedettes de paris

Le **Paris Iéna**

King of Naples, Sicily and Spain). Napoleon II (King of Rome) is buried in the crypt opposite his father the emperor. Two dramatic black figures holding up the entrance to the crypt, the red porphyry tomb, the ring of giant figures, and the friezes and texts eulogising the emperor's heroic deeds give the measure of the cult of Napoleon, cherished in France for ruling large swaths of Europe and for creating an administrative and educational system that endures to this day.

The Invalides complex also houses the enormous Musée de l'Armée, which is in effect several museums in one; allow a whole afternoon to visit it properly. Even if militaria are not your thing, the building is a splendour, and there's some fine portraiture, such as Ingres' *Emperor Napoleon on his Throne*. The Antique Armour wing is packed full of armour and weapons that look as good as new, many displaying the most staggering workmanship, from the superb 16th-century suit made for François I to cabinets full of swords, maces, crossbows, muskets and arquebuses. The Plans-Reliefs section is a collection of gorgeous 18th- and 19th-century scale models of French cities, used for military strategy; also here is a stunning 17th-century model of Mont St-Michel, made by a monk from playing cards.

The World War I rooms are moving, with the conflict brought into focus by uniforms, paintings, a scale model of a trench on the western front and, most sobering of all, white plastercasts of the hideously mutilated faces of two soldiers. The World War II wing takes in not just the Resistance, but also the Battle of Britain and the war in the Pacific (there's a replica of Little Boy, the bomb dropped on Hiroshima), alternating artefacts with film footage. Also included in the entry price is the Historial Charles de Gaulle (*see p140* **History Maker**).

Musée Maillol

59-61 rue de Grenelle, 7th (01.42.22.59.58/ www.museemaillol.com). M° Rue du Bac. **Open** 11am-6pm (last admission 5.15pm) Mon, Wed-Sun. **Admission** €8; €6 reductions; free under-16s. **Credit** *Shop* AmEx, MC, V. **Map** p405 G7. Dina Vierny was 15 when she met Aristide Maillol (1861-1944) and became his principal model for the next decade, idealised in such sculptures as *Spring, Air* and *Harmony*. In 1995 she opened this delightful museum, exhibiting Maillol's drawings, engravings, pastels, tapestry panels, ceramics and early Nabis-related paintings, as well as the sculptures and terracottas that epitomise his calm, modern classicism. Vierny also set up a Maillol Museum in the Pyrenean village of Banyuls-sur-Mer. This Paris venue also has works by Picasso, Rodin, Gauguin, Degas and Cézanne, a whole room of Matisse drawings, rare Surrealist documents and works by naïve artists. Vierny has also championed Kandinsky and Ilya Kabakov, whose *Communal Kitchen* installation recreates the atmosphere of Soviet domesticity. Monographic exhibitions are devoted to modern and contemporary artists.

Musée National Rodin

Hôtel Biron, 79 rue de Varenne, 7th (01.44.18.61. 10/www.musee-rodin.fr). M° Varenne. **Open** *Apr-Sept* 9.30am-5.45pm Tue-Sun (gardens until 6.45pm). *Oct-Mar* 9.30am-4.45pm Tue-Sun (gardens until 5pm). **Admission** €6; €4 reductions, all Sun; free under-18s, all 1st Sun of mth. PMP. *Exhibitions* €7; €5 18-25s. *Gardens* €1. **Credit** MC, V. **Map** p405 F6.
The Rodin museum occupies the *hôtel particulier* where the sculptor lived in the final years of his life. The *Kiss*, the *Cathedral*, the *Walking Man*, portrait busts and early terracottas are exhibited indoors, as are many of the individual figures or small groups that also appear on the *Gates of Hell*. Rodin's works are accompanied by several pieces by his mistress and pupil, Camille Claudel. The walls are hung with paintings by Van Gogh, Monet, Renoir, Carrière and Rodin himself. Most visitors have greatest affection for the gardens: look out for the *Burghers of Calais*, the elaborate *Gates of Hell*, and the *Thinker*.
▶ *Rodin fans can also visit the Villa des Brillants at Meudon (19 av Rodin, Meudon, 01.41.14.35.00), where the artist worked from 1895.*

★ Musée d'Orsay

1 rue de la Légion-d'Honneur, 7th (01.40.49. 48.14/recorded information 01.45.49.11. 11/www.musee-orsay.fr). M° Solférino/RER Musée d'Orsay. **Open** 9.30am-6pm Tue, Wed, Fri-Sun; 9.30am-9.45pm Thur. **Admission** €9.50; €7 reductions; free under-18s, all 1st Sun of mth. PMP. **Credit** *Shop* MC, V. **Map** p405 G6. *See p144* **Profile**.

WEST OF LES INVALIDES

The 7th & 15th arrondissements.

South-west of the Invalides is the huge **Ecole Militaire** (av de La Motte-Picquet, 7th), the military academy built by Louis XV to educate

---

INSIDE TRACK
SEGWAY SIGHTSEEING

City Segway Tours (01.56.58.10.54/ www.citysegwaytours.com) offers alternative guided excursions around the city's main sights on a contraption called an i2, a self-balancing, personal transportation device. The tours take place day and night, and last about four hours, including a 30-minute initiation session. Anyone over 12 can ride, but under-18s must be accompanied or have an insurance form filled in by an adult. Tours cost €70 and leave from the Eiffel Tower.

Profile Musée d'Orsay

A former railway station holds a fabulous collection of French art.

SIGHTS

The **Musée d'Orsay** (*see p143*) follows a chronological route, from the ground floor to the upper level and then to the mezzanine, showing links between Impressionist painters and their forerunners. Running down the centre of the tracks, a central sculpture aisle takes in monuments and maidens by Rude, Barrye and Carrier-Belleuse, but the outstanding pieces are by Carpeaux, including his controversial *La Danse* for the façade of the Palais Garnier. The Lille side, on the right of the central aisle, is dedicated to the Romantics and history painters: Ingres and Amaury-Duval contrast with the Romantic passion of Delacroix's North African period. Further on are early Degas canvases and works by Symbolists Moreau and Puvis de Chavannes.

The first rooms to the Seine side of the main aisle are given over to the Barbizon landscape painters: Corot, Daubigny and Millet. One room is dedicated to Courbet, with the *Artist and his Studio*, *Burial at Ornans* and *L'Origine du Monde*. This floor also covers pre-1870 works by the Impressionists, including Manet's *Olympia*.

Upstairs are the Impressionists, Pissarro, Renoir and Caillebotte, Manet's *Déjeuner sur l'Herbe*, Monet's paintings of Rouen cathedral and works by Degas. Among the Van Goghs are *Church at Auvers* and *Wheat Field with Crows*. You'll also find the primitivist jungle of Le Douanier Rousseau, the gaudy lowlife of Toulouse-Lautrec, the colourful exoticism of Gauguin's Breton and Tahitian periods, and Cézanne's still lifes, landscapes and the *Card Players*.

On the mezzanine are works by the Nabi painters – Vallotton, Denis, Roussel, Bonnard and Vuillard. Several rooms are given over to art nouveau decorative arts, including furniture by Majorelle, and Gallé and Lalique ceramics.

THREE TO SEE

Edouard Manet
Déjeuner sur l'Herbe (1863)

Gustave Caillebotte
Raboteurs de Parquet (1875)

Paul Cézanne
Baigneurs (c.1890)

the children of penniless officers; it would later train Napoleon. The severe neo-classical building, designed by Jacques Ange Gabriel, is still used by the army and closed to the public.

From the north-western side of the Ecole Militaire begins the vast Champ de Mars, a market garden converted into a military drilling ground in the 18th century. It has long been home to the most celebrated Paris monument of all, the **Eiffel Tower**. At the south-eastern end of the Champ de Mars stands the Mur pour la Paix ('wall for peace'), erected in 2000 to articulate hopes for peace. South-east of the Ecole are the Y-shaped **UNESCO** building, built in 1958, and the modernist Ministry of Labour. Fashionable apartments line broad avenue Bosquet and avenue Suffren, though there's much architectural eclecticism in the area: look at the pseudo-Gothic and pseudo-Renaissance houses on avenue de Villars; Lavirotte's fabulous art nouveau doorway at 27 avenue Rapp; and the striking, box-shaped **Notre Dame de l'Arche de l'Alliance** church (81 rue d'Alleray, 15th, 01.56.56.62.56), which was completed in 1998. For signs of life, visit the Saxe-Breteuil street market. The upper reaches of rue Cler contain classy food shops.

Les Egouts de Paris

Entrance opposite 93 quai d'Orsay, by Pont de l'Alma, 7th (01.53.68.27.81). M° Alma Marceau/RER Pont de l'Alma. **Open** 11am-4pm Wed-Sat (until 5pm May-Sept). Closed 3wks Jan. **Admission** €4.20; €3.40 reductions; free under-5s. **No credit cards. Map** p400 D5.
For centuries the main source of drinking water in Paris was the Seine, which was also the main sewer. Construction of an underground sewerage system began at the time of Napoleon. Today the Egouts de Paris constitutes a smelly museum; each sewer in the 2,100km (1,305-mile) system is marked with a replica of the street sign above. The Egouts can be closed after periods of heavy rain.

★ Eiffel Tower

Champ de Mars, 7th (01.44.11.23.45/recorded information 01.44.11.23.23/www.tour-eiffel.fr). M° Bir-Hakeim/RER Champ de Mars Tour Eiffel. **Open** *13 June-Aug* 9am-12.45am daily. *Sept-12 June* 9.30am-11.45pm daily. **Admission** *By stairs* (1st & 2nd levels, Sept-mid June 9.30am-6pm, mid June-Aug 9am-midnight) €4; €3.10 reductions. *By lift* (1st leve) €4.80; €2.50 reductions; (2nd level) €7.80; €4.30 reductions; (3rd level) €12; €6.70 reductions; free under-3s. **Credit** AmEx, MC, V. **Map** p404 C6.
No building better symbolises Paris than the Tour Eiffel. Maupassant claimed he left Paris because of it, William Morris visited daily to avoid having to see it from afar – and it was originally meant to be a temporary structure. The radical cast-iron tower

was built for the 1889 World Fair and the centenary of the 1789 Revolution by engineer Gustave Eiffel. Eiffel made use of new technology that was already popular in iron-framed buildings. Construction took more than two years and used some 18,000 pieces of metal and 2,500,000 rivets. The 300m (984ft) tower stands on four massive concrete piles; it was the tallest structure in the world until overtaken by New York's Empire State Building in the 1930s. Vintage double-decker lifts ply their way up and down; you can walk as far as the second level. There are souvenir shops, an exhibition space, café and even a post office on the first and second levels. The smart Jules Verne restaurant, on the second level, has its own lift in the north tower.
At the top (third level), there's Eiffel's cosy salon and a viewing platform with panels pointing out what to see. Views can reach 65km (40 miles) on a good day, although the most fascinating perspectives are of the ironwork itself. At night, for ten minutes on the hour, 20,000 flashbulbs attached to the tower provide a beautiful effect. To avoid the queues, come late at night.
▶ *The Jules Verne restaurant is now run by Alain Ducasse; see p218.*

FREE UNESCO

7 pl de Fontenoy, 7th (01.45.68.10.00/tours 01.45.68.16.42/www.unesco.org). M° Ecole Militaire. **Open** 9.30am-6pm Mon-Fri. *Tours* 3pm Mon-Fri (in English Wed). **Admission** free. **Map** p405 D7.
The Y-shaped UNESCO headquarters, built in 1958, is home to a swarm of international diplomats. It's worth visiting for the sculptures and paintings – by Picasso, Arp, Giacometti, Moore, Calder and Miró – and for the Japanese garden, with its contemplation cylinder by minimalist architect Tadao Ando.

FREE Village Suisse

38-78 av de Suffren or 54 av de La Motte-Picquet, 15th (www.villagesuisseparis.com). M° La Motte Picquet Grenelle. **Open** 10.30am-7pm Mon, Thur-Sun. **Map** p404 D7.
The mountains and waterfalls created for the Swiss Village at the 1900 Exposition Universelle are long gone, but the village lives on. Rebuilt as blocks of flats, the street level has been colonised by some 150 boutiques offering various high-quality, albeit pricey, antiques and collectibles.

Along the Seine

Downstream from the Eiffel Tower is the **Musée du Quai Branly**, the Chirac-sponsored museum of primitive arts which opened in 2006. A short way further on, the high-tech **Maison de la Culture du Japon** stands near Pont Bir-Hakeim on quai Branly. Beyond, the 15th arrondissement Fronts de Seine riverfront, with its tower-block developments, had some of the worst architecture of the 1970s inflicted upon it. This would-be brave new world of walkways, suspended gardens and tower blocks has no easily discoverable means of access. The adjacent Beaugrenelle shopping centre is more straightforward to get into, but remains dingy. Further west, things look up: the sophisticated former headquarters of the Canal+ TV channel (2 rue des Cévennes, 15th), designed by American architect Richard Meier, is surrounded by fine modern housing; and the pleasant **Parc André Citroën**, created in the 1990s on the site of the former Citroën car works, runs all the way down to the Seine quayside, where you'll find the occasional cruise ship and summer partygoers.

FREE Maison de la Culture du Japon

101bis quai Branly, 15th (01.44.37.95.00/www. mcjp.asso.fr). M° Bir-Hakeim/RER Champ de Mars Tour Eiffel. **Open** noon-7pm Tue, Wed, Fri, Sat; noon-8pm Thur. Closed Aug. **Admission** free. **Map** p404 C6.

Constructed in 1996 by the Anglo-Japanese architectural partnership of Kenneth Armstrong and Masayuki Yamanaka, this opalescent glass-fronted Japanese cultural centre screens films and puts on exhibitions and plays. It also contains a library, an authentic Japanese tea pavilion on the roof, where you can watch the tea ceremony, and a well-stocked book and gift shop.

★ Musée du Quai Branly

37-55 quai Branly, 7th (01.56.61.70.00/www. quaibranly.fr). RER Pont de l'Alma. **Open** 11am-7pm Tue, Wed, Sun; 11am-9pm Thur-Sat. **Admission** €8.50; €6 reductions; free under-18s. **Credit** AmEx, DC, MC, V. **Map** p404 C6.

Surrounded by trees on the banks of the Seine, this museum, housed in an extraordinary building by Jean Nouvel, is a vast showcase for non-European cultures. Dedicated to the ethnic art of Africa, Oceania, Asia and the Americas, it joins together the collections of the Musée des Arts d'Afrique et d'Océanie and the Laboratoire d'Ethnologie du Musée de l'Homme, as well as contemporary indigenous art. Treasures include a tenth-century anthropomorphic Dogon statue from Mali, Vietnamese costumes, Gabonese masks, Aztec statues, Peruvian feather tunics, and rare frescoes from Ethiopia.

FREE Parc André Citroën

Rue Balard, rue St-Charles or quai Citroën, 15th. M° Balard or Javel. **Open** 8am-dusk Mon-Fri; 9am-dusk Sat, Sun, public hols. **Map** p404 A9.

This park is a fun, postmodern version of a French formal garden, designed by Gilles Clément and Alain Prévost. It comprises glasshouses, computerised fountains, waterfalls, a wilderness and themed gardens featuring different coloured plants and even sounds. Stepping stones and water jets make it a garden for pleasure as well as philosophy. The tethered Eutelsat helium balloon takes visitors up for panoramic views. If the weather looks unreliable, call 01.44.26.20.00 to check the programme.

Musée du Quai Branly.

Beyond the Périphérique

Cultural riches and social challenges in the suburbs.

In 2008, President Sarkozy announced his 'Grand Paris' project, a proposed shake-up of the Parisian suburbs on a scale similar to Haussmann's reshaping of central Paris. Kicking off with a consultation process involving ten teams of international architects and city planners, among them Richard Rogers, the scheme is designed to revamp large swathes of the Seine St-Denis *département*, improve transport links across the greater Paris region, establish a science and technology district in the Essonne, and generally extend the administrative influence of the capital into its outlying towns. Further elements of the project, whose outline emphasises the desirability of 'powerful architectural statements', are to be announced in the spring of 2009. But for the forseeable future, the relationship between Paris and its suburbs looks set to remain as prolematic as ever.

No one doubts the ambitiousness of Sarkozy's plan, but its power to sow discord has already become apparent. Mayor Delanoë, a man with presidential ambitions, has criticised it, arguing that Sarkozy's dream of creating a Greater Paris to rival the economic muscle of Greater London is inappropriate; and Sarkozy's appointment of a special minister to oversee the plan, Christian Blanc, has led the Socialist mayor and Paris politicians of other stripes to accuse Sarkozy of bypassing the city's power to decide its own future. The rows are only just beginning.

Delanoë is, in any case, right to feel slighted, since closing the social, cultural and economic divide between Paris and its suburbs has been one of his key policies. Tangible evidence of this has been improved transport links. The recently inaugurated T3 tramway now runs alongside the southern edge of the Périphérique, which divides Paris and the *banlieue*, and the eight-lane ring road itself has also had sections covered over and landscaped. Meanwhile, district councils of the outer boroughs are signing co-operation agreements with the Mairie. One of the most recent, involving Ivry-sur-Seine, includes a plan for a local history museum to be built on a bridge across the river.

For many people, though, the suburbs still evoke memories of the violent 2005 riots. Much of the *banlieue* (especially the undesirable northern and eastern suburbs) remains poor and neglected: on certain estates, the fire brigade is attacked whenever it tries to extinguish blazes, attempts to reopen local shops are answered by chronic vandalism, and even the police are afraid to enter some areas without back-up.

But there are also numerous respectable residential districts, with their own self-contained, provincial atmosphere quite different from that of the capital. Other signs that things are beginning to change beyond the Périphérique include the arrival of **MAC/VAL**, the first permanent collection of contemporary art to open in suburban Paris, and other art venues and galleries are following suit.

LA DEFENSE

The skyscrapers and walkways of La Défense – named after a stand against the Prussians in 1870 – create a whole new world. The area has been a showcase for French business since the mid 1950s, when the CNIT hall was built to host trade shows, but it was the arrival of the

Grande Arche that gave the district its most dramatic monument. Today, more than 100,000 people work here, and another 35,000 live in the blocks of flats on the southern edge, served by the inevitable mall, a huge multiplex and leisure complex. In summer 2007, Jean-Christophe Choblet, the creator of Paris-Plage, created a series of outdoor cultural events to encourage workers to socialise in the neighbourhood rather than take the usual commuter train home. On the central esplanade are fountains and sculptures by Miró and Serra. None of the skyscrapers is especially distinguished, although together they are an impressive sight.

La Grande Arche de La Défense

92044 Paris La Défense (01.49.07.27.27/ www.grandearche.com). M° La Défense. **Open** *Apr-Sept* 10am-8pm daily. *Oct-Mar* 10am-7pm daily. **Admission** €10; €8.50 reductions; free under-6s. **Credit** MC, V.

Completed for the bicentenary of the Revolution in 1989, the Grande Arche was designed by Danish architect Johan Otto von Spreckelsen. Though it lines up neatly on the Grand Axe – from the Louvre, up the Champs-Elysées to the Arc de Triomphe – the building itself is skewed. A vertigo-inducing glass lift soars up through canvas 'clouds' to the roof, for a fantastic view over Paris.

▶ *Also here is the Musée de l'Informatique (08.20.21.02.30, www.museeinformatique.fr), which opened in 2008 and traces the story of computing with displays of old machines and multimedia displays.*

ST-DENIS & THE NORTH

North of Paris, the *département* of Seine St-Denis (and part of adjoining Val d'Oise) is the one that best fulfils the negative stereotype of the *banlieue*. It's a victim of its 19th-century industrial boom and the 20th-century housing shortage, when colossal estates went up in La Corneuve, Aulnay-sous-Bois and Sarcelles. It includes some of the poorest *communes* in all of France. Yet the *département* boasts a buzzing theatre scene, with the **MC93** in Bobigny (*see p342*), the **Théâtre Gérard-Philipe** (*see p342*) in St-Denis, and the Théâtre de la Commune in Aubervilliers, plus prestigious music festivals. Amid the sprawl stands one of the treasures of Gothic architecture: the **Basilique St-Denis**, final resting place for the majority of France's former monarchs.

Le Bourget, home to the city's first airport and still used for private business jets and an air fair, contains the **Musée de l'Air et de l'Espace** in its original passenger terminals and hangars. North-east of Paris, Pantin arrived on the cultural scene with the opening in 2004

of the **Centre National de la Danse** (*see p292*) in a cleverly rehabilitated office block. North-west of St-Denis, Ecouen, noted for its beautiful Renaissance château, now the **Musée National de la Renaissance**, allows for a glimpse of a more rural past.

★ Basilique St-Denis

1 rue de la Légion-d'Honneur, 93200 St-Denis (01.48.09.83.54). M° St-Denis Basilique/ tram 1. **Open** *Apr-Sept* 10am-6.15pm Mon-Sat; noon-6.15pm Sun. *Oct-Mar* 10am-5.15pm Mon-Sat; noon-5.15pm Sun. *Tours* 10.30am, 3pm Mon-Sat; 12.15pm, 3pm Sun. **Admission** €6.50; €4.50 reductions; free under-18s. PMP. **Credit** MC, V.

Legend has it that when St Denis was beheaded, he picked up his noggin and walked with it to Vicus Catulliacus (now St-Denis) to be buried. The first church, parts of which can be seen in the crypt, was built over his tomb in around 475. The present edifice was begun in the 1130s by Abbot Suger, the powerful minister of Louis VI and Louis VII. It is considered the first example of Gothic architecture, uniting the elements of pointed arches, ogival vaulting and flying buttresses. In the 13th century, master mason Pierre de Montreuil erected the spire and rebuilt the choir nave and transept. St-Denis was the burial place for all but three French monarchs between 996 and the end of the *ancien régime*, so the ambulatory is a museum of French funerary sculpture. It includes a fanciful Gothic tomb for Dagobert, the austere effigy of Charles V, and the sculpted Renaissance tomb of Louis XII and his wife Anne de Bretagne. In 1792 these tombs were desecrated, and the royal remains thrown into a pit.

★ Musée de l'Air et de l'Espace

Aéroport de Paris-Le Bourget, 93352 Le Bourget Cedex (01.49.92.71.99/recorded information 01.49.92.70.62/www.mae.org). M° Gare du Nord, then bus 350/RER Le Bourget, then bus 152. **Open** *Apr-Sept* 10am-6pm Tue-Sun. *Oct-Mar* 10am-5pm Tue-Sun. **Admission** €7; €5 reductions; free under-18s. *With Concorde & Boeing 747* €9.50; €3-€8 reductions; free under-4s. PMP. **Credit** MC, V.

INSIDE TRACK
BANLIEUE BOAT

Launched in 2008, **Voguéo** (www.vogueo.fr) is a new river service that links Paris and the eastern *banlieue*. The boats shuttle between Gare d'Austerlitz and Maisons-Alfort, with stops along the way at Bibliothèque François-Mitterrand, Parc de Bercy and Ivry-sur-Seine. Tickets cost €3.

La Grande Arche de La Défense.

The impressive air and space museum is set in the former passenger terminal at Le Bourget airport. The collection begins with the pioneers, including fragile-looking biplanes and the command cabin of a Zeppelin airship. On the runway are Mirage fighters, a US Thunderchief, and Ariane launchers 1 and 5. A hangar houses the prototype Concorde 001 and wartime survivors. A new scale models gallery opened in 2008.

Musée National de la Renaissance

Château d'Ecouen, 95440 Ecouen (01.34.38.38.50/www.musee-renaissance.fr). Train Gare du Nord to Ecouen-Ezanville then bus 269 or walk. **Open** *15 Apr-Sept 9.30am-12.45pm, 2-5.45pm Mon, Wed-Sun. Oct-14 Apr 9.30am-12.45pm, 2-5.15pm Mon, Wed-Sun.* **Admission** €4.50; €3 reductions, all on Sun; free under-18s, all on 1st Sun of mth. **Credit** MC, V.

The Renaissance château completed in 1555 for Royal Constable Anne de Montmorency and wife Margaret de Savoie is the setting for a collection of 16th-century decorative arts, arranged over three floors (some sections are open only at certain times – phone ahead). Best are the painted chimney pieces, decorated with biblical and mythological scenes.

VINCENNES & THE EAST

The more upmarket residential districts in the east surround the **Bois de Vincennes**, such as Vincennes, with its royal château, St-Mandé and Charenton-le-Pont. **Joinville-le-Pont** and **Champigny-sur-Marne** draw weekenders for the riverside *guinguette* dancehalls.

Château de Vincennes

Av de Paris, 94300 Vincennes (01.48.08.31.20/ www.chateau-vincennes.fr). M° Château de Vincennes. **Open** *May-Aug 10am-6pm daily. Sept-Apr 10am-5pm daily.* **Admission** *Short visit* €5; €3.50 reductions; free under-18s. *Long visit* €7.50; €4.80 reductions; free under-18s. **Credit** *Shop* MC, V.

An imposing curtain wall punctuated by towers encloses this medieval fortress, which is still home to an army garrison. The square keep was begun by Philippe VI and completed in the 14th century by Charles V, who added the curtain wall. Henry V died here in 1422, and Louis XIII used the château for hunting expeditions and had the Pavillon du Roi and Pavillon de la Reine built by Louis Le Vau, although any decorative elements disappeared when they became barracks. Construction began on the chapel in 1380, but wasn't finished until the 16th century.

★ MAC/VAL

Pl de la Libération, 94404 Vitry-sur-Seine (01.43.91.64.20/www.macval.fr). M° Porte de Choisy then bus 183/RER C Gare de Vitry-sur-Seine then bus 180. **Open** *noon-7pm Tue-Sun; noon-9pm Thur.* **Admission** €4; €2 reductions; free under-18s, students, all on 1st Sun of mth. **Credit** AmEx, V.

See p151 **Peripheral Vision**.

Pavillon Baltard

12 av Victor-Hugo, 94130 Nogent-sur-Marne (01.43.24.76.76/www.pavillonbaltard.fr). RER Nogent-sur-Marne. **Open** during exhibitions only.

When Les Halles was demolished, someone had the nous to save one of its Baltard-designed iron-and-glass market pavilions (no.8, eggs and poultry) and relocate it for the benefit of the suburbs.

BOULOGNE & THE WEST

The capital's most desirable suburbs lie to the west. La Défense, Neuilly-sur-Seine, Boulogne-Billancourt, Levallois-Perret and, over the river, Issy-les-Moulineaux have become accepted business addresses for Parisians. Neuilly-sur-Seine is where President Nicolas Sarkozy cut his political teeth as mayor in the early 1990s.

Boulogne-Billancourt is the main town and a lively centre in its own right. In 1320, the Gothic Eglise Notre-Dame was begun in tribute to a miraculous statue of the Virgin that washed up at Boulogne-sur-Mer. By the 18th century, Boulogne was known for its wines and laundries, then, early in the 20th century, for its artist residents (Landowski, Lipchitz, Chagall, Gris), whereas Billancourt was known for car manufacturing, aviation and its film studios.

In the 1920s and '30s, Boulogne-Billancourt was proud of its modernity: Tony Garnier built the elegant new town hall on avenue André-Morizet; a new post office, apartments and schools all went up in the modern style; and private houses were built by the leading avant-garde architects of the day – Le Corbusier, Mallet-Stevens, Perret, Lurçat, Pingusson and Fischer – notably on rue Denfert-Rochereau and rue du Belvédère. The **Musée des Années 30** focuses on artists and architects who lived or worked in the town at the time. The innovative glass-fronted apartment block by Le Corbusier – including the flat where he lived from 1933 to 1965 – can be visited each Wednesday morning at 24 rue Nungesser et Coli (reserve ahead with the Fondation Le Corbusier on 01.42.88.41.53, www.fondationlecorbusier.asso.fr).

The former Renault factory has sat in the Seine like a beached whale ever since it closed in 1992. In 2000, billionaire François Pinault decided to convert it into a contemporary art museum. Finally, in May 2005, frustrated by the inertia of the Boulogne-Billancourt council and the lack of investment on the site, Pinault abandoned the idea. The Fondation François Pinault still went ahead – but in a very different location: a *palazzo* on Venice's Grand Canal. Across the Seine, villas in large gardens surround the **Parc de St-Cloud**, one of the loveliest areas of open space around Paris.

In the 19th century, riverside towns such as **Chatou**, **Asnières** and **Argenteuil**, accessible by train, became places of entertainment – for promenades, *guinguettes* and rowing on the Seine – as depicted in many Impressionist paintings.

At Rueil-Malmaison, the romantic **Château de Malmaison** was loved by Napoleon and Josephine. Josephine had a second château, **La Petite Malmaison** (229bis av Napoléon-Bonaparte, 01.47.32.02.02, by appointment only), built nearby. The empress is buried in the Eglise St-Pierre St-Paul in the old centre, as is her daughter Hortense de Beauharnais, Queen of Holland and mother of Napoleon III.

Suresnes, across the Seine from the Bois de Boulogne, has been a wine-producing village since Roman times, and still celebrates the Fête des Vendanges grape harvest every autumn. The 162-metre (532-foot) Mont Valérien was a place of pilgrimage; one of the nearby streets is still named rue du Calvaire. In 1841, a huge fortress was built here to defend Paris. It was occupied by the German army during World War II; French *résistants* were brought here at night and shot. The fortress itself still belongs to the French army, and is the centre of its eavesdropping network. On the surrounding hill is the **American Cemetery** (190 bd de Washington), which contains the graves of American soldiers from World Wars I and II.

St-Germain-en-Laye is a smart suburb with a historic centre and a château. Henri II lived here with his wife Catherine de Médicis and his mistress Diane de Poitiers; it was here also that Mary Queen of Scots grew up, Louis XIV was born and the deposed James II lived for 12 years. Napoléon III turned the château into the **Musée des Antiquités Nationales**.

Château de Malmaison

Av du Château, 92500 Rueil-Malmaison (01.41.29.05.55/www.chateau-malmaison.fr). RER La Défense then bus 258. **Open** *Apr-Sept* 10am-5pm Mon-Fri; 10am-5.30pm Sat, Sun. *Oct-Mar* 10am-4.30pm Mon, Wed-Fri; 10am-5pm Sat, Sun. **Admission** €5-€7; €3.50 reductions, all Sun; free under-18s, all 1st Sun of mth. PMP. **Credit** AmEx, MC, V.
Napoleon and Josephine's love nest, bought by Josephine in 1799, was the emperor's favourite retreat during the Consulate (1800-03). After their divorce, Napoleon gave the château to his ex, who died here in 1814. The couple redesigned the entrance as a military tent; you can see Napoleon's office, the billiard room and Josephine's tented bedroom. Today, the château is often used for wedding receptions.

★ FREE Mémorial de la France Combattante

Rue du Professeur-Léon-Bernard, 92150 Suresnes (01.41.44.56.34/tour reservations 01.49.74.35.71). Train to Suresnes-Mont-Valérien/RER La Défense then bus 160, 360 or tram 2. **Open** (guided tour only) *Apr-Sept* 1.15pm, 4.30pm Sun. *Oct-Mar* 3pm Sun. By reservation Mon-Sat. **Admission** free.

Sixteen bronze relief sculptures by 16 artists represent France's struggle for liberation – from a Gaullist perspective. Behind an eternal flame, the crypt contains tombs of 16 heroes from 16 French battles in World War II (a 17th is left empty for the last liberation hero). The memorial was built on the site where members of the Resistance were brought from prisons in Paris. A staircase from within the crypt leads visitors inside the curtain wall, then up around the hill to the chapel where prisoners were locked before execution, and down to the Clairière des Fusillés, the clearing where they were shot. The chapel walls were covered in the prisoners' last, desperate graffiti (of which only a small patch remains); it also contains five of the wooden firing posts against which the condemned were tied. More than 1,000 men were shot here (women were deported); no one is known to have escaped. A monument by artist Pascal Convert lists the names of the victims, including Communist politician Gabriel Péri.

Musée des Années 30

Espace Landowski, 28 av André-Morizet, 92100 Boulogne-Billancourt (01.55.18.53.00/www.annees30.com). M° Marcel Sembat. **Open** 11am-6pm Tue-Sun. Closed 2wks Aug. **Admission** (incl Musée-Jardin Paul Landowski) €4.50; €3.50 reductions; free under-16s. **Credit** MC, V.

The Musée des Années 30 shows what a lot of second-rate art was produced in the 1930s, though there are decent modernist sculptures by the Martel brothers, graphic designs, and Juan Gris still lifes and drawings. The highlights are the designs by avant-garde architects Perret, Le Corbusier and Fischer.

Musée des Antiquités Nationales

Château St-Germain, pl Charles-de-Gaulle, 78105 St-Germain-en-Laye (01.39.10.13.00/www.musee-antiquitesnationales.fr). RER St-Germain-en-Laye. **Open** *May-Sept* 10am-6.15pm Mon, Wed-Sun. *Oct-Apr* 9am-5.15pm Mon, Wed-Sun. **Admission** €4.50; €3 reductions, all on Sun; free under-18s, all on 1st Sun of mth. **Credit** *Shop* MC, V.

This awe-inspiring museum traces France's rich archaeological heritage. The redesigned Neolithic galleries feature statue-menhirs, female figures and an ornate tombstone from Cys-la-Commune. Curiosities include the huge antlers from a prehistoric Irish deer and the 18th-century cork models of ancient sites.

Peripheral Vision

How MAC/VAL tries to make modern art accessible to all.

Today, the suburbs play host to a number of mainstream cultural venues, of which the most prominent is undoubtedly the **MAC/VAL** contemporary art museum (*see p149*) in the south-east suburb of Vitry-sur-Seine. MAC/VAL was opened in November 2005, just days after the *banlieue* riots ended, and has since earned itself a fearsome reputation for artistic savvy. The museum's main objective is to make art fun and accessible to people who don't normally visit galleries. To this end it has low admission prices and organises regular 'meet the artist' events.

In fact, unbeknown to most Parisians, the *département* of Val-de-Marne, which encompasses Vitry-sur-Seine, has been actively supporting and buying contemporary art for over 20 years, and MAC/VAL is the fruit of this investment. The museum's permanent collection offers a stunning snapshot of artistic creation in France from 1950 to the present, including installations by Gilles Barbier, Jesús Rafael Soto and Christian Boltanski. Vitry-sur-Seine also ranks third in France in terms of contemporary art installations in public spaces. The most famous of the town's open-air works is Jean Dubuffet's *Chaufferie avec cheminée* ('Boiler with chimney') on place de la Libération.

SIGHTS

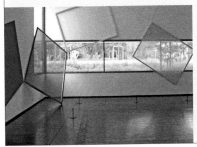

Consume

**Hôtel
Particulier
Montmartre.**
See p167.

Hotels

Boutique bargains mean cheap no longer has to mean nasty.

Paris remains one of the most visited cities in the world: 28 million tourists came here in 2007, a record figure for the city. But as the euro strengthens and people around the world tighten their belts, good-quality, affordable quality accommodation is increasingly of the essence. The longstanding luxury palaces remain popular, of course, at least with travellers on above-average budgets. But the good news is that the city's lower-end hoteliers have considerably bucked up their ideas, and there are now more decent bargain beds in Paris than ever before.

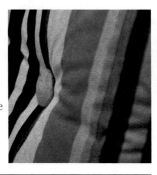

THE LOCAL SCENE

At the top end of the scale, long-established luxury palaces such as the **Crillon**, the **George V** and the **Bristol** are as much a part of Paris's scenery as the Eiffel Tower, and have rates to match. But if your idea of luxury has more to do with intimacy and exclusivity, old-timers like **L'Hôtel** and newcomers **Hôtel Particulier Montmartre** and **Jays Paris** offer guests the same attention and comfort levels as top-end hotels in rather cosier surroundings.

These grand old spots have been joined by a new breed of hotel in recent years, offering style on a shoestring. Take Franck Altruie's chain of boutique hotels, including **Quartier Bercy Square** and **Quartier Bastille**, Le Faubourg; and **Hôtel Amour** in the ninth, where beautiful people bed up on a budget amid artsy photos and cutting-edge decor. And if your wallet won't stretch to a hotel, check out the city's youth hostels, in particular the trendy newcomer **St Christopher's Inn** on the ever-gentrifying Canal de l'Ourcq. The selection in this chapter should provide options for everybody, whatever the budget – even for people who had feared that pitching a tent in the **Camping du bois de Boulogne** (2 allée du Bord-de-l'Eau, 16th, 01.45.24.30.31) would be their only choice.

Hotels are graded according to an official star rating system designed to sort the deluxe from the dumps – but we haven't followed it in this guide, as the ratings merely reflect room size and amenities such as lifts or bars, rather than other important factors such as decor, staff or atmosphere. Instead, we've divided the hotels by area, then listed them in four categories, according to the standard prices (not including seasonal offers or discounts) for one night in a double room with en suite shower/bath. For **Deluxe** hotels, you can expect to pay more than €350; for properties in the **Expensive** bracket, €220-€350; for **Moderate** properties, allow €130-€219; while **Budget** rooms go for less than €130. For **gay hotels**, *see p311*.

Note that all hotels in France charge a room tax (*taxe de séjour*) of around €1 per person per night, although this is sometimes included in the rate. Children under 12 often stay for free when sharing a room with parents (check when booking), and small pets usually cost between €10 and €20 extra per night. Hotels are often booked solid and cost more during the major trade fairs (January, May, September), and it's hard to find a good room during Fashion Weeks (January, March, July and October). At quieter times, hotels can often offer special deals at short notice; phone ahead or check their websites.

About the author

Anna Brooke is the author of four guidebooks to Paris and France, and also writes for publications including the Financial Times.

❶ Red numbers given in this chapter correspond to the location of each hotel as marked on the street maps. *See pp400-407.*

THE ISLANDS

Expensive

★ Hôtel du Jeu de Paume

54 rue St-Louis-en-l'Ile, 4th (01.43.26.14.18/
fax 01.40.46.02.76/www.jeudepaumehotel.com).
M° Pont Marie. **Rates** €275-€350 double.
Credit AmEx, DC, MC, V. **Map** p409 K7 ❶
With a discreet courtyard entrance, 17th-century
beams, private garden and a unique timbered breakfast room that was once a real tennis court built
under Louis XIII, this is a charming and romantic
hotel. These days it is filled with an attractive array
of modern and classical art, and has a coveted billiards table. A dramatic glass lift and catwalks
lead to the rooms and two self-catering apartments,
which are simple and tasteful, the walls hung with
Pierre Frey fabric.
Bar. Gym. Internet (€10/hr, wireless).
Room service.

Paris Yacht

Quai de la Tournelle, 5th (06.88.70.26.36/
www.paris-yacht.com). M° Maubert Mutualité.
Rates (incl breakfast) €300 double. **No credit**
cards. Map p409 K7 ❷
See p174 **Nautical but Nice**.
Internet (free, wireless). TV.

Moderate

Hôtel des Deux-Iles

59 rue St-Louis-en-l'Ile, 4th (01.43.26.13.35/fax
01.43.29.60.25/www.deuxiles-paris-hotel.com).

M° Pont Marie. **Rates** €189 double. **Credit**
AmEx, MC, V. **Map** p409 K7 ❸
This peaceful 17th-century townhouse offers 17
soundproofed, air-conditioned rooms kitted out in
toned down stripes, *toile de Jouy* fabrics and neo colonial-style furniture. Its star feature is a tiny courtyard off the lobby and a vaulted stone breakfast
area. All the rooms and bathrooms were freshened
up in 2007 (fortunately saving the lovely blue earth-
enware tiles on the bathroom walls).
Concierge. Internet (free, wireless). Room
service. TV.
▶ *The equally pleasant Hôtel le Lutèce (65 rue*
St-Louis-en-l'Ile, 01.43.26.23.52, www.paris-
hotel-lutece.com) is run by the same team.

Budget

Hospitel Hôtel Dieu

1 pl du Parvis-Notre-Dame, 4th (01.44.32.01.00/
fax 01.44.32.01.16/www.hotel-hospitel.com).
M° Cité or Hôtel de Ville. **Rates** €120 double.
Credit MC, V. **Map** p408 J7 ❹
If the thought of sleeping in a working hospital
doesn't put you off (half the rooms here are used by
families of the Hôtel Dieu hospital's in-patients and
staff), you can stay in one of 14 recently renovated,
spotless rooms with colourful contemporary decor,
right in the middle of Ile de la Cité in front of Notre-
Dame. A medical smell is present but not strong,
bathrooms are quite large, and you couldn't ask for
a better sightseeing base.
Disabled-adapted rooms. Internet (€4/hr,
wireless). No smoking throughout. Room
service. TV.

Hôtel Ritz. *See p157.*

CONSUME

THE LOUVRE & PALAIS-ROYAL

Deluxe

Hôtel Costes

*239 rue St-Honoré, 1st (01.42.44.50.00/fax 01.42.44.50.01/www.hotelcostes.com). M°
Concorde or Tuileries.* **Rates** €420-€750 double. **Credit** AmEx, DC, MC, V. **Map** p401 G5 ❺
Attitude definitely counts in this temple of notoriety – a place so trendy its website only contains contact details and an on-line boutique of its own *ultra-branché* products, and where innumerable A-listers still gravitate to the low-lit bar after all these years. The Costes boasts one of the best pools in Paris, a sybaritic, Eastern-inspired affair with an underwater music system. Rooms are a modern take on Napoleon III, designed by Jacques Garcia.
Bars (2). Business centre. Concierge. Disabled-adapted rooms. Gym. Internet (free, wireless). No-smoking rooms. Parking (€30). Pool (indoor). Restaurant. Room service. Spa. TV.
▶ *The same management is responsible for the sleek Hôtel Costes K (81 av Kléber, 16th, 01.44.05.75.75), which has a fabulous spa.*

Hôtel de Crillon

10 pl de la Concorde, 8th (01.44.71.15.00/fax 01.44.71.15.02/www.crillon.com). M° Concorde. **Rates** €750-€930 double. **Credit** AmEx, DC, MC, V. **Map** p401 F4 ❻

Le Meurice.

The Crillon lives up to its *palais* reputation with decor strong on marble, mirrors and gold leaf. The Michelin-starred Les Ambassadeurs (*see p190*) has an acclaimed chef, Jean-François Piège, and a brand new kitchen with a glassed-in private dining area for groups of no more than six who wish to dine amid the bustle of the 80-strong kitchen staff. If you have €10,500 to spare, opt for the Presidential Suite (the only one with a view over the American Embassy). The Winter Garden tearoom is a must.
Bar. Business centre. Concierge. Gym. Internet (free, wireless). No-smoking rooms. Parking (free). Restaurants (2). Room service. TV.

Hôtel Ritz

15 pl Vendôme, 1st (01.43.16.30.30/fax 01.43.16.31.78/www.ritzparis.com). M° Concorde or Opéra. **Rates** €730-€830 double. **Credit** AmEx, DC, MC, V. **Map** p401 G4 ❼
Chic hasn't lost its cool at the grande dame of Paris hotels, where each of the 162 bedrooms (of which 56 are suites), from the romantic Frédéric Chopin to the glitzy Impérial, ooze sumptuousness. But then what else can one expect from a hotel that has proffered hospitality to Coco Chanel, the Duke of Windsor, Proust, and Dodi and Di? There are plenty of corners in which to strike a pose or quench a thirst, from Hemingway's elegant cigar bar to the Ancient Greece-themed poolside hangout. *Photo p155.*
Bars (3). Business centre. Concierge. Gym. Internet (€28/day, wireless; €25/day, high speed). No-smoking rooms. Parking (€47). Pool (indoor). Restaurants (2). Room service. Spa. TV.

Hôtel Sofitel le Faubourg

15 rue Boissy-d'Anglas, 8th (01.44.94.14.14/fax 01.44.94.14.28/www.sofitel.com). M° Concorde or Madeleine. **Rates** €425-€530 double. **Credit** AmEx, DC, MC, V. **Map** p401 F4 ❽
This hotel is close to all the major couture boutiques, which is no surprise, as it used to house the *Marie Claire* offices. The rooms have Louis XVI armchairs, large balconies, walk-in wardrobes and Roger & Gallet goodies in the bathrooms; for shopping widowers, there's a small gym and a hammam. It's quiet too: the street has been closed to traffic since 2001 because the American embassy is on the corner.
Bar. Business centre. Concierge. Disabled-adapted rooms). Gym. Internet (€18/day high speed). No-smoking rooms. Parking (€30). Restaurant. Room service. TV.
Other locations Sofitel Arc de Triomphe, 14 rue Beaujon, 8th (01.53.89.50.50); Sofitel Champs-Elysées, 8 rue Jean Goujon, 8th (01.40.74.64.64); Hôtel Scribe, 1 rue Scribe, 9th (01.44.71.24.24).

★ Le Meurice

228 rue de Rivoli, 1st (01.44.58.10.10/fax 01.44.58.10.15/www.lemeurice.com). M° Tuileries. **Rates** €650-€830 double. **Credit** AmEx, DC, MC, V. **Map** p401 G5 ❾

CONSUME

With its extravagant Louis XVI decor, intricate mosaic tiled floors and clever, modish restyling by Philippe Starck, Le Meurice is looking grander than ever. All 160 rooms (kitted out with iPod-ready radio alarms) are done up in distinct historical styles; the Belle Etoile suite on the seventh floor provides 360-degree panoramic views of Paris from its terrace. You can relax in the Winter Garden to the strains of regular jazz performances; for more intensive intervention, head over to the lavishly appointed spa with treatments by Valmont.

Bar. Business centre. Concierge. Disabled-adapted rooms. Gym. Internet (€30/day, wireless). No-smoking rooms. Restaurants (2). Room service. Spa. TV: DVD.

▶ *Don't miss dinner at the hotel's three Michelin-starred restaurant, which has chef Yannick Alléno at the helm; see p187.*

Le Westin
3 rue de Castiglione, 1st (01.44.77.11.11/fax 01.44.77.14.60/www.westin.com/paris). M° Tuileries. **Rates** (incl breakfast) €390-€570 double. **Credit** AmEx, DC, MC, V. **Map** p401 G5 ❿

In the heart of shopping HQ, the Westin mixes belle epoque features with pale limestone walls, beautiful vintage-style furniture (inspired by the 1930s and '40s), a neoclassical fountain and patio. Its sleek modern bedrooms, decked out with top-end gadgets and the award-winning Heavenly Bed, sport balcony views over the Tuileries gardens. The bathrooms are sumptuous, and some have their own balconies. There's an excellent restaurant, Le First, with a sleek, deep purple and pearly grey, boudoir-like interior designed by Jacques Garcia.

Bar. Business centre. Concierge. Disabled-adapted rooms. Gym. Internet (€25/day, wireless). No-smoking rooms. Restaurant. Room service. Spa. TV.

Moderate

★ Hôtel Brighton
218 rue de Rivoli, 1st (01.47.03.61.61/fax 01.42.60.41.78/www.esprit-de-france.com). M° Tuileries. **Rates** €180-€290 double. **Credit** AmEx, DC, MC, V. **Map** p401 G5 ⓫

With several rooms overlooking the Tuileries gardens, the Brighton is great value, so book well ahead for a room with a view. Recently restored, it has a classical atmosphere, from the high ceilings in the rooms to the faux-marble and mosaic downstairs.

Bar. Concierge. Disabled-adapted rooms. Internet (€5/45mins, wireless). No-smoking rooms. Room service. TV.

Hôtel Mansart
5 rue des Capucines, 1st (01.42.61.50.28/fax 01.49.27.97.44/www.esprit-de-france.com). M° Madeleine or Opéra. **Rates** €190-€345 double. **Credit** AmEx, DC, MC, V. **Map** p401 G4 ⓬

This spacious hotel has real style, with a light, roomy lobby decorated with murals inspired by formal gardens. The 57 bedrooms feature pleasant fabrics, antiques and paintings; five of the rooms have an excellent view of place Vendôme.

Bar. Concierge. Internet (€5/45mins, wireless). Room service. TV.

Hôtel des Tuileries
10 rue St-Hyacinthe, 1st (01.42.61.04.17/fax 01.49.27.91.56/www.hotel-des-tuileries.com). M° Tuileries. **Rates** €180-€240 double. **Credit** AmEx, DC, MC, V. **Map** p401 G5 ⓭

The fashion pack adores this 18th-century hotel (the staircase is listed), located in prime shopping territory. Done out with ethnic rugs, a smattering of animal prints, bright art and antique furniture, the 26 comfy bedrooms feel more like they belong in an eccentric family home than a central Paris hotel.

Concierge. Internet (€10/hr, shared terminal or wireless). TV.

Le Relais du Louvre
19 rue des Prêtres St-Germain-l'Auxerrois, 1st (01.40.41.96.42/fax 01.40.41.96.44/ www.relaisdulouvre.com). M° Pont Neuf or Louvre-Rivoli. **Rates** €165-€212 double. **Credit** AmEx, MC, V. **Map** p402 H6 ⓮

The cellar of this characterful hotel, with its antiques and wooden beams, was once used by revolutionaries to print anti-royalist literature. It also inspired Puccini's Café Momus in *La Bohème*. The rooms are decorated in floral fabrics, and the front ones look out on to St-Germain-l'Auxerrois church. There's also a self-contained apartment for four people.

Concierge. Internet (free). No-smoking rooms. TV.

Budget

Hotel Lion d'Or
5 rue de la Sourdière, 1st (01.42.60.79.04/fax 01.42.60.09.14/www.hotel-louvre-paris.com). M° Tuileries. **Rates** €95-€115 double. **Credit** MC, V. **Map** p401 G5 ⓯

Simple, brightly coloured rooms and fully furnished studios (with kitchenettes) that can sleep up to five make the Golden Lion a popular choice for families and groups of friends. There's also a handy internet café next door.

Safety box (reception). TV (some rooms).

OPERA TO LES HALLES
Deluxe

Hôtel Ambassador
16 bd Haussmann, 9th (01.44.83.40.40/ fax 01.42.46.19.84/www.hotelambassador-paris.com). M° Chaussée d'Antin or Richelieu Drouot. **Rates** €260-€620 double. **Credit** AmEx, DC, MC, V. **Map** p401 H4 ⓰

Shipshape and Bristol Fashion

Cake and couture at Hôtel le Bristol.

Paris's image as the epicentre of luxury fashion is absolutely spot on. Timeless brands like Chanel, Yves Saint Laurent and Dior were born here, their sparkling boutiques still dotting the city's streets like pearls on a very expensive necklace. Paris's fashion shows are also some of the most prominent in the world, and every year designers and their entourages fly in from across the globe for a week of fashion fury and media hype.

But unlike the boutiques – where anyone can shop if they have the funds – it is not easy to catch a fashion show unless you know the dates and have the right connections. Which is where the **Hôtel le Bristol** (*see p163*) steps in: set on the exclusive rue du Faubourg St-Honoré, near luxury boutiques such as Christian Lacroix, Azzaro, Salvatore Ferragamo, Givenchy and Dolce & Gabbana, and with a loyal following of fashionistas and millionaires (usually both rolled into one), the hotel has teamed up with its haute couture neighbours to offer Thés à la Mode – a lip-smacking afternoon tea (most Saturdays 3.30-5pm) accompanied by a top-end fashion show for just €50. Guests are fed tea, cakes (the Bristol's head *pâtissier* Laurent Jeannin rises to the challenge with a different dessert each week, inspired by the designer on

show), gourmet sandwiches and a parade of models dressed in new collections by brands such as Céline, Givenchy, Ungaro, Versace and Christian Lacroix.

The whole show is satisfyingly sophisticated and surprisingly unpretentious. It's also a fine opportunity to check out the Bristol's new olfactive identity. As if a catwalk in the bar weren't quite enough, perfume designer Jean-Michel Duriez (from the Maison Jean Patou perfumery) has created a scent specifically for the hotel's communal areas (candles can also be bought for €30). It's a pleasant fragrance – the head note is light and floral, inspired by the hotel's famous garden (one of the largest hotel gardens in Paris); the base note is woody (mainly sandalwood), reflecting the hotel's history, traditional decor and antiques.

Keep an eye out for the Bristol's new wing in autumn 2009. The hotel purchased an adjacent building in 2007 (on the corner of avenue Matignon and rue du Faubourg St-Honoré), and 22 new rooms and four suites will be unveiled, all with views of the Eiffel Tower. The extension will also increase the size of the bar area – great news for the fashion shows, which, as word gets around, will undoubtedly attract an ever-increasing number of aficionados.

CONSUME

If you're looking for some vintage style but can't face another gilded Louis XIV interior, check into this historic, Haussmann-era hotel, which sets traditional furniture against contemporary decor in each of the 294 bedrooms. The low-lit Lindbergh Bar is named after the pilot who dropped in for a celebratory drink and cigar after his solo transatlantic flight in 1927. The hotel is ideally situated for shopping at the *grands magasins*.
Bar. Business centre. Concierge. Disabled-adapted rooms. Gym. Internet (€7/30mins, shared terminal; free, wireless). No-smoking rooms. Restaurant. Room service. TV.

Hôtel Concorde St-Lazare
108 rue St-Lazare, 8th (01.40.08.44.44/fax 01.42.93.01.20/www.concordestlazare-paris. com). M° St-Lazare. **Rates** €225-€500 double. **Credit** AmEx, DC, MC, V. **Map** p401 G3 **⑰**
Guests here are cocooned in soundproofed luxury. The 19th-century Eiffel-inspired lobby with jewel-encrusted pink granite columns is a historic landmark: the high ceilings, walls and sculptures look much as they have for over a century. Rooms are spacious, with double entrance doors and exclusive Annick Goutal toiletries; the belle époque brasserie, Café Terminus, and sexy Golden Black Bar were designed by Sonia Rykiel. Guests have access to a nearby fitness centre.
Bar. Business centre. Concierge. Internet (€10/day, shared terminal; free, wireless). No-smoking rooms. Parking (€25). Restaurant. Room service. TV.

Hôtel Westminster
13 rue de la Paix, 2nd (01.42.61.57.46/fax 01.42.60.30.66/www.warwickwestminsteropera. com). M° Opéra/RER Auber. **Rates** €350-€630 double. **Credit** AmEx, DC, MC, V. **Map** p401 G4 **⑱**
This luxury hotel near place Vendôme has more than a touch of British warmth about it, no doubt owing to the influence of its favourite 19th-century guest, the Duke of Westminster (after whom the hotel was named; the current Duke reportedly still stays here). The hotel fitness centre has a top-floor location, with a beautiful tiled steam room and views over the city, and the cosy bar features deep leather chairs, a fireplace and live jazz at weekends.
Bar. Concierge. Gym. Internet (€20/day, high speed or wireless). No-smoking rooms. Parking (€25). Restaurant. Room service. Spa. TV.

★ InterContinental Paris Le Grand
2 rue Scribe, 9th (01.40.07.32.32/fax 01.42.66.12.51/www.paris.intercontinental.com). M° Opéra. **Rates** €390-€640 double. **Credit** AmEx, DC, MC, V. **Map** p401 G4 **⑲**
This 1862 hotel is the chain's European flagship – but, given its sheer size, perhaps 'mother ship' would be more appropriate: this landmark establishment occupies the entire block (three wings, almost 500 rooms) next to the opera house; some 80 of the honey-coloured rooms overlook the Palais Garnier. The space under the vast *verrière* is one of the best oases in town, and the hotel's restaurant and elegant

Hôtel Amour. See p162.

CONSUME

coffeehouse, the Café de la Paix (*see p221*), poached its chef, Laurent Delarbre, from the Ritz. For a truly relaxing daytime break, head to the I-Spa for one of its seawater treatments.

Bar. Business centre. Concierge. Gym. Internet (€24/day, high speed; free, wireless). No-smoking rooms. Parking (€40). Restaurants (2). Room service. Spa. TV.

Moderate

★ Hôtel Amour

*8 rue Navarin, 9th (01.48.78.31.80/fax 01.48.74.14.09/www.hotelamour.com).
M° St-Georges.* **Rates** €130-€200 double.
Credit AmEx, MC, V. **Map** p402 H2 ❷⓪

Opened back in 2006, this boutique hotel is a real hit with the in crowd. Each of the 20 rooms is unique, decorated on the theme of love or eroticism by a coterie of contemporary artists and designers such as Marc Newson, M&M, Stak, Pierre Le Tan and Sophie Calle. Seven of the rooms contain artists' installations, and two others have their own private bar and a large terrace on which to hold your own party. The late-night brasserie has a coveted outdoor garden, and the crowd is young, beautiful and loves to entertain. *Photo p161.*

Bar. Internet (free, wireless). No-smoking rooms only. Restaurant.

Hôtel Arvor Saint Georges

8 rue Laferrière, 9th (01.48.78.60.92/fax 01.48.78.16.52/www.arvor-hotel-paris.com).

M° St-Georges. **Rates** €140-€170 double.
Credit AmEx, DC, MC, V. **Map** p402 H2 ❷①

Don't be put off by the slightly austere façade; the owner intended it this way to contrast with the homely atmosphere that reigns inside. Although you're right in the middle of the city, the hotel has the relaxing feel of a quiet country house. The decor is delicate and uncluttered, and most of the 30 spacious rooms, including six suites, overlook the rooftops (no.503 has the best view of the Eiffel Tower). The small terrace is the ideal spot to take a break from the Paris buzz.

Internet (free, wireless). No-smoking rooms. TV.

★ Hôtel Britannique

*20 av Victoria, 1st (01.42.33.74.59/fax 01.42.33.82.65/www.hotel-britannique.fr).
M° Châtelet, RER Châtelet-les-Halles.* **Rates** €185-€215 double. **Credit** AmEx, MC, V.
Map p408 J6 ❷②

Smiling staff in stripy waistcoats welcome you to this adorable hotel, where guest areas and rooms are cocooned in thick drapes, luscious carpets and a mishmash of British colonial-style furniture that make you feel like you've stepped into an English country cottage. Enjoy deeply delicious pastries in the warm, rustic breakfast room, or book a top floor *chambre* and eat them on your plant-filled balcony – a rare oasis of greenery for such a central and reasonably priced hotel.

Bar. Concierge. Internet (high speed & wireless). No-smoking rooms. TV.

Hôtel Particulier Montmartre. *See p167.*

Hôtel Langlois

63 rue St-Lazare, 9th (01.48.74.78.24/fax 01.49.95.04.43/www.hotel-langlois.com). M° Trinité. **Rates** €140-€150 double. **Credit** AmEx, DC, MC, V. **Map** p401 H3 ㉓

Built as a bank in 1870, this belle époque building became the Hôtel des Croisés in 1896. In 2001, after featuring in the Jonathan Demme film *Charade*, it changed its name to Hôtel Langlois in honour of the founder of the Cinémathèque Française. Its 27 spacious, air-conditioned bedrooms are decorated in art nouveau style; the larger ones have delightful hidden bathrooms.

Internet (free, wireless). Room service. TV.

Résidence Hôtel des Trois Poussins

15 rue Clauzel, 9th (01.53.32.81.81/fax 01.53.32.81.82/www.les3poussins.com). M° St-Georges. **Rates** €154-€189 double; €154-€237 studio with kitchenette. **Credit** AmEx, DC, MC, V. **Map** p401 H2 ㉔

Just off the beaten track in a pleasant *quartier*, and within walking distance (uphill) of Montmartre, the Résidence offers hotel accommodation in the traditional manner, and also has some rare self-catering studios for people who'd rather cook than eat out. Now completely redone, the decor is pleasantly traditional, with a preference for yellow.

Concierge. Disabled-adapted room. Internet (€4/hr, wireless). Room service (nighttime only). TV.

Budget

Hôtel Chopin

10 bd Montmartre or 46 passage Jouffroy, 9th (01.47.70.58.10/fax 01.42.47.00.70/www.hotel-chopin.com). M° Grands Boulevards. **Rates** €88-€102 double. **Credit** MC, V. **Map** p402 J4 ㉕

Handsomely set in a historic, glass-roofed arcade next door to the Grévin musuem, the Chopin's original 1846 façade adds to its old-fashioned appeal. The 36 rooms are quiet and functional, done out in either salmon and green or blue.

TV.

Hôtel du Cygne

3 rue du Cygne, 1st (01.42.60.14.16/fax 01.42.21.37.02/www.hotelducygne.fr). M° Etienne Marcel/RER Châtelet Les Halles. **Rates** €110-€145 double. **Credit** MC, V. **Map** p402 J5 ㉖

This traditional hotel in a 17th-century building has 20 compact, cosy and simple rooms embellished with touches such as antiques and home-made furnishings. It's on a pedestrian street in the bustling Les Halles district, so light sleepers might prefer the rooms overlooking the courtyard. The cheapest rooms have shared bathrooms.

Internet. TV.

Hôtel Madeleine Opéra

12 rue Greffulhe, 8th (01.47.42.26.26/fax 01.47.42.89.76/www.hotel-madeleine-opera.com). M° Havre-Caumartin or Madeleine. **Rates** €90-€95 double. **Credit** MC, V. **Map** p401 G4 ㉗

This bargain hotel is located just north of the Eglise de la Madeleine, in the heart of the city's theatre and *grands magasins* districts. Its sunny lobby sits behind a 200-year-old façade that was once a shopfront. The 23 rooms are perhaps a touch basic, but still nice enough, and breakfast is brought to your room every morning.

Internet (€5/45mins, wireless). Room service (morning). TV.

CHAMPS-ELYSEES & WESTERN PARIS

Deluxe

★ Four Seasons George V

31 av George V, 8th (01.49.52.70.00/fax 01.49.52.70.10/www.fourseasons.com/paris). M° Alma Marceau or George V. **Rates** €695-€1,090 double. **Credit** AmEx, DC, MC, V. **Map** p400 D4 ㉘

There's no denying that the George V is serious about luxury: chandeliers, marble and tapestries; over-attentive staff; glorious flower arrangements; divine bathrooms; and ludicrously comfortable beds in some of the largest rooms in all of Paris. The Versailles-inspired spa includes whirlpools, saunas and a menu of treatments for an unabashedly metrosexual clientele; non-guests can now reserve appointments. It's worth every euro.

Bar. Business centre. Concierge. Disabled-adapted rooms. Gym. Internet (€22/24hrs, high speed). No-smoking rooms. Parking (€40). Pool (indoor). Restaurants (2). Room service. Spa. TV.

Hôtel le A

4 rue d'Artois, 8th (01.42.56.99.99/fax 01.42.56.99.90/www.hotel-le-a.com). M° Franklin D. Roosevelt or St-Philippe-du-Roule. **Rates** €355-€444 double. **Credit** AmEx, DC, MC, V. **Map** p401 E4 ㉙

The black-and-white decor of this designer boutique hotel provides a fine backdrop for the models, artists and media types hanging out in the lounge bar area; the only splashes of colour come from the graffiti-like artworks by conceptual artist Fabrice Hybert. The 26 rooms all have granite bathrooms, and the starched white furniture slip covers, changed after each guest, make the smallish spaces seem larger than they are. The dimmer switches are a nice touch – as are the lift lights changing colour at each floor.

Bar. Concierge. Disabled-adapted rooms. Internet (€5/45mins, wireless). No-smoking rooms. Room service. TV.

CONSUME

★ Hotel le Bristol

112 rue du Fbg-St-Honoré, 8th (01.53.43.43.00/
fax 01.53.43.43.01/www.hotel-bristol.com).
Mº Champs-Elysées Clemenceau. **Rates** €730-
€830 double. **Credit** AmEx, DC, MC, V.
Map p401 E4 ⓾
See p159 **Shipshape and Bristol Fashion**.
Bar. Business centre. Concierge. Disabled-adapted
rooms. Gym. Internet (high speed & wireless).
No-smoking rooms. Parking (free). Pool (indoor).
Restaurant. Room service. Spa. TV.

Hôtel Daniel

8 rue Frédéric-Bastiat, 8th (01.42.56.17.00/
fax 01.42.56.17.01/www.hoteldanielparis.com).
Mº Franklin D. Roosevelt or St-Philippe-du-Roule.
Rates €420-€490 double. **Credit** AmEx, DC,
MC, V. **Map** p401 E4 ⓛ
A romantic hideaway close to the monoliths of the
Champs-Elysées, the city's new Relais & Châteaux
is decorated in chinoiserie and a palette of rich
colours, with 26 rooms cosily appointed in *toile de
Jouy* and an intricately hand-painted restaurant that
feels like a courtyard. At about €50 a head, the gastronomic restaurant Le Lounge, run by chef Denis
Fetisson, is a good deal for this neighbourhood; the
bar menu is served at all hours.
Bar. Concierge. Disabled-adapted rooms. Internet
(free, wireless). No-smoking rooms. Parking
(€25). Restaurant. Room service. TV.

Hôtel Fouquet's Barrière

46 av George V, 8th (01.40.69.60.00/fax
01.40.69.60.05/www.fouquetsbarriere.com).
Mº George V. **Rates** €690-€910 double.
Credit AmEx, DC, MC, V. **Map** p400 D4 ⓜ
This grandiose five-star is built around the famous
fin-de-siècle brasserie Le Fouquet's. Five buildings
form the hotel complex, housing 107 rooms (including 40 suites), upmarket restaurant Le Diane, the
Sparis spa, indoor pool and a rooftop terrace for
hire. Jacques Garcia, of Hôtel Costes and Westin
fame, was responsible for the interior design, which
retains the Empire style of the exterior while incorporating luxurious modern touches inside – flat-
screen TVs and mist-free mirrors in the marble
bathrooms. And, of course, it's unbeatable for location – right at the junction of avenue George V and
the Champs-Elysées.
Bar. Business centre. Concierge. Disabled-adapted
rooms. Gym. Internet (free, high speed &
wireless). No-smoking rooms. Parking (€45). Pool
(indoor). Restaurants (2). Room service. Spa. TV.

Hôtel Plaza Athénée

25 av Montaigne, 8th (01.53.67.66.67/fax
01.53.67.66.66/www.plaza-athenee-paris.com).
Mº Alma Marceau. **Rates** €740-€945 double.
Credit AmEx, DC, MC, V. **Map** p400 D5 ⓝ
This palace is ideally placed for power shopping at
Chanel, Louis Vuitton, Dior and other avenue

Montaigne boutiques. Material girls and boys will
enjoy the high-tech room amenities such as remote-
controlled air con, internet and video-game access
on the TV via infrared keyboard, and mini hi-fi.
Bar. Business centre. Concierge. Disabled-adapted
rooms. Gym. Internet (€15/hr, high speed &
wireless). No-smoking rooms. Parking (€25).
Restaurants (2; 4 in summer). Room service. TV.
▶ *Make time for a drink in the Bar du Plaza,*
a cocktail bunny's most outré fantasy, with
flattering lighting, high chairs for maximum
leg-crossing opportunities and ridiculous drinks.

Hôtel de Sers

41 av Pierre-1er-de-Serbie, 8th (01.53.23.75.75/
fax 01.53.23.75.76/www.hoteldesers.com).
Mº Alma Marceau or George V. **Rates** €480-
€650 double. **Credit** AmEx, DC, MC, V.
Map p400 D4 ⓞ
Behind its stately 19th-century façade, the Hôtel de
Sers calls itself a baby palace, displaying an ambitious mix of minimalist contemporary furnishings
(often in deep reds and mauves, nothing too austere),
with a few pop art touches. Original architectural
details, such as the grand staircase and reception,
complete the picture. The large top floor apartment
affords dreamy views over Paris's rooftops.
Bar. Concierge. Disabled-adapted rooms.
Gym. Internet (free, high speed & wireless).
No-smoking rooms. Parking (€50). Restaurant.
Room service. TV.

★ Hôtel de la Trémoille

14 rue de la Trémoille, 8th (01.56.52.14.00/
fax 01.40.70.01.08/www.hotel-tremoille.com).
Mº Alma-Marceau. **Rates** €475-€620 double.
Credit AmEx, DC, MC, V. **Map** p400 D4 ⓟ
New manager Olivier Lordonnois has pushed the
Trémoille to another level. The recent opening of a
new restaurant-bar-lounge and improved spa and
fitness facilities have made this four-star deluxe a
serious competitor to the other palaces nearby. The
93 flawless rooms are decorated to evoke no fewer
than 31 different 'atmospheres', and the bathrooms
are filled with Molton Brown products. A unique feature is the 'hatch', which enables room service to
deliver your meal without disturbing you.
Bar. Business centre. Concierge. Disabled-
adapted rooms. Gym. Internet (free, high speed).
No-smoking rooms. Restaurant. Room service.
Spa. TV.

Hôtel de Vigny

9-11 rue Balzac, 8th (01.42.99.80.80/fax
01.42.99.80.40/www.hoteldevigny.com).
Mº George V. **Rates** €440-€520 double.
Credit AmEx, DC, MC, V. **Map** p400 D3 ⓠ
One of only two Relais & Châteaux in the city,
this hotel has the feel of a private, plush townhouse. Although it's just off the Champs-Elysées,
the Vigny pulls in a discerning, low-key clientele.

CONSUME

Its 37 rooms and suites are decorated in tasteful stripes or florals, with marble bathrooms. Enjoy dinner in the art deco Baretto restaurant, or a cup of tea in the library.
Bar. Concierge. Internet (€7/hr, high speed). No-smoking rooms. Parking (€23). Restaurant. Room service. TV.

★ Jays Paris

6 rue Copernic, 16th (01.47.04.16.16/fax 01.47.04.16.17/www.jays-paris.com). M° Kléber or Victor Hugo. **Rates** €420-€590 suite. **Credit** MC, V. **Map** p400 C4 ③⑦
Introducing a new concept on the Paris hotel scene, Jays is a luxurious *boutique-apart* hotel that trades on a clever blend of antique furniture, modern design and high-tech equipment. The marble staircase, lit entirely by natural light filtered through the glass atrium overhead, gives an instant feeling of grandeur, and leads to five suites, each with a fully equipped kitchenette. A cosy salon is available to welcome in-house guests and their visitors.
Bar. Concierge. Internet (free, high speed & wireless). No smoking throughout. Parking (€15). Room service. TV.

Pershing Hall

49 rue Pierre-Charron, 8th (01.58.36.58.00/ fax 01.58.36.58.01/www.pershinghall.com). M° George V. **Rates** €450-€540 double. **Credit** AmEx, DC, MC, V. **Map** p400 D4 ③⑧
The refreshing mix of 19th-century grandeur and contemporary comfort makes Pershing Hall feel quite large, but this luxury establishment is really a cleverly disguised boutique hotel with just 26 rooms. Fashionable locals frequent the stylish bar and restaurant terrace. Designed by Andrée Putman, the neat bedrooms emphasise natural materials, with stained grey oak floors and fine mosaic-tiled bathrooms with geometric styling and copious towels.
Bar. Concierge. Gym. Internet (free, high speed; pay as you go, wireless). No-smoking rooms. Restaurant. Room service. Spa. TV.

Le Sezz

6 av Frémiet, 16th (01.56.75.26.26/fax 01.56. 75.26.16/www.hotelsezz.com). M° Passy. **Rates** €330-€460 double. **Credit** AmEx, DC, MC, V. **Map** p404 B6 ③⑨
Le Sezz opened its doors in 2005 with 27 sleek, luxurious rooms and suites – the work of acclaimed French furniture designer Christophe Pillet. The understated decor represents a refreshingly modern take on luxury, with black parquet flooring, rough-hewn stone walls and bathrooms partitioned off with sweeping glass façades. The bar and public areas are equally sleek and chic.
Bar. Concierge. Internet (free wireless). No-smoking rooms. Parking (€20). Room service. Spa. TV.

Expensive

Hôtel Keppler

10 rue Keppler, 16th (01.47.20.65.05/fax 01.47.23.02.29/www.hotelkeppler.com). M° Georges V or M°/RER Charles-de-Gaulle Etoile. **Rates** €300-€490 double. **Credit** AmEx, DC, MC, V. **Map** p400 C4 ④⓪
This newly renovated boutique is a family-run treasure, decorated with striped wallpaper, funky mirrors, animal prints and various knick-knacks. None of the 39 rooms is huge, but all are cleverly thought through, so that lack of space is never an issue and the whole experience is pleasantly cosy. The top floor suites have their own (large) balcony – perfect for an alfresco breakfast or aperitif – and views over Paris's rooftops towards the Eiffel Tower.
Bar. Concierge. Internet (wireless). Gym. No-smoking rooms. Room service. Sauna. TV.

Hôtel Pergolèse

3 rue Pergolèse, 16th (01.53.64.04.04/fax 01.53.64.04.40/www.hotelpergolese.com). M° Argentine. **Rates** €220-€672 double. **Credit** AmEx, DC, MC, V. **Map** p400 B3 ④①
The Pergolèse was one of the first designer boutique hotels in town, but still looks contemporary a decade or so after being kitted out by Rena Dumas-Hermès with art deco-style furniture by Philippe Starck and rugs by Hilton McConnico. Rooms feature pale wood details and cool, white-tiled bathrooms.
Bar. Concierge. Internet (pay as you go, wireless). No-smoking rooms. Room service. TV.

★ Hôtel Regent's Garden

6 rue Pierre-Demours, 17th (01.45.74.07.30/fax 01.40.55.01.42/www.hotel-paris-garden.com). M° Charles de Gaulle Etoile or Ternes. **Rates** €190-€590 double. **Credit** AmEx, DC, MC, V. **Map** p400 C2 ④②
This elegant hotel – built for Napoleon III's physician – features appropriately Second Empire high ceilings and plush upholstery, and a lounge overlooking a lovely walled patio. There are 39 large bedrooms, some with gilt mirrors and fireplaces. It's an oasis of calm ten minutes from the Champs-Elysées, and the first hotel in Paris to receive an Ecolabel, for its recycling and energy- and water-saving efforts.
Concierge. Internet (€5/hr, shared terminal; free, wireless). No-smoking rooms. Parking (€14). Room service (daytime only). TV.

Hôtel Square

3 rue de Boulainvilliers, 16th (01.44.14.91.90/ fax 01.44.14.91.99/www.hotelsquare.com). M° Passy/RER Avenue du Pdt Kennedy. **Rates** €300-€380 double. **Credit** AmEx, DC, MC, V. **Map** p404 A7 ④③
Located in the upmarket 16th, this courageously modern hotel has a dramatic yet welcoming interior, and attentive service that comes from having to

look after only 22 rooms. They're decorated in amber, brick or slate colours, with exotic woods, quality fabrics and bathrooms seemingly cut from one huge chunk of Carrara marble. View the exhibitions in the atrium gallery or mingle with the media types at the hip Zebra Square restaurant and DJ bar. *Bar. Concierge. Disabled-adapted rooms. Internet (free, wireless). No-smoking rooms. Parking (€25). Restaurant. Room service. TV.*

Moderate

Hôtel Elysées Ceramic

34 av de Wagram, 8th (01.42.27.20.30/fax 01.46.22.95.83/www.elysees-ceramic.com). M° Charles de Gaulle Etoile. **Rates** €220 double. **Credit** AmEx, DC, MC, V. **Map** p400 D3
Situated between the Arc de Triomphe and place des Ternes, this comfortable hotel has one of Paris's finest art nouveau ceramic façades dating from 1904; inside, the theme continues with a ceramic cornice around the reception. All 57 rooms have been renovated in sophisticated chocolate or pewter tones with modern, art nouveau-inspired wallpaper and light fixtures. Outside is a terrace garden perfect for taking afternoon tea or evening cocktails. *Bar. Concierge. Internet (€10/hr, shared terminal; €8/hr, wireless). Room service (breakfast only). TV.*

MONTMARTRE & PIGALLE

Deluxe

★ Hôtel Particulier Montmartre

23 av Junot, 18th (01.42.58.00.87/fax 01.42. 58.00.87/www.hotel-particulier-montmartre.com). M° Lamarck Caulaincourt. **Rates** €400-€600 suite. **Credit** MC, V. **Map** p401 H1
Visitors lucky (and wealthy) enough to manage to book a suite at the Hôtel Particulier Montmartre will find themselves in one of the city's hidden gems. Nestled in a quiet passage off rue Lepic, in the heart of Montmartre and opposite a mysterious rock known as the *Rocher de la Sorcière* (witch's rock), this sumptuous *Directoire*-style house is dedicated to art, with each of the five luxurious suites personalised by an avant-garde artist. The private garden conceived by Louis Bénech (famous for the Tuileries renovation) adds the finishing touch to this charming hideaway. *Photo p162.*
Concierge. Internet (free, wireless). No-smoking rooms. Room service. TV.

Expensive

Kube Rooms & Bar

1-5 passage Ruelle, 18th (01.42.05.20.00/fax 01.42.05.21.01/www.kubehotel.com). M° La Chapelle. **Rates** €300-€400 double. **Credit** AmEx, DC, MC, V. **Map** p402 K1

Hôtel Eldorado. *See p169.*

CONSUME

The younger sister of the Murano Urban Resort (*see p169*), Kube is a more hip and affordable design hotel. Like the Murano, it sits behind an unremarkable façade in an unlikely neighbourhood, the ethnically diverse Goutte d'Or. The Ice Kube bar serves vodka in glasses that, like the bar itself, are carved from ice. Also on the menu are 'apérifood' and 'snackubes' by Pierre Auge. Access to the 41 rooms is by fingerprint identification technology.
Bars (2). Concierge. Disabled-adapted rooms. Gym. Internet (free, wireless). No-smoking rooms. Parking (€30). Restaurant. Room service. TV.

Terrass Hotel

12-14 rue Joseph-de-Maistre, 18th (01.46.06.72.85/fax 01.44.92.34.30/www.terrass-hotel.com). M° Place de Clichy. **Rates** €270-€345 double. **Credit** AmEx, DC, MC, V. **Map** p401 H1 ㊼
There's nothing spectacular about this classic hotel, but for people willing to pay top euro for the best views in town, it fits the bill. Ask for room 704 and you can lie in the bath and look at the Eiffel Tower (and people up the Eiffel Tower can – in theory – see you in the bath). Julien Rocheteau, trained by Ducasse, is at the helm of gastronomic restaurant Diapason; in fine weather, opt for a table on the seventh-floor terrace, open from June to September.
Bar. Concierge. Disabled-adapted rooms. Internet (€3/hr, shared terminal; free, wireless). No-smoking rooms. Restaurant. Room service. TV.

Moderate

Hôtel Royal Fromentin

11 rue Fromentin, 9th (01.48.74.85.93/fax 01.42.81.02.33/www.hotelroyalfromentin.com). M° Blanche or Pigalle. **Rates** €159 double. **Credit** AmEx, DC, MC, V. **Map** p401 H2 ㊽
Wood panelling, art deco windows and a vintage glass lift echo the hotel's origins as a 1930s cabaret hall; its theatrical feel attracted Blondie and Nirvana. It's just down the road from the Moulin Rouge, and many of its 47 rooms overlook Sacré-Coeur. Rooms have been renovated in French style, with bright fabrics and an old-fashioned feel.
Bar. Concierge. Internet (free, shared terminal & wireless). No-smoking rooms. TV.

Timhotel Montmartre

11 rue Ravignan, 18th (01.42.55.74.79/fax 01.42.55.71.01/www.timhotel.fr). M° Abbesses or Pigalle. **Rates** €130-€160 double. **Credit** AmEx, DC, MC, V. **Map** p401 H1 ㊾
The location adjacent to picturesque place Emile-Goudeau makes this one of the most popular hotels in the Timhotel chain. It has 59 rooms, comfortable without being plush; try to bag one on the fourth or fifth floor for stunning views over Montmartre. Special offers are often available at quieter times of the year; ring for details.
Internet (€7/hr, wireless). No-smoking rooms. TV.

Budget

Hôtel des Arts

5 rue Tholozé, 18th (01.46.06.30.52/fax 01.46.06.10.83/www.arts-hotel-paris.com). M° Abbesses or Blanche. **Rates** €85-€165 double. **Credit** MC, V. **Map** p401 H1 ㊿
The wagging tail of Caramel the black labrador welcomes guests to this Montmartre gem, pleasantly decorated in oriental rugs, wooden bookcases and Provençal-style furniture. Rooms are simple but inviting, some affording views of the hidden roof gardens and windmills of the *Butte*. Art by local artists is displayed in the basement breakfast room.
Bar. Concierge. Internet (wireless).

Hôtel Eldorado

18 rue des Dames, 17th (01.45.22.35.21/fax 01.43.87.25.97/www.eldoradohotel.fr). M° Place de Clichy. **Rates** €50-€70 double. **Credit** AmEx, DC, MC, V. **Map** p401 G1 (51)
This eccentric hotel is decorated with flea market finds. The Eldorado's winning features include a wine bar, one of the best garden patios in town and a loyal fashionista following. The cheapest rooms have shared bathrooms and toilets. *Photo p167.*
Bar. Internet (free, wireless). Restaurant.

Hôtel Ermitage

24 rue Lamarck, 18th (01.42.64.79.22/fax 01.42.64.10.33/www.ermitagesacrecoeur.fr). M° Lamarck Caulaincourt. **Rates** (incl breakfast) €94 double. **No credit cards. Map** p402 J1 (52)
This 12-room townhouse hotel stands on the calm, non-touristy north side of Montmartre, only five minutes from Sacré-Coeur. Rooms are large and endearingly overdecorated, with bold floral wallpaper; those higher up have fine views.
No-smoking rooms. Parking (€15). Room service (morning only).

BEAUBOURG & THE MARAIS

Deluxe

★ Murano Urban Resort

13 bd du Temple, 3rd (01.42.71.20.00/fax 01.42.71.21.01/www.muranoresort.com). M° Filles du Calvaire or Oberkampf. **Rates** €350-€650 double. **Credit** AmEx, DC, MC, V. **Map** p409 L5 (53)
Behind this unremarkable façade is a super cool and supremely luxurious hotel, popular with the fashion set for its slick lounge-style design, excellent restaurant and high-tech flourishes – including coloured light co-ordinators that enable you to change the mood of your room at the touch of a button. The handsome bar has a mind-boggling 140 varieties of vodka to sample, which can bring the op art fabrics in the lift to life and make the fingerprint access to

CONSUME

the hotel's 43 rooms and nine suites (two of which feature private pools) a late-night godsend.
Bar. Concierge. Gym. Internet (free, wireless). No-smoking rooms. Parking (€35). Restaurant. Room service. TV.

Expensive

Hôtel Bourg Tibourg
19 rue du Bourg-Tibourg, 4th (01.42.78.47.39/ fax 01.40.29.07.00/www.hotelbourgtibourg.com). Mº Hôtel de Ville. **Rates** €230-€260 double. **Credit** AmEx, DC, MC, V. **Map** p409 K6 ⑤④
The Bourg Tibourg has the same owners as Hôtel Costes (*see p157*) and the same interior decorator – but don't expect this jewel box of a boutique hotel to look like a miniature replica. Aside from its enviable location in the heart of the Marais and its fashion-pack fans, here it's all about Jacques Garcia's neo-Gothic-cum-Byzantine decor – impressive and imaginative. Exotic, scented candles, mosaic-tiled bathrooms and luxurious fabrics in rich colours create the perfect escape from the outside world. There's no restaurant or lounge – posing is done in the neighbourhood bars.
Concierge. Disabled-adapted rooms. Internet (free, wireless). Room service. TV.

★ Hôtel du Petit Moulin
29-31 rue de Poitou, 3rd (01.42.74.10.10/ fax 01.42.74.10.97/www.hoteldupetitmoulin. com). Mº St-Sébastien Froissart. **Rates** €190-€350 suite. **Credit** AmEx, DC, MC, V. **Map** p409 L5 ⑤⑤

Within striking distance of the Musée Picasso and the hip shops situated on and around rue Charlot, this listed, turn-of-the-century façade masks what was once the oldest *boulangerie* in Paris, lovingly restored as a boutique hotel by Nadia Murano and Denis Nourry. The couple recruited no lesser figure than fashion designer Christian Lacroix for the decor, and the result is a riot of colour, trompe l'oeil effects and a savvy mix of old and new. Each of its 17 exquisitely appointed rooms is unique, and the walls in rooms 202, 204 and 205 feature swirling, extravagant drawings and scribbles taken from Lacroix's sketchbook.
Bar. Concierge. Internet (€5/45mins, wireless). Parking (free). Room service. TV.

Les Jardins du Marais
74 rue Amelot, 11th (01.40.21.20.00/fax 01.47.00.82.40/www.homeplazza.com). Mº Bastille. **Rates** €224-€455 double. **Credit** AmEx, DC, MC, V. **Map** p409 L5 ⑤⑥
The centrepiece of this ultra-swish hotel is a vast courtyard, filled with tables, potted plants and lampposts that wouldn't look out of place in Narnia. The decor inside is smart and modern; the lobby looks tastefully trendy in its steely black and white marble, with purple furnishings and chairs by Philippe Starck. Rooms are less daring, with traditional fabrics and furniture.
Bar. Concierge. Disabled-adapted facilities. Gym. Internet (free wireless). No-smoking rooms. Restaurant. Room service. TV.
► *The in-house restaurant is a favourite with the local media crowd.*

L'Hôtel. *See p175.*

CONSUME

Moderate

★ Hôtel de la Bretonnerie

*22 rue Ste-Croix-de-la-Bretonnerie, 4th
(01.48.87.77.63/fax 01.42.77.26.78/www.
bretonnerie.com). M° Hôtel de Ville.* **Rates** €125-
€160 double. **Credit** MC, V. **Map** p409 K6 ⑤⑦
With its combination of wrought ironwork, exposed
stone and wooden beams, the labyrinth of corridors
and passages in this 17th-century *hôtel particulier* is
full of atmosphere. Tapestries, rich colours and the
occasional four-poster bed give the 29 suites and
bedrooms individuality. Location is convenient too.
*Concierge. Disabled-adapted room. Internet
(free, wireless). TV.*

Hôtel Duo

*11 rue du Temple, 4th (01.42.72.72.22/fax
01.42.72.03.53/www.duoparis.com). M° Hôtel de
Ville.* **Rates** €200-€340 double. **Credit** AmEx,
DC, MC, V. **Map** p406 K6 ⑤⑧
Formerly the Axial Beaubourg, this stylish boutique
hotel, decorated with white marble floors, mud-
coloured walls, crushed velvet sofas and exposed
beams, is close to the Centre Pompidou. Rooms are
not large, but exude refinement and comfort.
*Bar. Concierge. Disabled-adapted rooms. Gym.
Internet (free, high speed). Sauna. TV.*

Hôtel St-Louis Marais

*1 rue Charles V, 4th (01.48.87.87.04/fax
01.48.87.33.26/www.saintlouismarais.com). M°
Bastille or Sully Morland.* **Rates** €115-€140 double.
Credit AmEx, DC, MC, V. **Map** p409 L7 ⑤⑨

Built as part of a 17th-century Célestin convent, this
peaceful hotel had its bathrooms redone and Wi-Fi
access installed in 2005. Rooms are compact and
cosy, with wooden beams, tiled floors and simple,
traditional decor.
*Concierge. Internet (€5/hr, wireless). No-smoking
rooms. Parking (€20). Room service (breakfast
only). TV.*
Other locations Hôtel St-Louis Bastille,
114 bd Richard Lenoir, 11th (01.43.38.29.29);
Hôtel St-Louis Opéra, 51 rue de la Victoire, 9th
(01.48.74.71.13).

Hôtel St-Merry

*78 rue de la Verrerie, 4th (01.42.78.14.15/fax
01.40.29.06.82/www.hotelmarais.com). M°
Châtelet or Hôtel de Ville.* **Rates** €160-€230
double. **Credit** AmEx, MC, V. **Map** p406 K6 ⑥⓪
The Gothic decor of this former presbytery attached
to the Eglise St-Merry is ideal for a Dracula set, with
wooden beams, stone walls and plenty of iron;
behind the door of room nine, an imposing flying
buttress straddles the carved antique bed. On the
downside, the historic building has no lift, and only
the suite has a TV.
*Concierge. Internet (€2/day, wireless). No-
smoking rooms. Room service. TV (suite only).*
Other locations Hôtel Saintonge Marais, 16 rue
de Saintonge, 3rd (01.42.77.91.13).

Budget

Grand Hôtel Jeanne d'Arc

*3 rue de Jarente, 4th (01.48.87.62.11/fax
01.48.87.37.31/www.hoteljeannedarc.com). M°
Chemin Vert or St-Paul.* **Rates** €89-€116 double.
Credit MC, V. **Map** p409 L6 ⑥①
This hotel's strong point is its location on a quiet
road close to pretty place du Marché-Ste-Catherine.
Recent refurbishment has made the reception area
striking, with a huge mirror adding the illusion of
space. Rooms are colourful and comfortable.
Internet (€1/hr, wireless). No-smoking rooms. TV.

Hôtel Paris France

*72 rue de Turbigo, 3rd (01.42.78.00.04/fax
01.42.71.99.43/www.paris-france-hotel.com).
M° Temple.* **Rates** €89-€129 double. **Credit**
AmEx, DC, MC, V. **Map** p402 L5 ⑥②
A great central location, sweet lift, spruce staff and
clean, pleasant rooms are on offer here. The attic has
views of Montmartre and (if you lean out far enough)
the Eiffel Tower.
*Bar. Internet (free, wireless). No-smoking
rooms. TV.*

Hôtel du Septième Art

*20 rue St-Paul, 4th (01.44.54.85.00/fax
01.42.77.69.10/www.paris-hotel-7art.com). M°
Pont Marie or St-Paul.* **Rates** €90-€145 double.
Credit AmEx, DC, MC, V. **Map** p409 L7 ⑥③

CONSUME

A good address for film freaks on a budget. Ideally located in a lively part of the Marais, the quaint façade hides a treasure trove of movie memorabilia, which takes up most of the reception space. Exposed brick walls and devoted staff make for a friendly, cosy atmosphere. The decor in the bedrooms isn't exactly groundbreaking, but everything is clean and well equipped. There's no lift.
Bar. Gym. Internet (€5/hr, shared terminal; free, wireless). TV.

BASTILLE & EASTERN PARIS
Expensive

Hôtel Marceau Bastille
13 rue Jules César, 12th (01.43.43.11.65/fax 01.43.41.67.70/www.hotelmarceaubastille.com).
M° Bastille. **Rates** €350-€450 double. **Credit** AmEx, DC, MC, V. **Map** p409 M7 🅖🄰
This slick boutique hotel has 55 rooms divided into two different styles: urban or *écolo* (eco-friendly), some with a balcony. The bar-lounge, overlooking a pleasant, bamboo-planted patio, is surrounded by a gallery that exhibits works of contemporary artists.
Bar. Concierge. Disabled-adapted rooms. Gym. Internet (free, wireless). No-smoking rooms. Room service (6pm-midnight). TV.

Moderate

Le Pavillon Bastille
65 rue de Lyon, 12th (01.43.43.65.65/fax 01.43.43.96.52/www.pavillonbastille.com).
M° Bastille. **Rates** €195 double. **Credit** AmEx, DC, MC, V. **Map** p407 M7 🅖🄵
The best thing about this hotel is its location between the Bastille opera and the Gare de Lyon. The 25 rooms may be small, but you're a stone's throw from the Viaduc des Arts, where an elevated garden has replaced the railroad's tracks and arty boutiques now occupy the arches.
Bar. Disabled-adapted room. Internet (€12/hr, wireless). No-smoking rooms. TV.

Standard Design Hotel
29 rue Taillandiers, 11th (01.48.05.30.97/ fax 01.47.00.29.26/www.standard-hotel.com).
M° Ledru Rollin. **Rates** €170-€195 double. **Credit** AmEx, DC, MC, V. **Map** p407 M6 🅖🄶
The Standard's black and white interior, with the occasional splash of colour, is satisfyingly generic and a winner with visitors looking for a break from the sometimes heavy atmosphere of older, more traditional hotels. The rooms have all mod cons, the breakfast room awakens the senses with bold stripes, and you can roll into bed after a night out in Bastille's cool bars and restaurants.
Bar. Internet (free, wireless). No-smoking rooms. TV.

Budget

★ Mama Shelter
109 rue de Bagnolet, 20th (01.43.48.48.48/ fax 01.44.54.38.66/www.mamashelter.com).
M° Alexandre Dumas, Maraîchers or Porte de Bagnolet. **Rates** €89-€209 double.
Credit AmEx, DC, MC, V.
See *p180* **Chic on the Cheap**.
Bar. Internet (free, wireless). No-smoking rooms. Restaurant. TV.

Le Quartier Bastille, Le Faubourg
9 rue de Reuilly, 12th (01.43.70.04.04/fax 01.43.70.96.53/www.lequartierhotelbf.com).
M° Faidherbe Chaligny or Reuilly-Diderot.
Rates €118-€148 double. **Credit** AmEx, DC, MC, V. **Map** p407 P7 🅖🄷
Within walking distance of Bastille and the hip 11th arrondissement, the Quartier Bastille (a branch of Franck Altruie's chain of budget design hotels) flashes funky, neo-1970s furniture and just the right amount of colour. Rooms are minimalist but more than comfortable.
Disabled-adapted rooms. Internet (free, wireless). No-smoking rooms. Parking (€18). TV.

★ Le Quartier Bercy Square
33 bd de Reuilly, 12th (01.44.87.09.09/fax 01.43.07.41.58/www.lequartierhotelbs.com).
M° Daumesnil or Dugommier. **Rates** €125-€150 double. **Credit** AmEx, DC, MC, V.
Map p407 P9 🅖🄸
You'd never think that lime green and brown stripes would match bold silver and white replica 19th-century wallpaper, but they do at this boutique hotel (another of Franck Altruie's design addresses) in the heart of the ever more trendy 12th arrondissement. Rooms are small but inviting, often using coloured light to create atmosphere.
Bar. Internet (free, wireless). No-smoking rooms. TV.

NORTH-EAST PARIS
Moderate

Le Général Hôtel
5-7 rue Rampon, 11th (01.47.00.41.57/fax 01.47.00.21.56/www.legeneralhotel.com).
M° République. **Rates** €275-€205 double.
Credit AmEx, DC, MC, V. **Map** p402 L5 🅖🄹
A fashionable find near the nightlife action of the 11th, Le Général was one of Paris's first boutique bargains when it opened back in 2003. It is still notable for its remarkably moderate rates and sleek, neutral-toned interior.
Bar. Business centre. Concierge. Disabled-adapted rooms. Gym. Internet (free, wireless). No-smoking rooms. Sauna. TV.

CONSUME

Nautical but Nice

Spend a few nights on the Seine.

The **Paris Yacht** (*see p155*) has to be the city's quirkiest place to sleep – as long as you don't get seasick. Bobbing peacefully on the Left Bank opposite the Ile St-Louis and five minutes' walk from Notre-Dame, this two-cabin houseboat was built in 1933, and has been in service everywhere from Bastia to the Canal de Bourgogne. Now converted to accommodate up to four guests (welcomed with a bottle of champagne from the owners), the boat is equipped with everything from central heating to high-speed internet.

During the summer, the terrace on the upper deck provides the perfect Seine-side setting for dinner. But if you fancy eating on *terra firma*, you can join the landlubbers at the famous and famously expensive Tour d'Argent (15-17 quai de la Tournelle, 5th, 01.43.54.23.31) for its classic numbered duck – and point out 'your' yacht to fellow diners. Reservations for Paris Yacht are for between three and six nights, but it's possible to extend your stay if you get used to life on the waves.

Budget

Hôtel Beaumarchais

3 rue Oberkampf, 11th (01.53.36.86.86/fax 01.43.38.32.86/www.hotelbeaumarchais.com). M° Filles du Calvaire or Oberkampf. **Rates** €110-€130 double. **Credit** AmEx, MC, V. **Map** p409 L5 ⓱
This contemporary hotel is in the Oberkampf area, not far from the Marais and Bastille. Its 31 rooms are brightly decorated with colourful walls, bathroom mosaics and wavy headboards; breakfast is served on the tiny garden patio or in your room. *Concierge. Internet (free, high speed & wireless). Room service. TV.*

Hôtel Garden Saint-Martin

35 rue Yves Toudic, 10th (01.42.40.17.72/ fax 01.42.02.59.66/www.hotel-gardensaint martin-paris.com). M° Jacques Bonsergent. **Rates** €85-€88 double. **Credit** MC, V. **Map** p402 L4 ⓲
The trendy shops, cafés and bars along the Canal St-Martin draw visitors to this hotel, where creature comforts are guaranteed at an excellent rate. No prizes will be won for the ordinary decor, but there is a very pleasant patio garden, and the staff are helpful. *Internet (free, wireless). No-smoking rooms. TV.*

THE LATIN QUARTER & THE 13TH

Moderate

★ Five Hôtel

3 rue Flatters, 5th (01.43.31.74.21/fax 01.43.31.61.96/www.thefivehotel.com). M° Les Gobelins or Port Royal. **Rates** €179-€322 double. **Credit** AmEx, MC, V. **Map** p406 J9 ⓳

The rooms in this stunning boutique hotel may be small, but they're all exquisitely designed, with Chinese lacquer and velvety fabrics. Fibre optics built into the walls create the illusion of sleeping under a starry sky, and you can choose from four different fragrances to subtly perfume your room (the hotel is entirely non-smoking). Guests staying in the suite have access to a private garden with a jacuzzi. *Concierge. Internet (free, wireless). No smoking throughout. TV.*

Hôtel la Demeure

51 bd St-Marcel, 13th (01.43.37.81.25/fax 01.45.87.05.03/www.hotel-paris-lademeure.com). M° Les Gobelins. **Rates** €165-€262 double. **Credit** AmEx, DC, MC, V. **Map** p406 K9 ⓴
This comfortable, modern hotel on the edge of the Latin Quarter is run by a friendly father and son. It has 43 air-conditioned rooms with internet access, plus suites with sliding doors to separate sleeping and living space. The wrap-around balconies of the corner rooms offer lovely views of the city, and bathrooms feature either luxurious tubs or shower heads with elaborate massage possibilities. *Internet (€8/hr; free, wireless). No-smoking rooms. Parking (€17). TV.*

★ Hôtel de la Sorbonne

6 rue Victor-Cousin, 5th (01.43.54.58.08/ fax 01.40.51.05.18/www.hotelsorbonne.com). M° Cluny La Sorbonne/RER Luxembourg. **Rates** €70-€210 double. **Credit** AmEx, DC, MC, V. **Map** p408 J8 ㉔
It's out with the old at this charming, freshly renovated hotel, whose new look is very much a modern take on art nouveau, with bold, designer wallpapers, floral prints, lush fabrics and quotes from French literature woven into the carpets. Rooms are all equipped with iMac computers. *Concierge. Internet (free, wireless). No-smoking rooms. TV.*

Select Hôtel

1 pl de la Sorbonne, 5th (01.46.34.14.80/fax 01.46.34.51.79/www.selecthotel.fr). M° Cluny La Sorbonne. **Rates** (incl breakfast) €169-€225 double. **Credit** AmEx, DC, MC, V. **Map** p408 J8 ⓱

Located at the foot of the Sorbonne, this 68-room hotel delivers pure, understated chic with its clever blend of modern art deco features, traditional stone walls and wooden beams. The winter garden and airy common areas have recently been redone in a sleek, contemporary style.
Bar. Concierge. Internet (wireless). No-smoking rooms. Room service (until 10pm). TV.

Budget

Familia Hôtel

11 rue des Ecoles, 5th (01.43.54.55.27/fax 01.43.29.61.77/www.hotel-paris-familia.com). M° Cardinal Lemoine or Jussieu. **Rates** (incl breakfast) €99-€129 double. **Credit** AmEx, DC, MC, V. **Map** p406 K8 ⓰

This old-fashioned Latin Quarter hotel has balconies hung with tumbling plants and walls draped with replica French tapestries. Owner Eric Gaucheron extends a warm welcome, and the 30 rooms have personalised touches such as sepia murals, cherry-wood furniture and stone walls. The Gaucherons also own the Minerve next door – book in advance for both.
Concierge. Internet (free, wireless). Parking (€20). TV.
Other locations Hôtel Minerve, 13 rue des Ecoles, 5th (01.43.26.26.04).

★ Hôtel les Degrés de Notre-Dame

10 rue des Grands-Degrés, 5th (01.55.42.88.88/fax 01.40.46.95.34/www.lesdegreshotel.com). M° Maubert-Mutualité or St-Michel. **Rates** (incl breakfast) €115-€170 double. **Credit** MC, V. **Map** p406 J7 ⓱

On a tiny street across the river from Notre-Dame, this vintage hotel is an absolute gem. Its ten rooms are full of character, with original paintings, antique furniture and exposed wooden beams (nos.47 and 501 have views of the cathedral). It has an adorable restaurant and, a few streets away, two studio apartments that the owner rents to preferred customers only.
Bar. Internet (free, wireless). No-smoking rooms. Restaurant. Room service (noon-midnight). TV.

Hôtel du Panthéon

19 pl du Panthéon, 5th (01.43.54.32.95/fax 01.43.26.64.65/www.hoteldupantheon.com). M° Cluny La Sorbonne or Maubert Mutualité/ RER Luxembourg. **Rates** €90-€255 double. **Credit** AmEx, DC, MC, V. **Map** p408 J8 ⓱

The 36 rooms of this elegant hotel are beautifully decorated with classic French *toile de Jouy* fabrics, antique furniture and painted woodwork. Some enjoy impressive views of the Panthéon; others squint out on to a hardly less romantic courtyard, complete with chestnut tree.
Internet (free, wireless). No-smoking rooms. TV.

Hôtel Résidence Gobelins

9 rue des Gobelins, 13th (01.47.07.26.90/fax 01.43.31.44.05/www.hotelgobelins.com). M° Les Gobelins. **Rates** €75-€85 double. **Credit** AmEx, MC, V. **Map** p406 K10 ⓱

A tiny lift leads to colourful rooms, equipped with satellite TV and telephone. The breakfast room overlooks a private garden, and there's free internet at the reception. The hotel is entirely non-smoking.
Internet (free, shared terminal). No smoking throughout. TV.

Hôtel Résidence Henri IV

50 rue des Bernardins, 5th (01.44.41.31.81/fax 01.46.33.93.22/www.residencehenri4.com). M° Cardinal Lemoine. **Rates** €90-€310 double. **Credit** AmEx, DC, MC, V. **Map** p406 K7 ⓮

This belle époque style hotel has a mere eight rooms and five apartments, so guests are assured of the staff's full attention. Peacefully situated next to leafy square Paul-Langevin, it's just minutes away from Notre-Dame. The four-person apartments come with a handy mini-kitchen featuring a hob, fridge and microwave – although you may be reduced to eating on the beds in the smaller ones.
Concierge. Internet (free, wireless). No-smoking rooms. TV.

ST-GERMAIN-DES-PRES & ODEON

Deluxe

★ L'Hôtel

13 rue des Beaux-Arts, 6th (01.44.41.99.00/fax 01.43.25.64.81/www.l-hotel.com). M° Mabillon or St-Germain-des-Prés. **Rates** €255-€640 double. **Credit** AmEx, DC, MC, V. **Map** p408 H6 ⓰

Guests at the sumptuously decorated L'Hôtel are more likely to be models and film stars than the starving writers who frequented it during Oscar Wilde's last days (the playwright died on the ground floor in November 1900). Under Jacques Garcia's careful restoration, each room has its own special theme: Mistinguett's *chambre* retains its art deco mirror bed, and Oscar's tribute room is appropriately clad in green peacock murals. *Photo p170.*
Bar. Concierge. Internet (shared terminal, wireless). Pool (indoor). Restaurant. Room service (until 11pm). Sauna. TV.
► *Don't miss out on dinner in the fabulously decadent one-star restaurant, run by talented chef Philippe Bélisse (see p213).*

Hôtel Lutetia

45 bd Raspail, 6th (01.49.54.46.46/fax 01.49.54.46.00/www.lutetia-paris.com). M° Sèvres Babylone. **Rates** €400-€600 double. **Credit** AmEx, DC, MC, V. **Map** p405 G7 ㉜
This historic Left Bank hotel is a masterpiece of art nouveau and early art deco architecture that dates from 1910. It has a plush jazz bar and lively brasserie. Its 250 rooms, revamped in purple, gold and pearl grey, maintain a 1930s feel. Big-name guests in years gone by have included Picasso, Josephine Baker and de Gaulle. It was also Abwehr HQ during the Nazi occupation.
Bar. Business centre. Concierge. Gym. Internet (€18/day, high speed; free, wireless). No-smoking rooms. Restaurants (2). Room service. TV.

Villa d'Estrées

17 rue Gît-le-Coeur, 6th (01.55.42.71.11/fax 01.55.42.71.00/www.villadestrees.com). M° St-Michel. **Rates** €365-€405 double. **Credit** AmEx, DC, MC, V. **Map** p408 J7 ㉝
Jewel colours, sumptuous fabrics, stripes and patterns are the hallmarks of this polished boutique hotel; there's nothing at all minimalist about Villa d'Estrées, which was designed by Jacques Garcia. Each of the ten rooms and suites is individually decorated, all with a nod to Empire style and a crisp, slightly masculine feel.
Bar. Concierge. Internet (free, wireless). No-smoking rooms. Restaurant. Room service (until 10pm). TV.

Expensive

★ Hôtel de l'Abbaye Saint Germain

10 rue Cassette, 6th (01.45.44.38.11/fax 01.45.48.07.86/www.hotelabbayeparis.com). M° Rennes or St-Sulpice. **Rates** (incl breakfast) €251-€367 double. **Credit** AmEx, MC, V. **Map** p405 G7 ㉞
A monumental entrance opens the way through a courtyard into this tranquil hotel, originally part of a convent. Wood panelling, well-stuffed sofas and an open fireplace in the drawing room make for a relaxed atmosphere, but, best of all, there's a surprisingly large garden where breakfast is served in the warmer months. The 43 rooms and duplex apartment are tasteful and luxurious.
Bar. Concierge. Internet (€12/2hrs; free, shared terminal). Room service. TV.

Le Placide

6 rue St-Placide, 6th (01.42.84.34.60/fax 01.47.20.79.78/www.leplacidehotel.com). M° Sèvres-Babylone, St-Placide or Vanneau. **Rates** €300-€390 double. **Credit** AmEx, DC, MC, V. **Map** p405 G7 ㉟
With only ten rooms, the Placide is about as bijou as it gets. White, chrome and neutral tones reign throughout (as does bark- or bamboo-inspired wall-paper), broken only by the occasional funky cushion. All the bedrooms have large bathrooms and their own sitting area. The stylish ground-floor duplex has been designed for disabled guests.
Bar. Concierge. Disabled rooms. Internet (shared terminal; free, wireless). Room service. TV.

★ Relais Saint-Germain

9 carrefour de l'Odéon, 6th (01.43.29.12.05/ fax 01.46.33.45.30/www.hotel-paris-relais-saint-germain.com). M° Odéon. **Rates** (incl breakfast) €285-€370 double. **Credit** AmEx, DC, MC, V. **Map** p408 H7 ㊿
The rustic, wood-beamed ceilings remain intact at the Relais Saint-Germain, a 17th-century hotel bought and renovated by much-acclaimed chef Yves Camdeborde (originator of the *bistronomique* dining trend) and his wife Claudine. Each of the 22 rooms has a different take on eclectic Provençal charm, and the marble bathrooms are huge by Paris standards.
Bar. Concierge. Internet (free, high speed & wireless). No-smoking rooms. Restaurant. Room service (until 10pm). TV.
▶ *Guests get first dibs on a highly sought-after seat in the 15-table Le Comptoir restaurant next door; see p212.*

La Villa

29 rue Jacob, 6th (01.43.26.60.00/fax 01.46.34.63.63/www.villa-saintgermain.com). M° St-Germain-des-Prés. **Rates** €265-€410 double. **Credit** AmEx, DC, MC, V. **Map** p408 H6 ㊲
Refreshingly modern and stylish, the charismatic La Villa features cool faux crocodile skin on the bedheads and crinkly taffeta over the taupe-coloured walls. Wonderfully, your room number is projected on to the floor outside your door; very useful for any drunken homecomings.
Bar. Concierge. Internet (€5/30mins, high speed; €12/hr, wireless). No-smoking rooms. Room service (until midnight). TV.

Moderate

Le Clos Médicis

56 rue Monsieur-le-Prince, 6th (01.43.29.10.80/ fax 01.43.54.26.90/www.closmedicis.com). M° Odéon/RER Luxembourg. **Rates** €205-€255 double. **Credit** AmEx, DC, MC, V. **Map** p408 H8 ㊳

CONSUME

Designed more like a stylish, private townhouse than a hotel, Le Clos Médicis is located by the Luxembourg gardens – perfect if you fancy starting the morning with a stroll among the trees. The hotel's decor is refreshingly modern, with rooms done out with taffeta curtains and chenille bedcovers, and antique floor tiles in the bathrooms. The cosy lounge has a working fireplace.
Bar. Concierge. Internet (free, high speed & wireless). No-smoking rooms. TV.

Grand Hôtel de l'Univers
6 rue Grégoire-de-Tours, 6th (01.43.29.37.00/ fax 01.40.51.06.45/www.hotel-paris-univers.com). M° Odéon. **Rates** €130-€280 double. **Credit** AmEx, DC, MC, V. **Map** p408 H7 **89**
Making the most of its 15th-century origins, this hotel features exposed wooden beams, high ceilings, antique furnishings and toile-covered walls. Manuel Canovas fabrics lend a posh touch, but there are also useful services such as a laptop for hire.
Bar. Concierge. Internet (€8/hr, shared terminal; free, wireless). No-smoking rooms. TV.
▶ *The same team runs the Hôtel St-Germain-des-Prés (36 rue Bonaparte, 6th, 01.43.26.00.19), which has a medieval-themed room and the sweetest attic in Paris.*

Hôtel du Globe
15 rue des Quatre-Vents, 6th (01.43.26.35.50/ fax 01.46.33.62.69/www.hotel-du-globe.fr). M° Odéon. **Rates** €160-€170 double. **Credit** MC, V. **Map** p408 H7 **90**

The Hôtel du Globe has managed to retain much of its 17th-century character – and very pleasant it is too. Gothic wrought-iron doors open into the florid corridors, and an unexplained suit of armour supervises guests from the tiny salon. The rooms with baths are somewhat larger than those with showers, and if you're an early booker you might even get the room with the four-poster bed (ask when reserving).
Internet (free wireless). TV.

Hôtel des Saints-Pères
65 rue des Sts-Pères, 6th (01.45.44.50.00/fax 01.45.44.90.83/www.espritfrance.com). M° St-Germain-des-Prés. **Rates** €170-€225 double. **Credit** AmEx, MC, V. **Map** p405 G7 **91**
Built in 1658 by one of Louis XIV's architects, this hotel has an enviable location near St-Germain-des-Prés' designer boutiques. It boasts a charming garden and a sophisticated, if small, bar. The most coveted room is no.100, with its fine 17th-century ceiling by painters from the Versailles School; it also has an open bathroom, so you can gaze at scenes from the myth of Leda and the Swan while you scrub.
Bar. Concierge. Internet (€10/hr, shared terminal & wireless). TV.

Hôtel Villa Madame
44 rue Madame, 6th (01.45.48.02.81/fax 01.45.44.85.73). M° St-Sulpice. **Rates** €190-€280 double. **Credit** AmEx, MC, V. **Map** p408 G7 **92**
This newly revamped hotel (formerly the Regents) located in a quiet street is a lovely surprise, its courtyard garden used for breakfast in the summer

CONSUME

Hôtel Aviatic.

months. Honey- and chocolate-coloured woods mix with warm-toned velvets to make the rooms (all with plasma screens) feel cosy and inviting; some even have small balconies with loungers.
Concierge. Room service (breakfast only). TV.

Budget

Hôtel de Nesle
7 rue de Nesle, 6th (01.43.54.62.41/fax 01.43.54.31.88/www.hoteldenesleparis.com). M° Odéon. **Rates** €75-€110 double. **Credit** MC, V. **Map** p408 H6 ⓫
Only nine of the 20 rooms are en suite, but all are decorated with colourful murals, and many overlook a charming garden courtyard.
Internet (€15, shared terminal). Parking (€15).

MONTPARNASSE

Expensive

Hôtel des Académies et des Arts
15 rue de la Grande Chaumière, 6th (01.43.26.66.44/fax 01.40.46.86.85/www.hotel-des-academies.com). M° Notre-Dame des Champs, Raspail or Vavin. **Rates** €187-€285 double. **Credit** AmEx, DC, MC, V. **Map** p405 G8 ⓬
Reopened in early 2007 after a full refurbishment, this small boutique hotel scores highly on style. There are cosy salons, fireplaces and an extensive collection of art books. The 20 immaculate rooms are individually designed around four themes (Paris, Actor, Man Ray or Rulhmann), and offer wonderful views over the rooftops or down on to the spectacular Jérôme Mesnager mural in the courtyard.
Concierge. Disabled-adapted room. Internet (free, shared terminal & wireless). TV.

Moderate

★ Hôtel Aviatic
105 rue de Vaugirard, 6th (01.53.63.25.50/fax 01.53.63.25.55/www.aviatic.fr). M° Duroc, Montparnasse Bienvenüe or St-Placide. **Rates** €169-€249 double. **Credit** AmEx, DC, MC, V. **Map** p405 F8 ⓭
This historic hotel has masses of character, from the Empire-style lounge and garden atrium to the bistro-style breakfast room and polished marble floor in the lobby. New decoration throughout, in beautiful steely greys, warm reds, elegant, striped velvets and *toile de Jouy* fabrics, lends an impressive touch of glamour, and the service is consistently with a smile.
Concierge. Internet (€15/hr, wireless). Parking (€27). TV.
▶ *For lunch on the hop, staff will pack up a picnic so you can eat in the nearby Luxembourg gardens.*

Hôtel Delambre
35 rue Delambre, 14th (01.43.20.66.31/fax 01.45.38.91.76/www.hoteldelambre.com). M° Edgar Quinet or Vavin. **Rates** €140-€170 double. **Credit** AmEx, MC, V. **Map** p405 G9 ⓮
Occupying a narrow slot in a small street between Montparnasse and St-Germain, this hotel was home to surrealist André Breton in the 1920s. Today it's modern and friendly, with cast-iron details in the 13 rooms and newly installed air-conditioning. The mini suite in the attic, comprising two separate rooms, is particularly pleasant and sleeps up to four.
Disabled-adapted room. Internet (€9/hr, wireless). No-smoking rooms. TV.

Hôtel Istria Saint-Germain
29 rue Campagne-Première, 14th (01.43.20.91.82/fax 01.43.22.48.45/www.istria-paris-hotel.com). M° Raspail. **Rates** €150-€270 double. **Credit** AmEx, DC, MC, V. **Map** p405 G9 ⓯
Behind this unassuming façade is the place where the artistic royalty of Montparnasse's heyday – the likes of Man Ray, Marcel Duchamp and Louis Aragon – once lived. The Istria Saint-Germain has been modernised since then, but it still has plenty of charm, with 26 bright, simply furnished rooms, a cosy breakfast room and a comfortable communal area.
Concierge. Disabled-adapted room. Internet (€6/hr, wireless). No-smoking rooms. Parking (€20). Room service. TV.
▶ *Film fans take note: the artists' studios next door featured in Godard's A Bout de Souffle.*

THE 7TH & WESTERN PARIS

Deluxe

★ Le Bellechasse
8 rue de Bellechasse, 7th (01.45.50.22.31/fax 01.45.51.52.36/www.lebellechasse.com). M° Assemblée Nationale or Solférino/RER Musée d'Orsay. **Rates** (incl breakfast) €340-€390 double. **Credit** AmEx, MC, V. **Map** p405 F6 ⓰
A former *hôtel particulier*, the Bellechasse fell into the hands of Christian Lacroix, already responsible

---

THE BEST HOTEL RESTAURANTS

For Michelin-starred exclusivity
Les Ambassadeurs at Hôtel de Crillon. *See p158.*

For casual exclusivity
Le Lounge at Hôtel Daniel. *See p165.*

For cultural history
Café de la Paix at InterContinental Paris Le Grand. *See p161.*

CONSUME

CONSUME

Chic on the Cheap

Paris's best budget beds.

For some people, a hotel is much more than a simple base in which to smarten up before exploring the city. It's the make or break of the holiday. And no matter how blue the sky, crispy the baguette or short the queue into the Louvre, if the room's not right, neither is Paris. So what do you do if you can't splurge on a top-notch hotel? Until recently, not a lot; but nowadays a growing number of hoteliers are filling the budget market with good value accommodation that looks smart, feels comfortable and is full of mod cons.

In 2008, two more excellent budget addresses hit the scene. The newest may sound like a refuge for overstressed Italian mums, but **Mama Shelter** (*see p173*), owned by Club Med founders the Trigano family and philosopher Cyril Aouizerate, is in fact Philippe Starck's latest design commission. It's set a stone's throw east of Père Lachaise, and its decor appeals to the young-at-heart with Batman and Incredible Hulk light fittings, dark walls, polished wood and splashes of bright fabrics. Every room comes with an iMac computer, TV, free internet access and a CD and DVD player (there's even a kettle in some rooms – something even French four-stars don't usually provide); and when hunger strikes, there's a brasserie with a romantic terrace. If you're sure of your dates, book online and take advantage of the saver's rate, which is non-exchangeable and non-refundable, but guarantees the lowest price.

If a hotel room is still too expensive and you don't mind bunking up with others, you could try **St Christopher's Inn** (*see p182*). The Paris branch of the English youth hostel chain is housed in a former boat hangar on the ever-gentrifying Canal de l'Ourcq, and offers beds from €12 (plus a women's only floor and a few private rooms). The decor in the bedrooms has a distinct sailor's cabin feel, with round, colourful mirrors, bubble-pattern wallpaper and 1950s-inspired cabin furniture. The hostel really comes into its own in its bar Belushi's, where the usual backpack brigade are joined by Parisians bent on taking advantage of the canalside setting, satellite sports, lunchtime brasserie and some of the cheapest drinks in the capital (from €2.50 for a glass of wine).

Mama Shelter.

for the makeover of the Hôtel du Petit Moulin (*see p170*). It reopened in July 2007, duly transformed into a trendy boutique hotel. Only a few steps away from the Musée d'Orsay, it offers 34 splendid – though rather small – rooms, in seven different decorative styles. It's advisable to book early, as the Bellechasse remains *the* hotel of the moment.
Bar. Internet (free, shared terminal & wireless). No-smoking rooms. TV.

★ Le Montalembert
3 rue Montalembert, 7th (01.45.49.68.68/ fax 01.45.49.69.49/www.montalembert.com). M° Rue du Bac. **Rates** €370-€470 double. **Credit** AmEx, DC, MC, V. **Map** p405 G6 89
Grace Leo-Andrieu's impeccable boutiqu is a benchmark of quality and service. It has everything that *mode* maniacs (who flock here for Fashion Week) could want: bathrooms stuffed with Molton Brown toiletries, a set of digital scales and plenty of mirrors with which to keep an eye on their figure. Decorated in pale lilac, cinnamon and olive tones, the entire hotel has Wi-Fi access, and each room is equipped with a flat-screen TV. Clattery two-person stairwell lifts are a nice nod to old-fashioned ways in a hotel that is otherwise *tout moderne*.
Bar. Concierge. Internet (free, shared terminal; €29/day, wireless). No-smoking rooms. Restaurant. Room service. TV: DVD.

Expensive

Hôtel Duc de Saint-Simon
14 rue de St-Simon, 7th (01.44.39.20.20/fax 01.45.48.68.25/www.hotelducdesaintsimon.com). M° Rue du Bac. **Rates** €225-€290 double. **Credit** AmEx, DC, MC, V. **Map** p405 G6 100
A lovely courtyard leads the way into this popular hotel situated on the edge of St-Germain-des-Prés. Of the 34 romantic bedrooms, four have terraces over a closed-off, leafy garden. It's perfect for lovers, though if you can do without a four-poster bed there are more spacious rooms than the Honeymoon Suite.
Bar. Concierge. Internet (free, shared terminal & wireless). No-smoking rooms. Room service. TV.

Moderate

Hôtel La Bourdonnais
111-113 av de La Bourdonnais, 7th (01.47.05.45.42/fax 01.45.55.75.54/www. hotellabourdonnais.com). M° Ecole Militaire. **Rates** €153-€220 double. **Credit** AmEx, DC, MC, V. **Map** p404 D7 101
The Bourdonnais feels more like a traditional French bourgeois townhouse than a hotel, with 56 bedrooms decorated in rich colours, antiques and Persian rugs. The main lobby opens on to a jungle-like winter garden and patio, where guests take breakfast.
Concierge. Internet (€10/hr, shared terminal). Parking (€15). TV.

Hôtel Lenox
9 rue de l'Université, 7th (01.42.96.10.95/fax 01.42.61.52.83/www.lenoxsaintgermain.com). M° St-Germain-des-Prés. **Rates** €130-€220 double. **Credit** AmEx, DC, MC, V. **Map** p405 G6 102
Its location may be in the seventh, but this venerable literary and artistic haunt is unmistakeably part of St-Germain-des-Prés. The a,rt deco-style Lenox Club Bar, open to the public, features comfortable leather club chairs and jazz instruments on the walls. Bedrooms, reached by an astonishing glass lift, have more traditional decor and city views.
Bar. Concierge. Internet (€10/hr, shared terminal & wireless). No-smoking rooms. Room service (from 5.30pm). TV.

Budget

Hôtel Eiffel Rive Gauche
6 rue du Gros-Caillou, 7th (01.45.51.24.56/fax 01.45.51.11.77/www.hotel-eiffel.com). M° Ecole Militaire. **Rates** €105-€155 double. **Credit** MC, V. **Map** p404 D6 103
The Provençal decor and warm welcome make this a nice retreat. For the quintessential Paris view at a bargain price, ask to stay on one of the upper floors: you can see the Eiffel Tower from nine of the 29 rooms. All feature Empire-style bedheads and modern bathrooms. Outside, there's a tiny, tiled courtyard with a bridge.
Concierge. Internet (€6/30mins, shared terminal; free, wireless). TV.
▶ *If this is fully booked, try sister hotel Eiffel Villa Garibaldi (48 bd Garibaldi, 15th, 01.56.58.56.58), which has equally reasonable rates.*

YOUTH ACCOMMODATION

Auberge Internationale des Jeunes
10 rue Trousseau, 11th (01.47.00.62.00/fax 01.47.00.33.16/www.aijparis.com). M° Ledru-Rollin. **Rates** (incl breakfast, per person) €16-€20. **Credit** AmEx, MC, V. **Map** p407 N7 104
Cleanliness is a high priority at this large, 120-bed hostel close to Bastille and within easy distance of the Marais. Rooms accommodate between two and four people, and the larger ones have their own shower and toilet. With the lowest hostel rates in central Paris, the place does tend to fill up fast in summer, but advance reservations can be made. Although the hostel is open all hours without any late-night curfew, the rooms are closed for cleaning every day between 10am and 3pm. Under-35s only.
Internet (€6/hr, shared terminal). Microwave.

Auberge Jules-Ferry
8 bd Jules-Ferry, 11th (01.43.57.55.60/fax 01.43.14.82.09/www.hihostels.com). M° République. **Rates** (incl breakfast & linens, per person) €20.50. **Credit** MC, V. **Map** p402 M4 105

CONSUME

This friendly IYHF hostel has 100 beds in rooms for two to six. There's no need – indeed, no way – to make advance bookings. There's no curfew, though rooms are closed between 10am and 2pm. *Internet (€6/hr, shared terminal).*

BVJ Paris/Quartier Latin
44 rue des Bernardins, 5th (01.43.29.34.80/fax 01.53.00.90.91/www.bvjhotel.com). M° Maubert Mutualité. **Rates** (incl breakfast, per person) €28 dorm; €32 double. **No credit cards.** Map p406 J7 ⓛ

The BVJ hostel has 121 beds with homely tartan quilts in clean but bare modern dorms (for up to ten), and rooms with showers. There's also a TV lounge and a work room in which to write up your journal. *Internet (€4/hr, shared terminal).*

Other locations BVJ Paris/Louvre, 20 rue Jean-Jacques-Rousseau, 1st (01.53.00.90.90).

★ MIJE
6 rue de Fourcy, 4th (01.42.74.23.45/fax 01.40.27.81.64/www.mije.com). M° St-Paul. **Rates** (incl breakfast, per person; €2.50 obligatory membership) €29 dorm (18-30s); €34 double. **No credit cards.** Map p409 L6 ⓛ

MIJE runs three 17th-century Marais residences – one is a former convent – that provide the most attractive hostel sleeps in Paris. Its plain, clean rooms have snow-white sheets and sleep up to eight people; all have a shower and basin. The Fourcy address has its own restaurant (evenings only). The curfew is 1am unless you arrange otherwise with reception. *Internet (€6/hr, shared terminal).*

Other locations (same phone) 12 rue des Barres, 4th; 11 rue du Fauconnier, 4th.

St Christopher's Inn
159 rue de Crimée, 19th (01.40.34.34.40/www.st-christophers.co.uk/paris-hostels). M° Crimée, Jaurès, Laumière or Stalingrad. **Rates** €12-€36 dorm; €37.50-€50 double. **Credit** AmEx, MC, V. Map p403 N1 ⓛ

See p180 **Chic on the Cheap.** *Bar. Internet (free, wireless). No-smoking rooms. Restaurant.*

BED & BREAKFAST
Alcove & Agapes
Le Bed & Breakfast à Paris, 8bis rue Coysevox, 18th (01.44.85.06.05/fax 01.44.85.06.14/ www.bed-and-breakfast-in-paris.com).

This B&B booking service offers over 100 *chambres d'hôte* (€75-€295 for a double, including breakfast; three-, four- and five-bed rooms available too) with hosts who range from artists to grannies. Extras can include anything from dinner to cooking classes or tours of Paris.

Good Morning Paris
43 rue Lacépède, 5th (01.47.07.28.29/fax 01.47.07.44.45/www.goodmorningparis.fr).

This company has 100 rooms in the city. Prices range from €69 to €79 for doubles, and €106 for an apartment that sleeps two to four people. There's a minimum stay of two nights.

APART-HOTELS & FLAT RENTAL
A deposit is usually payable on arrival. Small ads for private short-term lets run in the fortnightly anglophone mag *FUSAC* (01.43.40.50.00, www.fusac.fr); or check out www.frenchconnections.co.uk, which has a selection of furnished apartments for four or more people, and www.apartmentservice.com.

Citadines Apart'hotel
Central reservations 01.41.05.79.79/fax 01.41.05.78.87/www.citadines.com. **Rates** €110-€615. **Credit** AmEx, DC, MC, V.

The 16 modern Citadines complexes across Paris tend to attract a mainly business clientele. Room sizes vary from slightly cramped studios to quite spacious two-bedroom apartments.

Paris Appartements Services
20 rue Bachaumont, 2nd (01.40.28.01.28/ fax 01.40.28.92.01/www.paris-apts.com). M° Sentier. **Open** 9am-6pm Mon-Fri. *Key pick-up 24hrs.* **Rates** (min 5 nights) €83-€214. **Credit** AmEx, MC, V.

This organisation specialises in short-term rentals, offering furnished studios and one-bedroom flats in the first to fourth arrondissements.

Swell Apartments
11 rue Duhesme, 18th (+44 (0)7725 056 421/ www.swell-apartments.co.uk). M° Lamarck Caulincourt. **Rates** €120-€150 (min 3 nights). **Credit** MC, V. Map p401 H1

Don't be put off by the tatty entrance; this one-bedroom flat on the north side of Montmartre (sleeps two) is lovely. The bedroom, with duck-egg blue and white walls, has a crystal chandelier and marble fireplace. The cosy lounge has elegant furniture.

Restaurants

There are great restaurants galore in Paris, but they come at a price.

Finding good food in Paris is easy. Finding the means to eat good food in Paris is trickier. The haute cuisine spots are wildly expensive; and at the bottom end, the bargain bistro has all but vanished, making way for a more ambitious style of bistro where a three-course meal costs at least €30 a head. Add to this the cost of wine, mineral water and coffee, all marked up sharply, and you'll be lucky to get out for less than €100 for two. It can add up over the course of a few days, so it makes sense to plan before you go. Which, we hope, is where this selection of more than 100 terrific Paris eateries will come in handy.

EATING IN PARIS

Despite the expensive nature of life in Paris, you can save money by choosing when you eat with care. Most restaurants offer cheaper lunch menus; you may have a more limited choice, and the dishes might appear simpler than those on the *carte*, but they are likely to draw on the freshest ingredients from the market.

Among the best of the lunch menus is the €27 three-course deal at **Au Bon Accueil**, where the food is of haute cuisine quality. At **La Table Lauriston**, an à la carte meal costs about €50 per person, but there's a lunch menu for €25. And at **Rech**, the chic Alain Ducasse seafood house, you can have lunch for €34. Further up the scale, the kind of haute cuisine restaurants at which you can easily spend €200 or more a head for dinner often have lunch menus for €75 to €80 – still a lot of money, but you'll be treated to a full-blown experience, from *amuse-bouches* to *mignardises*.

Another approach is to explore the city's thriving international restaurants, where you can still find some bargain prices. You're unlikely to come across Indian food that can compare to what you might get in the UK, but Paris has worthy North African, Chinese, Japanese and Laotian restaurants (Italian food, though popular, is usually overpriced). Near

Palais-Royal and the Palais Garnier, rue Ste-Anne and the small surrounding streets are a goldmine of Japanese noodle houses, where a sink-sized bowl of ramen or udon with a plate of *gyoza* (pork dumplings) on the side will set you back no more than €10. Dig a little deeper and you'll also find good Taiwanese and Korean food in this area. For Chinese, Laotian and Vietnamese food, take métro line 14 to the new Olympiades station, which is in the heart of Chinatown, or wander the multicultural streets of Belleville, where couscous restaurants jostle for space with Vietnamese noodle joints. Best avoided are the *traiteurs* all over Paris selling microwaved Asian food of unknown origin.

As Parisians grow more health-conscious and also have less to spend on lunch, soup, sandwich and juice bars are becoming a viable option. Many have jumped on the bandwagon with no attention to the quality of ingredients, but one reliable chain is the French-run **Cojean** (www.cojean.fr), and the British-influenced **Rose Bakery** and **Bread & Roses** are teaching the French the benefits of organic ingredients. And there's nothing wrong with a classic *jambon-beurre* sandwich from a traditional bakery, either.

Despite these changes, the bistro continues to reign in Paris. Young chefs have found a

About the author
Rosa Jackson *writes about Paris and Provence for publications around the world, and runs a custom food itinerary service; see www.edible-paris.com for details.*

❶ Blue numbers given in this chapter correspond to the location of each restaurant on the street maps. *See pp400-409.*

CONSUME

winning formula – a small space, a limited menu, often a long, shared table and a counter for quick meals – and are sticking to it, to the delight of Parisians who appreciate this more convivial approach to dining and the variety of dishes offered during the year. Three perfect examples are the recently opened **Hide** near the Champs-Elysées, **Itinéraires** in the Latin Quarter, and **Le Gaigne** in the Marais.

Just as they're drinking less wine of better quality, Parisians are going out less frequently but eating better. A popular alternative to the three-course bistro meal is offered at wine bars such as **Racines**, where you can order a top-notch cheese or charcuterie plate or perhaps a comforting stew with mashed potatoes.

Except for the very simplest restaurants, it's wise to book ahead. This can usually be done on the same day as your intended visit, although really top-notch establishments require bookings weeks in advance and confirmation the day before. If you've failed to get a reservation, you can try putting yourself on a waiting list a couple of days ahead, as last-minute cancellations are common.

All listings have been checked at the time of going to press but are liable to change. Many venues close for their annual break in August, and some also close at Christmas. Restaurants in this chapter are presented by area. For more restaurant reviews, refer to *Time Out Paris Eating & Drinking*, available at www.timeout.com/shop.

With our reviews, we give the average price for a standard main course chosen from the à la carte menu. If 'Main courses' is not listed, only prix fixe options are available. 'Prix fixe' indicates the price of the venue's set menu at lunch and/or dinner. All bills include a service charge, but an additional tip of a few euros (for the whole table) is polite unless you're unhappy with the service. Budget eateries are marked **€**.

THE ISLANDS

Brasserie de l'Ile St-Louis
55 quai de Bourbon, 4th (01.43.54.02.59). *M° Pont Marie.* **Open** noon-midnight Mon, Tue, Thur-Sun. Closed Aug. **Main courses** €20. **Credit** MC, V. **Map** p409 K7 ❶ Brasserie
Happily, this old-fashioned brasserie soldiers on while exotic juice bars on the Ile St-Louis come and go. The terrace has one of the best summer views in Paris and is invariably packed; the dining room exudes shabby chic. Nicotined walls make for an authentic Paris mood, though nothing here is gastronomically gripping: a well-dressed *frisée aux lardons* and a more successful pan of warming tripes.

Mon Vieil Ami
69 rue St-Louis-en-l'Ile, 4th (01.40.46.01.35/ www.mon-vieil-ami.com). M° Pont Marie. **Open** noon-2.30pm, 7-11.30pm Wed-Sun. Closed 3wks Jan & 1st 3wks Aug. **Main courses** €22. **Prix fixe** €41. **Credit** AmEx, DC, MC, V. **Map** p409 K7 ❷ Bistro

Antoine Westermann from the Buerehiesel in Strasbourg has created a true foodie destination here. Starters such as tartare of finely diced raw vegetables with sautéed baby squid on top impress with their deft seasoning. Typical of the mains is a cast-iron casserole of roast duck with caramelised turnips and couscous. Even the classic room has been successfully refreshed with black beams, white perspex panels and a long *table d'hôte* down one side.

THE LOUVRE
& PALAIS-ROYAL

★ L'Ardoise

28 rue du Mont-Thabor, 1st (01.42.96.28.18/ www.lardoise-paris.com). M° Concorde or Tuileries. **Open** noon-2.30pm, 6.30-11pm Tue-Sat; 6.30-11pm Sun. Closed 1st 3wks Aug. **Main courses** €19. **Prix fixe** €32. **Credit** MC, V. **Map** p401 G5 ❸ **Bistro**

One of the city's finest modern bistros, L'Ardoise is regularly packed with gourmets eager to sample Pierre Jay's reliably delicious cooking. A wise choice might be six oysters with warm chipolatas and a pungent shallot dressing; equally attractive are a gamey hare pie with an escalope of foie gras nestling in its centre. A lightly chilled, raspberry-scented Chinon, from a wine list arranged by price, is a perfect complement. Unusually, it's open on Sundays.

Chez La Vieille

37 rue de l'Arbre-Sec, 1st (01.42.60.15.78). M° Louvre Rivoli. **Open** noon-2.30pm,

7.30-9.45pm Mon, Tue, Thur, Fri; noon-2.30pm Wed. Closed Aug. **Main courses** €25. **Prix fixe** *Lunch* €25. **Credit** AmEx, MC, V. **Map** p406 J5 ❹ **Bistro**

The rustic ground floor of this bistro bursts with well-rounded regulars, whereas upstairs is plain and bright. A wondrous ad-lib selection of starters might include hot *chou farci* and home-made *terrine de foie gras*. Equally impressive is *foie de veau*, coated in a pungent reduction of shallots and vinegar and served with potato purée. Puddings follow the same cornucopian principle as the starters. Opening hours are limited and booking ahead is essential, but the lunchtime prix fixe is a bargain.

Chez Vong

10 rue de la Grande-Truanderie, 1st (01.40.26.09.36/www.chez-vong.com). M° Etienne Marcel or Les Halles. **Open** noon-2.30pm, 7-10.30pm Mon-Sat. Closed 3wks Aug. **Main courses** €20. **Prix fixe** *Lunch* €24. **Credit** AmEx, DC, MC, V. **Map** p402 J5 ❺ **Chinese**

The staff at this cosy Chinese restaurant take pride in its excellent cooking. From the greeting at the door to the knowledgeable, trilingual service (Cantonese, Mandarin and French), each part of the experience is thoughtfully orchestrated. Any doubts about authenticity are extinguished with the arrival of the beautifully presented dishes. Expertly cooked spicy shrimp glistens in a smooth, characterful sauce of onions and ginger, and *ma po* tofu melts in the mouth, its spicy and peppery flavours melding with those of the fine pork mince.

Brasserie de l'Ile St-Louis.

CONSUME

BOUILLON
Racine

Located in the heart of the LatinQuarter,
the Bouillon Racine combines art nouveau charm
and exceptionally tasty food.

Open daily noon-11pm (last order)
Live jazz 1st & 3rd Tuesdays of the month

3 rue Racine, 6th. M° Odéon.
Tel: 01.44.32.15.60
Email.bouillon.racine@wanadoo.fr
www.bouillonracine.com

Les Fines Gueules

43 rue Croix-des-Petits-Champs, 1st (01.42.61. 35.41). M° Bourse or Sentier. **Open** 2.30-4pm, 7.30-11pm daily. **Main courses** €16. **Credit** MC, V. **Map** p402 H5 ❻ **Bistro/wine bar**
At first glance, Les Fines Gueules might seem like an ordinary corner café, but a closer look at the menu reveals unusual attention to ingredients at this mini wine bar/bistro. Even if you've never heard of Hugo (Desnoyer, star butcher and supplier to some of the city's finest restaurants) or Jean-Luc (Poujauran, a celebrity Paris baker), you can taste the difference when the pedigree steak tartare arrives with a salad of baby leaves dressed in truffle oil. There are just a few seats around the bar, but upstairs is a buzzy dining room that attracts a mix of smoochy couples and business suits. A good selection of 'natural' and organic wines comes by the glass and the bottle.

Le Grand Véfour

17 rue de Beaujolais, 1st (01.42.96.56.27/www. relaischateaux.com). M° Palais Royal Musée du Louvre. **Open** 12.30-1.30pm, 8-9.30pm Mon-Thur; 12.30-1.30pm Fri. Closed 1wk Apr, Aug, 1wk Dec. **Main courses** €74. **Prix fixe** *Lunch* €78. **Credit** AmEx, DC, MC, V. **Map** p402 H5 ❼ **Haute cuisine**
Opened in 1784 (as the Café de Chartres), this is one of the oldest and most historic restaurants in Paris. An à la carte meal begins with a fantasia suite of delicacies: tiny frogs' legs, for example, arranged within a circle of sage sauce; a first course of creamed Breton sea urchins served in their spiny shells with a quail's egg and topped with caviar. Fish dishes may be a touch overcooked, and the adventurous desserts are not always successful, but you'll forgive all after a glass of vintage armagnac.

Kaï

18 rue du Louvre, 1st (01.40.15.01.99). M° Louvre Rivoli. **Open** noon-2pm, 7-10.30pm Tue-Sat; 7-10.30pm Sun. Closed 1wk Apr & 3wks Aug. **Main courses** €27. **Prix fixe** *Lunch* €38. *Dinner* €65, €110. **Credit** AmEx, MC, V. **Map** p402 H5 ❽ **Japanese**
This Japanese restaurant has developed a following among fashionable diners. The 'Kai-style' sushi is a zesty take on a classic: marinated and lightly grilled yellowtail is pressed on to a roll of *shiso*-scented rice. Not to be outdone, the grilled aubergine with miso, seemingly simple, turns out to be a smoky, luscious experience, best enjoyed with a small spoon. A generous main of breaded pork lacks the finesse and refinement of the starters, but is nonetheless satisfying. Thoroughly French desserts come courtesy of celebrity pastry chef Pierre Hermé.

★ Le Meurice

Hôtel Meurice, 228 rue de Rivoli, 1st (01.44.58. 10.10/www.meuricehotel.com). M° Tuileries. **Open** 12.30-2pm, 7.30-10pm Mon-Fri. Closed 2wks Feb & Aug. **Main courses** €100. **Prix fixe** *Lunch* €90. *Dinner* €220. **Credit** AmEx, DC, MC, V. **Map** p401 G5 ❾ **Haute cuisine**
Yannick Alléno, chef here since 2003, has really hit his stride and is doing some glorious, if rather understated, contemporary cooking. Alléno has a light touch, teasing the flavour out of every leaf, frond, fin or fillet. Turbot is sealed in clay before cooking and then sauced with celery cream and a coulis of flat parsley, and Bresse chicken stuffed with foie gras and served with truffled *sarladais* potatoes is breathtakingly good. A fine cheese tray comes from Quatrehomme, and the pastry chef amazes with his signature millefeuille. *Photo p191.*

★ Restaurant du Palais-Royal

110 galerie Valois, 1st (01.40.20.00.27/www. restaurantdupalaisroyal.com). M° Bourse, Musée du Louvre or Palais Royal. **Open** noon-2pm, 7-10pm Mon-Sat. Closed 19 Dec-10 Jan. **Main courses** €28. **Prix fixe** €60. **Credit** AmEx, DC, MC, V. **Map** p401 H5 ❿ **Bistro**
There can be few more magical places to dine on a summer evening than the terrace of this restaurant. Inside is memorable too: you sit in a red dining room alongside the commissars of arts and letters who work at the ministry of culture a few doors down. Risotto is a speciality and the Black, Black and Lobster is tremendous; rice simmered in rich squid ink is served al dente, topped with tender but fleshy pink lobster, sun-dried tomato and spring vegetables. Don't miss out on the *baba au rhum*.

Zen

8 rue de l'Echelle, 1st (01.42.61.93.99). M° Louvre Rivoli. **Open** noon-3pm, 7-10.30pm daily. Closed Aug. **Main courses** €12. **Prix fixe** €20-€50. **Credit** MC, V. **Map** p401 H5 ⓫ **Japanese**
There's no shortage of Japanese restaurants in this neighbourhood, but the recently opened Zen is refreshing in a couple of ways. First, there is no pale wood in sight – the colour scheme here is sharp white, green and yellow for a cheerful effect. Second, the menu has a lot to choose from – bowls of ramen, sushi and chirashi, hearty dishes such as chicken with egg on rice or tonkatsu – yet no detail is neglected. A perfect choice if you're spending a day at the Louvre – you can be in and out in 30 minutes.

OPERA TO LES HALLES

€ Bioboa

3 rue Danielle-Casanova, 1st (01.42.61.17.67). M° Pyramides. **Open** 10am-6pm Mon-Sat. **Main courses** €11.50. **Prix fixe** €13. **Credit** V. **Map** p401 G4 ⓬ **Organic**
The fact that this place describes itself as a 'food spa' shows how it's embracing the organic ('bio' in French) revolution. There's a high-concept air about the place: white designer chairs and tables; a beautiful bird fresco that winds through it; and a mam-

CONSUME

Counter Culture

Forget table service: Paris has found a new way of eating.

In the past few years, eating at the bar has become an increasingly popular trend – one that suits solo diners, office workers and people who have grown jaded after too many leisurely three-course meals. This new way of eating caught the attention of Paris diners a few years ago, when Joël Robuchon came out of 'retirement' to open **L'Atelier** (5 rue Montalembert, 7th, 01.42.22.56.56, www.joel-robuchon.com), which is organised more like a sushi bar than a traditional French restaurant. Seating is at tall red stools around a lacquered wood bar that looks on to the open kitchen, demystifying the haute cuisine experience and creating a more convivial atmosphere: it's almost impossible not to get into conversation with your neighbours here.

Other haute cuisine chefs followed suit, notably Pierre Gagnaire, who added a counter to his seafood annexe **Gaya Rive Gauche** (*see p216*). Anyone who might be intimidated by the high prices or the hushed atmosphere at his eponymous restaurant off the Champs-Elysées can taste a slightly toned-down version of his experimental style here, without having to linger all afternoon. Similarly forward-thinking is Alain Senderens, who radically modernised the former Lucas Carton (now

Senderens) and added a tapas-meets-sushi bar, Le Passage (*see p193*), where sophisticated small plates are served at relatively reasonable prices.

Long before Robuchon opened L'Atelier, though, an Englishman and a Scot understood that Parisians might be ready for a new way of eating. Mark Williamson and Tim Johnston founded **Willi's Wine Bar** (13 rue des Petits Champs, 1st, 01.42.61.05.09, www.williswinebar.com) in 1980, and today this chic bistro near the Palais-Royal seems as modern as ever. The key to its success has been the long oak bar at the front, where people can stop in for a glass of wine and a plate of cheese or a contemporary dish from the kitchen.

Counters are rapidly becoming *de rigueur* in the new breed of market-inspired bistros. The advantage for the restaurateur is obvious: diners don't linger as long, which allows them to keep prices down. One bistro – Christian Constant's **Les Cocottes** (*see p216*) – has done away with tables altogether to serve at one long bar with no reservations; and chef Sylvain Sendra – who ran a thriving little bistro with a counter, Le Temps au Temps, before moving to spacious new premises in 2008 – has made the bar a feature of his new restaurant **Itinéraires** (*see p206*).

L'Atelier.

moth fridge overflowing with expensive mineral waters, exotic smoothies and colourful takeaway salads for the fabulously busy. A healthy feast here might consist of soft-boiled eggs with sweet roasted autumn vegetables, or a juicy tofu burger with organic ketchup – one of Bioboa's staples.

★ € Bistrot Victoires

6 rue de la Vrillière, 1st (01.42.61.43.78).
M° Bourse. **Open** noon-3pm, 7-11pm daily.
Main courses €11. **Credit** MC, V. **Map**
p402 H5 ⑬ **Bistro**
Bistros with vintage decor serving no-nonsense food at generous prices are growing thin on the ground in Paris, so it's no surprise that this gem is packed to the gills with bargain-loving office workers and locals every day. The *steak-frites* are exemplary, featuring a slab of entrecôte topped with a smoking sprig of thyme, but *plats du jour* such as *blanquette de veau* (veal in cream sauce) are equally comforting. The wines by the glass can be rough, but the authentic buzz should make up for any flaws.

La Bourse ou la Vie

12 rue Vivienne, 2nd (01.42.60.08.83). M°
Bourse. **Open** noon-10pm Mon-Fri. Closed 1wk
Aug & 1wk Dec. **Main courses** €20. **Credit**
AmEx, MC, V. **Map** p402 H4 ⑭ **Bistro**
After a career as an architect, the round-spectacled owner of La Bourse ou la Vie has a new mission in life: to revive the dying art of the perfect *steak-frites*. The only decision you'll need to make is which cut of beef to order with your chips, unless you pick the cod. Choose between ultra-tender *coeur de filet* or a huge, surprisingly tender *bavette*. Rich, creamy pepper sauce is the speciality here, but the real surprise is the chips, which gain a distinctly animal flavour from the suet in which they are cooked.

★ Chez Miki

5 rue de Louvois, 2nd (01.42.96.04.88). M°
Bourse. **Open** noon-10pm Tue-Sat, 6-10pm
Sun. **Main courses** €15. **Prix fixe** €30, €35.
Credit MC, V. **Map** p402 H4 ⑮ **Japanese**
There are plenty of Japanese restaurants to choose from along nearby rue Ste-Anne, but none is as original – nor as friendly – as this tiny bistro run entirely by women, next to the square Louvois. The speciality here is bento boxes, which you compose yourself from a scribbled blackboard list (in Japanese and French). For €15 you can choose two small dishes – marinated sardines and fried chicken wings are especially popular – and a larger dish, such as grilled pork with ginger. Don't miss the inventive desserts, which might include lime jelly spiked with alcohol.

Drouant

18 rue Gaillon, 2nd (01.42.65.15.16/www.
drouant.com). M° Pyramides or Quatre Septembre.
Open noon-2.30pm, 7pm-midnight daily. **Main**

courses €20-€30. **Prix fixe** *Lunch* €43-€60.
Dinner (10.30pm-midnight) €55-€60. **Credit**
AmEx, DC, MC, V. **Map** p401 H4 ⑯ **Brasserie**
Star chef Antoine Westermann has whisked this landmark 1880 brasserie into the 21st century with bronze-coloured banquettes and butter-yellow fabrics. Westermann has dedicated this restaurant to the art of the hors d'oeuvre, served in themed sets of four ranging from the global (Thai beef salad with brightly coloured vegetables, coriander, and a sweet and spicy sauce) to the nostalgic (silky leeks in vinaigrette). The bite-sized surprises continue with the main course accompaniments – four of them for each dish – and the multiple mini-desserts.

▶ *Westermann also runs the successful Ile*
St-Louis **bistro** *Mon Vieil Ami (see p184).*

Au Gourmand

17 rue Molière, 1st (01.42.96.22.19/www.
augourmand.fr). M° Palais Royal or Pyramides.
Open 7.30-10pm Mon; 12.30-2pm, 7.30-10pm
Tue-Fri; 7.30-10pm Sat. **Main courses** €28.
Prix fixe *Lunch* €28, €32. *Dinner* €30, €36.
Credit MC, V. **Map** p401 H5 ⑰ **Bistro**
Ochre walls and red velvet curtains give this restaurant an almost too grown-up feel, but it's worth looking beyond that to the inventive fare coming out of the kitchen. Vegetables from celebrity market gardener Joël Thiébaut star alongside meat in dishes such as juicy pork cheek wrapped in caul fat under a heap of colourful spring vegetables. Vegetarians can also find contentment, perhaps in a thick slice of grilled aubergine topped with diced cucumber, tomato and ricotta. But a disastrous rum-spiked avocado mousse for dessert shows the chef's creativity with vegetables does have its limitations.

€ Higuma

32bis rue Ste-Anne, 1st (01.47.03.38.59).
M° Pyramides. **Open** 11.30am-10pm daily.
Main courses €8. **Prix fixe** €10.50-€12.50.
Credit MC, V. **Map** p401 H4 ⑱ **Japanese**
Higuma's no-nonsense food and service makes it one of the area's most popular destinations. On entering, customers are greeted by plumes of aromatic steam emanating from the open kitchen-cum-bar, where a small team of chefs ladle out giant bowls of noodle soup piled with meat, vegetables or seafood. You can slurp at the counter or sit at a plastic-topped table.

★ Liza

14 rue de la Banque, 2nd (01.55.35.00.66/www.
restaurant-liza.com). M° Bourse. **Open** 12.30-2pm,
8-10.30pm Mon-Thur; 12.30-2pm, 8-11pm Fri; 8-
11pm Sat; noon-4pm Sun. **Main courses** €25.
Prix fixe *Lunch* €18, €23. *Dinner* €42. **Credit**
AmEx, MC, V. **Map** p402 H4 ⑲ **Lebanese**
Liza Soughayar's restaurant showcases the style and superb food of contemporary Beirut. Lentil, fried onion and orange salad is delicious, as are the *kebbe* (minced seasoned raw lamb) and grilled halloumi

CONSUME

cheese with home-made apricot preserve. Main courses such as minced lamb with coriander-spiced spinach and rice are light, flavoursome and well presented. Try one of the excellent Lebanese wines, and finish with the halva ice-cream with carob molasses. Although there's no prix fixe menu at lunchtime, prices are cheaper at €17-€32.

Racines
8 passage des Panoramas (01.40.13.06.41). M° Bourse or Bonne Nouvelle. **Open** noon-midnight Mon-Fri. **Main courses** €15. **Credit** MC, V. **Map** p402 J4 ❷⓿ **Wine bar**
The 19th-century passage des Panoramas contains an eclectic collection of shops and restaurants – among them this wildly popular wine bar opened by the former owners of La Crèmerie in St-Germain. The menu is limited to superb-quality cheese and charcuterie plates, plus a couple of hot dishes, perhaps pork cheeks stewed in red wine or braised lamb, and a few comforting desserts. Many of the intense-tasting wines are biodynamic, and despite the rather hectic atmosphere lingering over an extra glass or two is cheerfully tolerated.

★ La Tour de Montlhéry (Chez Denise)
5 rue des Prouvaires, 1st (01.42.36.21.82). M° Les Halles/RER Châtelet Les Halles. **Open** noon-3pm, 7.30pm-5am Mon-Fri. Closed 15 July-15 Aug. **Main courses** €24. **Credit** MC, V. **Map** p402 J5 ❷⓵ **Bistro**
At the stroke of midnight, the place is packed, jovial and hungry. Savoury traditional dishes, washed down by litres of the house Brouilly, are the order of the day. Les Halles was the city's wholesale food market, and game, beef and offal still rule here. Diners devour towering rib steaks served with marrow and a heaped platter of chips, among the best in town. Brave souls can try *tripes au calvados*, grilled *andouillette* (lamb's brain), or go for a stewed venison, served with celery root and home-made jam.

CHAMPS-ELYSEES & WESTERN PARIS

Alain Ducasse au Plaza Athénée
Hôtel Plaza Athénée, 25 av Montaigne, 8th (01.53.67.65.00/www.alain-ducasse.com). M° Alma Marceau. **Open** 7.45-10.15pm Mon-Wed; 12.45-2.15pm, 7.45-10.15pm Thur, Fri. Closed mid July-mid Aug & 2wks Dec. **Prix fixe** €220-€320. **Credit** AmEx, DC, MC, V. **Map** p400 D5 ❷❷ **Haute cuisine**
The sheer glamour factor would be enough to recommend this restaurant, Alain Ducasse's most lofty Paris undertaking. The dining room ceiling drips with 10,000 crystals. An *amuse-bouche* of a single langoustine in a lemon cream with a touch of Iranian caviar starts the meal off beautifully, but other dishes can be inconsistent: a part-raw/part-cooked salad

of autumn fruit and veg in a red, Chinese-style sweet-and-sour dressing, or Breton lobster in an overwhelming sauce of apple, quince and spiced wine. Cheese is predictably delicious, as is the *rum baba comme à Monte-Carlo*.

★ Les Ambassadeurs
Hôtel de Crillon, 10 pl de la Concorde, 8th (01.44.71.16.17/www.crillon.com). M° Concorde. **Open** 7-10.30am, 12.30-1.45pm, 7.30-9.45pm Tue-Sat; noon-3pm Sun. Closed 1st wk Jan & Aug. **Main courses** €90. **Prix fixe** *Lunch* (Tue-Sat) €75. *Dinner* €200. *Brunch* (Sun) €66-€72. **Credit** AmEx, DC, V. **Map** p401 F4 ❷❸ **Haute cuisine**
Since the arrival of chef Jean-François Piège, the experience of eating at Les Ambassadeurs has become sublime. In a main of Rossini-style bluefin tuna, a tube of foie gras is magically embedded in the tuna's raw centre, and crunchy-soft veal sweetbreads come with fresh morel mushrooms and tiny roasted potatoes. A succession of bright ideas makes the meal memorable: bite-sized ice-creams arrive straight after the mains, followed by tiny citrus-flavoured *madeleines* and pineapple macaroons.

Astrance
4 rue Beethoven, 16th (01.40.50.84.40). M° Passy. **Open** 12.15-1.30pm, 8-9.30pm Tue-Fri. Closed 1wk Feb, 4wks Aug, 1wk Oct & 1wk Dec. **Prix fixe** *Lunch* €70. *Dinner* €170. **Credit** AmEx, DC, MC, V. **Map** p404 B6 ❷❾ **Haute cuisine**
When Pascal Barbot opened Astrance, he was praised for creating a new style of Paris restaurant – refined, yet casual and affordable. A few years later, this small, slate-grey dining room feels just like an haute cuisine restaurant. Most customers, having reserved at least a month ahead, give free rein to the chef with the 'Menu Astrance' (€170). Barbot has an original touch, combining foie gras with slices of white mushrooms and a lemon condiment, or sweet lobster with candied grapefruit peel, a grapefruit and rosemary sorbet, and raw baby spinach. Wines by the glass are reasonably priced.

Le Bistrot Napolitain
18 av Franklin D. Roosevelt, 8th (01.45.62.08.37). M° St-Philippe-du-Roule. **Open** noon-2.30pm, 7.15-10.30pm Mon-Fri. Closed 1wk July, Aug &

INSIDE TRACK
HAUTE FOR LESS

Les Ambassadeurs' majestic dining room (*see p190*) serves the ravishing haute cuisine of chef Jean-François Piège. A la carte starters cost around €80, but the same amount will buy you a four-course meal – with no skimping on ingredients – at lunchtime.

Le Meurice. See p187.

1wk Dec. **Main courses** €25. **Credit** MC, V.
Map p401 E4  **Italian**

This chic Italian bistro is as far from a tourist joint
as it is possible to be. On weekday lunchtimes it is
full of suave Italianate businessmen. Generosity
defines the food – not just big plates, but lashings
of the ingredients that others skimp on, such as the
slices of tangy parmesan piled high over rocket on
the tender beef carpaccio. The pizzas are very good:
the Enzo comes with milky, almost raw *mozzarella
di bufala* and tasty tomatoes. For pasta you can
choose between dried and fresh, with variations
such as fresh saffron tagliatelle.

Goupil le Bistro

*4 rue Claude-Debussy, 17th (01.45.74.83.25).
Mº Porte de Champerret.* **Open** noon-2pm, 8-
11.30pm Mon-Fri. Closed Aug. **Main courses**
€23. **Credit** AmEx, V. **Map** p400 C1 **Bistro**

On the outer edge of the 17th, Goupil is everything
you imagine a traditional French bistro to be, with
its burgundy-and-cream colour scheme, wooden
tables and chairs, bunches of flowers and scribbled
blackboard menu. The menu is seasonal and short.
A *tarte fine aux maquereaux* makes the most of the
fish, layering the mackerel fillets on buttery puff
pastry topped with tastebud-tingling mustard sauce.
Beetroot carpaccio with *mâche* (lamb's lettuce) and
egg mimosa again employs humble ingredients to
great effect. Finish with a classic such as *île flottante*.

★ Granterroirs

*30 rue de Miromesnil, 8th (01.47.42.18.18/www.
granterroirs.com). Mº Miromesnil.* **Open** 9am-
8pm Mon-Fri. *Food served* noon-3pm Mon-Fri.
Closed 3wks Aug. **Main courses** €21. **Prix fixe**
€39, €49. **Credit** MC, V. **Map** p401 F3 **Bistro**

This *épicerie* with a difference is the perfect remedy
for anyone for whom the word 'terroir' conjures up
visions of grease-soaked peasant food. Here, the
walls heave with more than 600 enticing specialities
from southern France, including Périgord foie gras,
charcuterie from Aubrac and a fine selection of
wines. Great gift ideas – but why not sample some
of the goodies by enjoying the midday *table d'hôte*
feast? Come in early to ensure that you can choose
from the five succulent *plats du jour* (such as marinated salmon with dill on a bed of warm potatoes).

€ Le Hide

*10 rue du Général-Lanrezac, 17th
(01.45.74.15.81/www.lehide.fr). Mº Charles de
Gaulle Etoile.* **Open** noon-3pm, 7.30-10.30pm
Mon-Fri; 7.30-10.30pm Sat. **Main courses**
€16. **Prix fixe** €22, €29. **Credit** MC, V.
Map p400 C3 **Bistro**

Ever since it opened, this snug bistro has been
packed with a happy crowd of bistro-lovers who
appreciate Japanese-born chef Hide Kobayashi's
superb cooking and good-value prices. Expect
dishes such as duck foie gras terrine with pear-and-

CONSUME

The Real Paris

Rendez vous in St Germain des Prés: These are the hidden gems of Paris! Chic and authentic, you will experience the food and atmosphere like true Parisians...

Restaurant Chez Fernand
13 rue Guisarde
Paris 6e
Tél.01.43.54.61.47

Boucherie Roulière
Restaurant & Grill
24 rue des Canettes Paris 6e
Tél. 01. 43.26.25.70

Comme à Savonnières
Bistrot
18 rue Guisarde Paris 6e
Tél.01.43.29.52.18

O Mantra
Bar, Night Club & Restaurant
7 rue Grégoire de Tours.
Paris 6e
Tél. 01.43.54.50.59

thyme compôte to start, followed by tender faux-filet steak in a light foie gras sauce or skate wing with a lemon-accented beurre noisette. Desserts are excellent: perfect tarte tatin comes with crème fraîche from Normandy. Good, affordable wines explain the merriment, including a glass of the day for €2.

Maxan

37 rue de Miromesnil, 8th (01.42.65.78.60/ www.rest-maxan.com). Mᵒ Miromesnil. **Open** noon-2.30pm Mon; noon-2.30pm, 7.30-10.30pm Tue-Fri; 7.30-10.30pm Sat. Closed Aug. **Prix fixe** €38. **Credit** MC, V. **Map** p401 F3 ㉙ **Bistro**
This is a welcome new-wave bistro in an area where eating options tend to be fashion haunts, grand tables or tourist traps. Owner-chef Laurent Zajac uses quality seasonal ingredients, giving them a personal spin in dishes such as scallops with curry spices and artichoke hearts, classic veal sweetbreads with wild asparagus, and an exotic take on *île flottante*. Popular with ministry of interior types at lunch, quieter by night.

★ Mini Palais

Pont Alexandre III, av Winston Churchill, 8th (01.42.56.42.42/www.minipalais.com). Mᵒ Champs-Elysées Clemenceau. **Open** 8.30am-1am Mon-Fri; 10.30am-1am Sat, Sun. **Main courses** €25. **Credit** AmEx, DC, MC, V. **Map** p401 E5 ㉚ **Bistro**
Museum restaurants rarely feel cosy – the noisy, high-ceilinged dining room of this one in the Grand Palais certainly doesn't – but the 80-seater terrace is positively majestic. At the helm is Gilles Choukroun, proud inventor of the *crème brûlée de foie gras aux cacahuètes*, which he presents in its original version here. Otherwise, his cooking is restrained compared to what he once served at Angl'Opéra: you might even find a classic *gigot de sept heures* (slow-cooked lamb) or roast beef fillet with black truffle-scented *farfalle* on the pricey menu.

Pierre Gagnaire

6 rue Balzac, 8th (01.58.36.12.50/www.pierre-gagnaire.com). Mᵒ Charles de Gaulle Etoile or George V. **Open** noon-1.30pm, 7.30-9.30pm Mon-Fri, Sun. Closed 1wk Apr & Aug. **Main courses** €105. **Prix fixe** *Lunch* €95, €245. *Dinner* €245. **Credit** AmEx, MC, V. **Map** p400 D3 ㉛ **Haute cuisine**
At Pierre Gagnaire most starters alone cost over €90, which seems to be the price of culinary experimentation. The €90 lunch menu is far from the experience of the *carte*: the former is presented in three courses, whereas the latter involves four or five plates for each course. Even the *amuse-bouches* fill the table: an egg 'raviole', ricotta with apple, fish in a cauliflower jelly, and glazed monkfish. The best thing about the lunch menu is that it includes four very indulgent desserts: clementine, raspberry and vanilla, chocolate, and passion fruit.

Rech

62 av des Ternes, 17th (01.45.72.29.47/www. rech.fr). Mᵒ Ternes. **Open** noon-2pm, 6.30-10pm. Closed 3wks Aug. **Main courses** €28. **Prix fixe** *Lunch* €34. **Credit** AmEx, MC, V. **Map** p400 C2 ㉜ **Bistro**
Alain Ducasse's personal touches are everywhere in this art deco seafood restaurant, which he took over in spring 2007, from the Japanese fish prints on the walls of the upstairs dining room to the blown glass candleholders on the main floor tables. The kitchen turns out the kind of precise, Mediterranean-inspired cooking you would expect from Ducasse: glistening sardine fillets marinated with preserved lemon, silky lobster ravioli and octopus carpaccio painted with pesto. As the fish dishes are light, you can justify indulging in a perfectly aged camembert and the XL éclair, an event in itself.

★ Restaurant L'Entredgeu

83 rue Laugier, 17th (01.40.54.97.24). Mᵒ Porte de Champerret. **Open** noon-2pm, 7.30-11pm Tue-Sat. Closed 1wk Apr, 1st 3wks Aug & 1wk Dec. **Prix fixe** *Lunch* €22, €30. *Dinner* €30. **Credit** DC, MC, V. **Map** p400 C2 ㉝ **Bistro**
Reading the menu here will make you seriously doubt your capacity for pudding. But have no fear. The heartiness belies refined, perfectly gauged cooking, served in civilised portions. Table turnover is fast, but this is not a place to linger smoochily in any case – you'll be too busy marvelling at the sharp *gribiche* sauce cutting through the milky crisp-battered oysters, the depth and aroma of the saffron-infused fish soup, the perfect layered execution of the caramelised pork belly, and the delicate desserts. The wine list is creative and assured.

Senderens

9 pl de la Madeleine, 8th (01.42.65.22.90/www. senderens.fr). Mᵒ Madeleine. **Open** noon-3pm, 7.30-11.30pm daily. Closed 3wks Aug. **Main courses** €39. **Prix fixe** €110-€150 (with wine). **Credit** AmEx, DC, MC, V. **Map** p401 G4 ㉞ **Haute cuisine**
Alain Senderens reinvented his art nouveau institution (formerly Lucas Carton) a few years ago with a *Star Trek* interior and a mind-boggling fusion menu. Now, you might find dishes such as roast duck foie gras with a warm salad of black figs and liquorice powder, or monkfish steak with Spanish mussels and green curry sauce. Each dish comes with a suggested wine, whisky, sherry or punch (to match a rum-doused *savarin* with slivers of ten-flavour pear), and although these are perfectly chosen, the mix of flavours and alcohols can prove overwhelming.

★ Stella Maris

4 rue Arsène-Houssaye, 8th (01.42.89.16.22/ www.stellamarisparis.com). Mᵒ Charles de Gaulle Etoile. **Open** noon-2.30pm, 7.30-10.30pm Mon-Fri; 7.30-10.30pm Sat. Closed 2wks Aug. **Main**

CONSUME

CONSUME

Le Petit Marché. See p198.

courses €50. **Prix fixe** *Lunch* €43, €99.
Dinner €99, €130. **Credit** AmEx, DC, MC, V.
Map p400 D3 **㉟ Haute cuisine**
Tateru Yoshino has divided his life between Paris
and Tokyo for many years. Trained by Robuchon
and Troisgros, he turns out food that is resolutely
French. The service is at times faltering, but charm-
ingly so, and the space is beautiful. You might float
your way through foie gras with carrots, truffles and
pistachio oil, pan-fried sea bass with saffron risotto,
and a perfectly lopsided Grand Marnier soufflé. The
exquisite, powdery blandness of the tasting menu
going-home present, *cake aux marrons glacés*, brings
it all softly, dreamily, back next morning at breakfast. Expensive but wonderful.

La Table de Lauriston
129 rue de Lauriston, 16th (01.47.27.00.07).
M° Trocadéro. **Open** noon-2.30pm, 7-10.30pm
Mon-Fri; 7-10.30pm Sat. Closed 3wks Aug &
1wk Dec. **Main courses** €23. **Prix fixe** *Lunch*
€25. *Dinner* €40, €61. **Credit** AmEx, MC, V.
Map p400 B5 **㊱ Bistro**
Serge Barbey's dining room has a refreshingly feminine touch. The emphasis here is firmly on ingredients, expertly prepared to show off their freshness.
In spring, stalks of asparagus from the Landes are
expertly trimmed to avoid any stringiness and
served with the simplest *vinaigrette d'herbes*. More
extravagant is the *foie gras cuit au torchon*, in which
the duck liver is wrapped in a cloth and poached in
a bouillon. Skip the crème brûlée, which you could
have anywhere, and order a dessert with attitude:
the giant *baba au rhum*.

Taillevent
15 rue Lamennais, 8th (01.44.95.15.01/www.
taillevent.com). M° George V. **Open** 12.15-
1.30pm, 7.15-9.30pm Mon-Fri. Closed Aug. **Main
courses** €75. **Prix fixe** *Lunch* €70, €140, €190.
Dinner €140, €190. **Credit** AmEx, DC, MC, V.
Map p400 D3 **㊲ Haute cuisine**
Prices here are not as shocking as in some restaurants at this level; there's a €70 lunch menu.
Rémoulade de coquilles St-Jacques is a technical feat,
with slices of raw, marinated scallop wrapped in a
tube shape around a finely diced apple filling, encir-
cled by a mayonnaise-like *rémoulade* sauce. An
earthier and lip-smacking dish is the trademark
épeautre – an ancient wheat – cooked 'like a risotto'
with bone marrow, black truffle, whipped cream and
parmesan, and topped with sautéed frog's legs.
Ravioli au chocolat araguani is a surprising and
wonderful dessert.

MONTMARTRE & PIGALLE
Chez Toinette
20 rue Germain-Pilon, 18th (01.42.54.44.36).
M° Abbesses or Pigalle. **Open** 7.30-11.30pm Mon-
Sat. Closed last 3wks Aug. **Main courses** €17.
Credit MC, V. **Map** p401 H2 **㊳ Bistro**
This stalwart purveyor of bistro fare behind the
Théâtre de Montmartre has steadily upped its prices
in line with its burgeoning success. However, the
blackboard menu is still good value. As you squeeze
into the seats, the amiable waiter describes each dish
with pride, then presents an appetiser of olives, ripe
cherry tomatoes and crisp radishes. Of the starters,

194 Time Out Paris

try the red-blooded wild boar terrine or the soufflé-like asparagus quiche. Carnivorous mains include *mignon de porc*, spring lamb and assorted steaks. Round it off with armagnac-steeped prunes.

Le Ch'ti Catalan

*4 rue de Navarin, 9th (01.44.63.04.33). M°
Notre-Dame-de-Lorette.* **Open** noon-3pm, 7.30-11pm Mon-Fri; 7.30-11pm Sat. **Main courses** €15. **Credit** MC, V. **Map** p402 H2 ❸ **Bistro**
It's unconventional, to say the least, to pair ingredients such as endives, bacon and eel, commonly found in the north of France, with the sunny flavours of French Catalan cooking. But that's what two friends have done in this ochre-painted bistro. The amazing thing is, it works. *Anchoïade* – red peppers with tangy anchovies – is fresh and tasty; tender pork cheeks served in a casserole with melting white beans are succulent; and the *gueule noire* (black face) – crushed spice biscuits with crème fraîche and egg – refers to the slang for miners in northern France.

Le Moulin de la Galette

83 rue Lepic, 18th (01.46.06.84.77). M° Notre-Dame-de-Lorette. **Open** noon-2.45pm, 7.30-11pm Tue-Fri. Closed Aug. **Main courses** €30. **Credit** AmEx, MC, V. **Map** p402 H1 ❹ **Bistro**
The Butte Montmartre was once dotted with windmills, and this survivor houses a chic modern restaurant with a few tables in the cobbled courtyard. It's hard to imagine a more picturesque setting in Montmartre, but the kitchen makes an effort nonetheless with dishes such as foie gras with melting beetroot cooked in lemon balm and juniper or suckling pig alongside potato purée. Desserts, such as figs caramelised with muscovado sugar, look like a painter's tableau. If you're on a budget, stick to the set menus and order carefully from the wine list.

★ € Pétrelle

34 rue Pétrelle, 9th (01.42.82 11.02). M° Anvers.
Open 8-10pm Tue-Sat. Closed 4wks July/Aug & 1wk Dec. **Main courses** €25. **Prix fixe** €29. **Credit** MC, V. **Map** p402 J2 ❺ **Bistro**
Jean-Luc André is as inspired a decorator as he is a cook, and the quirky charm of his dining room has made it popular with fashion designers and film stars. But behind the style is some serious substance. André seeks out the best ingredients from local producers, and the quality shines through. The €29 no-choice menu is huge value for money (marinated sardines with tomato relish, rosemary-scented rabbit with roasted vegetables, deep purple poached figs) – or you can splash out with luxurious à la carte dishes such as tournedos Rossini.

€ Rose Bakery

*46 rue des Martyrs, 9th (01.42.82.12.80).
M° Notre-Dame-de-Lorette.* **Open** 9am-7pm Tue-Fri; 10am-5pm Sat, Sun. Closed 2wks Aug

& 1wk Dec. **Main courses** €14. **Credit** AmEx, MC, V. **Map** p402 H2 ❷ **British**
This English-themed café run by a Franco-British couple stands out for the quality of its ingredients – organic or from small producers – as well as the too-good-to-be-true puddings: carrot cake, sticky toffee pudding and, in winter, a chocolate-chestnut tart. The DIY salad plate is crunchily satisfying, but the thin-crusted *pizzettes*, daily soups and occasional risottos are equally good choices. Don't expect much beyond scones in the morning except at weekends, when brunch is served to a packed-out house. The dining room is minimalist but welcoming.

★ Spring

*28 rue de la Tour d'Auvergne, 9th
(01.45.96.05.72). M° Anvers or Cadet.* **Open** 8.30pm Tue, Wed; 1pm & 8.30pm Thur, Fri. Closed Aug & 1wk Dec. **Prix fixe** €42. **Credit** MC, V. **Map** p402 J2 ❸ **Bistro**
Where do Michelin inspectors go on their day off? To Spring, where young American chef Daniel Rose has wowed the critics since opening this sleek 16-seat bistro a few years ago. He serves a no-choice four-course menu that changes every day according to what he finds at the place des Fêtes market. On a late spring day this might result in a velvety cauliflower soup (made without cream), chunky octopus salad with potatoes, radishes and herbs, poached guinea hen with root vegetables, and baked apple with French toast. Reserve months ahead.

BEAUBOURG & THE MARAIS

404

*69 rue des Gravilliers, 3rd (01.42.74.57.81).
M° Arts et Métiers.* **Open** noon-2.30pm, 8pm-midnight Mon-Fri; noon-4pm (brunch), 8pm-midnight Sat, Sun. **Main courses** €19. **Prix fixe** *Brunch* €21. *Lunch* €17. **Credit** AmEx, DC, MC, V. **Map** p409 K5 ❹ **North African**
However much others try to copy Algerian-born Momo's formula, they can't replicate the unique atmosphere of his Paris and London restaurants. Book for the late sitting if you like to dance on the tables: before you've finished your mint cocktails, the waiters will already be gyrating on the bar. Starters include *salade méchouia* (a refreshing combination of diced tomato, red peppers and garlic), *zalouk* (aubergine and garlic) or stuffed sardines. Of the mouthwatering tagines the chicken with pear is a winner, but the real revelation is the fish tagine absolutely bursting with flavour.

★ L'Ambassade d'Auvergne

*22 rue du Grenier-St-Lazare, 3rd (01.42.72.31.22/
www.ambassade-auvergne.com). M° Arts et
Métiers.* **Open** noon-2pm, 7.30-10pm daily. **Main courses** €18. **Prix fixe** €30, €40, €55, €65. **Credit** AmEx, MC, V. **Map** p409 K5 ❺ **Bistro**

This rustic *auberge* is a fitting embassy for the hearty fare of central France. An order of cured ham comes as two hefty, plate-filling slices, and the salad bowl is chock-full of green lentils cooked in goose fat, studded with bacon and shallots. The *rôti d'agneau* arrives as a pot of melting chunks of lamb in a rich, meaty sauce with a helping of tender white beans. Dishes arrive with the flagship *aligot*, the creamy, elastic mash-and-cheese concoction. Of the regional wines (Chanturgue, Boudes, Madargues), the fruity AOC Marcillac makes a worthy partner.

€ Breizh Café
109 rue Vieille-du-Temple, 3rd (01.42.72.13.77/ www.breizhcafe.com). M° Filles du Calvaire. **Open** noon-11pm Wed-Sun. Closed 3wks Aug. **Main courses** €10. **Credit** MC, V. **Map** p409 L5 ⓐ **Crêperie**

With its modern interior of pale wood and its choice of 15 artisanal ciders, this outpost of a restaurant in Cancale, Brittany is a world away from the average crêperie. For the complete faux-seaside experience, you might start with a plate of creuse oysters from Cancale before indulging in an inventive buckwheat *galette* such as the Cancalaise, made with potato, smoked herring from Brittany and herring roe. The choice of fillings is fairly limited, but the ingredients are of high quality – including the use of Valrhona chocolate with 70 per cent cocoa solids in the dessert crêpes.

★ € Chez Hanna
54 rue des Rosiers, 4th (01.42.74.74.99). M° St-Paul. **Open** noon-midnight daily. **Main courses** €10. **Credit** MC, V. **Map** p409 K6 ⓐ **Jewish**

By noon on a Sunday a queue forms outside every felafel shop along rue des Rosiers. Long-established L'As du Fallafel a little further up the street still reigns supreme, whereas Hanna remains something of a locals' secret, quietly serving up felafel and shawarma sandwiches to rival any in the world. A pitta sandwich bursting with crunchy chickpea-and-herb balls, tahini sauce and vegetables costs €4 if you order from the takeaway window, €8 if you sit at one of the tables in the buzzy dining room overlooking the street. Either way, you can't lose.

Chez Julien
1 rue du Pont Louis-Philippe, 4th (01.42.78.31.64). M° Pont Marie. **Open** noon-3pm, 7-11pm Mon-Sat. **Main courses** €25. **Credit** MC, V. **Map** p409 K6 ⓐ **Bistro**

Thierry Costes discreetly took over this vintage bistro overlooking the Seine in spring 2007. The zebra banquette near the loo upstairs is most reminiscent of the Costes style, but the 1920s dining room is also unmistakeably chic with plum walls, a big chandelier and red banquettes, and the terrace outside now stretches across the cobbled pedestrian street. The food is predictable and pricey – crab salad, steak with shoestring fries, roast Bresse chicken with mini-potatoes – but it's hard not to enjoy this slice of Paris life.

★ € Chez Omar
47 rue de Bretagne, 3rd (01.42.72.36.26). M° Arts et Métiers or Temple. **Open** noon-2.30pm, 7-10.30pm Mon-Sat; 7-10.30pm Sun. **Main courses** €16. **No credit cards**. **Map** p409 L5 ⓐ **North African**

CONSUME

Le Bistrot Paul Bert. *See p199.*

The once-fashionable Omar doesn't take reservations, and the queue can stretch the length of the zinc bar and through the door. Everyone is waiting for the same thing: couscous. Prices range from €11 (vegetarian) to €24 (*royale*); there are no tagines or other traditional Maghreb mains, only a handful of French classics (duck, fish, steak). Overstretched waiters slip through the crowds with mounds of semolina, vats of vegetable-laden broth and steel platters heaving with meat, including the stellar *merguez*. Even on packed nights, there's an offer of seconds – gratis – to encourage you to stay a little while longer. **Other locations** Café Moderne, 19 rue Keller, 11th (01.47.00.53.62).

Le Gaigne

12 rue Pecquay, 4th (01.44.59.86.72/www. restaurantlegaigne.fr). M° Rambuteau. **Open** 12.15-2.30pm, 7.30-10.30pm Mon, Wed, Thur; 12.15-2.30pm, 7.30-11pm Fri, Sat; 7.30-10.30pm Sun. **Main courses** €24. **Prix fixe** *Lunch* €16, €22. *Dinner* €39, €54. **Credit** AmEx, MC, V. **Map** p409 K6 **⑩ Bistro**
It's a familiar story: young chef with haute cuisine credentials opens a small bistro in an out-of-the-way street. Here, the restaurant is even tinier than usual with only 20 seats and the cooking is unusually inventive. Chef Mickaël Gaignon previously worked with Pierre Gagnaire, and it shows in dishes such as *l'oeuf bio* – three open eggshells filled with creamed spinach, carrot and celeriac – or roast monkfish with broccoli purée and a redcurrant emulsion.

The dining room is pleasantly modern and staff are eager to please.

Le Hangar

12 impasse Berthaud, 3rd (01.42.74.55.44). M° Rambuteau. **Open** noon-2.30pm, 7.30-11pm Tue-Sat. Closed Aug. **Main courses** €17. **No credit cards**. **Map** p409 K5 **⑪ Bistro**
It's worth making the effort to find this bistro by the Centre Pompidou, with its terrace tucked away in a hidden alley and excellent cooking. A bowl of tapenade and toast is supplied to keep you going while choosing from the comprehensive *carte*. It yields, for starters, tasty and grease-free *rillettes de lapereau* (rabbit) alongside perfectly balanced pumpkin and chestnut soup. Main courses include pan-fried foie gras on a smooth potato purée made with olive oil.

Le Petit Marché

9 rue de Béarn, 3rd (01.42.72.06.67). M° Chemin Vert. **Open** noon-3pm, 7.30pm-midnight Mon-Fri; noon-4pm Sat, Sun. **Main courses** €17. **Prix fixe** *Lunch* €20.50. **Credit** AmEx, MC, V. **Map** 409 L6 **⑫ Bistro**
Petit Marché's menu is short and modern with Asian touches. Raw tuna is flash-fried in sesame seeds and served with a Thai sauce, making for a refreshing starter; crispy-coated deep-fried king prawns have a similar oriental lightness. The main vegetarian risotto is rich in basil, coriander, cream and al dente green beans. Pan-fried scallops with lime are precision-cooked and accompanied by a good purée and more beans. There's a short wine list. *Photo p194.*

Le Train Bleu. See p203.

BASTILLE & EASTERN PARIS

★ € A la Biche au Bois

45 av Ledru-Rollin, 12th (01.43.43.34.38).
M° Gare de Lyon. **Open** 7-11pm Mon; noon-
2pm, 7-11pm Tue-Fri. Closed 4wks July-
Aug & Christmas wk. **Main courses** €15.
Prix fixe €25. **Credit** AmEx, DC, MC, V.
Map p407 M8 ❸ **Bistro**

However crowded it gets here, it doesn't matter
because everyone always seems so happy with the
food and the convivial atmosphere. It's impossible
not to be enthusiastic about the more than generous
portions offered with the €24.90 prix fixe menu.
Mains might include tasty portions of wild duck in
blackcurrant sauce, partridge with cabbage or wild
venison stew. If you can still do dessert, go for one
of the home-made tarts laden with seasonal fruits.
The wine list has a reputation as one of the best-
value selections in town. Book in advance, but
expect to wait anyway.

★ Le Bistrot Paul Bert

18 rue Paul-Bert, 11th (01.43.72.24.01).
M° Charonne or Faidherbe Chaligny. **Open**
noon-2pm, 7.30-11pm Tue-Thur; noon-2pm,
7.30-11.30pm Fri, Sat. Closed Aug. **Main
courses** €21. **Prix fixe** *Lunch* €16. *Dinner*
€32. **Credit** MC, V. **Map** p407 N7 ❺ **Bistro**

This heart-warming bistro gets it right almost
down to the last crumb. A starter salad of *ris de
veau* illustrates the point, with lightly browned veal
sweetbreads perched on a bed of green beans and
baby carrots with a sauce of sherry vinegar and
deglazed cooking juices. A roast shoulder of suckling pig and a thick steak with a raft of golden,
thick-cut *frites* look inviting indeed. Desserts are
superb too, including what may well be the best *île
flottante* in Paris. If you're in the area at lunchtime,
bear in mind that the prix fixe menu is remarkable
value. *Photo p197.*

Bofinger

*5-7 rue de la Bastille, 4th (01.42.72.87.82/
www.bofingerparis.com).* *M° Bastille.* **Open**
noon-3pm, 6.30pm-12.30am Mon-Fri; noon-
12.30am Sat, Sun. **Main courses** €24.50.
Prix fixe €30.50. **Credit** AmEx, DC, MC, V.
Map p409 L7 ❻ **Brasserie**

Bofinger draws big crowds for its authentic art
nouveau setting and its brasserie atmosphere.
Downstairs is the prettiest place in which to eat, but
the upstairs room is air-conditioned. An à la carte
selection might start with plump, garlicky escargots or a well-made langoustine terrine, followed by
an intensely seasoned salmon tartare, a generous (if
unremarkable) cod steak, or calf's liver accompanied by cooked melon. Alternatively, you could
have the foolproof brasserie meal of oysters and
fillet steak, followed by a pungent plate of munster

cheese and bowl of cumin, washed down by the fine
Gigondas at €35.50 a bottle.

€ L'Encrier

55 rue Traversière, 12th (01.44.68.08.16).
M° Gare de Lyon or Ledru-Rollin. **Open** noon-
2.15pm, 7.30-11pm Mon-Fri; 7.30-11pm Sat.
Closed Aug & Christmas wk. **Main courses**
€14. **Prix fixe** *Lunch* €14. *Dinner* €19, €23.
Credit MC, V. **Map** p407 M7 ❻ **Bistro**

Through the door and past the velvet curtain, you
find yourself face to face with the kitchen – and a
crowd of locals, many of whom seem to know the
charming boss personally. Start with fried rabbit
kidneys on a bed of salad dressed with raspberry
vinegar, an original and wholly successful combination, and follow with goose *magret* with honey – a
welcome change from the usual duck version and
served with crunchy, thinly sliced sautéed potatoes.
To end, share a chocolate cake, or try the popular
profiteroles. The fruity Chinon is a classy red.

La Gazzetta

*29 rue de Cotte, 12th (01.43.47.47.05/www.
lagazzetta.fr).* *M° Ledru-Rollin.* **Open** 11.30am-
3pm, 6.30pm-1am Tue-Sun. Closed Aug. **Main
courses** €25. **Prix fixe** *Lunch* €14, €16.
Dinner €37, €49. **Credit** AmEx, DC, MC, V.
Map p407 N7 ❼ **Bistro**

Opened by the team behind bar Le Fumoir, La
Gazzetta has a similarly moody feel, with dim
lighting, a long zinc bar and retro decor. Chef Petter
Nilssen is Swedish, but made his name in the
south of France, and his food shows a Scandinavian
influence in dishes such as bonito in a sweet-salty
marinade with caraway, borage leaves, radish
and pomelo or new potatoes from the island of
Noirmoutier off the Atlantic coast with seaweed
butter and dill. The €34 menu is a good bet with four
courses and not too many decisions to make.

★ Le Souk

*1 rue Keller, 11th (01.49.29.05.08/www.
lesoukfr.com).* *M° Bastille or Ledru-Rollin.*
Open 7.30-11.30pm Tue-Fri; 11.30am-2.30pm,
7.30pm-12.30am Sat; 11.30am-2.30pm, 7.30pm-
11.30am Sun. **Main courses** €18. **Prix
fixe** €27. **Credit** DC, MC, V. **Map** p407 N7 ❻
North African

Potted olive trees mark the entrance to this lively
den of Moroccan cuisine. Start with savoury *b'stilla*,
a pasty stuffed with duck, raisins and nuts,
flavoured with orange-blossom water and sprinkled
with cinnamon and powdered sugar. Don't fill up,
though, as the first-rate tagines and couscous are
enormous. The *tagine canette* (duckling stewed with
honey, onions, apricots, figs and cinnamon, then
showered with toasted almonds) is terrific. For
dessert, try the excellent millefeuille with fresh figs,
while sweet mint tea is poured in a long stream
by a *djellaba*-clad waiter.

CONSUME

Profile Truffles

How to sniff out the finest tubers.

CONSUME

There's no mistaking the scent of a fresh truffle: potent, earthy and even slightly feral, it grabs you by the nostrils and draws you in. Yet all too often this intoxicating hit can prove elusive, even in a luxury-loving city like Paris. If a truffle is of poor quality or has been improperly stored, it will prove perfectly tasteless no matter how many shavings are showered on your food, so it makes sense to be cautious when paying a premium for this precious tuber.

First, consider the season. The charcoal-black *tuber melanosporum* or *truffe du Périgord*, France's most prized truffle, is in season from November to March, but the flavour reaches its peak in January. No matter how tempting it might be to indulge during the festive season, it pays to wait a few more weeks. Summer truffles, also known as *tuber aestivum* or *truffe de la St-Jean d'été*, are cream striped with grey rather than charcoal-black – they should be more affordable, and are ideal for people who find *tuber*

melanosporum overwhelming. In autumn, you might also come across the slightly more fragrant *truffe de Bourgogne* – the name of a variety (*tuber uncinatum*) rather than an indication of its origin. The white Alba truffle from Italy, the most expensive (at up to €5,000 per kg) and perhaps the most dizzyingly scented of all truffles, comes to Paris from October to December and can be found in luxury restaurants.

Watch out for the Chinese truffle, a completely flavourless *melanosporum* look-alike, and no matter what the time of year, be wary of preserved truffles, truffle oils and all other truffle preparations such as *boudin blanc truffé*, fluffy veal sausage sold at Christmas that usually contains no more than a few crumbs of preserved truffle.

Preserved truffles sold in jars are a poor substitute for fresh, and truffle oils nearly always get their scent from a chemical compound rather than the real thing: partly for cost reasons, but also because natural truffle flavour is notoriously hard to extract. Knowing that the word 'truffle' sells, many chefs have no scruples about using inexpensive fake truffle oil (though you wouldn't know it from the cost of the dish), even drizzling it on fresh truffles to strengthen their flavour.

Whether you're buying fresh truffle to take home or treating yourself in a restaurant, don't be afraid to ask questions and sniff before you buy. When chefs are using fresh truffles in

prime condition, they will be proud to bring them to your table before shaving them on to your dish. Tasteless truffles pop up even in the most expensive restaurants; ordering the truffle menu is no guarantee of a sublime experience. Still, here's a list of stores and restaurants that usually deliver.

Le Comptoir Corrézien
8 rue des Volontaires, 15th (01.47.83.52.97).
This little shop dedicated to products from southwest France is where chefs go to buy fresh black truffles in season.

Guy Savoy
18 rue Troyon, 17th (01.43.80.40.61/ www.guysavoy.com).
Few chefs know how to handle truffles like Guy Savoy, who is famed for his artichoke soup with truffles, served with brioche and truffle butter.

Un Jour à Peyrassol
13 rue Vivienne, 2nd (01.42.60.12.92/ www.peyrassol.com).
This chic offshoot of the Commanderie de Peyrassol, a picturesque wine-producing castle in the Var, has a blackboard menu full of truffle treats as well as an *épicerie*.

Maison de la Truffe
19 pl de la Madeleine, 8th (01.42.65.53.22).
Founded in 1932, this deluxe *épicerie* sells fresh truffles, truffle oils and preserves, and other luxury foodstuffs.

Michel Rostang
20 rue Rennequin, 17th (01.47.63.40.77/ www.michelrostang.com).
This haute cuisine chef was the first to serve a truffle sandwich – country bread, salted butter, shaved *tuber melanosporum* and a sprinkling of Noirmoutier salt – in a luxury restaurant. It's still on the menu in winter, or you can go for his full-blown truffle menu.

Restaurant Pierre
10 rue de Richelieu, 1st (01.42.96.09.17).
For a truly sensual experience, try the roast camembert filled with fresh truffles and other truffle *plats du jour*.

Terres de Truffes
21 rue Vignon, 8th (01.53.43.80.44/ www.terresdetruffes.com).
A truffle shop and restaurant run by chef Clément Bruno, who has a celebrated truffle restaurant in the Provençal town of Lorgues.

CONSUME

FAJITAS

MEXICAN RESTAURANT

*"Miguel cooks deliciously fresh northern Mexican dishes
with some southern specials among the starters (...).
The signature fajitas with beef and chicken are a
magnificent main."*
Time Out Paris Penguin Guide 2002

OPEN DAILY NOON-11PM
CLOSED MONDAY

15 RUE DAUPHINE, 6TH - M° ODEON OR PONT NEUF
TEL: 01.46.34.44.69
WWW.FAJITAS-PARIS.COM

Le Train Bleu

Gare de Lyon, pl Louis-Armand, 12th (01.43.43.09.06/www.le-train-bleu.com). M° Gare de Lyon. **Open** 11.30am-3pm, 7-11pm daily. **Main courses** €26. **Prix fixe** *Lunch* €48. *Dinner* €48, €96. **Credit** AmEx, DC, MC, V. **Map** p407 M8 🟠 **Brasserie**

This listed dining room – with vintage frescoes and big oak benches – exudes a pleasant air of expectation. Don't expect cutting-edge cooking, but rather fine renderings of French classics. Lobster served on walnut oil-dressed salad leaves is a generous, beautifully prepared starter, as is the pistachio-studded *saucisson de Lyon* with a warm salad of small *ratte* potatoes. Mains of veal chop topped with a cap of cheese, and *sandre* (pike-perch) with a 'risotto' of *crozettes* are also pleasant. A few reasonably priced wines would be welcome. *Photo p198.*

Unico

15 rue Paul-Bert, 11th (01.43.67.68.08/ www.resto-unico.com). M° Faidherbe-Chaligny. **Open** 12.30-2.30pm, 8-10.30pm Tue-Sat. **Main courses** €20. **Credit** MC, V. **Map** p407 N7 🟠 Argentinian

Architect Marcelo Joulia and photographer Enrique Zanoni were wise enough to retain the vintage 1970s decor of this former butcher's shop when they opened their temple to Argentinian beef. Orange tiles and matching light fixtures provide the backdrop for the fashionable, black-dressed crowd that comes here for thick slabs of meat grilled over charcoal and served with a selection of sauces. If you find yourself hesitating, opt for the *lomo* (fillet) with *chimichurri*, a mild salsa – and don't forget to wash it down with Argentinian wine, a rarity in Paris.

★ Au Vieux Chêne

7 rue du Dahomey, 11th (01.43.71.67.69). M° Faidherbe-Chaligny. **Open** noon-2pm, 8-10.30pm Mon-Fri; 8-10.30pm Sat. Closed 1wk July & 2wks Aug. **Main courses** €20. **Prix fixe** *Lunch* €13. *Dinner* €29. **Credit** MC, V. **Map** p407 N7 🟠 **Bistro**

Although everyone loves the the zinc-capped bar by the door when you come in, and the tiled floor, what makes this bistro so special is its desire to please. A starter of langoustines encased in fine crunchy angel hair and garnished with slices of fresh mango is delicious and refreshing, and chilled tomato soup is garnished with mint, a ball of tomato sorbet and a drizzle of olive oil. Stéphane Chevassus is a gifted game cook too, as proved by the tender roast pigeon sautéed with Chinese cabbage.

NORTH-EAST PARIS

★ € Le Baratin

3 rue Jouye-Rouve, 20th (01.43.49.39.70). M° Pyrénées. **Open** 12.15-3pm, 8-11pm Tue-Fri; 8-11pm Sat. **Main courses** €15. **Prix fixe** *Lunch* €15. **Credit** MC, V. **Map** p403 N3 🟠 **Bistro**

Star pastry chef Pierre Hermé visits this cheerful little bistro high up in Belleville at least every two weeks to fill up on Raquel Carena's homely cooking with the occasional exotic twist. Typical of her style, which draws on her native Argentina, are tuna carpaccio with cherries, roast Basque lamb with new potatoes and spinach, and hazelnut pudding. If the food weren't so fantastic, it would still be worth coming for the mostly organic wines. Le Baratin attracts gourmands from all over Paris – so be sure to book.

Atelier Maître Albert. *See p205.*

CONSUME

€ A la Bière
104 av Simon-Bolivar, 19th (01.42.39.83.25).
M° Colonel Fabien. **Open** noon-3pm, 7pm-1.30am
daily. **Main courses** €11. **Prix fixe** €13.40.
Credit V. **Map** p403 M2 ❸ **Brasserie**
A la Bière looks like one of those nondescript corner
brasseries, but what makes it stand out is an amaz-
ingly good-value €13.40 prix fixe full of fine bistro
favourites. White tablecloths and fine kirs set the
tone; starters of thinly sliced pig's cheek with a nice
French dressing on the salad, and a home-made rabbit terrine exceed expectations. The mains live up to
what's served before: charcoal-grilled entrecôte with
hand-cut chips, and juicy Lyonnais sausages with
potatoes drenched in olive oil, garlic and parsley.
This is one of the few bargains left in Paris.

Le Cambodge
10 av Richerand, 10th (01.44.84.37.70/www.
lecambodge.fr). M° Goncourt or République.
Open noon-2.30pm, 8-11.30pm Mon-Sat. Closed
1 Aug-15 Sept, 24 Dec-1 Jan. **Main courses** €13.
Credit MC, V. **Map** p402 L4 ❻ **Cambodian**

The system at Le Cambodge is simple: you write
your order on a piece of paper, including preferences
such as 'no coriander', 'no peanuts' or 'extra rice',
and after a short wait the dishes appear. Two
favourites are the *bobun spécial*, a hot and cold mix
of sautéed beef, noodles, salad, bean sprouts and
imperial rolls, and *banhoy*, a selection of the same
ingredients to be wrapped in lettuce and mint leaves
and dipped in a sauce. They also serve soups, salads and curries including stewed pork in a fragrant
coconut sauce.

★ Le Chateaubriand
129 av Parmentier, 11th (01.43.57.45.95). M°
Goncourt. **Open** noon-2pm, 8-11pm Tue-Fri; 8-
11pm Sat. Closed 3wks Aug, 1wk Dec. **Prix fixe**
Lunch €19. *Dinner* €40. **Credit** AmEx, MC, V.
Map p403 M4 ❻ **Bistro**
Self-taught Basque chef Iñaki Aizpitarte runs this
stylish bistro. Come at dinner to try the cooking at
its most adventurous, as a much simpler (albeit
cheaper) menu is served at lunch. Dishes have been
deconstructed down to their very essence and put

Le Pré Verre. *See p206.*

CONSUME

back together again. You'll understand if you try starters such as chunky steak tartare garnished with a quail's egg or asparagus with tahini foam and little splinters of sesame-seed brittle. The cooking's not always so cerebral – Aizpitarte's Spanish goat's cheese with stewed apple jam is brilliant. Be sure to book a few days ahead.

★ € Dong Huong

14 rue Louis-Bonnet, 11th (01.43.57.18.88). Mº Belleville. **Open** noon-10.30pm Mon, Wed-Sun. Closed 2wks Jan & 3wks Aug. **Main courses** €7. **Credit** MC, V. **Map** p403 N4 ⑥⑨ Vietnamese
The excellent food at this Vietnamese noodle joint attracts a buzzy crowd. The delicious *bành cuón*, steamed Vietnamese ravioli stuffed with minced meat, mushrooms, bean sprouts, spring onions and deep-fried onion, are served piping hot. *Com ga lui*, chicken kebabs with tasty lemongrass, though not as delicate, come with tasty rice. *Bò bùn chà giò* (noodles with beef and small *nem* topped with onion strips, spring onion and crushed peanuts) makes a meal in itself. For dessert, the mandarin, lychee and mango sorbets are tasty and authentic.

Ile de Gorée

70 rue Jean-Pierre-Timbaud, 11th (01.43.38.97.69). Mº Goncourt. **Open** 7pm-midnight daily. **Main courses** €15. **Credit** MC, V. **Map** p403 M4 ⑥⑦ African & Indian Ocean
Gorée Island is a 15-minute ferry ride off the Senegal coast. As for its namesake, mango and peach punch and live kora music set the mood. Simple but very well-prepared *boudin créole* (black pudding with cinnamon) and *aloco* (sautéed plantains) with sweet tomato relish can be followed with a hearty *dem farci* (stuffed mullet) in brown sauce or *thiou poisson* (whole fish) with tomatoes, bell peppers, carrots, potatoes and basmati rice. Muomuo, the friendly house cat, will happily lap up the rest of your rum-raisin ice-cream from the bowl. An enchanted isle indeed.

Kazaphani

122 av Parmentier, 11th (01.48.07.20.19). Mº Goncourt or Parmentier. **Open** noon-3pm, 7pm-midnight Tue-Fri, Sun; 7pm-midnight Sat. Closed 2wks Aug. **Main courses** €16. **Prix fixe** *Lunch* €18, €29, €35. **Credit** MC, V. **Map** p403 M4 ⑥⑧ Cypriot
The atmosphere at this family-run Cypriot restaurant is so relaxed that you might feel you've walked into someone's home. The €32 meze menu brings dish after dish of food; highlights include the octopus in olive oil, lemon and garlic; wonderfully lemony mushrooms; and a tasty paste of broad beans. Next arrive plates of calamares, deep-fried whitebait and huge, aniseed-flavoured *gambas*. Meat dishes are excellent quality too, particularly

THE BEST PUDDINGS

For rich rum baba
Alain Ducasse au Plaza Athénée. *See p190.*

For fancy chocolate fondant
Le 21. *See p211.*

For classic clafoutis
L'Agassin. *See p215.*

the crisp meatballs and stuffed pork. You can match the food with any of the good red wines on offer – Hatzimichalis, say, or Nemea.

€ La Madonnina

10 rue Marie-et-Louise, 10th (01.42.01.25.26). Mº Goncourt or Jacques Bonsergent. **Open** noon-2.30pm, 8-10.30pm Mon-Thur; noon-2.30pm, 8-11pm Fri; 8-11pm Sat. Closed 2wks Aug. **Main courses** €14. **Prix fixe** *Lunch* €12. **Credit** MC, V. **Map** p402 L4 ⑥⑨ Italian
La Madonnina flirts with kitsch so skilfully that it ends up coming off as cool. With its candles, mustard yellow walls and a smattering of red-checked tablecloths, this is the perfect place for a romantic night out. La Madonnina describes itself as a *trattoria napoletana*, but most of the dishes are pan-southern Italian. The extremely short menu changes monthly; don't miss the home-made pastas, such as artichoke and ricotta ravioli. The *cassata*, an extremely sweet Sicilian version of cheesecake, is authentic and unusual to see on menus outside Italy.

THE LATIN QUARTER & THE 13TH

Atelier Maître Albert

1 rue Maître-Albert, 5th (01.56.81.30.01/ www.ateliermaitrealbert.com). Mº Maubert Mutualité or St-Michel. **Open** noon-2.30pm, 6.30-11.30pm Mon-Wed; noon-2.30pm, 6.30pm-1am Thur, Fri; 6.30pm-1am Sat; 6.30-11.30pm Sun. **Main courses** €25. **Prix fixe** *Lunch* €29. **Credit** AmEx, DC, MC, V. **Map** p406 K7 ⑦⓪ Bistro
This Guy Savoy outpost in the fifth has slick decor by Jean-Michel Wilmotte. The indigo-painted, grey marble-floored dining room with open kitchen and rôtisseries on view is attractive but very noisy at night. The short menu lets you have a Savoy classic or two to start with, including oysters in seawater *gelée* or more inventive dishes such as the ballotine of chicken, foie gras and celery root in a chicken-liver sauce. Next up, perhaps, tuna served with tiny iron casseroles of dauphinois potatoes, and cauliflower in béchamel sauce. *Photo p203.*

CONSUME

L'Avant-Goût
26 rue Bobillot, 13th (01.53.80.24.00). M° Place d'Italie. **Open** noon-2pm, 7.45-10.45pm Tue-Sat. Closed 3wks Aug. **Main courses** €16.50. **Prix fixe** *Lunch* €14. *Dinner* €31. **Credit** MC, V. **Bistro**
Self-taught chef Christophe Beaufront has turned this nondescript street on the edge of the villagey Butte-aux-Cailles into a foodie destination. Typical of Beaufront's cooking is his *pot-au-feu de cochon aux épices*, a much-written-about dish that has been on his menu for years. He now presents the pork, sweet potato and fennel garnished with deep-fried ginger on a plate with a glass of bouillon to drink on the side. It's good, if not earth-shaking; however, a starter of piquillo pepper stuffed with smoked haddock rillettes does illustrate his talent.
▶ *Beaufront's food is available to take away at the épicerie across the street, complete with cast-iron cooking pots (to be returned).*

€ Le Bambou
70 rue Baudricourt, 13th (01.45.70.91.75). M° Olympiades or Tolbiac. **Open** noon-3.30pm, 7-10.30pm Tue-Sun. **Main courses** €10. **Credit** MC, V. **Vietnamese**
The Vietnamese fare here is a notch above what is normally served in Paris. Seating is elbow to elbow and, should you come on your own, the waiter will draw a line down the middle of the paper tablecloth and seat a stranger on the other side. That stranger might offer pointers on how to eat certain dishes, such as the no.42: grilled marinated pork to be wrapped in lettuce with beansprouts and herbs and eaten by hand, dipped into the accompanying sauce (no.43 is the same thing, but with pre-soaked rice paper wrappers).

Le Buisson Ardent
25 rue Jussieu, 5th (01.43.54.93.02). M° Jussieu. **Open** noon-2pm, 7.45-10pm Mon-Fri; 7.45-10pm Sat. Closed Aug. **Main courses** €19. **Prix fixe** €32. **Credit** MC, V. **Map** p406 K8 **⓲ Bistro**
This bistro's square front dining room with its red banquettes and painted glass panels dating from 1923 has a quintessentially Paris charm, especially when compared to the surrounding kebab shops. There is plenty for adventurous eaters on chef Stéphane Maubuit's menu, such as pan-fried squid with chorizo and quinoa or white bean and pig's ear salad with pan-fried foie gras, but he also does conventional dishes (chestnut velouté with spice bread croûtons) very well. Desserts are less remarkable, but this is one of the area's best finds for the price.

★ Itinéraires
5 rue de Pontoise, 5th (01.46.33.60.11). M° Maubert Mutualité. **Open** noon-2pm, 8-11pm Tue-Sat. **Main courses** €22. **Prix fixe** *Lunch* €18. *Dinner* €34. **Credit** MC, V. **Map** p406 K7 **⓲ Bistro**

Chef Sylvain Sendra played to a full house every night at his little bistro Le Temps au Temps near the Bastille before moving to this larger space near Notre Dame. The sleek space brings together all the elements that make for a successful bistro today: a long *table d'hôtes*, a bar for solo meals or quick bites, and a reasonably priced, market-inspired menu. Not everything is a wild success, but it's hard to fault a chef who so often hits the mark, in dishes such as squid-ink risotto with clams, *botargo* (dried mullet roe) and tomato.

L'Ourcine
92 rue Broca, 13th (01.47.07.13.65). M° Glacière or Les Gobelins. **Open** noon-2pm, 7-10.30pm Tue-Thur; noon-2.30pm, 7-11pm Fri, Sat. Closed 4wks July-Aug. **Prix fixe** *Lunch* (Tue-Fri) €22. *Dinner* €22, €30. **Credit** MC, V. **Map** p406 J10 **⓲ Bistro**
This restaurant near Gobelins is a wonderful destination for anyone who really loves Basque and Béarnais cooking. Start with *pipérade*, succulent chorizo or a spread of sliced beef tongue with piquillo peppers; then try the sautéed baby squid with parsley, garlic and Espelette peppers, or the *piquillos* stuffed with puréed cod and potato. Service is friendly, and an appealing atmosphere is generated by a growing band of regulars. The wine list is quite short but does offer several pleasant Southwestern bottles. The homely desserts include *gâteau basque.*

Le Pré Verre
8 rue Thénard, 5th (01.43.54.59.47/www.lepreverre.com). M° Maubert Mutualité. **Open** noon-2pm, 7.30-10.30pm Tue-Sat. Closed 3wks Aug & 2wks Dec. **Main courses** €18. **Prix fixe** *Lunch* €13.50. *Dinner* €28.50. **Credit** MC, V. **Map** p408 J7 **⓲ Bistro**
Philippe Delacourcelle knows how to handle spices like few other French chefs. He also trained with the late Bernard Loiseau, and learned the art of French pastry at Fauchon. Salt cod with cassia bark and smoked potato purée is a classic: what the fish lacks in size it makes up for in rich, cinnamon-like flavour and crunchy texture, and smooth potato cooked in a smoker makes a startling accompaniment. Spices have a way of making desserts seem esoteric rather than decadent, but the roast figs with olives are an exception to the rule. *Photo p204.*

★ Ribouldingue
10 rue St-Julien-le-Pauvre, 5th (01.46.33.98.80). M° St-Michel. **Open** noon-2pm, 7-11pm Mon-Sat. **Prix fixe** €27. **Credit** MC, V. **Map** p408 J7 **⓲ Bistro**
This bistro facing St-Julien-le-Pauvre church is the creation of Nadège Varigny, who spent ten years working with Yves Camdeborde before opening a restaurant inspired by the food of her childhood in Grenoble. It's full of people, including critics and chefs, who love simple, honest bistro fare, such as

CONSUME

Bread & Roses. *See p211.*

Decoding the Menu

From potage to île flottante.

MEALS (REPAS)
petit déjeuner breakfast. **déjeuner** lunch. **dîner** dinner. **souper** late dinner, supper.

PREPARATION (LA PREPARATION)
en croûte in a pastry case. **farci** stuffed. **au four** baked. **flambé** flamed in alcohol. **forestière** with mushrooms. **fricassé** fried and simmered in stock, usually with creamy sauce. **fumé** smoked. **garni** garnished. **glacé** frozen or iced. **gratiné** topped with breadcrumbs or cheese and grilled. **à la grècque** vegetables served cold in the cooking liquid with oil and lemon juice. **grillé** grilled. **haché** minced. **julienne** (vegetables) cut into matchsticks. **lamelle** very thin slice. **mariné** marinated. **pané** breaded. **en papillote** cooked in a packet. **parmentier** with potato. **pressé** squeezed. **râpé** grated. **salé** salted.

COOKING TYPE (LA CUISSON)
cru raw. **bleu** practically raw. **saignant** rare. **rosé** (of lamb, duck, liver, kidneys) pink. **à point** medium rare. **bien cuit** well done.

BASICS (ESSENTIELS)
ballotine stuffed, rolled-up piece of meat or fish. **crème fraîche** thick, slightly soured cream. **épices** spices. **feuilleté** 'leaves' of (puff) pastry. **fromage** cheese. **fruits de mer** shellfish. **galette** round flat cake of flaky pastry, potato pancake or buckwheat savoury crêpe. **gelée** aspic. **gibier** game. **gras** fat. **légume** vegetable. **maison** of the house. **marmite** small cooking pot. **miel** honey. **noisette** hazelnut; small, round portion of meat. **noix** walnut. **noix de coco** coconut. **nouilles** noodles. **oeuf** egg; – **en cocotte** baked egg; – **en meurette** egg poached in red wine; – **à la neige** *see île flottante*. **parfait** sweet or savoury mousse-like mixture. **paupiette** slice of meat or fish, stuffed and rolled. **timbale** dome-shaped mould, or food cooked in one. **tisane** herbal tea. **tourte** covered pie or tart, usually savoury.

MEAT (VIANDE)
agneau lamb. **aloyau** beef loin. **andouillette** sausage made from pig's offal. **bavette** beef flank steak. **biche** venison. **bifteck** steak. **boudin noir/blanc** black (blood)/white pudding. **boeuf** beef; – **bourguignon** beef cooked Burgundy style, with red wine, onions and mushrooms; – **gros sel** boiled beef with vegetables. **carbonnade** beef stew with onions and stout or beer. **carré d'agneau** rack of lamb. **cassoulet** stew of white haricot beans, sausage and preserved duck. **cervelle** brains. **châteaubriand** thick fillet steak. **chevreuil** young roe deer. **civet** game stew. **cochon de lait** suckling pig. **contre-filet** sirloin steak. **côte** chop; – **de boeuf** beef rib. **croque-madame** sandwich of toasted cheese and ham topped with an egg. **croque-monsieur** sandwich of toasted cheese and ham. **cuisses de grenouille** frogs' legs. **daube** meat braised in red wine. **entrecôte** beef rib steak. **escargot** snail. **estouffade** meat that's been marinated, fried and braised. **faux-filet** sirloin steak. **filet mignon** tenderloin. **foie** liver; – **de veau** calf's liver. **gigot d'agneau** leg of lamb. **hachis parmentier** shepherd's pie. **jambon** ham; – **cru** cured raw ham. **jarret** ham shin or knuckle. **langue** tongue. **lapin** rabbit. **lard** bacon. **lardon** small cube of bacon. **lièvre** hare. **marcassin** wild boar. **merguez** spicy lamb/beef sausage. **mignon** small meat fillet. **moelle** bone marrow; **os à la** – marrowbone. **navarin** lamb and vegetable stew. **onglet** cut of beef, similar to *bavette*. **pavé** thick steak. **petit salé** salt pork. **pied** foot (trotter). **porc** pork. **porcelet** suckling pig. **pot-au-feu** boiled beef with vegetables. **queue de boeuf** oxtail. **ragoût** meat stew. **rillettes** potted pork or tuna. **ris de veau** veal sweetbreads. **rognons** kidneys. **rôti** roast. **sang** blood. **sanglier** wild boar. **saucisse** sausage. **saucisson sec** small dried sausage. **selle** (*d'agneau*) saddle (of lamb). **souris d'agneau** lamb knuckle. **tagine** slow-cooked North African stew. **tartare** raw minced steak

CONSUME

(also tuna or salmon). **tournedos** small slices of beef fillet, sautéd or grilled. **travers de porc** pork spare ribs. **veau** veal.

POULTRY (VOLAILLE)
aiguillettes (*de canard*) thin slices (of duck breast). **blanc** breast. **caille** quail. **canard** duck; **confit de** – preserved duck. **coquelet** baby rooster. **dinde** turkey. **faisan** pheasant. **foie gras** fattened goose or duck liver. **gésiers** gizzards. **magret** duck breast. **oie** goose. **perdrix** partridge. **poulet** chicken. **suprême** (*de poulet*) fillets (of chicken) in a cream sauce.

FISH & SEAFOOD (POISSONS & FRUITS DE MER)
anguille eel. **bar** sea bass. **belon** smooth, flat oyster. **bisque** shellfish soup. **bouillabaisse** Mediterranean fish soup. **brochet** pike. **bulot** whelk. **cabillaud** fresh cod. **carrelet** plaice. **colin** hake. **coquille** shell. **coquilles St-Jacques** scallops. **crevettes** prawns (UK), shrimp (US). **crustacé** shellfish. **daurade** sea bream. **eglefin** haddock. **escabèche** sautéed and marinated fish, served cold. **espadon** swordfish. **fines de claire** crinkle-shelled oysters. **flétan** halibut. **hareng** herring. **homard** lobster. **huître** oyster. **langoustine** Dublin Bay prawns, scampi. **limande** lemon sole. **lotte** monkfish. **maquereau** mackerel. **merlan** whiting. **merlu** hake. **meunière** fish floured and sautéed in butter. **moules** mussels; – **à la marinière** cooked with white wine and shallots. **morue** dried, salted cod; **brandade de** – cod puréed with potato. **oursin** sea urchin. **palourde** type of clam. **poulpe** octopus. **raie** skate. **rascasse** scorpion fish. **rouget** red mullet. **St-Pierre** John Dory. **sandre** pike-perch. **saumon** salmon. **seîche** squid. **truite** trout.

VEGETABLES (LEGUMES)
aligot mashed potatoes with melted cheese and garlic. **asperge** asparagus. **céleri** celery. **céleri rave** celeriac. **cèpe** cep mushroom. **champignon** mushroom; – **de Paris** button mushroom.

chanterelle small, trumpet-like mushroom. **choucroute** sauerkraut; – **garnie** with cured ham and sausages. **ciboulette** chive. **citronelle** lemongrass. **coco** large white bean. **cresson** watercress. **échalote** shallot. **endive** chicory (UK), Belgian endive (US). **épinards** spinach. **frisée** curly endive. **frites** chips (UK), fries (US). **gingembre** ginger. **girolle** small, trumpet-like mushroom. **gratin dauphinois** sliced potatoes baked with milk, cheese and garlic. **haricot** bean; – **vert** green bean. **mâche** lamb's lettuce. **morille** morel mushroom. **navet** turnip. **oignon** onion. **oseille** sorrel. **persil** parsley. **pignon** pine kernel. **poivre** pepper. **poivron** red or green (bell) pepper. **pomme de terre** potato. **pommes lyonnaises** potatoes fried with onions. **riz** rice. **truffes** truffles.

FRUIT (FRUITS)
ananas pineapple. **cassis** blackcurrants; blackcurrant liqueur. **citron** lemon; – **vert** lime. **fraise** strawberry. **framboise** raspberry. **groseille** redcurrant; – **à maquereau** gooseberry. **myrtille** bilberry, blueberry. **pamplemousse** grapefruit. **pomme** apple. **prune** plum. **pruneau** prune. **quetsche** damson.

DESSERTS & CHEESE (DESSERTS & FROMAGE)
bavarois moulded cream dessert. **beignet** fritter or doughnut. **chèvre** goat; goat's cheese. **clafoutis** batter filled with fruit. **crème brûlée** creamy custard dessert with caramel glaze. **crème chantilly** sweetened whipped cream. **fromage blanc** smooth cream cheese. **glace** ice-cream. **île flottante** whipped egg white floating in vanilla custard. **réglisse** liquorice. **tarte aux pommes** apple tart. **tarte Tatin** warm, caramelised apple tart cooked upside down.

SOUPS & SAUCES (SOUPES & SAUCES)
aïoli garlic mayonnaise. **anchoïade** spicy anchovy and olive paste. **béarnaise** sauce of butter and egg yolk. **blanquette** 'white' stew made with eggs and cream. **potage** soup. **velouté** stock-based white sauce; creamy soup. **vichyssoise** cold leek and potato soup.

CONSUME

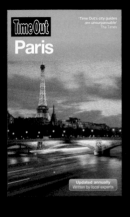

daube de boeuf or seared tuna on a bed of melting aubergine. If you have an appetite for offal, go for the gently sautéed brains with new potatoes or veal kidneys with a perfectly prepared potato gratin. For dessert, try the fresh ewe's cheese with bitter honey.

★ € Rouammit & Huong Lan

103 av d'Ivry, 13th (01.45.85.19.23). M°
Corvisart. **Open** noon-3pm, 7-11pm Tue-Fri;
noon-4pm Sat, Sun. Closed 1wk Aug. **Main**
courses €8.90, €10.80, €11.90. Laotian
Fans of South-east Asian food eventually learn to seek out Laotian holes-in-the-wall in Paris rather than splurge on flashier Thai restaurants. A perfect example is this Chinatown joint, easy to spot thanks to the queue outside the door. The food is cheap and delicious, and the service friendly. Among the highlights are *lap neua*, a tongue-tickling, chilli-spiked salad made with slivers of beef and tripe; *khao nom kroc*, Laotian ravioli filled with shrimp; and sweet, juicy prawns stir-fried with Thai basil. Even the sticky rice is exceptional.

Toustem

12 rue de l'Hôtel Colbert, 5th (01.40.51.99.87).
M° Maubert-Mutualité or St-Michel. **Open**
noon-2.30pm, 7-11pm Mon-Sat. **Main courses**
€24. **Prix fixe** Lunch €24. **Credit** MC, V.
Map p406 J7 🍷 **Bistro**
This oddly decorated outpost of Hélène Darroze's empire is contributing to the gastronomic revival of the Latin Quarter. Darroze is from southwest France, and this little bistro, with heavy wood beams, is where you'll find her cooking at its most generous. Foie gras features prominently on the menu, perhaps in a strongly seasoned terrine or in big, pan-fried chunks with penne in a creamy mushroom sauce. Vegetables such as multicoloured tomatoes come from star market gardener Joël Thiébault, and desserts such as a strawberry *vacherin* (fresh strawberries, vanilla ice cream and meringue) come in big glass *coupes*.

ST-GERMAIN-DES-PRES & ODEON

Le 21

21 rue Mazarine, 6th (01.46.33.76.90)
M° Odéon. **Open** noon-2pm, 8-10.30pm
Tue-Sat. **Main courses** €30. **Credit** MC, V.
Map p408 H6 🍷 **Bistro**
This clubby restaurant in St-Germain-des-Prés is a big hit with a *beau monde* crowd of antiques dealers, book editors and politicians. Chef Paul Minchelli's original minimalist style has evolved towards more homely preparations, as seen in a delicious sauté of flaked cod, potatoes, onions and green peppers or squid in a squid ink sauce with black rice. To keep the waistline-watching regulars happy, a few of his old classics are also still offered,

including grilled red mullet. Don't miss the chocolate fondant cake for dessert, and don't be shy about asking for help with the pricey wine list.

Bread & Roses

7 rue de Fleurus, 6th (01.42.22.06.06). M° St-
Placide. **Open** 8am-8pm Mon-Sat. Closed Aug &
1wk Dec. **Main courses** €18. **Credit** AmEx,
MC, V. **Map** p405 G8 🍞 **Bakery/café**
Come for a morning croissant and you might find yourself staying on for lunch, so tempting are the wares at this Anglo-influenced *boulangerie/épicerie/* café. Giant wedges of cheesecake sit alongside French pastries, and huge savoury puff-pastry tarts are perched on the counter. Attention to detail shows even in the authentically pale taramasalata, which is matched with buckwheat-and-seaweed bread. Prices reflect the quality of the often organic ingredients, but that doesn't seem to deter any of the moneyed locals, who order towering birthday cakes here for their snappily dressed offspring. *Photo p207.*

Le Comptoir

Hôtel Le Relais Saint-Germain, 9 carrefour
de l'Odéon, 6th (01.43.29.12.05). M° Odéon.
Open noon-6pm, 8.30-midnight (last orders
9pm) Mon-Fri; noon-11pm Sat, Sun. Closed 3wks

La Coupole. See p214.

CONSUME

Aug. **Main courses** €15. **Prix fixe** *Dinner* (Mon-Fri) €45. **Credit** AmEx, DC, MC, V. **Map** p408 H7 ⑦ **Brasserie**

Yves Camdeborde runs the bijou 17th-century Hôtel Le Relais Saint-Germain, whose art deco dining room, modestly dubbed Le Comptoir, serves brasserie fare from noon to 6pm and on weekend nights, and a five-course prix fixe feast on weekday evenings. The single dinner sitting lets the chef take real pleasure in his work. On the daily menu, you might find dishes like rolled saddle of lamb with vegetable-stuffed 'Basque ravioli'. The catch? The prix fixe dinner is booked up as much as six months in advance.

★ L'Epigramme

9 rue de l'Eperon, 6th (01.44.41.00.09). Mº Odéon. **Open** noon-2.30pm, 7-11.30pm Tue-Sat; noon-2pm Sun. **Prix fixe** *Lunch* €22. *Dinner* €28. **Credit** MC, V. **Map** p408 H7 ⑧ **Bistro**

The recently opened L'Epigramme is a pleasantly bourgeois dining room with terracotta floor tiles, wood beams, a glassed-in kitchen and comfortable chairs. Like the decor, the food doesn't aim to innovate but sticks to tried and true classics with the occasional twist. Marinated mackerel in a mustardy dressing on toasted country bread gets things off to a promising start, but the chef's skill really comes through in main courses such as perfectly seared lamb with glazed root vegetables and intense jus. It's rare to find such a high standard of cooking at this price, so be sure to book.

La Ferrandaise

8 rue de Vaugirard, 6th (01.43.26.36.36/www. laferrandaise.com). Mº Odéon/RER Luxembourg. **Open** noon-2.30pm, 7-10.30pm Tue-Thur; noon-2.30pm, 7pm-midnight Fri; 7pm-midnight Sat. **Main courses** €14. **Prix fixe** *Lunch* €24, €32. *Dinner* €32, €40. **Credit** MC, V. **Map** p408 H7 ㉛ **Bistro**

This bistro has quickly established a faithful following. In the modern bistro tradition, the young, northern French chef serves solid, classic food with a twist. A platter of excellent ham, sausage and terrine arrives as you study the blackboard menu, and the bread is crisp-crusted, thickly sliced sourdough. Two specialities are the potato stuffed with escargots in a camembert sauce, and a wonderfully flavoured, slightly rosé slice of veal. Desserts might include intense chocolate with rum-soaked bananas and a layered glass of mango and meringue. Wines start at €14.

Huîtrerie Régis

3 rue de Montfaucon, 6th (01.44.41.10.07). Mº Mabillon. **Open** 11am-midnight Tue-Sun. Closed mid July-Sept. **Main courses** €32. **Prix fixe** €21.50, €30. **Credit** MC, V. **Map** p408 H7 ㉜ **Oyster bar**

Paris oyster fans are often obliged to use one of the city's big brasseries to get their fix of shellfish, but what if you just want to eat a reasonably priced platter of oysters? Enter Régis and his 14-seat oyster bar. The tiny room feels pristine and the tables are properly laid. Here you can enjoy the freshest oysters

Le Restaurant.

CONSUME

from Marennes for around €25 a dozen. The bread and butter is fresh and wines are well-chosen. Hungry souls can supplement their feast with a slice of home-made apple tart or the cheese of the day.

Lapérouse
51 quai des Grands-Augustins, 6th (01.43.26.68.04). Mº St-Michel. **Open** noon-2.30pm, 7.30-10pm Mon-Fri; 7.30-10pm Sat. Closed 1wk Jan & Aug. **Main courses** €40. **Prix fixe** *Lunch* €45, €105. *Dinner* €105. **Credit** AmEx, DC, MC, V. **Map** p408 J6 🤫 **Brasserie**

One of the most romantic spots in Paris, Lapérouse was formerly a clandestine rendezvous for French politicians and their mistresses; the tiny private dining rooms upstairs used to lock from the inside. Chef Alain Hacquard does a modern take on classic French cooking: his beef fillet is smoked for a more complex flavour; a tender saddle of rabbit is cooked in a clay crust, flavoured with lavender and rosemary and served with ravioli of onions. The only snag is the cost, especially of the wine – a half-bottle of Pouilly-Fuissé is nearly €35.

★ Le Restaurant
L'Hôtel, 13 rue des Beaux-Arts, 6th (01.44.41.99.01/www.l-hotel.com). Mº St-Germain-des-Prés. **Open** 12.30-2pm, 7.30pm-10pm Tue-Sat. **Main courses** €39. **Prix fixe** *Lunch* €42, €85. *Dinner* €85, €145. **Credit** AmEx, DC, MC, V. **Map** p408 H6 🤫 **Haute cuisine**

Since being taken over by Oxford-based Cowley Manor, L'Hôtel has rechristened its restaurant (formerly Le Belier) and put the talented Philippe Bélisse in charge of the kitchen. You can choose from a short seasonal menu with dishes such as pan-fried tuna, John Dory or suckling pig. But for the same price you can also enjoy the marvellous four-course *menu dégustation* (€74) or, even better, the *menu surprise* at €125. Highlights of the autumn menu were the wild Breton crab stuffed with fennel, avocado and *huile d'Argan*, and a main course of pigeon on a bed of beetroot.

La Taverna degli Amici
16 rue du Bac, 6th (01.42.60.37.74). Mº Assemblée Nationale or Solférino. **Open** noon-2.30pm, 7.30-11pm Mon-Fri; 7.30-11pm Sat. Closed Aug & 1wk Dec. **Main courses** €16. **Prix fixe** *Lunch* €18. **Credit** MC, V. **Map** p401 G6 🤫 **Italian**

The ideal spot for a quick business lunch or a big, rumbustious dinner with friends. Occupying two floors, the yellow-walled rooms are well lit and airy. Run by the exceptionally friendly Notaro family, who own, manage and cook, the restaurant is constantly bustling. Don't miss the mixed bruschette, which includes three vegetable toppings, such as grilled courgettes marinated in olive oil, lemon and parsley. Pastas feature fresh, tasty toppings, such as their most popular dish, penne with *caccioricotta* (made with ewe's milk) and rocket. Most of the regulars finish with home-made tiramisu. *Photo p215.*

Le Timbre
3 rue Ste-Beuve, 6th (01.45.49.10.40). Mº Vavin. **Open** noon-1.30pm, 7.30-10.30pm Tue-Sat. Closed Aug & 1wk Dec. **Main courses** €17. **Prix fixe** *Lunch* €26. *Dinner* (Sat) €30. **Credit** MC, V. **Map** p405 G8 🤫 **Bistro**

Chris Wright's restaurant, open kitchen included, might be the size of the average student garret, but this Mancunian aims high. Typical of his cooking is a plate of fresh green asparagus elegantly cut in half lengthwise and served with dabs of anise-spiked sauce and balsamic vinegar, and a little crumbled parmesan. Main courses are also pure in presentation and flavour – a thick slab of pork, pan-fried but not the least bit dry, comes with petals of red onion that retain a light crunch.

MONTPARNASSE & BEYOND

★ La Cerisaie
70 bd Edgar Quinet, 14th (01.43.20.98.98). Mº Edgar Quinet or Montparnasse. **Open** noon-2pm, 7-10pm Mon-Fri. Closed Aug & 1wk Dec. **Main courses** €15. **Credit** MC, V. **Map** p405 G9 🤫 **Bistro**

Nothing about La Cerisaie's unprepossessing red façade hints at the talent that lurks inside. With a simple starter of white asparagus served with

CONSUME

preserved lemon and drizzled with bright green parsley oil, chef Cyril Lalanne proves his ability to select and prepare the finest produce. On the daily changing blackboard menu you might find *bourride de maquereau*, a thrifty take on the garlicky southern French fish stew, or *cochon noir de Bigorre*, an ancient breed of pig that puts ordinary pork to shame. *Baba à l'armagnac*, a variation on the usual rum cake, comes with stunningly good chantilly.

La Coupole

102 bd du Montparnasse, 14th (01.43.20.14.20/ www.flobrasseries.com/coupoleparis). M° Vavin. **Open** 8am-1am Mon-Fri; 8.30am-1am Sat, Sun. **Main courses** €40. **Prix fixe** €19.90, €30.50. **Credit** AmEx, DC, MC, V. **Map** p405 G9 🟡 **Brasserie**
La Coupole still glows with some of the old glamour. The people-watching remains superb, inside and out, and the long ranks of linen-covered tables, professional waiters, 32 art deco columns painted by different artists of the epoch, mosaic floor and sheer scale of the operation still make coming here an event. The set menu offers unremarkable steaks, foie gras, fish and autumn game stews, but the real treat is the shellfish, displayed along a massive counter. Take your pick from the *claires*, *spéciales* and *belons*, or go for a platter brimming with crabs, oysters, prawns, periwinkles and clams. *Photo p211.*

L'Opportun

64 bd Edgar Quinet, 14th (01.43.20.26.89). M° Edgar Quinet. **Open** noon-3pm, 7-11.30pm Mon-Sat. **Main courses** €19. **Prix fixe** (until 10pm) €21. **Credit** AmEx, DC, MC, V. **Map** p405 G9 🟡 **Bistro**
Owner-chef Serge Alzérat is passionate about Beaujolais, dubbing his convivial cream and yellow restaurant a centre of 'beaujolaistherapy' and a place for 'the prevention of thirst'. He's also an advocate for good, honest Lyonnais food. Thus his menu is littered with the likes of *sabodet* (thick pork sausage) with a purée of split peas, duck skin salad, *tête de veau* (a favourite of ex-president Chirac, whose photo graces the walls) and meat – lots of it. *Fromage* fans should skip dessert and try the st-marcellin by master cheesemaker Hervé Mons.

L'Ostréade

11 bd de Vaugirard, 15th (01.43.21.87.41/ www.ostreade.com). M° Montparnasse-Bienvenüe. **Open** noon-3pm, 7-10pm daily. **Prix fixe** €26-€36. **Credit** AmEx, DC, MC, V. **Map** p405 F9 🟡 **Seafood**
From the outside, L'Ostréade (sandwiched between Gare Montparnasse and a Quick fast-food joint), might look like a tourist trap, but is in fact a chic address, dressed up like a luxury yacht, coveted by seafood aficionados hooked on big 'n' juicy oysters and perfect fish. If they're in season, try the Part-Ar-Cum oysters, fresh from the Finistère in Brittany,

renowned for their hazelnut-like flavour; then the sea bass served with saffron sauerkraut; and a crackly-topped passionfruit crème brûlée.

Le Plomb du Cantal

3 rue de la Gaîté, 14th (01.43.35.16.92). M° Gaîté. **Open** noon-midnight Mon-Fri, Sat, Sun. **Main courses** €15. **Prix fixe** *Lunch* €19. **Credit** MC, V. **Map** p405 G9 🟡 **Bistro**
This lively homage to the Auvergne may suffer from its 1980s decor, but with food like this, who cares? *Aligot* (potato puréed with fresh tomme cheese) and *truffade* (potatoes sautéed with tomme) are scraped out of copper pots on to plates at the table, the shoestring fries arrive by the saucepan-load, and the omelettes are made with three eggs, 300 grams of potatoes, and, if you're really hungry, a supplement of tomme. The roast chestnut-based *salade corrézienne* is delicious and, like all salads here, too enormous to finish. Wines are generally good and the service is friendly.

THE 7TH & WESTERN PARIS

Le 144 Petrossian

18 bd de La Tour-Maubourg, 7th (01.44.11.32.32/www.petrossian.fr). M° La Tour Maubourg. **Open** noon-2.30pm, 7.30-10.30pm Tue-Sat. **Main courses** €40. **Prix fixe** *Lunch* €35, €90. *Dinner* €45, €90. **Credit** AmEx, DC, MC, V. **Map** p401 E5 🟡 **Russian**
Young Senegalese-French chef Rougui Dia directs the kitchen of this famed caviar house. You'll find Russian specialities such as blinis, salmon and caviar (at €39 an ounce) from the Petrossian boutique downstairs, but Dia has added preparations and spices from all over the world. You might start with a divine risotto made with carnaroli rice, codfish caviar and crisp parmesan. In a similar Med-meets-Russia vein are main courses of lamb 'cooked for eleven hours' on a raisin-filled blini, and roast sea bream with a terrific lemon-vodka sauce. At dinner bottles of wine start at €40.

Afaria

15 rue Desnouettes, 15th (01.48.56.15.36). M° Convention. **Open** noon-2pm, 7-11pm Tue-Sat. **Prix fixe** *Lunch* €19. *Dinner* €27. **Credit** MC, V. **Map** p404 C10 🟡 **Bistro**
Instead of the usual starter, main course and dessert categories, Basque-born chef Julien Duboué has divided his menu into sections such as 'les sudistes' for southern French-inspired cooking, and 'les petits appetits' for lighter dishes. Several dishes are for sharing, in particular a caveman-sized duck *magret* with balsamic fig vinegar, served on a terracotta roof tile with potato gratin perched on a bed of twigs. Other creations such as oysters with bulgur, hummus and preserved lemon show that Duboué is not just another Basque bistro chef, but a traveller who happily borrows ingredients from around the world.

L'Agassin

8 rue Malar, 7th (01.47.05.94.27). M° Ecole Militaire. **Open** noon-2.30pm, 7-11pm Tue-Sat. Closed Aug. **Prix fixe** *Lunch* €23, €34. *Dinner* €34. **Credit** AmEx, DC, MC, V. **Map** p405 D6 **94** **Bistro**

André Le Letty left Anacréon – a bistro in the 13th – to open this restaurant in the heart of aristocratic Paris. It's a curious mix of contemporary and classic, with occasional old-fashioned touches in the cooking (skate in butter and caper sauce served with steamed potatoes) but a modern spirit. Several dishes come with supplements of €2 to €10, but these are often worth the extra cost – the *girolle* mushrooms in season are beautifully firm and juicy. The prune *clafoutis* is unusually light, with armagnac ice-cream the perfect accompaniment.

★ L'Ami Jean

27 rue Malar, 7th (01.47.05.86.89). M° Ecole Militaire. **Open** noon-2pm, 7pm-midnight Tue-Sat. Closed Aug. **Main courses** €27. **Prix fixe** €32. **Credit** MC, V. **Map** p405 D6 **95** **Bistro**

This long-running Basque address is an ongoing hit thanks to chef Stéphane Jégo. Excellent bread from baker Jean-Luc Poujauran is a perfect nibble when slathered with a tangy, herby *fromage blanc* – as are starters of sautéed baby squid on a bed of ratatouille. Tender veal shank comes de-boned with a lovely side of baby onions and broad beans with tiny cubes of ham, and house-salted cod is soaked, sautéed and doused with an elegant vinaigrette. There's a great wine list, and some lovely Brana *eau de vie* should you decide to linger. *Photo p217.*

CONSUME

La Taverna degli Amici. *See p213.*

★ L'Arpège

*84 rue de Varenne, 7th (01.47.05.09.06/www.
alain-passard.com). M° Varenne.* **Open** noon-
2.30pm, 8-10.30pm Mon-Fri. **Main courses** €70.
Credit AmEx, DC, MC, V. **Map** p405 F6 ❾❺
Haute cuisine

Assuming you can swallow an exceptionally high
bill – €42 for a potato starter – chances are you'll
have a spectacular time at chef Alain Passard's Left
Bank establishment. His attempt to plane down and
simplify the haute experience – the chrome-armed
chairs look like something from the former DDR –
seems a misstep; but then something edible comes
to the table, such as tiny smoked potatoes served
with a horseradish mousseline. A main course of
sautéed free-range chicken with a roasted shallot, an
onion, potato *mousseline* and pan juices is the apoth-
eosis of comfort food. Desserts are elegant.

€ Le Bistro

*17 rue Pérignon, 15th (01.45.66.84.03).
M° Ségur.* **Open** 8am-10pm daily.
Main courses €11. **Credit** MC, V.
Map p405 E8 ❾❼ **Bistro**

At first glance there is nothing to distinguish this
corner bistro from hundreds of other cafés in Paris.
In the front room with its wood-panelled ceiling are
a plastic-topped bar and a few bare tables with black
banquettes, and in the back is a larger room with
red-and-white checked tablecloths. Then you see the
plates going by, each one – from the goat's cheese
salad to the *pavé de rumsteak* – loaded with golden
fried potato rounds or hand-cut chips. This is the
kind of neighbourhood bistro you had almost given
up hope of finding in Paris.

★ Au Bon Accueil

*14 rue de Monttessuy, 7th (01.47.05.46.11).
M° Alma Marceau.* **Open** noon-2.30pm, 7.30-
10.30pm Mon-Fri. Closed 2wks Aug. **Main
courses** €20. **Prix fixe** *Lunch* €27. *Dinner*
€31. **Map** p404 D6 ❾❽ **Bistro**

Jacques Lacipière runs Au Bon Accueil, and
Naobuni Sasaki turns out the beautiful food.
Perhaps most impressive is his elegant use of little-
known fish such as grey mullet and meagre (*mai-
gre*), rather than the usual endangered species. The
€27 lunch menu might highlight such posh ingredients as *suprême de poulet noir du Cros de la Géline*,

---

**INSIDE TRACK
LUNCH ON THE HOP**

For the perfect *jambon-beurre* sandwich,
head to a *boulangerie* for a *baguette
à l'ancienne* and a *charcuterie* for some
jambon à l'os – ham sliced off the bone.
Don't forget the thick slathering of
Normandy butter. Picnic perfection.

---

free-range chicken raised on a farm run by two former cabaret singers. But the biggest surprise comes
with desserts, worthy of the finest Paris pastry
shops. In summer book a table on the pavement terrace with its view of the Eiffel Tower.

Les Cocottes

*135 rue St-Dominique, 7th (no reservations). M°
Ecole Militaire/RER Pont de l'Alma.* **Open** 8am-
10pm Mon-Fri. **Main courses** €15. **Credit** MC,
V. **Map** p404 D6 ❾❾ **Bistro**

Christian Constant has found the perfect recipe for
pleasing Parisians at his new bistro: non-stop service and a flexible menu of salads, soups, *verrines*
(light dishes served in jars) and *cocottes* (served in
cast-iron pots), all at bargain prices – for this neighbourhood. Service is swift and the food satisfying,
though the *vraie salade César Ritz*, which contains
hardboiled egg, shouldn't be confused with US-style
Caesar salad. Soups such as an iced pea velouté are
spot-on, and *cocottes* range from sea bream with
ratatouille to potatoes stuffed with pig's trotter.

D'Chez Eux

*2 av de Lowendal, 7th (01.47.05.52.55/www.
chezeux.com). M° Ecole Militaire.* **Open** noon-
3pm, 7-10.30pm Tue-Sat. Closed Aug. **Main
courses** €25. **Credit** MC, V. **Map** p405 E7 ❿⓿⓿
Bistro

Arm yourself with stamina for a meal at this jovial
southwestern *auberge*, which looks touristy with its
red-and-white checked tablecloths but attracts *bons
vivants* from the neighbourhood, including the likes
of Jacques Chirac. First come the help-yourself lyon-
nais-style 'salads' (cooked beetroot, lentils, celeriac
rémoulade, ratatouille, etc), before hearty main dishes such as cassoulet or calf's liver with sherry vinegar, which are tasty and generous if not exactly
refined. The heaving dessert cart (think help-yourself chocolate mousse and rice pudding) will ensure
that you waddle out overfed but happy.

Gaya Rive Gauche

*44 rue du Bac, 7th (01.45.44.73.73/www.
pierre-gagnaire.com). M° Rue du Bac.*
Open noon-2.30pm, 7.30-10.45pm Mon-Fri.
Main courses €30. **Credit** AmEx, MC, V.
Map p405 G6 ❿⓿❶ **Seafood**

Superchef Pierre Gagnaire runs this comparatively
affordable fish restaurant. The menu enumerates
ingredients without much clue as to how they are
put together, though the helpful waiters will explain
if you don't like a surprise. But then surprises are
what Gagnaire is famous for. The Fats Waller, for
instance, turns out to be a soup of grilled red peppers with a bloody mary sorbet in the centre and
daubs of quinoa, basmati rice and Chinese spinach.
For the mains, diners are treated like sophisticated
children – everything has been detached from
the bone or carapace. Light desserts complete the
successful formula.

CONSUME

Le Gorille Blanc

*11bis rue Chomel, 7th (01.45.49.04.54). Mº
Sèvres-Babylone.* **Open** noon-2.30pm, 7-10.30pm
Mon-Fri; 7-10.30pm Sat. **Main courses** €18.
Prix fixe *Lunch* €19.50. **Credit** AmEx, MC, V.
Map p405 G7 ⓶ **Bistro**

There are not many inspiring places to eat near
Le Bon Marché, so this bistro is quite a find. Crisp-
skinned duck confit with sautéed potatoes is a sure
bet here, but the kitchen also turns out sprightly fish

dishes such as tapenade-coated sea bream fillet
wrapped in filo pastry and served with tomato and
aubergine confit. Desserts are simple but tasty.

Le Grand Pan

*20 rue Rosenwald, 15th (01.42.50.02.50).
Mº Convention.* **Open** 12.30-2.30pm, 7.30-
11pm Mon-Fri; 7.30-11pm Sat. **Main courses**
€40. **Prix fixe** *Lunch* €30. **Credit** MC, V.
Map p405 D10 ⓷ **Bistro**

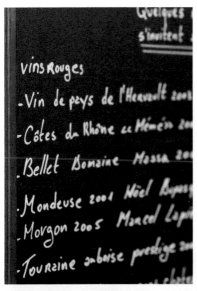

L'Ami Jean. *See p215.*

CONSUME

Young chef Benoît Gauthier trained with Christian Etchebest at the nearby Le Troquet, and he's come up with a clever formula that surfs the current Paris preference for great produce simply cooked. At dinner, a complimentary starter of soup is served – maybe courgette or white bean – and then you choose from the selection of grilled meats and lobster, many of which are designed for two people. Everything comes with a delicious mountain of homemade chips and green salad. Desserts run to homely choices like strawberry crumble or rice pudding with caramel sauce.

★ Jules Verne

Pilier Sud, Eiffel Tower, 7th (01.45.55.61.44/ www.lejulesverne-paris.com). M° Bir Hakeim or RER Tour Eiffel. **Open** 12.15-1.30pm, 7-9.30pm daily. **Main courses** €75. **Prix fixe** *Lunch* €75. *Dinner* €190. **Credit** AmEx, DC, MC, V. **Map** p404 C6 **104** **Haute cuisine**
You have to have courage to take on an icon like the Eiffel Tower, but superchef and entrepreneur Alain Ducasse has done just that in taking over the Jules Verne, perched in its spectacular eyrie 123 metres above the city. He has transformed the cuisine and brought in his favourite designer, Patrick Jouin. Ducasse protégé Pascal Féraud updates French classics, combining all the grand ingredients you'd expect with light, modern textures and sauces. Try dishes like lamb with artichokes, turbot with champagne zabaglione, and a fabulous ruby grapefruit soufflé. Reserve well ahead, and come for lunch if you want to make the most of the views.

Les Ombres

27 quai Branly, 7th (01.47.53.68.00). M° Alma-Marceau. **Open** noon-2.30pm, 7-10.30pm daily. **Main courses** €30. **Prix fixe** *Lunch* €38. *Dinner* €95. **Credit** AmEx, MC, V. **Map** p404 D5 **105** **Bistro**
The full-on view of the Eiffel Tower at night would be reason enough to come to this glass-and-iron restaurant on the top floor of the Musée du Quai Branly, but young chef Arnaud Busquet's food also demands that you sit up and take notice. The influence of Joël Robuchon – a mentor to Busquet's mentor – shows in dishes such as thin green asparagus curved into a nest with tiny *lardons* and topped with a breaded poached egg, ribbons of parmesan and meat *jus*. There is a reasonable prix fixe at lunch.

Il Vino

13 bd de La Tour-Maubourg, 7th (01.44.11.72.00/ www.ilvinobyenricobernardo.com). M° La Tour-Maubourg. **Open** noon-2pm, 7-10pm Tue-Sat. **Prix fixe** *Lunch* €50, €74. *Dinner* €95. **Credit** AmEx, DC, MC, V. **Map** p401 E5 **106** **Italian**
Enrico Bernardo, youngest-ever winner of the World's Best Sommelier award, runs this restaurant where, for once, food plays second fiddle to wine. You are presented with nothing more than a wine list. Each of 15 wines by the glass is matched with a surprise dish, or the chef can build a meal around the bottle of your choice. Best for a first visit is one of the blind tasting menus for €75, €100 or (why not?) €1,000. The impeccably prepared food shows a strong Italian influence.

Jules Verne.

CONSUME

Cafés & Bars

Paris is brimming with places to sip in style.

Quite aside from the gratification of quaffing coffee and cake, people-watching in Paris's cafés is a genuine joy. For Parisians, many of whom live in spatially challenged apartments, the local café is a home from home, with its unwritten rule of 'table rent' – once you've bought a drink, the table is yours for as long as you stay. It's this laid-back attitude that's made the capital's cafés so popular with writers; the likes of Hemingway and Orwell were frequent lingerers. People are still drawn to Left Bank literary classics **Les Deux Magots** and **Café de Flore**, although 'table rent' at these famous spots is now beyond the means of many aspiring authors.

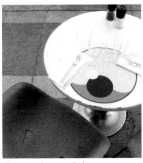

Decor-wise, traditional Paris is getting harder and harder to find. Although landmark addresses such as **La Palette**, with its art deco tiles and leafy terrace, and **Le Cochon à l'Oreille**, a remnant of Les Halles' heyday as the city's food market, do still exist, classic red banquettes and zinc bars are rapidly being replaced by the sort of slick haute design one might find in New York or London.

Nowhere is this more in evidence than in the city's bars. Stroll around the once working-class neighbourhoods of Oberkampf, Ménilmontant and Belleville – where nightlife is at its most exciting – and you'll notice an ever-increasing number of venues with the new sleek look. And interiors aren't the only things to have evolved: the traditional boundaries between bar, club, restaurant and dancehall are diminishing, with hybrid spaces such as **La Bellevilloise** (a former Paris co-operative) and **La Maroquinerie** (previously a leather factory) housing restaurant, bar, music venue and exhibition space all under one roof.

Urban regeneration is pulling punters ever northwards, beyond the Canal St-Martin in the tenth (home to fashionable boho bars and satisfying brunch spots) into the now ultra-trendy 19th, along the Canal de l'Ourcq (*see p224* **Northern Soul**). Other Right Bank hotspots include the Marais (and its north-west overspill around Etienne Marcel and Arts et Métiers métro stations) and the picturesque, village-like area in and around Abbesses in Montmartre. And over on the Left

Bank, St-Germain-des-Prés and Montparnasse continue to trade on a proud, if overplayed, literary heritage, and the Butte-aux-Cailles, in the 13th, has some of the last surviving cheap student haunts.

France has banned smoking inside public venues, turning the terraces into open-air ashtrays – especially in summer when sun worshipping frequently equates to cigarette smoking. Non-smokers grin and bear it.

Wine in three colours is ubiquitous, and coffee comes as a strong espresso unless otherwise requested. The sturdy brasserie and noble bistro provide food with formality akin to a restaurant, so if you're just there for a drink, you'll pay more for the social nicety of aproned and waistcoated service. You can usually run a tab, and tipping is optional.

THE LOUVRE & PALAIS-ROYAL

★ Angelina
226 rue de Rivoli, 1st (01.42.60.82.00).
M° Tuileries. **Open** 8am-7pm Mon-Fri;
9am-7pm Sat, Sun. **Credit** MC, V. **Map**
p401 G5 ❶

> ❶ Green numbers in this chapter correspond to the location of each café and bar as marked on the street maps.
> *See pp400-409.*

Angelina is home to some of the most scrumptious desserts Paris has to offer – all served in the faded grandeur of a belle époque salon just steps from the Louvre. The hot chocolate is pure decadence; try the speciality 'African', a velvety potion so thick that you need a spoon to consume it. Epicurean delights include the Mont Blanc dessert, a ball of meringue covered in whipped cream and sweet chestnut, and a particularly luxurious millefeuille. The tearoom is very popular at weekends, so be prepared to queue.

Le Café des Initiés

*3 pl des Deux-Ecus, 1st (01.42.33.78.29). M°
Louvre Rivoli or Les Halles.* **Open** 7am-2am
daily. **Credit** AmEx, MC, V. **Map** p402 H5 ❷
Friendly staff and a central location have turned this
designer hangout into a top spot for a trendy tipple.
The main room is lined with aerodynamic red banquettes, a long zinc bar provides character, and sleek,
black, articulated lamps peer down from the ceiling.
When hunger strikes, homely favourites such as
shoulder of lamb baked in honey or tartare of salmon
never fail to please.

Café Marly

*93 rue de Rivoli, cour Napoléon, 1st
(01.49.26.06.60). M° Palais Royal Musée du
Louvre.* **Open** 8am-2am daily. **Credit** AmEx,
DC, MC, V. **Map** p401 H5 ❸
A class act, this, as you might expect of a Costes café
whose lofty, arcaded terrace overlooks the Louvre's
glass pyramid. Reached through the passage
Richelieu (the entrance for advance Louvre ticket
holders), the prime location comes at a price: it's €6
for a Heineken – so you might as well splash out €12
on a chocolate martini or a Shark of vodka, lemon-
ade and grenadine. Most wines are under €10 a glass,
and everything is impeccably served by razor-sharp
staff. Brasserie fare and sandwiches are on offer too.

L'Entr'acte

*47 rue de Montpensier, 1st (01.42.97.57.76).
M° Pyramides or Palais Royal Musée du Louvre.*
Open noon-midnight daily. **Credit** MC, V.
Map p402 H5 ❹
A little detour off avenue de l'Opéra, down an 18th-
century staircase, and you find an unexpected con-
gregation spread across the pavement: half are here
for this little bar near the Comédie Française, half for
the adjoining Sicilian pizzeria. There's food to be had
at L'Entr'acte too – €10 plates of cheese and charcuterie, standard pastas and so on – but most come to
enjoy an early evening glass of house Bourgueil. The
interior is tiny, with an equally poky basement, but
there's free Wi-Fi and even laptop loans.

Le Fumoir

*6 rue de l'Amiral-de-Coligny, 1st
(01.42.92.00.24/www.lefumoir.fr). M° Louvre
Rivoli.* **Open** 11am-2am daily. Closed 2wks Aug.
Credit AmEx, MC, V. **Map** p402 H6 ❺

Café Marly.

This elegant bar facing the Louvre has become a
local institution: neo-colonial fans whirr lazily and
oil paintings adorn the walls. A sleek crowd sips
martinis or reads papers at the long mahogany bar
(originally from a Chicago speakeasy), giving way
to young professionals in the restaurant and pretty
things in the library. It can feel a touch try-hard and
well behaved, but expertly mixed cocktails should
take the edge off any evening, and food is top notch.

★ La Garde Robe

*41 rue de l'Arbre-Sec, 1st (01.49.26.90.60).
M° Louvre Rivoli.* **Open** noon-3pm, 6-10.30pm
Wed-Sat. **Credit** MC, V. **Map** p402 J5 ❻
This tiny wine bar (its name means wardrobe),
where bottles line the walls like books in a library,
is perfect for an end-of-the-day snifter, preferably
accompanied by one of the platters of delicious
parma ham, cheese or oysters. Organic and biodynamic wines stand their ground next to vintages
from around the world.

Kong

*1 rue du Pont-Neuf, 1st (01.40.39.09.00/www.
kong.fr). M° Pont Neuf.* **Open** noon-2am Mon-
Thur, Sun; noon-3am Fri, Sat. **Credit** AmEx,
MC, V. **Map** p408 J6 ❼
Set on the top two floors of the Kenzo building
overlooking the Pont Neuf, this Philippe Starck-
designed bar was once one of the city's hottest cocktail venues. But the bright, manga-inspired interior,

CONSUME

decked out in a mishmash of neon and Hello Kitty, is looking past its quirky best. It's still fun to flirt with the too-beautiful-to-bartend staff and order an excellent Vodkatini, though it's not the place to come for a bargain. At weekends, there's a tiny dancing space.

▶ *There are more appealing Starck designs at Le Meurice; see p157.*

OPERA TO LES HALLES

Le Brébant
32 bd Poissonnière, 9th (01.47.70.01.02). M° Grands Boulevards. **Open** 7.30am-6am daily. **Credit** MC, V. **Map** p402 J4 ❽
Proof that change has swept the Grands Boulevards comes in the form of this prominent, round-the-clock bar-bistro. There's a permanently busy terrace below a colourful, stripy awning, and the cavernous, split-level interior is all bare bulbs and wrought iron. Prices are steep, so push the boat out and opt for an expertly made fruit daiquiri, or a Bonne Nouvelle of Bombay Sapphire gin and Pisang Ambon. There are rarer bottled beers too – Monaco, Picon and sundry brews from Brabant. A board advertises a decent range of proper eats: *burger-frites* (€14) and so on.

Le Café Noir
65 rue Montmartre, 2nd (01.40.39.07.36). M° Sentier. **Open** 8am-2am Mon-Fri; 4pm-2am Sat. **Credit** DC, MC, V. **Map** p402 J5 ❾

This enticingly kitsch corner bar might be Noir by name, but is definitely scarlet in tone – and attitude. A framed Gainsbourg portrait fights for attention among leopard-spotted bicycles, reindeer-antlered fish heads and papier-mâché light shades – and all crammed into a space the size of a swimming pool changing cubicle. The regulars give this place its nice-and-naughty boho buzz, with giggling emanating from the banquettes and prized pavement tables. There's a modest lunchtime menu.

★ Café de la Paix
12 bd des Capucines, 9th (01.40.07.36.36/www. cafedelapaix.fr). M° Opéra. **Open** 7am-midnight daily. **Credit** AmEx, DC, MC, V. **Map** p401 G4 ❿
Lap up every detail – this is once-in-a-holiday stuff. Whether you're out on the historic terrace or looking up at the ornate stucco ceiling, you'll be sipping

---

THE BEST TERRACES

For drinking in history
Café de la Paix. *See p221.*

For Seine-side cocktails
Palais de Tokyo. *See p225.*

For Left Bank posing
Les Deux Magots. *See p235.*

in the footsteps of the likes of Oscar Wilde, Josephine Baker, Emile Zola, and Bartholdi and the Franco-American Union (as they sketched out the Statue of Liberty). Let the immaculate staff bring you a kir (€12) or, for an afternoon treat, the vanilla mille-feuille – possibly the best in Paris.

★ Le Cochon à l'Oreille

15 rue Montmartre, 1st (01.42.36.07.56).
M° Les Halles. **Open** 11am-2am Mon-Sat.
No credit cards. Map p402 J5 ⓫
More than 50 wines await you at this impeccably preserved *bistrot à vins*. Its ornate glass panelled doors open on to a café with its original features fully intact. The antique public telephone, the imposing zinc counter and the cosy wooden booths are charming reminders of Les Halles' heyday as the city's celebrated food market – note the tiles that depict scenes of the market in all its chaotic splendour. Le Cochon à l'Oreille is obviously proud of its heritage, and guests are encouraged to record their impressions in notebooks tucked away in little nooks. Join the locals for a bite to eat from the concise, meat-oriented menu.

De la Ville Café

34 bd de Bonne-Nouvelle, 10th (01.48.24.48.09/ www.delavillecafe.com). M° Bonne Nouvelle.
Open 11am-2am daily. **Credit** MC, V.
Map p402 J4 ⓬
De la Ville has brought good news to Bonne-Nouvelle. A major expansion and refurbishment (it used to be a *maison close*) have upped the ante, bringing the Marais in-crowd to this otherwise ignored quarter. Inside, the distressed walls and industrial-baroque feel remain, but the curvy club section at the back has become very cool. A grand staircase leads to a first-floor lounge and exhibition space.
▶ *The café was opened by the crew behind Café Charbon; see p231.*

Dédé la Frite

135 rue Montmartre, 2nd (01.40.41.99.90).
M° Sentier or Bourse. **Open** 8am-2am daily.
Credit MC, V. **Map** p402 J4 ⓭
The food at Dédé's is reminiscent of an American diner (burgers, fries, ketchup on the bar, etc), but the look (distressed walls, bustling smoking terrace) and the attitude to food presentation is thankfully French through and through (pink-in-the-middle burgers and delicious hand-cut fries). It's popular with young suits from the nearby Bourse who flock here for after-work cocktails (€7) and beers (€3.50), before giving into the tempting wafts emanating from the kitchen. After hours, the music is cranked up and the party really starts.

★ Harry's New York Bar

5 rue Daunou, 2nd (01.42.61.71.14/www.harrys-bar.fr). M° Opéra. **Open** 10am-4am daily. **Credit** AmEx, DC, MC, V. **Map** p401 G4 ⓮

The city's most stylish American bar is an institution beloved of expats, visitors and hard-drinking Parisians. The white-coated bartenders mix some of the most sophisticated cocktails in town, from the trademark bloody mary (invented here, so they say) to the *Pétrifiant*, an aptly named elixir of half a dozen spirits splashed into a beer mug. They can also whip up personalised creations that will have you swooning in the downstairs piano bar, where Gershwin composed *An American in Paris*.

La Jungle

56 rue d'Argout, 2nd (01.40.41.03.45/www.la-jungle.com). M° Sentier. **Open** 10am-2am Mon-Fri; 4pm-2am Sat, Sun. **Credit** AmEx, MC, V.
Map p402 J5 ⓯
Set inside a former bordello, the Jungle runs a programme of live afro-jazz on Wednesdays and Fridays (€2 extra on drinks), DJs on Saturdays, and jazz and blues on Sundays. Come for the exotic cocktails (€6), plus dishes with a Cameroonian bent and Flag beer from Senegal.

Le Tambour

41 rue Montmartre, 2nd (01.42.33.06.90/ http://restaurantletambour.com). M° Sentier.
Open 6pm-6am daily. **Credit** MC, V. **Map** p402 J5 ⓰
The Tambour is a classic nighthawk's bar decked out with vintage public transport paraphernalia, its slatted wooden banquettes and bus stop-sign bar stools occupied by chatty regulars who give the 24-hour clock their best shot. Neither tatty nor threatening, there's a long dining room memorable for its métro map from Stalingrad station.

Le Truskel

10 rue Feydeau, 2nd (01.40.26.59.97/www.truskel.com). M° Bourse. **Open** 8pm-3am Tue, Wed; 8pm-5am Thur-Sat. Closed Aug. **Credit** MC, V. **Map** p402 H4 ⓱
The formula is quite simple at this pub-cum-disco – an excellent selection of beers slakes your thirst while an extensive repertoire of Britpop (sometimes live) assaults your ears. The back area is set aside for dancing (ex-Pulp man and Paris resident Jarvis Cocker has been known to splice the night here). As

---

INSIDE TRACK
HISTORY ON TAP

Although staid, the Hôtel Raphaël's **Bar Anglais** (17 av Kléber, 16th, 01.53.64. 32.00) is the stuff of history. Eisenhower toasted the Liberation here, and Ava Gardner, Marlon Brando and Cary Grant all popped in for a *verre* at various times. Serge Gainsbourg even wrote several of his songs while propping up the bar.

CONSUME

CONSUME

Northern Soul

Two arrondissements come of age on the Paris boozing map.

Although 'north-east drag' might sound like a private club for trannies from Chez Michou (*see p281*), it's actually the nickname given to the rows of bars that have recently sprung up in the 11th and 19th arrondissements. Whether you're in the market for extended happy hours, swift aperitifs or after-dinner tipples, there are plenty of places to while away the night or fall over with flair.

Oberkampf (11th) has always attracted bar crawlers, but nowadays night owls in the know flock here for three funky new bars: **L'Oxyd Bar** (26 av Jean Aicard, 11th, 01.48.06.20.81, www.oxydbar.com), with its ethnic loft-style decor and cool flow of live jazz; **Place Verte** (105 rue Oberkampf, 11th, 01.43.57.34.10), a vast space complete with library, terrace, cocktails, a decent restaurant and a cool 1970s vibe; and the **Folies Bar** (24 rue de la Folie Méricourt, 11th, 01.40.21.88.25, www.foliebar.com), the newest kid on the block, with top-notch wines, gastronomic tapas and cool, minimalist decor.

Meanwhile, in the 19th, five new bars have sprung up along the Canal de l'Ourcq. **25° Est** (10 pl de Stalingrad, 19th, 01.42.09.66.74) has taken over an arcaded building near Ledoux's iconic 18th-century rotunda, thus endowing itself with some of the best views of the canal and a flat roof for summer drinking and winter smoking. The canteen-style food (think meat platters and chips) is cheap, hearty and perfect for lining the stomach. Upstream, **Le Bastringue** (67 quai de Seine, 19th, 01.41.09.89.27) caters to early birds with decent wine, tasty grub and a pleasant setting overlooking a nearby riverboat theatre. **Belushis** (159 rue de Crimée, 19th, 01.40.34.34.40, www.st-christophers.co.uk/paris-hostels), in the brand new St Christopher's Inn (*see p182*), wins the prize for the cheapest drinks and best sports screenings; the **Okay Café**, just across the bridge (41bis quai de la Loire, 19th, 01.42.01.56.04), is set inside a converted hangar and doubles as a pub and crêperie; and finally, **Au Gout du Jour** (2 rue de Nantes, 19th, 01.46.07.16.78), near La Villette, draws the local bobo crowd with its shabby-chic interior and reasonable prices.

a cheeky touch, a bar bell rings for no reason whatsoever, causing first-time visitors from the UK to down their drinks in one and dive for the bar.

CHAMPS-ELYSEES & WESTERN PARIS

Charlie Birdy
124 rue La Boétie, 8th (01.42.25.18.06/www. charliebirdy.com). M° Franklin D. Roosevelt. **Open** 11am-5am daily. **Credit** AmEx, V. **Map** p401 E4 ⓳
Take a New York loft and meld it with a colonial English gentleman's club and you're looking at Charlie Birdy – a large 'pub' with a live music agenda of jazz, soul and funk that's worth listening to. If you're in a hurry, stay away – the service can be aggravatingly slow. But if you take your time choosing from the 50-strong cocktail menu, sink into a comfy chesterfield and let the evening wash over you, it'll be worth it. Food is reasonably priced.

Le Dada
12 av des Ternes, 17th (01.43.80.60.12). M° Ternes. **Open** 6am-2am Mon-Sat; 6am-10pm Sun. **Credit** AmEx, MC, V. **Map** p400 C3 ⓲

Perhaps the hippest café in this stuffy part of town, Le Dada is best known for its well-placed, sunny terrace. Inside, the wood-block carved tables and red walls provide a warm atmosphere for a crowd that tends towards the well-heeled, well-spoken and, well, loaded. That said, the atmosphere is friendly; if terracing is your thing, you could happily spend a summer's day here.

Flute l'Etoile
19 rue de l'Etoile, 17th (01.45.72.10.14/www. flutebar.com). M° Ternes. **Open** 5pm-2am Tue-Sat; 6am-10pm Sun. **Credit** AmEx, MC, V. **Map** p400 C3 ⓴
With a menu of some 23 different champagnes and designer decor (slick wooden panelling, blue walls and red velvet), Paris's first champagne lounge certainly looks the part. Indeed the only indication that it's not French (it's American) is the sneaky appearance of a Californian sparkler on the champagne list. For drinkers wishing to sample different vintages without buying a whole glass (from €9), the small tasting glasses (from €5) are a nice touch. And for anyone 'bored' by plain old bubbly, cocktails such as champagne sangria and Rossini-Tini (champagne, raspberry juice, liqueur and Grey Goose vodka) are a sophisticated alternative.

Impala Lounge

2 rue de Berri, 8th (01.43.59.12.66). M° George
V. **Open** noon-2am Mon, Sun; noon-5am Tue-Sat.
Credit AmEx, MC, V. **Map** p400 D4 ㉑
Dubbed the 'African Bar' by regulars, this wannabe-
hip spot hams up the colonial with zebra skins,
masks and a throne hewn from a tree trunk. Beer,
wine, tea and standard favourites can all be had, but
best are the cocktails, one of which claims to boost
a waning libido with its mystery mix of herbs and
spices. DJs rock Sunday afternoon away, and the
snack-and-mains menu includes ostrich.

★ Ladurée

75 av des Champs-Elysées, 8th (01.40.75.08.75/
www.laduree.fr). M° George V or Franklin D.
Roosevelt. **Open** 7.30am-12.30am daily. **Credit**
AmEx, DC, MC, V. **Map** p400 D4 ㉒
Decadence permeates this elegant tearoom, from
the 19th century-style interior and service to the
labyrinthine corridors that lead to the toilets. While
you bask in the warm glow of bygone wealth,
indulge in tea, pastries (the pistachio pain au chocolat is heavenly) and, above all, the hot chocolate. It's
a rich, bitter, velvety tar that will leave you in the
requisite stupor for any lazy afternoon.
► *The original branch at 16 rue Royale (8th,*
01.42.60.21.79) is famed for its macaroons.

Libre Sens

33 rue Marbeuf, 8th (01.53.96.00.72). M°
Franklin D. Roosevelt. **Open** 9am-3am daily.
Credit MC, V. **Map** p400 D4 ㉓
Unusually for this part of town, Libre Sens is reasonably priced and down to earth. The design is
slick, with low lighting and comfortable seating –
particularly attractive are the large booths – which
accommodates groups and couples. The crowd is
made up mostly of Parisians here for a drink after
work, and rightly so – the happy hour, between
6.30pm and 8.30pm, includes champagne for €6 and
cocktails for €7.

★ Palais de Tokyo

13 av du Président-Wilson, 16th (01.47.20.00.29/
www.palaisdetokyo.com). M° Iéna. **Open** noon-
1am Tue-Sun. **Credit** AmEx, MC, V. **Map**
p400 C5 ㉔
The Palais de Tokyo is one of the hippest destinations in the overwhelmingly staid 16th. The majestic neo-classical building has a stripped-back interior
and stunning outdoor terrace overlooking the Seine.
The Palais has hosted everything from contemporary art exhibits to haute couture fashion shows, but
its bar still manages to put together quirky cocktails
for €9. The Brazilian-themed Rio Bamako with
cachaça, lime and ginger is particularly tempting.
DJs play an eclectic mix from 10pm, but it really
packs in a crowd at weekends. In summer, when the
bar moves outside, the terrace throngs with beautiful people. *See also p233* **Night at the Museum***.*

Le Rival

20 av George V, 8th (01.47.23.40.99). M°
George V. **Open** 7am-2am daily. **Credit** MC, V.
Map p400 D4 ㉕
Stylish but low key, this four-star contemporary bar
makes a mean martini: fresh fruit, Polish or Detroit,
with a wellyful of Zubrowka or Krupnik chucked in
for good measure. A decent glass of Brouilly or
Chablis sets you back €7 – but heaven knows how
they can charge €18 for a cheeseburger and hash
browns. Still, the shopaholic and business clientele
seem happy to stump up.

Sir Winston

5 rue de Presbourg, 16th (01.40.67.17.37). M°
Charles de Gaulle Etoile. **Open** 9am-3am Mon-
Wed, Sun; 9am-4am Thur-Sat. **Credit** AmEx, V.
Map p400 C4 ㉖
A bit of an anomaly, this. Grand and imperial, and
located within sight of high-end glitz, Sir Winston
does a nice line in jazz and gospel brunches on a
Sunday. Colonial knick-knacks, chesterfields and
chandeliers make up the decor, with Winnie himself
framed behind a sturdy bar counter. A battalion of
whiskies stands guard beside him, and the wine list
is equally *recherché*. Where this place falters is in
its somewhat sissy cocktail menu. A Sir Winston
Breezer of Bacardi, melon liqueur, pineapple and
banana juice? Harrumph!

MONTMARTRE & PIGALLE

La Divette de Montmartre

136 rue Marcadet, 18th (01.46.06.19.64).
M° Lamarck Caulaincourt. **Open** 5pm-1am
Mon-Sat; 5-11pm Sun. **Credit** MC, V.
Tucked away among Montmartre's hilly back-
streets, this cavern of colourful nostalgia is run
by Serge and serves as his *Recherche du temps*
perdu in the shape of album covers, posters and
table football. Beatles and Rolling Stones sleeves
bedeck the bar, interrupted by *yé-yé* pop tat, St-
Etienne football paraphernalia and an old red telephone box. On tap are Wieckse Witte, Afflighem,
Pelforth and gossip from the days when Manu Chao
were regulars.
► *On Friday nights, come for live operetta, jazz,*
pop or whatever else takes Serge's fancy.

La Fourmi

74 rue des Martyrs, 18th (01.42.64.70.35).
M° Pigalle. **Open** 8.30am-2am Mon-Thur;
8.30am-4am Fri, Sat; 10am-2am Sun. **Credit**
MC, V. **Map** p402 H2 ㉗
Set on the cusp of the ninth and 18th arrondissements, La Fourmi is an old bistro that has been converted for today's tastes, with picture windows
lighting the spacious, roughshod interior. The classic zinc bar counter is crowned by industrial lights,
and an excellent music policy and cool clientele –
although they'd have to go some to beat the bar staff

CONSUME

– ensure a pile of flyers. As good a place as any to find out what's happening in town.

Poussette Café
6 rue Pierre Sémard, 9th (01.78.10.49.00/ www.lepoussettecafe.com). M° Poissonnière or Cadet. **Open** 10.30am-6.30pm Tue-Sat. **Map** p402 J3 ㉘
Fed up with the impracticalities of pushing her pram (*poussette*) into the local café, mother of two Laurence Constant designed her own parent-friendly establishment. This upmarket *salon de thé* caters for the harassed parent (herbal teas, smoothies, quiches and salads) and demanding baby (purées, solids and cuddly toys).
▶ *You can sign up for magic shows and parenting workshops via the café's website.*

Au Rendez-vous des Amis
23 rue Gabrielle, 18th (01.46.06.01.60). M° Abbesses. **Open** 8.30am-2am daily. **Credit** MC, V. **Map** p402 H1 ㉙
Considering its proximity to the honeypot that is Sacré Coeur, this café/bar is still cheap, making it popular with locals and foreign students, and the odd tourist. During happy hour (8pm to 10pm), a kir or glass of wine will set you back a very reasonable €2.50. There are cosy nooks round the back with plenty of upholstered spots to choose from.

★ Rouge Passion
14 rue Jean-Baptiste Pigalle, 9th (www.rouge-passion.fr). M° St Georges or Pigalle. **Open** noon-3pm Mon; noon-3pm, 6pm-1am Tue-Fri; 6pm-1am Sat. **Credit** MC, V. **Map** p401 G2 ㉚
Two bright upstarts (Anne and Sébastien) determined to make their mark on Paris's bar scene are behind this new venture – and they're going about it the right way. Offering a long list of wines (from just €3), free *assiettes apéros* (peanuts, olives and tapenades on toast) and decor that is satisfyingly vintage (red banquettes and beige walls), the formula is spot on. A small but mouthwatering selection of hot dishes, salads, cheese and *saucisson* platters help soak up *le vin* (set lunch menu €20, mains from €15). Look out for the wine tasting classes, given by a guest sommelier.

Le Sancerre
35 rue des Abbesses, 18th (01.42.58.08.20). M° Abbesses. **Open** 7am-2am Mon-Thur; 7am-4am Fri, Sat; 9am-2am Sun. **Credit** MC, V. **Map** p402 H1 ㉛
This popular Montmartre institution (with original zinc bar) is home to a frenzied mix of alcohol-fuelled transvestites, tourists, lovers and bobo (bohemian-bourgeois) locals, who all come for the cheap beer (under €4), trashy music and buzzy terrace. The decor inside is dark and scruffy, the service undeniably slow and the food (omelettes, *steak-frites*) nothing special; yet there is something irresistibly

refreshing about the no-frills approach that makes this bar stand out from the multitude of try-hard cafés in the area.

BEAUBOURG & THE MARAIS

★ Andy Whaloo
69 rue des Gravilliers, 3rd (01.42.71.20.38). M° Arts et Métiers. **Open** 5.30pm-2am Tue-Sat. **Credit** AmEx, MC, V. **Map** p409 K5 ㉜
Andy Whaloo, created by the people behind its neighbour 404 and London's Momo and Sketch, is Arabic for 'I have nothing'. Bijou? This place brings new meaning to the word. The formidably fashionable crowd fights for coveted 'seats' on upturned paint cans; from head to toe, it's a beautifully designed venue, crammed with Moroccan artefacts and a spice rack of colours. It's quiet early on, with a surge around 9pm, and the atmosphere heats up as the night gets longer.

L'Apparemment Café
18 rue des Coutures St-Gervais, 3rd (01.48.87.12.22). M° St-Sébastien Froissart. **Open** noon-2am Mon-Fri; 4pm-2am Sat; 12.30pm-midnight Sun. **Credit** MC, V. **Map** p409 L6 ㉝
The 'Apparently' feels more like a communal living room than a café. The low lighting, cosy nooks and board games (Trivial Pursuit and Taboo, both in French) make for an excellent place to while away an afternoon. The location is perfect for shoppers too, being just off the rue Vieille-du-Temple. Lunches consist of simple DIY platters of meats, cheeses and salads, but at €15 for the basic version they're a bit rudimentary for the price. Eating is obligatory during busy periods, when it's definitely advisable to book.

Le Baromètre
17 rue Charlot, 3rd (01.48.87.04.54). M° Arts et Métiers. **Open** 8am-11pm Mon-Sat. **Credit** MC, V. **Map** p409 L5 ㉞
This unpretentious wine bar is popular with the area's craftsmen and artisans. Lunchtimes are heaving, so unless you're after the sit-down *menu du jour* (€13) served at the back, you're better off coming for a lazy afternoon. Order a plate of cheese or the house speciality, bacon and andouillette gratin, and choose from the 20-strong selection of wines by the glass, most under €3.50.

L'Estaminet d'Arômes et Cépages
39 rue de Bretagne, 3rd (01.42.72.28.12/ www.aromes-et-cepages.com). M° Temple. **Open** 9am-8pm Tue-Sat; 9am-2pm Sun. **Credit** MC, V. **Map** p409 L5 ㉟
L'Estaminet d'Arômes et Cépages is tucked away in the Marché des Enfants-Rouges, a charming neighbourhood market and one of the city's oldest. The café

has a warm interior, with a grandfather clock in the corner and guests eating €13 *plats du jour* off Limoges porcelain. Wines from around €4 a glass.
▶ *Wine distributor Arômes et Cépages, which owns L'Estaminet, has a shop around the corner at 33bis rue Charlot, 3rd (01.42.72.34.85).*

★ L'Etoile Manquante

34 rue Vieille-du-Temple, 4th (01.42.72.48.34/ www.cafeine.com). M° Hôtel de Ville or St-Paul. **Open** 9am-2am daily. **Credit** MC, V. **Map** p409 K6 ⑯

The hippest of Xavier Denamur's merry Marais bars. Cocktails are punchy, traditional tipples just as good, and the salads and snacks are reasonably priced and tasty – but it's the design and buzz that are the main draws. The decor is trendy but comfortable, embellished with interesting art. As in all Denamur's places, no visit is complete without a trip to the toilets: here, an electric train shuttles between cubicles, starlight beams down from the ceiling, and a hidden camera films you washing your hands. Just watch the small screen on the wall behind you.

Lizard Lounge

18 rue du Bourg-Tibourg, 4th (01.42.72.81.34/ www.cheapblonde.com). M° Hôtel de Ville. **Open** noon-2am daily. **Credit** MC, V. **Map** p409 K6 ⑰

An anglophone favourite deep in the Marais, this loud and lively (hetero) pick-up joint provides lager in pints (€6), plus cocktails (€7) and a viewing platform for beer-goggled oglers. Bare brick and polished woodwork are offset by the occasional lizard and a housey soundtrack. Bargain boozing

(cocktails €5) kicks off at 5pm; from 8pm to 10pm there's another happy hour in the sweaty cellar bar (complete with miniscule dance floor); on Mondays it lasts all day. A popular weekend brunch of bacon, sausages and eggs benedict caters to the homesick.

Le Loir dans la Théière

3 rue des Rosiers, 4th (01 42 72 90 61). M° St-Paul. **Open** 11.30am-7pm Mon-Fri; 10am-7pm Sat, Sun. **Credit** V. **Map** p409 L6 ⑱

Le Loir is named after the unfortunate dormouse who gets dunked in the pot at the Mad Hatter's tea party. Its squishy sofas are the perfect complement to its comfort food: it specialises in baked goods, and its famed lemon meringue and chocolate fondant are divine. At weekends it's packed out with tourists in search of brunch; long lines of people looking enviously at your plate, plus occasionally patchy service, can mar the experience. Come early or be prepared to queue.

La Perle

78 rue Vieille-du-Temple, 3rd (01.42.72.69.93). M° Chemin Vert or St-Paul. **Open** 6am-2am Mon-Fri; 8am-2am Sat, Sun. **Credit** MC, V. **Map** p409 L6 ⑲

With an old locomotive over the bar and sleek rows of grey chairs, the Pearl achieves a rare balance between all-day and late-night venue, and also has a good hetero/homo mix. It feels like a neighbourhood bar; labourers and screenwriters rub elbows with young dandies, keeping one eye on the mirror and an ear on the electro-rock. The menu runs from omelettes to *salade marine*. Expect a DJ later on.

CONSUME

Café Charbon. *See p231.*

Le Petit Fer à Cheval

*30 rue Vieille-du-Temple, 4th (01.42.72.47.47/
www.cafeine.com). M° St-Paul.* **Open** 9am-2am
daily. **Credit** MC, V. **Map** p409 K6
Even a miniature Shetland pony would be pushed
to squeeze his hoof into this *fer à cheval* (horseshoe)
– this adorable little café has one of France's smallest bars. Tucked in behind the glassy façade is a
friendly dining room lined with reclaimed métro
benches; if you want scenery, the tables out front
overlook the bustle of rue Vieille-du-Temple. In
business for more than 100 years, the café enjoyed
a retro makeover by Xavier Denamur in the 1990s,
and today sports vintage film posters with an
ornate mirror backdrop.

Stolly's

*16 rue Cloche-Perce, 4th (01.42.76.06.76/www.
cheapblonde.com). M° Hôtel de Ville or St-Paul.*
Open 4.30pm-2am daily. **Credit** MC, V. **Map**
p409 K6 ⑪
This seen-it-all drinking den has been serving a
mainly anglophone crowd for nights immemorial.
The staff make the place what it is, and a summer
terrace eases libation, as do the long happy hours;
but don't expect anyone at Stolly's to faff about
with food. There's football on TV and a plastic shark
to compensate.

Wini June

*16 rue Dupetit-Thoars, 3rd (01.44.61.76.41).
M° Temple.* **Open** 6pm-2am daily. **Credit** MC,
V. **Map** p409 L5 ⑫
Wini June's virtual living room has become a
favourite haunt of Paris fashionistas and designers,
who lounge on the Empire-style or contemporary
furnishings. Wine (which is served up in crystal
glasses) is accompanied by a selection of nibbles
proffered by the attentive staff. The pint-sized
terrace is an outdoor version of the interior, flanked
with bamboo.

BASTILLE
& EASTERN PARIS

Le Baron Rouge

*1 rue Théophile-Roussel, 12th
(01.43.43.14.32). M° Ledru-Rollin.* **Open**
10am-3pm, 5-10pm Tue-Thur; 10am-10pm
Fri, Sat; 10am-3pm Sun. **Credit** AmEx,
MC, V. **Map** p407 N7 ⑬
It sells wine, certainly – great barrels of the stuff are
piled high and sold by the glass at very reasonable
prices. But the Red Baron is not just a wine bar –
more a local chat room, where regulars congregate
to yak over their *vin*, along with a few draught beers
and perhaps a snack of sausages or oysters. Despite
its lack of seating (there are only four tables), it's a
popular pre-dinner spot, so arrive early and don't
expect much elbow room; drinkers often spill out
on to the pavement.

★ Chez Prosper

*7 av du Trône, 11th (01.43.73.08.51).
M° Nation.* **Open** 8.30am-1am daily.
Credit MC, V. **Map** p407 Q8 ⑭
Chez Prosper welcomes punters all day long with
that simplest of pleasures: a smile. Yes, even when
squeezing past people queuing for a spot on the sun
terrace, the waiters are positively beaming. The traditional dining/drinks area – tiled floor, large mirrors, wooden furniture – is run with military
precision, and orders arrive promptly. The *steak-
frites* and *croques* (served on Poîlane bread) are
hearty, and the naughty Nutella tiramisu is worth
crossing town for.

Le Fanfaron

*6 rue de la Main-d'Or, 11th (01.49.23.41.14).
M° Ledru-Rollin.* **Open** 6pm-2am Mon-Sat.
Closed 2wks Aug. **No credit cards**.
Map p407 N7 ⑮
On a small backstreet, Le Fanfaron (named after
Dino Risi's 1962 movie) is the favoured haunt
for musically inclined retro dudes. Owner Xavier's

Chez Jeanette. *See p231.*

enviable collection of rare film soundtracks, the cheap (€2.70) beer and crackle of needle on vinyl pack in the punters. The decor is kitsch-cool, with Stones and Iggy memorabilia, second-hand furniture and '60s movie posters. There are reasonably priced goat's cheese and *saucisson* bar snacks too.

★ Les Furieux

74 rue de la Roquette, 11th (01.47.00.78.44/ www.lesfurieux.fr). M° Bastille or Voltaire. **Open** 4pm-2am Tue-Thur; 4pm-5am Fri, Sat; 7pm-2am Sun. **Credit** MC, V. **Map** p407 M6 ④⑥

Just when it looked like 'lounge attitude' would contaminate every bar on rue de la Roquette, Les Furieux fought back with a healthy dose of rock and metal, padded red walls, faux-leather banquettes, black paint, and rotating exhibitions of photography on the walls. Locals flock here for the happy hour (6pm to 8pm), when cocktails with rockin' names like Grunge, Scud, and, er, Boris are half price. Diehards can pay tribute to Paris's hedonistic heyday with 12 different absinthes.

Le Motel

8 passage Josset, 11th (01.58.30.88.52). M° Ledru-Rollin. **Open** 6pm-1.45am Tue-Sun. Closed Aug. **Credit** MC, V. **Map** p407 M7 ④⑦

Le Motel is the latest addition to the city's growing indie scene. It has a simple formula: cheap drinks and excellent music. During happy hour (6pm to 9pm) a pint of *blonde* costs €3.50 and cocktails €3. With DJs almost every night, the music ranges from cutting-edge indie to contemporary neo-folk and rock classics, with the odd Motown hit thrown in for good measure. Friendly twentysomethings cluster around faux Louis XVI armchairs or try their luck in the Sunday pop quiz.

L'Opa

9 rue Biscornet, 12th (01.46.28.12.90/ www.opa-paris.com). M° Bastille. **Open** 8pm-2am Tue-Thur; 9pm-6am Fri, Sat. **Credit** V. **Map** p409 M7 ④⑧

Late opening and Eric Perier's diverse range of nightly entertainment – DJs (weekends), videos, live acts (Tuesday to Thursdays) and the odd open mic event – are the attractions here, along with free admission and reasonable drinks prices. A couple of comfortable sofas take the edge off the institutional interior, with a modest stage in one corner and an upstairs chill-out space and separate bar.

Pause Café

41 rue de Charonne, 11th (01.48.06.80.33). M° Ledru-Rollin. **Open** 8am-2am Mon-Sat; 9am-8pm Sun. **Credit** MC, V. **Map** p407 M7 ④⑨

Featured in Cedric Klapisch's 1996 film *Chacun Cherche son Chat*, which was shot on location in the neighbourhood, the Pause Café has managed to prolong its hour of glory thanks to its large terrace on the corner of rues Charonne and Keller. Inside, the modern salons benefit from a smattering of primary colours with ornately plastered ceilings and lots of light. Having been immortalised on celluloid, the friendly staff occasionally let fame go to their heads: service can be excruciatingly slow. The food – French café fare – is not bad, but you might be waiting for a while; best to order a well-mixed cocktail to pass the time.

Le Temps des Cérises

31 rue de la Cerisaie, 4th (01.42.72.08.63). M° Bastille. **Open** 9am-9pm Mon-Fri. **Credit** MC, V. **Map** p409 L7 ⑤⓪

Not to be confused with several other cafés of the same name, this one-room *bistro à vins* has changed very little over the years. Faded net curtains, Duralex tumblers behind the zinc bar and prices from €2.30 for a *vin* or beer are reminiscent of a bygone age. The blackboard wine list is limited but always well chosen, and food is old-fashioned and hearty (think beef stew and *blanquette de veau*). The general banter is football-centred, so get ready to rumble with the natives about PSG.

NORTH-EAST PARIS

L'Alimentation Générale

64 rue Jean-Pierre-Timbaud, 11th (01.43.55.42.50/www.alimentation-generale.net). M° Parmentier. **Open** 5pm-2am Wed, Thur, Sun; 5pm-4am Fri, Sat. **Credit** AmEx, MC, V. **Map** p403 M5 ⑤①

The 'Grocery Store' is rue Jean-Pierre-Timbaud's answer to La Mercerie (*see p232*): it, too, is a big old space filled with junk. Cupboards of kitsch china and lampshades made from kitchen sponges are an inspired touch. The beer is equally well chosen – Flag, Sagres, Picon and Orval by the bottle – and the unusual €8 house cocktail involves basil and figs. DJs rock the joint: expect a €5 cover price for big names or live bands (including open-mic nights). Oh yes – and it has the most brazen toilet walls this side of town.

★ Ave Maria

1 rue Jacquard, 11th (01.47.00.61.73). M° Parmentier. **Open** 6.30pm-2am daily. **No credit cards**. **Map** p403 M5 ⑤②

Unlike some places that eschew good food for alcohol and a funky interior, colourful Ave Maria scores highly for all three. The kitsch interior is decked out in a canopy of chinoiserie parasols and a vast collection of Hindu gods. Music, a combination of reggae, funk, soul and dub, is cool but unobtrusive. Strangers sharing wooden benches devour exotic dishes from the menu, which combines meat, spices, lentils, rice and fruit. The cocktails are equally quirky; a jug of Agua Borabora – a mix of mango, kiwi, rosé, vodka and champagne for two – will set you back €14.

CONSUME

CONSUME

La Flèche d'Or. *See p232*.

Bar Ourcq

68 quai de la Loire, 19th (01.42.40.12.26).
Mº Laumière. **Open** 3pm-midnight Wed, Thur;
3pm-2am Fri, Sat; 3-10pm Sun. *Summer* 5-9.30pm
Wed-Fri, Sun; 3pm-2am Sat. **No credit cards.**
Map p403 N1 ⑤
This was one of the first hip joints to hit the Canal
de l'Ourcq, with an embankment broad enough to
accommodate *pétanque* games (ask at the bar) and
a cluster of deckchairs. It's a completely different
scene from the crowded bustle along Canal St-
Martin – more discerning and less self-satisfied. The
cabin-like interior is cosy, and drinks are listed in a
hit parade of prices, starting with €2.40 for a *demi*
or glass of red. Pastas at €8, exhibitions and a regular DJ spot keep the cool clientele sated. Closed on
rainy weekdays in summer.

La Bellevilloise

*19 rue Boyer, 20th (01.46.36.07.07/www.la
bellevilloise.com). Mº Gambetta.* **Open** 5.30pm-
2am Wed-Fri; 11am-2am Sat, Sun. **Credit** V.
Map p403 P4 ⑤
The Bellevilloise is the latest incarnation of a building that once housed the capital's very first workers' co-operative. Now it competently multi-tasks as
a bar, restaurant, club and exhibition space, hosting
regular film and music festivals on the top level (last
year a lawn for punters to sit on was sewn inside).
Enjoy brunch in the *halle aux oliviers* or decent
views of the *quartier* from the charming terrace;
downstairs the club-cum-concert venue has launched
some of Paris's most exciting new bands.

★ Café Charbon

*109 rue Oberkampf, 11th (01.43.57.55.13/
www.nouveaucasino.net). Mº Parmentier or
Ménilmontant.* **Open** 9am-2am Mon-Thur,
Sun; 9am-4am Fri, Sat. **Credit** MC, V.
Map p403 N5 ⑤
The bar contained within this beautifully restored
belle époque building sparked the Oberkampf
nightlife boom. Its booths, mirrors and adventurous
music policy put trendy locals at ease, capturing the
essence of café culture spanning each end of the 20th
century. After more than 15 years, the formula still
works – and is copied by nearby bars. *Photo p227.*
▶ *The management run the popular Nouveau
Casino nightclub next door (see p329) and the
groovy De la Ville Café (see p223) in the tenth.*

Café Chéri(e)

*44 bd de la Villette, 19th (01.42.02.02.05/
http://cafecherie.blogspot.com). Mº Belleville.*
Open 8am-2am daily. **Credit** MC, V.
Map p403 M3 ⑤
This splendid DJ bar has expanded its brief and its
opening hours to become an all-day café – without
compromising any of the cool that keeps it well
ahead of the pack after dark. Music comes from all
over, and runs from electro, rock, funk, hip hop,

indie, dance and jazz to golden oldies and ghetto-
inspired grooves. The interior sparkles with wit and
invention – note the marvellous mural alluding to
the personal sacrifices made for a life of coupledom.
There's a front terrace if you need a smoke or con-
versational respite from the BPM.
▶ *There's music from Thursdays to Saturdays
after 10pm; see p327.*

Le Café des Sports

94 rue de Ménilmontant, 20th (01.46.36.48.18).
Mº Gambetta. **Open** 10am-1.30am daily. Closed
Aug. **Credit** MC, V. **Map** p403 P4 ⑤
Le Café des Sports' fine and eclectic music pro-
gramme ranges from electro (Saturdays), to pop or
chanson (Tuesdays and Thursdays) to world dub.
Beer and wine are fabulously cheap (€2 from 6pm
to 8pm) and there's even free couscous with your
drink on Mondays. Unlike its sprawling neighbours,
Le Café des Sports has just one room to call home.
DJs play in the space around the back.

★ Chez Jeanette

47 rue du Fbg-St Denis, 10th (01.47.70.30.89).
Mº Strasbourg St-Denis or Château d'Eau.
Open 8am-2am daily. **Map** p402 K3 ⑤
When she sold her café back in March 2007, Jeanette
handed over to the young team from Chez Justine
because they promised not to change a thing. Now
the monstrous 1940s lights, tobacco-stained wallpaper depicting the Moulin Rouge and PVC-covered
banquettes have been rewarded with a Fooding
prize for decor, and the café is quickly becoming one
of Paris's hippest spots for an aperitif. There's a *plat
du jour* at lunch and plates of cheese and charcuterie
at night; at 8pm, the fluorescent lights go off and
candlelight takes over, to a cheer. *Photo p228.*

Chez Prune

36 rue Beaurepaire, 10th (01.42.41.30.47).
Mº Jacques Bonsergent. **Open** 8am-2am Mon-
Sat; 10am-2am Sun. **Credit** AmEx, MC, V.
Map p402 L4 ⑤
Chez Prune is an excellent lunch spot, and still one
of the best places to spend an evening on the Canal
St-Martin. The local bobo HQ, this traditional café,
with high ceilings and low lighting, sticks to a simple formula: groups of friends crowd around the
cosily ordered banquettes, picking at moderately
priced cheese or meat platters. Mostly, though, they
come for a few leisurely drinks or an *apéro* before
heading to one of the late night venues in the area.

Le Cinquante

50 rue de Lancry, 10th (01.42.02.36.83).
Mº Jacques Bonsergent. **Open** *Sept-July*
5.30pm-2am daily. *Aug* 5.30pm-2am Tue-Sun.
No credit cards. Map p402 L3 ⑥
Just down from the Canal St-Martin, the bare brick,
Formica and framed '50s ads of this funky venue
attract an inner circle of regulars. These days it's

CONSUME

established enough to produce its own T-shirts and customised bar stools. Reasonable prices – half-litre pitchers of sauvignon, Brouilly and Chablis in the €10 range – attract a mixed bag of tastes and generations. The two rooms behind the main bar are set aside for dining (affordable classics) and music (generally acoustic). Sunday is open-mic night.

La Flèche d'Or
102bis rue de Bagnolet, 20th (01.44.64.01.02/ www.flechedor.fr). M° Alexandre Dumas or Gambetta. **Open** 8pm-2am Mon-Thur, Sun; 8pm-6am Fri, Sat. **Credit** MC, V. **Map** p407 Q6 ⑥①
The Flèche, housed in a disused station hall, straddles the abandoned *petite ceinture* railway that encircles Paris. Closer in style to urban venues in Berlin and New York, it has carved itself a reputation as a launch pad for new bands by hosting indie and electro acts most nights (free entry; *see also p321*). You can get a €5.50 *demi* from the bar or a €14.50 cheeseburger from the restaurant. *Photo p230.*

La Gouttière
96 av Parmentier, 11th (01.43.55.46.42). M° Parmentier. **Open** 8am-2am Mon-Fri; 3pm-2am Sat. **Credit** V. **Map** p403 M4 ⑥②
Far enough (five minutes) from rue Oberkampf to feel off the beaten track, the Gutter is not out-and-out libertine, but you're on the right lines. Certainly, a come-what-may approach to music, drinking and eye contact abounds in the crowded venue. Decor, assuming you can see it, consists of a few LP covers and the kind of colour scheme often put to good use in adventure playgrounds. Reasonably priced lunches, the occasional live band and animated seduction techniques complete the picture.

★ L'Ile Enchantée/Wash Bar
65 bd de la Villette, 10th (01.42.01.67.99/ www.washbar-lg.com). M° Colonel Fabien. **Open** 8am-2am Mon-Fri; 5pm-2am Sat. *Wash Bar* 10am-8pm Mon-Fri; 4-8pm Sat. **Credit** MC, V. **Map** p403 M3 ⑥③
This house/electro DJ bar has made the bizarre decision to turn its entire first floor over to Korean conglomerate LG, which has installed the aptly named Wash Bar. Grab a cocktail (€6.50) downstairs in the retro-chic bar, then head upstairs to your choice of interactive zones. There's the 'bureau' (surf the net), the 'lounge' (watch TV) or the 'launderette' – a high-tech installation of LG's latest washing machines, all free to use. It's the only excuse to get your knickers off in the bobo HQ that is the Canal St-Martin, and has pulled in the punters at the Enchanted Island, making it more popular than ever.

★ Le Mange Disque
58 rue de la Fontaine-au-Roi, 11th (01.58.30.87.07). M° Goncourt. **Open** 11am-3pm, 5pm-2am Tue-Sat. Closed Aug. **No credit cards. Map** p403 M4 ⑥④

This remarkably cool bar shows just what you can do with a little art, a fine taste in music, the most mundane of furniture and the right connections. If you want to launch a CD, introduce a DJ or simply imbue your bash with cool, do it here. Savvy owner Hubert has brought in choice wines from little-known producers in south-west France, but only charges €2 to €3 a glass; likewise, the snacks cost under €10. Stacks of vinyl are left out for browsing, and with the constant traffic of events and launches, no two evenings are the same.

La Maroquinerie
23 rue Boyer, 20th (01.40.33.35.05/www.la maroquinerie.fr). M° Gambetta. **Open** 6pm-2am daily. Closed Aug. **Credit** MC, V. **Map** p403 P4 ⑥⑤
La Maroquinerie's former life as a leather factory is little in evidence these days. It's now a bright café and bar. The food is excellent – you can eat your way through the menu quite reasonably for around €25 – and wine sourced from across France starts at €3 a glass. The interior, with exposed brick, is atmospheric, and in summer chirpy locals invade the shaded terrace.
▶ *The downstairs stage hosts the occasional literary debate and a wealth of cool music acts; see p321.*

La Mercerie
98 rue Oberkampf, 11th (01.43.38.81.30/www. lamercerie.net). M° Parmentier. **Open** 5pm-2am daily. **Credit** MC, V. **Map** p403 N5 ⑥⑥
Opposite the landmark Charbon (*see p231*) and infinitely more grungy, the spacious Mercerie has bare walls (bare everything, in fact) and room for the usual Oberkampf shenanigans of death-wish drinking against a backdrop of loud, eclectic music. A DJ programme is lipsticked on the back bar mirror. Happy hour is from 7pm to 9pm, so you can cane the house vodkas (apricot, mango, honey) and still have enough euros to finish the job after dusk. The back area, with its tea lights, provides intimacy if that's where your evening's headed.

Mon Chien Stupide
1 rue Boyer, 20th (01.46.36.25.49). M° Gambetta. **Open** 6pm-2am Tue-Sun. **Credit** MC, V. **Map** p403 P4 ⑥⑦
As the action moves relentlessly eastwards from Oberkampf, the once-distant outposts of Gambetta and Bagnolet appear on the radar of the discerning bar-hopper. Colourful and humorous, My Stupid Dog is a bar for grown-ups; an undercurrent of jazzy sounds drifts along nicely. It's commendably unsympathetic to canines – note the 'Dog Paste' sign by the bar.

Le Panier
32 rue Ste-Marthe, 10th (01.42.01.38.18). M° Belleville. **Open** 10am-2am daily. **No credit cards. Map** p403 M3 ⑥⑧

Night at the Museum

Where culture and cocktails collide.

Museums are usually daytime destinations, places of discovery that welcome their guests at some civilised hour before noon and politely expel them well before dusk. However, several of Paris's museums have begun boldly defying the convention by incorporating late-opening bars and even top-notch dining. And who are the punters? Parisians, of course, mainly the kind who frequent museums in the daylight hours, returning to savour the refined atmosphere and take advantage of some of the best views in the city. Join the *parigots* in their quest for night-time fulfilment and visit the following museum bars.

For a cultivated cocktail, head to **Le Saut du Loup** (107 rue de Rivoli, 1st, 01.42.25.49.55, www.lesautduloup.com) in the Musée des Arts Décoratifs, with its sober mix of black, white and grey reflective surfaces, a well-heeled crowd and prices to match. It's the only bar in Paris to overlook the Tuileries gardens – the perfect spot for a consistently delicious drink at dusk.

For fun art world drinking, the bar inside the **Palais de Tokyo** fits the bill perfectly (13 av du Président-Wilson, 16th, 01.47.20.00.29, www.palaisdetokyo.com). The decor – all industrial concrete and bright, trendy tables – is as wacky as the drinks menu, which includes the likes of cotton candy-flavoured champagne. For culture vultures, the museum itself stays open until midnight.

The *m'as-tu vu* crowd head up to **Georges** – the famously avant-garde bar-restaurant on the top of the Centre Pompidou (rue St-Martin, 4th, 01.44.78.12.33, www.centrepompidou.fr). The spectacular views alone make it worth the trip up the glass-encased escalators; once at the top you pay for the privilege of a sunset *apéro* or an after-dinner tipple, but it's worth the investment.

Turning it up a notch, the Musée de l'Homme's **Café de l'Homme** (17 pl du Trocadéro, 16th, 01.44.05.30.15, www.restaurant-cafedelhomme.com) has established itself as one of the Chaillot area's best hangouts, thanks to its breathtaking terrace with views of the Palais de Chaillot's golden 1930s statues and the Eiffel Tower. Bring your dancing shoes for the DJ nights (from 11.30pm, when the restaurant closes), which last well into the small hours.

CONSUME

Palais de Tokyo.

CONSUME

The cobbled rue Ste-Marthe buzzes with the energy of *ateliers*, restaurants and bars. Le Panier enjoys a prominent position on a blissfully shaded square, and has a vast terrace at its centre. So much space is a rarity in Paris, and so this is a choice spot in summer. The food (served all day) is hit and miss, and service can be as relaxed as the atmosphere. Best just to opt for a cheese plate and a glass of wine.

Au Passage
1bis passage St-Sébastien, 11th (01.43.55.07.52). Mº St-Sébastien Froissart. **Open** 9am-midnight daily. **Credit** MC, V. **Map** p409 M5 ⑥⑨
A strange find, this, tucked down a long, narrow alleyway off rue Amelot, opposite the back entrance of Pop In – look out for the green Stella sign. Inside it's red and black and bohemian all over. Artists cluster around the corner bar, passing over the €2 bottles of Tsingtao beer for glasses of teeth-staining *vin rouge*, perhaps dipping into a plate of meat or cheese nibbles (€5/€8). There's art on the far wall, some retro cookbooks, and a feeling that entire decades could pass without anyone really noticing.

★ Au P'tit Garage
63 rue Jean-Pierre-Timbaud, 11th (01.48.07.08.12). Mº Parmentier. **Open** 6pm-2am daily. **Credit** AmEx, MC, V. **Map** p403 M4 ⑦⓪
As sweetly tuned as Chuck Berry's cherry-red '53, this quite marvellous rock 'n' roll bar is the pick of the bunch on rue Jean-Pierre-Timbaud. Not that the owners have fitted it with Americana or waitresses on rollerskates; the L'il Garage is as basic as the real car-fit business a few doors down the road. Stuffing bursts out of the bar stools and skip-salvage chairs accompany wobbly tables of ill-matched colours. Regulars cluster around the twin decks at the bar, while music-savvy Frenchettes giggle and gossip at the back.

Le Pure Café
14 rue Jean-Macé, 11th (01.43.71.47.22). Mº Faidherbe-Chaligny or Charonne. **Open** 7.30am-2am daily. **Credit** MC, V. **Map** p407 N7 ⑦①

INSIDE TRACK
COFFEE CULTURE

A word about coffee in France. If you ask for *un café*, you'll be given an espresso. Ask for it '*serré*' if you prefer it more concentrated, and '*allongé*' if you're craving an American-style coffee. A *crème* is made with milk, but good, frothy cappuccino is rare. If you just want a dash of frothy milk in your espresso, ask for a '*noisette*'. And if you want a skinny decaf? Head to Starbucks.

This place should satisfy film buffs and foodies alike; Le Pure Café was the setting for a rendezvous between Julie Delpy and Ethan Hawke in the movie *Before Sunset*. The bright interior is a world away from the sombre style of some traditional bistros, and it manages to revive traditional food equally well by using quality ingredients assembled with a twist. A main course will set you back around €18; a glass of wine €4.

Le Verre Volé
67 rue de Lancry, 10th (01.48.03.17.34). Mº Jacques Bonsergent. **Open** 10.30am-2.30pm, 7pm-2am Tue-Sun. Closed Aug. **Credit** MC, V. **Map** p402 L4 ⑦②
This organic-only *cave à vins* doubles up as a wine bar and restaurant. Although wine (around €4 per glass) is the focus at Le Verre Volé, you're obliged to eat; a hearty sausage and mash will set you back around €15 (other mains up to €20). Purists who would prefer a simple snack to complement their *bon vin* should opt for a plate of charcuterie and cheese at €12. The small dimensions, chatter and slightly hyperactive service give the place a bubbly energy that some might find a little boisterous.

THE LATIN QUARTER & THE 13TH
★ Le Crocodile
6 rue Royer-Collard, 5th (01.43.54.32.37/www.lecrocodile.fr). RER Luxembourg. **Open** 10pm-late Mon-Sat. Closed Aug. **Credit** MC, V. **Map** p408 J8 ⑦③
Ignore the apparently boarded-up windows at Le Crocodile; if you're here late, then it's open. Friendly young regulars line the sides of this small, narrow bar and try to decide what to drink – not easy, given the length of the cocktail list: at last count there were 312 varieties. The generous €6-per-cocktail happy hour (Monday to Thursday before midnight) will allow you to start with a champagne *accroche-coeur*, followed up with a Goldschläger (served with gold leaf) before moving on to one of the other 310.

Le Merle Moqueur
11 rue de la Butte aux Cailles, 13th (no phone). Mº Place d'Italie. **Open** 5pm-2am daily. **No credit cards.**
Amid semi-faded pseudo-tropical decor, the Teasing Blackbird – a Butte-aux-Cailles institution – tantalises students and nostalgic thirtysomethings with its splendid selection of rums (over 20) and a long list of cocktails. The atmosphere gets raucous after 10pm – get in early to grab one of the three tables.

Le Pantalon
7 rue Royer-Collard, 5th (no phone). RER Luxembourg. **Open** 5.30pm-2am Mon-Sat. **No credit cards. Map** p408 J8 ⑦④

Le Pantalon is a local café that seems familiar yet is utterly surreal. It has the standard fixtures, including the old soaks at the bar – but the regulars and staff are enough to tip the balance firmly into eccentricity. Friendly and very funny French grown-ups and foreign students chat in a mishmash of languages; drinks are cheap enough to make you tipsy without the worry of a cash hangover.

Pop Corner

16 rue des Bernadins, 5th (01.44.07.12.47).
Mº Maubert-Mutualité. **Open** 6pm-2am Tue-Thur; 6pm-4am Fri, Sat. **Credit** MC, V. **Map** p406 K7 ⑦⑤

This successful marriage of music bar and Brit pub, set between St-Germain-des-Prés and the river, attracts a mix of young professional Parisiennes and anglophone expats unloosening their ties – postwork, pre-shag stuff (there's even a bed in the corner). Abstract art on bare brick and €5 Poptions Magiques cocktails (Indi Pop: vodka and honey) add alternative touches – but both sexes are here to sink pints and peruse the possibilities.

Sputnik

14 rue de la Butte aux Cailles, 13th
(01.45.65.19.82/www.sputnik.fr). Mº Place
d'Italie. **Open** 2pm-2am Mon-Sat; 4pm-midnight Sun. **Credit** MC, V.

A hip young crowd gathers in this rock-oriented bar, which doubles as a sports bar during important football and rugby fixtures, and trebles as an internet café at other times. Ever-changing art exhibitions add interest to the walls, and live music once a month draws an indie crowd.

ST-GERMAIN-DES-PRES & ODEON

Le Bar

27 rue de Condé, 6th (01.43.29.06.61).
Mº Odéon. **Open** 8pm-late Mon-Sat. **No credit cards. Map** p408 H7 ⑦⑥

Le Bar is one of those places that you only ever visit when it's very, very late and you're very, very drunk. It's almost completely dark, has a shrine-type affair at the back and gravel on the floor, everyone talks in whispers, and the drinks are exceedingly strong. Once you've been here you'll be strangely drawn back at inappropriate times when you really should be going home, and at least one member of the party is guaranteed to fall asleep on the comfy banquettes.

★ Le Bar Dix

10 rue de l'Odéon, 6th (01.43.26.66.83).
Mº Odéon. **Open** 6pm-2am daily. **No credit cards. Map** p408 H7 ⑦⑦

Generations of students have glugged back jugs of the celebrated home-made sangría (€3 a glass in happy hour) while squeezed into the cramped upper bar, tattily authentic with its Jacques Brel record sleeves, Yves Montand handbills and pre-war light fittings. Spelunkers and hopeless romantics negotiate the hazardous stone staircase to drink in the cellar bar, with its candlelight and century-old advertising murals. Can someone please come and slap a preservation order on the place?

★ Le Bar du Marché

75 rue de Seine, 6th (01.43.26.55.15).
Mº Mabillon or Odéon. **Open** 8am-2am daily.
Credit MC, V. **Map** p408 H7 ⑦⑧

The matter in question is the Cours des Halles, the bar a convivial corner café opening on to the pleasing bustle of St-Germain-des-Prés. Simple dishes like a ham omelette or a plate of herring in the €7 range, and Brouilly or muscadet at €4-€5 a glass, are proffered by beret-topped waiters. It couldn't be anywhere else in the world. Locals easily outnumber tourists, confirming Rod Stewart's unusually astute observation that Paris gives the impression that no one is ever working.

Café de Flore

172 bd St-Germain, 6th (01.45.48.55.26/
www.cafe-de-flore.com). Mº St-Germain-des-Prés.
Open 7.30am-1.30am daily. **Credit** AmEx, DC,
MC, V. **Map** p408 H6 ⑦⑨

Bourgeois locals crowd the terrace tables at lunch, eating club sandwiches with knives and forks as anxious waiters frown at couples with pushchairs or single diners occupying tables for four. This historic café, former HQ of the Lost Generation intelligentsia, attracts tourists and, yes, celebrities from time to time. But a *café crème* is €4.60, a Perrier €5 and the omelettes and *croque-monsieurs* are best eschewed in favour of the better dishes on the menu (€15-€25).

▶ *There are play readings on Mondays and philosophy debates on the first Wednesday of the month, both at 8pm, in English.*

★ Chez Georges

11 rue des Canettes, 6th (01.43.26.79.15).
Mº Mabillon. **Open** noon-2am Tue-Sat.
Closed Aug. **Credit** MC, V. **Map** p408 H7 ⑧⓪

Belonging to a dying breed of *cave-bars* associated with the Latin Quarter, Chez Georges is beloved of students, professionals and neighbourhood eccentrics. Regulars pop in during the day to sip wine over a game of chess, and at night the *cave* fills up with people dancing to *chanson*, pop classics and even the odd Bar Mitzvah track. The heat generated is mascara-melting, and it's not for the claustrophobic – but it's a great way to meet new people.

Les Deux Magots

6 pl St-Germain-des-Prés, 6th (01.45.48.55.25/
www.lesdeuxmagots.com). Mº St-Germain-des-Prés. **Open** 7.30am-1am daily. **Credit** AmEx,
DC, MC, V. **Map** p408 H7 ⑧①

CONSUME

If you stand outside Les Deux Magots, you have to be prepared to photograph tourists wanting proof of their encounter with French philosophy. The former haunt of Sartre and de Beauvoir now draws a less pensive crowd that can be all too *m'as-tu vu*, particularly at weekends. The hot chocolate is still good (and the only item served in generous portions) – but, like everything else, it's pricey. Visit on a weekday afternoon when the editors return, manuscripts in hand, to the inside tables, leaving enough elbow room to engage in some serious discussion.

Les Editeurs

4 carrefour de l'Odéon, 6th (01.43.26.67.76/ www.lesediteurs.fr). M° Odéon. **Open** 8am-2am daily. **Credit** AmEx, MC, V. **Map** p408 H7 ㉜
It's no surprise to see row upon row of books in the bright, modern interior of Les Editeurs. A café with literary leanings, it sits on the lovely carrefour de l'Odéon, a crossroads that leads to the Luxembourg gardens. Bask in the glory of literary greats as portraits of authors and their editors look down on you. Brunch on Saturday and Sunday is good value at €25; in the evening, main courses come in at €22, and sandwiches are €14 throughout the day.

★ J'Go

Rue Clément, 6th (01.43.26.19.02/www. lejgo.com). M° Mabillon or Odéon. **Open** 11am-midnight daily. **Credit** MC, V. **Map** p408 H7 ㉝
As its name suggests, J'Go (pronounced *gigot*) is all about lamb – well, meat actually: a buzzing Toulouse-style wine bar in the Marché St-Germain

by day, it becomes a *rôtisserie* at meal times, serving its speciality spit-roasted lamb from Quercy, black pig from Bigorre, and whole roasted chickens. The €35 set menu is well worth the splurge, offering a whole jar of pâté, a giant bowl of salad, and lamb with creamy stewed *haricots blancs*. If you'd rather stick to wine and tapas, sidle up to one of the great wooden barrels, choose your poison (blindly if necessary – at €4 a glass all wines are good) and share a plate of charcuterie or foie gras *tartines* (€9).

★ La Palette

43 rue de Seine, 6th (01.43.26.68.15). M° Odéon. **Open** 9am-2am Mon-Sat. Closed Aug. **Credit** MC, V. **Map** p408 H6 ㉞
La Palette is the café-bar of choice for the very beau Beaux-Arts students who study at the venerable institution around the corner, and young couples who steal kisses in the wonderfully preserved art-deco back room decorated with illustrations. It ain't cheap – a glass of Chablis sets you back €6, a demi €4.50 – but you're paying for the prime location once frequented by such luminaries as Jim Morrison, Picasso and Ernest Hemingway. Grab a spot on the leafy terrace if you can – there's formidable competition for seats.

Le Rostand

6 pl Edmond-Rostand, 6th (01.43.54.61.58). RER Luxembourg. **Open** 8am-2am daily. **Credit** MC, V. **Map** p408 H8 ㉟
Le Rostand has a truly wonderful view of the Jardin du Luxembourg from its classy interior, decked out with oriental paintings, a long mahogany bar and

La Palette.

CONSUME

wall-length mirrors. It's a terribly well-behaved place; consider arriving draped in furs or sporting the latest designer eyewear if you want to fit in with the well-heeled clientele. Whiskies and cocktails are pricey, as is the brasserie menu, but the snack menu serves delicious omelettes and *croques* for around €8 (salad €4 extra). Perfect for a civilised drink after a stroll round the gardens.

MONTPARNASSE

Le Café Tournesol
9 rue de la Gaîté, 14th (01.43.27.65.72).
M° Gaîté. **Open** 8.30am-1.30am Mon-Sat;
9.30am-1.30am Sun. **Credit** AmEx, MC, V.
Map p405 G9
Off the beaten track, the Tournesol is young and vibrant. There's outdoor seating in the shadow of the Tour Montparnasse, and an exposed brick interior with a soul, funk and electro soundtrack. A *croque-monsieur* will set you back €6, a steak €12, and a *demi* of Stella €2.90. An abstract tableau presides over a well-organised back space and leaves plenty of seating for groups.

Le Select
99 bd du Montparnasse, 6th (01.45.48.38.24).
M° Vavin. **Open** 7am-2am Mon-Thur, Sun; 7am-4am Fri, Sat. **Credit** MC, V. **Map** p405 G8
For a decade between the wars, the junction of boulevards Raspail and du Montparnasse was where Man Ray, Cocteau and Lost Generation Americans hung out in the vast, glass-fronted cafés. Eight decades on, Le Select is the best of these inevitable tourist

haunts. Sure, its pricey menu is big on historical detail and short on authenticity, but by and large it manages to hold on to its heyday with dignity.

THE 7TH & WESTERN PARIS

★ Le Bardélo
64 av Bosquet, 7th (01.44.18.01.25/
www.lebardelo.com). M° Ecole Militaire.
Open 6pm-2am Tue-Sat. **Credit** MC, V.
Map p404 D6
This former cigar bar has swapped its outlawed tobacco for jazz, whisky, cocktails and fine wines. Leather sofas, exposed stone walls and plenty of dark wood create a smart setting for the moneyed clientele: a mix of young professionals and middle-aged bourgeois folk, all with one thing in common – a love of the performing and gustative arts. Wine-tasting sessions occur throughout the year.
▶ *Live jazz and café-théâtre take place in the downstairs cellar most Saturdays.*

Le Café du Marché
38 rue Cler, 7th (01.47.05.51.27). M° Ecole
Militaire. **Open** 7am-midnight Mon-Sat; 7am-5pm Sun. **Credit** MC, V. **Map** p405 D6
This well-loved address is frequented by trendy locals, shoppers hunting down a particular type of cheese and tourists who've managed to make it this far from the Eiffel Tower. Le Café du Marché really is a hub of neighbourhood activity. Its *pichets* of decent house plonk go down a treat, and mention must be made of the food – such as the huge house salad featuring lashings of foie gras and Parma ham.

Café Thoumieux
4 rue de la Comète, 7th (01.45.51.50.40/
www.thoumieux.com). M° La Tour Maubourg.
Open noon-2am Mon-Fri; 5pm-2am Sat.
Closed 3wks Aug. **Credit** AmEx, MC, V.
Map p405 E6
Café Thoumieux is a laid-back destination for cocktails, tapas and big-screen sport. Banquettes snake around the room, and spiky Aztec-pattern lamps light up the faces of the pretty young locals who have made this place their own. The flavoured vodkas are delicious, and include vanilla, caramel and banana; just watch out for the treacherous, extra-high bar stools (the banquettes are definitely the safest option) and the monstrous, pebble-dashed sink in the toilets – it's real.

CONSUME

Shops & Services

High class or boho, the Paris look is yours for the taking

Although a strong euro means that shopping in Paris won't reward your pocket, it is, and ever will be, a sensual pleasure. Whether you're trying on clothes behind the velvet curtains of Lanvin or tasting cheeses at an open-air market, the joy is in experiencing the pursuit of perfection for which the French are famous. Whereas we have window-shopping, they have window-licking (*lèche-vitrine*). Big departments stores and global chains have their roles to play, but there are also plenty of small independent boutiques, which combine to make shopping here a unique experience.

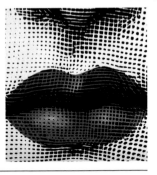

CONSUME

PARIS FASHION

On the fashion front, French prêt-à-porter is enjoying a renaissance, with a host of young brands pushing the old names to the sidelines. **Manoush**, **Iro**, **ba&sh**, **Les Prairies de Paris** and **April 77** are among the affordable labels to have opened own-name stores this year; others can be found in the *tendance* (trend) sections of **Printemps**, **Galeries Lafayette** and **Le Bon Marché**.

In addition, an increasing number of multi-brand boutiques have sprung up, presenting a cherry-picked selection of the season's offerings. **Dolls**, **Les Belles Images** and genre pioneer **Shine** are ones to watch, as well as the clothing concept store **LE33** which has injected street style into the Champs-Elysées. For avant-garde and 'intelligent' (read: Belgian) designers, **Maria Louisa** and **L'Eclaireur** (*see p257* Fashion Scouts) still come up trumps.

In the designer league, French creators are also cresting a wave, with **Robert Normand** and **Lefranc.ferrant** two of the most original labels to open their own boutiques in the past

year. Meanwhile, Martine Sitbon has made a comeback with her new brand **Rue du Mail**. Last winter also saw an obscene number of facelifts among the luxury labels. **Yves Saint Laurent**, **Sonia Rykiel**, **Lanvin**, **Givenchy** and renowned label boutique **Colette** all launched refitted or new stores in the luxury heartlands of rue du Fbg-St-Honoré, the 'golden triangle' (avenues Montaigne, George V and the Champs-Elysées), and St-Germain-des-Prés.

The vintage scene also goes from strength to strength. **Gabrielle Geppert** and **Marie Louise de Monterey** are two of our favourite new discoveries, both with a very distinct style.

HOW TO SHOP

Different areas have different specialities. There are clusters of antiques shops in the seventh arrondissement, and second-hand and rare book outlets in the fifth; crystal and porcelain manufacturers still dot rue de Paradis in the tenth; furniture craftsmen as well as children's clothes shops inhabit rue du Fbg-St-Antoine; bikes and cameras are clustered on boulevard Beaumarchais; and the world's top jewellers can be found on place Vendôme. The historic covered passages in the second and ninth are also fun places in which to shop, with chic stores such as cosmetics line **By Terry** mixed in with philatelists and booksellers.

Family-run food shops have thankfully not been eroded by supermarket culture, and tend to cluster in 'market streets' such as rue des Martyrs and rue Mouffetard, as well as around the many covered and open-air food markets. Here everything from a vintage bottle of

**INSIDE TRACK
TAX BACK**

Non-EU residents can claim a refund or *détaxe* (around 12 per cent) on VAT if they spend over €175 in any one day in one shop, and if they live outside the EU for more than six months in the year (*see also p369*).

armagnac to a single praline chocolate is lovingly presented, served and wrapped. Informed discussion is still very much part of the purchasing process, and beautiful, old-style shops (*see p268* **Bread of Heaven**), unchanged for decades, add to the pleasure.

If designer labels and homogenous high street shops turn you off, there are still plenty of independent traders in the city's markets. Paris's flea markets are truly epic, in size and in the variety of curiosities on offer. The sprawling **Marché aux Puces de Clignancourt** is the daddy of them all; the tree-lined **Marché de Vanves** and contemporary design market **Les Puces du Design** are more modest in scale.

Shops are generally open from 10am to 7pm Monday to Saturday, with specialist boutiques closing for an hour at lunch. Some are closed on Monday mornings. Sunday opening is found in the Marais, on the Champs-Elysées, at Bercy Village and in the Carrousel du Louvre. Many shops on the Champs-Elysées stay open until midnight, and Thursday is late closing at department stores. Small corner grocery stores open late for essentials.

General

DEPARTMENT STORES

The revamped *grands magasins* have brought in trendy designers and luxury spaces in a concerted attempt to lure shoppers away from independent boutiques.

BHV (Bazar de l'Hôtel de Ville)
52-64 rue de Rivoli, 4th (01.42.74.90.00/DIY hire 01.42.74.97.23/www.bhv.fr). M° Hôtel de Ville. **Open** 9.30am-7.30pm Mon, Tue, Thur-Sat; 9.30am-9pm Wed. **Credit** AmEx, MC, V. **Map** p406 J6.
Homeware heaven: there's even a Bricolage Café with internet access. Upper floors have a good range of men's outdoor wear, upmarket bed linen, toys, books, household appliances – and a large space devoted to every type of storage utility.

★ Le Bon Marché
24 rue de Sèvres, 7th (01.44.39.80.00/www.bonmarche.fr). M° Sèvres Babylone. **Open** 10am-7.30pm Mon-Wed; 10am-9pm Thur; 10am-8pm Fri; 9.30am-8pm Sat. **Credit** AmEx, DC, MC, V. **Map** p405 G7.
The city's oldest department store, opened in 1848, is also its most swish and user-friendly, thanks to an extensive redesign by LVMH. Luxury boutiques, Dior and Chanel among them, take pride of place on the ground floor; escalators designed by Andrée Putman take you up to the fashion floor, which has an excellent selection of global designer labels, from Lanvin to APC. Designer names also abound in Balthazar, the prestigious men's section.
▶ *For top-notch nibbles, try the adjoining Grande Epicerie food hall (01.44.39.81.00, www.lagrande epicerie.fr, 8.30am-9pm Mon-Sat).*

Galeries Lafayette
40 bd Haussmann, 9th (01.42.82.34.56/ fashion shows 01.42.82.30.25/fashion advice 01.42.82.35.50/www.galerieslafayette.com).

Printemps. *See p240.*

PRINTEMPS

PARIS

M° Chaussée d'Antin/RER Auber. **Open** 9.30am-8pm Mon-Wed, Fri, Sat; 9.30am-9pm Thur. **Credit** AmEx, DC, MC, V. **Map** p401 H3.
The store is launching a massive renovation programme over the next three years, with the opening in October 2008 of its Espace Luxe on the first floor, featuring luxury prêt-à-porter and accessories and nine avant-garde designers. The men's fashion space on the third floor, Lafayette Homme, has natty designer corners and a 'Club' area with internet access. On the first floor, Lafayette Gourmet has exotic foods galore, and a vast wine cellar.
► *Lafayette Maison over the road has five floors of home furnishings and interior design products.*
Other locations Centre Commercial Montparnasse, 14 rue du Départ, 14th (01.45.38.52.87).

★ Printemps

64 bd Haussmann, 9th (01.42.82.50.00/www.printemps.com). M° Havre Caumartin/RER Auber. **Open** 9.35am-8pm Mon-Wed, Fri, Sat; 9.35am-10pm Thur. **Credit** AmEx, DC, MC, V. **Map** p401 G3.
In the magnificently appointed Printemps you'll find everything you didn't even know you wanted and English-speaking assistants to help you find it. But fashion is where it really excels; an entire floor is devoted to shoes, and the beauty department stocks more than 200 brands. In all, there are six floors of men's and women's fashion. In Printemps de la Mode, French designers Paul & Joe and APC sit alongside all the big international designers. The Fashion Loft offers a younger but equally stylish take on current trends. Along with furnishings, Printemps de la Maison stocks everything from everyday tableware to design classics. *Photo p239.*
► *For fast refuelling, Printemps has a tearoom, sushi bar and Café Be, an Alain Ducasse bakery.*

Tati

4 bd de Rochechouart, 18th (01.55.29.52.20/www.tati.fr). M° Barbès Rochechouart. **Open** 10am-7pm Mon-Fri; 9.15am-7pm Sat. **Credit** MC, V. **Map** p402 J2.
Expect to find anything from T-shirts to wedding dresses, as well as bargain children's clothes and household goods at this discount heaven. It's unbeatably cheap, but don't expect high quality.
Other locations throughout the city.

SHOPPING MALLS

Bercy Village

Cour St Emilion, 12th (08.25.16.60.75/www.bercyvillage.com). M° Cour St Emilion. **Open** 11am-9pm daily. **Credit** AmEx, DC, MC, V. **Map** p407 P10.
This retail and leisure development housed in old wine warehouses is a relaxed place to shop, with the advantage of late and Sunday opening. Squarely

aimed at tourists and out-of-towners, the shops include Agnès b, Nature et Découvertes, Andaska and Pacific Adventure sports shops, L'Occitane, Oliviers & Co and Résonances for gifts, and Omnisens spa and Sephora for beauty. There are also cafés, restaurants, a park and multiplex.

Drugstore Publicis

133 av des Champs-Elysées, 8th (01.44.43.79.00/www.publicisdrugstore.com). M° Charles de Gaulle Etoile. **Open** 8am-2am Mon-Fri; 10am-2am Sat, Sun. **Credit** MC, V. **Map** p400 D4.
A 1960s legend, Drugstore Publicis was clad with neon swirls by architect Michele Saee following a renovation in 2004; a glass-and-steel café stretches out on to the pavement. On the ground floor there's a newsagent, pharmacy, bookshop and upmarket deli full of quality olive oils and elegant biscuits. The basement is a macho take on Colette, keeping selected design items and lifestyle mags, and replacing high fashion with fine wines and a cigar cellar.

Forum des Halles

rue Pierre-Lescot & rue Rambuteau, 1st (01.44.76.96.56/www.forumdeshalles.com) M° Les Halles/RER Châtelet Les Halles. **Open** 10am-8pm Mon-Sat. **Map** p402 J5.
The Forum des Halles is Paris's biggest and least pleasant shopping mall, although a facelift due for completion in 2012 should improve matters. Extending three levels underground, it incorporates métro stations, multiplex, gym, swimming pool and numerous restaurants, and is truly labyrinthine. High street retailers dominate: Mango, Zara, Kookaï, H&M, Bershka, Naf-Naf, Bodum, Habitat, Sephora, Yves Rocher and a flagship Fnac are all here.

La Galerie du Carrousel du Louvre

99 rue de Rivoli, 1st (01.43.16.47.10/www.lecarrouseldulouvre.com). M° Palais Royal Musée du Louvre. **Open** 10am-8pm daily. **Credit** AmEx, MC, V. **Map** p406 J6.
This massive underground centre – open every day of the year – is home to more than 35 shops, mostly big-name chains vying for your attention and cash. The Petit Prince boutique and Réunion des Musées Nationaux shops are great for last-minute gifts.

La Vallée Village

3 cours de la Garonne, 77700 Serris (01.60.42.35.00/www.lavalleevillage.com). Eurostar/TGV Marne La Vallée-Chessy-Parc Disneyland/RER Val d'Europe. **Open** 10am-7pm Mon-Sat; 11am-7pm Sun. Closed 1 Jan, 1 May, 25 Dec. **Credit** AmEx, MC, V.
Now directly linked to London via Eurostar, La Vallée, near Disneyland, is discount shopping heaven. Its 90 stores feature all the usual suspects – Armani, Hilfiger and Burberry – as well as French brands Agnès b, Zadig & Voltaire and Antik Batik.

▶ *Avoid the RER and splurge on a VIP Shopping Out of the City trip, complete with limo, champagne and goodie bags. From €750 for a group of four; reservations 08.26.10.26.75.*

Specialist

BOOKS & MAGAZINES

Bouquinistes

Along the quais, especially quai de Montebello & quai St-Michel, 5th. Mᵒ St-Michel. **Open** times vary from stall to stall, generally Tue-Sun. **No credit cards. Map** p406 J7.

The green, open-air boxes along the *quais* are one of the city's institutions. Most sell second-hand books – rummage through boxes packed with ancient paperbacks for something Existential.

Gibert Joseph

26 bd St-Michel, 6th (01.44.41.88.88/www.gibert joseph.com). Mᵒ St-Michel. **Open** 10am-8pm Mon-Sat. **Credit** MC, V. **Map** p408 J7.

Formed back in 1929, this string of bookshops is normally packed out with students.

▶ *Further up bd St-Michel (nos.30, 32 & 34) are branches specialising in stationery, CDs, DVDs and art materials.*

★ La Hune

170 bd St-Germain, 6th (01.45.48.35.85). Mᵒ St-Germain-des-Prés. **Open** 10am-11.45pm Mon-Sat; 11am-7.45pm Sun. **Credit** AmEx, MC, V. **Map** p405 G7.

This Left Bank institution boasts a global selection of art and design books, and a magnificent collection of French literature and theory.

English-language

Brentano's

37 av de l'Opéra, 2nd (01.42.61.52.50/www. brentanos.fr). Mᵒ Opéra or Pyramides. **Open** 10am-7.30pm Mon-Sat. **Credit** (€45 minimum) AmEx, DC; (€17 minimum) MC, V. **Map** p401 G4.

Brentano's is a good place to head for American classics, modern fiction and bestsellers, and also stocks a decent range of business titles. There is a children's section in the basement.

Galignani

224 rue de Rivoli, 1st (01.42.60.76.07). Mᵒ Tuileries. **Open** 10am-7pm Mon-Sat. **Credit** MC, V. **Map** p401 G5.

Opened in 1802, this was the first English-language bookshop in mainland Europe. Today it stocks fine art books, French and English literature, philosophical tomes and magazines.

CONSUME

Au Nain Bleu.
See p245.

I Love My Blender
*36 rue du Temple, 3rd (01.42.77.50.32/www.
ilovemyblender.fr). M° Hôtel de Ville.* **Open**
10am-7.30pm Tue-Sat. **Credit** AmEx, MC, V.
Map p405 K6.
Christophe Persouyre left a career in advertising to
share his passion for English and American literature: all the books he stocks were originally penned
in English, and here you can find their mother-
tongue and translated versions.

Red Wheelbarrow
*22 rue St-Paul, 4th (01.48.04.75.08/www.thered
wheelbarrow.com). M° St Paul.* **Open** 10am-6pm
Mon; 10am-7pm Tue-Sat; 2-6pm Sun. **Credit** MC,
V. **Map** p407 L7.
Penelope Fletcher Le Masson and Abigail Altman
run this friendly literary bookshop in the Marais,
which also has an excellent children's section.

★ Shakespeare & Company
*37 rue de la Bûcherie, 5th (01.43.25.40.93/www.
shakespeareandcompany.com). M° St-Michel.*
Open 10am-11pm Mon-Sat; 11am-11pm Sun.
Credit MC, V. **Map** p408 J7.
See p244 **Shakespeare & Company**.

Village Voice
*6 rue Princesse, 6th (01.46.33.36.47/
www.villagevoicebookshop.com). M° Mabillon.*
Open 2-7.30pm Mon; 10am-7.30pm Tue-Sat;
noon-6pm Sun. **Credit** AmEx, DC, MC, V.
Map p405 H7.
New fiction, non-fiction and literary magazines in
English, plus literary events and poetry readings.

WH Smith
*248 rue de Rivoli, 1st (01.44.77.88.99/www.
whsmith.fr). M° Concorde.* **Open** 9am-7.30pm
Mon-Sat; 1-7.30pm Sun. **Credit** AmEx, MC, V.
Map p401 G5.
With 70,000 English-language titles and extensive
magazine shelves, this is a home from home for Brits
craving a fix of their native periodicals; the first floor
has books, DVDs and audiobooks.

CHILDREN
Fashion

Children's fashion is clustered on rue Bréa
(6th), rue Vavin (6th) and rue du Fbg-St-Antoine
(12th). **Monoprix** (www.monoprix.fr) is
a good source of inexpensive children's
clothes, with some branches stocking Petit
Bateau basics. For chic at a snip, try the
Bonpoint (42 rue de l'Université, 7th,
01.40.20.10.55) and **Cacharel** (114 rue d'Alésia,
14th, 01.45.42.53.04) stock shops; it may be
last season's stuff, but your five-year-old is
never going to know.

Bonton
*82 rue de Grenelle, 7th (01.44.39.09.20/www.
bonton.fr). M° Rue du Bac.* **Open** noon-7pm
Mon; 10am-7pm Tue-Sat. Closed 2wks Aug.
Credit AmEx, DC, MC, V. **Map** p405 F6.
At this concept store for kids and trendy parents,
T-shirts and trousers come in rainbow colours, and
at pretty steep prices. Furniture and accessories are
also available, as is a children's hairdresser.
Other locations 118 rue Vieille-du-Temple, 3rd
(01.42.72.34.69).
▶ *In addition to the abovementioned branches,
the Bonton Bazar store (122 rue du Bac, 7th,
01.42.22.77.69) offers cute kids' homeware for
bedroom, bathroom, kitchen and 'library'.*

Jacadi
*116 rue d'Alésia, 14th (01.40.44.51,87/
www.jacadi.fr). M° Alésia.* **Open** 11am-7pm
Mon; 10am-7pm Tue-Sat. **Credit** MC, V.
Map p405 E10.
Jacadi's well-made clothes for babies and children –
pleated skirts, smocked dresses, dungarees and Fair
Isle knits – are a hit with well-to-do parents. The rue
d'Alésia store is the largest.
Other locations throughout the city.

★ Du Pareil au Même
*120-122 rue du Fbg-St-Antoine, 12th
(01.43.44.67.46/www.dpam.com). M° Ledru-
Rollin.* **Open** 10am-7pm Mon-Sat. **Credit**
AmEx, MC, V. **Map** p407 N7.
Bright, cleverly designed basics for children aged
three months to 14 years, at low prices. The Bébé
branch, with fashionable accessories and clothing
for kids up to two years, is a good source of gifts.
Other locations throughout the city.

Petit Bateau
*26 rue Vavin, 6th (01.55.42.02.53/
www.petit-bateau.com). M° Vavin.* **Open**
10am-7pm Mon-Sat. **Credit** AmEx, MC, V.
Map p405 G8.
Widely renowned in the city and beyond for its comfortable, well-made cotton T-shirts, vests and other
separates, Petit Bateau carries an equally coveted
teen range.
Other locations throughout the city.

★ Six Pieds Trois Pouces
*222 bd St-Germain, 7th (01.45.44.03.72/
www.sixpiedstroispouces.com). M° Solférino.*
Open 10.30am-7pm Mon-Sat. **Credit** AmEx,
DC, MC, V. **Map** p405 F6.
The excellent array of children's and teens' shoes
runs from Start-rite and Aster to Timberland and
New Balance, alongside the shop's own brand.
Other locations 19 rue de la Monnaie,
1st (01.40.41.07.79); 85 rue de Longchamp,
16th (01.45.53.64.21); 78 av de Wagram,
17th (01.46.22.81.64).

CONSUME

Shakespeare & Company

A Left Bank literary institution.

Despite the relentless march of the mammoth international book retailers, Paris is home to a healthy number of maverick booksellers. Of these, the most famous is **Shakespeare & Company** (*see p243*), once described by Henry Miller as a 'wonderland of books'.

The first Shakespeare & Company was founded in rue de l'Odéon in 1919 by Sylvia Beach, and rapidly became a literary hub. In 1922, Beach was the first to publish Joyce's *Ulysses*, before eventually being closed down during the German occupation in 1941. Ten years later, American Francophile George Whitman moved his extensive personal collection of European and American literature into a little shop on rue de la Bûcherie and opened his own literary den, in much the same vein as Beach's original. When Sylvia died in 1962, Whitman's store adopted the name Shakespeare & Company.

George Whitman is now in his nineties, and his daughter Sylvia (named after Beach, of course) has taken over the business, which continues to boast the best selection of English language books in the city, and hosts regular readings and workshops. Upstairs, the 'Tumbleweed Hotel' (every room crammed to the rafters with books) provides temporary lodgings for literary travellers, who can earn their keep by helping out in the shop.

In recent years Sylvia and her team have pulled off something of a coup by setting up the Shakespeare & Company Literary Festival (www.festivalandco.com). The biennial four-day event (next edition set for June 2010) is no small-time affair: at last count attracted over 5,000 visitors.

Paul Auster and Siri Hustvedt were the headliners in 2008, together with Jeanette Winterson, Alain de Botton, Jung Chang, Victoria Glendinning, Amélie Nothomb and Catherine Millet.

'We don't put them up in posh hotels, but they love to come,' Sylvia says. 'It's completely different from other literary festivals. Here we have a glass of wine in the bookshop and you glance round and see Paul Auster chatting to an unknown writer. They love that aspect of the festival, and of course, they love to come to Paris.' Most of the readings and debates are held in a marquee in square René Viviani next to the store, with some special events in locations such as the Hôtel de Ville.

Back in the shop, it's as if modern life left this place behind: books from floor to ceiling, a dusty piano, and Colette the dog. From his room above the shop, George can still be seen looking out of the window, keeping an eye on his old friends – many of them literary luminaries who might pop by to pick up a rare edition, chat with Sylvia or give a reading.

Zef

*15 rue Debelleyme, 3rd (01.42.76.09.65/
www.zef.eu). M° St-Sébastien Froissart.*
Open 11am-7.30pm Mon-Sat. **Credit** AmEx,
DC, MC, V. **Map** p409 L5.
Zef's designer is the daughter of fashion photographer Paolo Reversi. The trendy children's separates
have a classic Italian look, in soft muted colours with
adorable details like elbow patches on the jackets.
Boots, sheepskin gilets and hats are part of the look.
Other locations 32 rue de Richelieu, 1st
(01.42.60.61.04); 55bis rue des Sts-Pères, 6th
(01.42.22.02.93; babies and toddlers 01.42.22.45.22).

Toys & books

Traditional toyshops abound; department
stores (*see p239*) go overboard at Christmas.
For children's books in English, try **WH Smith**
(*see p243*) or **Brentano's** (*see p242*).

Arche de Noé

*70 rue St-Louis-en-l'Île, 4th (01.46.34.61.60).
M° Pont Marie.* **Open** 10.30am-7pm daily.
Credit AmEx, MC, V. **Map** p409 K7.
'Noah's Ark' is a great place for Christmas shopping,
with traditional wooden toys from eastern Europe,
games, jigsaws and finger puppets.

Fnac Junior

*19 rue Vavin, 6th (01.56.24.03.46/www.eveilet
jeux.com). M° Vavin.* **Open** 10am-7.30pm Mon-
Sat. **Credit** AmEx, MC, V. **Map** p405 G8.
Fnac carries books, toys, DVDs, CDs and CD-Roms
for the under-12s. Storytelling and other activities
(Wed, Sat) take place for three-year-olds and up.
Other locations throughout the city.

★ Au Nain Bleu

*5 bd Malesherbes, 8th (01.42.65.20.00/www.au
nainbleu.com). M° Madeleine.* **Open** 2-7pm
Mon; 10am-7pm Tue-Sat. **Credit** AmEx, MC, V.
Map p401 F4.
The city's best toyshop, decorated like a circus tent,
draws gasps of wonder from children. Wooden doll's
houses, pirate ships and gorgeous dolls are made to
last more than one generation. *Photo p242.*

Robopolis

*107 bd Beaumarchais, 3rd (01.44.78.01.18/
www.robopolis.com). M° Filles du Calvaire.*
Open 11am-1pm, 2-7pm Tue-Sat. **Credit** AmEx,
MC, V. **Map** p409 L5.
This is the only store in France devoted entirely to
our friends robotic, and as such it attracts gizmo-
lovers of all ages. It's as much a showroom as a shop,
with displays including dancing humanoids, white
iPod rabbits that sing and read, and even robotic
vacuum cleaners. Models such as Roboreptile and
Meccano's 'build-your-own' robot sit at the top of
kids' (and big kids') Christmas lists.

Village Joué Club

*3-5 bd des Italiens, 2nd (01.53.45.41.41/
www.joueclub.fr). M° Richelieu Drouot.* **Open**
10am-8pm Mon-Sat. **Credit** AmEx, MC, V.
Map p402 H4.
Village Joué Club, the largest toy store in Paris, is
spread out on ground level in and around passage
des Princes.

FASHION

All the world's big-name designers have
their own-label stores in Paris. In addition
to international fashion juggernauts Mango,
H&M and Zara, the high street has its fair share
of Gallic cheapies: think **Etam**, Jennyfer and
Pimkie. The highest density is in the **Forum
des Halles** (*see p240*), on nearby rue de Rivoli,
between the métro stations of Châtelet and
Louvre Rivoli, and around Galeries Lafayette
and Printemps.

Designer

A-poc

*47 rue des Francs-Bourgeois, 4th
(01.44.54.07.05). M° Rambuteau or St-Paul.*
Open 11am-7pm Mon-Sat. Closed 3wks Aug.
Credit AmEx, MC, V. **Map** p409 L6.
Issey Miyake's lab-style boutique takes a highly
conceptual approach to fashion. Alongside ready-
to-wear cotton Lycra ensembles are rolls of wool
jersey cut *sur mesure*; Miyake's assistants will be
happy to advise.
▶ *Miyake's original shop (3 pl des Vosges, 4th,
01.48.87.01.86) is now home to the creations of
Naoki Takizawa, protégé of the old master.*

Azzedine Alaïa

*7 rue de Moussy, 4th (01.42.72.19.19). M° Hôtel
de Ville.* **Open** 10am-7pm Mon-Sat. **Credit**
AmEx, DC, MC, V. **Map** p409 K6.
Ringing the doorbell gains you entry to the factory-
style showroom in the same building as Alaïa's
headquarters and apartment, where the 72-year-old
Tunisian creator continues to astound with his orig-
inality. Stunning haute couture creations are in the
back room, and sexy shoes bordering on fetish are
scattered among the mannequins and rails.

Balenciaga

*10 av George V, 8th (01.47.20.21.11/www.
balenciaga.com). M° Alma Marceau or George V.*
Open 10am-7pm Mon-Sat. **Credit** AmEx, DC,
MC, V. **Map** p400 D5.
With Nicolas Ghesquière at the helm, the Spanish
fashion house is ahead of Japanese and Belgian
designers in the hip stakes. Floating fabrics contrast
with dramatic cuts, producing a sophisticated urban
style that the fashion *haut monde* can't wait to slip
into. Bags and shoes are also available.

CONSUME

GALERIES Lafayette

THE DEPARTMENT STORE CAPITAL OF FASHION*

*Le grand magasin, capitale de la mode.

GALERIES LAFAYETTE - 40, BD HAUSSMANN 75009 PARIS.
METRO CHAUSSÉE D'ANTIN-LA FAYETTE
OPEN MONDAY THROUGH SATURDAY
FROM 9.30 AM TO 8 PM.
LATE NIGHT OPENING EVERY THURSDAY UNTIL 9 PM.
TEL.: 01 42 82 36 40 - galerieslafayette.com

Carlos Miele

380 rue St-Honoré, 1st (01.42.97.53.66/
www.carlosmiele.com.br). M°Concorde. **Open**
10am-7pm Mon-Sat. **Credit** AmEx, MC, V.
Map p402 H5.
The Brazilian designer favoured by Sandra Bullock,
Heidi Klum and J Lo brings luxury with a conscience
to the rue St-Honoré. He works with several cooper-
atives in *favelas* and with Amazonian Indians, hon-
ing traditional techniques like crochet, knotting,
embroidery and featherwork.

★ Chanel

31 rue Cambon, 1st (01.42.86.28.00/www.
chanel.com). M° Concorde or Madeleine. **Open**
10am-7pm Mon-Sat. **Credit** AmEx, DC, MC, V.
Map p401 G4.
Fashion legend Chanel has managed to stay relevant, thanks to Karl Lagerfeld. Coco opened her first
boutique in this street, at no.21, in 1910, and the tradition continues in this elegant interior. Lagerfeld
has been designing for Chanel since 1983, and keeps
on revamping the classics – the little black dress and
the Chanel suit – with great success.
Other locations 42 av Montaigne, 8th
(01.47.23.74.12).

Comme des Garçons

54 rue du Fbg-St-Honoré, 8th (01.53.30.27.27).
M° Concorde or Madeleine. **Open** 11am-7pm Mon-
Sat. **Credit** AmEx, DC, MC, V. **Map** p401 F4.
Rei Kawakubo's design ideas and revolutionary mix
of materials have influenced fashions of the past two
decades, and are showcased in this fibreglass store.
► *Comme des Garçons Parfums (23 pl du*
Marché-St-Honoré, 1st, 01.47.03.15.03) provides
a futuristic setting for the brand's fragrances.

Dior

26-30 av Montaigne, 8th (01.40.73.73.73/
www.dior.com). M° Franklin D. Roosevelt.
Open 10am-7pm Mon-Sat. **Credit** AmEx, DC,
MC, V. **Map** p400 D5.
The Dior universe is here on avenue Montaigne,
from the main prêt-à-porter store and jewellery,
menswear and eyewear to Baby Dior, where rich
infants are coochy-cooed by drooling assistants.
Other locations throughout the city.

Gaspard Yurkievich

43 rue Charlot, 3rd (01.42.77.55.48/www.
gaspardyurkievich.com). M° Filles du Calvaire.
Open 11am-7pm Tue-Sat. **Credit** MC, V.
Map p402 L5.
The first boutique of this native Parisian fashion
missile. Hot men's and women's designs and a dangerous line of shoes are all on display.

★ Givenchy

28 rue du Fbg-St-Honoré, 8th (01.42.68.31.00/
www.givenchy.com). M° Madeleine or Concorde.

Open 10am-7pm Mon-Sat. **Credit** AmEx, DC,
MC, V. **Map** p401 F4.
In March 2008, Givenchy opened this new flagship
Fbg-St-Honoré store for men's and women's prêt-à-
porter and accessories. Designed by Jamie Fobert,
who worked on the Tate, it incorporates surreal
rooms within rooms – cut-out boxes filled with
white, black or mahogany panelling – providing a
contemporary art gallery setting for Givenchy's
cutting-edge, sculptural and monochrome designs.

Hermès

24 rue du Fbg-St-Honoré, 8th (01.40.17.47.17/
www.hermes.com). M° Concorde or Madeleine.
Open 10.30am-6.30pm Mon-Sat. **Credit** AmEx,
DC, MC, V. **Map** p401 F4.
The fifth generation of the family directs the Hermès
empire from its 1930s building. Originally – and
still – a saddler, it is no also-ran in the fashion stakes,
with Jean-Paul Gaultier at the reins. Most of its
clients, however, are tourists after a horsey scarf.

★ Jay Ahr

2-4 rue du 29 Juillet, 1st (01.42.96.95.23/www.
jayahr.com). M° Tuileries. **Open** 11am-7pm
Mon-Sat. **Credit** AmEx, MC, V. **Map** p401 G5.
Former jewellery designer Jonathan Riss opened this
shop as a fashion stylist in 2004, and struck gold
with simple, figure-flaunting, '60s-inspired dresses.
Think plunging necklines and Bianca Jagger in her
heyday, with Ali McGraw and Anita Pallenberg in
the mix. There are no price tags on the dresses, so
you have to ask; they start at around €500.

Jean-Paul Gaultier

6 rue Vivienne, 2nd (01.42.86.05.05/www.
jeanpaulgaultier.com). M° Bourse. **Open**
10.30am-7pm Mon-Fri; 11am-7pm Sat. **Credit**
AmEx, DC, MC, V. **Map** p402 H4.
Having celebrated his 30th year in the fashion business, Gaultier is still going strong. His boudoir boutique with its peach taffeta walls stocks men's and
women's ready-to-wear and the reasonably priced
JPG Jeans lines.
Other locations 44 av George V, 8th
(01.44.43.00.44).
► *The haute couture department (01.42.97.48.12)*
is by appointment, and is located above the store.

John Galliano

384-386 rue St-Honoré, 1st (01.55.35.40.40/
www.johngalliano.com). M° Concorde or
Madeleine. **Open** 11am-7pm Mon-Sat.
Credit AmEx, DC, MC, V. **Map** p401 G4.
It's hard to imagine how he manages it all, but
Dior chief Galliano still has his own range and a
reputation as one of the UK's most original designers. You can admire the small but diverse collection
of flamboyant and feminine delights through the
showcase window, or from the Louis XVI-style
chairs inside.

CONSUME

Kenzo

*1 rue du Pont Neuf, 1st (01.73.04.20.03/
www.kozen.com). M° Pont Neuf.* **Open**
10am-7pm Mon-Sat. **Credit** AmEx, DC, MC, V.
Map p402 J6.
Kenzo has long been a friend of Paris, having
dressed the city itself in its various extravagant publicity campaigns. The flagship store has three floors
of men's and women's fashion, and is crowned with
the Bulle Kenzo spa and Philippe Starck-designed
Kong restaurant on the fifth floor.
Other locations throughout the city.

Lagerfeld Gallery

*40 rue de Seine, 6th (01.55.42.75.50/www.
karllagerfeld.com). M° Odéon.* **Open** 11am-7pm
Tue-Sat. Closed Aug. **Credit** AmEx, DC, MC, V.
Map p408 H6.
Andrée Putman helped create this shrine to King
Karl's brand of stylish minimalism where Lagerfeld's
fashion creations and photography are on display.
You could sneak in just to browse the latest fashion,
beauty and art publications, scattered across a hand-
some round table at the front of the gallery.

★ Lanvin

*22 rue du Fbg St-Honoré, 8th (01.44.71.31.73/
www.lanvin.com). M° Concorde or Madeleine.*
Open 10am-7pm Mon-Sat. **Credit** AmEx, DC,
MC, V. **Map** p401 F4.
The couture house that began in the 1920s with
Jeanne Lanvin has been reinvented by the talented
and indefatigable Albert Elbaz. In October 2007 he
unveiled this, the revamped showroom that set new
aesthetic standards for luxury fashion retailing.
Lanvin has an exhibition room devoted to her in
the Musée des Arts Décoratifs, and this apartment-
boutique comes close, incorporating original furniture from the Lanvin archive that has been restored.
All this would be nothing, of course, if the clothes
themselves were not exquisite.

Lefranc.ferrant

*22 rue de l'Echaudé, 6th (01.44.07.37.96/www.
lefranc-ferrant.fr). M° St-Germain-des-Prés.*
Open 11am-7pm Tue-Sat and by appointment.
Credit AmEx, MC, V. **Map** p408 H7.
The opening of this boutique has been eagerly
awaited by keen followers of the talented Paris
duo Béatrice Ferrant and Mario Lefranc. Their
trademark is a surreal approach to tailoring, as in
a strapless yellow evening gown made like a pair
of men's trousers – complete with flies. Prices are
in the €1,000, range and they love to undertake
bespoke commissions.

Louis Vuitton

*101 av des Champs-Elysées, 8th (08.10.81.00.10/
www.vuitton.com). M° George V.* **Open** 10am-
8pm Mon-Sat; 11am-7pm Sun. **Credit** AmEx,
DC, MC, V. **Map** p400 D4.

The 'Promenade' flagship sets the tone for Vuitton's
global image, from the 'bag bar', bookstore and new
jewellery department to the women's and men's
ready-to-wear. Contemporary art, videos by Tim
White Sobieski and a pitch-black elevator by Olafur
Eliasson complete the picture. Accessed by lift, the
Espace Vuitton hosts temporary art exhibits – but
the star of the show is the view over Paris.
Other locations 6 pl St-Germain-des-Prés, 6th;
22 av Montaigne, 8th.

★ Marc Jacobs

*56 galerie de Montpensier, 1st (01.55.35.02.60/
www.marcjacobs.com). M° Palais Royal Musée
du Louvre.* **Open** 11am-8pm Mon-Sat. **Credit**
AmEx, DC, MC, V. **Map** p402 H5.
By choosing the Palais-Royal for his first signature
boutique in Europe, Marc Jacobs brought new life –
and an influx of fashionistas – to these elegant clois-
ters. Stocking womenswear, menswear, accessories
and shoes, it has already become a place of pilgrimage for the designer's legion of admirers, who are
snapping up his downtown New York style.

Martin Grant

*10 rue Charlot, 3rd (01.42.71.39.49/www.martin
grantparis.com). M° Temple.* **Open** 10am-6pm
Mon-Fri. Closed 3wks Aug. **Credit** MC, V.
Map p406 K6.
This high-end shop is tucked away in a second-
floor Marais apartment. If you're a stickler for steady
cuts, pure textiles and unfussy designs, Australian
designer Martin Grant's interpretation of couture
is for you.

Martin Margiela

*23 & 25bis rue de Montpensier, 1st
(womenswear 01.40.15.07.55/menswear
01.40.15.06.44/www.maisonmartinmargiela.
com). M° Palais Royal Musée du Louvre.* **Open**
11am-7pm Mon-Sat. **Credit** AmEx, DC, MC, V.
Map p402 H5.
The first Paris outlet for the JD Salinger of fashion
is a pristine, white, unlabelled space. His collection
for women (Line 1) has a blank label but is recognisable by external white stitching. You'll also find
Line 6 (women's basics) and Line 10 (menswear),
plus accessories for men and women and shoes.
Other locations 13 rue de Grenelle, 7th
(01.45.49.06.45).

Miu Miu

*219 rue St-Honoré, 1st (01.58.62.53.20/www.
miumiu.com). M° Tuileries.* **Open** 11am-7pm
Mon; 10am-7pm Tue-Sat. **Credit** AmEx, DC,
MC, V. **Map** p401 G5.
Prada's younger sister has this rue St-Honoré store
as its main boutique, selling its quirky women's
fashions, shoes and bags.
Other locations 16 rue de Grenelle, 7th
(01.53.63.20.30).

★ Paul & Joe
64 rue des Sts-Pères, 7th (01.42.22.47.01/ www.paulandjoe.com). M° Rue du Bac or St-Germain-des-Prés. **Open** 10am-7pm Mon-Sat. **Credit** AmEx, DC, MC, V. **Map** p405 G6.

International fashionistas have taken a shine to Sophie Albou's retro-styled creations. The latest collection dresses leggy young things in a range of winter shorts, colourful mini dresses and voluminous trousers, with their intellectual paramours in slouchy woollens, tailored jackets and chunky boots. **Other locations** *Men* 56 rue Vieille-du-Temple, 3rd (01.42.72.42.06); 62 rue des Sts-Pères, 7th (01.42.22.98.98). *Women* 46 rue Etienne-Marcel, 2nd (01.40.28.03.34); 2 av Montaigne,

8th (01.47.20.57.50); 123 rue de la Pompe, 16th (01.45.53.01.08).

Paule Ka
223 rue St-Honoré, 1st (01.42.97.57.06/ www.pauleka.com). M° Tuileries. **Open** 11am-7pm Mon; 10am-7pm Tue-Sat. **Credit** AmEx, DC, MC, V. **Map** p401 G4.

Serge Cajfinger's '60s couture-influenced collections continue to gather a loyal following. With the opening of his rue St-Honoré boutique, he now has a foot in each of the city's fashion districts. **Other locations** 20 rue Malher, 4th (01.40.29.96.03); 192 bd St-Germain, 6th (01.45.44.92.60); 45 rue François 1er, 8th (01.47.20.76.10).

Sonia Rykiel. *See p250.*

CONSUME

CONSUME

Paul Smith

3 rue du Fbg-St-Honoré, 8th (01.42.68.27.10/
www.paulsmith.co.uk). M° Concorde. **Open** 11am-
7pm Mon; 10am-7pm Tue-Sat. **Credit** AmEx,
DC, MC, V. **Map** p401 F4.

A 'so British' atmosphere is cultivated with '40s
wallpaper, antiques, old books and bric-a-brac,
much of it for sale along with the colourful shirts
and knitwear in which Smith excels. Collections
for men, women and children, along with eyewear
and accessories, are all gathered in this elegant
Haussmann apartment.

Other locations *22-24 bd Raspail, 7th*
(01.42.84.15.30).

Prada

10 av Montaigne, 8th (01.53.23.99.40/www.
prada.com). M° Alma Marceau. **Open** 11am-
7pm Mon; 10am-7pm Tue-Sat. **Credit** AmEx,
DC, MC, V. **Map** p400 D5.

The high priestess of European chic, Miuccia
Prada's elegant stores pull in fashion followers of all
ages. Handbags of choice are complemented by the
coveted ready-to-wear range.

Other locations *5 rue de Grenelle, 6th*
(01.45.48.53.14); 6 rue du Fbg-St-Honoré, 8th
(01.58.18.63.30).

Rick Owens

130 galerie de Valois, 1st (01.40.20.42.52/
www.owenscorp.com). M° Palais Royal Musée du
Louvre. **Open** noon-7pm Mon; 10am-7pm Tue-
Sat. **Credit** AmEx, DC, MC, V. **Map** p402 H5.

The LA designer and rock star favourite brings his
glamour-meets-grunge style to the Palais-Royal,
with hoods, zips and asymmetrical wrappings for
men and women. It's not for animal lovers – the
upstairs has a dedicated mink section.

★ Robert Normand

149-150 galerie de Valois, 1st (www.robert
normand.com). M° Palais Royal/Musée du
Louvre. **Open** 1-7pm Mon; 10.30am-7pm Tue-
Sat. **Credit** AmEx, DC, MC, V. **Map** p402 H5.

Normand is a new addition to the Palais-Royal. The
38-year-old designer, who has collaborated with
Lanvin, Pucci and Christophe Lemaire, launched his
own label in 2000 – an exuberant combination of pop
art patterns with gangsta cuts, satin puffballs in peacock colours and blousons made of the kind of
baroque fabrics favoured by African potentates. The
man is treading the line between madness and genius.

Rue du Mail

5 rue du Mail, 2nd (01.42.60.19.20/www.
ruedumail.com). M° Bourse. **Open** noon-5pm
Mon-Fri. **Credit** AmEx, MC, V. **Map** p402 J4.

Martine Sitbon's sexy new collection is a hit with
Cate Blanchett, Sofia Coppola, Scarlett Johansson et
al. Swooping V necklines, flirty hemlines, black satin
and fruity chiffons define the look.

Sonia Rykiel

175 bd St-Germain, 6th (01.49.54.60.60/www.
soniarykiel.com). M° St-Germain-des-Prés or
Sèvres Babylone. **Open** 10.30am-7pm Mon-Sat.
Credit AmEx, DC, MC, V. **Map** p405 G6.

The queen of St-Germain celebrated the 40th birthday of her flagship store with a glamorous black and
smoked glass refit perfect for narcissists: tons of mirrors reflect the flowing gowns of her current '70s
throwback look. Menswear is across the street, and
two newer boutiques stock the younger, more affordable Sonia by Sonia Rykiel range (59 rue des Sts-
Pères, 6th, 01.49.54.61.00) and kids' togs (4 rue de
Grenelle, 6th, 01.49.54.61.10). *Photo p249.*

▶ *For something on the wild side, Rykiel Woman*
(6 rue de Grenelle, 6th, 01.49.54.66.21), on the
site of her original 1966 shop, stocks a range of
designer sex toys.

Other locations throughout the city.

★ Yohji Yamamoto

25 rue du Louvre, 1st (01.42.21.42.93/www.
yohjiyamamoto.co.jp). M° Les Halles or Sentier.
Open 10.30am-7pm Mon-Sat. **Credit** AmEx, DC,
MC, V. **Map** p405 G7.

One of the few true pioneers working in fashion
today, Yamamoto is a master of cut and finish, both
strongly inspired by the kimono and traditional
Tibetan costume. His dexterity with form makes for
unique shapes and styles, largely black. But when
he does colour, it's a blast of brilliance.

▶ *Find the men's boutique at 25 rue du Louvre,*
1st (01.45.08.82.45).

Yves Saint Laurent

6 pl St-Sulpice, 6th (01.43.29.43.00/www.ysl.
com). M° St-Sulpice. **Open** 11am-7pm Mon;
10.30am-7pm Tue-Sat. **Credit** AmEx, DC,
MC, V. **Map** p408 H7.

The memory of the founding designer, who died in
2008, lives on in this elegant boutique, which was
splendidly refitted in red in the same year. You'll
find menswear at no.12 (01.43.26.84.40).

Other locations *Men 32 rue du Fbg-St-Honoré,*
8th (01.53.05.80.80). Women 38 rue du Fbg-St-
Honoré, 8th (01.42.65.74.59).

Boutique & concept

★ AB33 and N°60

33 & 60 rue Charlot, 3rd (01.42.71.02.82/
01.44.78.91.90). M° Filles du Calvaire. **Open**
11am-8pm Tue-Sun. **Credit** AmEx, MC, V.
Map p409 L5.

AB33, the original boutique run by fashion addict
Agathe Buchotte, has become a must in every like-
minded woman's address book for its eclectic mix
of pieces from smaller brands like Odd Molly and
Laundry Industry. Up the road, the younger N°60
revels in a more rock 'n' roll attitude, courtesy of
labels such as McQ, Chalayan and April 77.

★ Anikalena Skärström

16 rue du Pont aux Choux, 3rd (01.44.59.32.85/
www.anikalena.com). M° St-Sébastien Froissart.
Open 11am-7pm Mon-Fri; noon-7pm Sat. Closed
2wks Aug. **Credit** MC, V. **Map** p402 J2.
Clean lines and streamlining are the guiding aesthetic for Anikalena's collections of sporty, sexy
day and evening dresses and separates, with the
occasional wow piece like the grass-green suede
coat of 2008. A word to the wise: check the finish.

April 77

49 rue de Saintonge, 3rd (01.40.29.07.30/
www.april77.fr). M° Filles du Calvaire. **Open**
11am-7pm Tue-Sat. **Credit** MC, V. **Map** p402 J2.
The cult skinny jeans brand has acquired its own
boutique, designed by Steven Thomas, to show off
their collection inspired by the mid-'80s music scene.

Base One

47bis rue d'Orsel, 18th (01.73.75.37.10/www.
baseoneshop.com). M° Anvers. **Open** 12.30-
8pm Tue-Sat; 3.30-8pm Sun. Closed 2wks Aug.
Credit MC, V. **Map** p402 J2.
Clubland duo Princesse Léa and Jean-Louis Faverole
squeeze items from little-known local and international designers (Shai Wear, Li-Lei, Drolaic, OK47),
plus small, established brands (Fenchurch, Motel,
Consortium) into their boutique. Massive gold piggy
banks from Present Time add un-Parisian bling.

Les Belles Images

74 rue Charlot, 3rd (01.42.76.93.61/www.
myspace.com/lesbellesimages). M° Filles du
Calvaire. **Open** 11am-7.30pm Tue-Sat.
Credit MC, V. **Map** p402 L5.
A retro '60s vibe reigns at this boutique (women's
and men's), where owner Sandy Bontout showcases
items from current collections of obscure and big-
name French and international labels, such as Ambali
separates, Walk that Walk shoes and editor's picks
from Veronique Leroy and Vivienne Westwood.

Colette

213 rue St-Honoré, 1st (01.55.35.33.90/www.
colette.fr). M° Pyramides or Tuileries. **Open**
11am-7pm Mon-Sat. **Credit** AmEx, DC, MC, V.
Map p401 G4.

INSIDE TRACK
SALE RAIL

Twice a year, in January and July,
boutiques sell off seasonal stock at
reduced prices to make way for incoming
collections. The nationwide dates for
the *soldes* (sales) are imposed by
the state-run consumer office; call
01.40.27.16.00 for more details.

The renowned and much-imitated one-stop concept
and lifestyle store stationed a mobile 'superette' outside while it went into rehab in summer 2008. Expect
the same highly eclectic selection of must-have
accessories, fashion, books, media, shiny new gadgets, and hair and beauty brands själ, Kiehl's and
uslu airlines, all in a swanky new space.

Dolls

56 rue de Saintonge, 3rd (01.44.54.08.21).
M° Filles du Calvaire. **Open** 11am-7.30pm
Tue-Sat. Closed 2wks Aug. **Credit** DC, MC, V.
Map p401 G4.
This hot new address for the Marais style crowd
concentrates on a few well-chosen brands: Valentine
Gaulthier (France), By Malene Birger (Denmark),
Sass & Bide (Australia), NDC shoes (Belgium) and
Citizens of Humanity jeans.

★ L'Eclaireur

3ter rue des Rosiers, 4th (01.48.87.10.22/www.
leclaireur.com). M° St-Paul. **Open** 11am-7pm Mon-
Sat. **Credit** AmEx, DC, MC, V. **Map** p409 L6.
See p257 **Fashion Scouts**.
▶ *Men are catered for separately at L'Eclaireur*
Homme (12 rue Malher, 4th, 01.44.54.22.11).
Other locations 10 rue Hérold, 1st
(01.40.41.09.89); 12 rue Malher, 4th (01.44.54.22.11);
10 rue Boissy d'Anglas, 8th (01.53.43.03.70); 26 av
des Champs-Elysées, 8th (01.45.62.12.32).

Galerie Simone

124 rue Vieille-du-Temple, 3rd (01.42.74.21.28).
M° St-Sébastien Froissart. **Open** noon-7pm Tue-
Sat; 1.30-6pm Sun. **Credit** AmEx, DC, MC, V.
Map p409 L5.
Simone Gaubatz sources and cultivates talented
young designers from around the world, displaying
their most eye-catching creations on mannequins in
this gallery-style space.

Jack Henry

25 rue Charlot, 3rd (01.42.78.93.51/www.jack
henry.fr). M° Filles du Calvaire. **Open** 11am-
7.30pm Tue-Sun. **Credit** AmEx, MC, V.
Map p409 L5.
The work of this Paris-trained American designer
has real intellectual heft to it, but you only have to
touch the silky soft cotton and wool jersey from
Japan to want his finely crafted, beautifully conceived tunics, skirts and jackets. Luxurious leather
bags and jewellery from designers including
Théodora Gabrielli, alias Dorothée, who patiently
creates new pieces while serving in the shop, are also
on display.

Joseph

147 bd St-Germain, 6th (01.55.42.77.56/www.
joseph.co.uk). M° St-Germain-des-Prés. **Open**
11am-7pm Mon, Sat; 10.30am-7pm Tue-Fri.
Credit AmEx, DC, MC, V. **Map** p405 G6.

CONSUME

Taking a cue from its London store, Joseph has opened a multi-brand shop boasting pieces by Ann Demeulemeester, Dries van Noten and Bruno Pieters, as well as accessories by Bijoux de Sophie and handbags by Jérôme Dreyfuss.

Kitsuné

52 rue de Richelieu, 1st (01.42.60.34.28/www. kitsune.fr). M° Palais Royal, Musée du Louvres or Pyramides. **Open** 11am-7.30pm Mon-Sat. **Credit** MC, V. **Map** p402 H4.

The London/Paris style collective has finally got its own boutique, which offers the entire catalogue of music compilations, as well as branded clothing that takes a back-to-basics approach using quality producers. You'll find Scottish cashmere, Japanese jeans and Italian shirts, together with items made in collaboration with Pierre Hardy, Scheisser underwear and James Heeley.

Kokon To Zai

48 rue Tiquetonne, 2nd (01.42.36.92.41/www. kokontozai.co.uk). M° Etienne Marcel. **Open** 11.30am-7.30pm Mon-Sat. **Credit** AmEx, DC, MC, V. **Map** p402 J5.

Always a spot-on spotter of the latest creations, this tiny style emporium is sister to the Kokon To Zai in London. The neon-lit club feel of the mirrored interior matches the dark glamour of the designs. Unique pieces straight off the catwalk share space with creations by Marjan Peijoski, Noki, Raf Simons, Ziad Ghanem and new Norwegian designers.

★ LE66

66 av des Champs-Elysées, 8th (01.53.53.33.96/ www.myspace.com/lesoixantesix). M° George V. **Open** 11am-8pm daily. **Credit** AmEx, DC, MC, V. **Map** p400 D4.

Exchewing the glass cabinet approach of Colette, this fashion concept store is youthful and accessible, with an ever-changing selection of hip brands including Puma Black Label. Assistants, who are also the buyers and designers, make for a motivated team. The store takes the form of three transparent modules, the first a book and magazine store run by Black Book of the Palais de Tokyo, and the second two devoted to fashion. It even has its own vintage store, in collaboration with Come On Eline and Kiliwatch.

Margo Milin

1 rue Charles François Dupuis, 3rd (06.61.77. 14.76/www.margomilin.com). M° République or Temple. **Open** 11.30am-7.30pm Mon-Sat. **No credit cards. Map** p401 G4.

Looking like a model herself, St Martin's graduate Marguerite Milin studied theatrical design and produces kimono-influenced wrap-around jumpers and party dresses that play with a contrast of textures and pattern versus plain. A fun, girly atmosphere is always found in the boutique, as customers take turns in the tiny changing room.

Maria Luisa

7 rue Rouget de Lisle, 1st (01.47.03.96.15). M° Concorde. **Open** 10.30am-7pm Mon-Sat. **Credit** AmEx, DC, MC, V. **Map** p401 G4.

Venezuelan Maria Luisa Poumaillou was one of the city's first stockists of Galliano, McQueen and the Belgians, and has an eye for rising stars such as Bernhard Willhelm, Eley Kishimoto, Undercover and Emma Cook. She has now pooled all the womenswear – previously split up into small boutiques – in this new minimalist flagship.

▶ *Poumaillou's menswear store can be found at 38 rue du Mont-Thabor, 1st (01.42.96.47.81).*

Me

29 rue du Dragon, 6th (01.53.63.02.52). M° St-Germain-des-Prés. **Open** 10am-7pm Mon-Sat. **Credit** AmEx, MC, V. **Map** p405 G7.

Oversized dolls are the mannequins at Me, the most youthful division of Issey Miyake, created by his disciples as an offshoot of Pleats Please. Washable, pleated stretch tops make up 80 per cent of the range.

Les Prairies de Paris

23 rue Debelleyme, 3rd (01.40.20.44.12/www. lesprairiesdeparis.com). M° St-Sébastien Froissart. **Open** 11am-7.30pm, 2.30-7pm Mon-Sat. **Credit** AmEx, MC, V. **Map** p409 L5.

Laeticia Ivanez opened this installation space/ boutique in the Marais in July 2008. The whole of the ground floor is given over to art shows, gigs and happenings, with an original Peter Colombo leather chair placed centre left. Downstairs the '60s theme continues, with a cocoon-like setting in which to commune with the disco-glam separates and cute children's collection.

Other locations 6 rue du Pré aux Clercs, 7th.

★ Set Galerie

7 rue d'Uzès, 2nd (01.40.16.56.49/www. stephaneplassier.com). M° Grands Boulevards. **Open** 11am-7pm Mon-Sat. **Credit** AmEx, MC, V. **Map** p402 H1.

Multitalented Stéphane Plassier already has a name for himself as an interior designer, branding consultant and *metteur en scène*. Now he's opened his own concept store above the design control room of his business. Fashion lines include Dessus-Dessous (underwear), Beautiful Jacket (jackets for men) and Set in Black, a range of black dresses. The converted industrial space also hosts a brilliant collection of books and objects, including a section devoted to religious kitsch.

Shine

15 rue de Poitou, 3rd (01.48.05.80.10). M° Filles du Calvaire. **Open** 11am-7.30pm Mon-Sat. **Credit** AmEx, MC, V. **Map** p407 M7.

See By Chloe, Marc by Marc Jacobs and Acne Jeans, plus Repetto shoes and Véronique Branquino, are among the goodies in this glossy showcase.

CONSUME

Surface 2 Air

*68 rue Charlot, 3rd (01.44.61.76.27/www.
surface2aiparis.com). Mᵒ St-Sébastien Froissart.*
Open 11am-7.30pm Mon-Sat. **Credit** MC, V.
Map p409 L5.
This non-concept concept store also acts as an art
gallery and graphic design agency. The cult clothing
selection takes in Alice McCall's sassy frocks, Fifth
Avenue Shoe Repair jeans and printed dresses by
Wood Wood. For men, labels include Marios, Wendy
& Jim and F-Troupe.

Womenswear

Agnès b

*2, 3, 6 & 19 rue du Jour, 1st (men
01.42.33.04.13/women 01.45.08.56.56/
www.agnesb.com). Mᵒ Les Halles.* **Open** *Oct-
Apr* 10am-7pm Mon-Sat. *May-Sept* 10am-
7.30pm Mon-Sat. **Credit** AmEx, MC, V.
Map p402 J5.

Agnès b rarely wavers from her design vision: pure
lines in fine quality cotton, merino wool and silk.
Best buys are shirts, pullovers and cardigans that
keep their shape for years. Her mini-empire of men's,
women's, children's, travel and sportswear shops is
compact; see the website for details.
Other locations throughout the city.

★ Antoine et Lili

*95 quai de Valmy, 10th (01.40.37.41.55/
www.antoineetlili.com). Mᵒ Jacques Bonsergent.*
Open 11am-7pm Mon, Sun; 11am-8pm Tue-
Fri; 10am-8pm Sat. **Credit** AmEx, DC, MC, V.
Map p402 L3.
Antoine et Lili's fuchsia-pink, custard-yellow and
apple-green shopfronts are a new raver's dream. The
bobo designer's clothes, often in wraparound styles,
adapt to all sizes and shapes. The Canal St-Martin
'village' comprises womenswear, a kitsch home decoration boutique and childrenswear. *Photo p258.*
Other locations throughout the city.

LE66.

CONSUME

ba&sh

22 rue des Francs-Bourgeois, 3rd
(01.42.78.55.10/www.ba-sh.com). M° Jacques
Bonsergent. **Open** 11am-7pm Mon, Sun; 11am-
8pm Tue-Fri; 10am-8pm Sat. **Credit** AmEx,
DC, MC, V. **Map** p402 L3.
This fresh, Paris-based label created by Barbara
Boccara and Sharon Krief now has 350 outlets
around the world, including five Paris boutiques.
You'll find dresses, skirts and blouses with ethnic
touches on one side and drapey jersey on the other.
Other locations throughout the city.

COS

4 rue des Rosiers, 4th (www.cosstores.com).
M° St-Paul. **Open** 10.30am-7.30pm Mon-Sat.
Credit AmEx, MC, V. **Map** p402 J5.
After its London launch, H&M's upmarket brand
Collection of Style (COS) now has a Paris outpost,
designed by William Russell, in rue des Rosiers,
causing some consternation among those who'd
rather have kept this a chain-free zone.

Firmaman

200 bd Perèire, 17th (01.44.09.71.32/www.
firmaman.com). M° Porte Maillot. **Open**
11am-7pm Tue-Sat. **Credit** AmEx, DC, MC, V.
Map p400 B2.
Realising that pregnant women have long been
scouring regular boutiques for a more fashionable
maternity look, Marguerite Pineau Valencienne has
chosen appropriate clothes from the likes of Isabel
Marant, Bash and Citizens of Humanity, displayed
alongside maternity wear by Blossom, Pietro Brunelli
and Virginie Castaway. The city's first maternity
concept store, it also has lingerie, well-being products and gifts for new mums, dads and babies.

★ Iro

53 rue Vieille-du-Temple, 4th (01.42.77.25.09/
www.iro.fr). M° St-Paul. **Open** 10.30am-7.30pm
Mon-Sat. **Credit** AmEx, MC, V. **Map** p409 K6.
Fashion editors have tipped designers Laurent and
Arik Bitton for stardom with what they call 'basic
deluxe': skinny knits, skinny jeans, babydoll dresses
and the 'perfecto' mini leather jacket that was the hit
of winter 2007. With a background in music, the

brothers know how to hit just the right note between
trendy and fashion victim, for a French silhouette.
Other locations 68 rue des Sts-Pères, 7th
(01.45.48.04.06).

Isabel Marant

16 rue de Charonne, 11th (01.49.29.71.55/
www.isabelmarant.tm.fr). M° Ledru-Rollin.
Open 10.30am-7.30pm Mon-Sat. **Credit** AmEx,
MC, V. **Map** p407 M7.
Marant's style is easily recognisable in her ethno-
babe brocades, blanket-like coats and decorated
sweaters. It's a favourite among young trendies.
Other locations 47 rue de Saintonge, 3rd
(01.42.78.19.24); 1 rue Jacob, 6th (01.43.26.04.12).

Manoush

217 rue St Honoré, 1st (01.40.20.04.44/
www.manoush.com). M° Tuileries. **Open**
10am-7pm Mon-Sat. **Credit** AmEx, DC, MC, V.
Map p400 D4.
Manoush, which means 'gypsy' in French slang, has
proved more than a flash-in-the-pan leftover from
the boho craze of 2005 and now has four boutiques
touting designer Frédérique Trou-Roy's kitsch and
kooky vision.
Other locations throughout the city.

Vanessa Bruno

25 rue St-Sulpice, 6th (01.43.54.41.04/www.
vanessabruno.com). M° Odéon. **Open** 10.30am-
7.30pm Mon-Sat. **Credit** AmEx, DC, MC, V.
Map p408 H7.
Mercerised cotton tanks, flattering trousers and feminine tops have à Zen-like quality that stems from
Bruno's stay in Japan, and they somehow manage
to flatter every figure type. She also makes great
bags; the ample Lune was created to mark ten years
in the business.
Other locations 12 rue de Castiglione, 1st
(01.42.61.44.60); 100 rue Vieille-du-Temple, 3rd
(01.42.77.19.41).

Zadig & Voltaire

42 rue des Francs-Bourgeois, 3rd
(01.44.54.00.60/www.zadig-et-voltaire.com).
M° Hôtel de Ville or St-Paul. **Open** 10.30am-
7.30pm Mon-Sat; 1.30-7.30pm Sun. **Credit**
AmEx, DC, MC, V. **Map** p409 K6.
Z&V's relaxed, urban collection is a winner. Popular
separates include cotton tops, shirts and faded jeans;
its winter range of cashmere jumpers is superb.
▶ *The more upmarket Zadig & Voltaire De Luxe*
is at 18 rue François 1er (01.40.70.97.89).
Other locations throughout the city.

Menswear

Shops in **Streetwear & clubwear** (*see p255*)
stock more casual clothes; many brands listed
in **Designer** (*see p245*) also cater for men.

THE BEST
FASHION BOUTIQUES

For designer toddlers
Dior. *See p247.*

For classic couture
Lanvin. *See p248.*

For cool concept
LE66. *See p252.*

APC

38 rue Madame, 6th (01.42.22.12.77/www.
apc.fr). M° St-Placide. **Open** 11am-7.30pm
Mon-Sat. **Credit** AmEx, MC, V. **Map** p405 G8.
The look here is simple but stylish: think perfectly
cut basics in muted tones. Hip without trying too
hard, its jeans are a big hit with denim aficionados
– the skinny version caused a stampede when they
came out.
Other locations 5 rue de Marseille, 10th
(01.42.39.84.46); 112 rue Vieille-du-Temple,
3rd (01.42.78.18.02).

★ La Chemiserie

21 rue d'Uzès, 2nd (01.42.36.47.80/www.
cacharel.fr). M° Grands Boulevards. **Open** 11am-
7.30pm Mon-Sat. **Credit** AmEx, DC, MC, V.
Map p402 J4.
Cacharel is behind this concept shirt store in a loft-
style space. Cool, masculine and nonchalant, the
shirts, which start at €45, have that Gallic panache
for which the brand is famous, and are joined by a
small selection of suits, velvet and cord blazers
and cashmere scarves.
► *In the same street, check out the jackets and*
underwear at Set Galerie (see p252).

Christophe Lemaire

28 rue de Poitou, 3rd (01.44.78.00.09/www.
lemaireonline.com). M° St-Sébastien Froissart.
Open 11am-7.30pm Mon-Sat. **Credit** AmEx,
DC, MC, V. **Map** p409 L6.
Creative director for Lacoste for seven years, Lemaire
opened his own boutique in an old pharmacy. It's decorated like a fantasy apartment: the salon, in '70s
gold and glitz, stocks his own-label menswear and
womenswear in high-tech Japanese textiles, and
leads into a soundproofed music room with a wall of
old speakers where you can buy collectable Lacoste
and Lemaire's own fave CDs. Next door the seductive 'Japanese salon' holds the jeans range. You can
also buy the vintage lighting on display here.

★ Eglé Bespoke

26 rue du Mont-Thabor, 1st (01.44.15.98.31/
www.eglebespoke.com). M° Concorde. **Open**
11am-7pm Mon-Sat & by appointment. **Credit**
MC, V. **Map** p401 G5.
Two young entrepreneurs are reviving bespoke
for a new generation in this tiny shop. Custom shirts
start from €119 and can be delivered in a week or
so; they will also make or copy shirts for women
and produce made-to-order jeans for both sexes.
Laser-printed buttons from South America are
perfect for stamping your beloved's shirt with a
saucy message.

Jacenko

38 rue de Poitou, 3rd (01.42.71.80.38). M° St-
Sébastien Froissart. **Open** 11am-7.30pm Tue-
Sat; 2-7pm Sun. **Credit** MC, V. **Map** p402 J5.

A tasteful little boutique whose owner has a faultless eye for shirts, jackets, woollens and accessories
that are dandy but not downright gay. McQ, Viktor
& Rolf, Givenchy and John Smedley all appear.

Madelios

23 bd de la Madeleine, 1st (01.53.45.00.00/
www.madelios.com). M° Madeleine. **Open**
10am-7pm Mon-Sat. **Credit** AmEx, DC, MC, V.
Map p401 G4.
A one-stop shop for men's fashion, with two floors
and more than 100 labels. Suits by Kenzo, Paul
Smith and Givenchy, plus shoes and accessories.

Nodus

22 rue Vieille-du-Temple, 4th (01.42.77.07.96/
www.nodus-boutique.com). M° Hôtel de Ville or
St-Paul. **Open** 10.45am-2pm, 3-7.30pm Mon-
Sat; 1-7.30pm Sun. **Credit** AmEx, DC, MC, V.
Map p409 K6.
Under the wooden beams of this cosy men's shirt
specialist are neat rows of striped, checked and plain
dress shirts, stylish silk ties with subtle graphic
designs, and silver-plated crystal cufflinks.
Other locations throughout the city.

Pull-In Underwear

8 rue Française, 2nd (01.42.36.91.06/www.pull-
in.com). M° Etienne Marcel. **Open** 10am-7.30pm
Mon-Sat. **Credit** AmEx, MC, V. **Map** p402 H5.
Hailing from south-west France, Pull-In is the official
underwear supplier to the French rugby team. The
ultra-trendy brand makes swimwear, but its boxers
in wacko patterns have now supplanted Calvin Kleins
as *the* visible waistband for Gallic hip hoppers.

Streetwear & clubwear

American Apparel

31 pl du Marché-St-Honoré, 1st (01.42.60.03.72/
www.americanapparel.net). M° Opéra, Pyramides
or Tuileries. **Open** 10.30am-7.30pm Mon-Sat.
Credit AmEx, DC, MC, V. **Map** p401 G4.
Paris has acquired a taste for American Apparel's
sweatshop-free, unisex cotton basics.
Other locations throughout the city.

Clery Brice

11 rue Pierre-Lescot, 1st (01.45.08.58.70/www.
clerybrice.com). M° Les Halles/RER Châtelet Les
Halles. **Open** 11am-12.30pm, 1.30-8pm Mon-Sat.
Credit MC, V. **Map** p402 J5.
Here you pay lofty prices to get limited editions of
the coolest trainers six months before the rest of the
world even finds out they should be wearing them.

Ekivok

39 bd de Sébastopol, 1st (01.42.21.98.71/
www.ekivok.com). M° Les Halles/RER Châtelet
Les Halles. **Open** 11am-7.30pm Mon-Sat.
Credit MC, V. **Map** p402 J5.

CONSUME

In Ekivok's graffiti-covered boutique you'll find major brands Bullrot, Carhartt, Hardcore Session and Juicy Jazz for men, and Golddigga, Punky Fish, Skunk Funk, Emilie the Strange and Hardcore Session for women, plus Eastpak accessories.

Kiliwatch

64 rue Tiquetonne, 2nd (01.42.21.17.37//http:// espacekiliwatch.fr). M° Etienne Marcel. **Open** 2-7pm Mon; 11am-7.30pm Tue-Sat. **Credit** AmEx, MC, V. **Map** p402 J5.

The trailblazer of the rue Etienne-Marcel revival is filled with hoodies, casual shirts and washed-out jeans. Brands such as Gas, Edwin and Pepe Jeans accompany pricy, good-condition second-hand garb.

Royal Cheese

24 rue Tiquetonne, 2nd (01.40.28.06.56/www. royalcheese.com). M° Etienne Marcel. **Open** 11am-1pm, 2-8pm Mon-Sat. **Credit** AmEx, DC, MC, V. **Map** p402 J5.

Clubbers hit Royal Cheese to snaffle up hard-to-find imports: Stüssy, Cheap Monday and Lee for the boys; Insight, Sessun, Edwin and Lazy Oaf for the girls. Prices are hefty: Japanese jeans cost €200. **Other locations** 3 rue Mandar, 2nd (01.44.82.04.85).

★ Y-3

47 rue Etienne-Marcel, 3rd (01.45.08.82.45/ www.y-3.com). M° Bourse. **Open** 11am-7pm Mon-Sat. **Credit** AmEx, MC, V. **Map** p402 J5.

The first Paris boutique for this successful collaboration between Yohji Yamamoto and Adidas gives regular sportswear a kick, with high-tech fabrics, oversized pockets and elegant design.

Used & vintage

See also p268 **Antiques & flea markets**.

Adrenaline

30 rue Racine, 6th (01.44.27.09.05). M° Odéon. **Open** 11am-7pm Mon-Sat. **Credit** AmEx, MC, V. **Map** p408 H7.

This *dépot-vente* specialises in vintage luggage and handbags. Iconic Vuitton suitcases and Kelly and Birkin bags command enormous prices, but there are some slightly more affordable pieces and a small collection of '60s couture.

La Belle Epoque

10 rue de Poitou, 3rd (06.80.77.71.32). M° St-Sébastien Froissart. **Open** 1.30-6.30pm Tue-Sat. **Credit** MC, V. **Map** p409 L5.

Ex-model and theatrical costumier Philippe will happily spend many hours rhapsodising about the joys of vintage. In the shop you'll find everything from the blue velours Grace Jones ensemble by Yves Saint Laurent to a selection of inexpensive '70s shirts and fake fur coats.

Come On Eline

16-18 rue des Taillandiers, 11th (01.43.38.12.11). M° Ledru-Rollin. **Open** *Sept-July* 11am-8.30pm Mon-Fri; 2-8pm Sun. *Aug* 2-8pm Mon-Fri. **Credit** DC, MC, V. **Map** p407 M7.

The owners of this three-floor vintage wonderland have an eye for what's funky, from cowboy gear to 1960s debutantes frocks, though prices are high.

★ Didier Ludot

20-24 galerie de Montpensier, 1st (01.42.96.06.56/www.didierludot.com). M° Palais Royal Musée du Louvre. **Open** 10.30am-7pm Mon-Sat. **Credit** AmEx, DC, MC, V. **Map** p402 H5.

Didier Ludot's temples to vintage haute couture appear in Printemps, Harrods and New York's Barneys. The prices are steep, but the pieces are stunning: Dior, Molyneux, Balenciaga, Pucci, Féraud and, of course, Chanel, from the 1920s onwards. Ludot also curates exhibitions, using the exclusive shop windows around the Palais-Royal as a gallery. ▶ *Didier Ludot stocks his own line of vintage little black dresses, also available at La Petite Robe Noire (125 galerie de Valois, 1st, 01.40.15.01.04).*

Free 'P' Star

8 rue Ste-Croix-de-la-Bretonnerie, 4th (01.42.76.03.72). M° St-Paul. **Open** noon-11pm Mon-Sat; 2-10pm Sun. **Credit** MC, V. **Map** p409 K6.

Late-night shopping is fun at this Aladdin's cave of retro glitz, ex-army wear and glad rags that has provided fancy dress for many a Paris party.

Gabrielle Geppert

31 & 34 galerie Montpensier, 1st (01.42.61.53. 52/www.gabriellegeppert.com). M° Palais Royal Musée du Louvre. **Open** 10am-7.30pm Mon-Sat. **Credit** AmEx, DC, MC, V. **Map** p402 H5.

If Didier Ludot is too intimidating, visit Gabrielle Geppert's shop, where much fun can be had rummaging in the back room or trying on the outrageous collection of '70s sunglasses (about €380 a pop, but they will get you into any party worth going to). A new exclusive room dedicated to accessories by the likes of Hermès and Manolo Blahnik can be opened on request, and she also carries a range of original costume jewellery by Elisabeth Ramuz.

★ Marie Louise de Monterey

1 rue Charles-François-Dupuis, 3rd (01.48.04.83.88/www.marielouisedemonterey. com). M° Temple. **Open** noon-7pm Tue-Sat. **Credit** MC, V. **Map** p409 L5.

Australian Maria Vrisakis has a great eye for vintage that echoes current fashion trends, and her crisply ironed pieces are displayed in a refreshingly airy and uncluttered space. There is an adorable babywear collection and vintage Prada shoes in Cinderella sizes.

Fashion Scouts

L'Eclaireur's esoteric boutiques put the art into shopping.

Paris's fashion-savvy consumers have a few reliable staples up their designer sleeves for a day of perfect spending: the Carrousel du Louvre for future looks, Hôtel Costes for cocktails to soften the blow to the wallet, and, always top of the agenda for cutting-edge trends and unique finds, **L'Eclaireur** (see p251). This touchstone for fashionistas takes the form of five distinctive boutiques, and can make or break a designer merely by stocking his creations or relegating them to the sale rail. Although each store is different, all five are unified by their determination to sniff out new finds; L'Eclaireur (which means scout) certainly lives up to its name.

The women's collections are still handpicked by Martine Hadida, the other half of entrepreneur Armand. As the youngest in a Moroccan Jewish family of ten, Armand started out as a shop assistant, and went on to open the first L'Eclaireur boutique in the Galerie des Champs-Elysées arcade. Starting with Marithé and François Girbaud, the pair soon stocked the shop with Vivienne Westwood, John Galliano, Moschino and the Belgians, 'who no one wanted at the time'. Each season they went against the grain, daring to do long silhouettes in the face of cinched waists and shoulder pads.

Hadida's talent turned out to be as much for location scouting as for sourcing designer gear; in 1990 he bought 3 rue des Rosiers, which has since become one of Paris's most sought-after fashion streets. It was a precursor to today's concept stores, displaying clothes alongside Dyson's revolutionary vacuum cleaners, Alain Ducasse's stove, and designs by Philippe Starck and Jean Nouvel. The store is now devoted to womenswear, with menswear nearby at rue Malher (no.12, 4th, 01.44.54.22.11). It was also here that the couple's partnership with Barnaba Fornasetti, son of the Surrealist Piero, began. Their newest boutique, on rue Boissy-d'Anglas (no.8), which leans more towards couture, fulfils a dream to create a Fornasetti-themed restaurant (01.53.43.09.99), which includes a corner decorated with his erotic drawings.

If you go to just one L'Eclaireur, make it the rue Hérold boutique (no.10), where ringing the doorbell is the open sesame to a hidden cave of treasures. Head along the dark corridor lined with casts of Roman statues, then enter the main chamber for the personal shopping treatment from the energetic Nathalie. Among the clothes – with cutting-edge creations by Gustav Olins, Under Cover and Carol Christian Poell – are housed a bizarre selection of curios, the likes of which an 18th-century explorer might have brought back from his travels: an enormous globe, stuffed exotic birds, antique mirrors, and hunting decoys that look like Picasso sculptures. Another room is devoted to furniture. You'll find Winnie Lui's chandeliers, hung with doll's houses and beads, next to a life-size giraffe's head sticking out of the wall, and Piet Hein Eek's huge tables and standard lamps, made from reclaimed wood and metal, the result of a long-running collaboration.

Hadida's claim that he wants to 'share, not to sell' may be pushing it, but a visit to rue Hérold remains an experience more akin to visiting a secret museum than the mere acquisition of fancy frocks.

CONSUME

Studio W

*6 rue du Pont-aux-Choux, 3rd (01.44.78.05.02).
Mº St-Sébastien Froissart.* **Open** 2-7.30pm Tue-
Sat. **Credit** MC, V. **Map** p409 L5.
Aesthete William Moricet's tiny shop is simply
exquisite, from the vintage Courrèges and Yves
Saint Laurent couture on mannequins to the glossy
golden retriever who lounges among crocodile and
patent leather shoes and bags.

FASHION ACCESSORIES & SERVICES

Eyewear

Get an eye test at an *ophtalmologiste*, then take
along your prescription for cool French specs.

★ Alain Mikli

*74 rue des Sts-Pères, 7th (01.45.49.40.00/www.
mikli.fr). Mº Sèvres Babylone or St-Sulpice.* **Open**
10am-7pm Mon-Sat. **Credit** AmEx, DC, MC, V.
Map p405 G7.
Cult French designer Mikli uses cellulose acetate, a
blend of wood and cotton sliced from blocks. At his
flagship Starck-designed boutique, frames are laid
out in a glass counter like designer sweeties.
Other locations throughout the city.

Anne et Valentin

*4 rue Ste-Croix-de-la-Bretonnerie, 4th
(01.40.29.93.01/www.anneetvalentin.com).
Mº Hôtel de Ville or St-Paul.* **Open** noon-8pm
Tue-Sat. Closed 12-22 Aug. **Credit** AmEx, DC,
MC, V. **Map** p409 K6.

This modish French eyewear firm occupies a cosy
three-floor Marais boutique. A&V design chic unisex frames: light titanium models have names like
Tarzan and Truman; coloured acetate frames have
inventive details and colour combinations.

Hats & gloves

★ Maison Fabre

*128 galerie de Valois, 1st (01.42.60.75.88/
www.maisonfabre.com). Mº Palais Royal Musée
du Louvre.* **Open** 11am-7pm Mon-Sat. **Credit**
AmEx, MC, V. **Map** p402 H5.
This glovemaker from Millau, which was founded
in 1924, has capitalised on its racy designs from the
sports car eras of the 1920s and '60s, opening a sexy
little boutique. Classic gloves made from the softest
leather (€100) come in 20 wild colours. Then there
are the variations: crocodile, python, coyote, fur-
trimmed, fingerless. But the ultimate lust object is
the patent leather 'Auto' glove fastened with a
massive button – somewhere between the cool of
The Avengers and the kook of *Austin Powers*.

Maison Michel

*65 rue Ste-Anne, 2nd (01.42.96.89.77/www.
michel-paris.com). Mº Pyramides.* **Open** by
appointment. **Credit** MC, V. **Map** p401 H4.
One of the specialist businesses saved from extinc-
tion by Chanel, Maison Michel has been making hats
since 1936 and supplies haute couture designers and
the Paris opera. They can create the perfect panama
or a flamboyant creation for the races, and also
launched a prêt-à-porter range in 2006 with a range
of sexy, shiny, '60s-inspired cloches and caps.

Antoine et Lili. *See p254.*

Marie Mercié
23 rue St-Sulpice, 6th (01.43.26.45.83).
M° Odéon. **Open** 11am-7pm Mon-Sat.
Credit AmEx, MC, V. **Map** p408 H7.
Mercié's creations make you wish you lived in an era when hats were de rigueur. Step out in one shaped like curved fingers (complete with shocking-pink nail varnish and pink diamond ring) or a beret like a face with red lips and turquoise eyes. Ready-to-wear starts at €30; *sur mesure* takes ten days.

Jewellery

Dotted in and around place Vendôme, the key *joailliers* define the luxurious spirit of Paris. The Marais is home to a number of fashion and costume jewellery boutiques.

Boucheron
26 pl Vendôme, 1st (01.42.61.58.16/www.boucheron.com). M° Opéra. **Open** 10.30am-7pm Mon-Sat. **Credit** AmEx, DC, MC, V. **Map** p401 G4.
Boucheron was the first to set up shop on place Vendôme, attracting celebrity custom from the nearby Ritz hotel. Owned by Gucci, the grand jeweller produces stunning pieces, using traditional motifs with new accents: take, for example, its fabulous chocolate-coloured gold watch.
Other locations 78 rue Sts-Pères, 7th (01.44.39.10.29).

★ Cartier
13 rue de la Paix, 2nd (01.58.18.53.00/www.cartier.com). M° Opéra. **Open** 10.30am-7pm Mon-Sat. **Credit** AmEx, DC, MC, V. **Map** p401 G4.
This iconic French jeweller and watchmaker has impressive landmark headquarters. Downstairs, pearls, panthers and the Trinity ring jostle for attention among historic pieces commissioned by crowned heads; the upper salons house perfumer Mathilde Laurent's bespoke scents, starting at around €60,000.
Other locations throughout the city.

Casoar
29 galerie de Montpensier, 1st (01.42.96.39.54/www.cartier.com). M° Opéra. **Open** 10.30am-7pm Mon-Sat. **Credit** AmEx, DC, MC, V. **Map** p401 G4.
This elegant outpost of the fashion editors' favourite jewellery shop displays intricate re-editions of Napoleon III, belle époque and art deco jewellery such as intaglio rings and earrings in *pâte de verre*.

Chanel Joaillerie
18 pl Vendôme, 1st (01.55.35.50.05/www.chanel.com). M° Opéra or Tuileries. **Open** 11am-7pm Mon-Sat. **Credit** AmEx, DC, MC, V. **Map** p401 G4.
Chanel launched its fine jewellery in the 1990s, reissuing the single collection – big on platinum and diamonds – that Coco herself designed some 60

years previously. The current line reinterprets the motifs – camellias, stars and comets – to create a collection of contemporary classics.

Dior Joaillerie
8 pl Vendôme, 1st (01.42.96.30.84/www.dior.com). M° Opéra or Tuileries. **Open** 11am-7pm Mon, Sat; 10.30am-7pm Tue-Fri. **Credit** AmEx, DC, MC, V. **Map** p401 G4.
The unabashed bling of Victoire de Castellane's designs is responsible for the fad of semi-precious coloured stones and runaway success of the 'Mimi Oui', a ring with a tiny diamond on a slim chain.
Other locations 28 av Montaigne, 8th (01.47.23.52.39).

KarryO'
62 rue des Sts-Pères, 6th (01.45.48.94.67/www.karryo.com). M° St-Germain-des-Prés. **Open** 11am-7pm Mon-Sat. **Credit** MC, V. **Map** p405 G7.
Paris socialites come here to source their vintage jewellery, as well as modern gems by owner Karine Berrebi. Her adjacent gallery, Unique, features one-of-a-kind finds, from jewels and decorative objects to Hermès bags and the occasional Schiaparelli fur.

Viveka Bergström
23 rue de la Grange aux Belles, 10th (01.40.03.04.92/www.viveka-bergstrom.com). M° Colonel Fabien. **Open** 1-7pm Tue-Fri; noon-7pm Sat. **Credit** AmEx, MC, V. **Map** p402 L3.
The daughter of Saab's aeroplane designer in the 1950s, Viveka Bergström makes slinky tassel necklaces, oversized beaten gold rings and brooches, and conversation starters like the angel-wing bracelet and a necklace featuring a map of Paris.

Lingerie & swimwear

For swimwear, *see also p271* **Sport & fitness**.

★ Alice Cadolle
4 rue Cambon, 1st (01.42.60.94.22/www.cadolle.com). M° Concorde or Madeleine. **Open** 10am-1pm, 2-6.30pm Mon-Sat. Closed Aug. **Credit** AmEx, MC, V. **Map** p401 G4.
Five generations of lingerie-makers are behind this boutique, founded by Hermine Cadolle, who claimed to be the inventor of the bra. Great-great-granddaughter Poupie Cadolle continues the tradition in a cosy space devoted to a luxury ready-to-wear line of bras, panties and corsets.
▶ *For a special treat, Cadolle Couture (255 rue St-Honoré, 1st, 01.42.60.94.94) will create indulgent bespoke lingerie (by appointment only).*

Erès
2 rue Tronchet, 8th (01.47.42.28.82/www.eres.fr). M° Madeleine. **Open** 10am-7pm Mon-Sat. **Credit** AmEx, DC, MC, V. **Map** p401 G4.

Erès's beautifully cut swimwear has embraced a sexy '60s look complete with buttons on the low-cut briefs. The top and bottom can be purchased in different sizes, or you can buy one piece of a bikini. **Other locations** 4bis rue du Cherche-Midi, 6th (01.45.44.95.54); 40 av Montaigne, 8th (01.47.23.07.26); 6 rue Guichard, 16th (01.46.47.45.21).

Etam Lingerie
139 rue de Rennes, 6th (01.45.44.16.88/www. etam.com). M° Montparnasse-Bienvenüe. **Open** 10am-7pm Mon-Sat. **Credit** AmEx, DC, MC, V. **Map** p401 G4.
Etam, which started out in lingerie in 1916, has now opened the largest lingerie store in Europe. It may be quantity over quality, but who can resist the 'bar à culottes' or the 'hot and spicy corner'?

★ Fifi Chachnil
231 rue St-Honoré, 1st (01.42.61.21.83/www. fifichachnil.com). M° Tuileries. **Open** 11am-7pm Mon-Sat. **Credit** AmEx, MC, V. **Map** p401 G4.
Chachnil has a new approach to frou-frou underwear in the pin-up tradition. Her chic mixes – deep red silk bras with boudoir pink bows, and pale turquoise girdles with orange trim – will have ladies and their male admirers purring in delight. The transparent black babydoll negligées with an Empire-line bust are classic saucy retro.
Other locations 68 rue Jean-Jacques-Rousseau, 1st (01.42.21.19.98).

Princesse Tam-Tam
52 bd St-Michel, 6th (01.42.34.99.31/www. princessetam-tam.com). M° Cluny La Sorbonne. **Open** 1.30-7pm Mon; 10am-7pm Tue-Sat. **Credit** AmEx, MC, V. **Map** p408 J7.
This inexpensive underwear and swimwear brand now has traffic-stopping promotions. Bright colours and sexily transparent and sporty gear are in. **Other locations** throughout the city.

Sabbia Rosa
73 rue des Sts-Pères, 6th (01.45.48.88.37). M° St-Germain-des-Prés. **Open** 10am-7pm Mon-Sat. **Credit** AmEx, MC, V. **Map** p405 G7.
Let Moana Moatti tempt you with feather-trimmed satin mules, or satin, silk and chiffon negligées in fine shades of tangerine, lemon, mocha or pistachio. All sizes are medium, others are made *sur mesure*; prices are just the right side of stratospheric.

Vannina Vesperini
4 rue de Tournon, 6th (01.56.24.32.72/www. vanninavesperini.com). M° Odéon. **Open** 11am-7pm Mon-Sat. **Credit** AmEx, MC, V. **Map** p408 J7.
Only the finest silk satin is used for this designer's underwear, camisoles and sophisticated nightwear. The new boutique has a made-to-measure *atelier*.

Yoba
11 rue du Marché-St-Honoré, 1st (01.40.41. 04.06/www.yobaparis.com). M° Tuileries. **Open** 11am-8pm Mon-Wed, Fri; 11am-9pm Thur; noon-8pm Sat. **Credit** MC, V. **Map** p401 G5.
One for the liberated ladies, this smart boutique stocks items from wispy lingerie to cheeky sex toys.

Shoes & bags

An entire floor of footwear, including designer labels, can be found at **Printemps** (*see p240*). Rue du Dragon, rue de Grenelle and rue du Cherche-Midi form the backbone of an area which is a must for shoe and accessory addicts.

Bruno Frisoni
34 rue de Grenelle, 6th (01.42.84.12.30/www. brunofrisoni.fr). M° Rue du Bac. **Open** 10.30am-7pm Tue-Sat. **Credit** AmEx, V. **Map** p405 G7.
Innovative Frisoni's shoes have a cinematic, pop edge: modern theatrics for the unconventional.

★ Christian Louboutin
19 rue Jean-Jacques-Rousseau, 1st (01.42.36. 05.31/www.christianlouboutin.com). M° Palais Royal Musée du Louvre. **Open** 10.30am-7pm Mon-Sat. Closed 3wks Aug. **Credit** AmEx, MC, V. **Map** p402 J5.
Every fashionista, WAG and shoe fiend worth her salt owns or hankers after a pair of Louboutin's trademark red-soled creations. The sculptural form of each design is displayed to maximum advantage in an individual frame. There's a made-to-measure service.
Other locations 38 rue de Grenelle, 7th (01.42.22.33.07); 68 rue du Fbg-St-Honoré (01.42.68.37.65).

★ Hervé Chapelier
1bis rue du Vieux-Colombier, 6th (01.44.07. 06.50/www.hervechapelier.fr). M° St-Germain-des-Prés or St-Sulpice. **Open** 10.15am-7pm Mon-Sat. **Credit** AmEx, MC, V. **Map** p407 G7.
Bag yourself a classic, chic, hard-wearing, bicoloured tote at Hervé Chapelier. Sizes and prices range from a dinky purse at €22 to a weekend bag at €130. **Other locations** throughout the city.

Iris
28 rue de Grenelle, 7th (01.42.22.89.81/www.iris-shoes.it). M° Rue du Bac or St-Sulpice. **Open** 10.30am-7pm Mon-Sat. **Credit** AmEx, MC, V. **Map** p405 F7.
This white boutique stocks shoes by Marc Jacobs, John Galliano, Proenza-Schouler and Viktor & Rolf.

Jamin Puech
61 rue de Hauteville, 10th (01.40.22.08.32/www. jamin-puech.com). M° Poissonnière. **Open** 11am-7pm Mon-Fri; noon-7pm Sat. **Credit** AmEx, DC, MC, V. **Map** p402 K3.

CONSUME

The complete collection of Isabelle Puech and Benoît Jamin's dazzling handbags is displayed in a bohemian setting complete with antler-horn chairs. **Other locations** throughout the city.

Moss
22 rue de Grenelle, 7th (01.42.22.01.42). M° Rue du Bac or St-Sulpice. **Open** 10.30am-7pm Mon-Sat. **Credit** AmEx, MC, V. **Map** p405 F7.
The three sisters who run this boutique pride themselves on sourcing cutting-edge shoes, that can be hard to find elsewhere, such as creations by former Celine stylist Avril Gau and signature designs by Laurence Dacade, Duccio del Duca and Hartian Bourdin. You'll also find scarves by Octavio Pizzaro and jewellery by Karry O', the fourth sister.

Peggy Huyn Kinh
9-11 rue Coëtlogon, 6th (01.42.84.83.82/www.phk.fr). M° St-Sulpice. **Open** 11am-7pm Mon-Sat. **Credit** AmEx, MC, V. **Map** p405 G7.
Once creative director at Cartier, Peggy Huyn Kinh now makes bags of boar skin and python, as well as silver jewellery.

Pierre Hardy
156 galerie de Valois, 1st (01.42.60.59.75/ www.pierrehardy.com). M° Palais Royal Musée du Louvre. **Open** 11am-7pm Mon-Sat. **Credit** AmEx, DC, MC, V. **Map** p402 H5.
This classy black-and-white shoebox is home to Hardy's range of superbly conceived footwear – with a price tag to match – for men and women.

★ Repetto
22 rue de la Paix, 2nd (01.44.71.83.20/www.repetto.com). M° Opéra. **Open** 9.30am-7.30pm Mon-Sat. **Credit** AmEx, MC, V. **Map** p401 G4.
This ballet shoe-maker struck gold when it decided to reissue its dance shoes with pavement soles. The prowly *ballerines* and showbiz dance boots in black, metallic and spangly finishes are fun, stylish and exceptionally comfortable. They are sold alongside the full range of real balletwear; you can try out your *pointes* on a red carpet with a *barre* if you want to show off. **Other locations** 51 rue du Four, 6th (01.45.44.98.65).

Rodolphe Menudier
14 rue de Castiglione, 1st (01.42.60.86.27/ www.rodolphemenudier.com). M° Concorde or Tuileries. **Open** 11am-7.30pm Mon; 10.30am-7.30pm Tue-Sat. **Credit** AmEx, MC, V. **Map** p401 G5.
This boutique makes the perfect backdrop for Menudier's racy designs. Open, silver-handled drawers display his stilettos in profile, as well as outrageous thigh-high boots with Plexiglass soles; more demure customers can opt for a pair of pumps.

Roger Vivier
29 rue du Fbg-St-Honoré, 8th (01.53.43.00.85/ www.rogervivier.com). M° Concorde or Madeleine. **Open** 11am-7pm Mon-Sat. **Credit** AmEx, DC, MC, V. **Map** p401 F4.
The fashion editors' shoeman of choice, Vivier is credited with inventing the stiletto.

FOOD & DRINK

You could spend a lifetime sampling the breads, pastries, chocolate and cheeses available in Paris. Open-air markets continue to beckon with their fresh, seasonal produce, and **Galeries Lafayette** and **Le Bon Marché** (for both, *see p239*) have luxury food halls.

Bakeries

★ Arnaud Delmontel
39 rue des Martyrs, 9th (01.48.78.29.33/www.arnaud-delmontel.com). M° St-Georges. **Open** 7am-8.30pm Mon, Wed-Sun. **No credit cards**. **Map** p402 H2.
With its crisp crust and chewy crumb shot through with irregular holes, Delmontel's Renaissance bread is one of the finest in Paris. He puts the same skill into his unsurpassable almond croissants and *tarte au citron à l'ancienne*, available in individual portions. **Other locations** 57 rue Damrémont, 18th (01.42.64.59.63).

L'Autre Boulange
43 rue de Montreuil, 11th (01.43.72.86.04). M° Faidherbe Chaligny or Nation. **Open** 7.30am-1.30pm, 3.30-7.30pm Tue-Sat. Closed Aug. **Credit** MC, V. **Map** p407 P7.
Michel Cousin bakes up to 23 different types of organic loaf in his wood-fired oven – varieties include the *flutiot* (rye bread with raisins, walnuts and hazelnuts), the *sarment de Bourgogne* (sourdough and a little rye) and a spiced cornmeal bread.

Le Boulanger de Monge
123 rue Monge, 5th (01.43.37.54.20/www.leboulangerdemonge.com). M° Censier Daubenton. **Open** 7am-8.30pm Tue-Sun. **Credit** MC, V. **Map** p406 K9.

THE BEST FOOD SHOPS

For squishy st-marcellin
Fromagerie Quatrehomme. *See p262.*

For cardamom ganache
Christian Constant. *See p262.*

For 1945 Mouton-Rothschild
Lavinia. *See p263.*

CONSUME

Dominique Saibron uses spices to give inimitable flavour to his organic sourdough *boule*. Every day about 2,000 bread-lovers visit this boutique, which also produces one of the city's best baguettes.

Moisan

5 pl d'Aligre, 12th (01.43.45.46.60). M° Ledru-Rollin. **Open** 8am-8pm Tue-Sat; 7am-2pm Sun. **No credit cards. Map** p407 N7.

Moisan's organic bread, *viennoiseries* and rustic tarts are outstanding. At this branch, situated by the market, there's always a healthy queue snaking out the door.
Other locations 4 av du Général-Leclerc, 14th (01.43.22.34.13).

★ Du Pain et des Idées

34 rue Yves Toudic, 10th (01.42.40.44.52/ www.dupainetdesidees.com). M° Jacques Bonsergent. **Open** 6.45am-8pm Mon-Fri. **No credit cards. Map** p402 L4.
See p268 **Bread of Heaven**.

★ Poilâne

8 rue du Cherche-Midi, 6th (01.45.48.42.59/ www.poilane.com). M° Sèvres Babylone or St-Sulpice. **Open** 7.15am-8.15pm Mon-Sat. **Credit** (€20 minimum) AmEx, DC, MC, V. **Map** p405 G7.

Apollonia Poilâne runs the family shop, where locals queue for fresh country *miches*, flaky-crusted apple tarts and buttery shortbread biscuits. *Photo p267.*
Other locations 49 rue de Grenelle, 15th (01.45.79.11.49).

Cheese

The sign *maître fromager affineur* denotes merchants who buy young cheeses from farms and age them on their premises; *fromage fermier* and *fromage au lait cru* signify farm-produced and unpasturised cheeses respectively.

★ Alléosse

13 rue Poncelet, 17th (01.46.22.50.45/www. fromage-alleosse.com). M° Ternes. **Open** 9am-1pm, 4-7pm Tue-Thur; 9am-1pm, 4.30-7pm Fri, Sat. **Credit** MC, V. **Map** p400 C2.

People cross town for these cheeses – wonderful farmhouse camemberts, delicate st-marcellins, a choice of *chèvres* and several rarities.

Fromagerie Dubois et Fils

80 rue de Tocqueville, 17th (01.42.27.11.38). M° Malesherbes or Villiers. **Open** 9am-1pm, 4-8pm Tue-Fri; 8.30am-7.45pm Sat; 9am-1pm Sun. Closed 1st wks Aug. **Credit** AmEx, MC, V. **Map** p401 E2.

Superchef darling Dubois stocks 80 types of goat's cheese, plus prized, aged st-félicien.

★ Fromagerie Quatrehomme

62 rue de Sèvres, 7th (01.47.34.33.45). M° Duroc or Vaneau. **Open** 8.45am-1pm, 4-7.45pm Tue-Thur; 8.45am-7.45pm Fri, Sat. **Credit** MC, V. **Map** p405 F8.

The award-winning Marie Quatrehomme runs this *fromagerie*. Justly famous for her comté fruité, beaufort and st-marcellin, she also sells specialities such as goat's cheese with pesto. *Photo p265.*
Other locations 9 rue du Poteau, 18th (01.46.06.26.03).

Marie-Anne Cantin

12 rue du Champ-de-Mars, 7th (01.45.50.43.94/ www.cantin.fr). M° Ecole Militaire or Latour Maubourg. **Open** 2-7.30pm Mon; 8.30am-7.30pm Tue-Sat; 8.30am-1pm Sun. **Credit** AmEx, MC, V. **Map** p404 D6.

Cantin, a defender of unpasteurised cheese and supplier to many posh Paris restaurants, offers aged *chèvres* and amazing morbier, mont d'or and comté.

Chocolate

Cacao et Chocolat

29 rue de Buci, 6th (01.46.33.77.63). M° Mabillon. **Open** 10.30am-2pm, 3-7.30pm daily. **Credit** AmEx, DC, MC, V. **Map** p405 H7.

This shop recalls chocolate's Aztec origins, with its choice of spicy fillings (honey and chilli, nutmeg, clove and citrus), chocolate masks and pyramids.
Other locations 63 rue St-Louis-en-l'Ile, 4th (01.46.33.33.33); 36 rue Vieille-du-Temple, 4th (01.42.71.50.06).

Christian Constant

37 rue d'Assas, 6th (01.53.63.15.15). M° Rennes or St-Placide. **Open** 8.30am-9pm Mon-Fri; 8.30am-8pm Sat, Sun. **Credit** MC, V. **Map** p405 G8.

A master chocolate-maker and *traiteur*, Constant scours the globe for new ideas. His *ganaches* are subtly flavoured with verbena, jasmine or cardamom.

★ Jean-Paul Hévin

3 rue Vavin, 6th (01.43.54.09.85/www. jphevin.com). M° Notre-Dame-des-Champs or Vavin. **Open** 10am-7pm Tue-Sat. Closed Aug. **Credit** AmEx, MC, V. **Map** p405 G8.

Hévin specialises in the beguiling combination of chocolate with potent cheese fillings, which loyal customers serve with wine as an aperitif.
Other locations 231 rue St-Honoré, 1st (01.55.35.35.96); 23bis av de La Motte-Picquet, 7th (01.45.51.77.48).

La Maison du Chocolat

120 av Victor-Hugo, 16th (01.40.67.77.83/ www.lamaisonduchocolat.com). M° Victor Hugo. **Open** 10am-7.30pm Mon-Sat; 10am-1pm Sun. **Credit** AmEx, MC, V. **Map** p400 B4.

Robert Linxe opened his first Paris shop in 1977, and has been inventing new chocolates ever since, using Asian spices, fresh fruits and herbal infusions. **Other locations** throughout the city.

Patrick Roger

108 bd St-Germain, 6th (01.43.29.38.42/www. patrickroger.com). Mº Odéon. **Open** 10.30am-7.30pm Mon-Sat. **Credit** MC, V. **Map** p408 H7.
Roger is shaking up the art of chocolate-making. Whereas other *chocolatiers* aim for gloss, Roger may create a brushed effect on hens so realistic you almost expect them to lay (chocolate) eggs. **Other locations** 45 av Victor-Hugo, 16th (01.45.01.66.71).

Richart

258 bd St-Germain, 7th (01.45.55.66.00/www. richart.com). Mº Solférino. **Open** 10am-7pm Mon-Sat. **Credit** AmEx, MC, V. **Map** p405 F6.
Each chocolate *ganache* has an intricate design, packages look like jewel boxes, and each purchase comes with a tract on how best to savour the stuff.

Drinks

Les Caves Augé

116 bd Haussmann, 8th (01.45.22.16.97). Mº St-Augustin. **Open** 1-7.30pm Mon; 9am-7.30pm Tue-Sat. Closed Mon in Aug. **Credit** AmEx, MC, V. **Map** p401 E3.
The oldest wine shop in Paris – Marcel Proust was a regular customer – is serious and professional.

Les Caves Taillevent

199 rue du Fbg-St-Honoré, 8th (01.45.61.14.09/ www.taillevent.com). Mº Charles de Gaulle Etoile or Ternes. **Open** 10am-7.30pm Tue-Sat. Closed 1st 3wks Aug. **Credit** AmEx, DC, MC, V. **Map** p400 D3.
Choose from half a million wines to go with your meal at the nearby Taillevent restaurant (*see p194*).

Julien, Caviste

50 rue Charlot, 3rd (01.42.72.00.94). Mº Filles du Calvaire. **Open** 9am-1.30pm, 3.30-7.30pm Tue-Sat; 10.30am-1.30pm Sun. Closed 3rd wk Aug. **Credit** AmEx, MC, V. **Map** p402 L5.
Julien promotes the small producers he has discovered, and often holds wine tastings on Saturdays.

★ Lavinia

3 bd de la Madeleine, 1st (01.42.97.20.20/ www.lavinia.fr). Mº Madeleine. **Open** 10am-8pm Mon-Fri; 9am-8pm Sat. **Credit** AmEx, DC, MC, V. **Map** p401 G4.
Lavinia is a thoroughly contemporary emporium that stocks a broad selection of French alongside many non-French wines; its glassed-in *cave* has everything from a 1945 Mouton-Rothschild at €22,000 to trendy and 'fragile' wines for under €10.

▶ *Have fun tasting wine with the dégustation machines on the ground floor, which allow customers to taste a sip of up to ten different wines each week for €10.*

Legrand Filles et Fils

1 rue de la Banque, 2nd (01.42.60.07.12/www. caves-legrand.com). Mº Bourse. **Open** 11am-7pm Mon; 10am-7.30pm Tue-Fri; 10am-7pm Sat. Closed Mon in July & Aug. **Credit** AmEx, MC, V. **Map** p402 H4.
Fine wines and brandies, teas and *bonbons,* and a showroom for regular wine tastings.

Ryst Dupeyron

79 rue du Bac, 7th (01.45.48.80.93/www. dupeyron.com). Mº Rue du Bac. **Open** 12.30-7.30pm Mon; 10.30am-7.30pm Tue-Sat. Closed 2wks Aug. **Credit** AmEx, MC, V. **Map** p405 F7.
The Dupeyrons have been selling armagnac for four generations, and still have bottles from 1868. Treasures here include 200 fine Bordeaux wines and an extensive range of vintage port.

Global

Les Délices d'Orient

52 av Emile-Zola, 15th (01.45.79.10.00). Mº Charles Michels. **Open** 8.30am-9pm Tue-Sun. **Credit** MC, V. **Map** p404 B8.
Shelves groan under stuffed aubergines, halva, falafel and all manner of Middle Eastern delicacies. **Other locations** 14 rue des Quatre-Frères-Peignot, 15th (01.45.77.82.93).

Izraël

30 rue François-Miron, 4th (01.42.72.66.23). Mº Hôtel de Ville. **Open** 9.30am-1pm, 2.30-7pm Tue-Fri; 9.30am-7pm Sat. Closed Aug. **Credit** MC, V. **Map** p409 K6.
A Marais fixture, this narrow shop stocks spices and other delights from Mexico, Turkey and India.

★ Jabugo Ibérico & Co

11 rue Clément-Marot, 8th (01.47.20.03.13). Mº Alma Marceau or Franklin D. Roosevelt. **Open** 10am-9pm Mon-Fri; 10am-8pm Sat. **Credit** AmEx, DC, MC, V. **Map** p400 D4.
Spanish hams here have the Bellota-Bellota label, meaning that the pigs have been allowed to feast on acorns. Manager Philippe Poulachon compares his cured hams (€98 a kilo) to the delicacy of truffles.
▶ *Restaurant Bellota-Bellota (18 rue Jean-Nicot, 7th, 01.53.59.96.96) also sells hams at its adjoining épicerie.*

Markets

The city council has made markets more accessible to working people by extending their opening hours. There are now more than 70 markets – including a handful of the covered variety – in Paris. The city council's website (www.paris.fr) has full details of each one; below is a selection of the best.

Marché Anvers
Pl d'Anvers, 9th. M° Anvers. **Open** 3-8pm Fri. **Map** p402 J2.

An afternoon market that adds to the village atmosphere of a peaceful *quartier* down the hill from Montmartre. Among its highlights are regional vegetables, hams from the Auvergne, lovingly aged cheeses and award-winning honey.

★ Marché Bastille
Bd Richard-Lenoir, 11th. M° Richard-Lenoir. **Open** 7am-2.30pm Thur; 7am-3pm Sun. **Map** p403 M5.

One of the biggest markets in Paris. A favourite of political campaigners, it's also a great source of local cheeses, farmers' chicken and excellent fish.

Marché Batignolles
Rue Lemercier, 17th. M° Brochant. **Open** 9am-2pm Sat. **Map** p401 F1.

Batignolles is more down to earth than the better-known Raspail organic market, with a quirky selection of stallholders, many of whom produce what they sell. Prices are higher here than at ordinary markets, but the goods are worth it.

Marché Beauvau
Pl d'Aligre, 12th. M° Ledru-Rollin. **Open** 8.30am-1pm, 4-7.30pm Tue-Sat; 8.30am-1.30pm Sun. **Map** p407 N7.

This market is proudly working class. Stallholders do their utmost to out-shout each other, and price-conscious shoppers don't compromise on quality.

★ Marché Monge
Pl Monge, 5th. M° Place Monge. **Open** 7am-2.30pm Wed, Fri; 7am-3pm Sun. **Map** p406 K8.

This pretty, compact market is set on a leafy square. It has a high proportion of producers and is much less touristy than nearby rue Mouffetard.

Marché Président-Wilson
Av Président-Wilson, 16th. M° Alma-Marceau or Iéna. **Open** 7am-2.30pm Wed; 7am-3pm Sat. **Map** p400 C5.

A classy market attracting the city's top chefs, who snap up ancient vegetable varieties.

Saxe-Breteuil
Av de Saxe, 7th. M° Ségur. **Open** 7am-2.30pm Thur; 7am-3pm Sat. **Map** p405 E8.

Saxe Breteuil has an unrivalled setting facing the Eiffel Tower, as well as the city's most chic produce. Look for farmer's goat's cheese, rare apple varieties, Armenian specialities, abundant oysters and a handful of dedicated small producers.

Pâtisseries

Arnaud Larher
53 rue Caulaincourt, 18th (01.42.57.68.08/ www.arnaud-larher.com). M° Lamarck Caulaincourt. **Open** 10am-7.30pm Tue-Sat. **Credit** MC, V. **Map** p401 H1.

Look out for the strawberry-and-lychee flavoured *bonheur* and the chocolate-and-thyme *récif*.

Finkelsztajn
27 rue des Rosiers, 4th (01.42.72.78.91/www. laboutiquejaune.com). M° St-Paul. **Open** 10am-7pm Mon, Wed-Sun. Closed 15 July-15 Aug. **Credit** (€20 minimum) AmEx, MC, V. **Map** p409 L6.

This motherly, yellow-fronted shop, in business since 1946, stocks dense Jewish cakes filled with poppy seeds, apples or cream cheese.

Gérard Mulot
76 rue de Seine, 6th (01.43.26.85.77/ http://gerard-mulot.com). M° Odéon. **Open** 6.45am-8pm Mon, Tue, Thur-Sun. Closed Easter & Aug. **Credit** V. **Map** p408 H7.

Gérard Mulot rustles up stunning pastries. Try the *mabillon*: caramel mousse with apricot marmalade. **Other locations** 93 rue de la Glacière, 13th (01.45.81.39.09).

★ Pierre Hermé
72 rue Bonaparte, 6th (01.43.54.47.77). M° Mabillon, St-Germain-des-Prés or St-Sulpice. **Open** 10am-7pm Tue-Fri, Sun; 10am-7.30pm Sat. Closed 1st 3wks Aug. **Credit** AmEx, DC, MC, V. **Map** p405 G7.

Fromagerie Quatrehomme. *See p262.*

Pastry superstar Hermé attracts connoisseurs from St-Germain and afar with his seasonal collections. **Other locations** 4 rue Cambon, 1st (01.58.62.43.17); 185 rue de Vaugirard, 15th (01.47.83.89.96).

Treats & *traiteurs*

Da Rosa
62 rue de Seine, 6th (01.45.21.41.30/www. restaurant-da-rosa.com). Mº Odéon. **Open** 10am-11pm daily. **Credit** AmEx, MC, V. **Map** p408 H7.
José Da Rosa sourced ingredients for top restaurants before filling his own shop with Spanish hams, Olivier Roellinger spices and Luberon truffles.

Fauchon
26 & 30 pl de la Madeleine, 8th (01.70.39.38.00/ www.fauchon.com). Mº Madeleine. **Open** No.26 8am-9pm Mon-Sat. No.30 9am-8pm Mon-Sat. **Credit** AmEx, MC, V. **Map** p401 F4.
The city's most famous food shop is worth a visit, particularly for the beautifully packaged gift items.

★ Hédiard
21 pl de la Madeleine, 8th (01.43.12.88.88/www. hediard.fr). Mº Madeleine. **Open** 8.30am-9pm Mon-Sat. **Credit** AmEx, DC, MC, V. **Map** p401 F4.
Hédiard's charming shop dates back to 1880, when they were the first to introduce exotic foods to Paris, specialising in rare teas and coffees, spices, jams and candied fruits.
▶ *Pop upstairs for a cuppa in the shop's posh tearoom, La Table d'Hédiard.*
Other locations throughout the city.

Huilerie Artisanale Leblanc
6 rue Jacob, 6th (01.46.34.61.55/www.huile-leblanc.com). Mº St-Germain-des-Prés. **Open** noon-7pm Tue-Fri; 10am-7pm Sat. Closed 2wks Aug. **No credit cards. Map** p405 H6.
The Leblanc family started making walnut oil before branching out to press pure oils from hazelnuts, almonds, pine nuts, grilled peanuts and olives.

Torréfacteur Verlet
256 rue St-Honoré, 1st (01.42.60.67.39/www. cafeverlet.com). Mº Palais Royal Musée du Louvre. **Open** 9.30am-6.30pm Mon-Sat. Closed Aug. **Credit** MC, V. **Map** p401 G5.
Eric Duchaussoy roasts rare coffee beans to perfection – sip a cup here or take some home to savour.

GIFTS

Florists

★ Culture(s)
46 rue de Lancry, 10th (01.48.03.58.71). Mº Jacques Bonsergent or République. **Open** 11am-2pm; 3-8pm Tue-Sat. **Credit** AmEx, MC, V. **Map** p402 L4.
In a loft-style studio, this unusual florist combines exotic flowers, trees and garden themed items, such as floral printed rain hats. Truly original.

Au Nom de la Rose
87 rue St-Antoine, 4th (01.42.71.34.24/www. aunomdelarose.fr). Mº St-Paul. **Open** *Sept-July* 10am-9pm daily. *Aug* 10am-9pm Mon-Sat. **Credit** AmEx, DC, MC, V. **Map** p409 L7.

CONSUME

Specialising in roses, Au Nom can supply a bouquet, as well as rose-based beauty products and candles. **Other locations** throughout the city.

Gifts & eccentricities

★ Diptyque
34 bd St-Germain, 5th (01.43.26.45.27/www. diptyqueparis.com). Mº Maubert Mutualité. **Open** 10am-7pm Mon-Sat. **Credit** V. **Map** p405 G6.
Diptyque's divinely scented candles are the quintessential gift from Paris. They come in 48 different varieties and are probably the best you'll ever find.

Galeries Laffitte
27 rue Laffitte, 9th (01.47.70.38.83). Mº Notre-Dame-de-Lorette. **Open** 9am-7pm Mon-Fri; 10am-6.30pm Sat. **Credit** MC, V. **Map** p402 H3.
The basement houses a regular *papeterie* filled with pens and notebooks, and the ground floor has art supplies and a selection of gifts, from quality leather bags to Italian pastel-coloured diary covers.

Paris-Musées
29bis rue des Francs-Bourgeois, 4th (01.42.74. 13.02). Mº St-Paul. **Open** 2-7pm Mon; 11am-1pm, 2-7pm Tue-Fri; 11am-7pm Sat; noon-7.30pm Sun. **Credit** AmEx, DC, MC, V. **Map** p409 L6.
Run by the museum federation, this shop sells reproduction lamps and ceramics from local museums.

★ Sennelier
3 quai Voltaire, 7th (01.42.60.72.15/www. magasinsennelier.fr). Mº St-Germain-des-Prés. **Open** 2-6.30pm Mon; 10am-12.45pm, 2-6.30pm Tue-Sat. **Credit** AmEx, DC, MC, V. **Map** p405 G6.
Old-fashioned colour merchant Sennelier sells oil paints, watercolours and pastels, rare pigments, primed canvases, varnishes and paper.
Other locations 4bis rue de la Grande-Chaumière, 6th (same phone).

HEALTH & BEAUTY
Cosmetics

★ L'Artisan Parfumeur
24 bd Raspail, 7th (01.42.22.23.32/www. artisanparfumeur.com). Mº Rue du Bac. **Open** 10.30am-7.30pm Mon-Sat. **Credit** AmEx, DC, MC, V. **Map** p405 G7.
Among scented candles, potpourri and charms, you'll find the best vanilla perfume Paris can offer – Mûres et Musc, a bestseller for two decades.
Other locations throughout the city.

By Terry
21 & 36 galerie Véro-Dodat, 1st (01.44.76.00.76/ www.byterry.com). Mº Palais Royal Musée du Louvre. **Open** 10.30am-7pm Mon-Sat. **Credit** AmEx, MC, V. **Map** p402 H5.

Terry de Gunzburg, who earned her reputation at Yves Saint Laurent, offers made-to-measure 'haute couleur' make-up by skilled chemists and colourists combining high-tech treatments and handmade precision. There's prêt-à-porter, too.
Other locations 30 rue de la Trémoille, 8th (01.44.43.04.04); 10 av Victor-Hugo, 16th (01.55.73.00.73).

Conceptual Scent
48-50 rue de l'Université, 7th (01.45.44.50.14). Mº Rue du Bac. **Open** 10am-7pm Mon-Sat. **Credit** AmEx, MC, V. **Map** p405 G6.
Invisible from the street, this minimal space is a temple to fragrance, selling its own delicious lines of perfumes, gels and candles. Sniff out the Eau Interdite, a curious, absinthe-scented eau de cologne.

Détaille 1905
10 rue St-Lazare, 9th (01.48.78.68.50/www. detaille.com). Mº Notre-Dame-de-Lorette. **Open** 11am-2pm, 3-7pm Tue-Sat. **Credit** MC, V. **Map** p401 H3.
Step back in time at this shop, opened, as the name suggests, in 1905 by war artist Edouard Détaille. Six fragrances (three for men and three for women) are made from century-old recipes.

Editions de Parfums Frédéric Malle
37 rue de Grenelle, 7th (01.42.22.76.40/ www.editionsdeparfums.com). Mº Rue du Bac or St-Sulpice. **Open** 1-7pm Mon; 11am-7pm Tue-Sat. **Credit** AmEx, DC, MC, V. **Map** p405 F6.
Choose from a range of eight perfumes by Frédéric Malle, former consultant to Hermès and Lacroix. Carnal Flower by Dominique Ropion is seduction in a bottle.
Other locations 21 rue du Mont-Thabor, 1st (01.42.22.77.22); 140 av Victor-Hugo, 16th (01.45.05.39.02).

★ Galerie Noémie
92 av des Champs-Elysées, 8th (01.44.76.06.26/ www.galerienoemie.com). Mº George V. **Open** 11am-7pm Mon-Thur; 11am-9pm Fri, Sat. **Credit** AmEx, DC, MC, V. **Map** p402 J5.
You can tell owner Noémie is a painter by the way all the make-up is set out in palettes. Little pots of gloss (starting from €7.50) in myriad colours triple as lip gloss, eyeshadow or blusher. Check out Noemie's blog at http://blog.galerienoemie.com.
Other locations Galeries Lafayette, 40 bd Haussmann, 9th (01.42.82.34.56).

Guerlain
68 av des Champs-Elysées, 8th (01.45.62.52.57/ www.guerlain.com). Mº Franklin D. Roosevelt. **Open** 10.30am-8pm Mon-Sat; 3-7pm Sun. **Credit** AmEx, DC, MC, V. **Map** p401 E4.

CONSUME

Poilâne. See p262.

The golden oldie of luxury beauty products and scents is looking as ravishing than ever. Head to the first floor to get the full measure of the history behind the house that created the mythic Samsara, Mitsouko and L'Heure Bleue.

★ Salons du Palais-Royal Shiseido

Jardins du Palais-Royal, 142 galerie de Valois, 1st (01.49.27.09.09/www.salons-shiseido.com). M° Palais Royal Musée du Louvre. **Open** 10am-7pm Mon-Sat. **Credit** AmEx, DC, MC, V. **Map** p401 H5.

Under the arcades of the Palais-Royal, Shiseido's perfumer Serge Lutens practises his aromatic arts. A former photographer at Paris *Vogue* and artistic director of make-up at Christian Dior, Lutens is a maestro of rare taste. Bottles of his concoctions – Tubéreuse Criminelle, Rahat Loukoum and Ambre Sultan – can be sampled by visitors. Look out for Fleurs d'Oranger, which the great man defines as the smell of happiness. Many of the perfumes are exclusive to the Salons; prices start at around €100.

Other locations 2 pl Vendôme, 1st (01.42.60.68.61); 29 rue de Sèvres, 6th (01.42.22.46.60); 66 bd du Montparnasse, 15th (01.43.20.95.40).

Sephora

70 av des Champs-Elysées, 8th (01.53.93.22.50/ www.sephora.fr). M° Franklin D. Roosevelt. **Open** *Sept-June* 10am-midnight daily. *July, Aug* 10am-1.30am. **Credit** AmEx, DC, MC, V. **Map** p401 E4.

The flagship of the cosmetic supermarket chain houses 12,000 brands of scent and slap. Sephora Blanc (14 cour St-Emilion, 12th, 01.40.02.97.79) features beauty products in a minimalist interior.

Other locations throughout the city.

Salons & spas

Anne Sémonin

Le Bristol, 108 rue du Fbg-St-Honoré, 8th (01.42.66.24.22/www.hotel-bristol.com). M° Champs-Elysées Clemenceau or Miromesnil. **Open** 10am-7pm Mon-Sat; by appointment Sun. **Credit** AmEx, DC, MC, V. **Map** p401 E3.

Facials involve delicious concoctions of basil, lavender, lemongrass, ginger and plant essences. Also on offer are reflexology and a selection of massage styles, from Thai to ayurvedic. Body treatments cost from €70 to €210. Sémonin's renowned seaweed skincare products and essential oils are also on sale.

Other locations 2 rue des Petits-Champs, 2nd (01.42.60.94.66).

Appartement 217

217 rue St-Honoré, 1st (01.42.96.00.96/ www.lappartement217.com). M° Tuileries. **Open** 10am-7pm Tue-Sat. **Credit** AmEx, DC, MC, V. **Map** p401 G5.

CONSUME

Opened by Stéphane Jaulin, the former beauty director of Colette, a beautiful feng-shuied Haussmannian apartment is the setting for facials using organic beauty guru Dr Hauschka's products and ayurvedic or deep tissue massages. The water has been decalcified, electrical currents are insulated, and the silky-soft kimonos are made from organic wood pulp.

Les Bains du Marais

31-33 rue des Blancs-Manteaux, 4th (01.44.61.02.02/www.lesbainsdumarais.com). M° St-Paul. **Open** *Men* 10am-11pm Thur; 10am-8pm Fri. *Women* 11am-8pm Mon; 10am-11pm Tue; 10am-7pm Wed. *Mixed (swimwear required)* 7-11pm Wed; 10am-8pm Sat; 10am-11pm Sun. Closed Aug. **Credit** AmEx, MC, V. **Map** p409 K6.

This hammam and spa mixes the modern and traditional (lounging beds and mint tea). Facials, waxing and essential oil massages (€70) are also available. The hammam and standard massage are €35 each.

La Bulle Kenzo

1 rue du Pont-Neuf, 1st (01.73.04.20.04/www. labullekenzo.com). M° Pont Neuf. **Open** 11.30am-8pm Mon-Sat. **Credit** AmEx, DC, MC, V. **Map** p406 J6.

Kenzo's flagship store houses a chic beauty salon. The two massage rooms offer different vibes: the Pétillante room has a disco ball, whereas the Japanese Zen cocoon room provides calmer pleasures.

L'Espace Payot

62 rue Pierre-Charon, 8th (01.45.61.42.08). M° George V. **Open** 7am-10pm Mon-Fri; 9am-7pm Sat; 10am-5pm Sun. **Credit** AmEx, MC, V. **Map** p400 D4.

Opened in 2006 by Dr Nadia Payot, one of the leading ladies in French skincare, this institute offers the entire gamut of luxurious face and body treatments. One of the largest spas in Paris, it has a gym, pool, sauna and steam bath, and health food bar. Prices range from €40 to €80, and a day pass is €150.

L'Esthétique de Demain

15 rue de la Grande-Truanderie, 1st (01.40.26.53.10). M° Châtelet or Etienne Marcel. **Open** 2-7pm Mon; 10am-8.30pm Tue-Fri; 10am-7pm Sat. **Credit** MC, V. **Map** p402 J5.

If you're looking to get the job done without a lot of hoopla, this low-key, low-cost salon specialising in hair removal is for you. Waxing for men and women starts at €9, facials from €28. Massages 'per minute' are also on offer (it's €10 for ten minutes).

★ Hammam de la Grande Mosquée

1 pl du Puits-de-l'Ermite, 5th (01.43.31.18.14/ www.la-mosquee.com). M° Censier Daubenton.

Bread of Heaven

Get your teeth into the delights from Du Pain et des Idées.

To look at the fluffy, golden croissants at **Du Pain et des Idées** (*see p262*) as they emerge steaming from the oven, you would never guess that French baking is in crisis – but it is. 'They don't even teach croissant making in bakery school any more,' says baker-owner Christophe Vasseur, 'and 80 per cent of the croissants you find in bakeries, even those that claim to be artisanal, are industrially made.' The lack of teaching is compounded by the lack of interest from students. 'Only one in ten who gets the diploma goes on to work in a bakery. There are easier things to do than get up at four every morning.'

But Vasseur, who worked in fashion PR before a career change at the age of 38 led to him winning the Gault-Millau prize for Best Bakery last year, traded lie-ins for the chance to follow his dream. He is motivated by fond childhood memories of baked goodies – like the *tendresse aux pommes*, a *flan brioché* filled with apples, raisins and cinnamon that his neighbour used to make; with

no recipe, he has since managed to 'find it through memory'. After three years of training, Vasseur set about putting into practice what he had learnt; months of trial and error have gone into every product at this most Proustian of bakeries.

Among his specialities are the nutty *pain des amis* to be shared among friends; even his *baguette tradition* rises for seven hours before going into the wood-fired oven. Other creations come from literature, such as Le Rabelais – *pain brioché* with saffron, honey and nuts from the recipe of the renaissance writer – and Le Pagnol aux Pommes. The latter, a bread studded with royal gala apple (with its skin on), raisins and orange flower water, is a special treat only available on Fridays, when it attracts a crowd eager to grab one straight from the oven at 11am.

The only possible quibble with Du Pain et des Idées is that it doesn't open at weekends. 'Even the most passionate baker needs a work-life balance,' says this modern artisan.

CONSUME

Open *Men* 2-9pm Tue; 10am-9pm Sun. *Women* 10am-9pm Mon, Wed, Sat; 2-9pm Fri. **Credit** MC, V. **Map** p406 K9.

The authentic hammam experience in this beautiful 1920s mosque has become popular with *parisiennes*, so avoid weekends when the volume of traffic makes it less relaxing than it should be. Follow a steam session with a *gommage* (exfoliation with a rough mitt), then a massage. The hammam is €15, *gommage* €10 and massage €10. Swimwear is compulsory. Towel and gown hire is also available.

★ Hammam Med Centre

43-45 rue Petit, 19th (01.42.02.31.05/www. hammammed.com). M° Ourcq. **Open** *Women* 11am-10pm Mon-Fri; 9am-7pm Sun. *Mixed (swimwear required)* 10am-9pm Sat. **Credit** MC, V. **Map** p403 N5.

This hammam is hard to beat – spotless mosaic-tiled surroundings, flowered sarongs and a relaxing pool. The exotic 'Forfait florale' option (€139) will have you enveloped in rose petals and massaged with *huile d'Argan* from Morocco, and the more simple hammam and *gommage* followed by mint tea and pastries is €39. Plan to spend a few hours here, as the soft-voiced staff take things at their own pace.

Spa Nuxe

32 rue Montorgueil, 1st (01.55.80.71.40/www. nuxe.com). M° Les Halles. **Open** 9am-9pm Mon-Fri; 9am-7.30pm Sat. **Credit** AmEx, MC, V. **Map** p402 J4.

This luxurious day spa housed in stone vaults with wooden cabins and safari-style tents offers massages and skin treatments using Nuxe's gentle, plant-based products. The facials, where you undress completely, begin with a short foot, tummy and neck message for total relaxation; from €70.

HOUSE & HOME

Antiques & flea markets

No trip to Paris is complete without a visit to one of the city's flea markets. The enormous **Marché aux Puces de Clignancourt** has an unrivalled abundance of junk and genuine design classics; in town, traditional antiques can be found in the **Louvre des Antiquaires**, and around Carré Rive Gauche (6th), Village Suisse and rue du Fbg-St-Honoré (1st). You'll find art deco in St-Germain-des-Prés, and retro by rue de Charonne (11th). For books, look at the **bouquinistes** (*see p242*).

Louvre des Antiquaires

2 pl du Palais-Royal, 1st (01.42.97.27.27/ www.louvre-antiquaires.com). M° Palais Royal Musée du Louvre. **Open** 11am-7pm Tue-Sun. Closed Sun in July & Aug. **Credit** varies. **Map** p406 H5.

This upmarket antiques centre houses 250 antiques dealers: perfect for Louis XV furniture, tapestries, porcelain, jewellery, model ships and tin soldiers.

Marché aux Puces d'Aligre

Pl d'Aligre, rue d'Aligre, 12th. M° Ledru-Rollin. **Open** 7.30am-1.30pm Tue-Sun. **Map** p407 N7.

The only flea market in central Paris, Aligre stays true to its junk tradition with a handful of *brocanteurs* peddling books, phone cards, kitchenware and oddities at what seem to be optimistic prices.

★ Marché aux Puces de Clignancourt

Av de la Porte de Clignancourt, 18th. M° Porte de Clignancourt. **Open** 7am-7.30pm Mon, Sat, Sun.

The biggest market in Europe; its sheer size may overwhelm the first-time visitor. Understanding how this Byzantine emporium is ordered is essential; there are 15 to 20 distinct markets amounting to around 2,000 stalls. Each market has at least one speciality; some are in malls, others are outdoors in a more rustic setting. Head straight for the rue des Rosiers, the main artery of the market.

Marché aux Puces de Vanves

Av Georges-Lafenestre & av Marc-Sangnier, 14th. M° Porte de Vanves. **Open** 7am-7.30pm Sun.

Vanves is the smallest and friendliest of the Paris flea markets, and infinitely more tranquil than its much bigger sister at Clingancourt. It's a favourite with serious collectors, so arrive early for the best pick of decent vintage clothes, dolls, costume jewellery and silverware, although not much in the way of furniture.

Le Village St-Paul

Rue St-Paul, rue Charlemagne & quai des Célestins, 4th. M° St-Paul. **Open** 10am-7pm Mon-Sat. **No credit cards.** **Map** p409 L7.

This colony of antiques sellers, housed in small, linking courtyards, is a source of retro furniture, kitchenware and wine gadgets.

Design & interiors

The vast **Lafayette Maison** (*see p239*) offers a selection of current design and homeware. Also great for modern furniture is the bi-annual **Les Puces du Design** (*see p278*) every June and October.

Astier de Villatte

173 rue St-Honoré, 1st (01.42.60.74.13/www. astierdevillatte.com). M° Palais Royal Musée du Louvre. **Open** 11am-7.30pm Mon-Sat. Closed 3wks Aug. **Credit** AmEx, MC, V. **Map** p401 G4.

Once home to Napoleon's silversmith, this ancient warren now houses ceramics inspired by 17th- and 18th-century designs, handmade by the Astier de Villatte siblings in their Bastille workshop.

CONSUME

★ Caravane Chambre 19

19 rue St-Nicolas, 12th (01.53.02.96.96/www.
caravane.fr). M° Ledru-Rollin. **Open** 11am-7pm
Tue-Sat. Closed 2wks Aug. **Credit** AmEx, MC,
V. **Map** p407 M7.

This offshoot of Françoise Dorget's original Marais
shop has goodies such as exquisite hand-sewn quilts
from west Bengal, crisp cotton and organdie tunics,
Berber scarves, lounging sofas and daybeds.
Other locations 6 rue Pavée, 4th
(01.44.61.04.20); 22 rue St-Nicolas, 12th
(01.53.17.18.55).

Christian Liaigre

42 rue du Bac, 7th (01.53.63.33.66/www.
christian-liaigre.fr). M° Rue du Bac. **Open**
10am-7pm Mon-Sat. Closed 3wks Aug.
Credit AmEx, MC, V. **Map** p405 G6.

This French interior decorator fitted out Marc
Jacobs' boutiques. His showroom displays his elegant lighting and furniture designs.
Other locations 61 rue de Varenne, 7th
(01.47.53.78.76).

Christophe Delcourt

47 rue de Babylone, 7th (01.42.71.34.84/
www.christophedelcourt.com). M° Jacques
Bonsergent. **Open** 9am-noon, 1-6pm Mon-
Fri. Closed Aug. **Credit** AmEx, DC, MC, V.
Map p401 G4.

Delcourt's art deco-influenced, geometrical lights
and furniture are given a contemporary spin by their
combination of stained wood and black steel.

CSAO

9 rue Elzévir, 3rd (01.42.77.66.42/www.csao.fr).
M° St-Paul. **Open** 11am-7pm Mon-Sat; 2-7pm
Sun. **Credit** AmEx, DC, MC, V. **Map** p409 L6.

This boutique offers African craftwork created
according to fair trade principles. The artisans often
fashion their objects out of recycled materials, such
as the funky furniture constructed from tins.

★ FR66

25 rue de Renard, 4th (01.44.54.35.36/www.
fr66.com). M° Hôtel de Ville. **Open** 10am-7pm
Mon-Sat. Closed 2-3wks Aug. **Credit** AmEx,
MC, V. **Map** p406 K6.

Somewhere between a gallery and a shop, this two-
level experimental space accommodates contemporary artists and designers who produce exciting and
original products for the home.

Galerie Patrick Seguin

5 rue des Taillandiers, 11th (01.47.00.32.35/
www.patrickseguin.com). M° Bastille or Ledru-
Rollin. **Open** 10am-7pm Tue-Sat. Closed 2wks
Aug. **Credit** AmEx, DC, MC, V. **Map** p407 M7.
Seguin specialises in French design from the 1950s:
items by Jean Prouvé and Charlotte Perriand are on
display in a showroom designed by Jean Nouvel.

Sentou Galerie

26 bd Raspail, 7th (01.45.49.00.05/www.sentou.
fr). M° Pont Marie. **Open** 2-7pm Mon; 10am-7pm
Tue-Sat. **Credit** AmEx, MC, V. **Map** p409 K7.

A trend-setting shop for colourful tableware and furniture: painted Chinese flasks, vases and so on.
Other locations 29 rue François-Miron, 4th
(01.42.78.50.60); 26 bd Raspail, 7th (01.45.49.00.05).

Silvera

41 rue du Fbg-St-Antoine, 11th (01.43.43.06.75/
www.silvera.fr). M° Bastille or Ledru-Rollin.
Open 10am-7pm Mon-Sat. Closed 2wks Aug.
Credit AmEx, MC, V. **Map** p407 M7.

The former Le Bihan was taken over by Silvera in
2005 and is now a three-floor showcase for modern
design. Look out for furniture and lighting from
Perriand, Pesce, Pillet, Morrison, Arad and others.
Other locations 58 av Kléber, 16th
(01.53.65.78.78).

Kitchen & bathroom

Bains Plus

51 rue des Francs-Bourgeois, 4th
(01.48.87.83.07). M° Hôtel de Ville. **Open**
2-7pm Mon, Sun; 11am-7.30pm Tue-Sat.
Credit AmEx, MC, V. **Map** p409 K6.

This is the ultimate gentlemen's shaving shop: stock
includes duck-shaped loofahs, seductive dressing
gowns, chrome mirrors, bath oils and soaps.

★ E Dehillerin

18 rue Coquillière, 1st (01.42.36.53.13/www.
e-dehillerin.fr). M° Les Halles. **Open** 9am-
12.30pm, 2-6pm Mon; 9am-6pm Tue-Sat.
Credit MC, V. **Map** p402 J5.

Suppliers to great chefs since 1820, this no-nonsense
warehouse stocks just about every kitchen utensil
ever invented. A saucepan from Dehillerin is for life.

Laguiole Galerie

1 pl Ste-Opportune, 1st (01.40.28.09.42/www.
forge-de-laguiole.com). M° Châtelet. **Open**
10.30am-1pm, 2-7pm Mon-Sat. **Credit** MC, V.
Map p406 J6.

Philippe Starck designed this chic boutique, a showcase for France's classic knife, the Laguiole.

MUSIC & ENTERTAINMENT
CDs & DVDs

Gibert Joseph (*see p242*) sells CDs and DVDs;
WH Smith (*see p243*) stocks DVDs in English.

★ Crocodisc

40-42 rue des Ecoles, 5th (01.43.54.47.95/
www.crocodisc.com). M° Maubert Mutualité.
Open 11am-7pm Tue-Sat. Closed 2wks Aug.
Credit MC, V. **Map** p408 J7.

The excellent albeit expensive range includes rock, funk, African, country and classical, in the form of new and second-hand vinyl and CDs. For jazz and blues, try sister shop Crocojazz.
Other locations Crocojazz, 64 rue de la Montagne-Ste-Geneviève, 5th (01.46.34.78.38).

Fnac Forum
Levels -1 to -3, Porte Lescot, Forum des Halles, 1st (08.25.02.00.20/ticket office 08.92.68.36.22/www. fnac.com). Mº Les Halles. **Open** 10am-7.30pm Mon-Sat. **Credit** AmEx, MC, V. **Map** p402 J5.
Fnac is a supermarket of culture: books, DVDs, CDs, audio kit, computers and photographic equipment. Most branches stock everything; others specialise, such as Fnac Music at 4 place de la Bastille. All branches operate as a concert box office.
▶ *Get discounts on large purchases by signing up for Fnac membership.*
Other locations throughout the city.

Monster Melodies
9 rue des Déchargeurs, 1st (01.40.28.09.39). Mº Les Halles. **Open** noon-7pm Mon-Sat. **Credit** MC, V. **Map** p402 J5.
The owners are very willing to help you hunt down your treasured tracks – and with more than 10,000 second-hand CDs of every variety, that's just as well.

Virgin Megastore
52-60 av des Champs-Elysées, 8th (01.49.53.50.00/www.virginmega.fr). Mº Franklin D. Roosevelt. **Open** 10am-midnight Mon-Sat; noon-midnight Sun. **Credit** AmEx, DC, MC, V. **Map** p401 E4.
The luxury of perusing CDs and DVDs till midnight makes this a choice spot, and the listening posts let you sample any CD by scanning its barcode. Tickets for concerts and sports events are available here too. This main branch has the best selection of books.
Other locations Carrousel du Louvre, 99 rue de Rivoli, 1st (01.44.50.03.10); 5 bd Montmartre, 2nd (01.40.13.72.13); 15 bd Barbès, 18th (01.56.55.53.70).

Musical instruments

Paris Accordéon
80 rue Daguerre, 14th (01.43.22.13.48/www. parisaccordeon.com). Mº Denfert Rochereau or Gaîté. **Open** 9am-noon, 1-7pm Tue-Fri; 9am-noon, 1-6pm Sat. **Credit** AmEx, MC, V. **Map** p405 G10.
Accordions, from simple squeezeboxes to beautiful tortoiseshell models, second-hand and new.

SPORT & FITNESS

Unless you need specialised equipment, you'll find what you want at **Go Sport** (www.go-sport.com) or **Décathlon** (www.decathlon.fr).

Citadium
50-56 rue de Caumartin, 9th (01.55.31.74.00/ www.citadium.com). Mº Havre Caumartin. **Open** 10am-8pm Mon-Wed, Fri, Sat; 10am-9pm Thur. **Credit** AmEx, DC, MC, V. **Map** p401 G3.
Cultish emporium of sporting goods, from hip watches to cross-country skis, on four themed floors.

Nauti Store
40 av de la Grande-Armée, 17th (01.43.80.28.28/ www.nautistore.fr). Mº Argentine. **Open** 10.30am-2pm, 3-7pm Mon-Sat. **Credit** DC, MC, V. **Map** p400 C3.
This shop stocks a vast range of sailing clothes and shoes from labels such as Helly Hansen and Sebago.

René Pierre
35 rue de Maubeuge, 9th (01.44.91.91.21/www. rene-pierre.fr). Mº Poissonnière. **Open** 10am-1pm, 2-6.30pm Mon-Sat. **Credit** MC, V. **Map** p402 H3.
France's finest table-football tables, ready for free delivery as far as Calais for UK buyers.

TICKETS

The easiest way to reserve and buy tickets for concerts, plays and matches is from a **Fnac** store. You can also reserve on www.fnac.com or by phone (08.92.68.36.22). **Virgin** has teamed up with Ticketnet to create an online ticket office (www.virginmega.fr). Tickets can also be purchased by phone (08.25.12.91.39) and sent to your home for a €5.50 fee.

Fnac Forum
Levels -1 to -3, Porte Lescot, Forum des Halles, 1st (08.25.02.00.20/www.fnac.com). Mº Les Halles/ RER Châtelet Les Halles. **Open** 10am-7.30pm Mon-Sat. **Credit** AmEx, MC, V. **Map** p402 J5.

Virgin Megastore
52-60 av des Champs-Elysées, 8th (01.49.53.50.00/www.virginmega.fr). Mº Franklin D. Roosevelt. **Open** 10am-midnight Mon-Sat; noon-midnight Sun. **Credit** AmEx, MC, V. **Map** p401 E4.

TRAVEL AGENTS
Nouvelles Frontières
13 av de l'Opéra, 1st (08.25.00.07.47/www. nouvelles-frontieres.fr). Mº Pyramides. **Open** 9am-9pm Mon-Sat; 9am-7pm Sun. **Credit** V.
Agent with 16 branches in Paris.

Thomas Cook
17 rue du Colisée, 8th (08.26.82.67.77/www. thomascook.fr). Mº Opéra. **Open** 9am-10pm Mon-Sat. **Credit** AmEx, DC, MC, V.
Travel agent with more than 30 branches in Paris.

CONSUME

Arts & Entertainment

Calendar

Sort the saint's days from the sporting events.

Paris is bursting with culture, from film festivals to world music. During summer, classical music moves outdoors, with many urban parks turning into alfresco concert venues. Among them is the lovely Parc Floral de Paris, which holds weekend concerts throughout the warmer months.

However, there are also plenty of less highbrow diversions, especially at Paris-Plage, the beach on the Seine. Elsewhere, Solidays, Rock en Seine, Festival des Inrockuptibles and the Techno Parade all attract top acts. And if sport fans don't manage to get tickets for the French Open or the Six Nations, there's always the Marathon de Paris and the finale of the Tour de France, for which tickets aren't required.

PUBLIC HOLIDAYS

On *jours fériés*, you can expect the banks, many museums, most businesses and some restaurants to close, with those remaining open often charging a premium; public transport runs a Sunday service. The annual holiday calendar is detailed below; dates vary by year unless stated.

New Year's Day (*Jour de l'An*)
Easter Monday (*Lundi de Pâques*)
May Day (*Fête du Travail*)
VE Day (*Victoire 1945*) – 8 May
Ascension Day (*Jour de l'Ascension*)
Whit Monday (*Pentecôte*)
Bastille Day (*Quatorze Juillet*) – 14 July
Feast of the Assumption (*Fête de l'Assomption*) – 15 Aug
All Saints' Day (*Toussaint*) – 1 Nov
Remembrance Day (*L'Armistice 1918*) – 11 Nov
Christmas Day (*Noël*), 25 Dec.

SPRING

Six Nations

Stade de France, 93210 St-Denis (08.92.70.09.00/ www.stadedefrance.fr). RER B La Plaine Stade de France or RER D Stade de France St-Denis. **Admission** varies. **Date** Feb-Mar.
Brits and Celts invade Paris for three big rugby weekends in spring. Log on to www.rbs6nations. com at least three months in advance for tickets.

Fashion Week

Various venues (www.modeaparis.com). **Date** Mar, July, Oct & Jan.
Paris presents its haute couture and prêt-à-porter collections at a variety of venues across town, but to invited guests only.

Le Printemps des Poètes

Various venues (01.53.80.08.00/www. printempsdespoetes.com). **Date** Mar.
Celebrating the centenary of poet René Char's birth, the 2008 edition of this popular national poetry festival had 'L'Eloge de l'Autre' as its theme.

Printemps du Cinéma

Various venues (www.printempsducinema.com). **Date** Mar.
Film tickets at a variety of cinemas all across the city are cut to a bargain €3.50 for this popular three-day film bonanza.

★ Banlieues Bleues

Various venues in Seine-St-Denis (01.49.22.10.10/www.banlieuesbleues.org). **Admission** €14-€20. **Date** Mar-Apr.
An annual five-week festival of quality French and international jazz, blues, R&B, soul, funk, flamenco and world music.
▶ *For more on music festivals in Paris and further afield, see p318.*

Le Chemin de la Croix

Square Willette, 18th (01.53.41.89.00). *Mᵒ Abbesses or Anvers.* **Date** Good Friday.

A crowd of pilgrims follows the Archbishop of Paris from the bottom of Montmartre up to Sacré-Coeur as he performs the Stations of the Cross.

Foire du Trône
Pelouse de Reuilly, 12th (www.foiredutrone.com). M° Porte Dorée. **Admission** free; rides €1.50-€4. **Date** late Mar-May.
France's biggest funfair: stomach-churning rides, bungee jumping and *barbe à papa* (candyfloss).

★ Marathon de Paris
Av des Champs-Elysées, 8th, to av Foch, 16th (01.41.33.15.68/www.parismarathon.com). **Date** 5 Apr 2009.
Perhaps the world's most picturesque marathon, with 35,000 runners heading from the Champs-Elysées along the Right Bank to the Bois de Vincennes, and back along the Left Bank to the Bois de Boulogne. The 2009 half-marathon takes place on 8 March.

Foire de Paris
Paris-Expo, pl de la Porte de Versailles (01.49.09.60.00/www.foiredeparis.fr). M° Porte de Versailles. **Admission** €12; €7 reductions; free under-7s. **Date** 29 Apr-10 May 2009.
This enormous lifestyle fair includes world crafts and foods, plus the latest health and house gizmos.

Fête du Travail
Date 1 May.
May Day is strictly observed. Key sights (the Eiffel Tower aside) close, and unions march in eastern Paris via Bastille. Sweet-smelling posies of lily of the valley (*muguet*) are sold on every street corner.

Printemps des Musées
Various venues (www.printempsdesmusees. culture.fr). **Date** early May.
For one Sunday in May, selected museums are free.

La Fête des Enfants du Monde
Various venues (www.koinobori.org). **Date** early May-June.
A Franco-Japanese festival with shows, exhibitions and concerts.

★ La Nuit des Musées
All over France (www.nuitdesmusees.culture.fr). **Admission** free. **Date** mid May.
For one night, museums open their doors late for special events and entertainment.

Festival de St-Denis
Various venues in St-Denis (01.48.13.12.10/ www.festival-saint-denis.com). M° St-Denis Basilique. **Admission** €9-€55. **Date** May-June.
The Gothic St-Denis basilica and other historic buildings in the neighbourhood host four weeks of top quality classical concerts.

Quinzaine des Réalisateurs
Forum des Images, Porte St-Eustache, Forum des Halles, 1st (01.44.89.99.99/www.quinzaine-realisateurs.com). M° Les Halles. **Admission** €5.50. **Date** May, June.
The Cannes Directors' Fortnight sidebar comes to Paris; 2009 is the 30th anniversary of this festival of screenings and events.

French Tennis Open
Stade Roland-Garros, 2 av Gordon-Bennett, 16th (01.47.43.48.00/www.frenchopen.org). M° Porte d'Auteuil. **Admission** €21-€75. **Date** 24 May-6 June 2009.
The glitzy Grand Slam tournament, whose tricky clay courts have been the downfall of many a champion, always attracts a selection of showbiz stars.

Le Printemps des Rues
Various venues (01.47.97.36.06/www. leprintempsdesrues.com). **Admission** free. **Date** late May or early June.
This annual two-day street-theatre festival has an experimental vibe.

SUMMER

Tous à Vélo
Across Paris (www.tousavelo.com). **Date** early June.
Cycling tours and activities as Paris's two-wheelers take to the streets.
▶ *To hire a bike or learn more about the Vélib free bike scheme, visit www.velib.paris.fr.*

Prix de Diane Hermès
Hippodrome de Chantilly, 16 av du Général-Leclerc, 90209 Chantilly (03.44.62.41.00/ www.france-galop.com). **Admission** €8; €4 reductions; free under-18s. **Date** 7 June 2009.
The French Derby draws the crème de la crème of high society to Chantilly, sporting silly hats and keen to have a flutter.

★ Fête de la Musique
All over France (01.40.03.94.70/www.fetede lamusique.fr). **Admission** free. **Date** 21 June.

THE BEST
SUMMER FESTIVALS

For a cycling tradition
Le Tour de France. *See p277.*

For pomp and circumstance
Bastille Day. *See p276.*

For a lazy afternoon on the beach
Paris-Plage. *See p277.*

ARTS & ENTERTAINMENT

La Nuit des Musées. *See p275.*

Free gigs (encompassing all musical genres) take place across the country as part of this festival on the summer solstice.

★ Gay Pride March
Information: Centre Gai et Lesbien (01.43.57.21.47/www.inter-lgbt.org). **Date** 27 June 2009.
Outrageous floats and flamboyant costumes parade towards Bastille; then there's an official fête and various club and nightlife events.
▶ *For more information on gay events in Paris, see p306.*

Festival Chopin à Paris
Orangerie de Bagatelle, Parc de Bagatelle, Bois de Boulogne, 16th (01.45.00.22.19/www.frederic-chopin.com). M° Porte Maillot, then bus 244. **Admission** €16-€37. **Date** June, July.
Candlelit evening recitals in the Bagatelle gardens.

Foire St-Germain
Pl St-Sulpice & venues in St-Germain-des-Prés, 6th (01.43.29.61.04/www.foiresaintgermain.org). M° St-Sulpice. **Admission** free. **Date** June, July.
St-Germain-des-Prés lets its hair down for a month of concerts, theatre and workshops.

★ Paris Jazz Festival
Parc Floral de Paris, Bois de Vincennes, 12th (39.75/www.parisjazzfestival2008.com.). M° Château de Vincennes. **Admission** *Park* €5; €2.50 reductions; free under-7s. **Date** June, July.
Two months of free jazz weekends at the Parc Floral.

La Goutte d'Or en Fête
Eglise St-Bernard, square St-Bernard, 18th (06.62.08.83.99/www.gouttedorenfete.org). M° Barbès Rochechouart. **Admission** free. **Date** late June-early July.
Established and local musicians play an eclectic mix of reggae, raï and rap.

Paris Cinéma
Various venues (01.55.25.55.25/www.paris cinema.org). **Admission** varies. **Date** early July.
Premieres, tributes and restored films make up the programme of this summer film-going initiative.

Solidays
Longchamp Hippodrome (01.53.10.22.22/www. solidays.com). M° Porte Maillot. **Admission** *Day* €25. *Weekend* €45. **Date** early July.
A three-day music festival, for the benefit of AIDS charities. *See also p318.*

Miss Guinguette
41 quai Victor Hugo, Ile du Martin-Pêcheur, 94500 Champigny-sur-Marne (information 01.49.83.03.02/www.guinguette.fr). RER Champigny-sur-Marne. **Admission** €7. **Date** 14 July.
A contest to find the light-footed queen of the open-air dancehall scene at this river island venue.

Le Quatorze Juillet (Bastille Day)
All over France. **Date** 14 July.
France's national holiday commemorates the events of 1789. The evening before, Parisians dance at place

Palm trees, huts, hammocks and around 2,000 tonnes of fine sand on both banks of the Seine bring a seaside vibe to the city. Not only this, there's a floating pool and a lending library too.

Le Cinéma en Plein Air
Parc de la Villette, 19th (01.40.03.75.75/ www.villette.com). M° Porte de Pantin.
Admission €2. **Date** mid July-end Aug.
A themed season of films screened under the stars on Europe's largest inflatable screen.

Festival Classique au Vert
Parc Floral de Paris, Bois de Vincennes, 12th (01.45.43.81.18). M° Château de Vincennes.
Admission €5; €2.50 reductions; free under-7s.
Date Aug, Sept.
Classical recitals in a park setting every weekend throughout August and September.

Fête de l'Assomption
Cathédrale Notre-Dame de Paris, pl du Parvis Notre-Dame, 4th (01.42.34.56.10). M° Cité/ RER St-Michel Notre-Dame. **Admission** free.
Date 15 Aug.
A national holiday. Notre-Dame becomes a place of religious pilgrimage for Assumption Day.

★ Rock en Seine
Domaine National de St-Cloud (08.92.68.08.92/ www.rockenseine.com). M° Porte de St-Cloud.
Admission Day €42. *3 days* €98. **Date** end Aug.
Three days, three stages, and one world-class line-up of rock and indie groups. *See also p318.*

AUTUMN
Jazz à la Villette
Parc de la Villette, 211 av Jean-Jaurès, 19th (01.44.84.44.84/www.jazzalavillette.com). M° Porte de Pantin. **Admission** €12-€30. **Date** early Sept.
The first fortnight in September brings one of Paris's best jazz festivals.

Festival Paris Ile-de-France
Various venues (www.festival-ile-de-france.com).
Tickets varies. **Date** early Sept-mid Oct.
Classical, contemporary and world music festival.

Techno Parade
www.technoparade.fr. **Date** mid Sept.
The Saturday parade (finishing at Bastille) marks the start of electro music fest Rendez-vous Electroniques.

Journées du Patrimoine
All over France (08.20.20.25.02/ www.jp.culture.fr). **Date** mid Sept.
Embassies, ministries, scientific establishments and corporate headquarters open their doors. The festive Soirée du Patrimoine takes place on the first Journée. Get *Le Monde* or *Le Parisien* for a full programme.

---

de la Bastille. At 10am on the 14th, crowds line up along the Champs-Elysées as the President reviews a full military parade. By night, the Champ de Mars fills for the fireworks display.

★ Le Tour de France
Av des Champs-Elysées, 8th (01.41.33.15.00/ www.letour.fr). **Date** July.
The ultimate cycling endurance test climaxes after some 3,500km (2,175 miles). Blink and you'll miss the winner flying past the finishing line on the Champs-Elysées.

Etés de la Danse
Grand Palais, Av Winston Churchill, 8th (08.92.68.71.00/www.lesetesdeladanse.com). M° Champs-Elysées Clemenceau or Franklin D. Roosevelt. **Tickets** €24-€65. **Date** early-late July.
An international festival featuring both classical and contemporary dance.

Paris, Quartier d'Eté
Various venues (01.44.94.98.00/www. quartierdete.com). **Admission** free-€15.
Date mid July-mid Aug.
A series of classical and jazz concerts, dance and theatre performances in outdoor venues.

★ Paris-Plage
Pont des Arts to Pont de Sully (08.20.00.75.75/ www.paris.fr). M° Châtelet, Hôtel de Ville, Louvre Rivoli, Pont Marie, Sully Morland. **Admission** free. **Date** mid July-mid Aug.

ARTS & ENTERTAINMENT

Vintage Paris

Drink in the atmosphere at Montmartre's harvest festival.

The **Fête des Vendanges de Montmartre** (*see below*) is perhaps the most quintessentially Gallic of the capital's annual festivals. The event takes place in Montmartre in the vicinity of Paris's very own vineyard, the tiny Clos Montmartre, which sits on the northern side of the Butte. Although the vines produce an average of just 1,000 bottles a year, the modest harvest is the pretext for a long weekend of Bacchanalian street parties. The cabarets and overpriced bars around the Sacré-Coeur become the backdrop to this village fête-style festival, complete with *chansons* to accompany the regional produce vendors, the costumed parades and congratulatory speeches.

A sip of the genuine Cru du Clos Montmartre is hard to come by, as almost the entire supply is auctioned off for charity; but stalls upon stalls selling wine from neighbouring vineyards and other epicurean delights amply compensate its absence. Pomp and ceremony to temper the hedonism are provided by the wine-tasting brotherhood, the Commanderie de Montmartre, who parade through the streets wearing red and blue, Paris's official colours. Other guests of honour include the city's mayor and the *parrains d'honneur*, the king and queen of the harvest, two celebrities who inaugurate the harvest parade.

In recent years the organisers have brought a cultural twist to the event by specifying an annual theme. For 2007, the focus was on singer Georges Brassens; 2008 celebrated the life and work of the heroes of French cinema who lived in the arrondissement.

Montmartre's wine-making past stretches back to Roman times, and wine has been produced on this site since the 12th century. By the 1850s, Montmartre was supplying wine all over Paris. However, a phylloxera outbreak destroyed a significant portion of crops, and the introduction of the railways meant that wine could be transported more cheaply from further afield. This makes the longevity of Montmartre's last vineyard all the more impressive, and its harvest well worthy of this unique celebration.

ARTS & ENTERTAINMENT

★ Festival d'Automne
Various venues. Information: 156 rue de Rivoli, 1st (01.53.45.17.00/www.festival-automne.com). **Admission** €3-€60. **Date** mid Sept-late Dec.
A major annual festival of challenging contemporary theatre, dance and modern opera, intent on bringing non-Western culture into the French consciousness. 'Autumn Festival' is a bit of a misnomer for this event, as some exhibitions run over the new year into January.

★ Nuit Blanche
Various venues (39.75/www.paris.fr). **Admission** free. **Date** early Oct.
Culture by moonlight: galleries and museums host special after-dark installations, and swimming pools, bars and clubs stay open late into the night.

Prix de l'Arc de Triomphe
Hippodrome de Longchamp, Bois de Boulogne, 16th (01.49.10.20.30/www.prixarcdetriomphe.com). M° Porte d'Auteuil, then free shuttle bus. **Admission** €8; €4 reductions; free under-18s. **Date** early Oct.
France's richest flat race attracts the elite of horse racing for a weekend of pomp and ceremony.

Mondial de l'Automobile
Paris-Expo, pl de la Porte de Versailles (01.56.88.22.40/www.mondial-automobile.com). M° Porte de Versailles. **Admission** €12; €6.45 reductions; free under-10s. **Date** early Oct.
A fortnight of automotive madness with cutting-edge vehicle design from all over the world.

Fête des Vendanges de Montmartre
Rue des Saules, 18th (01.30.21.48.62/www.fetedesvendangesdemontmartre.com). M° Lamarck Caulaincourt. **Date** mid Oct.
Paris's local wine festival takes place in Montmartre. *See above* **Vintage Paris**.

Les Puces du Design
Quai de la Loire, 19th (01.53.40.78.77/www.pucesdudesign.com). M° Jaurès. **Admission** free. **Date** mid Oct & June.
Having moved to the up-and-coming end of the canal, this weekend-long fair specialises in modern and vintage furniture, and design classics.

FIAC
01.47.56.64.20/www.fiacparis.com. **Admission** €25; €12.50 reductions. **Date** mid Oct.

The Louvre and the Grand Palais are the two venues for this week-long international contemporary art fair.

★ Festival des Inrockuptibles
Various venues (01.42.44.16.16/www.lesinrocks. com). **Admission** varies. **Date** early Nov.
This festival, curated by popular music mag *Les Inrockuptibles*, boasts top international indie, rock, techno and trip hop acts, and a discerning crowd.

Armistice Day
Arc de Triomphe, 8th. M° Charles de Gaulle Etoile. **Date** 11 Nov.
To commemorate French combatants who served in the World Wars, the President lays wreaths at the Tomb of the Unknown Soldier under the Arc de Triomphe. The *bleuet* (a cornflower) is worn.

Fête du Beaujolais Nouveau
Various venues (www.beaujolaisgourmand.com). **Date** late Nov.
The third Thursday in November sees cafés and wine bars buzz as patrons assess the new vintage.

WINTER

Africolor
Various venues in suburbs, including Montreuil, St-Denis & St-Ouen (01.47.97.69.99/ www.africolor.com). **Admission** €5-€15. **Date** late Nov-late Dec.
A month-long African music festival.

Paris sur Glace
Pl de l'Hôtel de Ville, 4th; M° Hôtel de Ville. Pl Raoul Dautry, 15th; M° Montparnasse Bienvenüe. Pl de la Bataille de Stalingrad, 19th;
M° Stalingrad. Information: 39.75/www.paris.fr. **Admission** free (skate hire €6). **Date** Dec-Mar.
These locations are turned into outdoor ice rinks.

Noël (Christmas)
Date 24, 25 Dec.
Christmas is a family affair in France, with a dinner on Christmas Eve (*le Réveillon*), normally after mass. Usually the only bars and restaurants open are the ones in the city's main hotels.

★ New Year's Eve/New Year's Day
Date 31 Dec, 1 Jan.
Jubilant crowds swarm along the Champs-Elysées letting off bangers. Nightclubs and restaurants hold expensive New Year's Eve soirées. And on New Year's Day the Grande Parade de Paris brings floats, bands and dancers.

Fête des Rois (Epiphany)
Date 6 Jan.
Pâtisseries sell *galettes des rois*, cakes with a frangipane filling in which a *fève*, or tiny charm, is hidden.

Mass for Louis XVI
Chapelle Expiatoire, 29 rue Pasquier, 8th (01.42.65.35.80). M° St-Augustin. **Date** Jan.
On the Sunday closest to 21 January – the anniversary of the beheading of Louis XVI in 1793 – right-wing crackpots mourn the end of the monarchy.

Nouvel An Chinois
Around av d'Ivry & av de Choisy, 13th. M° Porte de Choisy or Porte d'Ivry. Also av des Champs Elysées, 8th. **Date** 26 Jan 2009.
Lion and dragon dances, and lively martial arts demonstrations to celebrate the Chinese New Year.

Le Tour de France. *See p277.*

ARTS & ENTERTAINMENT

Cabaret, Circus & Comedy

Satisfy your inner artiste with big tops, bare legs and belly laughs.

Roll up, roll up for the leggy lovelies whose synchronised, topless dancing twangs to the rhythm of the cancan. True to their reputation, Paris's traditional cabarets still cater (surprisingly well) to the throngs of tourists and businessmen who come for an eyeful of boob-bouncing, posh nosh and champers.

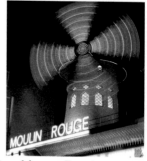

If the get-your-glitz-out-for-the-boys genre isn't your cup of tea, a Gallic giggle is still to be had in old-fashioned *café-théâtres*, where songs and sketches accompany dinner and a bottle of plonk. On the stand-up front, French comic Jamel Debbouze has opened **Le Comedy Club** – a launch pad for new French stand-up comics and a spinoff from his TV show *Le Jamel Comedy Club*. As for circus, Paris laps it up, from traditional ringmaster acts to avant-garde acrobatics and rib-tickling clowns.

ARTS & ENTERTAINMENT

CABARET & CAFE-THEATRE

The year the Eiffel Tower raised its final girders (1889), the Moulin Rouge was raising something of its own: skirts. The risqué, frock-lifting dance called *quadrille réaliste* (but later dubbed the can-can) became such a trademark that 120 years later, busty babes are still slinking across the cabaret stages of Paris.

These days, cabaret is an all-evening, smart-dress extravaganza, complete with pre-show meal and champagne. It may be touristy and pricey, but it's a fine spectacle. Male dancers, acrobats and magicians complement the foxy foxtrots; the dancing is perfectly synchronised, the costumes beautiful and the whole caboodle now perfectly respectable.

Cabaret

Crazy Horse Saloon
12 av George V, 8th (01.47.23.32.32/www.crazy horse.fr). M° Alma Marceau or George V. **Shows** 8.30pm, 11pm Mon-Fri, Sun; 7.30pm, 9.45pm, 11.50pm Sat. **Admission** *Show* (incl 2 drinks) €70. *Show* (incl champagne) €100-€120;

€50-€60 reductions. **Credit** AmEx, DC, MC, V. **Map** p400 D4.
More risqué than the other cabarets, the Horse, whose *art du nu* was invented in 1951 by Alain Bernadin, is an ode to feminine beauty: 13 lookalike dancers with identical body statistics (when standing, the girls' nipples and hips are all the same height) move around the stage, clad only in rainbow light and strategic strips of black tape. The girls put on some tantalising numbers, with titles such as 'God Save Our Bare Skin' (a sexy take on the Changing of the Guards) and 'Va Va Voom'.
▶ *Dinner prior to the show can be arranged for €175 per person (show included) at Fouquet's, Devez, Chez Francis or Bateaux Parisiens.*

Le Lido
116bis av des Champs-Elysées, 8th (01.40.76.56.10/www.lido.fr). M° Franklin D. Roosevelt or George V. **Lunch** 1pm. **Matinée** 3pm Tue, Sun (once a mth, dates vary). **Dinner** 7pm. **Shows** 9.30pm, 11.30pm daily. **Admission** *Matinée show* (incl champagne) €85. *Lunch & matinée show* (incl champagne) €125. *9.30pm show* (incl champagne) €100; €20 reductions. *11.30pm show* (incl champagne) €90; free under-

12s. *Dinner & show* €140-€280; €30 reductions.
Credit AmEx, DC, MC, V. **Map** p400 D4.
This is the largest cabaret of all: high-tech touches optimise visibility, and chef Philippe Lacroix provides fabulous gourmet nosh. On stage, 60 Bluebell Girls slink around, shaking their boobs with sequinned panache. For a special treat, opt for the Premier service (€280) with free cloakroom, the best tables in the house and free water and coffee with your meal.

★ Moulin Rouge
82 bd de Clichy, 18th (01.53.09.82.82/www. moulin-rouge.com). M° Blanche. **Dinner** 7pm.
Shows 9pm, 11pm daily. **Admission** *9pm show* (incl champagne) €99. *11pm show* (incl champagne) €89. *Dinner & show* €145-€175.
Credit AmEx, DC, MC, V. **Map** p401 G2.
Toulouse-Lautrec posters, glittery lampposts and fake trees lend tacky charm to this revue, while 60 Doriss dancers cavort with faultless synchronisation. Costumes are flamboyant and the *entr'acte* acts funny. The downer is the space, with tables packed in like sardines. There's also a twice-monthly matinee: lunch and show €125, show only €95.

Café-théâtre

Les Blancs Manteaux
15 rue des Blancs-Manteaux, 4th (01.48.87.15.84/ www.blancsmanteaux.fr). M° Hôtel de Ville. **Shows** from 7pm daily (phone for details). **Admission** *Show* €17; €13 students, under-25s; *2 shows* €26 (except Sat). *Dinner & 1 show* €32. *Dinner & 2 shows* €40. **No credit cards**. **Map** p409 K6.
For the last 36 years, this Marais institution has been launching new talent with weekly comedy platforms. With a dinner-and-show ticket, you can dine on Moroccan cuisine at nearby L'Arganier.

Chez Michou
80 rue des Martyrs, 18th (01.46.06.16.04/ www.michou.com). M° Pigalle. **Dinner** 8.30pm daily. **Shows** 10.30pm approx. **Admission** *Show* €40. *Dinner & show* €105 (incl wine).
Credit MC, V. **Map** p402 H2.
Drag, sparkling costumes, good food and wine: Michou's show is not quite as 'blue' as his azure attire suggests. Book ahead if you want to dine.

★ Au Lapin Agile
22 rue des Saules, 18th (01.46.06.85.87/www. au-lapin-agile.com). M° Lamarck Caulaincourt. **Shows** 9pm-2am Tue-Sun. **Admission** *Show* (incl 1 drink) €24; €17 reductions (except Sat & public hols). **No credit cards**. **Map** p402 H1.
The prices have gone up and they sell their own compilation CDs, but that's all that seems to have changed since this quaint, pink bar first opened in 1860. Tourists now outnumber the locals, but the Lapin harbours an echo of old Montmartre.

Le Petit Casino
17 rue Chapon, 3rd (01.42.78.36.50/www.lepetit casino.fr). M° Arts et Métiers or Rambuteau.

Moulin Rouge.

Dinner 8pm. **Shows** 9pm, 10.30pm daily (times may vary). **Admission** *Show* (2 acts) €18. *Dinner* €15 (€21 Sat & public hols). **Credit** MC, V. **Map** p406 K5.
Up-and-coming talents find precious stage space in this traditional *café-théâtre* devoted to one-man shows and cheap 'n' tasty nosh.

COMEDY & FRINGE THEATRE

Le Bout
62 rue Pigalle, 9th (01.42.85.11.88/www.lebout. com). M° Pigalle. **Shows** daily, times vary. **Admission** €15; €10 reductions. *2 shows* €20. **No credit cards. Map** p402 H2.
This *café-théâtre* school has been cramming them into its 40-seater venue since 1999. The emphasis is on newcomers, but not necessarily amateurs.

★ Café de la Gare
41 rue du Temple, 4th (01.42.78.52.51/www. cdlg.org). M° Hôtel de Ville. **Shows** 9pm Mon, Tue; 7pm, 8.30pm, 10pm Wed-Sat; 9pm Sun. **Admission** €20-€24; €10-€20 reductions. **Credit** MC, V. **Map** p406 K6.
Up and running since the revolutionary days of 1968, the most famous fringe theatre in Paris has 300 stage-hugging seats and hosts quality French stand-up and raucous, irreverent comedies.

Caveau de la République
1 bd St-Martin, 3rd (01.42.78.44.45/www. caveau.fr). M° République. **Shows** 8.30pm Thur-Sat; 3.30pm Sun. Closed Aug. **Admission** €30.50 Thur; €37 Fri-Sun; €15.75-€24.50 reductions. **Credit** MC, V.
This traditional *chanson* venue has been churning out political-satirical songs and sketches for more than a century. Nowadays stand-up comedy is the main draw, and the laughs are mostly wrung from current scandals.

Le Comedy Club
42 bd de Bonne Nouvelle, 10th (08.11.94.09.40/ www.lecomedyclub.fr). M° Bonne Nouvelle.

Shows days vary. **Admission** €20. **Credit** MC, V. **Map** p402 J4.
Jamel Debbouze, the comic known for his one-man shows and films such as *Le Fabuleux Destin d'Amélie Poulain*, gives the chuckle trade a helping hand with this theatre. Tuesdays and Wednesdays (7.30pm) are open mic nights. Saturdays are for the confirmed mirth merchants of Jamel's TV show.
► *For more on Jamel Debbouze's career, see pp46-50 Crossing the Divide.*

★ Le Point Virgule
7 rue Ste-Croix-de-la-Bretonnerie, 4th (01.42. 78.67.03/www.lepointvirgule.com). M° Hôtel de Ville. **Shows** *Mon-Wed, Sat, Sun* times vary. **Admission** €18; €14 reductions. *2 shows* €29, *3 shows* €39. *Children's show* €12; €10 children. **No credit cards. Map** p409 K6.
This small Marais theatre has become the ultimate launch pad for up-and-coming comedians, with daily shows, a *café-théâtre* school and an annual comedy festival in September.

CIRCUS

★ Cirque d'Hiver Bouglione
110 rue Amelot, 11th (01.47.00.28.81/www. cirquedhiver.com). M° Filles du Calvaire. **Shows** *Late Oct-late Feb* days vary. **Admission** €24.50-€46.30. **Credit** AmEx, MC, V. **Map** p409 L5.
This traditional circus has been in the same family for seven decades. It now has a brand new façade to match its revamped interior, and crowds flock for its twice-yearly seasons.

Cirque Pinder
Pelouse de Reuilly, Bois de Vincennes, 12th (01.45.90.21.25/www.cirquepinder.com). M° Porte de Charenton or Porte Dorée. **Shows** *Mid Nov-mid Jan* 2.30pm, 5.30pm, 8.30pm daily. **Admission** €13-€50; free under-2s. **Credit** AmEx, DC, MC, V.
Big cats are the stars of the show, but horses, elephants and monkeys also make Pinder the most traditional travelling circus in France.

2r2c (Coopérative de rue de cirque)
Various venues (01.46.22.33.71/www.2r2c.coop).
This collective organises circus throughout the year in the Paris region, including the excellent Village du Cirque on the Pelouse de Reuilly (Oct-Nov).

Espace Chapiteaux
Parc de La Villette, 19th (01.40.03.75.75/ www.villette.com). M° Porte de la Villette. **Shows** days vary. **Admission** varies. **Credit** MC, V. **Map** p403 inset.
This big top hosts companies such as Cirque Plume, Centre National des Arts du Cirque and aerialists Les Arts Saut.

ARTS & ENTERTAINMENT

Children

There is life beyond Mickey.

For all its agitation and commotion, the French capital offers a wealth of child-friendly attractions all year round. Parks, in particular, are an essential part of growing up in the capital – most Parisians raise their children in gardenless apartments – and nearly always incorporate a mini playground and concrete table-tennis tables (even posh place des Vosges offers some small slides and rocking horses). In big parks such as the **Jardin de Luxembourg** and **Buttes Chaumont**, many a childhood is whiled away on the backs of ponies, in sandpits, on swings, at puppet shows and by boating ponds. But there's also plenty to do outside of these lovely green spaces.

When the little ones are ready for a spot of sightseeing, the famous sights can be ticked off without much stress. However, it may be wise to head for the **Eiffel Tower** (*see p145*), the **Louvre** (*see p59*) and **Notre-Dame**'s towers (*p56*) early in the morning, when the queues are less disheartening. One of the most exciting ways for the family to take in the city is from a boat on the Seine. If you don't think your brood will sit still through an hour's commentated tour, the hop-on hop-off waterborne Batobus links eight prime sights, including the Eiffel Tower and Jardin des Plantes.

Most museums and attractions cultivate young eggheads by filling gaps in the academic schedule. Wednesdays, weekends and school holidays are packed with children's activities, from museum workshops to film screenings and theatre productions (you can often request an English speaker in advance). *Pariscope*, *L'Officiel des Spectacles*, *Figaroscope* (with Wednesday's *Le Figaro*) and *Télérama*'s *Sortir* supplement all have kids' sections. Look out for bi-monthly free magazine *Paris-Mômes*, distributed with daily newspaper *Libération* and in toy shops and public libraries. Children's attractions, shows, exhibitions and workshops are listed (in French) on websites such as www.cityjunior.com, www.commeundimanche. com, www.lamuse.net and www.paris.fr.

GETTING AROUND

Paris is a city made for strolling, so if you can, substitute the métro with a walk.

Métro-hopping with babies and toddlers is notoriously frustrating: two adults might manage a pushchair, but if you're travelling alone, a baby-carrier is a godsend when navigating the tight turnstiles and never-ending staircases. If you do take the challenge, don't expect help from passersby, and travel between 10.30am and 5pm to avoid the crowds. The driverless line 14 (St-Lazare to Olympiades) is a big hit with kids, who can sit at the front and peer down the tunnel as the train advances; the mostly overground lines six (Nation to Charles de Gaulle Étoile) and two (Nation to Porte Dauphine) offer attractive city views; a number of RER stations have lifts.

It's often easier, though, to take the bus. Some, such as nos.24, 63 and 95 (www.ratp.fr), pass numerous sights, and all have priority seats near the front for travelling with under-fours, who go free on public transport. Three- to 11-year-olds qualify for a half-price *carnet* (a book of ten tickets) for all transport, including the Montmartrobus minibus and Montmartre funicular. Taxi drivers will usually take a family of four (charging €1 to carry a pushchair and a little extra for the fourth person). If you're stuck, try **G7 taxis** (01.47.39.47.39), which has an English-speaking booking line.

For older kids, the recent addition of extra cycle paths across the centre (especially along the Seine, up the Canal St-Martin and along the Canal de l'Ourcq) makes a spin *en famille* an enjoyable way to get around the city while seeing the sights. The RATP rents hard-to-steal green and white bikes, plus junior bikes and

ARTS & ENTERTAINMENT

child seats, at a number of locations across the city (www.rouelibre.fr); and **Cyclo Pouce** (38 quai de Marne, 19th, 01.42.41.76.98) provides baby seats and equipment for disabled children. Short distances are also easily covered on the city's Vélib self-service scheme (www.velib.fr; *see p367*). For a day out in beautiful surroundings, the Bois de Vincennes in the east and the Bois de Boulogne in the west provide woodlands, picnic areas, boating lakes and cycle rental.

EATING OUT

Fun places to take your kids include the big belle époque dining room at affordable **Chartier** (7 rue du Fbg-Montmartre, 9th, 01.47.70.86.29, www.restaurant-chartier.com); **Tokyo Eat** at the Palais de Tokyo (13 av du Président-Wilson, 16th, 01 01.47.20.00.29, www.palaisdetokyo.com), with its wacky decor and round, family-sized tables; the tables at **Atelier Renault** (53 av des Champs-Elysées, 8th, 08.11.88.28.11, www.atelier. renault.com) that overlook the high-tech car showroom; and **Coco & Co** (11 rue Bernard Palissy, 6th, 01.45.44.02.52, www.cocoandco. fr), serving only egg dishes in an egg-themed dining room. The restaurants on the Cour St-Emilion near Parc de Bercy are good for traffic-free outdoor eating, and if you fancy browsing for baby clothes while slurping on a hot coffee, the **Poussette Café** (6 rue Pierre Sémard, 9th, 01.78.10.49.00, www.lepoussettecafe.com) is a haven, with parking space for buggies and milk-warming facilities. On Sundays, fashionable nightclub **Showcase** (*see p330*) puts on a family brunch, where children are entertained with games and make-up.

BABIES & TODDLERS

Nappy-changing facilities are a rarity, so always pack a portable changing mat. A facility worth remembering is the WC chalet in the Jardin du Luxembourg, where €0.50 gives you access to

---

THE BEST CHILD-FRIENDLY MUSEUMS

For budding explorers
Muséum National d'Histoire Naturelle. *See p287.*

For mini magicians
Musée de la Magie. *See p287.*

For water babies
Musée National de la Marine. *See p287.*

---

loos with a padded changing table; the **Galeries Lafayette** and **Printemps** (for both, *see p240*) department stores have clean, well-equipped nappy changing facilities, as does the **Poussette Café** (*see p226*). Breastfeeding in public is more common than ever, but still often frowned upon, so take a scarf for places where modesty is essential, or choose a quiet corner.

A city break with tots in tow doesn't have to mean missing out on the city's galleries and museums. Almost all of the main attractions have child-friendly activities or green spaces nearby – handy as a reward for good behaviour. There's a carefully tended garden by Notre-Dame, and the dignified **Musée Rodin** (*see p143*) has outdoor distractions such as a sandpit to dig in, a sculpture-filled garden to explore (free entry to parents with a pushchair) and a tempting ice-cream stand. And if the heady heights of the Eiffel Tower prove too daunting, more down-to-earth amusements can be found at the adjacent Champ de Mars, with its play areas and donkey rides; or there are old-style merry-go-rounds by the river.

Babysitting

Many hotels can organise babysitting (ask when you reserve). The **American Church in Paris** (65 quai d'Orsay, 7th, 01.40.62.05.00, www. acparis.org) has a noticeboard displaying ads from English-speaking babysitters and au pairs; **Baby Sitting Services** (01.46.21.33.16, www.babysittingservices.com) can organise babysitting at short notice.

MUSEUMS & SIGHTSEEING

Egyptian mummies at the Louvre; suits of armour at Les Invalides; dinosaur skeletons at the Galeries de Paléontologie at the **Muséum National d'Histoire Naturelle**; theatrically lit tribal masks, totems and American Indian cowhides at the Musée du Quai Branly; early flying machines, rockets and the chance to go inside Concorde at the Musée de l'Air et de l'Espace; live science experiments at the Palais de la Découverte; model boats at the **Musée National de la Marine**; the Argonaut submarine at the Cité des Sciences et de l'Industrie or fashion and jewellery at the Musée de la Mode et du Textile: there's plenty to feed a child's imagination.

Most museums offer children's workshops (in French) on Wednesday afternoons, at weekends and in the holidays. At the Louvre the programme for kids varies from storytelling to learning about Egyptian sculpture. Next door, the Museé des Arts Décoratifs offers hands-on art workshops for ages four to 12, plus

Little Chefs

Teach your kids the culinary arts.

If your nippers are showing early signs of culinary genius or, *au contraire*, don't know a spatula from their elbow, the **Ecole Ritz Escoffier** (38 rue Cambon, 1st, 01.43.16.31.50, www.ritzparis.com) at the Ritz has an army of master chefs ready to teach them the art of preparing and (the best bit) eating posh nosh.

Auguste Escoffier was the Ritz's first chef, famous not only for his mastery of haute cuisine but also for the recipes he left behind (especially desserts): peach melba and poire belle-hélène were two of his inventions, named after 19th-century Australian singer Nellie Melba and the hotel director's daughter Hélène Ellès.

In 1988, the Ritz decided to continue Escoffier's work by opening a school that 'teaches France's gastronomic traditions to professional and amateur food-lovers'. The result is a world-renowned culinary laboratory that instructs over 800 people a year, from 43 different countries. And guess what? They like them to start young. Great news for your six- to 11-year-olds, who can sign up for a two-and-a-half-hour lesson to become a Petit Marmiton du Ritz ('little Ritz kitchen hand') and learn how to cook scrumptious dishes such as handmade potato gnocchi with smoked salmon, Hallowe'en tart, cookies and

brownies, and marshmallow and marzipan models. The lessons are simple, fun and easy to follow, and students get to take home their creations at the end.

Although the food takes centre stage, children get a kick out of the pomp and circumstance surrounding it all. For a start, they get dressed up like real professionals, chef's hat and all (if you can't prise them out of the outfit, you can buy it for €100), non-French speakers get their own translator, and before heading into the kitchen *atelier* they get taken past the real working kitchens. Prices begin at €90 (reserve as far in advance as possible), which is nothing compared to the priceless meals they'll be preparing for you when you get home.

If money is an issue or you have older children, the **Ecole Lenôtre** (Pavillon Elysée, 10 av des Champs-Elysées, 8th, 01.42.65.97.60, www.lenotre.fr) cooking school on the Champs-Elysées runs special cooking classes most Wednesdays (Sept-June) for eight- to 17-year-olds, from €40. Younger kids' recipes stay simple (think cookies, fruit crumble and guacamole), but older children can test their skills on more complicated dishes such as herb-crusted cod with vegetable confit or tiramisu.

special tours tailored to different age groups. The Palais de Tokyo has inventive 'Tok Tok' workshops, often led by notable contemporary artists, and the Musée Rodin and Musée Bourdelle run children's clay workshops. In July and August the Musée Jacquemart-André runs a 'Family Fun' programme (2.30-5.30pm daily), where kids aged four to 12 are given a games book to guide them through the museum and get to dress up in old-fashioned costumes. Under-18s get free admission to the national museums, including the Louvre, Musée d'Orsay, Centre Pompidou, Musée du Quai Branly and Musée Rodin.

★ Centre Pompidou – Galerie des Enfants
Rue St-Martin, 4th (01.44.78.12.33/www. centrepompidou.fr/enfants). M° Hôtel de Ville or Rambuteau/RER Châtelet Les Halles. **Open** *Museum* 11am-10pm Mon, Wed-Sun (until 11pm Thur). *Workshops* most Wed & Sat afternoons & school hols. **Admission**

Museum €10; free under-18s. *Workshops* €10 (one child and one adult combined). **Credit** MC, V. **Map** p402 K5.
In the ground-floor gallery, well thought out exhibitions specially conceived by top artists and designers introduce children to aspects of modern art, design and architecture, often with interactive elements and the opportunity to touch. There are also hands-on workshops for six- to 12-year-olds, and family workshops one Sunday afternoon a month. Outside, look for the colourful Stravinsky fountain on the south side, designed by Niki de Saint Phalle and Jean Tinguely.

Cité de l'Architecture
Palais de Chaillot, 1 pl du Trocadéro, 16th (01.58.51.52.00/www.citechaillot.fr). **Open** 11am-7pm Mon, Wed-Sun (until 9pm Thur). **Admission** €8; €5 reductions; free under-18s. **Credit** MC, V. **Map** p400 B5.
This vast ode to French architecture is certainly eye-catching, with over 850 life-size copies of France's architectural treasures (including portions of great

cathedrals such as Chartres). To help kids understand the exhibits, colourful interactive games are dotted around the permanent displays, so they can try their hand at architecture and learn the concepts of Romanesque and Gothic as they create fantastical animal heads, design stained-glass windows or build a Romanesque arch. A family audio-guide in English is planned for 2009, so ask when you buy your tickets.

Etoiles du Rex

1 bd Poissonnière, 2nd (01.45.08.93.58/ www.legrandrex.com). M° Bonne Nouvelle. **Open** 10am-7pm Wed-Sun (tours leave every 5 mins). **Admission** €15.50; €13.50 reductions. **Credit** AmEx, MC, V. **Map** p402 J4.
The slick but cheesy 50-minute backstage tour of the glorious art deco Grand Rex cinema is a treat for any kids with acting aspirations. Be prepared to ham your heart out when, propelled by automatic doors, lifts and mystery voices, you visit the projection room, climb behind the giant screen and are thrust into a whirlwind of sound dubbing, special effects and an audition for *King Kong*.
▶ *If you're in Paris during the summer, don't miss the Cinéma en Plein Air season, with Europe's biggest inflatable screen (see p277).*

Grévin

10 bd Montmartre, 9th (01.47.70.85.05/ www.musee-grevin.com). M° Grands Boulevards. **Open** 10am-6.30pm (last admission 5.30pm) Mon-Fri; 10am-7pm (last admission 6pm) Sat, Sun & hols. **Admission** €19.50; €11.50-€16.50 reductions. **Credit** AmEx, DC, MC, V. **Map** p402 H4.
This kitsch version of Madame Tussauds is a hit with kids who can have their photo taken alongside waxwork doppelgangers of showbiz stars and personalities like Naomi Campbell, Zinédine Zidane, Brigitte Bardot, the Queen or Laurel and Hardy. Great historical moments, such as Neil Armstrong walking on the moon, are re-enacted in the 'snapshots of the 20th century' area, and a small gallery at the top of a spiral staircase near the end shows how waxworks are made, from the initial sculpture to fixing real hair strand by strand and choosing the right colour of eyeballs.

Musée de la Magie

11 rue St-Paul, 4th (01.42.72.13.26/www. museedelamagie.com). M° St-Paul or Sully-Morland. **Open** 2-7pm Wed, Sat, Sun (extra hours & days in school hols). **Admission** €9; €7 reductions. **No credit cards**. **Map** p409 L7.
Small kids love the distorting mirrors and putting their hands in the lion's mouth at this museum of magic and curiosities, housed in vaulted cellars. A short magic show is included in the visit – it's in French, but rabbits out of hats translate pretty well into any language.

★ Musée National de la Marine

Palais de Chaillot, 17 pl du Trocadéro, 16th (01.53.65.69.69/www.musee-marine.fr). M° Trocadéro. **Open** 10am-6pm Mon, Wed-Sun. **Admission** €8; €4 reductions; free under-6s. **Credit** *Shop* MC, V. **Map** p400 B5.
Sail your family back in time through 400 years of French naval history. Highlights include the *Océan*, a 19th-century sailing vessel equipped with an impressive 120 cannons; a gilded barge built for Napoleon; and some extravagant, larger-than-life figureheads, from serene-faced angels to leaping seahorses. There are also dozens of model boats, dating from the 18th to the 20th century, and a window through which you can watch the in-house restoration team at work.

★ Muséum National d'Histoire Naturelle

36 rue Geoffroy-St-Hilaire, 2 rue Bouffon, 57 rue Cuvier, 5th (01.40.79.30.00/www.mnhn.fr). M° Gare d'Austerlitz or Jussieu. **Open** *Nov-Mar* 10am-5pm Mon, Wed-Sun (10am-6pm Grande Galerie de l'Evolution). *Apr-Oct* 10am-6pm Mon, Wed-Sun. Last admission 45mins before closing. **Admission** *Grande Galerie de l'Evolution* €8; €6 reductions; free under-4s. *Galeries de Paléontologie et d'Anatomie Comparée or Galerie*

Stade de France.
See p288.

ARTS & ENTERTAINMENT

de Minéralogie et de Géologie €6; €4 reductions; free under-4s. *Combined ticket for all sites* €20; €15 reductions.**Credit** MC, V. **Map** p406 K9.

At the natural history museum's Grande Galerie de l'Evolution, stuffed creatures parade majestically through their various habitats. Animals of all kinds teach children about the diversity of nature and, in the endangered and vanished section, about the importance of protecting them. Also in the Jardin des Plantes complex are the small Ménagerie zoo (*see p289*), separate pavilions containing hunks of meteorites and crystals in the Galerie de Minéralogie et de Géologie, and the bony remains of fish, birds, monkeys, dinosaurs and humans in the Galerie de Paléontologie et d'Anatomie Comparée.

Musée de la Poupée

Impasse Berthaud, 3rd (01.42.72.73.11/www. museedelapoupeeparis.com). M° Rambuteau. **Open** 10am-6pm Tue-Sun. **Admission** €7; €3-€5 reductions; free under-3s. **No credit cards.** **Map** p406 L7.

This small, all-in-one private museum and doll hospital enchants little girls with some 400 dolls (mostly of French origin) their accompanying accessories and pets, arranged in thematic tableaux. A few teddies and quacking ducks are thrown in for young boys, and story-telling sessions are held at 2.30pm on Wednesdays (in French; reserve in advance).

★ Stade de France

Guided visits via entrance Porte H, Stade de France, Seine St-Denis (01.55.93.00.00/tours 08.92.70.09.00/www.stadefrance.fr). M° St-Denis

Porte de Paris/RER Stade de France St-Denis. **Tours** every hr 10am-5pm daily (French), 10.30am & 2.30pm daily (English). **Admission** €12; €8 reductions; free under-6s. **Credit** AmEx, DC, MC, V.

Football- and rugby-crazy kids will absolutely love the behind-the-scenes tours of France's handsome national sports stadium. After a quick scan of the museum (photos, football shirts, electric guitars from the rock stars who also play here), the tour begins by sitting in the stands and ends with a runout through the tunnel to the sound of applause. On the way, you can visit the changing and shower rooms and tour the on-site hospital and prison cells. On match or concert days, tours are not available. *Photo p287.*

AQUARIUMS, MENAGERIES & ZOOS

Cinéaqua

2 av des Nations Unies, 16th (01.40.69.23.23/ www.cineaqua.com). M° Trocadéro. **Open** 10am-8pm daily (5 July-31 Aug until 10pm). **Admission** €19.50; €12.50-€15.50 reductions; free under-3s. **Credit** MC, V. **Map** p400 B5.

Paris's first ever 'ocean entertainment centre' is a hybrid aquarium-cinema complex containing over 500 species of fish, invertebrates, sharks and coral, and several cinema screens. There are loads of kids' clubs with face-painting and games from 1pm to 5pm on Wednesdays, Saturdays and Sundays, plus a touch pool where nippers get the chance to stroke carp and sturgeon.

Disneyland Paris. *See p290.*

★ Ménagerie du Jardin des Plantes

57 rue Cuvier, 5th (01.40.79.37.94/www. mnhn.fr). M° Gare d'Austerlitz, Jussieu or Place Monge. **Open** 9am-6pm Mon-Sat; 9am-6.30pm Sun. **Admission** €7; €5 reductions; free under-4s. **Credit** AmEx, MC, V. **Map** p406 K8.

Heads rolled during the Terror, leaving many an aristocratic collection of exotic animals without a home. This *ménagerie* became the solution in 1794. Nowadays, its inhabitants include vultures, monkeys, orangutans, ostriches, flamingoes, a century-old turtle, a lovely red panda and lots of satisfyingly scary spiders and snakes. There's a petting zoo with farm animals for small kids, and older ones can zoom in on microscopic species in the Microzoo.

Palais de la Porte Dorée Aquarium Tropical

293 av Daumesnil, 12th (01.44.74.84.80/ www.aquarium-portedoree.org). M° Porte Dorée. **Open** 10am-5.15pm Tue-Fri; 10am-7pm Sat, Sun. **Admission** €4.50-€5.70; €6-€8 1 adult with 1 or 2 children under 12; €3-€4.20 reductions; free under-4s. **No credit cards**.

The basement of this art deco palace, built for the colonial exhibition in 1931, contains the small but much-loved city aquarium and its colonial crocodiles, brought from Dakar in 1948; other watery residents include cuttlefish, clownfish and sharks, and luminous deep-water species.

▶ *The Palais de la Porte Dorée is also home to the new Cité Nationale de l'Histoire de l'Immigration (see p106).*

Parc de Thoiry

78770 Thoiry-en-Yvelines (01.34.87.53.76/ www.thoiry.tm.fr). 45km (28 miles) west of Paris; by car A13, A12, then N12 towards Dreux until Thoiry. **Open** *July, Aug* 10am-6pm daily. *Sept-June* 10am-5pm Mon-Sat; 10am-6pm Sun. **Admission** Free under-3s. *Safari park, park & château* €24; €16.50 reductions. *Park & château* €18; €13 reductions. **Credit** MC, V.

As well as a beautiful château, the Parc de Thoiry houses one of Europe's first animal reserves. Follow the long safari park trail, accessible only by car, and see zebras rub their noses over your windscreen and bears amble down tracks. In the adjoining zoo, rarities include Siberian lynx and Tonkean macaques.

Parc Zoologique de Paris

53 av de St-Maurice, 12th (01.44.75.20.00/ www.mnhn.fr). M° Porte Dorée. **Open** *Summer* 9am-6pm Mon-Sat; 9am-6.30pm Sun & bank hols. *Winter* 9am-5pm Mon-Sat; 9am-5.30pm Sun & bank hols. **Admission** €5; free under-4s. **Credit** MC, V.

Located on the edge of the Bois de Vincennes, the main Paris zoo was founded in the 1930s and laid out with fake mountains, lakes and ditches to avoid

the use of cages where possible. Today it is in the midst of a huge transformation, creating a series of 'biozones' representing different ecosystems. In the interim the Grand Rocher is out of bounds, and some of the animals have been moved, but there are still plenty of acrobatic gibbons to keep children amused.

PERFORMING ARTS & SPORTS

Fairy tales, fables and folk stories are favourites at children's shows at the city's theatres and *café-théâtres* on Wednesday afternoons, at weekends and in the holidays. The varied programme at the **Théâtre Dunois** (7 rue Louise-Weiss, 13th, 01.45.84.72.00, www. theatredunois.org) is almost entirely geared towards children. For children's theatre in an unusual setting, the **Abricadabra Péniche-Antipod** (opposite 55 quai de Seine, 19th, 01.42.03.39.07, http://abricadabra.nerim. net, closed July, August) is a riverboat on the Canal de l'Ourcq with an appealing programme.

In general, children's films are dubbed into French, but you can see VO (*version originale*) screenings of the latest Hollywood hits at most venues across town. Keep a lookout for children's showings on Wednesdays and Saturday afternoons at the Cinémathèque Française and L'Ecran des Enfants (Oct-June 2.30pm Wed) at the Centre Pompidou. The IMAX cinema in La Villette's Géode will keep kids enthralled too.

Each winter, traditional circuses, complete with big cats, clowns and horses, pitch tent on the Pelouse de Reuilly or Bois de Boulogne; and the **Cirque Bouglione** (*see p283*) occupies the gorgeous Cirque d'Hiver with its annual extravaganza.

Waterbabies can choose between 35 public pools (www.paris.fr) including the floating **Piscine Josephine-Baker** (*see p341*), moored on the Seine and filled with purified water pumped from the river; the art nouveau Piscine de la Butte-aux-Cailles, with indoor and outdoor pools fed by artesian wells; and the recently restored Espace Sportif Pailleron, near Buttes-Chaumont, which has two pools and an ice rink (rollerskating in summer). At the indoor

ARTS & ENTERTAINMENT

Aquaboulevard (*see p340*), over-threes can splash down different slides and ride the waves (swimming hats are obligatory).

PARKS & THEME PARKS

Disneyland Paris/ Walt Disney Studios Park

Marne-la-Vallée (08.25.30.60.30/from UK 0870 503 0303/www.disneylandparis.com). 32km E of Paris. RER A or TGV Marne-la-Vallée-Chessy. By car, A4 exit 14. **Open** *Disneyland Paris* Sept-mid July 10am-8pm Mon-Fri; 9am-8pm Sat, Sun. Mid July-Aug 9am-11pm daily. *Studios Park* Winter 10am-6pm Mon-Fri; 9am-6pm Sat, Sun. Summer 9am-7pm daily. **Admission** 1 park €47; €39 reductions; free under-3s. 1-day hopper (both parks) €57; €49 reductions; free under-3s. Parking €8. **Credit** AmEx, MC, V.

Young ones will get a real kick out of Fantasyland, with its Alice maze, Sleeping Beauty's castle and teacup rides. Walt Disney Studios focuses on special effects and the tricks of the animation trade. *Photo p288.*

▶ *Disney's newest adrenalin ride, the Twilight Zone Tower of Terror, takes daredevils to the top of an old Hollywood hotel, then sends them plummeting down a 13-storey lift shaft.*

Jardin d'Acclimatation

Bois de Boulogne, 16th (01.40.67.90.82/www. jardindacclimatation.fr). M° Les Sablons. **Open** *May-Sept* 10am-7pm daily. *Oct-Apr* 10am-6pm daily. **Admission** €2.70; €1.35 reductions; free under-3s. **Credit** (€15 minimum) MC, V.

Founded in 1860, this amusement park and garden has bears, a Normandy-style farm and an aviary, as well as boat rides, a funfair with Chinese dragon rollercoaster, flying chairs, the Enchanted House for children aged two to four and two playgrounds. Older kids can visit the Explor@dome science and multimedia museum, steer radio-controlled boats or try out the mini car circuit and mini golf. The Musée en Herbe (01.40.67.97.66, www.musee-en-herbe.com, €4-€8) is a kids' museum that introduces under-12s to art and science. Many of the attractions cost €2.70 a go; others are free.

▶ *A miniature train runs from Porte Maillot through the Bois de Boulogne to the park entrance, and has space for pushchairs.*

INSIDE TRACK
WET WEDNESDAYS

On Wednesdays at 2.30pm, kiddies' cinema L'Ecran des Enfants, inside the **Centre Pompidou**, shows the best international children's cinema for five- to 13-year-olds (adults €3.50, kids €2).

Jardin du Luxembourg

Main access 2 rue Auguste Compte, 6th. M° Odéon/RER Luxembourg. **Open** summer 7.30am-dusk daily; winter 8am-dusk daily. **Map** p408 H8.

The 25-hectare park where an impoverished Ernest Hemingway staved off hunger by catching pigeons is a prized family attraction. Kids come from across the city for its pony rides, ice-cream stands, puppet shows, pedal karts, sandpits, metal swingboats and merry-go-round. The playground has an entrance fee but is more imaginative than most.

★ Parc Astérix

60128 Plailly (08.26.30.10.40/www.parcasterix. fr). 36km N of Paris. By coach from the Louvre or RER Roissy-Charles de Gaulle 1 (check website for times). By car, A1 exit Parc Astérix. **Open** *Apr-June* 10am-6pm daily. *July, Aug* 9.30am-7pm daily. *Sept-mid Nov* 10am-6pm Wed, Sat, Sun. Closed mid Nov-Mar except during Christmas hols. **Admission** €39; €27 reductions; free under-3s. Parking €7. **Credit** MC, V.

The park is split into Ancient Greece, the Roman Empire, the Land of the Vikings and the indomitable Gaulish Village. Thrill-seekers can defy gravity on Goudurix, Europe's largest rollercoaster, while younger kids get wet on the Grand Splatch log flume. For some serious handshaking, Astérix, Obélix and friends wander around and a jamboree of live acts pumps up the pace. The park's newest attraction is Le Défi de César, a virtual reality ride.

Parc des Buttes-Chaumont

Rue Botzaris, rue Manin, rue de Crimée, 19th. M° Buttes Chaumont. **Open** *Oct-Apr* 7am-8.15pm daily. *May, mid Aug-Sept* 7am-9.15pm daily. *June-mid Aug* 7am-10.15pm daily. **Map** p407 N2.

This area, which was formerly mined for gypsum, was turned into a sumptuous park under Napoleon III. Spectacular in every way (including the views over Paris), it is a family magnet with Punch and Judy stands, pony rides, sandpits, waterfalls, picnic and games areas and drinks stands.

★ Parc de la Villette

Av Corentin-Cariou, 19th (01.40.03.75.75/www. villette.com). M° Porte de la Villette. Av Jean-Jaurès, 19th. M° Porte de Pantin. **Map** p403 (insert).

Aside from a children's science museum, a music museum, an IMAX cinema, theatres, various concert and exhibition venues and outdoor seasonal festivals, the city's former abattoir district is made up of a succession of gardens and playgrounds for families to explore. Jardin des Voltiges has climbing ropes and balancing games, and the modern Jardin des Dunes et Vents has pedal windmills, waves of bouncy tubes and giant hamster wheels.

▶ *The little known Jardins Passagers (open after 3pm Apr-Sept) are a collection of gardens that teach children about flora and fauna.*

Dance

Take your seats for the ballet or perform your very own tango in Paris.

As befits its status as the self-styled capital of culture, Paris is home to a thriving dance scene, a rich programme of major international companies and home-grown talent. In 2009, the **Théâtre de la Ville** and **Théâtre National de Chaillot** will see the return of such luminaries as Pina Bausch and William Forsythe. There's no shortage of ballet productions at the **Théâtre du Châtelet** and **Palais Garnier**, with Frederick Ashton's delightful *La Fille Mal Gardée* on the bill in June 2009. And the **Festival d'Automne** will again feature an impressive line-up of innovative dance.

There's more of interest outside the centre of town. Now in its fifth year as the HQ for over 600 regional companies, the **Centre National de la Danse** in Pantin, reaches out to its audience with a well-devised series of performances, and smaller dance 'laboratories' such as Ménagerie de Verre and Regard du Cygne showcase new work by smaller companies. Dance centres and festivals in the *banlieue* are also determined to draw audiences to their suburban locations, with a distinct mix of styles and cultures.

ARTS & ENTERTAINMENT

INFORMATION AND RESOURCES

For listings, *see Pariscope* and *L'Officiel des Spectacles*. For events coverage, look out for two monthlies: *La Terrasse* (distributed free at major dance venues) and the glossy *Danser*.

For shoes and equipment, **Sansha** (52 rue de Clichy, 9th, 01.45.26.01.38, www.sansha.com) has a good reputation, and **Repetto** (22 rue de la Paix, 2nd, 01.44.71.83.06, www.repetto.com) supplies the Opéra with pointes and slippers; **Menkes** (12 rue Rambuteau, 3rd, 01.40.27.91.81, www.menkes.es) sells serious flamenco gear as well as outsize glam-rock boots.

FESTIVALS

The year starts with **Faits d'Hiver** (01.42. 74.46.00, www.faitsdhiver.com) and hip hop festival **Suresnes Cité Danse** (01.46.97. 98.10, www.theatre-suresnes.fr) in January. May and June bring with them the **Rencontres Chorégraphiques de Seine-St-Denis** (01.55.82.08.10, www.rencontres choregraphiques.com), the **IRCAM Agora** festival (01.44.78.12.40, www.ircam.fr) and **Onze Bouge** (01.53.27.13.68, www.

festivalonze.org). The **Rencontres de la Villette** (01.40.03.75.75, www.rencontres villette.com) dishes up street dance at various suburban locations every October. You'll also find smaller dance festivals at the **Maison des Arts de Créteil**, and at the **Ménagerie de Verre** in the 11th. *See also pp274-279* **Calendar**.

Les Etés de la Danse

Grand Palais, av Winston Churchill, 8th (01.42.68.22.14/www.lesetesdeladanse.com). M° Champs-Elysées Clemenceau. **Date** late July-early Aug.

Founded in 2005, this festival *(photo above)* puts the spotlight on one company or choreographer, with a month of performances in the Grand Palais. Shows are accompanied by workshops and activities.

★ Festival d'Automne

Information: 156 rue de Rivoli, 1st (01.53.45.17.00/www.festival-automne.com). **Date** *mid Sept-late Dec.*

For 35 years, the Festival d'Automne has shown the way forward in the performing arts. With a focus on leading French experimental companies, the festival also invites big-name choreographers from around the world.

THE BEST
SPECIALIST STAGES

For tutu classics
Palais Garnier. See p292.

For alternative dance
Regard du Cygne. See p293.

For a raggajam refresher
Studio Harmonic. See p293.

Paris quartier d'été

01.44.94.98.00/www.quartierdete.com.
Date mid July-mid Aug.
With 60,000 visitors in 2008, this popular festival features eclectic programmes and free outdoor performances in Paris and its outskirts. Public rehearsals and talks give audiences the chance to meet prestigious international choreographers.

MAJOR DANCE VENUES

Centre National de la Danse

1 rue Victor-Hugo, 93507 Pantin (01.41.83.27.27/box office 01.41.83.98.98/ www.cnd.fr). *M° Hoche/RER Pantin.* **Open** *Box office* 10am-7pm Mon-Fri. **Admission** €6-€14. **Credit** AmEx, MC, V.
This centre first opened in 2004, with the mission to bridge the divide between stage and spectator. It invites audiences to its quarterly 'Grandes leçons de danse', contemporary dance master classes. It also offers an expertly curated selection of performances presented in the studios, exhibitions, and a phenomenal archive of films and choreographic material.

Maison des Arts de Créteil

Pl Salvador-Allende, 94000 Créteil (01.45.13.19.19/www.maccreteil.com). *M° Créteil-Préfecture.* **Open** *Box office* 1-7pm Tue-Sat. Closed mid July-Aug. **Admission** €8-€30. **Credit** MC, V.
This suburban arts centre has an eclectic programme of contemporary performances. One to watch is the Bill T Jones/Arnie Zane Dance Company, which made a splash in the 2008 season with *Chapel/Chapter*. Don't miss the International Exit Festival.

★ Palais Garnier

Pl de l'Opéra, 9th (08.92.89.90.90/from abroad 01.72.29.35.35/www.opera-de-paris.fr). *M° Opéra.* **Open** *Box office* 10.30am-6.30pm Mon-Sat. *Telephone bookings* 9am-6pm Mon-Fri, 9am-1pm Sat. Closed 15 July-end Aug. **Admission** €7-€172; €5 reductions (90mins before show). **Credit** AmEx, MC, V. **Map** p401 G4.
The Ballet de l'Opéra National de Paris manages to tread successfully between classics and new productions, between the Opéra Bastille and lavish Palais Garnier. The New York City Ballet performed in 2008, and Frederick Ashton's *La Fille Mal Gardée* takes to the stage in 2009.

Théâtre du Châtelet

1 pl du Châtelet, 1st (01.40.28.28.00/www. chatelet-theatre.com). *M° Châtelet.* **Open** *Box office* July, Aug 1-6pm daily. Sept-June 11am-

Théâtre de la Ville.

7pm daily. **Admission** €10-€95. **Credit** AmEx, MC, V. **Map** p402 J6.

This classical music institution is strengthening its reputation in other live artistic disciplines. The new dance season will treat Paris audiences to performances by two mammoth American companies. The Martha Graham company will present two programmes revisiting some of Graham's core pieces, and a selection of work by Alvin Aley will celebrate the company's 50th birthday in July 2009.

Théâtre National de Chaillot

1 pl du Trocadéro, 16th (01.53.65.30.00/www. theatre-chaillot.fr). M° Trocadéro. **Open** *Box office* 11am-7pm Mon-Sat; 1-5pm Sun. *Phone bookings* 11am-7pm Mon-Sat. Closed July, Aug. **Admission** €27-€33; €12-€27 reductions. **Credit** MC, V. **Map** p400 C5.

The 2009 dance programme at Chaillot opens with Jean Montalvo and Dominique Hervieux. Russell Maliphant and Wayne McGregor's Random Dance will lead the March line-up.

★ Théâtre de la Ville

2 pl du Châtelet, 4th (01.42.74.22.77/ www.theatredelaville-paris.com). M° Châtelet. **Open** *Box office* 11am-8pm Mon-Sat. *Telephone bookings* 11am-7pm Mon-Sat. Closed July, Aug. **Admission** €12-€23; €12 reductions. **Credit** MC, V. **Map** p406 J6.

This leading venue has nurtured long-standing collaborations with international choreographers. The 2009 programme will see performances by the likes of Sasha Waltz, Sidi Larbi Cherkaoui and Anne Teresa De Keersmaeker.

▶ *Some performances take place at sister venue Théâtre des Abbesses (31 rue des Abbesses, 18th).*

OTHER DANCE VENUES

L'Etoile du Nord

16 rue Georgette-Agutte, 18th (01.42.26.47.47/ www.etoiledunord-theatre.com). M° Guy Môquet. **Open** *Box office* 2-6pm Mon-Fri. Closed July, Aug. **Admission** €19; €10-€14 reductions. **Credit** V.

This smaller venue splits its programme between theatre and contemporary multimedia dance. The Avis de Turbulences festival (end May-mid June) features a decent selection of mixed bills.

Ménagerie de Verre

12-14 rue Léchevin, 11th (01.43.38.33.44/www. menagerie-de-verre.org). M° Parmentier. **Open** *Box office* 10am-7pm Mon-Fri. Closed July, Aug. **Admission** €13; €10 reductions. **No credit cards**. **Map** p403 N5.

This multidisciplinary hothouse is rooted in the avant-garde, with contemporary dance and classes given by a succession of guest teachers.

★ Regard du Cygne

210 rue de Belleville, 20th (01.43.58.55.93/ bookings 09.71.34.23.50/www.leregarducygne. com). M° Télégraphe. **Open** *Box office* 1hr before show. Closed Aug. **Admission** €6-€15. **No credit cards**. **Map** p403 Q3.

This pared-down studio in Belleville is a great place to get a taste of the alternative dance scene.

▶ *The Spectacles Sauvages nights allow unknowns to show a ten-minute piece to the public.*

Théâtre de la Bastille

76 rue de la Roquette, 11th (01.43.57.42.14/ www.theatre-bastille.com). M° Bastille or Voltaire. **Open** *Box office* 10am-6pm Mon-Fri; 2-6pm Sat. Closed July, Aug. **Admission** €13-€20. **Credit** MC, V. **Map** p407 M6.

This small theatre showcases innovative contemporary dance and drama pieces. Worth checking out in April 2009 is Mark Tompkins' Lulu.

DANCE CLASSES

Dance classes are available to suit all tastes and levels. The open-air dancing on the banks of the Seine is particularly popular in summer.

Centre de Danse du Marais

41 rue du Temple, 4th (01.42.72.15.42/ 08.92.68.68.70/www.parisdanse.com). M° Hôtel de Ville or Rambuteau. **Open** 9am-9pm Mon-Fri; 9am-8pm Sat; 9am-7pm Sun. **Classes** €18. **Map** p402 K5.

There's a huge choice of classes here, with big-name teachers such as belly dance star Leila Haddad and ballet's Casati-Lazzarelli team. The five-class 'sampler' pass is a good deal at €68.

★ Studio Harmonic

5 passage des Taillandiers, 11th (01.48.07.13.39/ www.studioharmonic.fr). M° Bastille. **Open** *Office* 10am-5pm Mon-Fri. *Classes* 9.30am-10pm Mon-Fri; 9am-7.30pm Sat. Closed 3wks Aug. **Classes** €15-€16. **Map** p407 M7.

The rising star among Paris's dance schools. Studio Harmonic's claims to fame are teacher Laure Courtellemont and her trademark raggajam, a blend of hip hop and Afro-Caribbean dance.

INSIDE TRACK
DANCE BY THE SEINE

From May to September, the amphitheatres of the Seine-side **Jardin Tino Rossi** (5th) fill up with salsa, rock, tango, Irish, hip hop and just about any other dance form you can think of. Informal classes are held around 7pm or 8pm, then the *bal* begins.

Film

Good things happen after the lights go down.

The city that held the world's first public film screening still has a passion for the movies. More tickets per capita are bought here than anywhere else in Europe, and, in any given week, there's a choice of around 350 flicks – not counting festivals. New cinemas are added all the time; although they tend to be multiplexes (the next big addition is MK2's 14-screen behemoth in the 19th, due for completion in 2012), the old-fashioned *art et essai* venues that did so much to teach the likes of Truffaut and Tavernier about film after World War II, are – just – managing to get by.

MOVIEGOING IN PARIS

Happily, the rise of the multiplex hasn't meant a reduction in the choice and variety of films on offer. In Paris, multiplexes regularly show films from Eastern Europe, Asia and South America, and countless independent cinemas continue to screen a hugely eclectic assortment of cult, classic and just plain obscure films. As well as retrospectives and cut-price promotions, there are often visits from directors and stasr.

Local interest is strong enough to sustain several monthly movie magazines, and there's even a book fair, the **Salon du Livre, des Revues et du DVD de Cinéma**, devoted to writing on film. Launched in 2007, the annual **Salon du Cinéma** gives film buffs a chance to visit mocked-up movie sets and meet world-renowned directors and actors. Finally, French DVD labels produce some of the most expertly curated discs in the world. At **Fnac** and **Virgin Megastore** (for both, *see p271*), you're more than likely to find American and British titles otherwise unavailable in the US or UK.

INFORMATION AND TICKETS

New releases hit the screens on Wednesdays. Hollywood is well represented, of course, but Paris audiences have a balanced cinematic diet that satisfies their appetite for international films as well as shorts and documentaries. On top of this there are the 150-plus annual releases funded or part-funded with French money (the French film industry is still the world's third largest, after the US and India).

For venues, times and prices, consult one of the city's two main weekly listings magazines:

L'Officiel des Spectacles and *Pariscope. Films nouveaux* are new releases, *Exclusivités* are the also-showing titles, and *Reprises* means rep. For non-francophone flicks, look out for two letters somewhere near the title: VO (*version originale*) means a screening in the original language with French subtitles; VF (*version française*) means that it has been dubbed into French.

Buy tickets in the usual way at the cinema – for new blockbusters, especially at multiplexes, it pays to buy tickets at least one screening in advance. You can also phone **AlloCiné** (08.92.89.28.92, www.allocine.fr). Online booking may entail a booking fee. Seats are often discounted by 20 to 30 per cent at Monday or Wednesday screenings, and the Mairie sponsors cut-price promotions at cinemas throughout the year.

If you're in town for longer than a couple of weeks, you might want to pick up a *carte illimitée*, a season ticket that allows unlimited viewing: every multiplex chain offers one.

CINEMAS
Giant screens & multiplexes

La Géode
26 av Corentin-Cariou, 19th (08.92.68.45.40/ www.lageode.fr). Mº Porte de la Villette. **Admission** €10.50; €9 under-25s. **Credit** MC, V. **Map** p403 inset.

The IMAX cinema at the Cité des Sciences occupies a shiny geodesic sphere. The vast hemispheric screen lets you experience 3D plunges through natural scenery, and animated adventures where figures zoom out to grab you.

★ Le Grand Rex

1 bd Poissonnière, 2nd (08.92.68.05.96/
www.legrandrex.com). M° Bonne Nouvelle.
Admission €7-€8.50; €5.50-€6.90 students,
over-60s, under-12s. *Les Etoiles du Rex*
tour €9.80; €8 under-12s. **Credit** MC, V.
Map p402 J4.

With its wedding-cake exterior, fairy-tale interior
and the largest auditorium in Europe (2,750 seats),
this is one of the few cinemas to upstage whatever
it screens: no wonder it's a listed historic monument.
Its blockbuster programming (usually in French) is
suited to its vast, roll-down screen; it also hosts concerts and rowdy all-night compilation events. There
are six smaller screens too.

▶ *The Etoiles du Rex tour is a 50-minute,*
SFX-laden taste of movie magic.

Max Linder Panorama

24 bd Poissonnière, 9th (01.48.24.00.47/
www.maxlinder.com). M° Grands Boulevards.
Admission €8.50; €6.50 Mon, Wed, Fri, students
(except weekends), under-12s. **Credit** MC, V.
Map p402 J4.

This state-of-the-art cinema, with THX surround
sound and an 18m (60ft) screen, is named after the
dapper French silent comedian who owned it
between 1914 and 1925. The walls and 700 seats
are all black to prevent even the tiniest twinkle of
reflected light distracting the audience from what's
happening on the screen. Look for all-nighters and
one-off showings of rare vintage films or piano-
accompanied silents.

★ MK2 Bibliothèque

128-162 av de France, 13th (08.92.69.84.84/
www.mk2.com). M° Bibliothèque François
Mitterrand or Quai de la Gare. **Admission**
€9.80; €6.80 students and over-60s (except
weekends); €5.90 under-18s; €19.80 monthly
pass. **Credit** MC, V. **Map** p407 M10.

The MK2 chain's flagship offers an all-in-one
night out: 14 screens, three restaurants, a bar open
until 5am at weekends and two-person 'love seats'.
A paragon of imaginative programming, MK2 is
growing all the time; it has added ten more venues
in town, including two situated along the Bassin de
la Villette with decent waterside cafés attached. For
details of the Illimité season ticket, *see below* UGC
Ciné Cité Bercy.

UGC Ciné Cité Bercy

2 cour St-Emilion, 12th (08.92.70.00.00/
www.ugc. fr). M° Cour St-Emilion. **Admission**
€9.90; €6.50 students, over-60s (except Sat
& Sun before 7pm); €5.90 under-18s; €19.80
monthly pass. **Credit** MC, V. **Map** p407 P10.

This ambitious 18-screen development screens art
movies and mainstream fodder, and hosts regular
meet-the-director events. The 19-screen UGC Ciné
Cité Les Halles (7 pl de la Rotonde, Nouveau Forum
des Halles, 1st, 08.92.70.00.00) serves the same mix.

▶ *For €19.80 a month, the UGC/MK2 Illimité*
card offers film buffs unlimited screenings at any
UGC or MK2 venue, as well as some independents.
Also now available, at €35 a month, is the Illimité
2 card, which is valid for two people.

Le Grand Rex.

ARTS & ENTERTAINMENT

Le Balzac.

Showcases

Auditorium du Louvre

*Musée du Louvre, 99 rue de Rivoli, 1st
(01.40.20.55.55/www.louvre.fr). M° Palais Royal
Musée du Louvre.* **Admission** €9; €4 under-26s;
free under-18s. **Credit** MC, V. **Map** p402 H5.
This 420-seat auditorium was designed by IM Pei,
as part of the Mitterand-inspired renovation of the
Louvre. Film screenings are often related to the exhibitions; silent movies with live music are regulars.

Centre Pompidou

*Rue St-Martin, 4th (01.44.78.12.33/www.
centrepompidou.fr). M° Hôtel de Ville or
Rambuteau.* **Admission** €6; €4 students.
Credit MC, V. **Map** p406 K6.
The varied programme here features themed series,
experimental and artists' films, and a weekly docu-
mentary session. This is also the venue for the
Cinéma du Réel festival in March (www.cinereel.org).

Le Cinéma des Cinéastes

*7 av de Clichy, 17th (08.92.68.97.17/
www.cinema-des-cineastes.fr). M° Place de Clichy.*
Admission €8.70; €6.90 students, under-12s,
over-60s. **Credit** MC, V. **Map** p401 G2.
Done out to evoke the studios of old, this three-
screen showcase of world cinema holds meet-the-
director sessions and festivals of classic, foreign, gay
and documentary films. Also offers a monthly pass.

★ La Cinémathèque Française

*51 rue de Bercy, 12th (01.71.19.33.33/www.
cinematheque.fr). M° Bercy.* **Admission**
Exhibitions €2.50-€9. *Films* €6; €5 students, 13s-
18s; €3 under-12s; free for members. *Membership*
€10/month. **Credit** MC, V. **Map** p407 N9.
Relocated to Frank Gehry's striking, spacious cubist
building, the Cinémathèque Française now boasts
four screens, a bookshop, a restaurant, exhibition
space and the Musée du Cinéma, where it displays a
fraction of its huge collection of movie memorabilia.
In the spirit of its founder Henri Langlois, the
Cinémathèque hosts retrospectives, cult movies, classics, experimental cinema and Q&A sessions.

Forum des Images

*2 Grande Galerie, Porte St-Eustache, Forum
des Halles, 1st (01.44.76.63.00/www.forum
desimages. net). M° Les Halles.* **Open** 1-9pm Tue-
Sun. Closed 2wks Aug. **Admission** (per day)
€5.50; €4.50 students, under-26s. Membership
available. **Credit** AmEx, MC, V. **Map** p402 J5.
See p298 **French for Film**.

Arthouses

Accattone

*20 rue Cujas, 5th (01.46.33.86.86). M° Cluny La
Sorbonne/RER Luxembourg.* **Admission** €7; €6
Wed, students, under-20s (except Fri nights and
weekends). **No credit cards. Map** p408 J8.

Named after Pasolini's first film, this tiny Latin Quarter cinema has a clear preference for old Italian arthouse. That said, there's still plenty of room on the rolling weekly programme for the likes of Buñuel, Oshima, Roeg and Ken Russell. In the 1960s the cinema was managed by François Truffaut.

Action

Action Christine *4 rue Christine, 6th (01.43.225.85.78/www.actioncinemas.com). M°* *Odéon or St-Michel.* **Admission** €8; €6 students, under-20s. **No credit cards. Map** p408 J7.
Action Ecoles *23 rue des Ecoles, 5th (01.43.25.72.07). M° Maubert Mutualité.* **Admission** €8; €6 students, under-20s. **No credit cards. Map** p408 J8.
Grand Action *5 rue des Ecoles, 5th (01.43.54.47.62/www.legrandaction.com). M° Cardinal Lemoine.* **Admission** €8; €6.50 students, under-20s. **No credit cards. Map** p406 K8.
A Left Bank stalwart, the Action group is renowned for screening new prints of old movies. It's heaven for anyone who's nostalgic for Tinseltown classics and quality US independents.

★ Le Balzac

1 rue Balzac, 8th (01.45.61.10.60/www.cinema balzac.com). M° George V. **Admission** €9; €7 Mon, Wed, students, under-18s, over-60s; €5 under-12s. **No credit cards. Map** p400 D4.
Built in 1935 and boasting a mock ocean-liner foyer, Le Balzac scores highly for design and programming. Jean-Jacques Schpoliansky, the manager, is often found welcoming punters in person at the start of each screening. The Balzac awards prizes according to audience votes.

Le Champo

51 rue des Ecoles, 5th (01.43.54.51.60/www. lechampo.com). M° Cluny La Sorbonne or Odéon. **Admission** €7.50; €6 Wed, last screening Sun, lunchtime matinées, students, under-20s. **No credit cards. Map** p408 J7.
The two-screen Champo has been in operation for nearly seven decades, a venerable past recognised in 2000 when it was given historic monument status. In the 1960s it was a favourite haunt of *nouvelle vague* directors such as Claude Chabrol.

Le Cinéma du Panthéon

13 rue Victor-Cousin, 5th (01.40.46.01.21/ www.whynotproductions.fr/pantheon). RER Luxembourg. **Admission** €7; €5.50 Mon, Wed, students, 13-18s; €4 under-13s. **Credit** MC, V. **Map** p408 J8.
To celebrate its centenary in 2007, the city's oldest surviving movie house opened a tea room with interior design by Catherine Deneuve. It continues to screen new, often obscure international films and hosts meet-the-director nights and discussions.

★ Le Denfert

24 pl Denfert-Rochereau, 14th (01.43.21.41.01/ www.allocine.fr). M° Denfert Rochereau/RER Denfert Rochereau. **Admission** €6.50; €5 Mon, Wed, students, over-60s; €4.60 under-15s. **No credit cards. Map** p405 H10.
This charming little cinema offers a nicely eclectic repertory selection that ranges from François Ozon and Hayao Miyazaki to shorts and animation, as well as new-release foreign films.

L'Entrepôt

7-9 rue Francis-de-Pressensé, 14th (01.45.40.07.50/www.lentrepot.fr). M° Pernety or Plaisance. **Admission** €7; €5.60 students, over-60s; €4 under-12s. **No credit cards. Map** p405 F10.
A diverse array of documentaries, shorts, gay cinema and productions from developing nations are more common here than mainstream stuff.

Images d'Ailleurs

21 rue de la Clef, 5th (01.45.87.18.09). M° Censier Daubenton. **Admission** €6; €5.50 concessions; €4.70 under-12s, for all Mon. **No credit cards. Map** 406 K9.
Opened back in 1990, the Images d'Ailleurs cinema focuses on cinematic works from Africa and other rare movie treats.

Le Latina

20 rue du Temple, 4th (01.42.78.47.86/www. lelatina.com). M° Hôtel de Ville. **Admission** €8; €6.50 Mon, Tue, students, under-20s. **No credit cards. Map** p406 K6.
The exciting programming at this flag-bearer for Latin cultures runs the gamut from Argentinian to Romanian films. Latin dance features at the €17 film-dinner-dancing deals on Monday and Wednesday evenings.

INSIDE TRACK
TUBE TALES

The métro is, perhaps unsurprisingly, a popular Paris film location. These days, nearly all métro scenes in movies and advertising are shot in a disused station on line 3bis, **Porte des Lilas – Cinéma**, which is kept in working order by the RATP and hired out to production companies. It's currently open to the public only for the **Journées du Patrimoine** (*see p277*), but the Paris authorities are studying a proposal to dig a new tunnel linking line 3bis and 7bis, which would see Porte des Lilas – Cinéma returned to active transport duty in 2013.

ARTS & ENTERTAINMENT

Le Mac Mahon

5 av Mac-Mahon, 17th (01.43.80.24.81/www. cinemamacmahon.com). M° Charles de Gaulle Etoile. **Admission** €6.50; €4.50 students. **No credit cards. Map** p400 C3.

This single-screen, 1930s-era cinema has changed little since its 1960s heyday (tickets are still, delightfully, of the tear-off variety), when its all-American programming fostered the label '*mac-mahonisme*' among the buffs who haunted the place. Americana still makes up the bulk of what's on the screen.

★ La Pagode

57bis rue de Babylone, 7th (01.45.55.48.48). M° St-François-Xavier. **Admission** €8; €6.50 Mon, Wed, students, under-21s. **No credit cards. Map** p405 F7.

This glorious edifice is not, as local legend might have it, a block-by-block import, but a 19th-century replica of a pagoda by a French architect. Renovated in the late 1990s, this is one of the loveliest cinemas in the world.

Studio 28

10 rue Tholozé, 18th (01.46.06.36.07/www. cinemastudio28.com). M° Abbesses or Blanche. **Admission** €7.50; €6.30 students, under-18s. **No credit cards. Map** p401 H1.

Studio 28 was the venue for the first screening of Buñuel's scandalous *L'Age d'Or*, and this historic cinema also features in the more heartwarming *Amélie*. It offers a decent repertory mixture of classics and recent movies, complete with Dolby sound and a rather civilised bar for a pre- or post-screening tipple.

Studio Galande

42 rue Galande, 5th (01.43.54.72.71/www.studio galande.fr). M° Cluny La Sorbonne or St-Michel. **Admission** €7.80; €6 Wed, students. **No credit cards. Map** p408 J7.

Some 20 different films are screened in subtitled versions at this venerable Latin Quarter venue every week: international arthouse fare, combined with the occasional instalment from the *Matrix* series.

▶ *On Fridays and Saturdays, fans of The Rocky Horror Picture Show turn up in drag, equipped with rice and water pistols.*

FESTIVALS & EVENTS

The city plays host to a range of film festivals, some of them free, some taking place outdoors. *See also pp274-279* **Calendar**.

★ Salon du Cinéma

Parc des expos, Porte de Versailles, 15th (www.salonducinema.com). M° Porte de Versailles. **Date** Jan.

This event features behind-the-scenes reconstructions of movie sets, allowing the public to watch the work of make-up artists, cameramen and stuntmen.

Festival International de Films de Femmes

Maison des Arts, pl Salvador-Allende, 94040 Créteil (01.49.80.38.98/www.filmsdefemmes. com). M° Créteil-Préfecture. **Date** Mar.

A selection of retrospectives and new international films by female directors. The festival celebrated its 30th birthday in 2008.

French for Film

The Forum des Images returns home.

After three years of taking its eclectic film programming *hors les murs*, the hyperactive **Forum des Images** (*see p296*) resumed activities in its proper home in December 2008. A major facelift has given this cinephile's paradise a new, more open layout that makes it easier to move between the different spaces: five cinemas, bar, library and research centre.

Opened in 1988, the Forum was conceived partly as a screening venue for old and little known movies, and partly as an archive centre for every kind of moving picture featuring Paris; today the collection numbers over 6,500 documentaries, adverts, newsreels and films, from the work of the Lumière brothers to 21st-century reportage. They have all been painstakingly digitised.

The most exciting new addition is the Bibliothèque du Cinéma François-Truffaut, a public library where cinema buffs can consult and borrow film-related books, magazines, DVDs and CDs. Furthermore, the Forum's new glass-fronted entrance hall will give it greater visibility on rue du Cinéma, the new name given to the passage in the Forum des Halles that has the Forum des Images at one end and the UGC multiscreen complex at the other. Visitors can choose between blockbusters at the UGC and the Forum's programme of thought-provoking film cycles and wacky festivals: the Forum hosts Les Rencontres, the trash treats of L'Etrange Festival, films fresh from Cannes, and Pocket Films, a festival of films shot entirely on mobile phones.

ARTS & ENTERTAINMENT

Printemps du Cinéma
Various venues (www.printempsducinema.com).
Date Mar.
Three days of bargain €3.50-entry films at cinemas all across Paris.

Côté Court
Ciné 104, 104 av Jean-Lolive, 93500 Pantin (01.48.46.95.08/www.cotecourt.org). M° Eglise de Pantin. **Date** June.
A great selection of new and old short films shown at Ciné 104 and a handful of neighbouring venues.

Paris Cinéma
Various venues (01.55.25.55.25/www.paris cinema.org). **Date** July.
A programme of shorts and documentaries sponsored by the Mairie.

★ Cinéma au Clair de Lune
Various venues (01.44.76.63.00/www.forum desimages.net). **Date** Aug.
Night-time films on giant open-air screens in squares and public gardens around town: a party atmosphere is guaranteed.

3 Jours/3 Euros
All cinemas throughout Paris (www.paris.fr/ fr/culture/missioncinema). **Date** Aug.
This Mairie-sponsored promotion is timed to start getting kids into cinemas before the schools go back. For three days, every screening costs just €3.

★ L'Etrange Festival
Forum des Images (06.60.21.57.57/www.etrange festival.com). **Date** Sept. **Map** p404 J5.
Explicit sex, gore and weirdness in the screenings and 'happenings' at this annual feast of all things unconventional draw large crowds.

Salon du Livre, des Revues et du DVD de Cinéma
Cinémathèque Française, 51 rue de Bercy, 12th (www.cinemathequefrancaise.com). M° Bercy.
Date Oct. **Map** p407 N9.
European publishers of cinema-related books sell their wares; there are also round-table discussions and a chance to meet filmmakers.

Les Rencontres
Forum des Images (see p296). **Date** Nov, Dec.
Map p404 J5.
A global choice of new independent features, documentaries and short films.

BOOKSHOPS

Cinédoc
45-53 passage Jouffroy, 9th (01.48.24.71.36/ www.cine-doc.fr). M° Grands Boulevards. **Open** 10am-7pm Mon-Sat. **Credit** V. **Map** p402 J4.

Marcel Carné.

Finding what you're looking for isn't easy in this narrow bookshop. Ask the staff or take pot luck among the old photos, film magazines and books.

Ciné Reflet
14 rue Monsieur le Prince, 6th (01.40.46.02.72). M° Odéon. **Open** 1-8pm Mon-Sat; 3-7pm Sun.
Credit MC, V. **Map** p408 H7.
This sprawling shop is well stocked with old photos, posters, and new and second-hand books. The strong English-language selection includes the *Time Out Film Guide* and magazines like *Sight & Sound*.

★ Contacts
14 rue St-Sulpice, 6th (01.43.59.17.71/www. medialibrairie.com). M° Odéon. **Open** 10am-7pm Mon-Sat. **Credit** MC, V. **Map** p408 H7.
Truffaut's favourite *librairie* has been selling books on film for over 40 years. The stock is well organised, with a large and up-to-date selection of English-language titles. You'll also find *Film Comment* and *American Cinematographer*, plus a few videos.

Scaramouche
161 rue St-Martin, 3rd (01.48.87.78.58). M° Rambuteau. **Open** 11.30am-1pm, 2-8pm Mon-Sat. **Credit** MC, V. **Map** p402 K5.
This large-ish shop covers cinema and *gestuelle* (mime and puppetry). The film section includes a wide range of titles in English, plus a huge collection of publicity photos and portraits.

ARTS & ENTERTAINMENT

Galleries

The art of going global.

However patriotic the French may be when it comes to cuisine or idiomatic purity, they're wildly and enthusiastically international when it comes to contemporary art and design. In a world where artists use ever media imaginable, and travel to all corners of the globe to exhibit, Paris is as good a place as any to catch up on what's happening in the American and Asian art scenes as it is to discover artists emerging from eastern Europe. However, it's not just about the visiting talent: there are also plenty of noteworthy local artists here, working in a variety of genres.

GALLERIES IN PARIS

The commercial gallery scene is principally centred around the Marais. Essential stops include the immaculate **Galerie Emmanuel Perrotin** and **Yvon Lambert** for big international names, and **Chez Valentin** for witty conceptual projects. At the new **Espace Claude Berri** (www.espace-claudeberri.com), set up by the renowned film director, exhibitions of work from Berri's private collection will alternate with solo shows. Emerging artists can be found at **FAT Galeri**e and **Galerie Michel Rein**, and across the river in St-Germain-des-Prés, where **Galerie Kamel Mennour** and **in situ Fabienne Leclerc** occupy impressive new premises. There's also a number of galleries specialising in modern design (*see p304* **House Beautiful**).

In the 13th arrondissement, the area around rue Louise-Weiss has never quite fulfilled its promise of becoming Paris's Chelsea: spaces are too small and quality too varied. Even so, **Air de Paris** and **Art:Concept** are usually worth a look. At the opposite end of the spectrum, the Champs-Elysées area is home to a handful of galleries presenting big bankable names, among more classic *antiquaires* and early 20th-century art.

The **Galeries Mode d'Emploi** leaflet (also online at www.fondation-entreprise-ricard.com) provides detailed weekly listings, as does **www.paris-art.com**. At *vernissage* time, usually Saturday evenings, the city's artists, collectors, critics and curators do the rounds of what's opening. Most galleries close from mid July to late August and at Christmas.

Prix Marcel DuChamp

Conceived in 2000 by collectors' association the ADIAF and designed to raise the profile (and, no doubt, the profits) of the French art scene, the Prix Marcel Duchamp may have failed to create anything like the media frenzy of the Turner Prize, its British equivalent, but it does provide a pretty good survey of the mid-career scene. Past winners of the prize have included Thomas Hirschhorn, Dominique Gonzalez Foerster, Mathieu Mercier, Carole Benzaken, Claude Closky, Philippe Mayaux and Tatiana Trouvé; and the 2008 shortlist – Michel Blazy, Stéphane Calais, Laurent Grasso and Didier Marcel – features a group of individual practitioners working in media that range from film installation and computer imagery to painting and drawing.

The initial shortlist is presented at the **FIAC** art fair (*see p278*) in October. The winner, chosen by a jury of international critics and museum curators, wins €35,000 and a prestigious solo show at the Centre Pompidou the following summer.

BEAUBOURG & THE MARAIS

FAT Galerie
1 rue Dupetit-Thouars, 3rd (01.44.54.00.84/ www.fatgalerie.com). M° Temple. **Open** 11am-7pm Tue-Sat. **Map** p409 L5.
Making their mark in the cluster of new galleries in the Haut Marais, Aurélia Lanson and Séverine van Warsch combine shows by emerging artists – wall drawings by Cyprien Chabert, painter Lili Phung – with the pick of upcoming designers.

★ Galerie Alain Gutharc
*7 rue St-Claude, 3rd (01.47.00.32.10/www.
alaingutharc.com). Mº St-Sébastien Froissart.*
Open 2-7pm Tue-Fri; 11am-1pm, 2-7pm Sat.
Map p409 L6.
The last of the Bastille galleries has now moved
to the Marais. Gutharc talent-spots young French
artists, often giving them a first gallery show, and
also presents an annual art-design crossover.
Among recent discoveries, check out the dreamily
surreal paintings of Marlène Mocquet.

Galerie Almine Rech
*19 rue de Saintonge, 3rd (01.45.83.71.90/
www.galeriealminerech.com). Mº Filles
du Calvaire.* **Open** 11am-7pm Tue-Sat.
Map p409 L5.
Continuing the rue Louise Weiss exodus, Almine
Rech has returned to the Marais. Spread over two
floors, her new gallery has more of an apartment
feel in which to show off big international names.
Among regulars are light installations by James
Turrell, neo-minimalists John McCracken and
Anselm Reyle, and powerful films by French artist
Ange Leccia.

Galerie Anne de Villepoix
*43 rue de Montmorency, 3rd (01.42.78.32.24/
www.annedevillepoix.com). Mº Rambuteau.*
Open 10am-7pm Mon-Sat. **Map** p402 K5.
As well as pieces by such international names as
Doug Aitken and Erwin Wurm, Galerie Anne de
Villepoix features distinctive and varied talents on
the French scene, such as the bravura monochrome
paintings by Ming, witty conceptual pieces by Franck
Scurti and a politically loaded take on art history
by Kader Attia.

Galerie Chantal Crousel
*10 rue Charlot, 3rd (01.42.77.38.87/www.
crousel.com). Mº Filles du Calvaire.* **Open**
11am-1pm, 2-7pm Tue-Sat. **Map** p409 L5.
Crousel celebrated the 25th anniversary of her
gallery in 2005 with a move to this space in rue
Charlot's burgeoning design and fashion scene. She
was the first in France to show work by Mona
Hatoum and Tony Cragg. Hot younger talents
include Rikrit Tiravanija and Thomas Hirschhorn,
as well as Anri Sala and Melik Ohanian, two of
France's most exciting video artists.

★ Galerie Chez Valentin
*9 rue St-Gilles, 3rd (01.48.87.42.55/www.
galeriechezvalentin.com). Mº Chemin Vert.*
Open 11am-1pm, 2-7pm Tue-Sat. **Map** p409 L6.
Chez Valentin is a gallery at the experimental cutting edge, and shows here tend to be radically conceptual but often fun: look for pseudo-documentaries
by video-maker Laurent Grasso, photos by Nicolas
Moulin, installations by Pierre Ardouin and projects
by 2003 Prix Duchamp winner Mathieu Mercier.

Galerie Daniel Templon
*30 rue Beaubourg, 3rd (01.42.72.14.10/
www.danieltemplon.com). Mº Rambuteau.*
Open 10am-7pm Mon-Sat. **Map** p402 K5.
A Paris institution since the '60s and conveniently
located opposite the Centre Pompidou, Galerie T is
a favourite with the art establishment. It mainly
shows paintings – wall-friendly items for wealthy
private collectors. Jean-Michel Alberola, Gérard
Garouste, Philippe Cognée and Vincent Corpet all
feature on the list, along with the American David
Salle and German expressionist Jonathan Meese.

★ Galerie Dominique Fiat
*16 rue des Coutures-St-Gervais, 3rd
(01.40.29.98.80/www.galeriefiat.com).*
Mº St-Sébastien Froissart. **Open** 11am-7pm
Tue-Sat. **Map** p409 L6.
Fiat is part of a dynamic new generation of gal-
leries. Shows have included the word games and
art world parodies by novelist and artist Thomas
Lélu (who renamed the gallery Galerie Dominique
Fiat Panda for the occasion) and structures by
Laurent Saksik.

Prix Marcel Duchamp.

★ Galerie Emmanuel Perrotin
76 rue de Turenne, 3rd (01.42.16.79.79/www.
galerieperrotin.com). M° St-Sébastien Froissart.
Open 11am-7pm Tue-Sat. **Map** p409 L5.
Perrotin is one of the sharpest figures in town: not
content with owning a gallery in Miami and a glossy
magazine, he has recently jumped on the design
bandwagon with shows by Robert Stadler and Eric
Benqué. As well as the quirky Japanese set of
Takashi Murakami, Mariko Mori et al, and big
French names such as Sophie Calle, Xavier Veilhan,
Prix Marcel Duchamp winner Tatiana Trouvé and
Bernard Frize, he also features the radical Austrian
collective Gelatin.
▶ *In 2007, Perrotin added a spacious new*
annexe to his elegant Paris HQ, around the
corner at 10 impasse St-Claude.

Galerie Karsten Greve
5 rue Debelleyme, 3rd (01.42.77.19.37/www.
galerie-karsten-greve.com). M° St-Sébastien
Froissart. **Open** 11am-7pm Tue-Sat. **Map**
p409 L5.
The Cologne gallery's smart Paris outpost is the
venue for retrospective displays of top-ranking
artists: think big names rather than risk taking. Jannis
Kounellis, Louise Bourgeois, Pierre Soulages, John
Chamberlain and Dubuffet have all featured here.

★ Galerie Laurent Godin
5 rue du Grenier-St-Lazare, 3rd (01.42.71.10.66/
www.laurentgodin.com). M° Rambuteau. **Open**
11am-7pm Tue-Sat. **Map** p402 K5.

After running a public space in Lyon, Laurent
Godin has quickly made a name with his Paris
gallery, which features a diverse cross-generational
mix, ranging from New York neo-Pop artist Haim
Steinbach and waste-paper expert Wang Du to
promising installations by young French artist
Vincent Olinet.

Galerie Magda Danysz
78 rue Amelot, 11th (01.45.83.38.51/www.
magda-gallery.com). M° Filles du Calvaire. **Open**
11am-7pm Tue-Fri; 2-7pm Sat. **Map** p402 L5.
Magda Danysz has moved into a three-storey space
near the Cirque d'Hiver on the fringes of the Marais,
aiming to make contemporary art accessible. She
has a taste for artists influenced by graffiti and animation, as well as the hybrid art-design-science out-
put of the Ultralab cooperative.

Galerie Maisonneuve
22 rue de Poitou, 3rd (01.43.66.23.99/www.
galerie-maisonneuve.com). M° Filles du Calvaire.
Open 2-7pm Tue-Sat. **Map** p409 L5.
After starting in a flat in a Belleville tower block,
Maisonneuve has moved to a small apartment space
in the burgeoning Haut Marais. Artists represented
include Jan Kopp, Alexandre Périgot, Mathieu
Briand and Cecilia Tripp.

★ Galerie Marian Goodman
79 rue du Temple, 3rd (01.48.04.70.52/
www.mariangoodman.com). M° Rambuteau.
Open 11am-7pm Tue-Sat. **Map** p409 K6.

Galerie Lara Vincy. *See p305.*

ARTS & ENTERTAINMENT

This New York gallery owner has an impressive Paris presence in a beautiful 17th-century mansion, where the roster of established artists has included Gerhard Richter, William Kentridge, Eija-Liisa Ahtila and Steve McQueen.

Galerie Michel Rein

42 rue de Turenne, 3rd (01.42.72.68.13/ www.michelrein.com). M° Chemin Vert. **Open** 11am-7pm Tue-Sat. **Map** p409 L6.
Rein presents interesting multidisciplinary artists, such as Fabien Verschaere, Dora Garcia and Saadane Afif, and has recently picked up some of the talents emerging from eastern Europe, such as Dan Perjovschi and Mark Raidpere.

Galerie de Multiples

17 rue St-Gilles, 3rd (01.48.87.21.77/www.galerie demultiples.com). M° Chemin Vert. **Open** 2-7pm Tue-Sat. **Map** p409 L6.
Artist Mathieu Mercier was one of the founders of this gallery, where shows can take the form of anything from posters to soup ladles or pieces inspired by rock music by Saâdane Afif.

Galerie Nelson-Freeman

59 rue Quincampoix, 4th (01.42.71.74.56/www. galerienelsonfreeman.com). M° Hôtel de Ville or Rambuteau. **Open** 11am-1pm, 2-7pm Tue-Sat. **Map** p406 J6.
A tie-up with the New York dealer Peter Freeman has given a more North American slant to the Nelson stable, although it continues showing big European

names, such as photographer Thomas Ruff and Pedro Cabrita Reis, as well as representing late Fluxus maverick Robert Filliou.

Galerie Polaris

15 rue des Arquebusiers, 3rd (01.42.72.21.27/ www.galeriepolaris.com). M° St-Sébastien Froissart. **Open** 1-7pm Tue-Fri; 11am-1pm, 2-7pm Sat. **Map** p409 L6.
Polaris occupies an old gym, and shows artists mainly working in photo and video, names like Stéphane Couturier, known for his stunning, flattened perspective images of building sites.

★ Galerie Schleicher + Lange

12 rue de Picardie, 3rd (01.42.77.02.77/www. schleicherlange.com). M° Filles du Calvaire. **Open** 2-7pm Tue-Sat. **Map** p409 L5.
Shows put on by these two young Germans focus on artists yet to exhibit in Paris, alternating between upcoming London-based talents, such as Zoe Mendelson, and discoveries from eastern Europe. They also host Vidéo Surveillance, an occasional programme of video screenings.

Galerie Thaddaeus Ropac

7 rue Debelleyme, 3rd (01.42.72.99.00/ www.ropac.net). M° Filles du Calvaire. **Open** 10am-7pm Tue-Sat. **Map** p409 L5.
Ropac's main base is in Salzburg, but he also runs this attractive Paris gallery, featuring American Pop and neo-Pop by Warhol, Tom Sachs and Alex Katz, along with European artists such as Ilya Kabakov, Sylvie Fleury and Gilbert & George.

ARTS & ENTERTAINMENT

House Beautiful

Get on the design trail in St-Germain-des-Prés.

If native artists continue to be poorly represented on the world stage, French designers, deservedly, have a much higher profile. Among the art galleries and tribal specialists of St-Germain-des-Prés, a growing number of specialist design galleries have set up shop. One of them is the St-Germain design offshoot of **Jousse Entreprise** (*see p305*; 18 rue de Seine, 01.53.82.13.60, www.jousse-entreprise.com, open 2.30-7pm Mon, 11am-7pm Tue-Sat): find cult metal lamps by Serge Mouille and 1950s art pottery by George Jouve, as well as pieces by Roger Tallon, the designer of the TGV train.

A few doors down is **Galerie Jacques Lacoste** (12 rue de Seine, 01.40.20.41.82, open 11am-1pm, 2-7pm Tue-Sat), which champions the newly fashionable 1940s maestro Jean Royère and the sensually carved wooden bowls of Alexandre Noll.

Also on rue de Seine, **Galerie Downtown** (33 rue de Seine, 01.46.33.82.41, www.galeriedowntown.com, open 10.30am-1pm, 2-7pm Tue-Sat) draws on François Laffanour's reputation as one of the most respected dealers in Paris, with French and US modern classics by the Charlotte Perriand, Jean Prouvé, Charles Eames, George Nakashima et al, and collaborations

with contemporary designers Ron Arad and Byung Hoon Choi.

Cat-Berro (25 rue Guenégaud, 01.43.25.58.10, www.catberro.fr, open 2-6.30pm Tue-Sat) stands out for its one-offs by designers such as Mattia Bonetti, Olivier Gagnère, Christian Ghion and Pucci de Rossi, mixing modernity and the French craft tradition.

Exploring the common ground between functional and artistic design, Didier Krzentowski's **Galerie Kréo** (31 rue Dauphine, 01.53.10.23.00, www.galerie kreo.com, open 2-7pm Tue-Fri; 11am-7pm Sat), which has moved from the 13th to join the St-Germain design hub, commissions limited-edition pieces by leading contemporary designers. Look out for Marc Newson, Jasper Conran, Ron Arad, Hilla Jongerus and native talent such as the Bouroullec brothers and Martin Szekely.

Finally, the recently established **Perimeter Editions** (47 rue St-André-des-Arts, 01.55.42.01.22, www.perimeter-editions.com, open 2.30-7pm Tue-Sat) shows off Guillaume Bardet's extraordinary sculptural tables and Adrien Gardère's multifunctional furniture along with select vintage pieces, against a striking 17th-century interior of ancient parquet and high ceilings.

ARTS & ENTERTAINMENT

★ Galerie Yvon Lambert
108 rue Vieille-du-Temple, 3rd (01.42.71.09.33/ www.yvon-lambert.com). M° Filles du Calvaire. **Open** 10am-1pm, 2.30-7pm Tue-Fri; 10am-7pm Sat. **Map** p409 L5.
Lambert celebrated 30 years in the business in 2006, and remains a powerhouse of the French scene, with plenty of big-name stuff, a New York offshoot and a personal collection given museum status in Avignon. The gallery includes a dedicated area for video installations, and the main space shows leading international names – American bigwigs Andres Serrano, Sol LeWitt, Nan Goldin and Jenny Holzer, plus next-generation artists Douglas Gordon and Jonathan Monk. The street-front art bookshop has a window showcase and basement gallery for younger talents.

Galerie Zurcher
56 rue Chapon, 3rd (01.42.72.82.20/www.galerie zurcher.com). M° Arts et Métiers. **Open** noon-7pm Tue-Sat. **Map** p402 K5.

Among the Chinese wholesalers north of Beaubourg, Zurcher shows emerging artists with a fresh take on painting and video: Marc Desgrandschamps, Camille Vivier and Elisa Sighicelli. Mathilde Rosier and Eléonore de Montesquiou are also featured.

THE CHAMPS-ELYSEES
Galerie Jérôme de Noirmont
38 av Matignon, 8th (01.42.89.89.00/www.de noirmont.com). M° Miromesnil. **Open** 11am-7pm Mon-Sat. **Map** p401 E4.
Eye-catching shows from big names including AR Penck, Jeff Koons, Shirin Neshat, Bettina Rheims, kitsch duo Pierre et Gilles, and art-world personalities Eva and Adèle.

Galerie Lelong
13 rue de Téhéran, 8th (01.45.63.13.19/ www.galerie-lelong.com). M° Miromesnil. **Open** 11am-6pm Tue-Fri; 10am-4pm Sat. Closed Aug. **Map** p401 E3.

If you hanker after Miró, Tàpies, Bacon or Kounellis, Lelong is a safe bet, with its selection of bankable, postwar international names.

ST-GERMAIN-DES-PRES

Galerie Denise René
196 bd St-Germain, 7th (01.42.22.77.57/www. deniserene.com). M° Rue du Bac or St-Germain-des-Prés. **Open** 10am-1pm, 2-7pm Tue-Sat. Closed Aug. **Map** p406 G6.

Denise René has remained committed to kinetic art, Op art and geometrical abstraction by Soto et al, ever since Jean Tinguely first presented his machines here in the 1950s.

Other locations 22 rue Charlot, 3rd (01.48.87.73.94).

Galerie G-P et N Vallois
36 rue de Seine, 6th (01.46.34.61.07/www. galerie-vallois.com). M° Mabillon or Odéon. **Open** 10.30am-1pm, 2-7pm Mon-Sat. **Map** p408 H7.

Interesting conceptual work in all media includes the likes of American provocateur Paul McCarthy, Turner Prize winner Keith Tyson and a clutch of French thirty- and fortysomethings, including Alain Bublex and Gilles Barbier, as well as veteran *affichiste* Jacques Villeglé.

★ Galerie Kamel Mennour
47 rue St-André-des-Arts, 6th (01.56.24.03.63/ www.galeriemennour.com). M° Odéon or St-Michel. **Open** 11am-7pm Tue-Sat. **Map** p408 H7.

After bursting on to the St-Germain art scene with shows by fashion photography crossovers David LaChapelle and Ellen von Unwerth and filmmaker Larry Clark, and introducing emerging artists Kader Attia and Adel Abdessemed, Mennour has confirmed his presence on the gallery scene with a move to these grand new premises in a *hôtel particulier*. Expect shows from Daniel Buren and Claude Lévêque, France's representative at the 2009 Venice Biennale.
▶ *For more on Kamel Mennour's career, see pp46-50 Crossing the Divide.*

Galerie Lara Vincy
47 rue de Seine, 6th (01.43.26.72.51/www.lara-vincy.com). M° Mabillon, Odéon or St-Germain-des-Prés. **Open** 2.30-7pm Mon; 11am-1pm, 2.30-7pm Tue-Sat. **Map** p408 H7.

Liliane Vincy, daughter of the founder, is one of the few characters to retain something of the old St-Germain spirit and a sense of 1970s Fluxus-style happenings. Interesting theme and solo shows include master of the epigram Ben, as well as text-, music- and performance-related pieces.

Galerie Loevenbruck
40 rue de Seine, 6th (01.53.10.85.68/www. loevenbruck.com). M° Mabillon or Odéon. **Open** 2-7pm Tue-Sat. **Map** p408 H6.

Loevenbruck injected a dose of humour into St-Germain with artists – Virginie Barré, Bruno Peinado and Olivier Blankaert, and Philippe Mayeux – who treat conceptual concerns with a light touch.

★ in situ Fabienne Leclerc
6 rue du Pont-de-Lodi, 6th (01.53.79.06.12). M° Odéon or St-Michel. **Open** 11am-7pm Tue-Sat. **Map** p408 H6.

Fabienne Leclerc consistently impresses with the quality of installations from a set of highly individual artists, including Mark Dion, known for his interest in zoology and classification, Indian star Subodh Gupta and video maestro Gary Hill.

13TH ARRONDISSEMENT

Air de Paris
32 rue Louise-Weiss, 13th (01.44.23.02.77/www. airdeparis.com). M° Chevaleret. **Open** 11am-7pm Tue-Sat. **Map** p407 M10.

This gallery shows experimental, neo-conceptual and chaotic material. A hip international stable of artists includes Liam Gillick, Carsten Höller, Sarah Morris and Philippe Parreno.
▶ *Don't miss the 'Random Gallery' – displays in the shop window between Air de Paris and neighbour Praz-Delavallade.*

★ Art:Concept
16 rue Duchefdelaville, 13th (01.53.60.90.30/ www.galerieartconcept.com). M° Bibliothèque François Mitterrand or Chevaleret. **Open** 11am-7pm Tue-Sat. **Map** p407 M10.

Despite the cramped conditions, Art:Concept presents some interesting, electic work. Look out for installations by Michel Blazy, whose favourite materials include shaving foam, spaghetti and dog biscuits, and constructions by Richard Fauguet.

gb agency
20 rue Louise-Weiss, 13th (01.53.79.07.13/www. gbagency.fr). M° Chevaleret. **Open** 11am-7pm Tue-Sat. **Map** p407 M10.

The gb agency brought young artists Loris Gréaud and Elina Brotherus to the fore. Group shows predominate, with self-referential themes such as temporality, or the concept of the art exhibition itself.

Jousse Entreprise
24 & 34 rue Louise-Weiss, 13th (01.53.82.10.18/ www.jousse-entreprise.com). M° Bibliothèque François Mitterrand or Chevaleret. **Open** 11am-7pm Tue-Sat. **Map** p407 M10.

Philippe Jousse presents contemporary artists – such as Matthieu Laurette, Frank Perrin and challenging video artist Clarisse Hahn – alongside 1950s avant-garde furniture by Jean Prouvé, lights by Serge Mouille and ceramics by Georges Jouve.
▶ *There are more design classics in their sister gallery in the 6th; see p304 House Beautiful.*

ARTS & ENTERTAINMENT

Gay & Lesbian

From Delanoë down, gay men and lesbians thrive in Paris.

Paris is home to a thriving LGBT community, visibly involved in every walk of life – right at the top of the tree sits openly gay mayor Bertrand Delanoë, who came out two years before running for office. Local gays and lesbians say that they encounter very little, if any, discrimination in their day-to-day lives, and feel integrated into mainstream society. However, the annual **Gay Pride March**, held on the last Sunday in June, is a powerful reminder of what the gay rights movement has accomplished over the last 30 years, and of what is yet to be achieved.

GETTING OUT AND ABOUT

Gays and lesbians live in every part of the city, but **Beaubourg** and the '**gay Marais**' are particularly gay-friendly. Most of the dedicated venues are to be found in the area bounded by rue des Archives, rue Vieille-du-Temple and rue Ste-Croix-de-la-Bretonnerie. A light lunch, coffee or cocktail in the vicinity will provide ample opportunity to check out the talent, while a stroll through the nearby streets will yield a seductive selection of shops. Every fetish is catered for, along with funky fashion boutiques and even something for the bibliomaniacs: **Les Mots à la Bouche**, where you can peruse the international gay and lesbian press or pick up free monthly magazines listing the hottest events.

In the evening, kick off the action at a café or a restaurant before moving on to the bars and clubs, which don't really get going until after midnight. Start by mixing it up at **Le Mixer** or the nearby **Raidd Bar**, which is still confirmed red hot. The majestic **Bains-Douches** (*see p330*), domain of clubbing royalty David and Cathy Guetta, and the **Queen** on the Champs-Elysées remain clubbing institutions, as does the smaller and more intimate **L'Insolite**. The popular **La Scène Bastille** (*see p330*) is a relatively new trendsetter; on the other side of the coin is the oldest gay club in Paris, **Le Club 18**, whch is always fun and still draws a great crowd. Lesbians can find a few nice bars of their own on rue du Roi de Sicile, or chill at the popular and friendly Chez Moune near Pigalle.

Information and resources

Magazines *Têtu* (www.tetu.com) and *Préf* (www.preferencesmag.com) report on goings-on in gay life and have text in English; *La Dixième Muse* (www.ladixiememuse.com) provides similar information for lesbians. There are also several free bi-weekly publications, distributed in gay bookshops, bars and clubs; the most useful are *2 X-Paris* (www.2xparis.fr), *Tribumove* (www.tribumove. com) and *AgendaQ*. For the girls, there's *Barbi(e)turix* (www.myspace.com/barbieturix). Two excellent and informative websites provide regularly updated listings (in English) of all things gay and lesbian in the city: www.paris-gay.com and www.gayvox.com.

Centre Gai et Lesbien

63 rue Beaubourg, 3rd (01.43.57.21.47/www. cglparis.org). M° Arts et Métiers or Rambuteau. **Open** 6-8pm Mon; 3-8pm Tue, Thur; 12.30-8pm Wed, Fri, Sat; 4-7pm Sun. *Library* 2-6pm Fri, Sat. **Map** p402 K6.
After many years on rue Keller, the CGL has moved into more centrally located digs in the Marais. In addition to providing information on topics ranging from the sociopolitical (if you don't know what rights gays and lesbians have or don't have in France, find out here) to the biomedical (the latest developments in the treatment of HIV, where to get tested for free), this multifunctional centre and library also hosts meetings for a variety of support groups and associations.

About the author

Bob Vallier *is a writer and philosopher who divides his time between Paris and Chicago.*

Inter-LGBT

c/o Maison des Associations du 3ème, boîte 8,
5 rue Perrée, 75003 Paris (01.72.70.39.22/
www.inter-lgbt.org). **Map** p409 L5.
The Interassociative Lesbienne, Gaie, Bi & Trans is
an umbrella group of 50 French LGBT associations.
It organises the Printemps des Assoces in the Espace
des Blancs Manteaux (48 rue Vieille-du-Temple, 4th)
every April and the annual Gay Pride March.

SOS Homophobie

01.48.06.42.41/www.sos-homophobie.org.
Open 6-10pm Mon, Fri, Sun; 8-10pm Tue,
Wed, Thur, Sun; 2-4pm Sat.
Victims of and witnesses to homophobic crimes and
discrimination can report them to this confidential service, which offers support and publishes an annual
report on homophobia.

Gay Paris

BARS & CAFES

Le Bear's Den

6 rue des Lombards, 4th (01.42.71.08.20/www.
bearsden.fr). M° Châtelet or Hôtel de Ville. **Open**
4pm-2am Mon-Thur, Sun; 4pm-5am Fri, Sat.
Credit MC, V. **Map** p406 J6.
A friendly local for bears, muscle bears, chubbies
and their admirers. Visit the website for details on
comically named theme nights such as 'Charcuterie'.
See also p309 **Dare to Bear.**
▶ *Bears, wolves and men who love hairy men*
also gather at the nearby Wolf; see p308.

★ Le Café Arena

29 rue St-Denis, 1st (01.45.08.15.16). M°
Châtelet. **Open** 9am-6am daily. **Credit** MC, V.
Map p406 J5.
This bar-restaurant has a great terrace for people-
watching and friendly staff; it's still the hottest ren-
dezvous in Les Halles.

Café Cox

15 rue des Archives, 4th (01.42.72.08.00/
www.cox.fr). M° Hôtel de Ville. **Open** 1pm-2am
daily. **No credit cards. Map** p409 K6.
Beefy, hairy, shaven-headed men congregate on the
pavement in front of Café Cox for post-work drinks,
before moving on to more intimate surroundings.

Le Duplex

25 rue Michel-le-Comte, 3rd (01.42.72.80.86/
www.duplex-bar.com). M° Hôtel de Ville or
Rambuteau. **Open** 8pm-2am Mon-Thur, Sun;
8pm-4am Fri, Sat. **Credit** V. **Map** p409 K5.
This small bar just round the corner from the Centre
Pompidou caters to a thirtysomething crowd. It's a
popular meeting place for various gay associations,
with friendly staff and local art on the walls.

Eagle

33bis rue des Lombards, 1st 01.47.0067.15).
M° Les Halles. **Open** 6pm-4am Mon-Thur, Sun;
6pm-6am Fri, Sat; 5pm-4am Sun. **No credit**
cards. Map p402 J6.
Formerly the London, this old bar has found new
life since it changed direction, and has become a hit
with bears, daddies, leathermen, and the men who
admire them. Enjoy tea and cake on the patio early
on, a shot of Jack at the bar later, or penetrate deeper and enjoy the musky smell in the disco backroom.

★ L'Interface Bar

34 rue Keller, 11th (01.47.0067.15). M° Bastille,
Ledru-Rollin or Voltaire. **Open** 3pm-2am Mon-
Thur, Sun; 3pm-4am Fri, Sat. **No credit cards.**
Map p407 M6.
The small, unpretentious Interface is on the trendy
and *très* gay rue Keller. Friendly staff cater mostly
to thirtysomethings; this is a great place in which to
start the evening before heading off to the Scène
nightclub around the corner or the hardcore Keller
leather bar down the road.

Le Mixer

23 rue Ste-Croix-de-la-Bretonnerie, 4th
(01.48.87.55.44/www.mixerbar.com).
M° Hôtel de Ville. **Open** 5pm-2am daily.
Credit AmEx, MC, V. **Map** p409 K6.
A mixed, young and carefree crowd gathers at this
watering hole for cocktails before heading off to the
clubs. DJs spin techno and house to energise the
crowd. Some nights are strictly for girls. *Photo p309.*

★ Open Café

17 rue des Archives, 4th (01.42.72.26.18/
www.opencafe.fr). M° Hôtel de Ville or
Rambuteau. **Open** 11am-2am Mon-Thur, Sun;
11am-4am Fri, Sat. **Credit** MC, V. **Map** p409 K6.
Cruise and be cruised in the café everybody visits at
some point in the evening. Great staff and prompt
service help. Pop out on to the terrace, and enjoy the
people-watching at any time of the day or night.

★ Le Quetzal

10 rue de la Verrerie, 4th (01.48.87.99.07).
M° Hôtel de Ville. **Open** 5pm-5am daily.
Credit MC, V. **Map** p409 K6.
This bar is considered one of the 'musts' of the Marais,
as it's often filled with hot men and a few drag queens
who help to keep things lively. You might be able to
find some action in the small dark space upstairs.

Raidd Bar

23 rue du Temple, 4th (01.42.77.04.88/www.
raiddbar.com). M° Hôtel de Ville. **Open** 5pm-5am
daily. **Credit** (min €10) MC, V. **Map** p406 K6.
The Raidd is standing room only at street level,
with another bar down below. The hot, herculean
bartenders take turns in the wall-mounted shower
for nightly shows and the dancefloor is jam-packed.

★ Wolf

37 rue des Lombards, 1st (01.40.28.02.52/ www.wolfparis.com). M° Les Halles. **Open** 5pm-2am daily. **No credit cards. Map** p402 J6.
Popular with bears, wolves, otters and a variety of other species, mostly on the hairy side. Everyone is welcome, though, and the ambience is very laid-back. *See also below* **Dare to Bear**.

RESTAURANTS

Le Bar à Manger (BAM)

13 rue des Lavandières-Ste-Opportune, 1st (01.42.21.01.72). M° Les Halles. **Open** noon-5pm, 7-11pm Tue-Sat. **Credit** MC, V. **Map** p408 J6.
Excellent, creative cuisine in a pleasant, relaxed setting. There are *prix fixe* menus at lunch (€18) and dinner (€29).

Le Kofi du Marais

54 rue Ste-Croix-de-la-Bretonnerie, 4th (01.48.87.48.71). M° Hôtel de Ville. **Open** noon-11pm daily. **Credit** AmEx, MC, V. **Map** p406 K6.
Modern, simple cooking with an American twist is the speciality here. Club sandwiches, burgers and salads are menu staples. Prices are reasonable and the service is good too.

★ Aux Trois Petits Cochons

31 rue Tiquetonne, 2nd (01.42.33.39.69/www. auxtroispetitscochons.fr). M° Etienne Marcel. **Open** 7.30pm-midnight. **Credit** MC, V. **Map** p406 J5.
This gay-owned, gay-run restaurant serves up traditional French cuisine with a contemporary twist. The three-course menu (€33) changes daily and is based on the freshest ingredients available. It's a very popular place, so booking is recommended.
▶ *If it's too busy, try sister restaurant Pig'z, 5 rue Marie Stuart, 2nd (01.42.33.05.89).*

Ze Restoo

41 rue des Blancs-Manteaux, 3rd (01.42.74.10.29). M° Rambuteau. **Open** 7pm-1am Mon-Sat. **Credit** AmEx, MC, V. **Map** p409 K6.
This restaurant has become a popular place in which to eat with friends before heading out for a fun-filled evening. There's a very relaxed atmosphere, with good service and imaginative dishes.

CLUBS

As well as the venues listed below, a mixed but increasingly gay crowd mingles at **Les Bains Douches** (*see p330*), **Nouveau Casino** (*see*

ARTS & ENTERTAINMENT

Dare to Bear

If you go down to the woods today, you're sure of a big surprise…

Paris is the city where male grooming and 'metrosexuality' was in vogue before the New York set even knew it existed, which makes the capital's current gay trend all the more surprising. The waifish boy look? Over. Obsessive plucking and painful pruning? So last century. These days a man's most desirable attribute is manliness – hairy chests and sideburns with a burly broad-shouldered look. So now is the time to grow that '70s moustache you've always secretly wanted and stop waxing your back. That's right, the bear is back.

Bears (*ours* in French, or, if you want to be more cuddly, *nounours*) are, of course, larger-scale men, often in their mid 40s to late 50s, hairy (the hairier, the bearier), though often with shaved heads. Their younger admirers are known as cubs; their thinner, leaner cousins are wolves; wolves who swim are, of course, otters.

What this entire bestiary has in common is a self-assured pride in the hairy, musky, manly body. A whole culture has evolved around this group,

and where there's culture, there's money to be made. Shops devoted to bear culture (which frequently intersects with the leather scene) include **IEM** (*see p311*) and **JV Cuir** (18 rue des Gâtines, 20th, 01.47.97.79.72), both of which have a good selection of bear wares.

Bars and businesses have taken advantage of the bear market too: you'll find adverts for *soirées ours* everywhere, as well as signs in otherwise twinkish establishments saying *ours bienvenus*. In the last couple of years, a pack of bear bars have opened or reinvigorated themselves, including the laid-back **Bear's Den** (*see p307*), the **Eagle** (*see p307*) and the **Wolf** (*see above*). A few blocks away, in the heart of the Marais, the **CUD bar** (*see p309*) remains popular with bears and bear-lovers. Also in the centre is **L'Impact** (*see p307*), which was the first bar in Paris to go entirely nudist (head here if you like bare bears).

Up-to-date information is provided in English and French on *www.bearparisclub. com* or *www.bearprod.fr*. Yes, the bear is back, so go out and get mauled.

Le Mixer. *See p307.*

p329) and **La Scène Bastille** (*see p330*). Most gay clubs are very hetero-friendly.

★ Le Club 18
18 rue de Beaujolais, 1st (01.42.97.52.13/www. club18.fr). M° Palais-Royal or Pyramides. **Open** midnight-dawn Fri-Sun. **Admission** (incl 1 drink) €10. **Credit** *Bar* MC, V. **Map** p402 H5.
The oldest gay club in Paris attracts a young and beautiful clientele. It is not very big, and the decor isn't all that great, but the music is fun and there's a very laid-back vibe. Everyone is here to dance and have a good time.

Le CUD Bar
12 rue des Haudriettes, 3rd (01.42.71.56.60/ www.cud-bar.com). M° Rambuteau. **Open** 4pm-7am daily. **Credit** MC, V. **Map** p409 K5.
Upstairs is a laid-back bar, but downstairs in the old cellar is a dancefloor that can get very crowded, especially after 2am. The crowd is a mixed bunch, and it's popular with the bears.

Les Follivores & les Crazyvores
Bataclan, 50 bd Voltaire, 11th (01.43.14.00.30/ www.le-bataclan.com/http://follivore.free.fr). M° Oberkampf. **Open** 11.30pm-dawn. **Admission** (incl 1 drink) €17. **Credit** V. **Map** p407 M5.
Twice a month, the Bataclan concert hall transforms itself into a club to host these two hugely popular parties. Crazyvores features music from the 1970s and '80s, and at Follivores the DJs spin gay classics from all eras mixed up with cutting-edge techno.

These are big events with exuberant crowds; the drag queens put on their best ball-gowns and biggest wigs, and the men sport their tightest tops. Great fun.

L'Insolite
33 rue des Petits-Champs, 1st (01.40.20.98.59). M° Pyramide. **Open** 11pm-5am Mon-Thur, Sun; 11pm-6am Fri, Sat. **Admission** varies. **Credit** *Bar* MC, V. **Map** p401 H4.
Hidden away underneath an old courtyard, this small club is a fun and friendly spot; the music tends to be '80s disco hits and new wave with a few more recent club hits thrown in.

Queen
102 av des Champs-Elysées, 8th (01.53.89.08.90/ www.queen.fr). M° George V. **Open** midnight-7am Mon-Thur, Sun; midnight-8am Fri, Sat. **Admission** €15 Mon-Thur, Sun; €20 Fri, Sat. **Credit** *Bar* AmEx, MC, V. **Map** p400 D4.
One of the oldest and largest clubs, Queen's main gay nights are Saturday@Queen and Overkitsch on Sundays in the summer months, but every night is a little gay. Big-name DJs often spin here to a crowd peppered with VIPs.

★ Le Tango (La Boîte à Frissons)
13 rue au Maire, 3rd (01.42.72.17.78/www. boite-a-frissons.fr). M° Arts et Métiers. **Open** 8pm-2am Thur; 10.30pm-5am Fri, Sat; 6-11pm Sun. **Admission** €7; free Thur. **Credit** V. **Map** p409 K5.

Wacky crowd, Madonna songs and accordion tunes. At the Friday and Saturday Bal de la Boîte à Frissons, couples dance the foxtrot, tango, madison or *guinguette* in the early part of the evening, followed after midnight by music of every variety except techno. This unusual old dance hall never fails to entertain.

SEX CLUBS & SAUNAS

Le Bunker
150 rue St-Maur, 11th (01.53.36.78.87/ www.bunker-cruising.com). M° Goncourt. **Open** 4pm-2am Mon-Thur; 4pm-3.30am Fri; 4pm-4.30am Sat; 4pm-1am Sun. **Admission** €7; €6 under-26s. **Map** p403 M4.

This cruising club, located not far from the Oberkampf bar district in a remote corner of the 11th, is one of the hottest in Paris. It features all-naked and underwear-only nights during the week, and hardcore themes at the weekend. Friday is a very popular night, as is the first Saturday of the month, when Le Bunker hosts its S&M 'Red and Black Night' – not for the faint-hearted.

Le Deep
80 quai de l'Hôtel de Ville, 4th (01.42.78.88.49). M° Hôtel de Ville. **Open** 4pm-5am daily. **Admission** €5.70-€7.70 (incl 1 drink). **Credit** MC, V. **Map** p409 K6.

The Deep is located by the river just behind the Hôtel de Ville. The ground floor features a bar and occasional strippers; the other two floors are for cruising, and offer some private cubicles for when you find Mr Right Now. Not as popular as it once was.

Le Dépot
10 rue aux Ours, 3rd (01.44.54.96.96/www. suncity.com/depot). M° Etienne Marcel. **Open** 2pm-8am Mon-Sat; 2-9pm Sun. **Admission** €7.50 before 11pm, €10 after 11pm Mon-Thur, Sun; €12 (incl 1 drink) Fri, Sat. **Credit** MC, V. **Map** p402 K5.

A very busy dance club upstairs with a labyrinthine maze of cubicles, glory holes and darkrooms downstairs. The clients have a lot of attitude and pickpockets work the darkroom, so be careful.

★ IDM
4 rue du Fbg-Montmartre, 9th (01.45.23.10.03/ www.idm-sauna.com). M° Grands Boulevards. **Open** noon-1am Mon-Thur, Sun; noon-2am Fri, Sat. **Admission** €15 Mon-Fri; €17 Sat, Sun; €10 under-30s. **Credit** MC, V. **Map** p402 J4.

The city's best gay sauna has three levels and plenty of cabins and corridors to prowl. The wet sauna is on two levels, and the small relaxation pool and showers are always at the perfect temperature. A few times a month, there are also performances by drag queens and other singers.

Sun City
62 bd de Sébastopol, 3rd (01.42.74.31.41/ www.suncity.fr). M° Etienne Marcel. **Open**

Legay Choc.

INSIDE TRACK
GET NAKED

L'Impact (18 rue Greneta, 2nd, 01.42.21.94.34, www.impact-bar.com) is the city's first all-naked cruising club, and offers various theme nights, a plentiful supply of condoms and lube, and a 2am to 3am happy hour. Tuesdays are Horse Man Naked nights, where interested parties can be measured up. Should they exceed the 20cm (8in) benchmark, they're granted free admission.

noon-6am daily. **Admission** €18 Mon-Fri; €19.50 Sat, Sun; €11 under-26s. **Credit** MC, V. **Map** p402 J5.

A Bollywood-themed sauna where very pretty boys stand around and look uninterested. Owned and operated by the Dépôt team (*see p310*), it features dry saunas, jacuzzi, hammams, video rooms, a pool, a gym and a bar. The decor is lovely, if kitsch.

SHOPS & SERVICES

Boy'z Bazaar

5 rue Ste-Croix-de-la-Bretonnerie, 4th (01.42.71. 67.00/www.boyzbazaar.com). M° Hôtel de Ville or St-Paul. **Open** 2-10pm daily. **Credit** AmEx, MC, V. **Map** p409 K6.

The trendiest clothes for nightclubbers, fashionistas and urban hipsters in the heart of the gaybourhood. **Other locations** 5 rue des Guillemites, 4th (01.42.71.63.86).

Les Dessous d'Apollon

17 rue du Bourg-Tibourg, 4th (01.42.71.87.37/ www.lesdessousdapollon.com). M° Hôtel de Ville or St-Paul. **Open** 2-7.30pm Mon; noon-7.30pm Tue-Sat; 3-7pm Sun. **Credit** AmEx, DC, MC, V. **Map** p409 K6.

The most extensive selection of underwear – ranging from functional to downright eccentric – that you'll ever encounter, plus T-shirts and accessories.

IEM

16 rue Ste-Croix-de-la-Bretonnerie, 4th (01.42.74.01.61/www.iem.fr). M° Hôtel de Ville. **Open** 1-8pm Mon-Thur; 1-10pm Fri, Sat; 3-7pm Sun. **Credit** AmEx, MC, V. **Map** p403 M4.

This sex hypermarket emphasises the harder side of gay life. Videos, clothes and gadgets can all be had, with leather and rubber upstairs. **Other locations** 43 rue de l'Arbre Sec, 1st (01.42.96.05.74).

★ Legay Choc

45 rue Ste-Croix-de-la-Bretonnerie, 4th (01.48.87.56.88/www.legaychoc.fr). M° Hôtel

de Ville. **Open** 8am-8pm Mon, Tue, Thur-Sun. **No credit cards. Map** p409 K6.

Run by two brothers (one gay, one straight) whose surname just happens to be Legay, this Marais *boulangerie* and *pâtisserie* is very popular. The pastries are delightful, and the lunch-hour sandwiches are generous, so expect lengthy queues. A satellite store, serving only sandwiches, is at 17 rue des Archives (01.48.87.24.61).

▶ *For that special occasion, a penis-shaped loaf can be made to order.*

★ Les Mots à la Bouche

6 rue Ste-Croix-de-la-Bretonnerie, 4th (01.42.78. 88.30/www.motsbouche.com). M° Hôtel de Ville or St-Paul. **Credit** AmEx, MC, V. **Map** p409 K6.

An institution in the Marais, this bookshop has a large selection of gay fiction, non-fiction, magazines, and English-language books.

Nickel

48 rue des Francs-Bourgeois, 4th (01.42.77. 41.10/www.nickel.fr). M° Hôtel de Ville or Rambuteau. **Open** 11am-7.30pm Mon, Tue, Fri, Sat; 11am-9pm Wed, Thur. **Credit** AmEx, MC, V. **Map** p406 L6.

Body and skincare treatments, strictly for men. A one-hour facial is €45-€55, a manicure €13 and an hour-long massage €45. Staff are adept, friendly, and knowledgeable.

Plus Que Parfait

23 rue des Blancs-Manteaux, 4th (01.42.71. 09.05). M° Hôtel de Ville or St-Paul. **Open** 3-8pm Mon; noon-8pm Tue-Sat; 3-7pm Sun. *Clothes deposit* Mon-Fri. **Credit** MC, V. **Map** p409 K6.

This *dépôt vente*, where pristine, second-hand designer clothing is sold on commission, is a veritable treasure trove of men's fashion finds.

Space Hair

10 rue Rambuteau, 3rd (01.48.87.28.51). M° Rambuteau. **Open** noon-10pm Mon; 10am-11pm Tue-Fri; 9am-10pm Sat. **Credit** MC, V. **Map** p409 K6.

Space Hair is divided into two salons, Cosmic and Classic, with a 1980s kitsch feel, late opening hours and cute stylists; it's best to book ahead.

WHERE TO STAY

Hôtel Central Marais

2 rue Ste-Croix-de-la-Bretonnerie, 4th (01.48.87.56.08/www.hotelcentralmarais.com). M° Hôtel de Ville or St-Paul. **Rates** €89 single or double; €109 triple; €7 breakfast. **Credit** MC, V. **Map** p409 K6.

If location and affordable rates are more important than plush surroundings, this aptly named hotel is a good bet. The barmen of the Central bar (located below the hotel) act as receptionists from 5pm until 2am, and can keep you updated on the local nightlife. The place had been undergoing renovations in the late summer and early autumn of 2008.

Hôtel Duo
11 rue du Temple, 4th (01.42.72.72.22/ www.duoparis.com). M° Hôtel de Ville. **Rates** €200-€340 double. **Credit** AmEx, DC, MC, V. **Map** p406 K6.
The mixed but very gay-friendly Duo is a stylish place at which to rest your head. What's more, it has helpful staff at the reception – a rarity in this trendy area.

Lesbian Paris

Famous club Pulp is much missed, but the girlie scene continues to flourish, especially near the corner of rue du Roi de Sicile and rue des Ecouffes in the Marais. Most of the bars welcome men accompanied by women, but a few are women only. Some girl-only parties are staged at clubs such as **Le Tango** (*see p310*); see the free monthly magazine *Barbi(e)turix*.

Le 3W Kafé
8 rue des Ecouffes, 4th (01.48.87.39.26/www.3w-kafe.com) M° St-Paul. **Open** 6pm-2am daily. **Credit** MC, V. **Map** p409 K6.
A convivial place where beautiful women go to have a drink, meet other women and listen to good music. There's a small dance space in the basement, and a number of theme nights every month. The three Ws stand for 'women with women'.

★ La Champmeslé
4 rue Chabanais, 2nd (01.42.96.85.20). M° Bourse or Pyramides. **Open** 4pm-4am daily. **Credit** MC, V. **Map** p402 H4.
This veteran girl bar remains a popular venue for lesbian locals and visitors. Beer is the drink of choice; pull up a seat and enjoy the regular cabaret nights.

Chez Moune
54 rue Pigalle, 9th (01.45.26.64.64). M° Pigalle. **Open** 10.30pm Tue-Sat. **Credit** MC, V. **Map** p401 H2.
Probably the oldest lesbian cabaret in Paris, Chez Moune opened in 1936 and still has nightly shows. Saturdays are traditionally women only, but in the last year other phallo-friendly dance parties and cabaret shows have occasionally been held.

Le Day Off
10 rue de l'Isly, 8th (01.45.22.87.90). M° Gare St-Lazare. **Open** 11am-3pm, 5pm-3am Mon-Fri. **Credit** MC, V. **Map** p401 G3.
An apt name for this weekday-only pub-restaurant – heavy drinking enjoyed by work-weary lesbians. It gets crowded in the early evening.

Dollhouse
24 rue du Roi de Sicile, 4th (01.40.27.09.21/ www.dollhouse.fr). M° St-Paul. **Open** 2-8pm Mon, Sun; 1-8pm Tue-Sat. **Credit** MC, V. **Map** p409 L6.
This store, located close to 3W, specialises in lingerie and gadgets for girls. Upstairs you'll find a selection of sophisticated and sexy underwear; head downstairs for the sexcessories.

Les Jacasses
5 rue des Ecouffes, 4th (01.42.71.15.51). M° St-Paul. **Open** 6pm-2am daily. **Credit** MC, V. **Map** p409 K6.
This new, relaxed bar for women, just around the corner from the girlie bars on rue du Roi de Sicile, makes a welcome addition to the neighbourhood.

Le Nyx Café
30 rue du Roi de Sicile, 4th (no phone/www.nyxcafe.fr). M° St-Paul. **Open** 5pm-2am Tue-Fri; 5pm-4am Sat, Sun. **Credit** MC, V. **Map** p409 L6.
The Nyx is mostly a girl bar, but welcomes everyone. Recent theme nights have included live rock and drag queens.

O'Kubi Caffé
219 rue St-Maur, 10th (01.42.01.35.08/www.okubicaffe.com). M° Goncourt. **Open** noon-2am Tue-Sat; noon-11pm Sun. **Credit** MC, V. **Map** p403 M3.
O'Kubi recently celebrated its second anniversary and continues to grow in popularity. It also has a bar and serves light food.

★ Le Rive Gauche
1 rue du Sabot, 6th (01.40.20.43.23/www.lerivegauche.com). M° St-Germain-des-Prés. **Open** 11pm-dawn Fri, Sat. **Admission** €10-€15. **No credit cards. Map** p405 G7.
This weekend women-only nightclub is one of the hottest places on the lesbian scene. The decor is '70s and the music eclectic.

Le Troisième Lieu
62 rue Quincampoix, 4th (01.48.04.85.64). M° Rambuteau. **Open** 6pm-2am Mon-Sat. **Credit** MC, V. **Map** p406 K5.
Elaborate *tartines*, delicious desserts and strong drinks are the fare at this lesbian-run bar and restaurant. Despite its militant subtitle ('Cantine des Ginettes Armées'), the vibe is jovial. There are also areas devoted to music and dancing.

Unity Bar
176-178 rue St-Martin, 3rd (01.42.72.70.59/ http://unity.bar.free.fr). M° Rambuteau. **Open** 4pm-2am daily. **No credit cards. Map** p402 K5.
This ladies-only bar is more butch than lipstick, with pool tables and a good beer selection.

Music

It ain't over till the First Lady sings.

The French state has long been known for its desire to keep tabs on the country's pop production, the notorious law dictating that ten per cent of music broadcast in France must be sung in French being a case in point. However, president Nicolas Sarkozy has taken it to an entirely new level, with family members involved in two of the most durable genres in French music: *chanson* and rap. Thanks to Sarkozy, most visitors will be aware of at least one contemporary French artist: Carla Bruni, former model, purveyor of winsome, folky pop and, more recently, France's

First Lady. Fewer know that his son, Pierre, is a hip hop producer who trades under the name Mosey. Still, visitors in search of musical kicks needn't take their cue from the Elysée. There are many finer *chanteuses* to be discovered elsewhere in the capital, as well as a multitude of other musical styles alongside a vibrant, intriguing classical and opera circuit.

Classical & Opera

Important centenaries can galvanise the musical life of a country, and Paris hasn't held back in the celebrations of its most renowned 20th-century musical son, Olivier Messaien. Messaien's legacy, via his pupils Pierre Boulez and George Benjamin, remains a vibrant force in 21st-century music. The contemporary repertoire plays a growing role in the French capital, attracting a young audience eager to discover the music of our time. The revitalised *Carmen* under Sir John Eliot Gardiner in June 2009, was packed last year with an enthusiastic, student-driven crowd to hear a revival of Pascal Dusapin's abstract opera *Roméo et Juliette*. The **IRCAM** remains the most important European centre for electronic music research, and the **Ensemble Intercontemporain** is a driving force in contemporary performance. Even the **Opéra National de Paris**, under outgoing director Gerard Mortier (*see p315* **Out with the New,**

in with the Old**), produces a major world premiere each season – in 2009 *Yvonne, Princesse de Bourgogne* by Philippe Boesmans. Although universally acclaimed masterpieces are rare, the audiences are courageous, and risk-taking sponsorship is available to look confidently to the future.

New music in France tends to follow the Debussy-Messiaen-Boulez-Dusapin atonal axis, but Jean-Luc Choplin, director of the **Châtelet**, is making a commendable effort to discover a more inclusive strand of composition, which tries to mix popular music with classical composition. Welcome to the Voice in 2008 involved Elvis Costello and Sting, and Gérard Pesson's *La Pastorale* in June 2009 will mix variety performers with scholarly contemporary musicians.

Radio France is responsible for two of the city's main orchestras, the **Orchestre Philharmonique de Radio France** and the **Orchestre National de France**. While conductor Myung-Whun Chung has been kept busy with Messiaen at the Philharmonique, the National has been making friends with its new music director, Italian Daniele Gatti, who replaced the venerable Kurt Masur in September 2008. Meanwhile, the **Orchestre de Paris** has chosen Paavo Järvi as new music director from 2010, as it waits impatiently for the construction of Jean Nouvel's new

About the authors

Stephen Mudge *is the French correspondent for* Opera News, *and writes about music and food for the BBC.* **David McKenna** *divides his time between London and Paris, and co-presents the Rockfort French music show on Resonance FM.*

ARTS & ENTERTAINMENT

2,400-seat concert house, the Philharmonie de Paris, scheduled to open in 2012.

Early music is an abiding passion in Paris, sustained by strong CD sales and a seemingly inexhaustible supply of obscure, unrecorded Baroque works. The quest for authenticity and period instruments now extends to Mozart and even early Romantic music. **Les Arts Florissants**, under the Franco-American William Christie, and Jean-Claude Malgoire's ensemble based in the north of France, are in the vanguard with their performances of Lully and Rameau. The younger likes of Christophe Rousset and glamorous Emmanuelle Haïm are both respected international figures in the field, and leading French pianist Alexandre Tharaud makes an excellent case for exploring this repertoire on a modern instrument.

There's also plenty of early music going on in the churches. The **Festival d'Art Sacré** (01.44.70.64.10) presents church music in authentic settings in the run-up to Christmas; **Les Grands Concerts Sacrés** (01.48.24.16.97) and **Musique et Patrimoine** (01.42.50.96.18, www.ampconcerts.com) also offer concerts at various churches; and music in Notre-Dame cathedral is taken care of by **Musique Sacrée Notre-Dame** (01.44. 41.49.99, www.musique-sacree-notredame paris.fr, tickets also on sale at the cathedral).

The main music provider in summer is the **Paris Quartier d'Eté** festival (01.44.94.98.00, www.quartierdete.com), with concerts in gardens across the city. The **Festival de Saint-Denis** (01.48.13.06.07, www.festival-saint-denis.com) also offers top names in a spectacular setting. *See also pp274-279.*

INFORMATION AND TICKETS

For listings, see *L'Officiel des Spectacles* or *Pariscope*. Monthly magazines *Le Monde de la Musique* and *Diapason* also list classical concerts, and *Opéra Magazine* provides good coverage of all things vocal. Look out too for *Cadences* and *La Terrasse*, two free monthlies distributed outside concerts.

For the **Fête de la Musique** (21 June), all events are free, and year-round freebies crop up at the **Maison de Radio France** and the **Conservatoire de Paris**, as well as in certain churches.

ORCHESTRAS & ENSEMBLES

★ Les Arts Florissants

01.43.87.98.88/www.arts-florissants.com.
William Christie's 'Arts Flo' remains the country's leading Early Music group, and his conducting of Rameau and Lully have become benchmarks of authentic performance. The group has not neglected passing on the secrets of Baroque ornamentation to the next generation, with the Jardin des Voix busy cultivating new Baroque vocal talent.

★ Ensemble Intercontemporain

01.44.84.44.50/www.ensembleinter.com.
Glamorous Finnish conductor Susanna Mälkki is the musical director of this bastion of contemporary music, founded and still often conducted by Pierre Boulez. The exacting standard of the 31 soloists is beyond reproach, and the ensemble has an enviable international reputation. The 2008/09 season focuses on the 100th birthday of Elliot Carter and the centenary of Messiaen.

Ensemble Orchestral de Paris

08.00.42.67.57/www.ensemble-orchestral-paris.com.
After ten years of loyal service, John Nelson is leaving this orchestra, which often seems marginalised by more prestigious rivals. Nelson has undoubtedly raised the standard of playing, and brought a degree of professionalism to the ensemble that was often lacking. His successor will doubtless aim to build on this achievement.

Orchestre Colonne

01.42.33.72.89/www.orchestrecolonne.fr.
Often to be found at the Salle Gaveau, this orchestra led by composer Laurent Petitgirard has intelligent programming, with every concert teaming a contemporary work with more popular repertoire. The Eveil series of concerts provides bargain tickets for parents and children, making an ideal introduction to classical music.

Orchestre Lamoureux

01.58.39.30.30/www.orchestrelamoureux.com.
This worthy orchestra still suffers from insufficient funding, and its concert appearances in the capital are sparse, but musical director Yutaka Sado is a fine conductor, and his programming is uncompromising and prepared to take on the challenge of new and unusual repertoires.

Orchestre National de France

01.56.40.15.16/www.radiofrance.fr.
The successor to 80-year-old Kurt Masur is Daniele Gatti, who took over the reins of this national institution in September 2008. Masur's authoritative way with the core symphonies will be a tough act to follow, but the new musical director's theatrical style may open the doors to a more varied repertoire, with Italian flair and warmth set to replace German structure and rigour.

★ Orchestre de Paris

01.42.56.13.13/www.orchestredeparis.com.
The successor to Christoph Eschenbach in 2010 is to be Paavo Järvi, at the head of this orchestra that many consider the finest in France. Eschenbach has

Out with the New, In with the Old

Drama on both sides of the curtain at the Opéra de Paris.

It was Giuseppe Verdi who disparagingly referred to the **Opéra de Paris** (listings p317) as a '*grande boutique*', and holding the reins of this iconic institution always leaves the director open to fire from all sides. But the tenure of Flemish-born Gerard Mortier courted unprecedented unpopularity in the French capital. Having transformed La Monnaie in Brussels from a provincial siding to a top house, Mortier's next move was to the Salzburg Festival, where this quietly spoken man wrought havoc with the Karajan tradition, introducing avant-garde repertoire and controversial productions of the classic Mozart works, and generally upsetting the moneyed festival-goers. When he became director of the Opéra de Paris, Mortier dived straight in with German *regietheater*-style productions, with a heavy emphasis on challenging would-be contemporary relevance. Glamour and the popular Italian repertoire took a back seat.

Mortier aimed for vital, thought-provoking, 21st-century realism, using singers who acted as well as they sang. There were magnificent productions of Berg's *Wozzeck* by Christoph Marthaler, and stunning performances of Bartók's 'Bluebeard's Castle' from *La Fura dels Baus*. But scandals abounded: nobody will forget *The Magic Flute* performed on bouncy mattresses with a trite French

poem replacing the spoken dialogue; Krzysztof Warlikowski's take on Gluck's *Iphigénie* set in an old people's home; and the grim, politicised version of Verdi's *Simon Boccanegra* by Johan Simons.

Interviews, inveighing against the conservative public at the Opéra, were largely read by the very people Mortier was criticising, and did not help his public relations. For this reason, the government chose Nicolas Joel as Mortier's successor when the latter retires to go and shake up the New York City Opera at the end of the current season. Currently director of the Toulouse opera, Joel fulfils many a Paris opera-goer's dream: great voices and traditional repertoire. He is also known as a producer, but in Paris has promised to leave the staging to others. In true Paris style, those who booed the last regime will possibly take equal exception to a director who will be labelled as a peddler of fusty, old-fashioned production values.

Musically, things look to be on surer ground, with Philippe Jordan named as the new music director. Jordan, son of the great conductor Armin Jordan, has earned international operatic praise, and Joel will no doubt be ready to welcome back to the house singers whose talents are more obviously vocal than dramatic. Hopefully transcendent vocal style will bring its own dramatic reality.

ARTS & ENTERTAINMENT

Palais Garnier.

raised the standard of playing, and was instrumental in the decision to start building a new concert hall at La Villette. He is contributing some big-scale Mahler during the 2009 season, alongside concerts from Järvi and visits from Michael Tilson Thomas and the towering figure of Pierre Boulez. *Photo p319.*

Orchestre Pasdeloup

01.42.78.10.00/www.concertspasdeloup.com.
The Pasdeloup is the oldest orchestra in Paris, but the time when it premiered works by major composers, including Ravel and Bizet, has long passed. The theme for the 2009 season is 'folie', a collection of popular classical masterpieces.

Orchestre Philharmonique de Radio France

01.56.40.15.16/www.radiofrance.fr.
After a year when highly respected musical director Myung-Whun Chung seemed to have his eye off the ball, he returned with a blast to celebrate the Messiaen centenary – a challenging repertoire that suits the full-on style of the conductor, even if the standard of playing lags behind the Orchestre National.

VENUES

Auditorium du Louvre

Entrance through Pyramid, Cour Napoléon, Musée du Louvre, rue de Rivoli, 1st

(01.40.20.55.55/reservations 01.40.20.55.00/ www.louvre.fr). M° Palais Royal Musée du Louvre. **Box office** 9am-5.30pm Mon, Wed-Fri. Closed July, Aug. **Admission** €8-€30. **Credit** MC, V. **Map** p401 H5.
The Auditorium du Louvre packs a full programme with chamber music, lunchtime concerts and music on film. The 2009 season lacks strong thematic programming, but the growing number of concerts makes this a top venue for exploring a comprehensive range of chamber music, including a series of string quartet concerts based on the music of papa Haydn.

Châtelet – Théâtre Musical de Paris

1 pl du Châtelet, 1st (01.40.28.28.40/www. chatelet-theatre.com). M° Châtelet. **Box office** 11am-7pm daily. *By phone* 10am-7pm Mon-Sat. Closed July, Aug. **Admission** €10-€122.50. **Credit** AmEx, DC, MC, V. **Map** p408 J6.
Jean-Luc Choplin has radically changed the programming of this bastion of Paris music making. An attempt to rediscover the theatre's popular roots has been achieved at the expense of traditional fine music subscribers. The 2008/09 season kicked off with an Elvis Costello operatic adventure, and is rounded off by *La Pastorale*, a show whose aim is to combine new variety acts with contemporary opera. Good fun, but hardly a Wagner *Ring* cycle.

ARTS & ENTERTAINMENT

Cité de la Musique.

The concert programming is slimmed down, but with a more traditional repertoire, including an excellent series of piano recitals.

★ Cité de la Musique
221 av Jean-Jaurès, 19th (01.44.84.44.84/ www.cite-musique.fr). M° Porte de Pantin. **Box office** noon-6pm Tue-Sun. *By phone* 11am-7pm Mon-Sat; 10am-6pm Sun. **Admission** €25-€30. **Credit** MC, V. **Map** p403 (inset).
The energetic programming at the Cité de la Musique features a vast non-classical repertoire that includes ethnic music and jazz. Concerts are frequently split up into series with a pedagogic aim. Classical music programming still favours the Baroque and the contemporary, with only rare adventures into the intervening centuries. The museum has a smaller concert space.
▶ *The Conservatoire (01.40.40.45.45) is host to world-class performers and professors, and puts on many free concerts.*

IRCAM
1 pl Igor-Stravinsky, 4th (01.44.78.48.43/ www.ircam.fr). M° Hôtel de Ville. See website for concert venues, and details of courses and conferences. **Map** p406 K6.
The underground bunker next door to the Centre Pompidou, set up in 1969 by the avant-garde composer Pierre Boulez to create electronic microtonal music for the new century, is looking less redundant nowadays, with a full programme of courses and conferences. The building itself is mostly dedicated to educational work and electronic music research, but IRCAM sponsors concerts with a modernist theme across the city. Current director Frank Madlener has succeeded in raising the profile of the institution, which explores the links between science and artistic creation.

Maison de Radio France
116 av du Président-Kennedy, 16th (01.56.40.15.16/information 01.42.30.15.16/ www.radiofrance.fr). M° Passy/RER Avenue du Pdt Kennedy. **Box office** 11am-6pm Mon-Sat. **Admission** €5-€55. **Credit** AmEx, DC, MC, V. **Map** p404 A7.
State-owned radio station France Musique broadcasts a wide range of classical concerts from this huge cylindrical building on the banks of the Seine. The main auditorium (the Salle Olivier Messiaen) may be charmless, but the quality of music-making from the Orchestre National de France and the Orchestre Philharmonique de Radio France makes up for much. Watch out for free events here, as well as the enterprising *Présences* contemporary music festival, which is now split between several French cities – this year, Paris, Metz and Dijon.
▶ *The Passe Musique offers under-26s admission to four concerts for €18, or a year of concerts for €99.*

Musée National du Moyen Age
6 pl Paul-Painlevé, 5th (01.53.73.78.16/www. musee-moyenage.fr). M° Cluny La Sorbonne. **Admission** €16; €13 reductions. **Credit** AmEx, MC, V. **Map** p408 J7.
The museum presents a worthy programme of medieval concerts in which troubadours reflect the museum's collection.

★ Musée d'Orsay
62 rue de Lille, 7th (01.40.49.47.57/www.musee-orsay.fr). M° Solférino/RER Musée d'Orsay. **Admission** €6-€32. **Credit** MC, V. **Map** p405 G6.
The museum runs a full and enterprising series of lunchtime and evening concerts. The concerts at 12.30pm concentrate on promising young artists. For 2009 there is a fascinating cycle exploring the art of vocal accompaniment, featuring top artists such as French baritone François Le Roux and Dame Felicity Lott with pianist Graham Johnson, as well as some master classes on the subject.

Opéra National de Paris, Bastille
Pl de la Bastille, 12th (08.92.89.90.90/from abroad 01.72.29.35.35/www.operadeparis.fr). M° Bastille. **Box office** (130 rue de Lyon, 12th) 10.30am-6.30pm Mon-Sat. *By phone* 9am-6pm Mon-Fri; 9am-1pm Sat. **Admission** €5-€196. **Credit** AmEx, MC, V. **Map** p409 M7.
The modern building everyone loves to hate: even the exterior of the house is decaying, with netting protecting passers-by from fascia tiles since one fell in 1990. Restoration work is finally under way, and should take two years. If you want to make the administration squirm, just mention the unfinished *salle modulable* or the unflattering acoustics of the theatre. Director Gerard Mortier has introduced cutting-edge dramatic values, but disappointed those who enjoy spectacular singing and lavish period costumes. A rarity this season is a new staging of Polish composer Szymanowski's *King Roger*, produced by his compatriot Krzysztof Warlikowski, in June 2009.
▶ *For more about Mortier's successor, Nicolas Joel, see p315.*

★ Opéra National de Paris, Palais Garnier
Pl de l'Opéra, 9th (08.92.89.90.90/from abroad 01.72.29.35.35/www.operadeparis.fr). M° Opéra. **Box office** 10.30am-6.30pm Mon-Sat. *By phone*

ARTS & ENTERTAINMENT

9am-6pm Mon-Fri; 9am-1pm Sat. **Admission** €7-€172. **Credit** AmEx, MC, V. **Map** p401 G4.

The Palais Garnier, with its ornate, extravagant decor and ceiling by Marc Chagall, is the jewel in the crown of Paris music-making, as well as a glistening focal point for the Right Bank. The Opéra National often favours the high-tech Bastille for new productions, but the matchless acoustics of the Palais Garnier are superior to the new house. When the Bolshoi visited recently, it was the 19th-century glamour of Garnier that was chosen for its controversial production of Tchaikovsky's *Eugene Onegin*.

Péniche Opéra

Facing 46 quai de la Loire, 19th (01.53.35.07.77/ www.penicheopera.com). M° Jaurès or Laumière. **Box office** 10am-7pm Mon-Fri; 2-7pm Sat. **Admission** €12-€24; €8 reductions. **Credit** MC, V. **Map** p401 M1.

The Péniche Opéra is an enterprising, boat-based company that produces a programme of chamber-scale shows and concerts. They are directed by the indefatigable Mireille Larroche, and range from Baroque rarities to contemporary creations via charming revue-style shows concentrating on forgotten French comic opera and operetta.

Salle Cortot

78 rue Cardinet, 17th (01.47.63.85.72/www. ecolenormalecortot.com). M° Malesherbes. **No box office**. **Admission** phone for details. **Map** p401 E2.

This cosy concert hall in the Ecole Normale de Musique has excellent acoustics for chamber music events and master classes.

Salle Gaveau

45 rue La Boétie, 8th (01.49.53.05.07/www. sallegaveau.com). M° Miromesnil. **Box office** 10am-6pm Mon-Fri. **Admission** €10-€100. **Credit** MC, V. **Map** p401 E3.

Many of the small Paris orchestras have found refuge in the Salle Gaveau, but this delightful venue is underachieving, and the top-quality chamber music that used to be the hall's core repertoire is a rarity – a concert this season by pianist Ivo Pogorelich was one of the few highlights.

Salle Pleyel

252 rue du Fbg-St-Honoré, 8th (01.42.56.13.13/ www.sallepleyel.fr). M° Ternes. **Box office** noon-7pm Mon-Sat. *By phone* 11am-7pm Mon-Sat; 11am-5pm Sun. **Admission** €10-€160. **Credit** MC, V. **Map** p400 D3.

Home to the Orchestre de Paris, this restored concert hall looks splendid, but the improved acoustics are only partially successful. The Prokofiev cycle with the London Symphony Orchestra under Valery Gergiev reaches its climax in May 2009, and the hall has regained its prestigious status as the only venue dedicated to large-scale symphonic concerts in the capital until the completion of the new concert hall in 2012. The list of soloists reads like a who's who of classical music: the 2009 season includes pianists Lang Lang, Pollini and Brendel, violinist Vadim Repin, and appearances by divas Jessye Norman and Anna Netrebko.

La Sorbonne

Amphithéatre Richelieu, 17 rue de la Sorbonne, 5th (01.42.62.71.71/www.musique-en-sorbonne.org). M° Cluny La Sorbonne or Odéon. **Box office** by phone or at the door. **Admission** €18-€40. **Credit** MC, V. **Map** p408 J7.

Having ended 2008 strongly with the complete Beethoven string quartets played by the Arpeggione quartet, the university lecture theatres continue with a series of ambitious concerts featuring the orchestra and chorus of the Sorbonne. Standards may waver, but the setting is impressive.

★ Théâtre des Bouffes du Nord

37bis bd de la Chapelle, 10th (01.46.07.34.50/ www.bouffesdunord.com). M° La Chapelle. **Box office** *by phone or in person* 11am-6pm Mon-Sat. **Admission** €10-€26. **Credit** MC, V. **Map** p402 K1.

This elegant theatre, directed by Micheline Rozan and Peter Brook, boasts one of the most imaginative chamber music programmes in the capital. Soloists include pianist Kathryn Stott in a programme of trios with violinist Valeryi Sokolov and cellist Leonid Gorokhov, as well as appearances by the Talich and Prazák quartets.

Théâtre des Champs-Elysées

15 av Montaigne, 8th (01.49.52.50.50/www. theatrechampselysees.fr). M° Alma Marceau. **Box office** 1-7pm Mon-Sat. *By phone* 10am-noon, 2-6pm Mon-Fri. **Admission** €5-€160. **Credit** AmEx, MC, V. **Map** p400 D5.

This beautiful art nouveau theatre hosted the scandalous premiere of Stravinsky's *Le Sacre du Printemps* in 1913. It remains the favourite venue for visiting foreign orchestras, which this year include the Vienna Philharmonic, Dresden Staatskapelle, London Philharmonic and BBC Symphony. The prestigious line-up of visiting maestros includes Eska-Pekka Salonen, Valery Gergiev, Seiji Ozawa and controversial young Brit Daniel Harding. Mozart's *Nozze di Figaro* is the operatic highlight of early 2009, along with celebrity concerts from superstar tenors Roberto Alagna and Jonas Kaufmann.

Théâtre National de l'Opéra Comique

Pl Boieldieu, 2nd (08.25.01.01.23/www.opera-comique.com). M° Richelieu Drouot. **Box office** 11am-7pm Mon-Sat; 11am-5pm Sun. *By phone* 11am-7pm Mon-Sat; 11am-5pm Sun. **Admission** €6-€115. **Credit** AmEx, DC, MC, V. **Map** p402 H4.

Orchestre de Paris. *See p314.*

Its promotion to national theatre status has brought this jewel box of a theatre back to life. Mindful of a French repertoire largely ignored by other houses, Jérôme Deschamps' second season includes Auber's *Fra Diavolo*, Rameau's *Zoroastre,* and the first Paris performances of *Lady Sarashina,* a new opera by Peter Eötvös. The climax will be the return of Bizet's *Carmen* in June 2009 to the theatre where it was so calamitously created, conducted by Sir John Eliot Gardiner.

Théâtre du Tambour-Royal

94 rue du Fbg-du-Temple, 11th (01.48.06.72.34/ http://tambour.royal.monsite.wanadoo.fr). M° Belleville or Goncourt. **Box office** 6.30-8pm Tue-Fri; 3-8pm Sat, Sun. *By phone* 10am-8pm Mon-Sat. **Admission** €16-€21. **Credit** MC, V. **Map** p403 M4.

This charming venue is where Maurice Chevalier launched his career. Its programming includes occasional concerts of light repertoire and revue-style shows, including the popular *Best of Mozart.*

Théâtre de la Ville

2 pl du Châtelet, 4th (01.42.74.22.77/www.theatre delaville-paris.com). M° Châtelet. **Box office** 11am-7pm Mon; 11am-8pm Tue-Sat. **Admission** €12-€23. **Credit** MC, V. **Map** p408 J6.

Programming in this vertiginous concrete amphitheatre features hip chamber music outfits such as the Kronos and Takács Quartets, Early Music pioneer Fabio Biondi, and soloists such as up-and-coming pianist Aleksandar Madzar and tenor Werner Güra.

▶ *The season here spills over to performances at the Théâtre des Abbesses (see p346), which shares the same phone number and box office hours.*

Rock, Roots & Jazz

The last few years have brought a number of changes to Paris's musical life, with several gains but a few losses as well. Rock has been on the rise, and in areas like Bastille, small, rock-orientated venues have gradually usurped the funky Latino vibes that dominated a decade ago.

The trashy, rock 'n' roll aesthetic of dance labels like Ed Banger and Kitsuné has also helped blur the line between gig-goers and clubbers, and the hipster entities that have emerged are well catered for by the new *éminences grises* of the capital's music scene, La Clique – the team behind don't-miss venues such as **Le ParisParis**, **Le Baron** and new hit **Le Showcase**, with its unusual location (underneath Pont Alexandre III) and formula of live gigs followed by DJs.

On the flipside, one of Paris's mainstays, jazz, has been suffering. The past few years have seen keepers of the flame like Le Slow Club (once arguably one of the most famous jazz joints in Europe), Le Bilboquet and Les 7 Lézards struggling and finally giving up the ghost. It's not all doom and gloom, though: **Au Duc des Lombards** keeps the traditional standards high, and **Le Sunset/Le Sunside** has stayed on top of its game.

Paris is also a European leader for world music, particularly African and Arab acts, and the café culture that nurtures native *chansonniers* still survives – check recent arrival **La Bellevilloise** for proof. This is all in addition, of course, to the many UK and US

ARTS & ENTERTAINMENT

Festival Fever

Where to get in on the act.

Paris is home to three noteworthy rock festivals. The first, **Sous la Plage** (www.souslaplage.com), is free and takes place at Paris-Plage (*see p277*) from early July to mid September. **Solidays** (*see p276*), in mid July, features electro and dub, and leans more towards Gallic sounds than its more international rival **Rock en Seine** (*see p277*), which takes place in late August and hosted bands such as REM and the Raconteurs in 2008.

Further afield, try **Les Eurockéennes** (www.eurockeennes.com), **La Route du Rock** (www.laroutedurock.com) or

Les Transmusicales (www.lestrans.com). Les Eurockéennes takes place in early July, and confirmed its credentials in 2008 with the likes of Moby, Massive Attack, N*E*R*D and Gnarls Barkley taking to the stage. La Route du Rock takes place in mid August in the port town of St-Malo, and Les Transmusicales (www.lestrans.com) kicks off in early December. Rumour has it that 2009 will see the festival return to the town centre after years exiled to giant aircraft hangars outside Rennes; it's the hippest event of its size in France.

rock acts whose European tours inevitably include a Paris stopover. And don't forget that every 21 June, the whole place turns into one giant music venue for the **Fête de la Musique**, when a party in the street is guaranteed.

INFORMATION AND RESOURCES

If you're intending to spend any length of time in Paris, or even just planning ahead, visit www.gogoparis.com, which selects regular concert highlights and also features a decent gig list for the coming months, with all information provided in English and French; www.infoconcert.com is also well worth a look. The **Fnac** and **Virgin Megastore** ticket offices also display details of up-and-coming concerts. Depending on your tastes (and your French) radio can be useful for tip-offs: Nova (101.5FM) does electro, lounge and world, TSF (89.9FM) and FIP (105.1FM) cover jazz, and Le Mouv' (92.1FM) and OuiFM (102.3FM) are for rock fans.

Venue box offices are usually closed in the daytime, and most venues take a break in August. Prices for gigs vary according to a group or artist's pulling power, but several excellent venues, like **La Flèche d'Or**, host regular free nights – ideal if you're feeling adventurous and/or are on a budget. For concerts, it's best to turn up at the time stated on the ticket: strict noise curfews mean that start times are adhered to pretty closely.

ROCK, POP & WORLD

Stadium venues

Palais Omnisports de Paris-Bercy
8 bd de Bercy, 12th (08.92.39.01.00/ www.bercy.fr). M° Bercy. **Open** *Box office*

11am-6pm Mon-Sat. **Credit** AmEx, DC, MC, V. **Map** p407 N9.
The only place to play for rock and pop behemoths of any generation; Coldplay and Elton John were among the big draws last year, and Tina Turner and Lenny Kravitz have dates in March and May 2009 respectively.

Zenith
211 av Jean-Jaurès, 19th (www.zenith-paris. com). M° Porte de Pantin. **Open** times vary. **No credit cards. Map** p403 inset.
State-of-the-art sound and credible bands make this the large venue of choice. Snoop Dogg and Camille dropped in last year.

Bar and club venues

Le Bataclan
50 bd Voltaire, 11th (01.43.14.00.30/www.le-bataclan.com). M° Oberkampf. **Open** times vary. **No credit cards. Map** p403 M5.
Established in 1864, this highly distinctive venue is still standing after the odd facelift, and remains admirably discerning in its booking of rock, world, jazz and hip hop acts.

★ Batofar
Opposite 11 quai François-Mauriac, 13th (01.53.60.17.30/www.batofar.org). M° Bibliothèque François-Mitterrand or Quai de la Gare. **Open** 9pm-late Wed-Sat. **Admission** €5-€20. **Credit** MC, V. **Map** p407 N10.
This distinctively red and enduringly hip party boat lays on DJs, rappers and assorted underground noise-merchants for the benefit of an up-for-it crowd. It comes into its own in the summer, when the terrace opens at 7pm and concerts regularly spill out on to the riverbank.
▶ *For more on Batofar's club nights, see p329.*

Café de la Danse

5 passage Louis-Phillipe, 11th (01.47.00.57.59/ www.myspace.com/cafedeladanse). M° Bastille. **Open** times vary. Closed July, Aug. **No credit cards. Map** p407 M7.

Pristine sound and a certain rarefied ideal of pop and rock perfection typify this former dancehall. It's largely seated, but there's still room to shake a tail-feather down the front.

★ La Cigale/La Boule Noire

120 bd de Rochechouart,18th (01.49.25.81.75/ www.lacigale.fr). M° Anvers or Pigalle. **Open** times vary. **Credit** MC, V. **Map** p402 J2.

Easily one of Paris's finest venues, the lovely, horse-shoe-shaped theatre La Cigale is linked to more cosy venue La Boule Noire, good for catching cult-ish visiting acts.

La Dame de Canton

Opposite 11 quai François-Mauriac, 13th (01.44.06.96.45/www.damedecanton.com). M° Bibliothèque François-Mitterrand or Quai de la Gare. **Open** noon-2am Tue-Thur; until late Fri, Sat; noon-midnight Sun. **Admission** €5-€10. **Credit** MC, V.

Another rebranding for the floating venue in a Chinese junk, formerly the Guinguette Pirate and latterly Le Cabaret Pirate. The cult indie spirit of yore has evaporated, and now it's about DJs spreading good vibes and roots, folk and *chanson* performers.

Le Divan du Monde

75 rue des Martyrs, 18th (01.42.52.02.46/ www.divandumonde.com). M° Anvers or Pigalle. **Open** times vary. **Credit** MC, V. **Map** p402 H2.

Le Divan du Monde has come a long way since the days when Toulouse-Lautrec used to sup absinthe here, but the decadent spirit of old Montmartre has just about survived, and the majority of the nights, showcasing indie, hip hop and electro groups, as well as DJs, are free.

Elysée Montmartre

72 bd de Rochechouart, 18th (01.44.92.45.47/ www.elyseemontmartre.com). M° Anvers. **Open** *Bar* 11am-midnight daily. *Concerts* times vary. **Credit** *Bar* MC, V. **Map** p402 J2.

A reliable and spacious venue in Montmartre. Dancing girls once lifted their skirts here on a regular basis, but these days you're more likely to see mid-sized alternative rock acts or the likes of disco old-timers Chic, who passed through last year.
▶ *The Elysée also hosts some enduring party nights, including Le Bal (see p329).*

★ La Flèche d'Or

102bis rue de Bagnolet, 20th (01.44.64.01.02/ www.flechedor.fr). M° Alexandre Dumas. **Open** 8pm-2am Wed-Sat. *Concerts* times vary. **Admission** free. **Credit** MC, V. **Map** p403 Q5.

This much-loved indie and electro venue is a great place for free music, with three or four bands playing every night the venue is open. It also provides monthly residencies to local groups and DJs.

Le Gambetta

104 rue de Bagnolet, 20th (01.43.70.52.01/www. gambetta-bar.com). M° Gambetta. **Open** 10am-2am daily. *Concerts* 9pm Wed-Sat. **Admission** free-€5. **Credit** AmEx, DC, MC, V. **Map** p407 Q6.

A small, smoky joint that hosts DJs and sound systems every night, as well as rock, reggae, raï, funk and folk acts several night a week. Ignoring the official opening hours, weekend parties have been known to last all night.

Mains d'Oeuvres

1 rue Charles-Garnier, 93400 St-Ouen (01.40.11. 25.25/www.mainsdoeuvres.org). M° Garibaldi or Porte de Clignancourt. **Open** *Bar* 9.30am-midnight daily. *Concerts* 8.30pm, days vary. **Admission** €10. **Credit** *Bar* MC, V.

A hub for fringe musical and performance activity just outside Paris, the Mains d'Oeuvres is a huge former leisure centre for car factory workers that specialises in left-field electro, rock mavericks and multimedia artists.

La Maroquinerie

23 rue Boyer, 20th (01.40.33.35.05/www. lamaroquinerie.fr). M° Gambetta. **Open** *Box office* (in person only) 2.30-6.30pm Mon-Fri. *Concerts* 8pm Mon-Fri. Closed Aug. **Credit** MC, V. **Map** p403 P4.

Literary discussion and rock 'n' roll coexist contentedly at this happening locale. It's home to the Inrocks Indie Club nights, featuring up-and-coming Anglo and French rock acts, but there are still traces of its world music roots.

★ La Mécanique Ondulatoire

8 passage Thière, 11th (www.lamecond.com). M° Bastille or Ledru Rollin. **Open** 6pm-2am Mon-Sat. *Concerts* from 8pm Tue-Sat. **Admission** €3-€6. **Credit** MC, V. **Map** p407 M7.

Cementing Bastille's status as Paris's prime hangout for rockers, this exciting recent arrival has three levels and alternates eclectic DJs with live acts in the cellar, plus there's jazz on Tuesday nights. *See also p324* **Teenage Kicks**.

Le Motel

8 passage Josset, 11th (01.58.30.88.52/www. myspace.com/lemotel). M° Ledru Rollin. **Open** 6pm-2am Tue-Sun. **Closed** Aug. **Credit** MC, V. **Map** p407 M7.

This most Anglophile of Paris bars, with Stone Roses and Smiths posters adorning the walls, manages to fit plenty of live bands, including some of the best upcoming local talent, on to its tiny stage.
▶ *For more on Le Mo tel, see p229.*

Nouveau Casino

109 rue Oberkampf, 11th (01.43.57.57.40/
www.nouveaucasino.net). M° Ménilmontant,
Parmentier or St-Maur. **Open** *Concerts* times
vary. **Credit** *Bar* MC, V. **Map** p403 N5.
A bankable and loveable albeit rather commercial
venue run by the adjacent Café Charbon (*see p231*),
with fab acoustics, gigs and club nights featuring
rock, dub and garage, plus reasonable drinks prices.
Get sweaty on the floor or survey the action from
the balcony.

Olympia

28 bd des Capucines, 9th (08.92.68.33.68/
www.olympiahall.com). M° Opéra. **Open** *Box
office* 10am-9pm Mon-Sat; 10am-7pm Sun.
Concerts times vary. **Credit** AmEx, DC, MC, V.
Map p401 G4. **Map** p401 G4.
The Beatles, Frank Sinatra, Jimi Hendrix and Edith
Piaf have all performed here over the years; as did
Jacques Brel, who recorded two fabled live albums
here in the early '60s. Now it's mainly a home for
nostalgia and *variété*, with a smattering of contemporary sounds.

O'Sullivans by the Mill

*92 bd de Clichy, 18th (01.53.09.08.49/www.
osullivans-pubs.com). M Blanche.* **Open** noon-
5am Mon-Thur; noon-6am Fri-Sun. *Concerts*
times vary. **Credit** MC, V. **Map** p401 G2.
This Irish chain bar is all about late, late nights,
with grizzly weekend rock gigs that last until sun-
rise, DJs and open mic nights the first Wednesday
of the month.

★ Le ParisParis

*5 av de l'Opéra, 1st (01.42.60.64.45/www.
leparisparis.com). M° Pyramides.* **Open**
11pm-5am Tue-Sat. *Concerts* times vary.
Admission free. **Drinks** €10. **Credit** MC, V.
Map p401 H5.
This small, sweaty *boîte* has become a focus for 'cool'
Paris. It's great, albeit pricey, once you're in, but
you'll have to pass the door test first.
▶ *If you like ParisParis, you may also enjoy*
Le Showcase (see right) and Le Baron (see p330),
run by the same team.

Point Ephémère

200 quai de Valmy, 10th (01.40.34.02.48/
www.pointephemere.org). M° Jaurès or

INSIDE TRACK
GIG LISTINGS

The weekly magazine *Les Inrockuptibles*
is a valuable resource. Alternatively,
try reliable, bi-monthly gig bible *Lylo*,
free in bars and branches of Fnac.

Louis Blanc. **Open** noon-2am daily. *Concerts*
8.30pm daily. **Credit** AmEx, DC, MC, V.
Map p403 Q5.
This converted warehouse is a classy affair, bringing together up-and-coming local rock, jazz and
world gigs with a decent restaurant, plus dance and
recording studios and exhibitions.
▶ *Point Ephémère is the sister venue to Mains*
d'Oeuvres; see p321.

Le Reservoir

16 rue de la Forge-Royal, 11th (01.43.56.39.60/
www.reservoirclub.com). M° Faidherbe Chaligny
or Ledru-Rollin. **Open** 8pm-5am Tue-Sat;
11.30pm-4.30pm Sun. **Admission** free-€10.
Credit AmEx, DC, MC, V. **Map** p407 N7.
This classy, Anglo-inspired venue hosts regular
club nights and live indie acts, as well as low-key
performances from larger acts. Also serves up a 'jazz
brunch' on Sundays.

La Scène Bastille

2bis rue des Taillandiers, 11th (01.48.06.50.70/
www.la-scene.com). M° Bastille. **Open** midnight-
6am Wed-Sun. *Concerts* 7.30-10.45pm Mon-Fri.
Closed Aug. **Credit** MC, V. **Map** p407 M7.
This beautifully designed bar and restaurant offers
you the option of chilling out in alcoves or joining
the kids to groove to hip hop, funk and jazz.

★ Le Showcase

Underneath Pont Alexandre III, 8th
(01.45.61.25.43/www.showcase.fr). M° Champs-
Elysées-Clemenceau. **Open** *Concerts* 10pm Fri,
Sat. Closed Aug. **Credit** MC, V. **Map** p401 E5.
A little too flash for some, but there's no doubting
this brand new vaulted club by the Seine, and its
Sous le Pont events – live performance followed by
DJs – have been the big success story of the past
year. Just be prepared to queue.

Le Trabendo

211 av Jean-Jaurès, 19th (01.49.25.89.99/www.
trabendo.fr). M° Porte de Pantin. **Open** times
vary. **Credit** MC, V. **Map** p403 inset.
This quirky, minimal-futurist spot in the 19th has
carved out a niche in all things alternative, from
post-rock to drum 'n' bass, avant-garde hip hop to
modern jazz.

CHANSON

Chez Adel

10 rue de la Grange-aux-Belles, 10th
(01.42.08.24.61). M° Jacques Bonsergent. **Open**
noon-midnight Tue-Sun. *Concerts* 5pm Tue-Sun.
Admission free. **Credit** MC, V. **Map** p402 L3.
Patron Adel is probably the most renowned *chanson* café owner in Paris, and this fine address
attracts countless devotees with its repertoire of
chanson and Eastern European sounds.

Au Duc des Lombards. *See p325.*

Artiste-in-residence Marc Havet serenades punters with politically incorrect *chanson* at the weekend; you can also expect poetry events and exhibitions of photos and paintings.

Sentier des Halles
50 rue d'Aboukir, 2nd (01.42.61.89.96/ www.sentierdeshalles.fr). M° Sentier. **Open** 7pm-midnight Tue-Sat. *Concerts* 8-10pm Tue-Sat. Closed Aug. **No credit cards. Map** p402 J4.
Really more of a concert venue than a music bar, Le Sentier has developed beyond its traditional *chanson* base to embrace a variety of modern styles.

★ Le Vieux Belleville
12 rue des Envierges, 20th (01.44.62.92.66/ www.le-vieux-belleville.com) M° Pyrénées. **Open** *Concerts* 8pm Thur-Sat. Closed mid Aug. **Credit** MC, V. **Map** p403 N4.
If you desire an authentic Belleville rendezvous, there's no better location than this old-style café with terrace, where the traditions of accordion music and croaky-voiced *chanson* endure.

WORLD & TRADITIONAL MUSIC

Cité de la Musique
221 av Jean-Jaurès, 19th (01.44.84.44.84/ www.cite-musique.fr). M° Porte de Pantin. **Open** noon-6pm Tue-Sat; 10am-6pm Sun. *Concerts* Tue-Sat (times vary). **Admission** €17-€38. **Credit** MC, V. **Map** p403 inset.
This Villette venue welcomes prestigious names from all over the globe, and also does a fine line in contemporary classical, avant-jazz and electronica.
▶ *The Conservatoire (01.40.40.45.45) puts on many free concerts.*

★ La Bellevilloise
19-21 rue Boyer, 20th (01.46.36.07.07/www.la bellevilloise.com). M° Gambetta or Ménilmontant. **Open** 5.30pm-2am Wed-Fri; 11am-2am Sat, Sun. **Admission** free. **Credit** MC, V. **Map** p403 P4.
This historic site was reopened in 2005 as a beautifully relaxed, spacious venue with a folky bent.

Le Limonaire
18 Cité Bergère, 9th (01.45.23.33.33). M° Grands Boulevards. **Open** 7pm-2am Mon; 6pm-2am Fri-Sun. *Concerts* 10pm Tue-Sat; 7pm Sun. Closed Mon, Sun in July & Aug. **Credit** MC, V. **Map** p402 J4.
Serious *chanson* takes the limelight. Performances vary from piano-led chansonniers to cabarets.

Au Magique
42 rue de Gergovie, 14th (01.45.42.26.10/ www.aumagique.com). M° Pernety. **Open** 8pm-2am Wed-Sun. *Concerts* 9.30pm Wed, Thur; 10pm Fri, Sat. **No credit cards. Map** p405 F10.

Institut du Monde Arabe
1 rue des Fossés-St-Bernard, 5th (01.40.51.38.38/www.imarabe.org). M° Jussieu. **Open** 10am-6pm Tue-Sun. *Concerts* 8.30pm Fri, Sat. **Admission** varies. **Credit** MC, V. **Map** p409 K7.
This huge, plush auditorium attracts some of the biggest names in the world of Arab music.

Le Kibélé
12 rue de l'Echiquier, 10th (01.48.24.57.74/ www.kibele.fr). M° Bonne Nouvelle. **Open** noon-2pm, 7pm-midnight Mon-Sat. *Concerts* 9pm Mon-Sat. **Admission** free-€5. **Credit** AmEx, MC, V. **Map** p402 K4.
Music from across the Mediterranean and beyond, with a Turkish restaurant in the same building.

Satellit' Café
44 rue de la Folie-Méricourt, 11th (01.47.00.48.87/www.satellit-cafe.com). M° Oberkampf, Parmentier or St-Ambroise.

ARTS & ENTERTAINMENT

Teenage Kicks

The 11th is solid rock.

ARTS & ENTERTAINMENT

It's the Fête de la Musique, 21 June 2008, a blisteringly hot mid-afternoon concert in the grounds of Château de Vincennes, and the teenage girls down the front have just gone wild. It's time for Les BB Brunes, the all-male adolescent trio which has, to date, been the commercial apogee of France's new rock explosion. Following in the wake of groups like the Naast, Second Sex, Plasticines and the other *'bébés rockeurs'*, Les BB Brunes are the ones who have nailed the cute, punky, post-Libertines formula and delivered it to an apparently grateful teen audience. By the end of last year, they were playing one of Paris's mega-venues, the Zenith (*see p320*); all well and good, but if you want to get beyond the marketing and immerse yourself in the Paris rock scene, there are other places to investigate – like the 11th arrondissement, in and around Bastille.

Ten years ago, the area was dominated by funky, Latin-tinged club sounds. The sole outpost of rock culture was Le Pop In (105 rue Amelot, 11th), an eccentric English pub-meets-indie club right out on the edge of the 11th, but hugely influential on what has been happening in the Bastille since. With a dance area that made you feel like you were having a party in someone's garage, it set the tone with a largely anglophone, rock-leaning musical policy; not unlike a UK indie disco, but out on a limb as far as Paris was concerned. Many of the aforementioned teen groups may well have picked up a few ideas on nights out here; Plasticines dedicated a song, 'Pop In, Pop Out', to the place.

The first bar to follow Le Pop In's lead was Planète Mars (21 rue Keller, 11th) in 2004, this time with a location right in the heart of Bastille. It rapidly became a favoured haunt for musicians, and thus

the territory for Paris's most rock 'n' roll district was staked out. Two streets along from that, on passage Thière, you can now find **La Mécanique Ondulatoire** (*see p321*), a three-level bar with singles on the wall and an arched-ceiling concert room downstairs. The co-owner, Pascale Biville, who reckons that two-thirds of the acts they put on are French, says: 'The principle idea was to open a rock bar. We found the building charming – only afterwards did we find out that there were these other rock bars in the area.' Five minutes away in passage Josset, though, Remi Tettiravou of **Le Motel** (*see p321*) makes no bones about the choice of location. 'We're here because it's the 11th, absolutely. It has become the area for people who are into rock.' As a bar, it's as determinedly anglophile as Le Pop In (Stone Roses, Happy Mondays and Smiths posters adorn the walls); but, like La Mécanique, Le Motel and its tiny stage are providing a platform for up-and-coming Paris acts. Les BB Brunes may have the Zenith, but it's in this part of town that rock has really struck a chord.

La Mécanique Ondulatoire.

Open *Bar* 8pm-1am Tue, Wed; 8pm-3am or 5am Thur; 10pm-6am Fri, Sat. *Club* 11pm-6am Thur-Sat. *Concerts* 9pm Tue-Thur. **Admission** €10; €8 reductions. **Credit** *Bar* MC, V. **Map** p403 M5. This bar lends its sound system to all things global, but the focus is on traditional African music.

★ Théâtre de la Ville
2 pl du Châtelet, 4th (01.42.74.22.77/ www.theatredelaville-paris.com). M° Châtelet. **Open** *Box office* 11am-7pm Mon-Sat. *Concerts*

8.30pm Mon-Fri; 5pm Sun. **Admission** €17; €12 reductions. **Credit** MC, V. **Map** p408 J6. Music and dance of the highest order can be found at both sites, with jazz and music from just about anywhere you can think of (Iraq, Japan, Thailand, Brittany) amid the classical recitals.

La Vieille Grille
1 rue du Puits-de-l'Ermite, 5th (01.47.07.22.11/ vieille.grille.free.fr). M° Place Monge. **Open** *Concerts* 8.30pm Mon-Sat; 3pm, 5pm Sun.

Admission varies. Closed in Aug. **No credit cards**. **Map** p406 K8.
An intimate, artist-run venue, great for passionate, theatrical performances of tango, French songs and klezmer, as well as operettas, theatre, book readings and children's shows: fun for all the family.

JAZZ & BLUES

Le Baiser Salé
58 rue des Lombards, 1st (01.42.33.37.71/ www.lebaisersale.com). M° Châtelet. **Open** *Chanson concerts* 7pm daily. *Jazz concerts* 10pm daily. **Admission** *Chanson* €13; €8 in advance. *Jazz* €12-€17. **Credit** AmEx, DC, MC, V. **Map** p406 J6.
The 'salty kiss' divides its time between passing *chanson* merchants, world artists and jazzmen of every stripe, from trad to fusion.

Caveau de la Huchette
5 rue de la Huchette, 5th (01.43.26.65.05/www. caveaudelahuchette.fr). M° St-Michel. **Open** *Concerts* 9.30pm-2.30am Mon-Wed, Sun; 9.30pm-6am Thur-Sat. **Admission** €11 Mon-Thur, Sun; €13 Fri, Sat; €9 reductions. **Credit** MC, V. **Map** p408 J7.
This medieval cellar has been a mainstay for 60 years. The jazz shows are followed by early-hours performances in a swing, rock, soul or disco vein.

Caveau des Oubliettes
52 rue Galande, 5th (01.46.34.23.09/www. caveaudesoubliettes.com). M° St-Michel. **Open** 5pm daily. *Concerts* 10pm daily. **Admission** free. **Credit** MC, V. **Map** p408 J7.
A foot-tapping frenzy echoes in this medieval dungeon, complete with instruments of torture and underground passages. There are various jam sessions in the week, and on Sundays.

★ Au Duc des Lombards
42 rue des Lombards, 1st (01.42.33.22.88/www. ducdeslombards.com). M° Châtelet. **Open** *Concerts* 9pm Mon-Sat. Closed mid Aug. **Admission** €19-€25. **Credit** MC, V. **Map** p406 J6.
Some of the capital's venerated jazz spots, like Le Bilboquet, have lost the fight for survival in recent years. But this one has endured, and attracts a high class of performer. *Photo p323.*

Lionel Hampton Jazz Club
Hôtel Méridien Etoile, 81 bd Gouvion-St-Cyr, 17th (01.40.68.30.42/www.jazzclub-paris. com). M° Porte Maillot. **Open** 7am-2am. *Concerts* 10pm-2am Mon-Sat; 12.30pm Sun. **Admission** (incl 1 drink) €26. **Credit** MC, V. **Map** p400 B2.
This hotel venue has a strong US bias, with lots of R&B and gospel, but native acts get a look in as well. Not particularly progressive, but classy nonetheless.

New Morning
7-9 rue des Petites-Ecuries, 10th (01.45.23.51.41/ www.newmorning.com). Concerts 9pm daily. **Admission** €15-€21. **Credit** MC, V. **Map** p402 K3.
One of the best places for the latest cutting-edge jazz exponents, with a broad policy that also embraces *chanson*, blues, world and sophisticated pop.

★ Nouvelle Athènes
9 pl Pigalle, 9th (01.49.70.03.99). M° Pigalle. **Open** 10am-2am Mon-Sat. *Concerts* 10.30pm Tue-Sat. **Admission** varies. **Map** p401 H2.
Nouvelle Athènes has a weight of history behind it. It was the café in Degas' *L'Absinthe*, a striptease joint frequented by the Nazis and Liberation troops, then rock venue New Moon, before burning down in 2004. The place has been resurrected as Pigalle's first jazz venue for decades.

Parc Floral de Paris
Route de la Pyramide, Bois de Vincennes, 12th (01.49.57.24.84/www.parcfloraldeparis.com). M° Château de Vincennes. **Open** *Apr-Sept* 9.30am-8pm daily. *Oct-Mar* 9.30am-6pm daily. *Concerts* (May-July) 4.30pm Sat, Sun. **Admission** €1.50-€3. **No credit cards**.
The best and most reasonably priced bet for jazz in the summer, as the cream of the international jazz world congregates for afternoons in the park.

Le Petit Journal Montparnasse
113 rue du Commandant René-Mouchotte, 14th (01.43.21.56.70/www.petitjournal-montparnasse. com). M° Gaîté or Montparnasse-Bienvenüe. **Open** 8pm-2am daily. *Concerts* 10pm Mon-Sat. **Admission** (incl 1 drink) €25; €15 reductions. **Credit** MC, V. **Map** p405 F9.
A two-level jazz brasserie with Latin sounds, R&B and soul-gospel.

Le Sunset/Le Sunside
60 rue des Lombards, 1st (Sunside 01.40.26.21.25/Sunset 01.40.26.46.60/ www.sunset-sunside.com). M° Châtelet. **Open** *Concerts* 9pm, 10pm daily. **Admission** €8-€25. **Credit** MC, V. **Map** p406 J6.
A split-personality venue, with Sunset dealing in electric groups and Sunside hosting acoustic performances. Their renown pulls in big jazz names from both sides of the Atlantic.

Théâtre du Châtelet
1 pl du Châtelet (information 01.40.28.28.00/ booking 01.40.28.28.40/www.chatelet-theatre. com). M° Châtelet. **Open** times vary. **Admission** €16-€69. **Credit** AmEx, DC, MC, V. **Map** p406 J6.
This venerable theatre and classic music hall has another life as a jazz and *chanson* venue – old- and new-school jazzers, from Stacey Kent to Jamie Cullum, appeared last year.

ARTS & ENTERTAINMENT

Nightlife

From barges to washing machine showrooms, quirky venues abound.

Compared to other European cities, club life in Paris can be a bit of a riddle. Although large, ritzy discos are easy enough to find (wander around the Champs-Elysées), locating more unusual venues requires some insider knowledge. But help is at hand: many of the bars and venues that litter Bastille, the Marais, Oberkampf, the Grands Boulevards, Pigalle and Canal St-Martin provide flyers (try La Fourmi, Andy Whaloo and L'Ile Enchantée) and are ideal for pre-clubbing drinks; Once you've checked the options over a drink, you'll be all set for the night ahead.

ABOUT THE SCENE

Many artists and labels that found fame through the ongoing surge in popularity of French electronic music are now more likely to fill large venues than honour their origins by playing on small stages. For audiences, this translates as big, one-off events in venues such as **Rex** and **Point Ephémère**, with cool labels, DJs and crews – Tigersushi, Versatile, Kill the DJ, Bob Sinclar, David Guetta, Dirty Sound System – running their own show.

However, it's also worth remembering that the city's smaller venues often get the biggest DJs. It's not rare, for example, to catch star Berlin DJ M.A.N.D.Y at **Elysée Montmartre** or Jarvis Cocker at the **Nouveau Casino** – not to mention other bijou joints such as **Le Baron** and **La Boule Noire**.

Elsewhere, it's also worth keeping an eye on **Mains d'Oeuvres**, famed for its wild occasional parties and regular gigs; and **Social Club** (formerly Triptyque). **Les Bains Douches** is also back on form, drawing a mixed, fashionable crowd. And the section of the 13th arrondissement beside the river is fast becoming the Left Bank's hottest nightlife area (*see p331* **River Dance**).

For big-room clubbing, the **Mix** is still top dog, and the legendary **Queen** continues to pack in a mostly gay crowd. And if you don't know when to stop, there are various after-party options – although with clubbing activity starting in the wee hours, normal clubs can feel like an after-party and a night can feel like it's only just warming up at 5am. Parties

that don't stop until sundown can be found on the **Concorde Atlantique** during summer, and at smaller venues such as **Batofar** (the historic home of after-parties, though it hosts them less frequently these days), **Red Light** and Nouveau Casino. Look out for on flyers for events run by the Families organisation, which keeps crowds rocking 24 hours a day, and DJ Terry and the Freak 'n' Chic crew.

For listings, check www.flyersweb.com, www.novaplanet.com, www.radiofg.com and www.lemonsound.com. Radio stations FG (98.2FM) and Nova (101.5FM) also provide details on what's happening.

The last métro leaves at around 12.30am (an hour later on Fridays, Saturdays and the night before public holidays), and the first one gets rolling at 5.30am. Between those times, you'll have to take a night bus, taxi or Vélib (but don't drink and ride). However, central Paris is small, and you may well be able to walk to your next destination.

CLUB BARS

★ Andy Whaloo

69 rue des Gravilliers, 3rd (01.42.71.20.38). M° Arts et Métiers. **Open** 5pm-2am Tue-Sun. **Admission** free. **Drinks** €3-€12. **Credit** AmEx, MC, V. **Map** p409 K5.

Owned by the people behind Momo and Sketch in London, Andy Whaloo serves sumptuous snack food and is tastefully decorated with Moroccan artifacts. The seating is made from upturned paint cans, and the DJs play everything from hip hop to techno, stepping up the volume as the night gets longer.

★ Baxo
21 rue Juliette Dodu, 10th (01.42.02.99.71/ www.baxo.fr). M° Colonel Fabien. **Open** 9am-3pm, 7pm-2am Mon-Fri; 5pm-2am Sat, Sun. **Admission** free. **Drinks** €3-€10. **Credit** MC, V. **Map** p403 M3.
A spanking new hybrid venue that triples as a restaurant, bar and DJ lounge for an übercool, bobo clientele. Friday nights are for resident DJs, and Saturdays bring live bands and guest splicers. The food is satisfyingly innovative.

Café Chéri(e)
44 bd de la Villette, 19th (01.42.02.02.05). M° Belleville. **Open** 8am-2am daily. **Admission** free. **Drinks** €2.80-€7. **Credit** MC, V. **Map** p403 M3.
A popular DJ bar, especially in summer, when fashionistas flock to the terrace. Cool live music is played from Thursdays to Saturdays after 10pm. Expect anything from DJ Jet Boy's electro punk to rock, funk, hip hop, rare groove, indie, dance, jazz, and '80s classics.
► *Café Chéri(e) is also a chic daytime venue; see p231.*

Dépanneur Lounge
27 rue Fontaine, 9th (01.44.53.03.78/www. depanneurlounge.com). M° Blanche or Pigalle. **Open** 10am-2am Mon-Thur; 4am-2am Fri-Sun. **Admission** free. **Drinks** €2-€8.90. **Credit** MC, V. **Map** p401 H2.
Just below Montmartre, but away from the seedy Pigalle drag, this new arrival serves decent French cuisine and cocktails by the bucket-load. As the last dinner plates are cleared, the DJ sets up for a night of serious splicing.

★ La Fourmi
74 rue des Martyrs, 18th (01.42.64.70.35). M° Pigalle. **Open** 8.30am-2am Mon-Thur, Sun; 8am-4am Fri, Sat. **Admission** free. **Drinks** €1.60-€8. **Credit** MC, V. **Map** p402 H2.
La Fourmi was a precursor to the industrial-design, informal, music-led bars that have sprung up around Paris – and it's still very much a style leader, attracting everyone from in-the-know tourists to fashionable Parisians. Great throughout the day for coffees or a beer, it has a small seating area outside and an always busy bar with DJ decks. You can stay into the early hours at weekends, but it's also a handy pre-club rendezvous and flyer supplier.

L'Ile Enchantée
65 bd de la Villette, 10th (01.42.01.67.99). M° Colonel Fabien. **Open** 8am-2am Mon-Fri; 5pm-2am Sat, Sun. **Admission** free. **Drinks** €2.20-€6.50. **Credit** MC, V. **Map** p403 M3.
Downstairs this feels like a trendy gastropub; thanks to an up-to-date music policy, it makes for a good pre-club drinking venue. Upstairs is the Wash Bar, the LG company's washing machine showroom (*see p232*), where the occasional bijou disco is held, attracting trendy pre-club party people and late night launderette users.

Lizard Lounge
18 rue du Bourg-Tibourg, 4th (01.42.72.81.34/ www.cheapblonde.com). M° Hôtel de Ville or St-Paul. **Open** noon-2am daily. **Admission** free. **Drinks** €6-€9. **Credit** AmEx, MC, V. **Map** p409 K6.
This three-level, trendy Marais hangout has a boozer upstairs serving beer in pint glasses, a mezzanine for crowd voyeurs, and a more full-on DJ bar in the booth-filled basement – often full, thanks to its modest proportions. Local jocks play a variety of contemporary styles.

La Mezzanine de l'Alcazar
62 rue Mazarine, 6th (01.53.10.19.99/www. alcazar.fr). M° Odéon. **Open** 7pm-2am daily. **Admission** free. **Drinks** €6-€14. **Credit** AmEx, DC, MC, V. **Map** p406 H7.
The stylish, Conran-owned Mezzanine is the upstairs posher sister of the Wagg, which is intended to be a clubbier venue. Naturally, both have become well-heeled hangouts, but the Mezzanine remains the venue of choice for the suited and booted.

Le Troisième Lieu
62 rue Quincampoix, 4th (01.48.04.85.64/www. letroisiemelieu.com). M° Rambuteau. **Open** 6pm-5am Thur-Sat. **Admission** free. **Drinks** €2.50-€6. **Credit** MC, V. **Map** p402 K5.
Opened by Les Ginettes Armées, organisers of renowned Sunday lesbian and mixed events, the Troisième Lieu tends towards electro and house. The ground floor hosts DJs mixing eclectic sounds for chatting and relaxing to, whereas the basement is more dancefloor-oriented.

INSIDE TRACK CLUBBING COMMANDMENTS
When clubbing in Paris, certain rules apply:
- Clubbing generally happens late, so arrive at 1am or 2am.
- Check flyers in clothes shops and DJ bars for free or reduced entry.
- Talk loudly in English. Clubs like tourists because they have a tendency to spend more.
- Order a bottle of spirits at the door of upmarket clubs. It can get you ushered straight past the doorman, and is often cheaper than buying a round of drinks.
- Avoid turning up with lots of boozed-up mates. Drunks and gangs are almost guaranteed not to get in – unless they're all female.

Le Wax

15 rue Daval, 11th (01.40.21.16.16). M° Bastille.
Open 5pm-2am Tue-Thur; 5pm-5am Fri, Sat.
Admission free. **Drinks** €4.50-€10. **Credit** MC,
V. **Map** p407 M6.

During the week, the Wax – clad in 1970s psyche-
delic orange – is a funky bar where DJs play groove
until 2am. But at weekends it becomes a (tiny) nightclub that keeps a youthful crowd awake until 5am
with house and electro.

Le Zèbre de Belleville

*63 bd de Belleville, 20th (01.43.55.55.55/
www.lezebre.com). M° Belleville.* **Open** times vary.
Admission €6-€15. **Drinks** €5-€10. **No credit
cards. Map** p403 N4.

This stylish cabaret/theatre bar is used by Dan
Ghenacia and the Freak 'n' Chic posse for buzzy
after-parties on Sundays. It's usually a more traditional circus and cabaret venue, so check flyers for
event information.

COOL CLUBS

★ Bateau Concorde Atlantique

*Port de Solférino, 25 quai Anatole-France,
7th (01.47.05.71.03/www.concorde-atlantique.
com). M° Assemblée Nationale/RER Musée
d'Orsay.* **Open** 11pm-5am Mon-Fri; 5pm-5am
Sat; 6pm-5am Sun. Closed mid Sept-mid June.
Admission free-€10. **Drinks** €5-€8. **Credit**
MC, V. **Map** p401 F5.

Bateau Concorde Atlantique.

With its terrace and voluminous dancefloor, this two-level boat is a clubbing paradise in the summer. The celebrated Respect crew held a popular, fondly remembered Wednesday night here, and are still involved in putting on parties at the venue, along-side other cool crews like Ed Banger.

★ Batofar

Opposite 11 quai François-Mauriac, 13th (recorded information 01.53.60.17.30/ www.batofar.org). Mº Quai de la Gare. **Open** 11pm-6am Mon-Sat; 6am-noon 1st Sun of mth. **Admission** €5-€12. **Drinks** €3.50-€8. **Credit** MC, V. **Map** p407 N10.

In recent years the Batofar has gone through a rapid succession of management teams, with varying levels of success. The current managers have helped revive the venue's tradition of playing cutting-edge music, including electro, dub step, techno and dance-hall nights featuring international acts. It's also a destination for early morning clubbers determined to shun their beds.

Le Divan du Monde

75 rue des Martyrs, 18th (01.42.52.02.46/ www.divandumonde.com). Mº Abbesses or Pigalle. **Open** 8pm-2am Tue-Thur; 7.30pm-5am Fri, Sat. **Admission** €6-€30. **Drinks** €3.50-€8. **Credit** AmEx, MC, V. **Map** p402 H2.

After a drink in the Fourmi opposite (*see p327*), pop over to the Divan for one-off parties and regular events. The upstairs specialises in VJ events, and downstairs holds dub, reggae, funk and world music club nights.

Elysée Montmartre

72 bd de Rochechouart, 18th (01.44.92.45.36/ www.elyseemontmartre.com). Mº Anvers. **Open** midnight-6am Fri, Sat. **Admission** €10-€15. **Drinks** €4-€10. **Credit** *Bar* MC, V. **Map** p402 J2.

A gig venue and club, the Elysée hosts big nights by outside promoters, such as Open House, Panik and Nightfever, for young clubbers.

★ La Flèche d'Or

102bis rue de Bagnolet, 20th (01.44.64.01.02/ www.flechedor.fr). Mº Alexandre Dumas. **Open** 8pm-2am Mon-Thur; 8pm-6am Fri, Sat. **Admission** free. **Drinks** €4.50-€11. **Credit** MC, V. **Map** p403 Q6.

This converted railway station reopened under new management, and has won over the Paris muso crowd with its adventurous programming, covering every-thing from electro to punk and *nouvelle chanson*.

Folies Pigalle

11 pl Pigalle, 9th (01.48.78.55.25/www.folies-pigalle.com). Mº Pigalle. **Open** midnight-dawn Mon-Thur; midnight-noon Fri, Sat; 6pm-midnight Sun. **Admission** €20 (incl 1 drink); €7 Sun eve. **Drinks** €10. **Credit** AmEx, MC, V. **Map** p402 H2.

THE BEST LATE HANGOUTS

For mellow jazz
New Morning. See p333.

For an all-nighter
Batofar. See p329.

For A-list action
L'Etoile. See p332.

The racy Folies Pigalle's programme includes every-thing from dancehall and hip hop to techno and elec-tro, go-go dancers, striptease shows and Paris's only transsexual spectacle on Sunday evenings.

Le Gibus

18 rue du Fbg-du-Temple, 11th (01.47.00.78.88/ www.gibus.fr). Mº République or Temple. **Open** midnight-6am Fri, Sat. **Concerts** 8-11.30pm Fri. **Admission** €5-€20. **Drinks** €3-€8. **Credit** *Bar* MC, V. **Map** p402 L4.

A famous 1980s punk venue, Le Gibus has gone through plenty of style changes during its life. Today it takes in R&B, reggae, '80s pop and hip hop on dif-ferent evenings, plus the occasional *striptease mixte*.

Le Glaz'art

7-15 av de la Porte de la Villette, 19th (01.40. 36.55.65/www.glazart.com). Mº Porte de la Villette. **Open** 8.30pm-2am (sometimes 5am) on concert nights (check programme on website). **Admission** €8-€15. **Drinks** €3-€8. **Credit** MC, V. **Map** p403 inset.

This converted coach station is way out north-east, but its strong DJ nights and live acts pull punters in from central Paris. Dub step, breakbeat, electro and drum 'n' bass nights have made the venue a magnet for breaks fans, and it has a nocturnal garden too.

Mains d'Oeuvres

1 rue Charles-Garnier, 18th (01.40.11.25.25/ www.mainsdoeuvres.org). Mº Garibaldi. **Open** times vary. **Admission** €5-€15. **Drinks** €2-€5. **Credit** *Bar* MC, V.

A rehearsal space and live venue for new bands. Occasionally the whole building is turned into a club venue, with rooms devoted to different music styles. Look for flyers or keep an eye on the website.

Nouveau Casino

109 rue Oberkampf, 11th (01.43.57.57.40/ www.nouveaucasino.net). Mº Parmentier. **Open** midnight-5am Wed-Sat. **Admission** €5 before 1am, €10 after. **Drinks** €5-€10. **Credit** *Bar* MC, V. **Map** p403 M5.

Conveniently surrounded by the numerous bars of rue Oberkampf and tucked behind the legendary Café Charbon (*see p231*), Nouveau Casino is a concert

ARTS & ENTERTAINMENT

venue that also hosts some of the city's liveliest club nights. Local collectives, international names and record labels, such as Versatile, regularly host nights here; it's well worth checking the website for one-offs and after-parties.

★ Point Ephémère

200 quai de Valmy, 10th (01.40.34.02.48/www. pointephemere.org). M° Jaurès or Louis Blanc. **Open** 10am-2am daily. **Admission** varies. **Drinks** €3-€7. **Credit** AmEx, DC, MC, V. **Map** 402 L2.

This hunk of Berlin in Paris was only ever meant to be temporary, but thankfully it's still around. An uncompromising programming policy delivers some of the best electronic music in town; there's also a restaurant and bar with decks and a gallery, and terrace space by the canal in summer. *Photo p332.*

Red Light

34 rue du Départ, 15th (01.42.79.94.53/www. enfer.fr). M° Edgar Quinet or Montparnasse Bienvenüe. **Open** midnight-11am Fri, Sat. **Admission** (incl 1 drink) €20-€25. **Drinks** from €10. **Credit** MC, V. **Map** p405 F9.

The former Enfer ('Hell') remains a trance, techno and house dynamo with local and global DJs spinning to a young, up- for-it, often gay, well-groomed crowd. Expect a mixture of local and international DJs.

★ Rex

5 bd Poissonnière, 2nd (01.42.36.10.96/www. rexclub.com). M° Bonne Nouvelle. **Open** 11.30pm-6am Wed-Sat. **Admission** free-€15. **Drinks** €5-€15. **Credit** *Bar* MC, V. **Map** p402 J4.

The Rex's new sound system puts over 40 different sound configurations at the DJ's fingertips, and has proved to be a magnet for top turntable stars. Once associated with iconic techno pioneer Laurent Garnier, the Rex has stayed at the top of the Paris techno scene, and occupies an unassailable position as the city's serious club music venue.

La Scène Bastille

2bis rue des Taillandiers, 11th (01.48.06.50.70/ www.la-scene.com). M° Bastille. **Open** 7.30pm-midnight Mon-Thur; 7.30pm-6am Fri-Sun. Closed Aug. **Admission** €12. **Drinks** €4-€9. **Credit** *Bar* MC, V. **Map** p407 M7.

This tastefully decorated club-bar-restaurant complex holds regular rock concerts, as well as club events most Thursdays to Saturdays. The agenda here changes constantly, so check what's on. Popular gay nights too.

Showcase

Below Pont Alexandre III, 8th (01.45.61.25.43/ www.showcase.fr). M° Champs-Elysées Clemenceau. **Open** 10pm-dawn Fri, Sat; 11am-3pm Sun. **Admission** free-€15. **Drinks** €3.50-€8. **Credit** MC, V. **Map** p401 E5.

This vast venue, in converted boat hangars below Pont Alexandre III, is where music-crazed insomniacs come on weekends to discover up-and-coming bands and dance until daybreak.

▶ *Sunday brunches here are a hit with families (see p285).*

Le Social Club

142 rue Montmartre, 2nd (01.40.28.05.55). M° Bourse or Grands Boulevards. **Open** 11.30pm-3am Wed; 11pm-6am Thur-Sat. **Admission** free-€12. **Drinks** €4-€10. **Credit** AmEx, MC, V. **Map** p402 J4.

Set in the hub of club activity around Grands Boulevards, this extraordinary electro venue has some of the hippest acts from the French and international scene, thanks to its owner's multidisciplinary career as a producer and founder of the record label Uncivilized World.

Wagg

62 rue Mazarine, 6th (01.55.42.22.01/www. wagg.fr). M° Odéon. **Open** 11.30pm-6am Fri, Sat; 3pm-midnight Sun. **Admission** €12 Fri, Sat; €12 Sun (incl drink). **Drinks** €7-€10. **Credit** AmEx, DC, MC, V. **Map** p406 H7.

Refurbished as part of the Conran makeover of the Mezzanine upstairs, Wagg went through a period of attracting big name DJs, but has settled down as home to a well-to-do Left Bank crowd. Expect funk, house and disco, plus salsa lessons on Sundays.

GLITZY CLUBS

★ Les Bains Douches

7 rue du Bourg-l'Abbé, 3rd (01.48.87.01.80/ www.lesbainsdouches.net). M° Etienne Marcel. **Open** midnight-6am Wed-Sun (restaurant from 8pm). **Admission** €10-€20. **Drinks** €8-€10. **Credit** AmEx, DC, MC, V. **Map** p402 J5.

Once a global leader, Les Bains Douches lost its way in the 1990s, relying on its reputation to pull in tourists. This all changed recently, and now local star DJs like Busy P and international names such as Erol Alkan grace its decks. The clientele is increasingly, but not yet exclusively, gay.

▶ *There's a fancy restaurant here that serves a decent €39 set menu.*

Le Baron

6 av Marceau, 8th (01.47.20.04.01/www.club lebaron.com). M° Alma Marceau. **Open** times vary. **Admission** free. **Drinks** from €10. **Credit** MC, V. **Map** p400 D5.

This small but supremely exclusive hangout for the international jet set used to be an upmarket brothel, and has the decor to prove it. It only holds 150, most of whom are regulars you'll need to befriend in order to get past the door. But if you manage to get in, you'll be rubbing shoulders with celebrities and super-glossy people.

River Dance

There's plenty to float your boat in the 13th.

If you thought that Paris's nightlife could be reduced to sweat-drenched basement clubs or ultra-chic VIP haunts, think again. There's plenty of middle ground – it's just not always on the, er, ground. For the last few years, party boats – floating nightclubs that double as restaurants, bars and even concert venues – have been drawing the hippest clubbers to the quai François-Mauriac, at the foot of the Bibliothèque François-Mitterrand in the 13th.

It's set to continue in 2009, with the most hotly awaited party boat of them all – **Le Petit Bain** (below Bibliothèque François Mitterand, 13th, 01.43.49.67.12, www.petitbain.org). Having tantalised us for the last six years with their September Sous la Plage music festival (last year drawing in the likes of post-punkster Ebony Bones), the Petit Bain's founders have finally received permission to moor their new multidisciplinary barge in the 13th, offering a 400-capacity concert hall, restaurant, terrace and after-hours entertainment worthy of any nighthawk's attention.

Just along the quayside, the **Batofar** (*see p329*) already gratifies clubbers with an eclectic range of musical entertainment (along the lines of rap, electro, aerobeat, drum, hip hop and disco), with home-grown and international DJs. It comes into its own in the summer, when the terrace opens as a bar and canteen, and the Outdoor Summer Sessions festival (June-Aug) kicks in with dance *ateliers*, sewing classes, open-air concerts, club nights and after-parties.

For a spot of nosh, followed by live music (ska, reggae, pop, jazz or rock) and late-night dancing, the nearby **Dame de Canton** (Port de la Gare, 13th, 01.53.61.08.48, www.damedecanton.com) has attitude (combined with a cheeky soupçon of cheese) in a pirate-ship setting. Top-notch bands give it their all in front of a lively audience on the upper deck, while groups of alcohol-fuelled mates munch away on the lower deck before joining the upstairs throngs for an after-show spin on the dancefloor (weekends only).

ARTS & ENTERTAINMENT

Batofar.

Le Cab
2 pl du Palais-Royal, 1st (01.58.62.56.25/www.
cabaret.fr). M° Palais Royal Musée du Louvre.
Open 11.30pm-5am Wed-Sat. *Restaurant*
7.30-11.30pm Tue-Sat. **Admission** free; €20
Thur-Sat. **Drinks** €13. **Credit** AmEx, MC, V.
Map p402 H5.
Le Cab is owned by the management behind Club
Mix and Queen, and R&B and commercial house
dominate the playlist. The doormen are tough, and
if they don't like you, you won't get in (unless you've
booked for dinner).

L'Etoile
12 rue de Presbourg, 16th (01.45.00.78.70/
www.letoileparis.com). M° Charles de Gaulle
Etoile. **Open** 11pm-5am Tue-Sat. *Restaurant*
8-11pm Tue-Sat. **Admission** €20 (free for
women Tue). **Drinks** €16-€25. **Credit**
AmEx, DC, MC, V.
An A-list celebrity haunt where guests such as
Johnny Halliday, Pamela Anderson and Robbie
Williams have been known to show their faces. If
you're not A-list, it's seriously hard to get in.

MadaM
128 rue La Boétie, 8th (01.58.76.02.11/www.
madam.fr). M° Franklin D. Roosevelt or George
V. **Open** 7pm-2am Thur; midnight-6am Fri-Sat;
10.30pm-4am Sun. **Admission** free. **Drinks**
€20. **Credit** AmEx, DC, MC, V. **Map** p401 E4.

MadaM's late-night sessions (kicking in at 4am at
weekends) are renowned for the young, moneyed
crowd they attract. The music is mainly electro
and house (French), with several up to date international tunes thrown in for good measure.

VIP Room
188 rue de Rivoli, 1st (01.58.36.46.00/www.
viproom.fr). M° Palais-Royal or Tuilleries. **Open**
midnight-5am Tue-Sun. **Admission** free.
Drinks €20. **Credit** AmEx, DC, MC, V.
Map p401 H1.
The VIP has moved from its Champs-Elysées
address into the former Scala nightclub, but other
than that, nothing has changed. It's still a hit with
the people who also enjoy the VIP's sister venues in
Cannes and St Tropez during the summer, and the
music is still dance-oriented.

MAINSTREAM CLUBS
Club Med World
39 Cour St-Emilion, 12th (08.10.81.04.10/
www.clubmedworld.fr). M° Cour St-Emilion.
Open 11pm-2am Tue-Thur; 11.30pm-6am Fri,
Sat. **Admission** €15 Tue-Thur; €20 Fri, Sat;
free for women. **Drinks** €9. **Credit** AmEx,
MC, V. **Map** p407 N10.
Part of a massive conference, restaurant and club
complex in the Bercy Village, Club Med World hosts
popular disco, salsa and '80s nights at weekends.

Point Ephémère. *See p330.*

ARTS & ENTERTAINMENT

I Love Opéra
5 av de l'Opéra, 1st (01.75.43.50.50/
www.iloveopera.fr). M° Pyramides. **Open**
Bar 6pm-midnight daily. *Restaurant* 8pm-
midnight daily (restaurant). **Admission**
free. **Drinks** €8-€25. **Credit** AmEx, MC, V.
Map p401 H5.
I Love Opéra is having trouble attracting the glitterati of its previous incarnation, Paris Paris, but
it's getting there with a chic pink, black and white
dining room (menus from €36) open all day, after-
work cocktail parties (from 6pm), and nightly clubbing with house, R&B, rock and hip hop.

La Loco
90 bd de Clichy, 18th (01.53.41.88.89/www.
laloco.com). M° Blanche. **Open** 9pm-6am daily.
Admission €10-€20. **Drinks** €6-€8. **Credit**
MC, V. **Map** p401 G2.
La Loco has a substantial and youthful following
taking advantage of its three dancefloors, which
offer different musical genres: house, dance, hip-hop
and chart music on weekend nights, and metal and
goth concerts during the week.

★ Mix Club
24 rue de l'Arrivée, 15th (01.56.80.37.37/
www.mixclub.fr). M° Montparnasse Bienvenüe.
Open 11pm-6am Wed-Sat; 5pm-1am Sun.
Admission €12-€20. **Drinks** €8. **Credit** MC,
V. **Map** p405 F8.
The Mix has one of the city's biggest dancefloors.
Regular international visitors include Erick Morillo's
Subliminal and Ministry of Sound parties, and in-
house events include David Guetta's 'Fuck Me I'm
Famous', 'Hipnotic' and 'One Night With Paulette',
plus just about everyone else who's big in France –
or anywhere else in the world, for that matter.

Queen
102 av des Champs-Elysées, 8th (01.53.89.08.90/
www.queen.fr). M° George V. **Open** 11pm-5am
Mon; midnight-6am Tue-Thur, Sun; midnight-
8am Fri, Sat. **Admission** €15 Mon-Thur, Sun;
€20 Fri, Sat. **Drinks** €10. **Credit** *Bar* AmEx,
MC, V. **Map** p400 D4.
Once the city's most fêted gay club and the only venue
that could hold a torch to the Rex, with a roster of top
local DJs holding court, Queen's star faded a little in
the early noughties but is now starting to shine more
brightly again. Last year it introduced more themed
nights, and still packs 'em in seven nights a week.
▶ *For more on Queen's gay nights, see p310.*

WORLD, JAZZ
& ROCK 'N' ROLL

Le Cabaret Sauvage
59 bd Macdonald, 19th (01.42.09.03.09/
www.cabaretsauvage.com). M° Porte de la
Villette. **Open** 11pm-dawn, days vary.

Admission €10-€20. **Drinks** €4-€8. **Credit**
AmEx, MC, V. **Map** p403 inset.
Le Cabaret Sauvage is a stylish, big top-shaped
venue that's taken over by outside promoters for
occasional club nights. In the old days this often contained a world music element, but more recently
electronic and drum 'n' bass nights have begun to
be held here, and, since the demise of Pulp, techno
label Kill the DJ has started using the venue. DJ
Chloe launched her last album here. Check the website for details of one-off nights.

La Chapelle des Lombards
19 rue de Lappe, 11th (01.43.57.24.24/
http://chapelle.lombards.free.fr). M° Bastille.
Open 11.30pm-6am Tue-Sun. **Admission** free
Mon-Wed, Sun; €15 Thur; €20 Fri, Sat (free for
women Tue-Thur & before midnight Fri).
Drinks €6-€12. **Credit** MC, V. **Map** p407 M7.
With Afrojazz and Latino bands and DJs providing the music, Latinos and Africans lead the dancefloor in this popular world music venue. Note:
smart dress only.

★ Favela Chic
18 rue du Fbg-du-Temple, 11th (01.40.21.38.14/
www.favelachic.com). M° République. **Open** 8pm-
2am Tue-Thur; 8pm-4am Fri, Sat. **Admission**
free Tue-Thur; €10 (incl 1 drink) Fri, Sat. **Drinks**
€6-€19. **Credit** MC, V. **Map** p402 L4.
Past the usually steely-faced door attendants, the
Brazilian-themed Favela Chic attracts an up-for-it,
international and invariably dressy crowd for
some serious samba and other full-on Latin dancing. There are decent DJs, live acts, and Brazilian
food and drinks too. The opening of a sister bar in
London's Shoreditch has seen the Favela Chic
brand expand into other forms of music, such as
disco punk and electro.

La Java
105 rue du Fbg-du-Temple, 10th (01.42.02.20.52/
www.la-java.fr). M° Belleville or Goncourt. **Open**
9pm-3am Wed, Thur; 11pm-6am Fri, Sat; 2pm-
2am Sun. **Admission** €5-€10. **Drinks** €3-€7.
Credit MC, V. **Map** p403 M4.
Tucked inside the crumbling, disused Belleville
market, La Java plays rock, salsa and world music,
with live bands every weekend.

★ New Morning
7-9 rue des Petites-Ecuries, 10th (01.45.23.51.41/
www.newmorning.com). M° Château d'Eau.
Open times vary. **Admission** approx €10.
Drinks €3-€7. **Credit** MC, V. **Map** p402 K3.
Jazz fans crowd into this hip, no-frills joint to natter,
drink and boogie to the consistently excellent live
music. Low key it may be but it's still worth looking
out for the occasional A-lister – the likes of Spike
Lee and Prince have been known to grace the New
Morning with their presence.

Sport & Fitness

Soak up the Six Nations or swim in a Seine-side pool.

The modern Olympic Games, as well as football's FIFA, World Cup and European trophies, were all planned and developed in the boardrooms of the French capital, and the range of activities available in Paris does justice to the city's proud sporting history. Much is owed to the dynamic influence of the sports press, particularly the daily newspaper *L'Equipe* and bi-weekly *France Football*. Their fin-de-siècle forebear, *L'Auto*, introduced the world's biggest annual cycling event into the calendar: the **Tour de France** (www.letour.fr).

SPECTATOR SPORTS

The national stadium is the 80,000-capacity **Stade de France** (*see p288*), served by stations on the RER B (La Plaine Stade de France) and RER D (Stade de France St-Denis) lines just one stop from the Gare du Nord. It was built for the 1998 football World Cup and staged the final, in which the hosts beat Brazil 3-0 to claim the title for the first time. It also hosted the rugby World Cup final between England and South Africa in 2007.

Indoor events, including judo, basketball, handball and tennis, take place at the **Palais Omnisports de Paris-Bercy** (8 bd de Bercy, 12th, 08.92.39.01.00, www.popb.fr, M° Bercy). The **Stade Roland Garros** (Porte des Mousquetaires, 2 av Gordon-Bennett, 16th, 01.47.43.48.00, www.fft.fr/rolandgarros, M° Porte d'Auteuil) stages the French tennis open; the **Parc des Princes**, home of Paris St-Germain football club, also hosts rugby and other sporting events.

Despite recent doping scandals, the three-week **Tour de France** is still a national festival, and huge crowds flock to the Champs-Elysées every July to welcome the riders home. The 2008 race was won by Spaniard Carlos Sastre, beating Australian Cadel Evans by just 58 seconds. For details of this and other major sporting events, *see pp274-279* **Calendar**.

Tickets for many sports are sold online at www.ticketnet.fr, and at branches of **Fnac** and **Virgin Megastore** (for both, *see p271*). For football and rugby internationals held at the Stade de France, contact the respective national associations (www.fff.fr; www.ffr.fr).

Basketball

Paris-Levallois Basket
Stade Coubertin, 82 av Georges-Lafont, 16th (01.46.10.93.60/www.parislevallois.com). M° Porte de St-Cloud. **Tickets** from €8. **Credit** MC, V. *Palais des Sports Marcel-Cerdan, 141 rue Danton, 92300 Levallois (01.46.17.06.30/ www.parislevallois.com). M° Pont de Levallois.* **Tickets** from €8. **Credit** MC, V.
PL was born in 2007 following the merger of the region's two biggest clubs, Paris Basket Racing and Levallois Sporting Club Basket, but the plan to create a superpower fell flat: the club was relegated to the Pro B league (second division) in its first season. Games are played at the Paris and Levallois sites.

Football

Paris St-Germain
Stadium *Parc des Princes, 24 rue du Commandant-Guilbaud, 16th (01.47.43.71.71/ tickets & information 32.75/www.psg.fr). M° Porte de St-Cloud.* **Tickets** €25-€100. **Credit** MC, V.
Shops *27 av des Champs-Elysées, 8th (01.56.69.22.22). M° Franklin D. Roosevelt.* **Open** 10am-10pm Mon-Thur; 10am-midnight Fri, Sat; noon-8pm Sun. **Credit** AmEx, MC, V. *Parc des Princes.* **Open** 10am-7pm Mon-Sat & 2hrs after game on match days. **Credit** AmEx, MC, V.
A group of donors set up PSG by amalgamating local clubs in 1970. PSG bought top stars to win silverware in the 1980s and '90s, but their star has faded. The club's fans were recently at the heart of a racism scandal, and the team narrowly avoided relegation in 2008.
▶ *For tickets, book online and pick them up from any branch of Fnac (see p271).*

Horse racing

The full racing schedule, the *Calendrier des Courses*, is published by France Galop (www.france-galop.com). For information on trotting, France's most popular form of racing, consult www.cheval-francais.com. Tickets are €1.50-€8 (free for under-18s). All betting is done with the state-owned PMU, whose website (www.pmu.fr) provides details of races and odds. *Paris Turf* (www.paris-turf.com) is a useful source of tips.

Hippodrome d'Auteuil
Route des Lacs, 16th (01.40.71.47.47).
Mº Porte d'Auteuil.
Steeplechasing in the Bois de Boulogne. The biggest event is the Gras Savoye Grand Steeplechase de Paris on the last Sunday in May.

★ Hippodrome de Chantilly
16 av du Général-Leclerc, 60500 Chantilly
(03.44.62.44.00). Train from Gare du Nord.
Flat racing 40km (25 miles) from Paris. The fashion parade turns out in force for the Prix de Diane Hermès in June; the full length of the course is used for the Prix du Jockey Club the weekend before.

Hippodrome d'Enghien
Pl André-Foulon, 95230 Soissy-sous-Montmorency
(01.39.89.00.12). Train from Gare du Nord.
Steeplechasing and floodlit trotting at this course 18km (11 miles) north of Paris.

★ Hippodrome de Longchamp
Route des Tribunes, 16th (01.44.30.75.00).
Mº Porte d'Auteuil then free bus.
Flat racing in the Bois de Boulogne. This course hosts the racing season's most fashionable social event, the Prix de l'Arc de Triomphe Lucien Barrière. Women in wild hats get in for free.

Hippodrome de Maisons-Laffitte
1 av de la Pelouse, 78602 Maisons-Laffitte
(01.39.12.81.70). RER Maisons-Laffitte then bus.
Flat racing.

Hippodrome de Paris-Vincennes
2 route de la Ferme, 12th (01.49.77.17.17).
Mº Château de Vincennes/RER Joinville-le-Pont
then free bus.
Trotting in the Bois de Vincennes. Floodlights on winter evenings add to the atmosphere.

Hippodrome de St-Cloud
1 rue du Camp Canadien, 92210 St-Cloud
(01.47.71.69.26). RER Rueil-Malmaison.
Flat racing.

Rugby

★ Stade Français Paris
Stade Jean-Bouin, 26 av du Général-Sarrail,
16th (01.40.71.71.00/www.stade.fr). Mº Porte
d'Auteuil. **Tickets** €5-€42. **Credit** AmEx,
MC, V.
One of the top teams in France. Home matches tend to take place on Saturday evenings.
▶ *For more about the stadium's prize-winning design, see p43.*

Stade Français Paris.

ACTIVITIES & TEAM SPORTS

The Mairie manages many of the facilities across the capital, ensuring very reasonable entry prices. For details, consult its free annual *Parisports: Guide du Sport à Paris* or view the online version at www.sport.paris.fr. If you're looking for sportswear and equipment, head for the excellent **Décathlon** (www.decathlon.fr) or **Go Sport** (www.go-sport.com) chain stores.

Some venues require proof of health insurance, ID and passport-sized photos for membership. Note that joining a club or taking part in a competitive event (even a fun run) usually requires a medical certificate from a doctor.

All-round sports clubs

The **Standard Athletic Club** (route Forestière du Pavé de Meudon, 92360 Meudon-la-Forêt, 01.46.26.16.09, www.standac.com) is a private sports club aimed at English speakers. Full

ARTS & ENTERTAINMENT

THE BEST
SPORTING ACTIVITIES

For climbing the walls
MurMur. See p336.

For perfecting your swing
Golf du Bois de Boulogne. See p338.

For a swim by the Seine
Piscine Josephine-Baker. See p341.

membership costs €800 per year. There are tennis and squash courts, a heated outdoor pool and workout facilities.

Local multi-sports clubs include **Racing Club de France** (01.47.63.99.26, www.racingclubdefrance.org), **ASPTT de Paris** (01.45.69.01.01, www.asptparis.com), **Paris Université Club** (01.44.16.62.62, www.puc.asso.fr) and **Stade Français** (01.40.71.33.33, www.stadefrancais.com).

American football

There are about 15 teams in the suburbs, plus 'no-tackle' flag football teams for men and women, and cheerleader squads. Contact the **Fédération Française de Football Américain** (01.43.11.14.70, www.fffa.org).

Athletics & running

Paris has plenty of municipal tracks, open to individual runners for a modest monthly subscription; for details pick up the *Guide du Sport* (see p334). Joggers use the banks of the Seine and the parks (Jardin du Luxembourg, Tuileries and Parc de la Villette), as well as the expansive Bois de Boulogne and Bois de Vincennes. The Paris Marathon takes place in April (see p274-279 **Calendar**), and other classic road races include the Paris half-marathon in March and the Paris-Versailles in September (www.parisversailles.com). The **Hash House Harriers** organise weekly runs. Log on to parishhh.free.fr for details.

Baseball, softball & cricket

Most Paris teams practise in the Bois de Vincennes. The **Fédération Française de Baseball, Softball et Cricket** (01.44.68.89.30, www.ffbsc.org) has details. An English expat runs the **Château de Thoiry Cricket Club** (78770 Thoiry, 01.34.87.55.70), 40km (25 miles) from Paris. **Paris University Club** (01.44.16.62.62, www.pucbaseball.com) has baseball teams for all ages.

Basketball

Almost every municipal sports centre has a court and club. Contact the **Fédération Française de Basketball** (01.53.94.25.00, www.basketfrance.com) for details.

Boules, pool & bowling

Boules or *pétanque* pitches are scattered all over Paris. Contact the **Fédération Française de Pétanque** (04.91.14.05.80, www.petanque.fr).
Some pool venues require ID or a passport.

Bowling Mouffetard
73 rue Mouffetard, 5th (01.43.31.09.35). M° Place Monge. **Open** 3pm-2am Mon-Fri; 10am-2am Sat, Sun. **Admission** €2-€5.90 per set. *Shoe hire* €1.80. **Credit** AmEx, MC, V. **Map** p406 K9.
Centrally located venue with eight bowling lanes.

Cercle Clichy Montmartre
84 rue de Clichy, 9th (01.48.78.32.85/www. academie-billard.com). M° Place de Clichy. **Open** 11am-6am daily. **Admission** *Pool* from €12/hr. *Billiards* from €12/hr. **Credit** (€25 minimum) MC, V. **Map** p401 G2.
Historic venue decorated with frescoes, offering a huge bar and pool tables aplenty. No under-18s.

Climbing

To use any municipal climbing wall, you will need to obtain a personal ID card. Take a photo, your passport, proof of valid insurance and the fee (€4 per month) to the centre you want to use. For the real thing, try the superb boulder formations in the Forêt de Fontainebleau; **Grimporama** (www.grimporama.com) has full details, including maps, on its website. The **Club Alpin du pays de Fontainebleau** (01.64.22.67.18, caf77.free.fr) organises group climbs and weekend outings.

Centre Sportif Poissonnier
2 rue Jean-Cocteau, 18th (01.42.51.24.68). M° Porte de Clignancourt. **Open** 7am-10pm Mon-Sat; 8am-6pm Sun. **Admission** free. **No credit cards.**
The largest of the six municipal walls in Paris.

★ MurMur
55 rue Cartier-Bresson, 93500 Pantin (01.48.46.11.00/www.murmur.fr). M° Aubervilliers – Pantin Quatre Chemins. **Open** 9.30am-11pm Mon-Fri; 9.30am-6.30pm Sat, Sun. **Admission** €8-€15; €4-€7.50 reductions. *Joining fee* €15. **Credit** AmEx, MC, V.
One of Europe's best climbing walls, with 1,550sq m (16,000sq ft) of wall.
▶ *MurMur also has walls at Issy-les-Moulineaux and Epinay (see website for details).*

Cycling

City cycling is growing in popularity, thanks to Mayor Delanoë's expansion of bike lanes and the Vélib intiative. The **Fédération Française de Cyclisme** (01.49.35.69.00, www.ffc.fr) has details of the many local cycle clubs. The **Stade Vélodrome Jacques-Anquetil** (Bois de Vincennes, 12th, 01.43.68.01.27) is regularly open to amateur cyclists, and the circuits by the Hippodromes at **Vincennes** and **Longchamp** (*see p335*) attract large groups of road cyclists. **Mieux se Déplacer à Bicyclette** (01.43.20.26.02, www.mdb-idf.org) organises free rides for members (€30 per year).

    Mountain biking (VTT, or *vélo tout terrain*) is popular in the many forests on the outskirts of Paris, including the Forêt de Montmorency in the north and the Fôret de Meudon in the south.

★ Gepetto & Vélos
59 rue du Cardinal-Lemoine, 5th (01.43.54.19.95/www.gepetto-et-velos.com). M° Cardinal Lemoine. **Open** 9am-1pm, 2-7.30pm Tue-Sat; 10am-7pm Sun. **Credit** MC, V. **Map** p406 K8.
The excellent Gepetto & Vélos rents, sells and repairs all types of bicycles.
Other locations 46 rue Daubenton, 5th (01.43.37.16.17).

Vélo Bastille
22 rue Alphonse Baudin, 11th (01.48.87.60.01/ www.parisvelosympa.com). M° Richard Lenoir. **Open** 9.30am-1pm, 2-6pm Mon, Wed-Fri; 9am-1pm, 2-7pm Sat, Sun. **No credit cards**. **Map** p406 L7.
Vélo Bastille offers repairs, rentals and guided cycling tours of the city.

Diving

Courses for the French diving licence are offered at the **Club de Plongée du 5ème** (7bis rue Poliveau, 01.43.36.07.67), which makes use of the Piscine Jean-Taris (*see p340*) and runs trips to the Med. **Bleu Passion** (94 bd Poniatowski, 12th, 01.43.45.26.29, www.bleu-passion.fr) runs a diving school and sells equipment.

Fencing

For a list of clubs, consult www.escrime-ffe.fr. The fencing section at the **Racing Club de France** (5 rue Eblé, 7th, 01.45.67.55.86, www.racingclubdefrance.org) is suitable for leisure or competition, with 12 fencing masters and 18 pistes. All levels and ages are welcome.

MurMur.

Fitness clubs

Club Med (www.clubmedgym.fr) dominates the health club scene, with 22 branches in Paris and the western suburbs, including five Waou Clubs with spa facilities. Single visits cost €25, and annual memberships start at €760. Other leading fitness centres include **Vit'Halles** (*see p338*) and **Forest Hill** (www.forest-hill.com).

    The non-profit **La Gym Suédoise** (01.45.00.18.22, www.gymsuedoise.com) holds one-hour gym sessions in ten locations across Paris. Membership is €75-€110 per term, or €10 per session. Unlike most gyms, it runs free trials at specified locations.

    There are free weekly 'Sport Nature' sessions of outdoor stretching, aerobics and running, set up by the Mairie at 13 locations around town. Check the annual *Guide du Sport* (*see p334*) or visit www.sport.paris.fr.

Club Quartier Latin
19 rue de Pontoise, 5th (01.55.42.77.88/www. clubquartierlatin.com). M° Maubert Mutualité. **Open** 9am-midnight Mon-Fri; 9am-7pm Sat, Sun. **Admission** *Pool* from €3.70. *Gym* from €19; from €15 reductions. **Credit** MC, V. **Map** p406 K7.
Home to the Pontoise pool (*see p341*), this venerable centre off boulevard St-Germain houses no-frills fitness facilities, and has a room for step, aerobics, stretching and yoga classes. There's a sauna too.

★ Espace Vit'Halles

48 rue Rambuteau, 3rd (01.42.77.21.71/ www.vithalles.com). M° Rambuteau. **Open** 8am-10.30pm Mon-Fri; 9am-10pm Sat; 10am-7pm Sun. **Admission** €25/day. **Credit** AmEx, MC, V. **Map** p406 K5.

This sunken-level health club has Technogym fitness machines, a sauna and some of the best classes in the city, particularly for step and spinning; the classes cost extra.

Football

For information on the local amateur leagues, contact the **Ligue Ile-de-France de Football** (01.42.44.12.12, paris-idf.fff.fr). To join a weekend kickabout, try the Bois de Boulogne near Bagatelle, the Bois de Vincennes or the Champ de Mars.

Golf

The suburbs are full of courses suitable for all levels and budgets. Contact the **Fédération Française de Golf** (01.41.49.77.00, www.ffgolf.org) for more information.

Golf du Bois de Boulogne

Hippodrome d'Auteuil, 16th (01.44.30.70.00/ www.golfduboisdeboulogne.fr). M° Porte d'Auteuil. **Open** *Mid Sept-Apr* 8am-8pm daily. *May-mid Sept* 8am-9pm Mon-Fri; 8am-8pm Sat, Sun. **Admission** €5. **Credit** AmEx, MC, V.

This municipal site has putting greens and a practice area complete with bunkers and water obstacles. Lessons are available from €25 for 30 minutes. It's closed on horse-racing days, so check before you set off.

Golf National

2 av du Golf, 78280 Guyancourt (01.30.43.36.00/ www.golf-national.com). RER St-Quentin-en-Yvelines then taxi. **Open** 8am-7pm Mon-Fri; 8am-8pm Sat, Sun. **Admission** €25-€120; annual membership from €550. **Credit** MC, V.

The home of the French Open, this has two 18-hole courses and one nine-hole course.

Horse riding

To enjoy the horse-riding trails in the Bois de Boulogne or the Bois de Vincennes, you need to join a riding club such as **La Société d'Equitation de Paris** (Centre Hippique du Bois de Boulogne, 16th, 01.45.01.20.06, www.equitation-paris.com), the **Centre Hippique du Touring** (Bois de Boulogne, 16th, 01.45.01.20.88, www.chtcf.com) or the **Cercle Hippique du Bois de Vincennes** (8 rue de Fontenay, 94130 Nogent-sur-Marne, 01.48.73.01.28, www.chbv.fr). Beginners can

learn at the **Club Bayard Equitation** in the Bois de Vincennes (Centre Bayard, UCPA Vincennes, 12th, 01.43.65.46.87, www.clubbayard.com). During July and August, you can have one-off lessons (€21) or take a special five-day course for €291. Out near Versailles, the **Haras de Jardy** (boulevard de Jardy, 92430 Marnes-la-Coquette, 01.47.01.35.30, www.haras-de-jardy.com) is open every day and offers lessons by the hour for all ages, with no membership fee. Leisurely rides in the forests of Fontainebleau are run by **La Bleausière** (06.82.01.21.18, la.bleausiere.free.fr).

Ice skating

The most popular open-air skating rink is the free one in front of the Hôtel de Ville, which is open from December to February. Smaller wintertime rinks are also erected at the Tour Montparnasse and Bibliothèque François Mitterrand. *See also pp274-279* **Calendar**.

Patinoire de Boulogne

1 rue Victor-Griffuelhes, 92100 Boulogne-Billancourt (01.46.08.00.88/www.patinoire boulogne.com). M° Marcel Sembat. **Open** 3-6pm Wed; 10.30am-1pm, 3-6pm, 9pm-midnight Sat; 10am-1pm, 3-6pm Sun (open daily during school holidays). **Admission** €5.30; €4.40 reductions. **No credit cards.**

Year-round indoor rink with free skate rental.

Patinoire Pailleron

32 rue Edouard-Pailleron, 19th (01.40.40.27.70). M° Bolivar. **Open** noon-1.30pm, 4-10pm Mon, Tue, Thur; noon-10pm Wed; noon-1.30pm, 4pm-midnight Fri; noon-midnight Sat; 10am-6pm Sun. **Admission** €4; €3 reductions. **No credit cards. Map** p403 N2.

Reopened in 2006, this rink is part of a renovated art deco sports complex. Skaters can sign up for hockey and dance lessons on the ice.

Patinoire Sonja Henie

Palais Omnisports de Paris-Bercy (01.40.40.27.70/www.bercy.fr). M° Bercy. **Open** *Sept-mid June* 3-6pm Wed; 9.30pm-12.30am Fri; 3-6pm, 9.30pm-12.30am Sat; 10am-noon, 3-6pm Sun. **Admission** €3-€6. **No credit cards. Map** p407 N9.

Protection, helmets and skates for hire (€3).

In-line skating

You can hire skates from **Nomades** (37 bd Bourdin, 4th, 01.44.54.07.44, www.nomade shop.com). For lessons for all ages, try the **Roller Squad Institute** (01.56.61.99.61, www.rsi.asso.fr). For real in-line skating and skateboard acrobatics, head for **Rollerparc Avenue** (100 rue Léon-Geffroy, 01.47.18.19.19) in Vitry-sur-Seine, or the **Espace Glisse de Paris** (*see below* **Skateboarding**).

Rowing & watersports

Paris residents can row, canoe and kayak for free on Saturdays at the **Base Nautique de la Villette** (41bis quai de la Loire, 19th, 01.42.40.29.90). Reserve a week in advance and bring along proof of residence, two photos and a swimming certificate (obtainable at any pool). You can go waterskiing and wakeboarding at the **Club Nautique du 19ème** (Bassin de Vitesse de St-Cloud, 92100 Boulogne-Billancourt, 01.42.03.25.24). Serious rowers can join the annual Traversée de Paris. Contact the **Ligue Ile-de-France d'Aviron** (94736 Nogent-sur-Marne, 01.48.75.79.10). For a leisurely paddle, hire a boat at Lac Daumesnil or Lac des Minimes in the Bois de Vincennes, or at Lac Supérieur in the Bois de Boulogne.

Rugby

For a good standard of play, try the **Athletic Club de Boulogne** (Stade du Saut du Loup, av de la Butte-Mortemart, 16th, 01.46.51.11.91), which fields two teams. The **British Rugby Club of Paris** (58-60 av de la Grande-Armée, 17th, 01.40.55.15.15, www.brfcparis.com) fields two teams in the corporate league.

Skateboarding

In 2008, the Mairie inaugurated the **Espace Glisse de Paris** (*see below*), doubtless hoping to reduce skateboarding in public places. Nonetheless, the most popular skateboarding spots remain the riverfront courtyard at the **Palais de Tokyo**, known as 'Le Dôme', and the ledges and steps at **Trocadéro**. **La Défense** tends to be full of security guards, but is still worth exploring for smooth marble, ledges and rails; the **Palais Omnisports de Paris-Bercy** (*see p334*) has vast ledges and some almighty gaps.

A more relaxed scene is found at the **place des Innocents** (by the Forum des Halles, 1st), which has low ledges and smooth ground, and at the **Opéra Bastille** (11th), which has small steps. For equipment and advice, try **Street Machine** at Les Halles (12 rue des Halles, 1st, 01.40.26.47.90, www.streetmachine.fr).

Cosanostra Skatepark

18 rue du Tir, 77500 Chelles (01.64.72.14.04/ www.cosanostraskatepark.net). RER Chelles-Gournay. **Open** *July, Aug* 2-8pm Mon-Wed, Sat; 2-11pm Thur, Fri; 2-7pm Sun. *Sept-June*

4-11pm Tue, Thur, Fri; 2-8pm Sat; 2-7pm Sun. **Admission** €6. *Season ticket* €230; €215 reductions. **No credit cards**.
A huge indoor street course and micro-ramp, which hosts international competitions.

★ Espace Glisse de Paris

Stade des Fillettes, 54bis bd Neyn, 18th (01.55.26.97.92/www.espaceglisseparis18.com). M° Porte de la Chapelle. **Admission** free.
Opened in 2008, this covered complex provides urban sports fans with a vast space. There are bowls and street furniture, and a funbox and beginners area are due to open in 2009. Different time slots are allocated for skaters, bladers and BMXers, so check ahead first. Equipment can be hired on site. Note that the complex will close during the early part of 2009 as building work is completed.

Squash

No membership is necessary to play squash at the **Club Quartier Latin** (*see p337*), which charges €17.50-€26 per match (racket rental from €2.50). The **Standard Athletic Club** (*see p336*) also rents squash courts to members or on payment of a €185 seasonal fee.

Squash Montmartre

14 rue Achille-Martinet, 18th (01.42.55.38.30/ www.squash-montmartre.com). M° Lamarck Caulaincourt. **Open** 10am-11pm Mon-Fri; 10am-7pm Sat, Sun. **Admission** from €11. **Credit** V.
Period memberships available, plus equipment hire.

Swimming

Pools are plentiful and cheap. Most require a swimming cap and ban bermudas, and many are open late. Swimming to music is integral to

---

INSIDE TRACK
STREET SKATE

Skating is a sociable affair in Paris. Every Friday night, thousands meet by the Tour Montparnasse for **Friday Night Fever** (www.pari-roller.com), a free, fast-paced three-hour skate through the streets, open to anyone who can keep up. Cars have no choice but to grind to a halt as thousands of skaters fly by. Beginners can join the more sedate skate event run by **Roller et Coquillage** (www.rollers-coquillages.org), which sets off from boulevard Bourdon, by place de la Bastille, at 2.30pm on Sundays. The route covers about 20km (12 miles) over three hours.

ARTS & ENTERTAINMENT

Nuit Blanche in October (*see p278*). Times given below may change during school and national holidays.

Aquaboulevard
4 rue Louis-Armand, 15th (01.40.60.10.00/ www.aquaboulevard.com). M° Balard. **Open** 9am-11pm Mon-Thur; 9am-midnight Fri; 8am-midnight Sat; 8am-11pm Sun. **Admission** *6hrs* €25; €10 reductions. **Credit** AmEx, MC, V. **Map** p404 A10.
With year-round summer temperatures, this water park under a giant atrium is great fun for kids. An extra charge gets you a steam bath and three saunas.

Piscine Butte-aux-Cailles
5 pl Paul-Verlaine, 13th (01.45.89.60.05). M° Place d'Italie. **Open** 7-8am, 11.30am-1.30pm, 4.30-6.30pm Tue; 7am-7pm Wed; 7-8.30am, 11.30am-6.30pm Thur, Fri; 7-8am, 10am-6pm Sat; 8am-5.30pm Sun. **Admission** €2.60; €1.50 reductions. **Credit** AmEx, MC, V.

This listed complex, built in the 1920s, has one main indoor pool and two outdoor pools (open in the summer). The water is a warm 28°C, thanks to the natural sulphurous spring.

Piscine Georges-Vallerey
148 av Gambetta, 20th (01.40.31.15.20). M° Porte des Lilas. **Open** 11.45am-1.30pm Mon; 11.45am-1.30pm, 5.15pm-10pm Tue, Thur; 10am-1pm, 2-7pm Wed; 9am-5pm Sat, Sun. **Admission** €2.60; €1.50 reductions. **Credit** (€15 minimum) MC, V.
Built for the 1924 Olympics, this complex features a retractable Plexiglas roof, a 50m pool (often split into two 25m pools) and one for kids.

Piscine Jean-Taris
16 rue Thouin, 5th (01.55.42.81.90). M° Cardinal Lemoine. **Open** 7-8.30am, 11.30am-1pm Tue, Thur; 7-8.30am, 11.30am-6pm Wed; 7-8.30am, 11.30am-1.30pm, 5-8.30pm Fri; 7am-6pm Sat; 8am-6pm Sun. **Admission** €2.60; €1.50 reductions. **Credit** V. **Map** p406 J8.

Take a Hike

Vélib and the Métro have their fans, but walkers also have it their way in Paris.

Think of hiking in France and you probably don't think of Paris – yet the city has much to offer outdoor types. A number of the country's famed long-distance footpaths, the Grandes Randonnées (GR), venture into the capital and pass by Notre-Dame, the Kilomètre Zéro point from which all distances in France are traditionally measured. In total, Paris has some 130km of GR paths, waymarked by white and red flashes painted on trees, buildings and telegraph poles. Two routes – the GR1 and GR2 – wind their way through the city for some 20km before heading out to the woods and forests around Paris.

The GRs are maintained by the Fédération Française de la Randonnée Pédestre (French Hiking Federation), which in June 2008 inaugurated the rando Gaz de France, a free, organised 9km hike around Paris. Some 13,500 hikers took to the streets – which were closed to traffic – to walk the route from Bastille through the east of the city. The event is now set to become an annual rendezvous for hikers.

Another event launched in 2008 is more likely to appeal to experienced hikers or cross-country runners. Held in spring, the Eco-Trail de Paris Ile-de-France (www.traildeparis.com) offers participants two long-distance cross-country courses (21km and 80km) around the Paris region.

The longer (ultra-marathon) event makes good use of the Ile de France's forests and woods. First to cross the 2008 finish line, on the first floor of the Eiffel Tower, was 25-year-old Belgian Wouter Hamelinck in six hours 17 minutes.

If you're tempted by long-distance walking, but perhaps not at such speed, the Paris region hosts several organised nocturnal walks. The thought of hiking over 50km in the dark may not be to everyone's liking, but insomniac ramblers turn up in their thousands for Paris-Mantes in January and the Marche de la Bièvre (http://marche.bievre.org) in May. The former unites the capital with the north-western town of Mantes-la-Jolie and dates back to 1935, whereas the latter follows the route of Paris's underground river, the Bièvre, towards its source beyond Versailles. Setting off en masse at midnight, hikers are guided out of the city's sprawling suburbs before donning headlamps and following painted arrows through forests and farmland. Those who don't want to go the whole distance can choose from shorter courses, beginning around dawn. For equipment, advice and further information, head for the Salon des Randonnées (www.randonee-nature.com), a three-day hiking fair that takes place at Porte de Versailles every March.

This 25m pool has huge bay windows overlooking a sloping garden, with the Panthéon visible just above the trees. Mixed showers and locker area.

★ Piscine Josephine-Baker

Quai François-Mauriac, 13th (01.56.61.96.50). M° Quai de la Gare. **Open** 7-8.30am, 1-9pm Mon; 1pm-midnight Tue; 7-8.30am, 1-9pm Wed; noon-11pm Thur; 7-8.30am, 11am-8pm Sat; 10am-8pm Sun. **Admission** €2.60; €1.50 reductions. **Credit** MC, V. **Map** p407 M10.

Moored on the Seine by the Bibliothèque Nationale, the Piscine Josephine-Baker is back to shipshape, apparently cured of the technical problems that plagued it since opening in 2006. The revamped complex boasts a 25m main pool (with sliding glass roof), a paddling pool and café, and a busy schedule of exercise classes.

Piscine Keller

14 rue de l'Ingénieur Keller, 15th (01.45.71.81.00). M° Charles Michels. **Open** noon-10pm Mon; 7-8.30am, noon-10pm Tue, Thur; 7am-2pm Wed; noon-10pm Fri; 9am-9pm Sat; 9am-7pm Sun. **Admission** €2.60; €1.50 reductions. **Credit** V. **Map** p404 B8.

Fully renovated in 2008, this 50m pool features a retractable roof and uses an innovative, chlorine-free water treatment method. Lane-swimming is prioritised, and there's a 15m pool for kids.

★ Piscine Pontoise Quartier Latin

18 rue de Pontoise, 5th (01.55.42.77.88/www. clubquartierlatin.com). M° Maubert Mutualité. **Open** 7-8.30am, 12.15-1.30pm, 4.30-10pm Mon; 7-8.30am, 12.15-1.30pm, 4.30-7pm Tue, Thur; 7-8.30am, 11.30-7.30pm Wed; 7-8.30am, 12.15-1.30pm, 4.30-8pm Fri; 10am-7pm Sat; 8am-7pm Sun. **Admission** €3.70; €2.20 reductions; €9.50 for all 9-11.45pm. **No credit cards**. **Map** p406 K7.

A beautiful art deco pool with two mezzanine levels. It has private locker rooms, plus night swimming to underwater music. Small fee for lockers.

Piscine Suzanne-Berlioux

Forum des Halles, 10 pl de la Rotonde, 1st (01.42.36.98.44). M° Les Halles. **Open** 11.30am-11pm Mon; 11.30am-10pm Tue; 7-8.15am, 10am-11pm Wed; 11.30am-10pm Thur, Fri; 9am-7pm Sat, Sun. **Admission** €3.80; €3 reductions. **Credit** (€8 minimum) MC, V. **Map** p402 J5.

Although usually busy, this 50m pool with its own tropical greenhouse is good for lane swimming – but there are no lockers (check in your belongings with the attendants). It reopened in 2008 after renovation.

Tennis & table tennis

The Paris Tennis system (www.tennis.paris.fr) allows you to register a password and reserve a court online, €6.50 per hour, €12.50 for indoor

Tennis in the Jardin du Luxembourg.

courts. Among the 43 municipal courts, the six at the **Jardin du Luxembourg** (01.43.25.79.18) are convenient, but there's a better selection at the **Centre Sportif La Faluère** (113 route de la Pyramide, 12th, 01.43.74.40.93) in the Bois de Vincennes.

To find public table tennis in parks around town, consult the *Guide du Sport* (see p334).

Centre Sportif Suzanne-Lenglen

2 rue Louis-Armand, 15th (01.44.26.26.50). M° Balard. **Open** 7am-10pm Mon-Fri; 7am-7pm Sat, Sun. **Admission** from €3. **No credit cards**. **Map** p404 A10.

Fourteen courts, two of which are covered.

Club Forest Hill

4 rue Louis-Armand, 15th (01.40.60.10.00/ www.aquaboulevard.com). M° Balard/RER Bd Victor. **Open** 9am-9pm daily. **Admission** prices vary. **No credit cards**. **Map** p404 A10.

Tennis, table tennis and other racquet sports at most of the dozen branches in and around Paris.

Triathlon

The multi-discipline effort of triathlon (swim, bike, run) is one of Europe's fastest growing sports, and the Paris area hosts some of the sport's biggest clubs. Held in June, the **Paris Triathlon** (www.triathlondeparis.fr) comprises a 1.5km swim in the Seine, a 40km bike leg around the Bois de Boulogne, and a 10km run in the Hippodrome de Longchamp. For details of local clubs, contact the **Ligue Ile de France de Triathlon** (www.idftriathlon.com).

ARTS & ENTERTAINMENT

Theatre

Money's tight… but in playhouses across Paris, the show must go on.

There's no shortage of absurd, politically challenging drama in Paris – it's just the wrong kind. Since the new government cut subsidies to theatres, it's become increasingly hard for small troupes to collect the money they need to put on a show. It's a sorry state of affairs, but, at least for the time being, it's more obvious if you're a struggling actor than if you're a member of the audience. And while smaller companies and theatres struggle to make ends meet, larger troupes and playhouses continue to uphold the French theatrical tradition as best they can.

PARIS IN STAGES

Several stalwarts of the theatrical tradition are still going strong in the city. The **Comédie Française**, on the Right Bank, and the **Théâtre de la Huchette**, on the Left, offer repertoires that have defined French drama. Ionesco's absurdist *La Cantatrice Chauve* was premiered at the Huchette in 1950, for instance, and is still going strong after over 16,000 performances. Another survivor is the **Théâtre des Bouffes du Nord**; thanks to Brit-born Peter Brook, it's been spellbinding Paris theatregoers with impressive French classical repertoire since the 1970s.

Last year's tendency for theatre to grow global continues at the **Odéon, Théâtre de l'Europe**, which fills its revamped auditorium with performances in a multitude of European languages. The **MC93 Bobigny**, in the suburbs, also hosts international companies performing in their own tongues; and Parc de la Villette's **Le Tarmac** theatre (Parc de la Villette, behind the Grand Halle, 19th, 01.40.03.93.90, http://letarmac.fr) houses the TILF (Théâtre International de Langue Française), the only theatre in France dedicated to the French-speaking world, welcoming visiting troupes from Africa, Asia and Canada.

Extending the recent vogue for blockbuster musicals, this year brings the first French version of *Grease* to the **Théâtre Comédia**. But if 'Allez Allez Grease Lightning' isn't quite experimental enough for you, satisfaction can be found at the **Théâtre National de Chaillot, Théâtre du Rond Point, Théâtre de la Ville** and **Théâtre de la Bastille**

(76 rue de la Roquette, 11th, 01.43.57.42.14, www.theatre-bastille.com) where relentlessly new and exciting spectacles combine off-the-wall theatre with dance or music. In the Bois de Vincennes, a special theatre bus takes you to the **Cartoucherie**, a factory remade as a theatre commune that's home to five innovative companies, including Ariane Mnouchkine's award-winning **Théâtre du Soleil**.

ALTERNATIVE THEATRE

For something more unconventional, why not pop along to one of Paris's more eccentric venues? A handful of diehards are addressing the industry's financial shortcomings by turning anything they can get their hands on into theatres (disused factories, squats, washhouses and even psychiatric hospitals).

The bastion of alternative theatre in the north is the **Lavoir Moderne Parisien** (35 rue Léon, 18th, 01.42.52.09.14, www.rueleon. net), a converted washhouse whose shows tackle the recurring themes of immigration and identity. The **Point Ephémère** (*see p322*) and its gargantuan older brother, **Mains d'Oeuvres** (*see p321*), are cool urban arts centres (in former warehouses) that stage multidisciplinary performances by some of the most interesting troupes in town. **La Générale** (10-14 rue du Général Lasalle, 19th, 06.24.98.30.51) is an all-in-one cultural centre housed in an old factory, equipped with a café, recording and film studios, and a theatre.

Les Laboratoires d'Aubervilliers (41 rue Lécuyer, 93300 Aubervilliers, 01.53.56.15.90, www.leslaboratoires.org) churn out some wonderful, conceptualist productions that frequently mix and match play acting with the disciplines of other resident artists (video, sound, dance, etc); and, for a creepy experience, **Les Anciennes Cuisines de Ville-Evrard** (202 av Jean-Jaurès, 93330 Neuilly-sur-Marne, 01.43.09.35.58) are dilapidated kitchens set in an annexe building of the town's psychiatric hospital, where the troupe Vertical Détour performs contemporary creations that frequently explore the topics of insanity and happiness. For more, visit www.actesif.com.

SHOWS IN ENGLISH

Catching a play in English in Paris isn't as difficult as you might think. Productions in English, German, Spanish and Italian come to the Théâtre de l'Odéon, Théâtre des Bouffes du Nord, **Théâtre de la Cité Internationale**, MC93 Bobigny and the versatile stage at the Centre Pompidou (pl Georges-Pompidou, 4th, 01.44.78.12.33, www.cnac-gp.com).

Several companies offer a range of English-language shows and English translations of French works. Local improv troupe the **Improfessionals** (www.improfessionals.com) has been treading the boards of central Paris for the last seven years, offering off-the-cuff stuff; the **Mondays at 7** troupe (www.mondays at7.com) at the Sudden Théâtre (14bis rue Ste-Isaure, 18th, 01.42.62.35.00, www.sudden theatre.fr) puts on plays by British and Irish playwrights most Monday evenings; and in 2008, the **Théâtre en Anglais** group (4bis rue de Strasbourg, 92600 Asnières, 01.55.02.37.87,

http://theatre.anglais.free.fr) stages a well-crafted interpretation of Shakespeare's *Romeo and Juliet* at the Théâtre Silvia Monfort (106 rue Brancion, 15th, 01.56.08.33.88, www.theatresilviamonfort.com). Shakespeare is also performed in English every June at the Bois de Boulogne's Théâtre de Verdure du Jardin Shakespeare (01.40.19.95.33) by the **Tower Theatre Company** (+44 207 352 5700, www.towertheatre.org.uk).

TICKETS AND INFORMATION

L'Officiel des Spectacles and *Pariscope* show weekly listings. Tickets can be bought at the theatres, from **Fnac** or **Virgin Megastore** (for both, *see p271*) or online at www.theatre online.com. Check out www.theatresprives.com for half-price tickets to performances during the first week of a new show.

RIGHT BANK

Cartoucherie de Vincennes

Route du Champ de Manoeuvre, Bois de Vincennes, 12th. M° Château de Vincennes, then shuttle bus.
Théâtre de l'Aquarium *(01.43.74.99.61/ www.theatredelaquarium.com).*
Théâtre du Chaudron *(01.43.28.97.04/ www.theatreduchaudron.fr).*
Théâtre de l'Epée de Bois *(01.48.08.39.74/ www.epeedebois.com).*
Théâtre du Soleil *(01.42.74.87.63/ www.theatre-du-soleil.fr).*

Théâtre de la Bastille.

Théâtre de la Tempête *(01.43.28.36.36/*
www.la-tempete.fr).
Past the Château de Vincennes in the middle of the
woods, five independent theatres, each with its own
troupe, offer first-class, politically committed fare.
This drama-lover's heaven is housed in ex-army
munitions warehouses, where you will be met with
home-made soup and a forest backdrop.

Comédia
4 bd de Strasbourg, 10th (01.42.38.22.22/
www.theatrecomedia.com). M° Strasbourg
St-Denis. **Box office** 11am-7pm Mon-Sat.
Admission varies. **Credit** MC, V.
Map p402 K4.
Mistinguett and Maurice Chevalier used to perform
in this 19th-century music hall before it was demolished and rebuilt as a cinema in 1933. Now a theatre
again (since the '70s), it hosts musicals and operettas
as well as traditional French boulevard comedies,
and rents its space to anyone with a wallet and a
name. In 2008, that meant a French version of the
musical *Grease*.

★ Comédie Française
All *www.comedie-francaise.fr.*
Salle Richelieu *2 rue Richelieu, 1st*
(08.25.10.16.80/01.44.58.15.15). M° Palais
Royal Musée du Louvre. **Box office** 11am-
6.30pm daily. **Admission** €11-€37. *1hr before*
show €5 *for cheapest seats only;* €11 *under-28s*
(free on Mon at the door). **Credit** AmEx, MC, V.
Map p401 H5.
Studio-Théâtre *Galerie du Carrousel du*
Louvre, 99 rue de Rivoli, 1st (01.44.58.98.54/
01.44.58.98.58). M° Palais Royal Musée du
Louvre. **Box office** 2-5pm on performance
day. **Admission** €13-€17; €8-€13 reductions.
Credit MC, V. **Map** p401 H5.
Théâtre du Vieux Colombier *21 rue*
du Vieux Colombier, 6th (01.44.39.87.00/
01.44.39.87.01). M° St-Sulpice. **Box office**
1-6pm Mon, Sun; 11am-6pm Tue-Sat.
Admission €28. *45 mins before show* €13
under-28s. **Credit** MC, V. **Map** p405 G7.
The gilded mother of French theatres, the Comédie
Française turns out season after season of classics,

as well as lofty new productions. The red velvet and
gold-flecked Salle Richelieu is located right by the
Palais-Royal; under the same management are the
Studio-Théâtre, a black box inside the Carrousel du
Louvre, and the Théâtre du Vieux Colombier. The
line-up for 2009 includes Edmond Rostand's *Cyrano*
de Bergerac.

★ Théâtre des Bouffes du Nord
37bis bd de la Chapelle, 10th (01.46.07.34.50/
www.bouffesdunord.com). M° La Chapelle.
Box office 11am-6pm Mon-Sat. **Admission**
€12-€26; €10-€22 reductions. **Credit** MC, V.
Map p402 K2.
This recently renovated landmark theatre has been
Peter Brook's playground for more than 30 years. In
2009, expect epic delights such as *Love is My Sin*,
an amalgam of Shakespeare's sonnets and mono-
logues directed by Brook himself.
► *The Bouffes du Nord also has one of the*
best chamber music programmes in the capital;
see p318.

Théâtre de la Folie
6 rue de la Folie-Méricourt, 11th
(01.43.55.14.80/http://theatrepouvantail.free.fr).
M° St-Ambroise. **Box office** 10am-6pm Mon-Fri;
2-6pm Sat. **Admission** €13-€18 per show.
Credit MC, V. **Map** p403 M5.
Set in a hidden courtyard, the Folie is just a little
smaller, a little edgier and a little funkier than many
Paris theatres, showing three shows in one night:
the first (7pm) by a well-known author, the second
(8.30pm) a contemporary comedy, and the third
(10pm) a socially engaged piece – often experimental but always effervescent.

Théâtre Marigny
Av de Marigny, 8th (01.53.96.70.30/www.
theatremarigny.fr). M° Champs-Elysées
Clemenceau or Franklin D. Roosevelt.
Box office 11am-6.30pm Mon-Sat; 11am-3pm
Sun. **Admission** €33-€51. **Credit** MC, V.
Map p401 E4.
Théâtre Marigny is one of the most expensive nights
out for theatregoers in Paris. But then not many other
theatres can boast a location off the Champs-Elysées,
a deluxe interior conceived by Charles Garnier (of
Opéra fame), high-profile casts and an illustrious
pedigree stretching back 150 years. The French
adaptation of *Equus* had its debut here in 2008.

Théâtre National de Chaillot
1 pl du Trocadéro, 16th (01.53.65.30.00/
www.theatre-chaillot.fr). M° Trocadéro. **Box**
office 11am-7pm Mon-Sat. **Admission**
€17.50-€33; €10-€27 reductions. **Credit** MC, V.
Map p400 B4.
Get here early, grab a cocktail and gaze in awe at the
Eiffel Tower through the lobby window. Chaillot's
three auditoriums range from cosy and experimen-

INSIDE TRACK
CHEAP SEATS

Half-price theatre tickets for
performances the same day are sold
at the **Kiosque de la Madeleine** (15 pl
de la Madeleine, 8th, open 12.30-8pm
Tue-Sat, 12.30-4pm Sun) and the
Kiosque Montparnasse (parvis de la
Gare Montparnasse, 15th, open 12.30-
8pm Tue-Sat, 12.30-4pm Sun).

Behind the Lines

Who's who in French theatre.

From dark medieval plays to 17th-century tragicomedies and 20th-century absurdist theatre, the French have always known how to pack a punch with new acting styles and popular dramatic movements. Titles such as *Tartuffe*, *Le Cid* and *La Cantatrice Chauve* are well known; here we round up the creative talents behind them.

MOLIERE (1622-1673)
As the Sun King's official playwright and founder of the Comédie Française, Jean-Baptiste Poquelin (Molière) created powerful stories able to veer between farce and the darkest of dramas. He is associated with alexandrine, the 12-syllable-per-line metre that characterised much of 17th-century French theatre. Among Molière's best-known comedies are *L'Ecole des Femmes*, *Le Misanthrope*, *Tartuffe* and *Le Malade Imaginaire*.

PIERRE CORNEILLE (1606-1684)
Along with Molière and Racine, Corneille was one of France's great dramatists. Hailed as the 'founder of French tragedy', he turned out plays for over 40 years, including the world-famous *Le Cid* (based on Guillén de Castro's *Las Mocedades del Cid*) – a tale of honour, love, loss and war in medieval Spain.

JEAN RACINE (1639-1699)
Racine was educated by Jansenist monks, and his works are heavily influenced by Greek and Latin classics. Molière produced his second play, *La Thébaïde*, and his third, *Andromaque*, but Racine didn't enjoy the latter production and gave the text to the rival company at the Hôtel de Bourgogne. There he produced a string of successful tragedies such as *Britannicus*, which chronicles the story of Agrippina and her son Nero, and his magnum opus *Phèdre*, based on Euripides' *Hippolytus*, an exploration of a woman's passion for her stepson.

PIERRE DE MARIVAUX (1688-1763)
Marivaux's contribution to 18th-century French theatre was so great that the deft and witty bantering of his dialogues were given their own term, *marivaudage* (verbal preciousness). He wrote numerous comedies for the Comédie Française, including *La Surprise de l'Amour* and *Les Fausses Confidences*.

GEORGES FEYDEAU (1862-1921)
During his lifetime, Feydeau was frequently dismissed as a light entertainer. Now, he is considered one of the belle époque's greatest playwrights, and a precursor of surrealist and Dadaist theatre. His legacy of lively farces includes *La Dame de chez Maxim*, *L'Hôtel du Libre Echange* and *Hortense a dit: 'Je m'en fous!'*.

EUGENE IONESCO (1909-1994)
French-Romanian Ionesco is known for his absurdist pieces, his most famous being *La Cantatrice Chauve* (still played in the Théâtre de la Huchette; *see p346*). Ionesco's plays are famed for their characters caught in hopeless situations and forced to do repetitive or meaningless actions, with plenty of clichéd play on words and nonsense dialogue.

Molière.

ARTS & ENTERTAINMENT

tal to a 2,800-seater amphitheatre. In 2009, the season is well endowed in the dance department with performances by several visiting troupes, including William Forsythe's *Yes, We Can't*.

Théâtre du Rond Point

2bis av Franklin D. Roosevelt, 8th (01.44.95.98.21/www.theatredurondpoint.fr). M° Champs-Elysées Clemenceau or Franklin D. Roosevelt. **Box office** noon-7pm Tue-Sat; noon-4pm Sun. **Admission** €26-€33; €14 under-30s; €24 over-60s. **Credit** MC, V. **Map** p401 E4.

More than just a theatre, this historic venue multitasks as a bookshop, tearoom and restaurant. So once you've fed your mind on contemporary, avant-garde and sometimes politically slanted theatre, make a night of it and opt for dinner as well.

★ Théâtre de la Ville & Théâtre des Abbesses

01.42.74.22.77/www.theatredelaville-paris.com. **Box office** 11am-7pm Mon; 11am-8pm Tue-Sat. **Admission** €15-€26; €12-€13.50 reductions. **Credit** MC, V.

Théâtre de la Ville *2 pl du Châtelet, 4th. M° Châtelet.* **Map** p406 J6.

Théâtre des Abbesses *31 rue des Abbesses, 18th. M° Abbesses.* **Map** p402 H1.

At its two sites, the 'City Theatre' turns out the most consistently innovative programming in Paris. Instead of running a standard rep company, the house imports music, dance and theatre productions.

LEFT BANK

Le Lucernaire

53 rue Notre-Dame-des-Champs, 6th (01.45.44.57.34/www.lucernaire.fr). M° Notre-Dame-des-Champs or Vavin. **Box office** 10am-7pm daily. **Admission** €20-€30; €8-€15 reductions. **Credit** MC, V. **Map** p401 F4.

Three theatres, three cinemas, a restaurant and a bar make up this versatile cultural centre. Theatre-wise, Molière and other classic playwrights get a good thrashing, but so do contemporary authors.

★ Odéon, Théâtre de L'Europe

Pl de l'Odéon, 6th (01.44.85.40.00/bookings 01.44.85.40.40/www.theatre-odeon.fr). M° Odéon. **Box office** 11am-6.30pm Mon-Sat. **Admission** €7.50-€30; €6-€15 reductions. **Credit** MC, V. **Map** p408 H7.

In 2009 the main Odéon and its sister theatre, Les Ateliers Berthier (1 rue André Suarès, 17th), are showcasing a retrospective of the British dramatist and poet Howard Barker, followed by Feydeau's *La Dame de chez Maxim* at the Odéon.

Théâtre de la Cité Internationale

17 bd Jourdan, 14th (01.43.13.50.50/www.theatredelacite.com). RER Cité Universitaire.

Box office 2-7pm Mon-Sat. **Admission** €21; €5-€14 reductions. **Credit** MC, V.

A polished, professional theatre on the campus of the Cité Universitaire, the Théâtre de la Cité displays an international flair worthy of its setting. In addition to the main theatre and dance season, the prestigious Ecole du Théâtre National de Strasbourg occupies the stage for a short stint each summer.

Théâtre de la Huchette

23 rue de la Huchette, 5th (01.43.26.38.99/www.theatrehuchette.com). M° Cluny La Sorbonne or St-Michel. **Box office** 5-9pm Mon-Sat. **Admission** €19.50; €14.50 reductions; €30 double bill ticket. **Credit** MC, V. **Map** p408 J7.

Ionesco's absurdist classic *La Cantatrice Chauve* ('The Bald Soprano') has been playing here since 1957, running on a double bill with his *La Leçon*.

BEYOND THE PERIPHERIQUE

Culture doesn't end at the city ring road. A combination of measures designed to bring theatre to the masses and extortionate rental rates for independent productions inside Paris has led to the creation of several excellent out-of-town venues.

In the north-east, **MC93 Bobigny** (1 bd Lénine, 93000 Bobigny, 01.41.60.72.72, www.mc93.com) is a slick institution dedicated to promoting global cross-cultural exchange with visiting companies from across France and abroad. The **Théâtre Gérard-Philipe** (59 bd Jules-Guesde, 93207 St-Denis, 01.48.13.70.00, www.theatregerardphilipe.com), housed in a century-old building and run by Alain Ollivier, offers consistently good fare of an experimental nature, including the annual Et Moi Alors! festival for youngsters.

Just beyond La Défense's lofty towers, the **Théâtre Nanterre Amandiers** (7 av Pablo Picasso, 92022 Nanterre, 01.46.14.70.00, www.nanterre-amandiers.com, shuttle bus from RER Nanterre-Préfécture 1hr before show) provides an eclectic mix of probing modern theatre (often of a sticky political nature), as well as the great classics and occasional opera.

INSIDE TRACK
GET IN ON THE ACT

If you fancy grabbing a lesson or two while you're in Paris, check out the **Method Acting Center** (115 rue du Fbg-du-Temple, 10th, 01.42.49.78.13, www.methodacting.fr), which offers a wide range of classes for budding actors and seasoned professionals.

Escapes & Excursions

Fontainebleau.
See p353.

Escapes & Excursions

A world of handsome history awaits outside the capital.

The forests surrounding Paris were once the playground of royalty and aristrocracy, and their extravagant legacy is plain to see in sumptuous châteaux such as Fontainebleau and Versailles. Further afield, the vineyards of Champagne are less than two hours from the capital, and even the Med is only a few hours away by TGV.

In this chapter, divided into **Excursions** (day trips) and **Escapes** (destinations further afield), we've listed local tourist information centres, which have details about specific areas. For the main entries – cathedrals, châteaux and other big attractions – we've included details of opening times, admission and transport; but be aware that these can change without notice. Always phone in advance to check. For a list of mainline stations in Paris and their destinations, *see p366.*

Excursions

AUVERS-SUR-OISE

This rural retreat is where van Gogh spent his last weeks. His tiny attic room at the **Auberge Ravoux** is open to the public. Previous Auvers residents included fellow artists Camille Pissarro, Paul Cézanne and Charles-François Daubigny. Today you can explore **Daubigny's museum** (Manoir des Colombières, rue de la Sansonne, 01.30.36.80.20, www.musee-daubigny.com) and his studio (61 rue Daubigny, 01.34.48.03.03, www.atelier-daubigny.com), which is still decorated with his murals.

Another attraction is the **Absinthe Museum** (44 rue Callé, 01.30.36.83.26), a rather modest collection of art and artefacts related to the notorious drink. Banned in France since 1915, the green concoction is not available at the replica café-bar upstairs.

The local artistic legacy has not been overlooked by Auvers' main historical attraction, either. The 17th-century **Château d'Auvers** (rue de Léry, 01.34.48.48.45, www.chateau-auvers.fr) features a walk-through tour with an Impressionist theme.

Auberge Ravoux

1 pl de la Mairie, 95430 Auvers-sur-Oise (01.30.36.60.60/www.maisondevangogh.fr). **Open** 10am-6pm Wed-Sun. **Admission** €5. **Credit** *Shop & restaurant* AmEx, MC, V.

Where to eat & stay

You can always do as Van Gogh might have done, and dine at the **Auberge Ravoux** (*see above*). Otherwise, try **L'Impressionit' Café** (Château d'Auvers, rue de Léry, 01.34.48.48.48), which does cheap lunches. The **Hostellerie du Nord** (6 rue Général-de-Gaulle, 01.30.36.70.74, www.hostellerriedunord.fr, closed dinner Sun) has chef Joël Boilleaut running the kitchen; upstairs are eight double rooms (€98-€188).

Getting there

By car

35km (22 miles) north from Paris by A15, exit 7, then N184, exit Méry-sur-Oise for Auvers.

By train

From Gare du Nord, changing at St-Ouen L'Aumone (whole journey takes about 1hr).

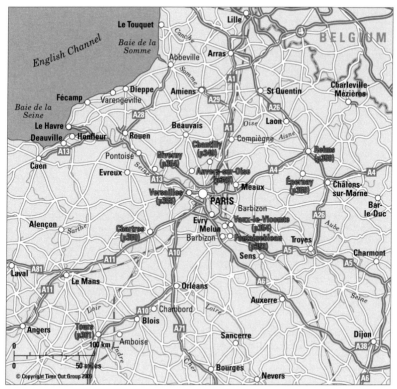

Tourist information

Office de Tourisme

Manoir des Colombières, rue de la Sansonne, 95430 Auvers-sur-Oise (01.30.36.10.06/www. auvers-sur-oise.com). **Open** *Apr-Feb* 9.30am-12.30pm, 2-6pm Tue-Sun. *Nov-Mar* 9.30am-12.30pm, 2-5pm Tue-Sun.

CHANTILLY & SENLIS

From the 14th century until 1897, the town of **Chantilly** was the domain of the Princes of Condé, the cousins of the French kings. As well as its impressive **château**, Chantilly has a rich equestrian history, with its hunting forests and prestigious horse-racing centres.

Much of the cream-coloured château, a fine example of French Renaissance architecture, was destroyed during the Revolution, leaving the main wing to be reconstructed in the 19th century by Henri d'Orléans, Duc d'Aumale. When the duke died in 1897, he bequeathed the Domaine de Chantilly – including the Grand Stables, the Hippodrome and the

61 square kilometre (23 square mile) forest – to the Institut de France on the condition that the château be opened to the public as the **Musée Condé**, and that none of the artworks would be moved or loaned to other museums. His remarkable collection is complemented by the surrounding **park**, beautifully landscaped by André Le Nôtre (of Versailles fame).

The Grandes Ecuries ('great stables') at the château were commissioned in 1719 by Prince Louis-Henri de Bourbon (who believed he would be reincarnated as a horse). Later, they became one of Napoleon's equestrian training grounds, having suffered only light damage during the Revolution. In 1982 the great horseman Yves Bienaimé restored the stables and turned them into the **Musée Vivant du Cheval**. The Bienaimé family has also restored the **Potager des Princes**, the princes' old vegetable garden.

The **Forêt de Chantilly** is full of hiking and cycling trails. A pleasant walk of around seven kilometres circles four small lakes, the Etangs de Commelles, and passes the Château de la Reine Blanche, a mill converted in the 1820s into a pseudo-medieval hunting lodge.

For trail details, ask at the Office National des Forêts (1 av de Sylvie, 03.44.57.03.88, www.onf.fr).

Senlis, not far east of Chantilly, is known as the birthplace of the French monarchy.

Château de Chantilly/ Musée Condée

Chantilly (03.44.27.31.80/www.chateaudechantilly. com). **Open** *Apr-Oct* 10am-6pm Mon, Wed-Sun. *Nov-Mar* 10.30am-5pm Wed-Sun. **Admission** *Château & park* €10; free under-18s. **Credit** MC, V. The major attraction here is the collection of paintings and drawings at the Musée Condé. It includes three paintings by Raphael, and the *Très Riches Heures du Duc de Berry*, a medieval book of hours, containing the most exquisite colours imaginable. If you thought the Middle Ages was dull, think again.

★ Château park

Open *Apr-Oct* 10am-8pm Mon, Wed-Sun. *Nov-Mar* 10.30am-6pm Mon, Wed-Sun. **Admission** *Park only* €5; free under-18s. *Combined ticket* (boat tour, carriage ride, mini-train rides) from €10. **Credit** MC, V.
The main section of the château's sprawling park, designed by royal landscape architect Le Nôtre, features traditional French formal parterres and an extensive canal system, which allows visitors to see the park from electric-powered boats. Get off the beaten path to explore the English Garden, the Island of Love, the kangaroo zoo and the original hamlet that inspired Marie-Antoinette to build her own version at Versailles.

Musée Vivant du Cheval

Les Grandes Ecuries, Chantilly (03.44.27.31.80/ www.museevivantducheval.fr). **Open** *Apr-Oct* 10am-6pm Mon, Wed-Fri; 10.30am-5.30pm Sat, Sun. *Nov-Mar* 1-6pm Mon, Wed-Fri; 1-5pm Sat, Sun. **Admission** €9; €7 reductions. **Credit** MC, V. This museum is an interactive affair, where kids can pet the ponies and everyone gets to learn how the horses are trained to perform in the ring. There are demonstrations every day.

Potager des Princes

Parc de la Faisanderie, 17 rue de la Faisanderie, Chantilly (03.44.57.39.66/www.potagerdes princes.com). **Open** *Apr-Nov* 2-7pm daily. **Admission** (last admission 5.30pm) €7.50; €6.50 reductions. **Credit** MC, V.
The restored princes' kitchen garden is a 19th-century English garden with vegetable plots, trained fruit trees, a small farmyard and an open-air theatre next to the lake.

Where to eat & stay

Try the home-style cooking at **Le Goutillon** (61 rue du Connétable, 03.44.58.01.00).

La Capitainerie (03.44.57.15.89, www. restaurantfp-chantilly.com) offers good French food in the old château kitchens. To sample Chantilly whipped cream, stop for tea at **Aux Goûters Champêtres** (03.44.57.46.21, closed mid Nov-mid Mar) in the *hameau* at the château.

One of the few hotels in the town centre is the **Hôtel du Parc Best Western** (36 av du Maréchal-Joffre, 03.44.58.20.00, www.hotel-parc-chantilly.com, doubles €110-€120).

Getting there

By car

40km (25 miles) from Paris by N16 (direct) or A1 (Chantilly exit).

By train

SNCF Chantilly-Gouvieux from Gare du Nord (30mins), then 5min walk to town, 20mins to château. Some trains stop at Creil, then loop back to Chantilly.

Tourist information

Office de Tourisme (Chantilly)

60 av Maréchal-Joffre, 60500 Chantilly (03.44.67.37.37/www.chantilly-tourisme.com). **Open** *Oct-Apr* 9.30am-12.30pm, 1.30-5.30pm Mon-Sat. *May-Sept* 9.30am-12.30pm, 1.30-5.30pm Mon-Sat; 10am-1.30pm Sun.

Office de Tourisme (Senlis)

Pl du parvis Notre-Dame, 60302 Senlis (03.44.53.06.40/www.ville-senlis.fr). **Open** *Mar-Oct* 10am-12.30pm, 2-6.15pm Mon-Sat; 10.30am-1pm, 2-6.15pm Sun. *Nov-Feb* 10am-12.30pm, 2-6.15pm Mon-Sat; 10.30am-1pm, 2-5pm Sun.

CHARTRES

Seen from a distance, the mismatched spires and dazzling silhouette of **Chartres cathedral** burst out of the Beauce cornfields and dominate the skyline of this modest town some 90 kilometres (56 miles) south-west of Paris. Chartres was a pilgrimage site long before the cathedral was built, ever since the Sacra Camisia (said to be the Virgin Mary's birthing garment) was donated in 876 by the king. The cathedral is one of the finest examples of Gothic architecture in the world; its doorways bristling with sculpture, along with its stained glass, embody a complete medieval world view.

The town of Chartres is an attractive tangle of narrow, medieval streets on the banks of the river Eure. Two sights merit a special mention: the **Musée des Beaux-Arts** (29 cloître

Jazz in the Country

Kick back among the beetroot fields at a unique music festival.

Every once in a while, if you're lucky, you get a chance to partake in one of life's privileged moments. And for lovers of jazz, one of those moments happens each month in a tiny hamlet called **Berlinval**, near Soissons (an hour north Paris), surrounded by nothing but beetroot fields and the occasional sheep.

Twenty five years ago, artist Richard Bréchet and his former wife, Marie-Edith, founded a jazz club called L'Alibi in Uzès, near Nîmes. It soon became the hottest jazz spot outside Paris, attracting big names from across the Atlantic, including trombonist Glenn Ferris (sidekick to Frank Zappa), the legendary Mal Waldron (composer and pianist with Billy Holiday) and saxophone star Archie Shepp.

Nowadays, Bréchet lives in Berlinval in a converted farmhouse that already doubles as an art gallery (La Galerie de Berlinval), but triples as L'Alibi – Mal Waldron/Archie Shepp Jazz Club once a month, when jazz greats jam and bop into the wee hours in his lounge. These are unique and deliciously surreal opportunities to listen to

and mingle with old and new A-listers such as Archie Shepp, pianist Kirk Lightsey (a former regular with Chet Baker), drummer Victor Lewis (who played for Stan Getz), double-bassist Santi Debriano, drummer John Betsch, pianist Tom McClung and saxophonist Adrien Varachaud. Concerts cost around €20 and you need to reserve in advance (03.23.59.01.32/galerie deberlinval@yahoo.fr). Accommodation can also be arranged from €10 (ask when you reserve). To receive the programme, email Bréchet on the address above.

Notre-Dame, 02.37.90.45.80), which houses a collection of 18th-century French paintings by Watteau and others; and the **memorial to Jean Moulin**, the legendary figure of the Resistance, a war-time prefect of Chartres until he was dismissed by the Vichy government after his refusal to co-operate with the Nazis. He became de Gaulle's man in France, and died under torture in Lyon in 1943. Moulin's memorial is a ten-minute walk west of the cathedral, at the corner of rue Collin d'Arleville and boulevard de la Résistance.

★ FREE Cathédrale Notre-Dame

Pl de la Cathédrale (02.37.21.72.07). **Open** *Cathedral* 8.30am-7.30pm daily. *Tower* May-Aug 9.30am-12.30pm, 2-6pm Mon-Sat; 2-6pm Sun. Sep-Apr 9.30am-12.30pm, 2-5pm Mon-Sat; 2-5pm Sun. **Admission** *Cathedral* free. *Tower* €6.50; €4.50 reductions; free under-18s. **No credit cards**.

The west front, or 'Royal Portal', of this High Gothic cathedral modelled in part on St-Denis has three sculpted doorways. Inside, there's another era of sculpture, represented in the 16th-century scenes of the life of Christ that surround the choir. In particular, note the circular labyrinth of black and white stones in the floor.

The cathedral is famed, above all, for its stained-glass windows depicting biblical scenes, saints and medieval trades in brilliant 'Chartres blue', punctuated by rich reds. During World War II the windows were removed and stored nearby for safety, only being reinstalled once the war was over. Climb the tower for a fantastic view over town and country. English-language tours by lecturer Malcolm Miller – one of the world's most knowledgeable and entertaining experts on the cathedral – take place twice daily for most of the year (noon & 2.45pm Mon-Sat, €10, €5 reductions); enquire in the gift shop. In his absence, audio-guides can be hired.

► *Malcolm Miller is also available for private tours of the cathedral (02.37.28.15.58, millerchartres@aol.com).*

Where to eat & stay

Tourists flock to the **Café Serpent** (2 cloître Notre-Dame, 02.37.21.68.81), in the shadow of the cathedral – if it's full, there are plenty of easy options nearby. For restaurant cuisine with a riverside view, try **L'Estocade** (1 rue de la Porte Guillaume, 02.37.34.27.17, closed all day Mon & Sun eve). For fireside treats, **La Vieille Maison** (5 rue au Lait, 02.37.34.10.67, ww.lavieillemaison.fr, closed Mon & Sun) has a cosy 14th-century dining room. For a local speciality, order some Chartres pâté at **Le Saint-Hilaire** (11 rue Pont St-Hilaire, 02.37.30.97.57).

Two perfectly serviceable chain hotels on the ring road, not far from the town centre, are the **Grand Monarque** (22 pl des Epars, 02.37.18.15.15, www.bw-grand-monarque.com, doubles €100-€175) and the more basic **Ibis Centre** (pl Drouaise, 02.37.36.06.36, www.ibishotel.com, doubles €79).

Getting there

By car
90km (56 miles) from Paris by A10, then A11.

By train
Direct from Gare Montparnasse (1hr).

Tourist information

Office de Tourisme
Pl de la Cathédrale, 28000 Chartres (02.37.18.26.26/www.chartres-tourisme.com). **Open** *Apr-Sept* 9am-7pm Mon-Sat; 9.30am-5.30pm Sun. *Oct-Mar* 10am-6pm Mon-Sat; 10am-1pm, 2.30-4.30pm Sun.

FONTAINEBLEAU

Home to 14 French kings since François I, Fontainebleau was once a sort of aristocratic club where gentlemen of the day came to hunt and learn the art of chivalry. The town grew up around the **château** in the 19th century, and is a pleasant place to visit.

The château is bite-sized compared to the sprawling grandeur of Versailles. The style adopted by the Italian artists brought in by François I is still visible, as are the additions by later rulers. The extensive château gardens, park and grand canal, all free for visitors to enter, are also worth exploring.

The 170 square kilometre (66 square mile) **Forêt de Fontainebleau** is part of the Gâtinais regional nature park, which has bizarre geological formations and diverse wildlife. It's the wildest slice of nature to be found near Paris. There are a number of well-marked trails, such as the GR1 from Bois-le-Roi train station, but more serious yompers are better off with an official map such as the TOP25 IGN series 2417-OT, which covers the entire forest, with climbing sites, campsites and picnic areas.

Trail maps are on sale at the **Fontainebleau tourist office**, which rents out bicycles (€20 per day) and has information on the nearby villages of Barbizon and Moret-sur-Loing. Bikes can also be hired from La Petite Reine

(32 rue Sablons, 01.60.74.57.57, www.la-petite-reine.fr). **La Bleausière** riding school (06.82.01.21.18, http://la.bleausiere.free.fr) in Barbizon offers year-round short and long guided tours for all ages and levels.

★ Château de Fontainebleau
Pl du Général-de-Gaulle (01.60.71.50.70/ www.musee-chateau-fontainebleau.fr). **Open** *Château* Apr-Sept 9.30am-6pm Mon, Wed-Sun. Oct-Mar 9.30am-5pm Mon, Wed-Sun. *Park & gardens* Mar, Apr, Oct 9am-6pm daily. May-Sept 9am-7pm daily. Nov-Feb 9am-5pm daily. **Admission** *Château* €8; €6 reductions; free under-18s. *Park & gardens* free. PMP. **Credit** AmEx, MC, V.

The Château de Fontainebleau, a former hunting lodge, is a real mix of styles. In 1528, François I brought in Italian artists and craftsmen to help architect Gilles le Breton transform a neglected lodge into the finest Italian Mannerist palace in France. This style, noted for its grotesqueries, contorted figures and crazy fireplaces, is still visible in the Ballroom and Long Gallery. Henri IV added a tennis court, Louis XIII built a double-horseshoe entrance staircase, and Louis XIV and XV added classical trimmings. Napoleon and Louis-Philippe also spent a fortune on redecoration. The château gardens include Le Nôtre's Grand Parterre and a carp pond in the Jardin Anglais. There is also an informal château park just outside. *Photo p351.*

Where to eat & stay

Rue Grande is lined with restaurants such as the stylish **Au Délice Impérial** (no.1, 01.64.22.20.70) and **Au Bureau** (no.12, 01.60.39.00.01), which has Tex-Mex specialities in a pub setting. At no.92, picnickers can find an array of local cheeses at the **Fromagerie Barthélémy** (01.64.22.21.64). For a blow-out meal, head for **Le Caveau des Ducs** (24 rue Ferrare, 01.64.22.05.05, www.caveaudesducs.com), with its traditional French cuisine.

Some of the dozen rooms at the charming, central **Hôtel de Londres** (1 pl du Général-de-Gaulle, 01.64.22.20.21, www.hoteldelondres.com, doubles €90-€150) have balconies overlooking the château. The elegant **Hôtel Napoléon** (9 rue Grande, 01.60.39.50.50, www.hotelnapoleon-fontainebleau.com, doubles €130-€250) overlooks an interior garden, and provides appropriately grand meals at its restaurant, **La Table des Maréchaux**.

Getting there

By car
60km (37 miles) from Paris by A6, then N7 (about 75mins). Be prepared for traffic jams when heading back to Paris on Sundays.

By train

Gare de Lyon to Fontainebleau-Avon (35mins), then bus AB (marked 'Château'). Ask for a 'Forfait Château de Fontainebleau' (€20.80; €7.70-€16 reductions) at the Gare de Lyon; it includes train fare, bus connection, château entrance and audio guide.

Tourist information

Office de Tourisme

4 rue Royale, 77300 Fontainebleau (01.60.74.99.99/www.fontainebleau-tourisme.com). **Open** *May-Oct* 10am-6pm Mon-Sat; 10am-1pm, 2-5.30pm Sun. *Nov-Apr* 10am-1pm Mon-Sat.

GIVERNY

In 1883, Claude Monet moved his mistress and their eight children into a quaint pink-brick house he had rented in bucolic Giverny, and spent as much time cultivating a beautiful garden here as painting the water lilies in it.

The leader of the Impressionist movement thrived on outdoor scenes, whether along the

Château de Fontainebleau. *See p353.*

ESCAPES & EXCURSIONS

ESCAPES & EXCURSIONS

Seine near Argenteuil or by the Thames in London. Having once seen the tiny village of Giverny from the window of a train, he was smitten. By 1890 he had bought his dream home and soon had a pond dug, bridges built and a tableau of greenery created. As Monet's eyesight began to fail, he produced endless impressions of his man-made paradise, each trying to capture how the leaves and water reflected light. He died here in 1926.

Of the hundreds of tourists who visit here every day, not all are art lovers; somewhat surprisingly, there are none of his original paintings on display here (though you will see the 32 Japanese woodblock prints collected by the artist). Most of the visitors are simply here for the lilies, and a good photo opportunity.

The garden is as much a masterpiece as any of Monet's paintins, its famous water-lily pond, weeping willows and Japanese bridge still remarkably intact from the master's day; and the charming house, the **Fondation Claude Monet** (*photo p356*), is dotted with touching mementos. But once you're back in the village, be prepared for difficulty finding a table at one of the scarce eating places, and long queues of impatient tourists almost everywhere you turn.

Get here early, or book ahead for dinner at the famous **Hôtel Baudy** museum-restaurant (81 rue Claude Monet, 02.32.21.10.03, closed Nov-Mar), where Monet's American disciples (such as Willard Metcalf and Dawson-Watson)

set up their easels for several decadent years, expanding the old hotel into an *art-atelier extraordinaire*, complete with ballroom, rose garden and tennis courts – Cézanne stayed for a month. Today, booking accommodation for Giverny is essential, but you'll be first to the Monet museum in the morning. Up the road, the **Musée d'Art Américain de Giverny** (99 rue Claude-Monet, 02.32.51.94.65, www.maag.org) houses works by the American Impressionist colony.

★ Fondation Claude Monet

84 rue Claude-Monet, 27620 Giverny (02.32.51.28.21/www.fondation-monet.com). **Open** 9.30am-6pm Tue-Sun. Closed Nov-Mar. **Admission** *House & garden* €5.50; €3-€4 reductions; free under-7s. **Credit** AmEx, MC, V.

Where to stay

For recommended hotels and B&Bs in the area, visit www.giverny.org. Pretty **Le Clos Fleuri** (5 rue de la Dîme, 02.32.21.36.51, doubles €80, closed Nov-Mar) is in Giverny, close to the Musée d'Art Américain and Monet's garden.

Getting there

By car

80km (50 miles) west of Paris by A13 to Bonnières, then D201.

Vaux-le-Vicomte.

By train

Gare St-Lazare to Vernon (45mins), then 5km taxi ride or bus from the station.

Tourist information

Comité Départemental du Tourisme de l'Eure

3 rue du Commandant-Letellier, BP 367, 27003 Evreux (02.32.62.04.27/www.cdt-eure.fr). **Open** 9am-12.30pm, 1.30-6pm Mon-Thur; 9am-1pm, 1.30-6pm Fri.

VAUX-LE-VICOMTE

This lavish country château has a valuable lesson to teach: never, ever out-do your king. When Nicolas Fouquet (1615-1680), Louis XIV's finance minister (and protégé of Cardinal Mazarin), decided to build an abode fit for his position, he had several hamlets moved away, called on three of France's most talented men (architect Louis Le Vau, painter Charles Lebrun and landscape gardener André Le Nôtre) and hired great sculptors such as Giradon, Lespagnandel and Nicolas Poussin to chip in with the decor. Its completion was celebrated in 1661 with a huge party for which Molière wrote a play and Lully composed music.

All would have gone swimmingly had it not been for one minor detail: Fouquet invited the king. Louis was disgusted at his minister's display of grandeur; soon after, Fouquet was given a show trial for the embezzlement of state funds. His personal effects were seized by the crown and he was put into exile, dying 19 years later in prison. But Fouquet's legacy did live on, as Louis hired Le Vau, Lebrun and Le Nôtre to work their magic on Versailles.

A self-guided tour of the interior includes Fouquet's personal suite, the servants' dining room, the huge basement and wine cellar, and the copper-filled kitchen. The dome with its unfinished ceiling – Lebrun only had time to paint the sky and one eagle before Fouquet was arrested – and roof are optional extras.

On the south side, a majestic staircase sweeps towards the gardens, divided into terraces whose boxed hedges and flowerbeds sweep into a vast expanse of lawns, grottoes, canals, lakes and fountains. Electric cars can be hired to help you cover the site. Entrance to the château includes the Musée des Equipages, where over 25 period carriages are on display in the former stables.

★ Vaux-le-Vicomte

77950 Maincy (01.64.14.41.90/www.vaux-le-vicomte.com). **Open** *Château* mid Mar-mid Nov 10am-1pm, 2-6pm daily. *Candlelight evenings* May-mid Oct 8pm-midnight Sat (July, Aug 8pm-

midnight Fri). Closed mid Nov to mid Mar. **Admission** €12.50 adults; €9.50-€10 reductions. *Candlelight evenings* €15.50 adults; €13.70 reductions. **Credit** MC, V.

Getting there

By car

55km (35 miles) from Paris by A5 (direction Troyes). Exit at first toll and then follow signs.

By train

Gare de Lyon to Melun (25mins) or RER D to Melun, then 6km taxi ride.

VERSAILLES

Centuries of makeovers have made **Château de Versailles** the most sumptuously clad château in the world – a brilliant, unmissable cocktail of extravagance. Architect Louis Le Vau first embellished the original building – a hunting lodge built during Louis XIII's reign – after Louis XIV saw Vaux-le-Vicomte, the impressive residence of his finance minister, Nicolas Fouquet (*see p354*). André Le Nôtre turned the boggy marshland into terraces, parterres, fountains and lush groves.

After Le Vau's death in 1670, Jules Hardouin-Mansart took over as principal architect, transforming Versailles into the château we know today. He dedicated the last 30 years of his life to adding the two main wings, the Cour des Ministres and the Chapelle Royale. In 1682 Louis moved in, accompanied by his court; thereafter, he rarely set foot in Paris. In the 1770s, Louis XV commissioned Jacques-Ange Gabriel to add the sumptuous Opéra Royal, used for concerts by the Centre de Musique Baroque (01.39.20.78.10). The expense of building and running Versailles cost France dear. With the fall of the monarchy in 1792, most of the furniture was lost – but the château was saved from demolition after 1830 by Louis-Philippe.

The **gardens** of Versailles are really works of art in themselves, their ponds and statues once more embellished by a fully working fountain system. On summer weekends, the spectacular jets of water are set to music, a

---

INSIDE TRACK
ON YOUR BIKE

One of the best ways to see **Versailles** is by bicycle. Conveniently, cycles can be hired from just outside the RER Versailles-Chantiers station (pl Raymond Poincaré, 01.39.20.16.60). Hire rates are €2 an hour or €12 a day.

---

prelude to the occasional fireworks displays of the Fêtes de Nuit.

Beyond the gardens are the Grand Canal and the wooded parkland and sheep-filled pastures of the estate's park. Outside the château gates are the **Potager du Roi** (the Sun King's vegetable garden), and stables which now house the **Académie du Spectacle Equestre**. The **Hall of Mirrors** – a 73-metre (240-foot) gallery overlooking the garden, hung with chandeliers – was commissioned in 1678 by Louis XIV and then decorated by Le Brun. It holds 357 mirrors.

In the town of Versailles, grab a *Historical Places* brochure free from the tourist office (*see p359*) and explore. The Quartier St-Louis opposite the Potager was developed by Louis XV around the Cathédrale St-Louis. Just off rue d'Anjou are the Carrés St-Louis, four market squares surrounded by 18th-century boutiques. North-east of the château is the Quartier Notre-Dame, part of the 'new town' designed by the Sun King himself. Eglise Notre-Dame is where members of the royal family were baptised and married. Around the corner is the Marché Notre-Dame, a market square dating back to 1671 and surrounded by restaurants and cafés. The covered market is closed on Mondays.

Académie du Spectacle Equestre

Grandes Ecuries, Château de Versailles (01.39.02.07.14/bookings 08.92.68.18.91/ www.acadequestre.fr).
Les Matinales des Ecuyers *(to watch riding practice & visit)* Viewings 10.30am, 11.15am Sun. Times vary for groups & during school hols; call for details. **Admission** €6; €5 reductions. **Credit** MC, V.
Reprise Musicale *(performance & visit)* Performances 8.30pm Sat; 3pm Sun. **Admission** *Daytime* €18; €10 reductions. *Evening* €25; €16-€21 reductions. **Credit** MC, V. Across from the château entrance are the Sun King's magnificent stables, restored in 2003. They house the Académie du Spectacle Equestre, which is responsible for the elaborate shows of tightly choreographed theatrics on horseback, run by famous horse trainer Bartabas.

★ Château de Versailles

78000 Versailles (01.30.83.78.00/advance tickets 08.92.68.46.94/www.chateauversailles.fr). **Open** *Apr-Oct* 9am-6.30pm Tue-Sun. *Nov-Mar* 9am-5.30pm Tue-Sun. **Admission** €13.50; €10 after 3pm; free under-18s. PMP, Passeport Versailles. **Credit** AmEx, DC, MC, V.

Versailles is a masterpiece – and usually packed with visitors. Allow yourself a whole day to appreciate the sumptuous State Apartments and the Hall of Mirrors, the highlights of any visit; and mostly accessible with a day ticket.

The Grand Appartement, where Louis XIV held court, consists of six gilded salons, all opulent examples of baroque craftsmanship. No less luxurious, the Queen's Apartment includes her bedroom, where royal births took place in view of the court. Hardouin-Mansart's showpiece, the Hall of Mirrors, where a united Germany was proclaimed in 1871 and the Treaty of Versailles signed in 1919, is flooded with natural light from its 17 vast windows. Designed to catch the last of the day's rays, it was here that the Sun King would hold extravagant receptions. Other apartments can be seen only as part of a guided tour.

Domaine de Versailles
Gardens Open *Apr-Oct* 7am-dusk daily. *Nov-Mar* 8am-dusk daily. **Admission** *Winter* free (statues covered over). *Summer* €3; €1.50 reductions; free under-10s. Passeport Versailles.
Grandes-Eaux Musicales *(01.30.83.78.88).* **Open** *Apr-Sept* Sat, Sun. **Admission** €7; €5.50 reductions; free under-10s. Passeport Versailles.
Credit AmEx, DC, MC, V.

Park Open dawn-dusk daily. **Admission** free. Sprawling across eight square kilometres, the carefully planned gardens consist of formal parterres, ponds, elaborate statues – many commissioned by Colbert in 1674 – and a spectacular series of fountains, served by an ingenious hydraulic system only recently restored to working order. On weekend afternoons in the spring and autumn, the fountains are set to music for the Grandes Eaux Musicales – and also serve as a backdrop, seven times a year, for the extravagant Fêtes de Nuit, capturing the regal splendour of the Sun King's celebrations with fireworks, music and theatre.

Grand Trianon/Petit Trianon/ Domaine de Marie-Antionette
01.30.83.77.43/weekend reservations 01.30.83.76.50. **Open** *Apr-Oct* noon-7pm daily. *Nov-Mar* noon-5.30pm daily. **Admission** *Summer* €9; €5 after 5pm; free under-18s. *Winter* €5; free under-18s. PMP, Passeport Versailles.
Credit AmEx, DC, MC, V.
In 1687 Hardouin-Mansart built the pink marble Grand Trianon in the north of the park, away from the protocol of the court. Here Louis XIV and his children's governess and secret second wife, Madame de Maintenon, could admire the intimate gardens

Fondation Claude Monet. *See p354.*

Time Travel

Get on the fast track and take the TGV out of town.

Thanks to the mighty TGV, you can cover a decent portion of the country in just a few hours – a godsend when you're hankering for a change of scenery. But where to go? Below are three cities at approximately one, two and three hours from Paris by TGV; ideal weekend and day-trip getaways (www.sncf.com).

1hr LILLE
www.lilletourism.com
Baroque and Flemish influences make the historic centre of this Flanders town very pretty indeed. Monuments to look out for include the 15th-century Palais Rihour (place Rihour), built for the dukes of Burgundy; the 17th-century arcaded stock exchange (Grande-Place) and the Palais des Beaux-Arts (place de la République, 03.20.06.78.00, www.pba-lille.fr), second only to the Louvre for its range of European art.

2hrs STRASBOURG
www.otstrasbourg.fr
Strasbourg is just three kilometres from the German border, and the Germanic influence is omnipresent, with sauerkraut and sausages the staple items on many restaurant menus. Its chocolate box centre is famed for its 16th- and 17th-century half-timbered houses (especially the Petite France district), one of the finest Gothic cathedrals in France, a Vauban dam, 14th-century defence towers, and an excellent modern and contemporary art museum with an entire section devoted to Gustave Doré (1 pl Jean-Hans Arp, 03.88.23.31.31, www.musees-strasbourg.org).

3hrs MARSEILLE
www.marseille-tourisme.com
This fast-paced, forward-thinking city has steep streets, tranquil squares and bustling 19th-century thoroughfares that provide a patchwork of backdrops for souk-like markets, chic shops and the colourful Vieux Port, where lively fishmongers sell their wares along the boat-lined quayside. For breathtaking views, climb up to the Notre-Dame de la Garde basilica, or stay grounded over a plate of *bouillabaisse* and go shopping around the vintage shops on Cours Julien. For more on the area, see *Time Out South of France* (£12.99 UK/$19.95 US).

Marseille

from the colonnaded portico. It retains the Empire decor of Napoleon, who stayed here with his second Empress, Marie-Louise.

The Petit Trianon, built for Louis XV's mistress Madame de Pompadour, is a wonderful example of neo-classicism. It later became part of the Domaine de Marie-Antoinette, an exclusive hideaway located beyond the canal in the wooded parkland. Given to Marie-Antoinette as a wedding gift by her husband Louis XVI in 1774, the domain also includes the chapel adjoining the Petit Trianon, plus a theatre, a neo-classical 'Temple d'Amour', and Marie-Antoinette's fairy-tale farm and dairy, known as the Hameau de la Reine. Here, the queen escaped from the discontent of her subjects and the revolutionary fervour of Paris by pretending to be a humble milkmaid. The Domaine opened to the public in summer 2006, and renovations were completed on the buildings in September 2008.

▶ *Enliven a stroll through the gardens by hiring hand-held digital PDA or iPod guides.*

Potager du Roi

10 rue Maréchal-Joffre (011.39.24.62.62/www. potager-du-roi.fr). **Open** *Apr-Oct* 10am-6pm Tue-Sun. *Nov-Mar* 10am-6pm Mon-Fri (by guided tour only). **Admission** *Mon-Fri* €4.50; €3 reductions; free under-6s. *Sat, Sun* €6.50; €3 reductions; free under-6s. **Credit** AmEx, DC, MC, V.

The Potager du Roi, the king's vegetable garden, features 16 small squares surrounded by 5,000 fruit trees espaliered into fabulous shapes.

Where to eat & stay

Set in a building dating back to the construction of the château, **Le Chapeau Gris** (7 rue Hoche, 01.39.50.10.81, www.auchapeaugris.com, closed dinner Tue, all day Wed) is the oldest restaurant in Versailles, and serves French country cuisine served under wooden beams. **Boeuf à la Mode** (4 rue au Pain, Marché Notre-Dame, 01.39.50.31.99) is an authentic 1930s brasserie serving steak and seafood specialities at mid-range prices. For a proper splurge, consider sampling **Gordon Ramsay**

> **INSIDE TRACK**
> **GORDON RAMSAY**
>
> If you fancy a drop of Gordon, you can now hire the chef's table overlooking the kitchens of his first French offshoot, **Gordon Ramsay au Trianon** near Versaille (01.30.84.55.55, www.gordon ramsay.com). For the not inconsiderable sum of €750 at lunch (€900 at dinner), you get canapés and a glass of champagne on arrival, plus a meal for six.

au Trianon (*see below*). Another long-established restaurant is the traditional **Brasserie du Théâtre** (15 rue des Réservoirs, 01.39.50.03.21), which stays open until 11.30pm for the after-show crowd from the Montansier theatre next door. You'll also find plenty of late-night bars around the Marché Notre-Dame.

The town centre has several reasonably priced hotels. One of the more historic is the **Hôtel du Cheval Rouge** (18 rue André-Chénier, 01.39.50.03.03, www.chevalrouge. fr.st, doubles €75-€92), built in Louis XIV's former stable overlooking the Marché Notre-Dame. Across from the château, the **Hôtel de France** (5 rue Colbert, 01.30.83. 92.23, www.hotelfrance-versailles.com, doubles from €141) is set in an 18th-century townhouse and has period decor.

Getting there

By car
20km (12.5 miles) from Paris by A13 or D10.

By train
For the station nearest the château, take the RER C5 (VICK or VERO trains) to Versailles-Rive Gauche; or take a Transilien SNCF train from Gare St-Lazare to Versailles-Rive Droit (10mins on foot to the château).

Tourist information

Office de Tourisme
2bis av de Paris, 78000 Versailles (01.39.24.88.88/www.versailles-tourisme.com). **Open** 11am-5pm Mon, Sun; 9am-6pm Tue-Sat.

Escapes

CHAMPAGNE COUNTRY

Named after the region in which it's produced, champagne – nearly all 300 million bottles a year of it – comes from the towns of **Reims** (nasally pronounced 'Ranse') and **Epernay**, some 25 kilometres (16 miles) apart. At less than two hours by train from Paris, both are ideal destinations for a day trip or a weekend break. Most champagne cellars give detailed explanations of how the drink is produced – from the grape varieties used to the strict name and quality controls – and guided tours finish with a sample. Don't forget your woollies when you visit, as the cellars are chilly and damp.

Epernay developed in the 19th century as expanding champagne houses moved out from Reims to acquire more space. Today, the aptly named avenue de Champagne is home to most major brands – but the best tours are at **Moët & Chandon** and **Mercier**.

In Reims, most of the major champagne houses are open by appointment only: Krug (03.26.84.44.20); Lanson (03.26.78.50.50); Louis Roederer (by appointment *and* recommendation only, 03.26.40.42.11) and Veuve Clicquot (03.26.89.53.90, www.veuve-clicquot.com). **Champagne Pommery** is set in an intriguing Elizabethan building.

Home of the coronation church of most French monarchs dating back to Clovis in 496, Reims was an important city even in Roman times. Begun in 1211, the present **Cathédrale Notre-Dame** (03.26.47.55.34, www.cathedrale-reims.com) has rich Gothic decoration that includes thousands of well-preserved figures on the portals. Look out, too, for the splendid stained-glass windows in the axial chapel, designed by Chagall. The statues damaged during heavy shelling in World War I can be seen next door in the former archbishop's palace, the Palais de Tau (2 pl du Cardinal-Luçon, 03.26.47.81.79).

L'Ancien Collège des Jésuites (1 pl Museux, 03.26.85.51.50, closed Tue, Sat & Sun am) is a classic example of 17th-century baroque architecture, housing a library decorated with religious carvings and paintings by Jean Hélart.

Champagne Pommery

5 pl du Général-Gouraud, 51100 Reims (03.26.61.62.55/www.pommery.com). **Open** *Mid Apr-mid Nov* 9.30am-7pm daily. *Mid Nov-mid Apr* (by appointment only) 10am-6pm daily. **Admission** (incl 1 glass) €7.50; (incl 2 glasses) €10. **Credit** MC, V.

Built in 1868, this unusual château was modelled on Elizabethan architecture. The visit takes place some 30m (98ft) underground, in 18km (11 miles) of tunnels linking 120 Gallo-Roman chalk quarries.

★ Mercier

68 av de Champagne, 51200 Epernay (03.26.51.22.22/www.champagne-mercier.fr). **Open** *Mid Mar-mid Nov* 9.30-11.30am, 2-4.30pm daily. *Mid Nov-mid Mar* 9.30-11.30am, 2-4.30pm Mon, Thur-Sun. **Admission** (incl 1 glass) €6.50; €3 reductions; free under-12s. **Credit** MC, V.

Some 7,000 tonnes of chalk were extracted to create the 18km (11 miles) of cellars at Mercier, opened in 1858. Note the 20-tonne champagne barrel at the entrance: it took 24 bulls and 18 horses to drag it all the way from Epernay to Paris for the 1889 Exposition Universelle. The interesting 45-minute underground tour takes place on a little train, and covers a stretch of tunnel that was used for mini-car races in the 1950s.

Moët & Chandon.

★ Moët & Chandon

20 av de Champagne, 51200 Epernay (03.26.51.20.00/www.moet.com). **Open** *Mid Mar-mid Nov* 9.30-11.30am, 2-4.30pm daily. *Mid Nov-mid Mar* 9.30-11.30am, 2-4.30pm Mon-Fri. **Admission** (incl 1 glass) €7.50; €4.50 reductions; free under-12s. **Credit** AmEx, DC, MC, V.
Moët & Chandon started life in 1743 as champagne supplier to Madame de Pompadour, and later supplied Napoleon and Alexander I of Russia. Since then it has kept pole position, with the largest domaine and more than 250 global outlets. In the hour-long tour, visitors are led through a section (under the grand house) of the 28km (17 miles) of tunnels. *Photo p.352.*

Where to eat & stay

In Reims, countless cafés and brasseries line lively **place Drouet d'Erlon**, as do many hotels. If you fancy staying at a working champagne domaine, contact **Ariston Fils Champagne** (4-8 Grande-Rue, 51170 Brouillet, 03.26.97.43.46, www.champagne-aristonfils.com, doubles €45-€48), which has three rooms and pampers its guests. To sleep like a king, book one of the luxuriously extravagant rooms at the **Château les Crayères** (64 bd Henry Vasnier, 03.26.82.80.80, www.chateaulescrayeres.com, doubles €275-€475), a grand country-house hotel set in lush grounds.

In Epernay, **La Cave à Champagne** (16 rue Gambetta, 03.26.55.50.70) does good traditional French food, as does **Théâtre** (8 pl Pierre-Mendès-France, 03.26.58.88.19, closed dinner Tue & Sun, all Wed & 15 Feb-2 Mar, 15 July-2 Aug & 22-28 Dec). Known for its champagnes, **Les Cépages** (16 rue Fauvette, 03.26.55.16.93, closed Wed & Sun and July & Christmas) serves homely food.

Set in a 19th-century red-brick mansion, **Le Clos Raymi** (3 rue Joseph-de-Venoge, 03.26.51.00.58, www.closraymi-hotel.com, doubles €100-€140) is a cosy mix of traditional and modern. Part of the international Best Western chain, the **Hôtel de Champagne** (30 rue Eugène-Mercier, 03.26.53.10.60, www.bw-hotel-champagne.com, doubles €90-€120) is comfy enough, and the **Hôtel Kyriad** (3bis rue de Lorraine, 03.26.54.17.39, doubles from €57) has basic, clean rooms.

Getting there

By car

150km (93 miles) from Paris by the A4. For Epernay, exit at Château Thierry and take the N3.

By train

From Gare de l'Est, trains take about 45mins for Reims and Epernay.

Tourist information

Office de Tourisme (Epernay)

7 av de Champagne, 51200 Epernay (03.26. 53.33.00/www.ot-epernay.fr). **Open** *Mid Apr-mid Oct* 9.30am-12.30pm, 1.30-7pm Mon-Sat; 11am-4pm Sun. *Mid Oct-mid Apr* 9.30am-noon, 1.30-5.30pm Mon-Sat.

Office de Tourisme (Reims)

2 rue Guillaume-de-Machault, 51100 Reims (03.26.77.45.00/www.reims-tourisme.com). **Open** *Easter-mid Oct* 9.30am-12.30pm, 1.30-7pm Mon-Sat; 11am-4pm Sun. *Mid Oct-Easter* 9am-6pm Mon; 11am-4pm Sun.

TOURS

Novelist Honoré de Balzac (1799-1850) once described his beloved birthplace as being 'more fresh, flowery and perfumed than any other town in the world', and Tours has a lot going for it today. In fact, it's a positively pleasant city, bursting with history, medieval quarters, a lively student population, colourful flower markets (Wednesday and Saturday on boulevard Béranger) and enticing bars and restaurants. Only an hour from Paris by TGV, it is the official gateway to the Loire Valley, and a choice place in which to refuel before overdosing on sumptuous Renaissance castles.

Sandwiched between the Loire (north) and the Cher (south) rivers, it began life as a fertile floodplain, prized by the Turones – a Celtic tribe that gave modern Tours its name. In 57 BC Julius Caesar conquered the city, modestly changing its name to Caesarodunum (Caesar's hill). Traces of the third-century Gallo-Roman city wall and amphitheatre can still be seen in the Musée des Beaux-Arts gardens (the left-hand tower of the Archbishop's palace and the curved wall to the east).

When Christianity arrived, St Martin, the founder of France's first monastery (in Ligugé in Poitou), became bishop of Tours. After his death in 397, his relics, laid to rest in the Roman **Basilique St-Martin**, were believed to have healing powers, drawing in thousands of pilgrims en route to Santiago de Compostela in Spain, and prompting the construction of Tours' medieval quarters.

Throughout the 15th and 16th centuries, the city vied with Paris as the seat of power: Charles VII, Louis XI (who instated Tours' silk industry), Charles VIII and François I all cherished Tours; Henry IV preferred Paris. Tours was bombarded by the Prussians in 1870 and suffered widespread damage in World War II, especially in the historic centre, which by the 1960s was a no-go zone of crumbling masonry.

Nowadays, after 40 years of regeneration, the medieval quarters contain some of Tours' most charming streets. Pedestrianised **place Plumereau**, with its exquisite half-timbered façades housing cafés, galleries and boutiques, is the hub of town. Wander down lanes like rue Briçonnet to find concealed courtyards, more half-timbered houses and the occasional crooked tower. In place de Châteauneuf, a lone Romanesque tower is the only intact segment of the original Basilique-St-Martin (sacked by the Huguenots in 1562). The neo-Byzantine **Basilique St-Martin** (02.47.05.63.87) houses St-Martin's shrine further up the road, opposite the ruined vestiges.

The east of Tours is dominated by the splendid **Cathédrale St-Gatien** (02.47.70.21.00). Work on it began in the 13th century and ended in the 16th century, demonstrating the French Gothic style in its entirety. The stained-glass windows inside are often compared to those of Sainte-Chapelle in Paris. Next door, the archbishop's palace and **Musée des Beaux Arts** (18 pl François-Sicard, 02.47.05.68.73, open 9am-12.45pm, 2-6pm Mon, Wed-Sun) has a surprisingly rich collection of paintings by Degas, Rembrandt and Delacroix, and several sculptures by Rodin and Bourdelle. Check out the enormous 200-year-old cedar of Lebanon in the garden, the branches of which are so heavy they have to be held up.

North of here, Tours' **Château Royal** looks over the Loire River with dishevelled majesty. You can best take in its assorted architecture by following the river: the **Tour de Guise** (look out for machicolations and a pepper-pot roof) was a 13th-century fortress, and the 15th-century **Logis des Gouverneurs** on the quay has gable dormers and a chunk of Gallo-Roman wall at its base.

Further west, the **Eglise St-Julien** has managed to insinuate a wine museum, the **Musée des vins de Touraine** (16 rue Nationale, 02.47.61.07.93, open 9am-noon, 2-6pm Mon, Wed-Sun), into its Gothic, monastic cells. And next door, the **Musée du Compagnonnage** (8 rue Nationale, 02.47.21.62.20, open 9am-noon, 2-6pm Mon, Wed-Sun, daily June-Sept) is a dinky museum, showcasing the handiwork of master craftsmen of the guilds.

Cross over rue Nationale (the main thoroughfare and shopping district) and you'll get to the fabulous **Hôtel Goüin**, a splendid Renaissance beauty that once belonged to a rich silk merchant, and which now contains the **Musée Archéologique de la Touraine** (25 rue de Commerce, 02.47.66.22.32, open 10am-1pm, 2-6pm Tue-Sun), devoted to the history of the Touraine region. Sadly, the only place still keeping the local silk industry alive is the

Manufacture Le Manach (35 quai Paul Bert, 02.47.54.45.78, www.lemanach.fr), on the right bank of the Loire. The weaving methods here have remained unchanged since the early 19th century, and it is one of the only manufacturers in France capable of reproducing authentic fabrics using patterns from the 17th century. Enquire at the tourist office if you fancy a visit.

Where to eat & stay

For dreamy regional dishes such as *crépine de dinde* (a giant turkey meatball cooked in red wine) and *poire tappé* (poached pear), head to **Le Petit Patrimoine** (58 rue Colbert, 02.47.66.05.81). If *moules-frites* is more your thing, the **Taverne de l'Homme Tranquille** has a large selection (22 rue du grand Marché, near pl Plumereau, 02.47.61.46.04).

For a few sneaky glasses of Touraine wine before you head back, **Au Chien Jaune** (74 rue Bernard Palissy, 02.47.05.10.17), a former brothel, is in a handy spot by the tourist office and railway station. Aside from the wine, it specialises in regional dishes.

If you're on a budget, a good, cheap option in a central location is **Hôtel Mondial** (3 pl de la Résistance, 02.47.05.62.68, www.hotelmondialtours.com, doubles €44-€70). For a touch more luxury, follow in the footsteps of Winston Churchill and try Tours' only four-star hotel, **L'Hôtel de l'Univers** (5 bd Heurteloup, 02.47.05.37.15, www.hotel-univers.fr, doubles €197-€398); or for somewhere a little more modest, with decent rooms and a pretty garden, the **Best Western Central Hôtel** (21 rue Berthelot, 02.47.05.46.44, www.bestwesterncentralhotel tours.com, doubles €76-€140), is more charming than the other chain hotels in Tours.

Getting there

By car
235km (146 miles) west from Paris by A10.

By train
From Gare Montparnasse to Tours centre (1hr).

Tourist information

Office de Tourisme
78-82 rue Bernard Palissy, 37042 Tours (02.47.70.37.37/www.ligeris.com). **Open** *Mid Apr-mid Oct* 8.30am-7pm Mon-Sat; 10am-12.30pm, 2.30-5pm Sun & bank hols. *Mid Oct-mid Apr* 9am-12.30pm, 1.30-6pm Mon-Sat; 10am-1pm Sun & bank hols.
If you're keen to see the châteaux but not to drive, the tourist office runs day trips from Paris to Azat-le-Rideau, Villandry, Chenonceau and Amboise.

Directory

Getting Around

ARRIVING & LEAVING

By air

Roissy-Charles-de-Gaulle airport
01.70.36.39.50/www.adp.fr.
Most international flights use
Roissy-Charles-de-Gaulle airport,
30km (19 miles) north-east of Paris.
Its two main terminals are some
way apart, so check which one
you need for your return flight.
The **RER B** (RATP helpline,
08.92.69.32.46, www.transilien.com)
is the quickest way to central Paris
(about 40mins to Gare du Nord;
45mins to RER Châtelet-Les Halles;
€8.40 single). A new station gives
direct access from Terminal 2;
from Terminal 1 you take the free
shuttle bus. RER trains run every
10-15mins, 4.56am-11.56pm daily
from the airport to Paris.
Air France buses
(08.92.35.08.20, www.cars-
airfrance.com; €14 single, €22
return, €7 under-11s, free under-2s)
leave every 15mins, 5.45am-11pm
daily, from both terminals, and stop
at porte Maillot and place Charles-
de-Gaulle (35-50min trip). Air
France buses also run to Gare
Montparnasse and Gare de Lyon
(€15 single, €24 return, €7.50 under-
11s, free under-2s) every 30mins (45-
60min trip), 7am-9pm daily; there's
a shuttle bus between Roissy and
Orly (€18 (no return), €9 under-11s,
free under-2s) every 30mins, 5.55am-
10.25pm daily from Roissy; 6.30am-
10.20pm Mon-Fri, 7am-10.30pm Sat,
Sun from Orly. The **RATP
Roissybus** (08.92.69.32.46,
www.ratp.fr; €8.90) runs every
15-20mins, 5.45am-11pm daily,
between the airport and the corner
of rue Scribe/rue Auber (at least
45mins); buy tickets on the bus.
Paris Airports Service
is a door-to-door minibus service
between airports and hotels, 24/7.
The more passengers on board, the
less each one pays. Roissy prices
go from €26 for one person to
€12.40 each for eight people,
6am-8pm (minimum €41, 4-6am,
8-10pm); book on 01.55.98.10.80,
www.parisairportservice.com.
Airport Connection
(01.43.65.55.55, www.airport-
connection.com; booking 7am-11pm)
runs a similar service, 4am-

midnight. Prices for Roissy are €28
per person, €47 for two, then €13
per extra person. A **taxi** to central
Paris can take 30-60mins depending
on traffic. Expect to pay €30-€50,
plus €1 per item of luggage.

Orly airport
01.70.36.39.50/www.adp.fr.
Domestic and international flights
use Orly airport, 18km (11 miles)
south of the city. It has two
terminals: Orly-Sud (mainly
international) and Orly-Ouest
(mainly domestic).
Air France buses
(08.92.35.08.20, www.cars-
airfrance.com; €10 single, €16
return, €5 under-11s, free under-2s)
leave both terminals every 30mins,
6.15am-11.15pm daily, and stop at
Invalides and Montparnasse (30-
45mins). The **RATP Orlybus**
(08.92.69.32.46, www.ratp.fr; €6.30)
runs between the airport and
Denfert-Rochereau every 15mins,
5.35am-11.05pm Mon-Fri, 5.35am-
12.05am Sat-Sun (30min trip); buy
tickets on the bus. The high-speed
Orlyval (www.orlyval.fr) shuttle
train runs every 4-7mins (6am-
11pm daily) to RER B station
Antony (€13.50 to Châtelet-les-
Halles) getting to central Paris
takes about 35mins. You could
also catch the **Paris par le train**
bus (€6.10) to Pont de Rungis,
where you can take the RER C into
central Paris. Buses run every
20mins, 5am-11.30pm daily; 35min
trip. Orly prices for the **Paris
Airports Service** and **Airport
Connection** door-to-door facility
(*see above*) are €25 for one person
and €5-€12 each for extra
passengers depending on numbers.
A **taxi** into town takes 20-40mins
and costs €16-€26, plus €1 per
piece of luggage.

Paris Beauvais airport
*08.92.68.20.66/www.aeroport
beauvais.com.*
Beauvais, 70km (44 miles) from
Paris, is served by budget airlines
such as **Ryanair** (08.92.23.23.75,
www.ryanair.com). Buses (€13)
leave for Porte Maillot 15-30mins
after each arrival; buses the other
way leave 3hrs 15mins before each
departure. Get tickets from arrival
lounge (information: 08.92.68.20.64)
or buy tickets on the bus.

Major airlines

Aer Lingus
08.21.23.02.67/www.aerlingus.com.
Air France
08.20.32.08.20/www.airfrance.fr.
American Airlines
01.55.17.43.41/
www.americanairlines.fr.
bmibaby
08.90.71.00.81/www.bmibaby.com.
British Airways *08.25.82.54.00/*
www.britishairways.fr.
British Midland
01.41.91.87.04/www.flybmi.com.
Continental *01.71.23.03.35/*
www.continental.com.
Easyjet
08.26.10.26.11/www.easyjet.com.
KLM & NorthWest
08.90.71.07.10/www.klm.com.
United
08.10.72.72.72/www.united.fr.

By car

Options for crossing the
Channel with a car include:
Eurotunnel (08.10.63.03.04,
www.eurotunnel.com); **Brittany
Ferries** (08.25.82. 88.28.
www.brittanyferries.com);
P&O Ferries (08.25.12.01.56,
www.poferries.com); and
SeaFrance (0044.8705.711.711,
www.seafrance.com).

Shared journeys

Allô-Stop *30 rue Pierre Sémard,
9th (01.53.20.42.42/www.allostop.
net). M° Poissonnière.* **Open** 10am-
1pm, 2-6pm Mon-Fri; 10am-1pm, 2-
4pm Sat. **Credit** MC, V. Call several
days ahead to be put in touch with
drivers. There's a fee (€5 under
250km, 155 miles; €8 over 250km),
plus a contribution towards the gas
expenses, paid to the driver (from
€5 under 100km, 62 miles, up to
€105 for over 2,000km, 1243 miles).

By coach

International coach services arrive
at the Gare Routière Internationale
Paris-Gallieni at Porte de Bagnolet,
20th. For reservations (in English),
call **Eurolines** on 08.92.89.90.91
(€0.34/min) or 01.44.63.00.66
(UK 01582 404 511), or visit
www.eurolines.fr. Fares start from
€11 for a single journey to Paris.

By rail

Eurostar services (01233 617 575, www.eurostar.com) to Paris depart from the dedicated terminal at St Pancras International. Thanks to the new high speed track, the journey from London to Paris now takes 2hrs 15mins direct, slightly longer for trains stopping at Ashford and Lille. Eurostar services from the new terminal at Ebbsfleet International, near junction 2 of the M25, take 2hrs 5mins direct. Fares start at £55/€77 for a London-Paris return ticket. Check in at least 30mins before departure time. Eurostar trains from London St Pancras arrive at Gare du Nord (08.92.35.35.39, www.sncf.fr), with easy access to public transport and taxi ranks.

Cycles can be taken as hand luggage if they are dismantled and carried in a bike bag. You can also check them in at the Eurodispatch depot at St Pancras (Esprit Parcel Service, 08705 850 850) or Sernam depot at Gare du Nord (01.55.31.58.40). Check-in must be done 24hrs ahead; a Eurostar ticket must be shown. The service costs £20/€25.

MAPS

Free maps of the métro, bus and RER systems are available at airports and métro stations. Other brochures from métro stations are *Paris Visite – Le Guide*, with details of transport tickets and a small map, and *Plan de Paris*, a fold-out one showing *Noctambus* night bus lines. A Paris street map (*Plan de Paris*) can be bought from newsagents. The blue *Paris Pratique* is clear and compact.

PUBLIC TRANSPORT

Almost all of the Paris public transport system is run by the **RATP** (Régie Autonome des Transports Parisiens; 08.92.69.32.46, www.ratp.fr): the bus, métro (underground) and suburban tram routes, as well as lines A and B of the RER (Réseau Express Régional) suburban express railway, which connects with the métro within the city centre. National rail operator **SNCF** (08.92.35.35.35, www.sncf.com) runs RER lines C, D and E, and serves the Paris suburbs (*Banlieue*), and French regions and abroad (*Grandes Lignes*).

Fares & tickets

Paris and suburbs are divided into six travel zones; zones 1 and 2 cover the city centre. RATP tickets and passes are valid on the métro, bus and RER. Tickets and *carnets* can be bought at métro stations, tourist offices and *tabacs* (tobacconists); single tickets can also be bought on buses. Hold on to your ticket in case of spot checks; you'll also need it to exit from RER stations.

● A single ticket *T+* costs €1.60, but it's more economical to buy a *carnet* of ten for €11.40.

● A one-day *Mobilis* pass costs from €5.80 for zones 1 and 2 to €16.40 for zones 1-6 (not including airports).

● A one-day *Paris Visite* pass for zones 1-3 is €8.50; a five-day pass is €27.50, with discounts on some attractions.

● One-week or one-month *Carte Orange* passes (passport photo needed) offer unlimited travel in the relevant zones; if bought in zones 1 or 2, each is delivered as a Navigo swipe card. A *forfait mensuel* (monthly *Carte Orange* valid from the first day of the month) for zones 1 and 2 costs €55.10; a weekly *forfait hebdomadaire* (weekly *Carte Orange* valid Mon-Sun inclusive) for zones 1 and 2 costs €16.80 and is better value than *Paris Visite* passes.

Métro & RER

The Paris **métro** is the fastest and cheapest way of getting around. Trains run 5.30am-12.40am Mon-Thur, 5.30am-1.30am Fri-Sun. Individual lines are numbered, with each direction named after the last stop. Follow the orange *Correspondance* to change lines. Some interchanges, such as Châtelet-Les-Halles, Montparnasse-Bienvenüe and République, involve long walks. The exit (*Sortie*) is indicated in blue. The driverless line 14 runs from Gare St-Lazare to Olympiades. Pickpockets and bag-snatchers are rife on the network – pay special attention as the doors are closing.

The five **RER** lines (A, B, C, D and E) run 5.30am-1am daily through Paris and out into the suburbs. Within Paris, the RER is useful for faster journeys – Châtelet-Les-Halles to Gare du Nord is one stop on the RER, and six on the métro. Métro tickets are valid for RER journeys within zones 1 and 2.

Buses

Buses run 6.30am-8.30pm, with some routes continuing until 12.30am, Mon-Sat; limited services operate on selected lines Sun and public holidays. You can use a métro ticket, a ticket bought from the driver (€1.60) or a travel pass. Tickets should be punched in the machine next to the driver; passes should be shown to the driver. When you want to get off, press the red request button.

Night buses

After the métro and normal buses stop running, the only public transport – apart from taxis – are the 42 **Noctilien** lines, between place du Châtelet and the suburbs (hourly 12.30am-5.30am Mon-Thur; half-hourly 1am-5.35am Fri, Sat); look out for the Noctilien logo on bus stops or the N in front of the route number. A ticket costs €1.60; travel passes are valid.

River transport

Batobus

(08.25.05.01.01/www.batobus.com). River buses stop every 15-25mins at: Eiffel Tower, Musée d'Orsay, St-Germain-des-Prés (quai Malaquais), Notre-Dame, Jardin des Plantes, Hôtel de Ville, Louvre, Champs-Elysées (Pont Alexandre III). They run Nov-Mar 10.30am-4.30pm; Mar-May & Sept-Nov 10am-7pm; June-Aug 10am-9.30pm. A one-day pass is €12 (€6, €8 reductions); two-day pass €14 (€7, €9 reductions); five-day pass €17 (€8, €11 reductions); season-ticket €55 (€35 reductions). Tickets can be bought at Batobus stops, RATP ticket offices and the **Office de Tourisme** (*see p381*).

Trams

Two modern tram lines operate in the suburbs, running from La Défense to Issy-Val de Seine and from Bobigny Pablo Picasso to St-Denis; a third runs between the Garigliano Bridge in the west of the city to Porte d'Ivry in the south-east. They connect with the métro and RER; fares are the same as for buses.

RAIL TRAVEL

Suburban destinations are served by the RER. Other locations farther from the city are served by the SNCF railway; the TGV high-speed train has slashed journey times and is being extended to all the main

DIRECTORY

regions. There are few long-distance bus services. Tickets can be bought at any SNCF station (not just the one from which you'll travel), SNCF shops and travel agents. If you reserve online or by phone, you can pay and pick up your tickets from the station or have them sent to your home. SNCF automatic machines (*billeterie automatique*) only work with French credit/debit cards. Regular trains have full-rate White (peak) and cheaper Blue (off-peak) periods. You can save on TGV fares by buying special cards. The *Carte 12/25* gives under-26s a 25-50 per cent reduction; even without it, under-26s are entitled to 25 per cent off. Buy tickets in advance to secure the cheaper fare. Before you board any train, stamp your ticket in the orange *composteur* machines located on the platforms, or you might have to pay a hefty fine.

SNCF reservations & tickets

National reservations/information 08.92.35.35.35 (€0.34 per min)/www.sncf.com. **Open** 7am-10pm daily. You can also dial 3635 and say 'billet' at the prompt.

Mainline stations

Gare d'Austerlitz Central and south-west France and Spain.
Gare de l'Est Alsace, Champagne and southern Germany.
Gare de Lyon Burgundy, the Alps, Provence and Italy.
Gare Montparnasse West France, Brittany, Bordeaux, the south-west.
Gare du Nord Eurostar, Channel ports, north-east France, Belgium and Holland.
Gare St-Lazare Normandy.

TAXIS

Paris taxi drivers are not known for their flawless knowledge of the Paris street map; if you have a preferred route, say so. Taxis can also be hard to find, especially at rush hour or early in the morning. Your best bet is to find a taxi rank (*station de taxis*, marked with a blue sign) on major roads, crossroads and at stations. A white light on a taxi's roof indicates the car is free; an orange light means the cab is busy. There is a service charge of €2.10. The rates are then based on zone and time of day: **A** (10am-5pm Mon-Sat central Paris, €0.82 per km); **B** (5pm-10am Mon-Fri, 5pm-midnight Sat, 7am-

midnight Sun central Paris; 7am-7pm Mon-Sat inner suburbs and airports, €1.10 per km); **C** (midnight-7am Sun central Paris; 7pm-7am Mon-Sat, all day Sun inner suburbs and airports; all times outer suburbs, €1.33 per km). Most journeys in central Paris cost €6-€12; there's a minimum charge of €5.60, plus €1 for each piece of luggage over 5kg or bulky objects, and a €0.70 surcharge from mainline stations. Most drivers will not take more than three people, although they should take a couple and two children. There is an additional charge of €2.75 for a fourth adult passenger.

Don't feel obliged to tip, although rounding up to the nearest euro is polite. Taxis are not allowed to refuse rides if they deem them too short and can only refuse to take you in a certain direction during their last half-hour of service (both rules are often ignored). If you want a receipt, ask for *un reçu* or *la note*. Complaints should be made to the **Bureau de la réglementation publique**, 36 rue des Morillons, 75732 Paris Cedex 15.

Phone cabs

These firms take phone bookings 24/7; you also pay for the time it takes your taxi to reach you. If you wish to pay by credit card, mention this when you order.

Airportaxis *to and from Paris airports, 01.41.50.42.50/ www.taxiparisien.fr.*
Alpha *01.45.85.85.85/ www.alphataxis.fr.*
G7 *01.47.39.47.39/ www.taxis-g7.fr.*
Taxis Bleus *08.91.70.10.10/ www.taxis-bleus.fr.*

DRIVING

If you bring your car to France, you must bring its registration and insurance documents.

As you come into Paris, you will meet the Périphérique, the giant ring road that carries traffic into, out of and around the city. Intersections, leading on to other main roads, are called *portes* (gates). Driving on the Périphérique is not as hair-raising as it might look, though it's often congested. Some hotels have parking spaces that can be paid for by the hour, day or by types of season tickets.

In peak holiday periods, the organisation Bison Futé hands out brochures at motorway *péages*

(toll gates), suggesting less crowded routes. French roads are categorised as *Autoroutes* (motorways, with an 'A' in front of the number), *Routes Nationales* (national 'N' roads), *Routes Départementales* (local, 'D' roads) and rural *Routes Communales* ('C' roads). *Autoroutes* are toll roads; some sections, including most of the area around Paris, are free.

Infotrafic *08.99.70.71.01 (€0.34 per minute)/ www.infotrafic.fr.*
Bison Futé *08.00.10.02.00/ www.bison-fute.equipement.gouv.fr*
Traffic information service for Ile-de-France *08.26.02.20.22/www.securite routiere.gouv.fr.*

Breakdown services

The AA and RAC do not have reciprocal arrangements with an equivalent organisation in France, so it's advisable to take out additional breakdown insurance cover, for example with a company like **Europ Assistance** (0870 737 5720/www.europ-assistance.co.uk). If you don't have insurance, you can still use its service (08.10.00.50.50, available 24/7), but it will charge you the full cost. Other 24-hour breakdown services in Paris include: **Action Auto Assistance** (01.45.58.49.58) and **Dan Dépann Auto** (01.40.06.06.53).

Driving tips

● At junctions where no signposts indicate right of way, the car coming from the right has priority. Many roundabouts now give priority to those on the roundabout. If this is not indicated (by road markings or a sign with the message *Vous n'avez pas la priorité*), priority is for those coming from the right.
● Drivers and all passengers must wear seat belts.
● Under-tens are not allowed to travel in the front of a car, except in baby seats facing backwards.
● You should not stop on an open road; you must pull off to the side.
● When drivers are flashing their lights at you, this often means they will not slow down and are warning you to keep out of the way.

Parking

There are still a few free on-street parking areas in Paris, but they're often full. If you park illegally, you risk getting your car clamped or towed away (*see below*). It's forbidden to park in zones marked for deliveries (*livraisons*) or taxis. Parking meters have now been replaced by *horodateurs*, pay-and-display machines, which take a special card (*carte de stationnement* at €10 or €30, available from *tabacs*). Parking is often free at weekends, after 7pm and in August.

Car hire

To hire a car, you must be 25 or over and have held a licence for at least a year. Some agencies accept drivers aged 21-24, but a supplement of €20-€25 per day is usual. Take your licence and passport with you. Bargain firms may have an extremely high charge for damage: read the small print.

Hire companies

Ada *01.48.06.58.13/ 08.25.16.91.69/www.ada.fr.*
Avis *01.44.18.10.54/ 08.20.05.05.05/www.avis.fr.*
Budget *01.41.22.19.30/ 08.25.00.35.64/www.budget.fr.*
EasyCar *01.70.61.85.52/ www.easycar.com.*
Europcar *01.53.64.16.24/ 08.25.35.83.58/www.europcar.fr.*
Hertz *01.39.38.38.38/ www.hertz.fr.*
Rent-a-Car *08.91.70.02.00/ www.rentacar.fr.*

Chauffeur-driven cars

Chauffeur Services Paris
(01.75.43.48.86/www.csparis.com).
Open 24hrs daily. **Prices** from €125 airport transfer; €240 for 4 hours. **Credit** AmEx, DC, MC, V.

CYCLING

In 2007, the mayor launched a free bike scheme – **Vélib** (www.velib. paris.fr). There are now over 20,000 bicycles available 24 hours a day, at nearly 1500 'stations' across the city. Just swipe your travel card to release the bikes from their stands. The *mairie* actively promotes cycling in the city and the Vélib scheme is complemented by the 372 km (231 miles) of bike lanes snaking their way around Paris.

The Itinéraires Paris-Piétons-Vélos-Rollers – scenic strips of the city that are closed to cars on Sundays and holidays – continue to multiply; www.paris.fr can provide an up-to-date list of routes and a downloadable map of cycle lanes. A free *Paris à Vélo* map can be picked up at any mairie or from bike shops. Cycle lanes (*pistes cyclables*) run mostly N-S and E-W. N-S routes include rue de Rennes, av d'Italie, bd Sébastopol and av Marceau. E-W routes take in the rue de Rivoli, bd St-Germain, bd St-Jacques and av Daumesnil. You could be fined (€22) if you don't use them. Cyclists are also entitled to use certain bus lanes (especially the new ones, set off by a strip of kerb stones); look out for traffic signs with a bike symbol.

Don't let the locals' blasé attitude to helmets and lights convince you it's not worth using them. Be confident and keep moving – and look out for scooter-mounted bag-snatchers.

Cycles & scooters for hire

Bike insurance may not cover theft.

Freescoot *63 quai de la Tournelle, 5th (01.44.07.06.72/ www.freescoot.com). M° Maubert Mutualité or St-Michel.* **Open** 9am-1pm, 2-9pm daily; closed Sun Oct-mid Apr. **Credit** AmEx, MC, V. Bicycles & scooters.
Other locations: 144 bd Voltaire, 11th (01.44.93.04.03).
Maison Roue Libre *1 passage Mondétour, 1st (01.44.76.86.43/ 08.10.44.15.34/www.rouelibre.fr). M° Châtelet.* **Open** 10am-6pm daily. **Credit** MC, V (weekends only). Bicycles.
Other locations: 37 bd Bourdon, 4th (01.42.71.54.54).

WALKING

Walking is the best way to explore Paris; just remember to remain vigilant at all times. Brits should be aware that traffic will be coming from the 'wrong' direction and that zebra crossings mean very little. By law, drivers are only obliged to stop at a red traffic light – even then, many will take a calculated risk.

TOURS

Bus tours

The following companies offer hop-on, hop-off bus tours of the city with commentary. Call or check online for precise routes. Prices are for one day only, but other fares (for multiple days) may be available.

Les Cars Rouges *01.53.95.39. 53/www.carsrouges.com.* **Tickets** €24; €12 4-11s.

Cityrama *01.44.55.61.00/www. pariscityrama.com.* **Tickets** €29; €15 4-11s.
Paris l'OpenTour *01.42.66. 56.56/http://paris-opentour.com.* **Tickets** €29; €15 4-11s.
Paris Vision *01.42.60.30.01/ http://fr.parisvision.com.* **Tickets** €22.

Bike tours

Fat Tire Bike Tours *01.56.58. 10.54/http://fattirebiketours.com/ paris.* **Tickets** €24. Bike tours of the city, with the main tour starting at the south leg of the Eiffel Tower. Tours run daily at 11am, with a 3pm tour added in summer. Check online for full details.

Boat tours

Cruising along the Seine is a delightful way to see Paris. The companies below all run a variety of tours on the river. Most boats depart from the quays in the 7th and 8th, and proceed to go on a circuit around the islands. Check online for full tour details and times: many companies operate more than one type of tour, though the basic tour usually runs every 20-60mins in summer. Rates are for one day only, though other tickets may be available.

Bateaux-Mouches *Pont de l'Alma, 8th (01.42.25.96.10/www. bateaux-mouches.fr). M° Alma-Marceau.* **Tickets** €10; €5 reductions; free under-4s.
Bateaux Parisiens *Port de la Boudonnais, 7th (01.76.64.14.45/ www.bateauxparisiens.com). RER Champ de Mars.* **Tickets** €11; €5 reductions; free under-3s.
Batobus Tour Eiffel *Various stops (08.25.05.01.01/www.batobus. com).* **Tickets** €12; €6 reductions.
Vedettes de Paris *Port de Suffren, 7th (01.44.18.19.50/www. vedettesdeparis.com). M° Bir-Hakeim.* **Tickets** €11; €5 reductions; free under-4s.
Vedettes du Pont-Neuf *Sq du Vert-Galant, 1st (01.46.33.98.38/ www.vedettesdupontneuf.com). M° Pont-Neuf.* **Tickets** €11; €6 under-12s; free under-4s.

Walking tours

Paris Walking Tours *01.48.09. 21.40/www.paris-walks.com.* **Tickets** €10; €5-€8 reductions. Led by long-term resident expats, daily walks (times vary by season) explore various city locales.

DIRECTORY

Resources A-Z

DIRECTORY

ADDRESSES

Paris arrondissements are indicated by the last two digits of the postal code: 75002 denotes the second, 75015 the 15th, and so on. The 16th arrondissement is divided into two sectors, 75016 and 75116. Some business addresses have a more detailed postcode, followed by a Cedex number, which indicates the arrondissement; *bis* or *ter* is the equivalent of 'b' or 'c' after a building number.

AGE RESTRICTIONS

For heterosexuals and homosexuals, the age of consent is 15. You must be 18 to drive, and to consume alcohol in a public place. Since 2003, you must be 16 to buy cigarettes.

ATTITUDE & ETIQUETTE

Parisians take manners seriously and are generally more courteous than their reputation may have led you to believe. If someone brushes you accidentally when passing, they will more often than not say '*pardon*'; you can do likewise, or say '*c'est pas grave*' (don't worry). In shops it is normal to greet the assistant with a '*bonjour madame*' or '*bonjour monsieur*' when you enter, and say '*au revoir*' when you leave. The business of '*tu*' and '*vous*' can be tricky for English speakers. Strangers, people significantly older than you and professional contacts should be addressed with the respectful '*vous*'; friends, relatives, children and pets as '*tu*'. When among themselves, young people will often launch straight in with '*tu*'.

BUSINESS

The best first stop in Paris for initiating business is the **CCIP** (*see p369*). Banks can refer you to lawyers, accountants and tax consultants.

Conventions & conferences

Paris is the world's leading centre for trade fairs.

CNIT *2 pl de la Défense, BP 321, 92053 Paris La Défense (01.72.72. 17.00/www.parisexpo.fr). Mº/RER Grande Arche de La Défense.* Mainly computer fairs.
Palais des Congrès
2 pl de la Porte-Maillot, 17th (01.40.68.00.05/www.palais-congres-paris.fr). Mº Porte-Maillot.
Parc des Expositions de Paris-Nord Villepinte
SEPENV 60004, 95970 Roissy-Charles-de-Gaulle (01.48.63.31.31/ www.expoparisnord.com). RER Parc des Expositions. Trade fair centre near Roissy airport.
Paris-Expo *Porte de Versailles, 15th (01.72.72.16.17/www.paris expo.fr). Mº Porte de Versailles.* The city's biggest expo centre.

Courier services

ATV *08.11.65.56.05/www.atoute vitesse.com.* **Open** 24hrs daily. **Credit** MC, V. Bike or van messengers 24/7. Rates rise after 8pm weekdays and at weekends.
Chronopost *Customer service: 08.25.80.18.01/www. chronopost.com.* **Open** 8am-8pm Mon-Fri; 9am-3pm Sat. **Credit** MC, V.
This overnight delivery offshoot of the state-run post office is the most widely used service for parcels.

UPS *34 bd Malesherbes, 8th (08.21.23.38.77/www.ups.com). Mº St-Augustin.* **Open** 8am-7pm Mon-Fri; 8am-1pm Sat. **Credit** AmEx, MC, V. International courier services.

Secretarial services

ADECCO International
28 rue Caumartin, 9th (01.45.24. 67.78/www.adecco.fr). Mº Havre-Caumartin. **Open** 8.30am-12.30pm, 2-6.30pm Mon-Fri. International employment agency specialising in bilingual secretaries and staff. **Other locations** throughout the city.

Translators & interpreters

Documents such as birth certificates, loan applications and so on must be translated by certified legal translators, listed at the CCIP (*see p369*) or embassies. For business translations there are dozens of reliable independents.

Association des Anciens Elèves de l'Esit
01.44.05.41.46/www.aaeesit.com. **Open** by phone only, 8am-8pm Mon-Fri; 8am-6pm Sat.
A translation and interpreting co-operative whose 1,000 members are graduates of the Ecole Supérieure d'Interprètes et de Traducteurs.
International Corporate Communication
3 rue des Batignolles, 17th (01.43. 87.29.29/www.iccparis.com). Mº Place de Clichy. **Open** 9am-1pm, 2-6pm Mon-Fri.
Translators of financial and corporate documents, plus simultaneous translation.

Useful organisations

American Chamber of Commerce *156 bd Haussmann, 8th (01.56.43.45.67/www.amcham france.org). M° Miromesnil.*
Closed to the public, calls only.

British Embassy Commercial Library *35 rue du Fbg-St-Honoré, 8th (01.44.51.31.00/www.amb-grandebretagne.fr). M° Concorde.* **Open** by appointment.
Stocks trade directories, and assists British companies that wish to develop or set up in France.

CCIP (Chambre de Commerce et d'Industrie de Paris) *27 av de Friedland, 8th (08.20.01.21.12/www.ccip.fr). M° Charles de Gaulle Etoile.* **Open** 8.30am-6.30pm Mon-Fri.
A variety of services for people doing business in France and is very useful for small businesses. Pick up the free booklet *Discovering the Chamber of Commerce* from its head office. There's also a legal advice line (08.92.70.51.00, 9am-4.30pm Mon-Thur, 9am-1pm Fri).
Other locations: Bourse du Commerce, 2 rue de Viarmes, 1st (has a free library and bookshop); 2 rue Adolphe-Jullien, 1st (support for businesses wishing to export goods and services to France).

INSEE (Institut National de la Statistique et des Etudes Economiques) *Salle de consultation, 195 rue de Bercy, Tour Gamma A, 12th (08.25.88.94.52/www.insee.fr). M° Bercy.* **Open** 9.30am-12.30pm, 2-5pm Mon-Thur; 9.30-12.30pm, 2-4pm Fri.
Source of seemingly every statistic to do with French economy and society.

US Commercial Service *Postal address: US Embassy, 2 av Gabriel, 8th. Visit: US Commercial Service, NEO Building, 14 bd Haussmann, 9th (01.43.12.70.57/www.buyusa.gov/france or www.amb-usa.fr). M° Richelieu Drouot.* **Open** by appointment 9am-6pm Mon-Fri. Helps American companies looking to trade in France. Advice by fax and email.

CONSUMER

In the event of a serious problem, try one of the following:

Direction Départementale de la Concurrence, de la Consommation et de la Répression des Fraudes *8 rue Froissart, 3rd (01.40.27.16.00). M° St-Sébastien Froissart.* **Open** 9am-noon, 2-5pm Mon-Fri.

Come here to file a consumer complaint concerning problems with Paris-based businesses.

Institut National de la Consommation *80 rue Lecourbe, 15th (08.92.70.75.92/www.conso.net). M° Sèvres Lecourbe.* **Open** by phone 9am-12.30pm Mon-Fri; recorded information at other times.
Questions on consumer, regulatory, housing and administrative issues.

CUSTOMS

Custom declarations are not usually necessary if you arrive from another EU country and are carrying legal goods for personal use. The amounts given below are guidelines only: if you come close to the maximums in several categories, you may still have to explain your personal habits to an interested but sceptical customs officer.

● 800 cigarettes, 400 small cigars, 200 cigars or 1kg loose tobacco.
● 10 litres of spirits (more than 22% alcohol), 90 litres of wine (less than 22% alcohol) or 110 litres of beer.
Coming from a non-EU country, you can bring:
● 200 cigarettes, 100 small cigars, 50 cigars or 250g tobacco.
● 1 litre of spirits (more than 22% alcohol) or 2 litres of wine or beer (more than 22% alcohol).
● 50g (1.76oz) of perfume.

Tax refunds

Non-EU residents can claim a refund or *détaxe* (around 12 per cent) on VAT if they spend over €175 in any one day in one shop and if they live outside the EU for more than six months in the year. At the shop concerned ask for a *bordereau de vente à l'exportation*, and when you leave France have it stamped by customs. Then send the stamped form back to the shop. *Détaxe* does not cover food, drink, antiques, services or works of art.

DISABLED TRAVELLERS

It's always wise to check up on a site's accessibility and provision for disabled access before you visit. There is general information (in French) available on the **Secrétaire d'Etat aux Personnes Handicapées** website: www.handicap.gouv.fr, telephone 08.20.03.33.33.

Association des Paralysés de France *13 pl de Rungis, 13th (01.53.80.92.98/www.apf.asso.fr). M° Place d'Italie.* **Open** 9am-12.30pm, 2-6pm Mon-Fri.
Publishes *Guide 98 Musées, Cinémas* (€3.81) listing accessible museums and cinemas, and a guide to restaurants and sights.

Fédération APAJH (Association pour Adultes et Jeunes Handicapés) *185 Bureaux de la Colline, 92213 St-Cloud Cedex (01.55.39.56.00/www.apajh.org). M° Marcel Sembat.*
Advice for disabled people living in France.

Plateforme d'Accueil et d'Information des Personnes Handicapées de la Mairie de Paris *08.00.03.37.48/01.43.47.77.99.*
Advice available in French to disabled persons living in or visiting Paris. The Office de Tourisme website (www.paris info.com) also provides useful information for disabled visitors.

Getting around

The métro and buses are not wheelchair-accessible, with the exception of métro line 14 (Méteor), stations Barbès-Rochechouard (line 2) and Esplanade de la Défense (line 1), and bus lines 20, 21, 24, 26, 27, 29, 30, 31, 38, 39, 43, 53, 54, 60, 62, 63, 64, 80, 81, 88, 91, 92, 94, 95, 96 and PC (Petite Ceinture) 1, 2 and 3. Forward seats on buses are intended for people with poor mobility. RER lines A, B, C, D and some SNCF trains are wheelchair-accessible in parts. For a full list of wheelchair-accessible stations: 08.10.64.64.64, www.infomobi.com. All Paris taxis are obliged by law to take passengers in wheelchairs.

Aihrop *3 av Paul-Doumer, 92508 Rueil-Malmaison Cedex (01.41.29.01.29/www.aihrop.com).* **Open** 9.30am-12.30pm, 1.30-5.30pm Mon-Fri. Closed Aug.
Transport for the disabled, anywhere in Paris and Ile-de-France; book 48 hours in advance.

DRUGS

French police have the power to stop and search anyone. It's wise to keep prescription drugs in their original containers and, if possible, to carry copies of the original prescriptions. If you're caught in possession of illegal drugs, you can expect a prison sentence and/or a fine. *See also below* **Health**.

DIRECTORY

ELECTRICITY & GAS

Electricity in France runs on 220V. Visitors with British 240V appliances can change the plug or use an adaptor (*adaptateur*). For US 110V appliances, you'll need to use a transformer (*transformateur*), available at BHV or branches of Fnac and Darty. Gas and electricity are supplied by the state-owned Electricité de France-Gaz de France. Contact EDF-GDF (08.20.82.13.33/ www.edf.fr/www.gazdefrance.com) about supply, bills, power failures and gas leaks.

EMBASSIES & CONSULATES

For a full list of embassies and consulates, see the Pages Jaunes (www.pagesjaunes.fr) under 'Ambassades et Consulats'. Consular services (passports, etc) are for citizens of that country only.

Australian Embassy *4 rue Jean-Rey, 15th (01.40.59.33.00/ www.france.embassy.gov.au). M° Bir-Hakeim.* **Open** *Consular services 9.15am-noon, 2-4.30pm Mon-Fri; Visas 10am-noon Mon-Fri.*
British Embassy *35 rue du Fbg-St-Honoré, 8th (01.44.51.31.00/ www.amb-grandebretagne.fr). M° Concorde. Consular services: 18bis rue d'Anjou, 8th. M° Concorde.* **Open** *9.30am-12.30pm, 2.30-4.30pm Mon-Fri. Visas: 16 rue d'Anjou, 8th (01.44.51.31.01).* **Open** *9.30am-noon by phone; 2.30-4.30pm.* British citizens wanting consular services (new passports, etc) should ignore the long queue stretching along rue d'Anjou for the visa department, and instead walk straight in at no.18bis.
Canadian Embassy *35 av Montaigne, 8th (01.44.43.29.00/ www.amb-canada.fr). M° Franklin D. Roosevelt.* **Open** *9am-noon, 2-5pm Mon-Fri. Consular services: 01.44.43.29.02.* **Open** *9am-noon Mon-Fri. Visas: 37 av Montaigne, 8th (01.44.43.29.16).* **Open** *8.30-11am Mon-Fri.*
Irish Embassy *12 av Foch, 16th. Consulate 4 rue Rude, 16th (01.44.17.67.00). M° Charles de Gaulle Etoile.* **Open** *Consular/visas 9.30am-noon Mon-Fri; by phone 9.30am-1pm, 2.30-5.30pm Mon-Fri.*
New Zealand Embassy *7ter rue Léonard-de-Vinci, 16th (01.45.01.43.43/www.nzembassy. com/france). M° Victor Hugo.* **Open** 9am-1pm, 2-5.30pm Mon-Fri (closes 4pm Fri). *July, Aug 9am-1pm, 2-4.30pm Mon-Thur; 9am-2pm Fri. Visas 9am-12.30pm Mon-Fri.* Visas for travel to New Zealand can be applied for on the website www.immigration.govt.nz.
South African Embassy *59 quai d'Orsay, 7th (01.53. 59.23.23/www.afriquesud.net). M° Invalides.* **Open** 8.30am-5.15pm Mon-Fri. *Consulate & visas* 8.30am-noon Mon-Fri.
US Embassy *2 av Gabriel, 8th (01.43.12.22.22/http://france. usembassy.gov). M° Concorde. Consulate & visas: 4 av Gabriel, 8th (08.10.26.46.26). M° Concorde.* **Open** *Consular services* 9am-12.30pm, 1-3pm Mon-Fri. *Visas* 08.92.23.84.72 or check website for non-immigration visas.

EMERGENCIES

Most of the following services operate 24 hours a day. In a medical emergency, such as a road accident, phone the Sapeurs-Pompiers, who have trained paramedics. *See also* **Health**: **Accident & Emergency; Doctors; Helplines**.

Ambulance (SAMU) 15
Police 17
Fire (Sapeurs-Pompiers) 18
Emergency (from a mobile phone) 112
GDF (gas leaks) 08.10.80.08.01/ www.gazdefrance.fr
EDF (electricity) 08.10.33.39 + number of arrondissement (01-20)
Centre anti-poison 01.40.05.48.48

GAY & LESBIAN

For information on HIV and AIDS, *see below* **Health**. *See also pp306-312* **Gay & Lesbian**.

HEALTH

Nationals of non-EU countries should take out insurance before leaving home. EU nationals staying in France can use the French Social Security system, which refunds up to 70 per cent of medical expenses. UK residents travelling in Europe require a European National Health Insurance Card (EHIC). This allows them to benefit from free or reduced-cost medical care when travelling in a country belonging to the European Economic Area (EEA) or Switzerland. The EHIC replaces the E111 form and is free of charge. For further information, refer to www.dh.gov.uk/travellers.

If you're staying for longer than three months, or working in France but you are still making National Insurance contributions in Britain, you will need form E128 filled in by your employer and stamped by the NI contributions office in order to get a French medical number. Consultations and prescriptions have to be paid for in full on the spot, and are reimbursed on receipt of a completed *fiche*. If you undergo treatment, the doctor will give you a prescription and a *feuille de soins* (bill of treatment). Stick the small stickers from the medication boxes on to the *feuille de soins*. Send this, together with the prescription and details of your EHIC card, to the local **Caisse Primaire d'Assurance Maladie** for a refund. For those resident in France, more and more doctors now accept the **Carte Vitale**, which lets them produce a virtual *feuille de soins* and you to pay only the non-reimbursable part of the bill. Information on health insurance can be found at www.ameli.fr. You can track refunds with Allosecu (08.11.90.09.07). See also the Ministry of Health's website at www.sante.gouv.fr.

Accident & emergency

Hospitals specialise in one type of emergency or illness – refer to the Assistance Publique's website (www.aphp.fr). In a medical emergency, call the Sapeurs-Pompiers or SAMU (*see* **Emergencies**). The following (in order of district) have 24hr accident and emergency services:

ADULTS
Hôpital Hôtel Dieu *1 pl du Parvis Notre-Dame, 4th (01.42.34.82.34).*
Hôpital St-Louis *1 av Claude-Vellefaux, 10th (01.42.49.49.49).*
Hôpital St-Antoine *184 rue du Fbg-St-Antoine, 12th (01.49.28.20.00).*
Hôpital de la Pitié-Salpêtrière *47-83 bd de l'Hôpital, 13th (01.42.16.00.00).*
Hôpital Cochin *27 rue du Fbg-St-Jacques, 14th (01.58.41. 41.41).*
Hôpital Européen Georges Pompidou *20 rue Leblanc, 15th (01.56.09.20.00).*
Hôpital Bichat-Claude Bernard *46 rue Henri-Huchard, 18th (01.40.25.80.80).*
Hôpital Tenon *4 rue de la Chine, 20th (01.56.01.70.00).*

CHILDREN:

Hôpital Armand Trousseau
*26 av du Dr Arnold-Netter,
12th (01.44.73.74.75).*
Hôpital St-Vincent de Paul
*74-82 av Denfert-Rochereau,
14th (01.58.41.41.41).*
Hôpital Necker *149 rue de
Sèvres, 15th (01.44.49.40.00).*
Hôpital Robert Debré *48 bd
Sérurier, 19th (01.40.03.20.00).*
**Private Hospitals
American Hospital in Paris**
*63 bd Victor-Hugo, 92200 Neuilly
(01.46.41.25.25/www.american-
hospital.org). M° Porte Maillot,
then bus 82.* **Open** 24hrs daily.
English-speaking hospital. French
Social Security refunds only a small
percentage of treatment costs.
**Hertford British
Hospital (Hôpital Franco-
Britannique)** *3 rue Barbès,
92300 Levallois-Perret
(01.46.39.22.22/www.
british-hospital.org). M° Anatole-
France.* **Open** 24hrs daily.
Most staff here speak English.

Complementary medicine

**Centre de Médecine
Naturelle** *2 rue d'Isly, 8th
(01.43.87.60.33). M° St-Lazare.*
Open by appointment 9am-8pm
Mon-Fri; 9am-1pm Sat.
Health services include
acupuncture, aromatherapy
and homeopathy.

Contraception & abortion

To get the pill (*la pilule*) or coil
(*stérilet*), you need a prescription,
available on appointment from the
two places listed below, from a
médecin généraliste (GP) or from a
gynaecologist. The morning-after
pill (*la pilule du lendemain*) can
be had from pharmacies without
prescription but is not reimbursed.
Condoms (*préservatifs*) and
spermicides are sold in pharmacies
and supermarkets, and there are
condom machines in most métro
stations, club lavatories and on
some street corners.

**Centre de Planification et
d'Education Familiales**
*27 rue Curnonsky, 17th (01.48.88.
07.28). M° Porte de Champerret.*
Open 9am-5pm Mon-Fri.
Free consultations on family
planning and abortion.
**MFPF (Mouvement Français
pour le Planning Familial)**
*10 rue Vivienne, 2nd (08.00.80.
38.03/01.42.60.93.20/www.
planning-familial.org). M° Bourse.*

Open 9.30am-5.30pm Mon, Tue,
Thur, Fri; 9.30am-7.30am Wed.
Phone for an appointment for
prescriptions and contraception
advice. For abortion advice, turn
up at the centre at one of the
designated time slots. The approach
here, however, is brusque.
Other locations: 94 bd Masséna,
13th (01.45.84.28.25).

Dentists

Dentists are found in the *Pages
Jaunes* under *Dentistes*. For
emergencies, contact:

**Hôpital de la Pitié-
Salpêtrière** (*see p370*) also offers
24hr emergency dental care.
SOS Dentaire *87 bd Port-Royal,
13th (01.43.36.36.00). M° Les
Gobelins/RER Port-Royal.* **Open**
by phone 9am-midnight.
A telephone service for emergency
dental care.

Doctors

You'll find a list of GPs in the
Pages Jaunes under *Médecins:
Médecine générale.* For a social
security refund, choose a doctor or
dentist who is *conventionné* (state
registered). Consultations cost €20
or more, of which a proportion can
be reimbursed. Seeing a specialist
costs more still.

Centre Médical Europe
*44 rue d'Amsterdam, 9th (01.42.
81.93.33). M° St-Lazare.* **Open**
8am-7pm Mon-Fri; 8am-6pm Sat.
Practitioners in all fields; modest
consultation fees.
SOS Médecins *36.24.* House
calls cost €35 before 7pm; from
€50 after and on holidays; prices
are higher if you don't have
French social security.
**Urgences Médicales de
Paris** *01.53.94.94.94.* Doctors
make house calls for €35 during
the day (€60 if you don't have
French social security); €50/€80
until midnight; €63.50/€90 after
midnight. Some English.

Opticians

Branches of **Alain Afflelou**
(www.alainafflelou.com) and
Lissac (www.lissac.com) stock
hundreds of frames and can make
prescription glasses within the
hour. For an eye test, you'll need to
go to an *ophtalmologiste* – ask the
optician for a list. Contact lenses
can be bought over the counter if
you have your prescription details.

Hôpital des Quinze-Vingts
*28 rue de Charenton, 12th
(01.40.02.15.20).*
Specialist eye hospital offers on-the-
spot consultations for eye problems.
SOS Optique *01.48.07.22.00/
www.sosoptique.com.*
24hr repair service for glasses.

Pharmacies

French *pharmacies* sport a green
neon cross. A rota of *pharmacies
de garde* operate at night and on
Sundays; see below for a list of
these night pharmacies. If closed,
a pharmacy will have a sign
indicating the nearest one open.
Staff can provide basic medical
services such as bandaging wounds
(for a small fee) and will indicate
the nearest doctor on duty.
Parapharmacies sell almost
everything pharmacies do but
cannot dispense prescription
medication. Toiletries and
sanitary products are often
cheaper in supermarkets.

**Grande Pharmacie de la
Nation** *13 pl de la Nation, 11th
(01.43.73.24.03). M° Nation.*
Open 8am-11pm daily.
Matignon *2 rue Jean-Mermoz,
8th (01.43.59.86.55). M°
Franklin D. Roosevelt.*
Open 8.30am-2am daily.
**Pharmacie des Champs-
Elysées** *84 av des Champs-
Elysées, 8th (01.45.62.02.41).
M° George V.* **Open** 24hrs daily.
**Pharmacie Européene de
la Place de Clichy** *6 pl de
Clichy, 9th (01.48.74.65.18). M°
Place de Clichy.* **Open** 24hrs daily.
Pharmacie des Halles *10 bd
de Sébastopol, 4th (01.42.72.03.23).
M° Châtelet.* **Open** 9am-midnight
Mon-Sat; 9am-10pm Sun.
Pharmacie d'Italie *61 av
d'Italie, 13th (01.44.24.19.72).
M° Tolbiac.* **Open** 8am-2am daily.
Pharma Presto *01.61.04.04.03/
www.pharma-presto.com.* **Open**
24hrs daily. Delivery (€40 8am-
6pm; €55 6pm-8am & weekends) of
medication.

STDs, HIV & AIDS

**Cabinet Médical
(Mairie de Paris)** *2 rue Figuier,
4th (01.49.96.62.70). M° Pont-
Marie.* **Open** 9am-5.30pm Mon,
Tue, Thur; noon-5.30pm Wed;
1.30-5.30pm Fri; 9.30-10.30am Sat.
Free, anonymous tests (*dépistages*)
for HIV, hepatitis B and C and
syphilis (wait one week for results).
Good counselling service, too.

DIRECTORY

DIRECTORY

Le Kiosque Infos Sida-
Toxicomanie *36 rue Geoffroy-l'Asnier, 4th (0148.04.95.20).*
M° St-Paul. **Open** 10am-7pm
Mon-Fri; 2-7pm Sat. Youth
association offering information
and counselling on AIDS, sexuality
and drugs
SIDA Info Service *08.00.84.*
08.00/www.sida-info-service.org.
Open 24hrs daily.
Confidential AIDS information in
French. English-speakers are
available 2-7pm Mon, Wed, Fri.

HELPLINES
**Alcoholics Anonymous
in English** *01.46.34.59.65/
www.aaparis.org.* 24hr recorded
message gives details of AA
meetings at the American Cathedral
or American Church (*see p376*).
Allô Service Public
39.39/www.service-public.fr. **Open**
8am-7pm Mon-Fri; 9am-2pm Sat.
A source of information and
contacts for all aspects of tax,
work and administration matters.
They even claim to be able to
help if you have problems with
neighbours. The catch: you can
only dial from inside France, and
operators speak only French.
Counseling Center
01.47.23.61.13.
English-language counselling
service, based at the American
Cathedral.
**Drogues Alcool Tabac
Info Service** *08.00.23.13.13/
www.drogues.gouv.fr.*
Phone service, in French, for help
with drug, alcohol and tobacco
problems.
Narcotics Anonymous
*01.43.72.12.72/
www.narcotiquesanonymes.org.*
The helpline is open daily 6-8pm.
Meetings in English are held three
times a week.
SOS Dépression
*01.40.47.95.95/
http://sos.depression.free.fr.*
Open 24hrs daily.
People listen and/or give advice.
Can send round a counsellor or
psychiatrist in case of a crisis.
SOS Help *01.46.21.46.46/
www.soshelpline.org.* **Open**
3-11pm daily.
English-language helpline.

ID
French law requires that some
form of identification be carried
at all times. Be prepared to produce
your passport or **EHIC** card
(*see p370*).

INSURANCE
See p370 **Health.**

INTERNET
ISPs

AOL *08.26.02.60.00/www.aol.fr.*
Club-Internet *08.05.50.05.55/
www.club-internet.fr.*
Free *08.92.13.51.51/www.free.fr.*
Neuf *08.00.97.59.75/
www.neuf.fr).*
Orange *32.20/www.orange.fr.*

Internet access

Many hotels offer internet access,
some from your own room – and
an increasing number of public
spaces are setting themselves
up as WiFi hotspots.

Milk *31 bd de Sébastopol, 1st
(08.20.00.10.00/www.milklub.com).
M° Châtelet or Rambuteau/
RER Châtelet Les Halles.*
Open 24hrs daily.
Other locations throughout
the city.

LANGUAGE
See p382 **Vocabulary**; for food
terms, *see p208* **Menu Lexicon**.

LEFT LUGGAGE
Gare du Nord
There are self-locking luggage
lockers (6.15am-11.15pm daily)
on Level -1 under the main
station concourse: small (€3.50),
medium (€7) and large (€9.50)
for 48 hours.
**Roissy-Charles-de-Gaulle
airport Bagages du Monde**
*(01.34.38.58.90/www.bagagesdumo
nde.com).* **Terminal 1** *Niveau
Départ, Porte 20 (01.34.38.58.82).*
Open 8am-8pm daily. **Terminal
2A** *Niveau Départ, Porte 2
(01.34.38.58.80).* **Open** 8am-8pm
daily. **Terminal 2F** *Niveau
Arrivée, Porte 4-5 (0134.38.58.81).*
Open 7am-7pm daily.
Company with counters in CDG
and an office in Paris (102 rue de
Chemin-Vert, 11th, 01.43.57.30.90,
open 2-6pm Mon; 9am-noon, 2-6pm
Tue-Thur; 10am-1pm Sat). Can ship
excess baggage anywhere in the
world, or store luggage.

LEGAL HELP
Mairies can answer some legal
enquiries; ask for times of their
free *consultations juridiques*.

Direction Départmentale
de la Concurrence, de la
Consommation et de la
Répression des Fraudes
*8 rue Froissart, 3rd
(01.40.27.16.00). M° St-Sébastien
Froissart.* **Open** 9am-noon, 2-5pm
Mon-Fri.
Part of the Ministry of Finance;
deals with consumer complaints.
**Palais de Justice Galerie de
Harlay** *Escalier S, 4 bd du Palais,
4th (01.44.32.51.51). M° Cité.*
Open 9am-noon Mon-Fri.
Free legal consultation. Arrive early
and obtain a ticket for the queue.
SOS Avocats *08.25.39.33.00.*
Open 7-11.30pm Mon-Fri. Closed
July, Aug.
Free legal advice by phone.

LIBRARIES
Every arrondissement has a
free public library. To get hold
of a library card, you need ID
and evidence of a fixed address
in Paris.

American Library *10 rue du
Général-Camou, 7th (01.53.59.
12.60/www.americanlibraryinparis.
org). M° Ecole-Militaire/RER
Pont de l'Alma.* **Open** 10am-7pm
Tue-Sat (shorter hours in Aug).
Admission day pass €12; annual
€100; discount for students.
A useful resource: this is the
largest English-language lending
library on the Continent. It receives
400 periodicals, as well as popular
magazines and newspapers
(mainly American).
**Bibliothèque Historique
de la Ville de Paris** *Hôtel
Lamoignon, 24 rue Pavée, 4th
(01.44.59.29.40). M° St-Paul.* **Open**
1-6pm Mon-Fri; 9.30am-6pm Sat.
Closed 1st 2wks Aug. **Admission**
free (bring passport photo and ID).
Books and documents on Paris
history in a Marais mansion.
**Bibliothèque Marguerite
Durand** *79 rue Nationale, 13th
(01.53.82.76.77). M° Tolbiac.*
Open 2-6pm Tue-Sat. Closed 3wks
Sept. **Admission** free.
40,000 books and 120 periodicals
on women's history. The feminism
collection includes letters of Colette
and Louise Michel.
**Bibliothèque Nationale de
France François Mitterrand**
*quai François-Mauriac, 13th
(01.53.79.59.59/www.bnf.fr).
M° Bibliothèque.* **Open** 10am-
8pm Tue-Sat; noon-7pm Sun.
Closed 2wks Sept & bank holidays.
Admission day pass €3.50;
annual €35.

Books, papers and periodicals, plus titles in English. An audio-visual room lets you browse photo, film and sound archives.

Bibliothèque Publique d'Information (BPI) *Centre Pompidou, 4th (01.44.78.12.33/ www.bpi.fr). Mº Hôtel de Ville/RER Châtelet Les Halles.* **Open** noon-10pm Mon, Wed-Fri; 11am-10pm Sat, Sun. Closed 1 May. **Admission** free.
Now on three levels, the Centre Pompidou's vast library has a huge global press section, reference books and language-learning facilities.

BIFI (Bibliothèque du Film) *51 rue de Bercy, 12th (01.71.19.32.32/www.bifi.fr). Mº Bercy.* **Open** 10am-7pm Mon-Fri. Closed 2wks Aug. **Admission** €3.50 day pass; €34 annual; €15 students annual.
Housed in the same building as the **Cinémathèque Française**. this world-class researchers' and film buffs' library offers books, magazines, film stills and posters, as well as films on video and DVD.

Documentation Française *29-31 quai Voltaire, 7th (01.40.15.71.10/www.la documentationfrancaise.fr). Mº Rue du Bac.* **Open** 9am-6pm Mon-Fri. Closed Aug & 1st wk Sept.
The official government archive and central reference library has information on French politics and economy since 1945.

LOCKSMITHS

Numerous round-the-clock repair services handle locks, plumbing and, sometimes, car repairs. Most charge a minimum €18-€20 call-out (*déplacement*) and €30 per hour, plus parts. Charges are higher on Sunday and at night.

Allô Serrurerie *01.42.29.44.68/ www.alloserrurerie.com.*
SOS Dépannage *08.20.22.23.33/www.okservice.fr.*
SOS Dépannage is double the price of most services, but claims to be twice as reliable.

LOST PROPERTY

Bureau des Objets Trouvés *36 rue des Morillons, 15th (08.21.00.25.25/www.prefecture-police-paris.interieur.gouv.fr). Mº Convention.* **Open** 8.30am-5pm Mon-Thur; 8.30am-4.30pm Fri.
Visit in person to fill in a form specifying details of the loss. This may have been the first lost

property office in the world, but it is far from the most efficient. Huge delays in processing claims mean that if your trip to Paris is short, you may need to nominate a proxy to collect found objects after you leave, although small items can be posted. If your passport was among the items lost, you'll need to go to your consulate to get a single-entry temporary passport in order to leave the country.

SNCF lost property
Some mainline SNCF stations have their own lost property offices.

MEDIA

See also p383 **Websites**.

Magazines

Arts & listings Two modest local publications compete for consumers of basic Wednesday-to-Tuesday listings: the handbag-sized **L'Officiel des Spectacles** (€0.35) and **Pariscope** (€0.40). Look out also for **Lylo**, a free bi-monthly booklet distributed around bars and clubs, for information on gigs and DJ nights. Affiliated to Radio Nova, monthly **Nova** gives multi-ethnic information on where to drink, dance and hang out. **Technikart** tries – not entirely successfully – to mix clubbing with the arts. Highbrow TV guide **Télérama** has superb arts coverage and comes with **Sortir**, a Paris listings insert. **Les Inrockuptibles** (fondly known as *Les Inrocks*) deals with contemporary music scenes at home and abroad; it has strong coverage of film and books too.

There are specialist magazines for every interest. The choice of film-related titles, in particular, is wide, and includes long-established intellectual heavyweights **Les Cahiers du Cinéma**, **Positif** and **Trafic**, fluffy **Studio** and celebrity-heavy **Première**.

Business Capital, its sister magazine **Management** and weightier **L'Expansion** are the notable monthlies. **Défis** has tips for the entrepreneur; **Initiatives** is for the self-employed.

English The **Time Out Paris Visitors' Guide** is on sale in newsagents across the city. **FUSAC** (France-USA Contacts) is a small-ads magazine that lists flat rentals, job ads and appliances for sale.

Gossip The French love gossip. **Public** gives weekly celebrity updates; **Oh Là!** (sister of Spain's *Hola!* and UK's *Hello!*) showcases celebs. **Voici** is the juiciest scandal sheet; **Gala** tells the same stories without the sleaze. **Paris Match** is a French institution founded in 1948, packed with society gossip, celeb interviews and regular photo scoops. **Point de Vue** specialises in royalty (no showbiz fluff). Monthly **Entrevue** aims to titillate and tends toward features on nonconformist sex.

News Weekly news magazines are an important sector in France, offering news and cultural sections as well as in-depth reports; they range from respected organs **L'Express**, **Le Point** and **Le Nouvel Observateur** to the sardonic, chaotically arranged **Marianne**. Weekly **Courrier International** publishes an interesting selection of articles, translated into French, from newspapers all over the world.

Women, men & fashion
Elle was a pioneer among women's mags and has editions across the globe. In France it's a weekly, and spot-on for interviews and fashion. Monthly **Marie-Claire** takes a more feminist, campaigning line. Both have design spin-offs (**Elle Décoration**, **Marie-Claire Maison**), and *Elle* has also spawned foodie **Elle à Table**. **DS** has lots to read and coverage of social issues. **Vogue**, bought for its fashion coverage and big-name guests, is rivalled during fashion week by **L'Officiel de la Mode**.

Meanwhile the underground prefers to buy more radical publications such as **Purple** (six-monthly art, literature and fashion tome), **Crash** and the new wave of fashion/lifestyle mags: **WAD** (stands for We Are Different), **Citizen K**, **Jalouse** and **Numéro**. Men's mags include the naughty-bizarre **Echo des Savanes** and French versions of lad bibles **FHM**, **Maximal** and **Men's Health**.

Newspapers

French national dailies, with relatively high prices and low print runs, are in dire straits. Only 20 per cent of France read a national paper; regional dailies dominate outside Paris. Serious, centre-left **Le Monde** is must-read material for business types, politicians and intellectuals, and despite its lofty reputation, subject matter is eclectic.

The conservative upper and middle classes go for daily broadsheet **Le Figaro**, which has a devotion to politics, shopping, food and sport. Taken over in 2004 by the head of the Dassault defence and media group, it steers clear of controversial industrial issues. Its sales are aided by pages of property and job ads and Wednesday's **Figaroscope** Paris listings. The Saturday edition has three magazines.

Founded in the aftershocks of 1968 by a group that included Sartre and de Beauvoir, **Libération**, once affectionately known as *Libé*, is shedding readers and yet to find a modern identity. In early 2005, its staff accepted a plan for financier Edouard de Rothschild to take a 39 per cent stake in the paper – only to go on a three-day strike when he later proposed 52 job cuts across the board. It is still the preferred read of the *gauche caviar* (champagne socialists) and worth buying for news and arts coverage.

For business and financial news, the French dailies **La Tribune**, **Les Echos** and the weekly **Investir** are the tried and trusted sources. The easy-read tabloid **Le Parisien** is strong on consumer affairs, social issues, local news, events and vox pops. Downmarket **France Soir** has gone tabloid. **La Croix** is a Catholic, right-wing daily. The Communist Party **L'Humanité** (shortened to *L'Huma*) struggles on. Sunday broadsheet **Le Journal du Dimanche** comes with **Fémina** mag and a Paris section.

L'Equipe is the doyen of European sports dailies – Saturday's edition comes with a magazine. Its sister bi-weekly **France Football** is the bible of world soccer. It was instrumental in setting up the game's top competitions during the golden age of French sports journalism after the war. **Paris-Turf** is for horse fans.

English-language papers

Paris-based **International Herald Tribune** is on sale throughout the city; British dailies, Sundays and **USA Today** are widely available on the day of issue at larger kiosks in the centre, though often without their supplements. The most popular (and many esoteric) English and

US newspapers and magazines can be found in central bookshops (*see pp242-243*).

Satirical papers

Wednesday institution **Le Canard Enchaîné** is the Gallic *Private Eye* – in fact it was the inspiration for the *Eye*. It's a broadly left-wing satirical weekly broadsheet that's full of in-jokes and breaks political scandals.

Radio

For a complete list of all Paris radio frequencies, go to www.bric-a-brac.org/radio. A mandatory state-defined minimum of 40 per cent French music has led to overplay of Gallic pop oldies and to the creation of dubious hybrids by local groups that mix words in French with a refrain in English. Trashy phone-in shows also proliferate. Frequencies are given in MHz.

87.8 France Inter Highbrow, state-run; jazz, international news and discussion slots aplenty.
90.4 Nostalgie As you'd expect.
90.9 Chante France 100 per cent French *chanson*.
91.3 Chérie FM Lots of oldies.
91.7 France Musiques State classical music channel: highbrow concerts and top jazz.
92.1 Le Mouv' New public station aimed at luring the young with pop and rock music.
93.1 Aligre From local Paris news to literary chat.
93.9 France Culture Talky state culture station.
94.8 RCJ/Radio J/Judaïque FM/Radio Shalom Shared wavelength for Jewish stations.
95.2 Ici et Maintenant/Neo New stations hoping to stir local public debate about current events.
96.0 Skyrock Pop station with loudmouth presenters. Lots of rap.
96.4 BFM Business and economics.
96.9 Voltage FM Dance music.
97.4 Rire et Chansons A non-stop diet of jokes and pop oldies.
97.8 Ado Music for teenagers.
98.2 Radio FG Beloved of clubbers for its on-the-pulse tips, this station ditched its all-gay remit back in 1999.
99.0 Radio Latina Great Latin and salsa music.
100.3 NRJ 'Energy' – geddit? National leader with the under-30s.
101.1 Radio Classique Top-notch, state-run classical music station.
101.5 Radio Nova Hip hop, trip hop, world, jazz.

101.9 Fun Radio Now embracing techno alongside Anglo pop hits.
102.3 Ouï FM Ouï will rock you.
103.9 RFM Easy listening.
104.3 RTL The most popular French station nationwide mixes music and talk programmes.
104.7 Europe 1 News, press reviews, sports, business, entertainment. Much the best weekday breakfast news broadcast, with politicians interviewed live.
105.1 FIP Traffic and weather information, what's on in Paris and a mix of jazz, classical, world and pop. 'Fipettes', female continuity announcers employed for their come-to-bed voices, are a much-loved feature.
105.5 France Info 24hr news, weather, economic updates and sports bulletins. Reports get repeated every 15 minutes: useful if you're learning French.
106.7 Beur FM North African music and discussion.

English You can receive the **BBC World Service** (648 KHz AM), with English-language news, current events, pop and drama; also on 198KHz LW, from midnight to 5.30am daily. At other times 198KHz LW carries **BBC Radio 4**, with British news, talk and *The Archers*. RFI (738 KHz AM; www.rfi.fr) has an English-language programme of news and music 7-8am, 2.30-3.30pm and 4.30-5pm daily. There's also the French capital's first all-English station, **Paris Live** (www.paris-live.com).

Television

In 2005, the choice of free TV channels in France more than doubled. Under the acronym TNT (Télévision Numérique Terrestre, or terrestrial digital television), seven new channels – available via the traditional rooftop aerial with a decoder that costs about €100, or automatically to cable and satellite customers – began broadcasting. For more information, go to www.tdf.fr or pick up a copy of weekly mag *Télérama*. The channels listed below are the six 'core' stations available on an unenhanced TV set:

TF1 *(www.tf1.fr)*. The country's biggest channel. Reality shows, soaps and football are staples.
France 2 *(www.france2.fr)*. This state-owned station mixes game shows, chat, documentaries and the usual cop series and films.

France 3 *(www.france3.fr)*. This, the more heavyweight of the two state channels, offers wildlife and sports coverage, debates, *Cinéma de Minuit* – classic films in V.O. *(version originale*, or original language) – and the endearing cookery show *Bon Appétit Bien Sûr*, fronted by Joël Robuchon.
Canal+ *(www.canalplus.fr)*. Subscription channel shows recent films, exclusive sport and late-night porn. A week's worth of the satirical puppets show *Les Guignols* is broadcast unscrambled on Sundays at 1.40pm.
Arte/France 5 *(www.arte-tv.com)*. The intellectual Franco-German hybrid Arte shares its wavelength with educational channel France 5 (3am-7pm).
M6 *(www.m6.fr)*. Dubbed US sci-fi series and made for TV movies, plus investigative reportage, popular science and kids' shows.

Cable TV & satellite

France offers a decent range of cable and satellite channels but content in English is still limited. CNN and BBC World offer round-the-clock news coverage. BBC Prime keeps you up to date on *EastEnders* (omnibus Sun 2pm), while Teva supplies comedy such as *Sex and the City*.

Numericable *(39.90/www. numericable.fr)*. The first cable provider to offer an interactive video service via the internet.

MONEY

The amount of currency visitors may carry is not limited. However, sums worth over €7,600 must be declared to customs when entering or leaving the country.

The euro

Non-French debit and credit cards can be used to withdraw and pay in euros, and currency withdrawn in France can be used subsequently all over the euro zone. Daylight robbery occurs, however, if you try to deposit a euro cheque from any country other than France in a French bank: they are currently charging around €15 for this service, and the European parliament has backed down on its original decision that cross-border payments should be in line with domestic ones across the euro zone. This is good news for the British, though: if you transfer money from the UK to France in euros, you will pay the same

charges as if Britain were within the euro zone (but it pays to watch the exchange rate carefully).

ATMs

Withdrawals in euros can be made from bank and post office automatic cash machines. The specific cards accepted are marked on each machine, and most can give instructions in English. Credit card companies charge a fee for cash advances, but rates are often better than banks.

Banks

French banks usually open 9am-5pm Mon-Fri (some close at lunch); some banks also open on Sat. All are closed on public holidays, and from noon on the previous day. Note that not all banks have foreign exchange counters. The commission rates vary between banks; the state-owned Banque de France usually offers good rates. Most banks accept travellers' cheques, but may be reluctant to accept personal cheques even with the Eurocheque guarantee card, which is not widely used in France.

Bank accounts

To open an account (*ouvrir un compte*), French banks require proof of identity, address and your income (if any). You'll probably be required to show your passport, an electricity, gas or phone bill in your name and a payslip/letter from your employer. Students need a student card and may need a letter from their parents. Of the major national banks (BNP, Crédit Lyonnais, Société Générale, Banque Populaire, Crédit Agricole), Société Générale tends to be the most foreigner-friendly. Most banks don't hand out a Carte Bleue/Visa card until several weeks after you've opened an account. A chequebook (*chéquier*) is usually issued in about a week. Payments made with a Carte Bleue are debited directly from your current account, but you can arrange for purchases to be debited at the end of every month. French banks are tough on overdrafts, so try to anticipate any cash crisis in advance and work out a deal for an authorised overdraft (*découvert autorisé*) or you risk being blacklisted as '*interdit bancaire*' – forbidden from having a current account – for anything up to ten years. Depositing foreign currency cheques can be slow, so

try to use wire transfer or a bank draft in euros to receive funds from abroad.

Bureaux de change

If you happen to be arriving in Paris early in the morning or late at night, you will be able to change money at the **American Express** bureaux de change in terminals 1 (01.48.16.13.26), 2A, 2B, 2C and 2D (01.48.16.48.40) and 2E (01.48.16. 63.81) at Roissy, and at Orly Sud (01.49.75.77.37); all open 6.30am-11pm daily. **Travelex** *(see p376)* has bureaux de change at the following train stations:

Gare Montparnasse
01.42.79.03.88. **Open** 8am-6.30pm daily.
Gare du Nord *01.42.80.11.50.* **Open** 6.30am-10pm daily.

Credit cards

Major international credit cards are widely used in France; Visa (more commonly known in France as *Carte Bleue*) is the most readily accepted. French-issued credit cards have a security microchip (*puce*) in each card. The card is slotted into a reader, and the holder keys in a PIN to authorise the transaction. Non-French cards work, but generate a credit slip to sign. In case of credit card loss or theft, call one of the following 24hr services which have English-speaking staff:

American Express
01.47.77.70.00.
Diners Club *01.49.06.17.50.*
MasterCard *01.45.16.65.65.*
Visa *08.92.70.57.05.*

Foreign affairs

American Express *11 rue Scribe, 9th (01.47.77.70.00/www. americanexpress.com). Mᵒ Opéra.* **Open** 9am-6.30pm Mon-Sat. Travel agency, bureau de change, *poste restante* (you can leave messages for other card holders), card replacement, travellers' cheque refund service, international money transfers and a cash machine for AmEx cardholders.
Barclays *6 rond-point des Champs-Elysées, 8th (08.10.09. 09.09/www.barclays.fr). Mᵒ Franklin D. Roosevelt.* **Open** 9.15am-4.30pm Mon-Fri. Barclays' international Expat Service handles direct debits, international transfer of funds, etc.

DIRECTORY

Citibank *15 rue Paul Cézanne, 8th (01.70.75.50.50/www.citibank. fr). M° St-Philippe-du-Roule.* **Open** 10am-5.30pm Mon-Fri. Bank clients get good rates for international money transfers, preferential exchange rates and no commission on travellers' cheques. **Travelex** *52 av des Champs-Elysées, 8th (01.42.89.80.33/ www.travelex.com/fr). M° Franklin D. Roosevelt.* **Open** 9am-10.30pm daily. Issues travellers' cheques and insurance; deals with bank transfers.

Western Union Money Transfer *www.westernunion. com.* Many post offices in town (*see below*) provide Western Union services. Transfers from abroad should arrive within 15 minutes; charges paid by the sender.

Tax

French VAT (*taxe sur la valeur ajoutée* or TVA) is arranged in three bands: 2.1 per cent for items of medication and newspapers; 5.5 per cent for food, books, CDs and DVDs; and 19.6 per cent for all other types of goods and services.

NATURAL HAZARDS

Paris has no natural hazards as such, though in recent years the town hall has produced evacuation plans to cover flooding. The deadly heatwave of 2003 led to *anti-canicule* measures for 2004, though these were ridiculed in the press. *See also p367* **Walking**.

OPENING HOURS

Standard opening hours for shops are 9/10am-7/8pm Mon-Sat. Some shops close on Monday. Shops and businesses often close at lunch, usually 12.30-2pm; many shops close in August. While Paris doesn't have the 24hr consumer culture beloved of some capitals, some branches of Monoprix stay open until 10pm. Also most areas have a local grocer that stays open into the night and will often open on Sundays and public holidays too.

24hr florist Elyfleur *82 av de Wagram, 17th (01.47.66.87.19). M° Wagram.* **Credit** MC, V. **24hr garage** Shell *6 bd Raspail, 7th (01.45.48.43.12). M° Rue du Bac.* This round-the-clock garage has an extensive array of supermarket

standards from the Casino chain. No alcohol sold 10pm-6am. **24hr newsagents** include: *33 av des Champs-Elysées, 8th, M° Franklin D. Roosevelt. 2 bd Montmartre, 9th, M° Grands Boulevards.* **Late-night** *tabacs* **Le Brazza** *86 bd du Montparnasse, 14th (01.43.35.42.65). M° Montparnasse-Bienvenüe.* **Open** 6am-2am daily. **La Favorite** *3 bd St-Michel, 5th (01.43.54.08.02). M° St-Michel.* **Open** 7am-2am daily.

POLICE

The French equivalent of 999 or 911 is **17** (**112** from a mobile), but don't expect a speedy response. That said, the Préfecture de Police has no fewer than 94 outposts in the city. If you're assaulted or robbed, report the incident as soon as possible. You'll need to make a statement (*procès verbal*) at the *point d'accueil* closest to the site of the crime. To find the nearest, call the Préfecture Centrale (08.91.01.22.22) or go to www. prefecture-police-paris.interieur. gouv.fr. Stolen goods are unlikely to be recovered, but you'll need a police statement for insurance.

POSTAL SERVICES

Post offices (*bureaux de poste*) are open 8am-7pm Mon-Fri; 8am-noon Sat, apart from the 24-hour one listed below. Details of all branches are included in the phone book: under 'Administration des PTT' in the *Pages Jaunes*; under 'Poste' in the *Pages Blanches*. Most post offices contain automatic machines (in French and English) that weigh your letter, print out a stamp and give change, thus saving you from wasting time in an enormous queue. You can also usually buy stamps and sometimes envelopes at a tobacconist (*tabac*). For more information refer to www.laposte.fr.

Main Post Office *52 rue du Louvre, 75001 Paris, 1st (01.40.28.20.00). M° Les Halles or Louvre Rivoli.* **Open** 24hrs daily for poste restante, telephones, stamps, faxes, photocopying and a modest amount of banking operations. This is the best place to arrange to have your mail sent to if you haven't got a fixed address in Paris. Mail should be addressed to you in block capitals, followed by Poste Restante, then the post office's address. There will be a charge of €0.50 for each letter received.

RECYCLING & RUBBISH

The city has a recently established system of colour-coded domestic recycling bins. A yellow-lidded bin can take paper, cardboard cartons, tins and small electrical items; a white-lidded bin takes glass. All other rubbish goes in the green-lidded bins, except for used batteries (shops that sell batteries should accept them), medication (take it back to a pharmacy), toxic products (call 08.20.00.75.75 to have them picked up) or car batteries (take them to an official tip or return to garages exhibiting the 'Relais Verts Auto' sign). Green, hive-shaped bottle banks can be found on many street corners. More information is available at www. environnement.paris.fr.

RELIGION

Churches and religious centres are listed in the *Pages Jaunes* under 'Eglises' and 'Cultes'. Paris has several English-speaking churches. The *International Herald Tribune*'s Saturday edition lists Sunday church services in English.

American Cathedral *23 av George V, 8th (01.53.23.84.00/ www.americancathedral.org). M° George V.*
American Church in Paris *65 quai d'Orsay, 7th (01.40.62. 05.00/www.acparis.org). M° Invalides.*
Emmanuel International Church of Paris *56 rue des Bons Raisins, Rueil-Malmaison (01.47.51.29.63/http://perso.orange. fr/ebcparis/). RER Reuil-Malmaison, then bus 244.*
Kehilat Gesher *10 rue de Pologne, 78100 St-Germain-en-Laye (01.39.21.97.19/www. kehilatgesher.org). RER St-Germain-en-Laye.* The Liberal English-speaking Jewish community has services in Paris and the western suburbs.
La Mosquée de Paris *2 pl du Puits de l'Ermite, 5th (01.45.35. 97.33/www.mosquee-de-paris.org). M° Place Monge.*
St George's Anglican Church *7 rue Auguste-Vacquerie, 16th (01.47.20.22.51/ www.stgeorgespans.com). M° Charles de Gaulle Etoile.*
St Joseph's Roman Catholic Church *50 av Hoche, 8th (01.42.27.28.56/ www.stjoeparis.org). M° Charles de Gaulle Etoile.*

St Michael's Church of England *5 rue d'Aguesseau, 8th (01.47.42.70.88/www.saint michaelsparis.org). M° Madeleine.*

RENTING A FLAT

Apartments are generally cheapest in northern, eastern and south-eastern Paris. You can expect to pay approximately €20 per square metre per month (which works out as, for example, €700 per month for a modest 35sq m apartment). Studios and one bedroom flats fetch the highest prices proportionally; the provision of lifts and cellars will also boost the rent.

Flat-hunting Given the scarcity of housing in Paris, it's a landlord's world; you'll need to search actively, or even frenetically, in order to find an apartment. The internet is a decent place to start: www.explorimmo.fr lists rental ads from *Le Figaro* and specialist real estate magazines; you can place a classified ad or check lettings on www.avendrealouer.fr. Thursday morning's *De Particulier à Particulier* (www.pap.fr) is a must for those who want to rent directly from the owner, but be warned – most flats go within hours. Fortnightly *Se Loger* (www .seloger.com) is also worth getting, though most of its ads are placed by agencies.

Landlords keen to let to foreigners advertise in the *International Herald Tribune* and English-language *FUSAC* (www.fusac.fr); rents tend to be higher than in the French press. There are also assorted free ad brochures that can be picked up from agencies. Private landlords often set a visiting time; prepare to meet hordes of other flat-seekers and have your documents and cheque book to hand.

There's also the option of flat-sharing – one that's been growing in popularity in recent years. To look for housemates, pick up a copy of *FUSAC* or browse the 3,000-odd weekly announcements found at www.colocation.fr, which also organises monthly soirée Le Jeudi de la Colocation, a chance to meet your potential future flatmates in the flesh.

Rental laws The minimum lease (*bail de location*) on an unfurnished flat is three years (though the tenant can give notice and leave before this period is up); furnished flats are generally let on one-year leases. During this period the landlord can only raise the rent by the official construction inflation index. At the end of the lease, the rent can be adjusted, but tenants can object before a rent board. Tenants can be evicted for non-payment, or if the landlord wishes to sell the property or use it as his own residence. It is illegal to throw people out in winter.

Landlords will probably insist you present a dossier with pay slips (*fiches de paie/bulletins de salaire*) showing income equivalent to three to four times the monthly rent, and for foreigners in particular, provide a financial guarantor (someone who will sign a document promising to pay the rent if you abscond). When taking out a lease, payments usually include the first month's rent, a deposit (*caution*) of the equivalent of two months' rent, and an agency fee, if applicable.

It's customary to have an inspection of the premises (*état des lieux*) at the start and end of the rental, the cost of which (around €150) is shared by landlord and tenant. Landlords may try to rent their flats *non-declaré* – without a written lease – and get rent in cash. This can make it hard for tenants to establish their rights – which is one reason why landlords do it.

Centre d'information et de défense des locataires
9 rue Severo, 14th (01.45.41.47.76). M° Pernety. **Open** *by appointment* 10am-12.30pm, 2.30-3.30pm Mon-Thur. Helps sort out problems with landlords, rent hikes, etc.

SAFETY & SECURITY

Beware of pickpockets, especially around crowded tourist hotspots. *See also p365* **Métro & RER** *and p376* **Police**.

SHIPPING SERVICES

Hedley's Humpers *6 bd de la Libération, 93284 St-Denis (01.48.13.01.02/www.hedleys humpers.com). M° Carrefour Pleyel.* **Open** 9am-1pm, 2-6pm Mon-Fri. Closed 2wks Aug. Specialist in transport of furniture and antiques.
In UK: 3 St Leonards Road, London NW10 6SX (020 8965 8733).
In USA: 21-41 45th Road, Long Island City, New York NY 11101 (1-718 433 4005).

SMOKING

Although smoking seems to be an essential part of French life (and death), the French state and public health groups have recently waged war against the cigarette on several fronts. Smoking is now banned in all enclosed public spaces, including bars, cafés, clubs, restaurants, hotel foyers and shops, as well as on public transport. Many bars, cafés and clubs offer smoking gardens or terraces. There are also increasingly strident anti-smoking campaigns. Health warnings on cigarette packets are unignorable, and prices have soared.

For information about stopping smoking, contact the Tabac Info Service (08.25.30.93.10/www.tabac-info.net). If you're a dedicated smoker, you'll soon learn that most *tabacs* close at 8pm (for a few that don't, *see p376* **Opening hours**). Some bars sell cigarettes behind the counter, generally only to customers who have a drink.

STUDY
Language

Most large multinational language schools, such as **Berlitz** (08.25.04.34.30/ www.berlitz.com), have at least one branch in Paris. **Konversando** (01.47.70.21.64/www.konversando. fr) specialises in international exchanges and talk.
Alliance Française *101 bd Raspail, 6th (01.42.84.90.00/ www.alliancefr.org). M° St-Placide.* The Alliance Française is a non-profit French-language school. Beginner and specialist courses start every month.
Ecole Eiffel *3 rue Crocé-Spinelli, 14th (01.43.20.37.41/www.ecole-eiffel.fr). M° Pernety.* Intensive classes, business French and phonetics.
Institut Catholique de Paris *12 rue Cassette, 6th (01.44.39.52.68/www.icp.fr/ilcf). M° St-Sulpice.* Courses in French culture and language. You must hold a *baccalauréat*-level qualification and be 18 or over (but you don't have to be Catholic).
Institut Parisien *29 rue de Lisbonne, 8th (01.40.56.09.53). M° Monceau.* Dynamic private school offering courses in language, French civilisation and business French.

La Sorbonne – Cours de Langue et Civilisation
47 rue des Ecoles, 5th (01.44.10.77.00/www.ccfs-sorbonne.fr). M° Cluny-La Sorbonne/RER Luxembourg. Classes for foreigners ride on the name of this eminent institution. Teaching is grammar-based.

University of London Institute in Paris
9-11 rue Constantine, 7th (01.44.11.73.83/www.ulip.lon.ac.uk). M° Invalides. Linked to the University of London, this 4,000-student institute offers English courses for Parisians, and French courses at university level.

Specialised

Many of the prestigious Ecoles Nationales Supérieures (including film schools La FEMIS and ENS Louis Lumière) offer summer courses in addition to their full-time degree courses – ask for *formation continue*.

Adult education courses
www.paris.fr or your local mairie. A huge range of inexpensive adult education classes is run by the city of Paris, including French as a foreign language, computer skills and applied arts.

American University of Paris
31 av Bosquet, 7th (01.40.62.07.20/www.aup.edu). M° Ecole-Militaire/RER Pont de l'Alma. International college awarding four-year American liberal arts degrees (BA/BSc).

Cordon Bleu
8 rue Léon-Delhomme, 15th (01.53.68.22.50/ www.cordonbleu.edu). M° Vaugirard. Courses range from three-hour sessions on classical and regional cuisine to a nine-month diploma for those starting a culinary career. Bon appetit!

Ecole du Louvre
Palais du Louvre, porte Jaugard, place du Carrousel, 1st (01.55.35.18.00/ www.ecoledulouvre.fr). M° Palais Royal Musée du Louvre. Art history and archaeology courses. Foreign students not wanting to take a degree can attend lectures.

INSEAD
bd de Constance, 77305 Fontainebleau (01.60.72.40.00/ www.insead.edu). Highly regarded international business school offering a ten-month MBA course in English as well as PhDs in a range of business subjects.

Parsons School of Design
14 rue Letellier, 15th (01.45.77.39.66/www.parsons-paris.com). M° La Motte-Picquet-Grenelle. Subsidiary of the New York art college offering BFA programmes in fine art, photography, fashion, marketing and interior design.

Ritz-Escoffier Ecole de Gastronomie Française
38 rue Cambon, 1st (01.43.16.30.50/www.ritz paris.com). M° Madeleine. Everything from afternoon demonstrations in the Ritz kitchens to diplomas. Courses are in French with English translation. *See also p286* **Little Chefs**.

Student life

Student & youth discounts
To claim a *tarif étudiant* (around €1.50 off cinema seats, up to 50 per cent off museums and standby theatre tickets), you must have a French student card or International Student Identity Card (ISIC), available from **CROUS** (*see above*), student travel agents and the **Cité Universitaire** (*see above*). ISIC cards are valid in France only if you are under 26. Under-26s can get up to 50 per cent off rail travel on some trains with the SNCF's Carte 12/25 and the same reduction on the RATP network with the Imagine R card.

Long-term visas & housing benefit
UK and other students from the EU may stay in France for as long as their passport is valid. To also work legally during their course in Paris, they can find out more information about their rights at www.droitsdes jeunes.gouv.fr.
Foreign students from outside the EU wishing to study in Paris for longer than three months must apply for a long-term visa through the French embassy in their particular country.

Student accommodation

The simplest budget lodgings for medium-to-long stays can be found at the **Cité Universitaire** or *foyers* (student hostels). There are some 37 halls of residence set in landscaped gardens, with sports facilities and a theatre (*see below*). Another option is a *chambre contre travail* – free board in exchange for childcare, housework or English lessons; for this, look out for ads at language schools

and the American Church. For cheap hotels and youth hostels, *see pp154-182*. As students often cannot provide proof of income, a *porte-garant* (guarantor) who will guarantee the payment of rent and bills is required.

Cité Universitaire
17 bd Jourdan, 14th (01.44.16.64.00/ www.ciup.fr). RER Cité Universitaire. **Open** *Offices* 8am-6pm Mon-Fri.
Foreign students enrolled on a university course, or interns who are also studying, can apply for a place at this campus of halls of residence (but be forewarned: only about ten per cent of the students who apply are actually successful). Rooms can be booked for a week, a month or for an entire academic year. Rents are approximately €300-€400 per month for a single room and €200-€300 per person for a double. UK citizens must apply to the Collège Franco-Britannique, and Americans to the Fondation des Etats-Unis.

CROUS (Centre Régional des Oeuvres Universitaires et Scolaires)
39 av Georges-Bernanos, 5th (01.40.51.36.00/ 08.92.25.75.75/www.crous-paris.fr). Service du Logement: (01.40.51.55.55). RER Port-Royal. **Open** 9am-5pm Mon-Fri.
Manages all University of Paris student residences, posts ads for rooms and has a list of hostels. Requests for rooms must be made by 1 April for the next academic year. CROUS also runs cheap canteens (listed on website) and is the clearing house for all *bourses* (grants) issued to foreign students. Call the Service des Bourses on 01.40.51.55.55.

UCRIF (Union des Centres de Rencontres Internationales de France)
27 rue de Turbigo, 2nd (01.40.26.57.64/www.ucrif.asso.fr). M° Etienne Marcel. **Open** 9am-6pm Mon-Fri.
UCRIF operates cheap, short-stay hostels from three help centres: 5th (01.43.29.34.80); 14th (01.43.13.17.00); 20th (01.40.31.45.45).

Working as a student

Foreign students can legally work up to 20 hours per week. Non-EU members studying in Paris must apply for an *autorisation provisoire de travail* from the DDTEFT. The job service at CROUS (01.40.51.37.52-57) finds part-time jobs for students.

DDTEFT (Direction Départementale du Travail, d'Emploi et de la Formation Professionelle) *109 rue Montmartre, 2nd (08.21.34.73.47/01.44.84.41.00/www.travail.gouv.fr). M° Bourse.*

Useful organisations

CIDJ (Centre d'Information et de Documentation Jeunesse) *101 quai Branly, 15th (08.25.09.06.30/01.44.49.12.00/www.cidj.com). M° Bir-Hakeim/RER Champ de Mars.* **Open** 10am-6pm Mon-Wed, Fri; 1-6pm Thur; 9.30am-1pm Sat.
The library gives students advice on courses and careers; the youth bureau of ANPE (Agence Nationale pour l'Emploi/www.anpe.fr) can assist with job applications.
Maison des Initiatives Etudiantes (MIE) *50 rue des Tournelles, 3rd (01.49.96.65.30/www.paris.fr).* **Open** 10am-10pm Mon-Fri; 2-9pm Sat.
Provides student associations with logistical assistance and Paris-based resources like meeting rooms, grants and computers. Radio Campus Paris, a radio station for students, has been broadcasting since September 2004.
Socrates-Erasmus Programme Britain: *UK Socrates-Erasmus Council, British Council, 10 Spring Gardens, London, SW1A 2BN (020 7389 4910/www.erasmus.ac.uk).* France: *Agence Socrates-Leonardo Da Vinci, 25 quai des Chartrons, 33080 Bordeaux Cedex (05.56.00.94.00/www.socrates-leonardo.fr).* The international Socrates-Erasmus scheme lets EU students with reasonable written and spoken French spend a year of their degree in the French university system. Applications must be made via the Erasmus co-ordinator at your home university. Non-EU students should find out from their university whether it has an agreement with the French university system.

American students can find out more from the following organisations:

MICEFA *26 rue du Fbg-St-Jacques, 14th (01.40.51.76.96/www.micefa.org).*

Relais d'accueil (Foreign students helpdesk) *Cité Universitaire, 17 bd Jourdan, 14th. RER Cité Universitaire. CROUS de Paris, 39 av Georges-Bernanos, 5th (01.40.51.36.00). RER Port-Royal.* **Open** *Sept-Nov* 8.30am-4pm Mon-Fri (Cité); 9am-4.30pm Mon-Fri (CROUS). Advice on housing, banking, visas, social security and university registration is available (by appointment) to foreign students at the addresses above.

TELEPHONES

Mobile phones

A subscription (*abonnement*) will normally get you a free phone if you sign up for at least one year. Two hours' calling time a month costs about €35 per month. International calls are normally charged extra – a lot extra. The three companies that rule the cell phone market in France are:

Bouyges Télécom *08.10.63.01.00/www.bouyguestelecom.fr.*
France Télécom/Orange *08.25.00.57.00/www.orange.fr.*
SFR *10.23/www.sfr.fr.*

Dialling & codes

All French phone numbers have ten digits. Paris and Ile-de-France numbers begin with 01; the rest of France is divided into four zones (02-05). Mobile phone numbers start with 06. 08 indicates a special rate (*see p380*); numbers beginning with 08 can only be reached from inside France. If you are calling France from abroad, leave off the 0 at the start of the ten-digit number. The country code is 33. To call abroad from France dial 00, then the country code, then the number. Since 1998 other phone companies have been allowed to enter the market, but France Télécom still has the monopoly on basic service. It has a useful website with information on rates and contracts: www.agence.francetelecom.com.

France Télécom English-Speaking Customer Service *(08.00.36.47.75/from abroad +33 1.55.78.60.56).* **Open** 9am-5.30pm Mon-Fri. Freephone information line in English on phone services, bills, payment, internet.

Public phones

Most public phones in Paris, almost all of which are maintained

by France Télécom, use *télécartes* (phonecards). Sold at post offices, *tabacs*, airports and train and métro stations, they cost €7.50 for 50 units and €15 for 120 units. For cheap international calls, you can also buy a *télécarte à puce* (card with a microchip) or a *télécarte pré-payée*, which features a numerical code you dial before making a call; these can be used on domestic phones too. Travelex's International Telephone Card can be used in more than 80 countries (available from **Travelex** agencies, *see p376*). Cafés have coin phones, while post offices usually have card phones. In a phone box, the display screen will read 'Décrochez'. Pick up the phone. When 'Introduisez votre carte' appears, put your card into the slot; the screen should read 'Patientez SVP'. 'Numérotez' is your signal to dial. 'Crédit épuisé' means you have no more units left. Hang up ('Raccrochez') – and don't forget your card. Some public phones take credit cards. If you're using a credit card, insert the card, enter your PIN number and 'Patientez SVP' will appear.

Operator services

Operator assistance, French directory enquiries (*renseignements*) 12.
To make a reverse-charge call within France, ask to make a call *en PCV*.
Airparif *01.44.59.47.64/www.airparif.asso.fr.* Information about pollution levels and air quality in Paris and Ile-de-France: invaluable for asthmatics.
International directory enquiries 32.12, then country code. €3 per call.
International news (France Inter recorded message, in French), *08.92.68.10.33* (€0.34 per min).
Telegram *all languages, international 08.00.33.44.11; within France 36.55.*
Telephone engineer 10.13.
Time 36.99.
Traffic news 08.26.02.20.22.
Weather *08.99.70.12.34* (€1.39 then €0.34 per min) for enquiries on weather in France and abroad, in French or English; you can also dial 08.92.68.02.75 (€0.34 per min) for a recorded weather announcement for Paris and region.

Telephone directories

Telephone books can be found in all post offices and most

cafés. The *Pages Blanches* (White Pages) list people and businesses alphabetically; the *Pages Jaunes* (Yellow Pages) list businesses and services by category order. Online versions can be found at www.pagesjaunes.fr.

Telephone charges

All local calls in Paris and Ile-de-France (to numbers beginning with 01) cost €0.11 for three minutes, standard rate and €0.04/min thereafter. This only applies to calls to other landlines. Calls beyond a 100km radius (*province*) are charged at €0.11 for the first 39 seconds, then €0.24 per minute.

International destinations are divided into 16 zones. Reduced-rate periods for calls within France and Europe are 7pm-8am during the week and all day Saturday and Sunday. Reduced-rate periods for the US and Canada are 7pm to 1pm Monday to Friday and all day Saturday and Sunday.

Cheap providers

Getting wise to the market demand, smaller telephone providers are becoming increasingly popular, as rates from giant France Télécom are not exactly bargain-basement. The following can offer alternative rates for calls – although you will still need to rent your telephone line from France Télécom to use them:

AT&T Direct (local access) *08.00.99.00.11.*
Free *www.free.fr.*
With the Freebox (Free's modem for ADSL connection), €29.99 per month gets you ten hours of free calls to landlines (additional calls cost €0.01 per minute), €0.19 per minute to mobiles and €0.03 per minute for most international calls.
IC Télécom *08.05.13.26.26/ www.ictelecom.fr.*
Neuf Télécom *08.92.79.00.19/ www.neuf.fr.*
Onetel *08.92.13.50.50/ www.onetel.fr.*
Télé 2 *www.tele2.fr.*

Special-rate numbers

0800 Numéro Vert
Freephone.
0810 Numéro Azur
€0.11 under three minutes, then €0.04/min.

0820 Numéro Indigo I
€0.118/min.
0825 Numéro Indigo II
€0.15/min.
0836.64/0890.64/0890.70
€0.112/min.
0890.71 €0.15/min.
0891.67/0891.70
€0.225/min.
0836/0892 €0.337/min.
This is for the likes of ticket agencies, cinema and transport information.
10.14 France Télécom information; free (except from mobile phones).

Minitel

France Télécom's Minitel, which was launched in the 1980s, is an enduring dinosaur: a videotext service available to any telephone subscriber. The internet has made it virtually redundant. However, if you come across one of these beige plastic boxes, type in 3611 for Minitel directory in English, wait for the beep, press 'Connexion', type MGS, then hit 'Envoi'. Then type 'Minitel en anglais' for the English service.

TIME & SEASONS

France is one hour ahead of Greenwich Mean Time (GMT). France uses the 24hr system (for example, 18h means 6pm).

TIPPING

A service charge of ten to 15 per cent is legally included in your bill at all restaurants, cafés and bars. However, it is polite to either round up the final amount for drinks, or to leave a cash tip of €1-€2 or more for a meal, depending on the restaurant and, of course, the quality of the service.

TOILETS

The city's automatic street toilets are not really as terrifying as they look. You put your coin in the slot, and open sesame. Each loo is completely washed down and disinfected after use, so don't try to avoid paying by sneaking in as someone is leaving: you'll get covered in bleach. Once inside, you have 15 minutes.

If a space age-style lavatory experience doesn't appeal, you can nip into the toilets of a café; although theoretically reserved for customers' use, a polite request

should win sympathy with the waiter – and you may find you have to put a €0.20 coin into a slot in the door-handle mechanism, customer or not. Fast-food chain toilets often have a code on their toilet doors that is made known to paying customers only.

TOURIST INFORMATION

Espace du Tourisme d'Ile de France
Carrousel du Louvre, 99 rue de Rivoli, 1st (08.26.16.66.66/ www.paris-ile-de-france.com). M° *Palais Royal Musée du Louvre or Pyramides.* **Open** 8.30am-7pm Mon-Fri.
This is the information showcase for Paris and the Ile-de-France.
Maison de la France
20 av de l'Opéra, 1st (01.42. 96.70.00/www.franceguide.com). M° *Opéra or Pyramides.* **Open** 10am-6pm Mon-Fri; 10am-5pm Sat.
The Maison de la France is the state organisation for tourism in France: information galore.
Office de Tourisme et des Congrès de Paris
Carrousel du Louvre, 99 rue de Rivoli, 1st (08.92.68.30.00 recorded information in English & French/www.parisinfo.com). M° *Palais Royal Musée du Louvre or Pyramides.* **Open** 9am-7pm daily.
Information on Paris and the suburbs, shop, bureau de change, hotel reservations, phonecards, museum cards, travel passes and tickets. Multilingual staff.
Other locations: *Gare de Lyon* 20 bd Diderot, 12th. M° Gare de Lyon. **Open** 8am-6pm Mon-Sat. *Gare du Nord* 18 rue de Dunkerque, 10th. M° Gare du Nord. **Open** 8am-6pm daily. *Montmartre* 21 pl du Tertre, 18th. M° Abbesses. **Open** 10am-7pm daily. *Opéra* 11 rue Scribe, 9th. M° Opéra. **Open** 9am-6.30pm Mon-Sat. *Pyramides* 25 rue des Pyramides, 1st, M° Pyramides. **Open** 9am-7pm daily. *Tour Eiffel* Champ de Mars, 7th. M° Bir-Hakeim. **Open** late Mar-Oct 11am-6.40pm daily.

VISAS

EU nationals don't need a visa to enter France, nor do US, Canadian, Australian, New Zealand or South African citizens for tays of up to three months. Nationals of other countries should enquire at the nearest French embassy or consulate before leaving home. If they are travelling to France from one of the countries in the Schengen agreement (most of the EU, but not Britain or Ireland), the visa from that country should be sufficient.

EU citizens may stay in France for as long as their passport is valid. For non-EU citizens who wish to stay for longer than three months, they must apply to the French embassy or consulate in their own country for a long-term visa. For more information, contact these two offices:

CIRA (Centre Interministeriel de Renseignements Administratifs)
0821.08.09.10 (0.12€/min)/ www.service-public.fr. **Open** 8am-7pm Mon-Fri; 8am-noon Sat. CIRA gives advice on most French administrative procedures via its premium-rate phone line.

Préfecture de Police de Paris Service Etrangers
7-9 bd du Palais, 4th (01.53.73.53.73/www.prefecture-police-paris.interieur. gouv.fr). Mº Cité. **Open** 9am-4pm Mon-Fri. This office can provide information on residency and work permits for foreigners.

WEIGHTS & MEASURES

France uses only the metric system; remember that all speed limits are in kilometres per hour. One kilometre is equivalent to 0.62 miles (1 mile = 1.6km). Petrol, like other liquids, is measured in litres (one UK gallon = 4.54 litres; 1 US gallon = 3.79 litres).

WHAT TO TAKE

Binoculars for studying high-altitude details of monuments, a pocket knife with corkscrew (for improvised picnics) and – vital – comfortable shoes.

WHEN TO GO

In July and August there are often deals on hotels and a good range of free events (such as Paris-Plage), but many family-run restaurants and shops close as the locals go off *en vacances.* Avoid October, with its fashion weeks and trade shows.

WOMEN

Though Paris is not especially threatening for women, the precautions you would take in any major city apply: be careful at night in areas like Pigalle, the rue St-Denis, Stalingrad, La Chapelle, Château Rouge, Gare de l'Est, Gare du Nord, the Bois de Boulogne and Bois de Vincennes. If you receive unwanted attention, a politely scathing *N'insistez pas!* (Don't push it!) makes your feelings clear. If things get too heavy, go into the nearest shop or café.

CIDFF (Centre d'Information et des Droits des Femmes et de la Famille) *7 rue du Jura, 13th (01.42.17.12.00). Mº Gobelins.* **Open** visits by appointment only. The CIDFF offers health, legal and professional advice for women.
Violence Conjugale: Femmes Info Service *01.40.33.80.60.* **Open** 7.30am-11.30pm Mon-Sat. Hotline for battered women, directing them towards medical aid or shelters.
Viols Femmes Informations *08.00.05.95.95.* **Open** 10am-7pm Mon-Fri. Freephone service. Help and advice available, in French, to rape victims.

WORKING IN PARIS

Most EU nationals can work legally in France, including UK and Irish citizens, but should apply for a French social security number. Some job ads can be found at branches of the French national employment bureau, the **Agence Nationale pour l'Emploi** (ANPE), or on its website (www.anpe.fr). Branches are also the place to sign up as a *demandeur d'emploi,* to be placed

on file as ready for work and possibly to qualify for French unemployment benefits.

Britons can only claim French unemployment benefit if they were already signed on before leaving the UK. Non-EU nationals need a work permit and cannot use the ANPE network without having valid work papers.

Club des Quatre Vents
1 rue Gozlin, 6th (01.43.29.60.20). Mº St-Germain-des-Prés. **Open** 9am-6pm Mon-Fri. Provides three-month work permits for US citizens at university or recent graduates.
Espace Emploi International (OMI et ANPE)
48 bd de la Bastille, 12th (01.53.02.25.50/www.emploi-international.org). Mº Bastille. **Open** 9am-5pm Mon, Wed-Fri; 9am-noon Tue. Provides work permits of up to 18 months for Americans aged 18-35.
Language Network
01.44.64.82.23. Helps native English speakers who wish to find work teaching.

Job ads

Help wanted advertisements sometimes appear in the *International Herald Tribune,* in *FUSAC* and on noticeboards at language schools and the **American Church** (*see p376*).

Bilingual secretarial/PA work is available for those with good written French. If you're looking for professional work, have your CV translated, including French equivalents for any qualifications. Most job applications require a photo and a handwritten letter.

THE LOCAL CLIMATE

Average temperatures and monthly rainfall in Paris.

	High (ºC/ºF)	Low (ºC/ºF)	Rainfall (mm/in)
Jan	7 / 45	2 / 36	53 / 2.1
Feb	10 / 50	2 / 36	43 / 1.7
Mar	13 / 55	4 / 39	49 / 1.9
Apr	17 / 63	6 / 43	53 / 2.1
May	20 / 68	9 / 48	65 / 2.6
June	23 / 73	12 / 54	54 / 2.1
July	25 / 77	15 / 59	62 / 2.4
Aug	26 / 79	16 / 61	42 / 1.7
Sept	23 / 73	12 / 54	54 / 2.1
Oct	20 / 68	8 / 46	60 / 2.4
Nov	14 / 57	4 / 39	51 / 2.0
Dec	7 / 45	3 / 37	59 / 2.3

Vocabulary

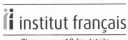
In French, the second person singular (you) has two forms. Phrases here are given in the more polite *vous* form. The *tu* form is used with family, friends, children and pets; you should be careful not to use it with people you do not know sufficiently well. Courtesies such as *monsieur, madame* and *mademoiselle* are generally used more than their English equivalents.

GENERAL

● **good morning/afternoon, hello** bonjour; **good evening** bonsoir; **goodbye** au revoir
● **OK** d'accord; **yes** oui; **no** non; **how are you?** comment allez vous?/vous allez bien?; **how's it going?** comment ça va?/ça va? (familiar)
● **sir/Mr** monsieur (M.); **madam/Mrs** madame (Mme); **miss** mademoiselle (Mlle)
● **please** s'il vous plaît; **thank you** merci; **sorry** pardon; **excuse me** excusez-moi; **I am going to pay** je vais payer
● **do you speak English?** parlez-vous anglais?; **I don't speak French** je ne parle pas français; **I don't understand** je ne comprends pas; **speak more slowly, please** parlez plus lentement, s'il vous plaît
● **it is** c'est; **it isn't** ce n'est pas; **good** bon/bonne; **bad** mauvais/mauvaise; **small** petit/petite; **big** grand/grande; **beautiful** beau/belle; **well** bien; **badly** mal; **a bit** un peu; **a lot** beaucoup; **very** très
● **with** avec; **without** sans; **and** et; **or** ou; **because** parce que
● **who?** qui?; **when?** quand?; **what?** quoi?; **which?** quel?; **where?** où?; **why?** pourquoi?; **how?** comment?; **at what time/when?** à quelle heure?
● **forbidden** interdit/défendu; **out of order** hors service (HS)/en panne; **daily** tous les jours (tlj)

ON THE PHONE

● **hello** allô; **who's calling?** c'est de la part de qui?/qui est à l'appareil?; **this is… speaking** c'est… à l'appareil; **I'd like to speak to…** j'aurais voulu parler à…; **hold the line** ne quittez pas; **please call back later** rappelez plus tard s'il vous plaît; **you must have the wrong number** vous avez dû composer un mauvais numéro

GETTING AROUND

● **where is the (nearest) métro?** où est le métro (le plus proche)?; **when is the next train for… ?** c'est quand le prochain train pour… ?; **ticket** un billet; **station** la gare; **platform** le quai; **entrance** entrée; **exit** sortie
● **left** gauche; **right** droite; **straight on** tout droit; **far** loin; **near** pas loin/près d'ici; **street map** un plan; **road map** une carte

SIGHTSEEING

● **museum** un musée; **church** une église; **exhibition** une exposition; **ticket** *(for museum)* un billet; *(for theatre, concert)* une place
● **open** ouvert; **closed** fermé; **free** gratuit; **reduced price** un tarif réduit

ACCOMMODATION

● **do you have a room (for this evening/for two people)?** avez-vous une chambre (pour ce soir/pour deux personnes)?; **full** complet; **room** une chambre; **bed** un lit; **double bed** un grand lit; **(a room with) twin beds** (une chambre à) deux lits; **with bath(room)/shower** avec (salle de) bain/douche; **breakfast** le petit déjeuner; **included** compris

AT THE CAFE OR RESTAURANT

● **I'd like to book a table (for three/at 8pm)** je voudrais réserver une table (pour trois personnes/à vingt heures); **lunch** le déjeuner; **dinner** le dîner

● **coffee** (espresso) un café; **tea** un thé; **wine** le vin; **beer** une bière; **mineral water** eau minérale; **tap water** eau du robinet/une carafe d'eau; **the bill, please** l'addition, s'il vous plaît

SHOPPING

● **cheap** pas cher; **expensive** cher; **how much?/how many?** combien?; **have you got change?** avez-vous de la monnaie?; **I'll take it** je le prends
● **I would like…** je voudrais…; **may I try this on?** est-ce que je pourrais essayer cet article?; **do you have a smaller/larger size?** auriez-vous la taille en-dessous/au dessus?; **I'm a size 38** je fais du 38

STAYING ALIVE

● **be cool** restez calme; **I don't want any trouble** je ne veux pas d'ennuis; **I only do safe sex** je ne pratique que le safe sex

NUMBERS

● **0** zéro; **1** un, une; **2** deux; **3** trois; **4** quatre; **5** cinq; **6** six; **7** sept; **8** huit; **9** neuf; **10** dix; **11** onze; **12** douze; **13** treize; **14** quatorze; **15** quinze; **16** seize; **17** dix-sept; **18** dix-huit; **19** dix-neuf; **20** vingt; **21** vingt-et-un; **22** vingt-deux; **30** trente; **40** quarante; **50** cinquante; **60** soixante; **70** soixante-dix; **80** quatre-vingts; **90** quatre-vingt-dix; **100** cent; **1000** mille; **10,000** dix mille; **1,000,000** un million

DAYS, MONTHS & SEASONS

● **Monday** lundi; **Tuesday** mardi; **Wednesday** mercredi; **Thursday** jeudi; **Friday** vendredi; **Saturday** samedi; **Sunday** dimanche
● **January** janvier; **February** février; **March** mars; **April** avril; **May** mai; **June** juin; **July** juillet; **August** août; **September** septembre; **October** octobre; **November** novembre; **December** décembre
● **spring** le printemps; **summer** l'été; **autumn** l'automne; **winter** l'hiver

DIRECTORY

Further Reference

BOOKS

Non-fiction

Petrus Abaelardus & Heloise *Letters* The full details of Paris' first great romantic drama.
Robert Baldick *The Siege of Paris* A gripping account of the Paris Commune of 1871.
Antony Beevor & Artemis Cooper *Paris after the Liberation* Rationing, freedom, Existentialism.
NT Binh *Paris au cinéma* Gorgeous coffee-table round-up of Paris sights on film.
Henri Cartier-Bresson *A propos de Paris* Classic black and white shots by a giant among snappers.
Vincent Cronin *Napoleon* A fine biography of the emperor.
Alastair Horne *The Fall of Paris* Detailed chronicle of the Siege and Commune 1870-71.
Andrew Hussey *Paris: A Secret History* Entertaining description of Paris through the ages.
J-K Huysmans *Croquis Parisiens* The world that Toulouse-Lautrec painted.
Ian Littlewood *Paris: Architecture, History, Art* Paris' history and its treasures.
Nancy Mitford *The Sun King; Madame de Pompadour* Great gossipy accounts of the courts of the *ancien régime*.
Noel Riley Fitch *Literary Cafés of Paris* Who drank what, where.
Virginia Rounding *Les Grandes Horizontales* Entertaining lives of four 19th-century courtesans.
Renzo Salvadori *Architect's Guide to Paris* Plans, maps and a guide to Paris's growth.
Simon Schama *Citizens* Epic, readable account of the Revolution.
William Shirer *The Collapse of the Third Republic* Forensic account of the reasons for France's humiliating 1940 defeat.

Fiction & poetry

Louis Aragon *Le Paysan de Paris* A great Surrealist view of the city.
Honoré de Balzac *Illusions perdues; La Peau de chagrin; Le Père Goriot; Splendeurs et misères des courtisanes* Many of the best-known novels in the 'Comédie Humaine' cycle are set in Paris.

Charles Baudelaire *Le Spleen de Paris* Prose poems, Paris settings.
Simone de Beauvoir *Les Mandarins* Paris intellectuals and idealists just after the Liberation.
Louis-Ferdinand Céline *Mort à crédit* Vivid, splenetic account of an impoverished Paris childhood.
Victor Hugo *Notre Dame de Paris* Romantic vision of medieval Paris. Quasimodo! Esmeralda! The bells!
Guy de Maupassant *Bel-Ami* Ruthless ambition in 19th-century Paris.
Gérard de Nerval *Les Nuits d'octobre* Late-night Les Halles and environs, mid 19th-century.
Georges Perec *La Vie, mode d'emploi* Cheek-by-jowl life in a Haussmannian apartment building.
Raymond Queneau *Zazie dans le Métro* Paris in the 1950s: bright and very *nouvelle vague*.
Nicolas Restif de la Bretonne *Les Nuits de Paris* The sexual underworld of Louis XV's Paris.
Jean-Paul Sartre *Les Carnets de la drôle de guerre* Existential angst as the German army takes over Paris.
Georges Simenon Maigret books.
Emile Zola *L'Assommoir; Nana; Le Ventre de Paris* Accounts of the underside of the Second Empire from the master Realist.

The ex-pat angle

Ernest Hemingway *A Moveable Feast* Chronicle of 1920s Paris.
Henry Miller *Tropic of Cancer* Love, lust, lice and low life: bawdy, yes. Funny, too.
George Orwell *Down and Out in Paris and London* Work in a Paris restaurant (it's hardly changed), hunger in a Paris hovel, suffering in a Paris hospital.

FILM

Luc Besson *Subway* Christophe Lambert goes underground. Hokum, but easy on the eye.
Marcel Carné *Hôtel du Nord* Arletty's finest hour.
Jean-Luc Godard *A Bout de Souffle* Belmondo, Seberg, Godard, the Champs-Elysées, the attitude, the famous ending. Essential.
Jean-Luc Godard *Une Femme est une femme* Belmondo and Karina, and Godard's first feature in colour

– the Grands Boulevards, the attitude, the music.
Edouard Molinaro *Un Témoin dans la ville* Lino Ventura on the run in 1950s nocturnal Paris. Superb *noir*.
Bertrand Tavernier *L.627* The drugs war in the 1990s, as seen from the cops' side. Gritty and polemic-making.
François Truffaut *Les 400 Coups* The first of the Antoine Doinel cycle.
Agnès Varda *Cléo de 5 à 7* The *nouvelle vague* heroine spends an anxious afternoon around Paris.
Claude Zidi *Les Ripoux (Le Cop)* Cops Philippe Noiret and Thierry Lhermitte scam the Goutte d'Or.

MUSIC

Air *Moon Safari* Relaxing, ambient beeps and sonics from that rara avis, a credible French pop group.
Serge Gainsbourg *Le Poinçonneur des Lilas* Classic early Gainsbourg.
Thelonious Monk *The Paris Concert* A blend of the experimental and the romantically gentle.

WEBSITES

www.culture.fr Current and forthcoming cultural events of all kinds, in Paris and other big French cities.
www.edible-paris.com Customised gastronomic itineraries in Paris by the editor of Time Out's *Eating & Drinking in Paris* guide.
www.gogoparis.com Online version of free monthly Anglo listings mag.
www.meteo.fr State weather forecasts.
www.pagesjaunes.fr The Paris yellow pages, with maps and multi-angle photos of every address in the city.
www.parissi.com Films, concerts and a strong calendar of clubbing events.
www.parisinfo.com Official site of the Office de Tourisme et des Congrès de Paris.
www.ratp.com Everything you'll need to know about using the buses, métro, RER and trams.
www.timeout.com/paris A pick of the best current events and good hotels, eateries and shops.

Index

INDEX

Advertisers' Index

Please refer to the relevant pages for contact details

Maps

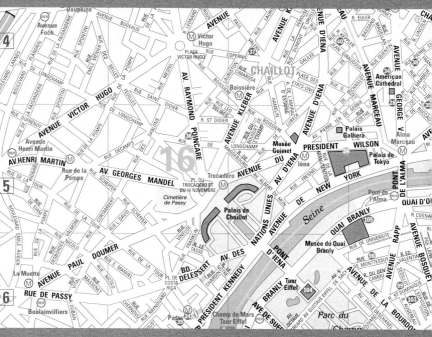

Place of interest and/or entertainment	
Hospital or college	
Railway station	
Park	
River	
Autoroute	=
Main road	
Pedestrian road	
Arrondissement boundary.	
Airport	✈
Church	✚
Métro station	Ⓜ
RER station	ⓇⒺⓇ
Area name . . . . LES HALLES	
Hotel	❶
Restaurant	❶
Cafés & Bars	❶

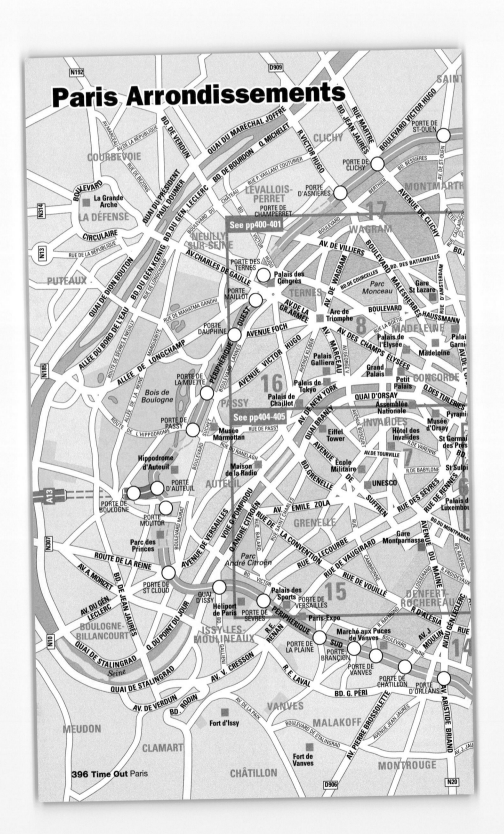

Paris Arrondissements

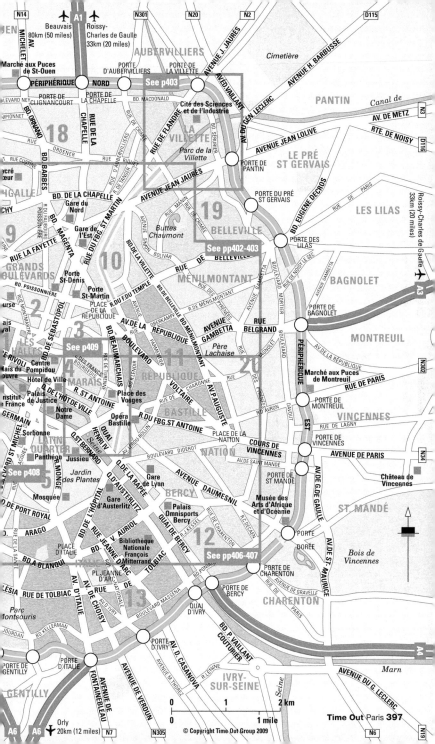

Paris by Area

PIGALLI

WESTERN PARIS

CHAILLOT

THE 7TH &
WESTERN PARIS

ST GERMAIN
DES PRES

ODEON

MONTPARNASSE

© Copyright Time Out Group 2009

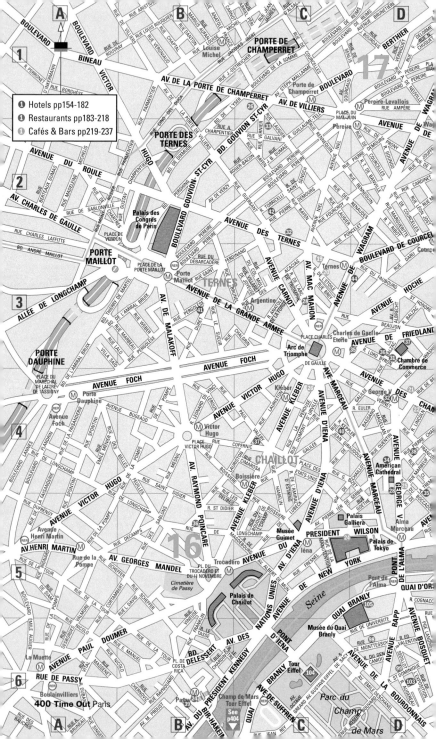

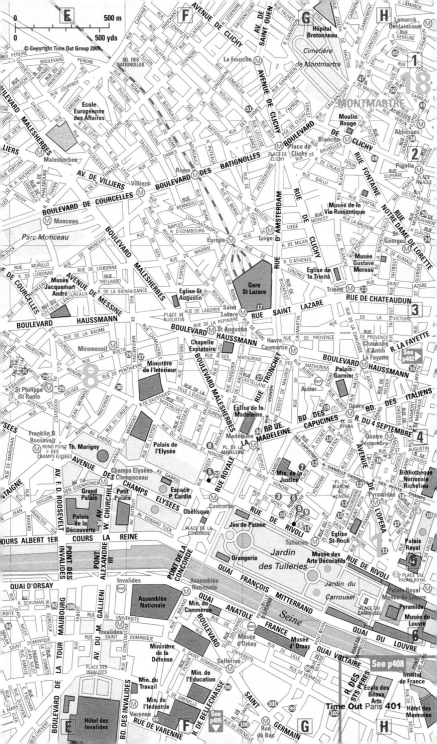

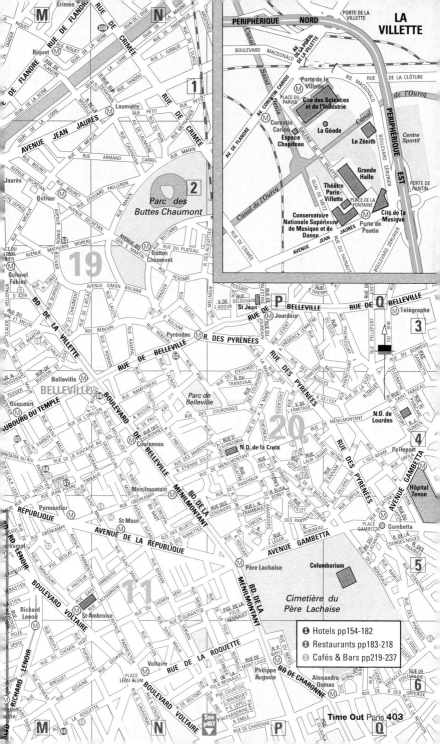

LA VILLETTE

PERIPHERIQUE NORD

PORTE DE LA VILLETTE

BOULEVARD MACDONALD

Cité des Sciences et de l'Industrie

La Géode

Espace Chapiteau

Le Zénith

Grande Halle

Théâtre Paris-Villette

Conservatoire Nationale Supérieure de Musique et de Danse

Cité de la Musique

Centre Sportif

PORTE DE PANTIN

Parc des Buttes Chaumont

BELLEVILLE

Parc de Belleville

Cimetière du Père Lachaise

Columbarium

❶ Hotels pp154-182

❶ Restaurants pp183-218

❶ Cafés & Bars pp219-237

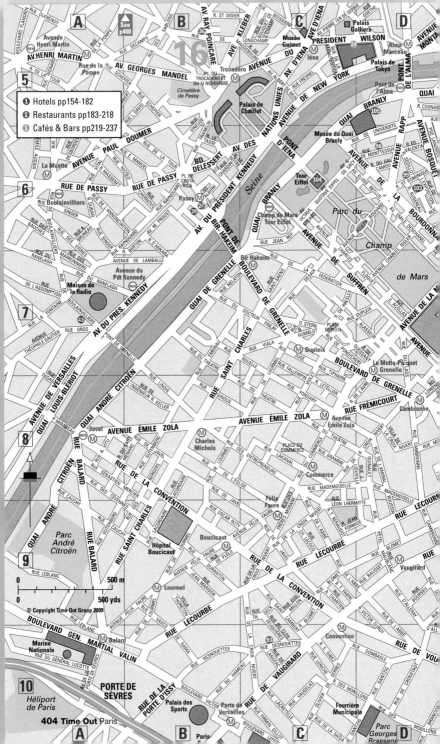

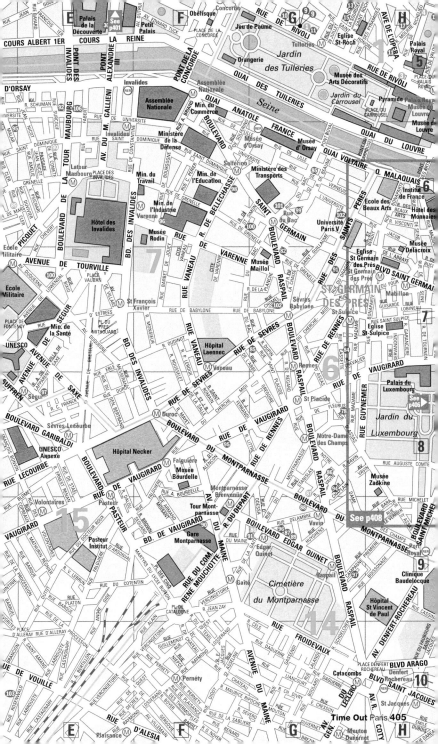

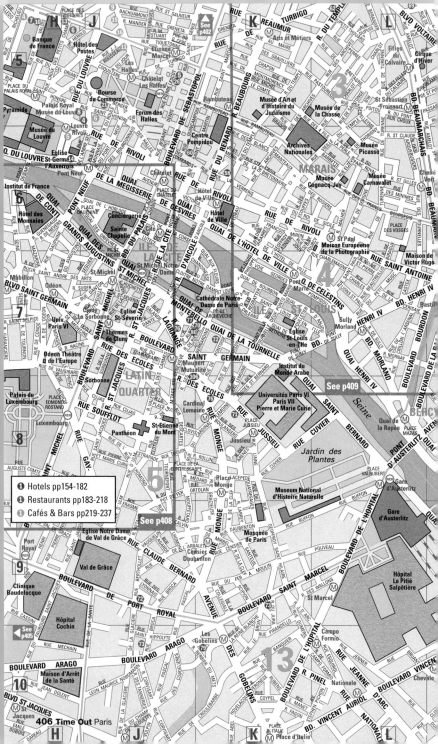

See p402

MARAIS

ÎLE DE LA CITÉ

ÎLE ST LOUIS

LATIN QUARTER

See p409

BERCY

Jardin des Plantes

❶ Hotels pp154-182
❶ Restaurants pp183-218
❶ Cafés & Bars pp219-237

See p408

See p405

13

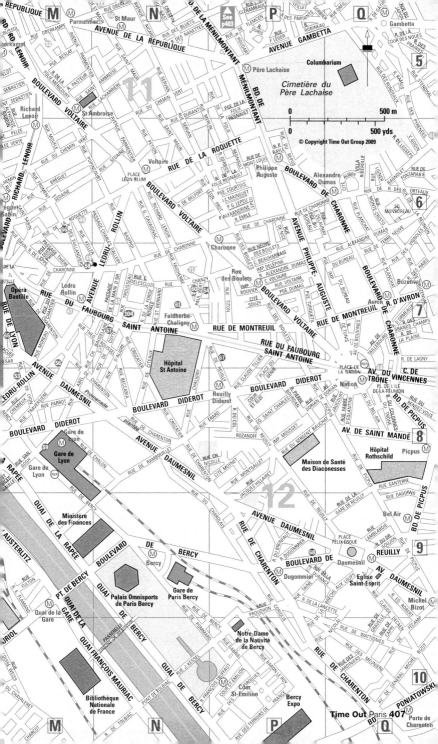

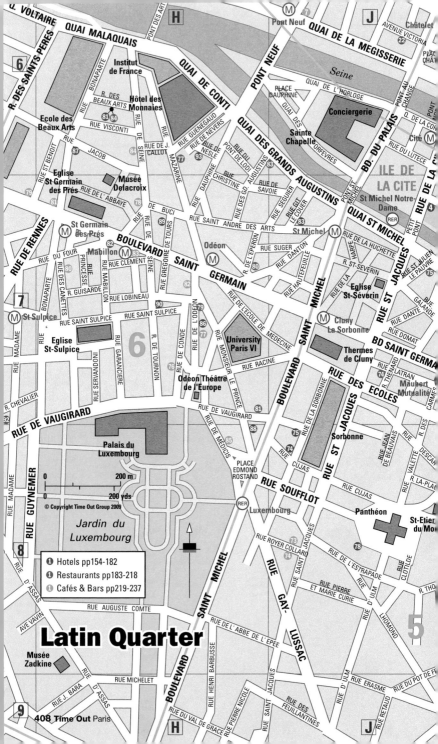

Latin Quarter

❶ Hotels pp154-182
❶ Restaurants pp183-218
❶ Cafés & Bars pp219-237

© Copyright Time Out Group 2009

0   200 m
0   200 yds

Jardin du Luxembourg

Palais du Luxembourg

Musée Zadkine

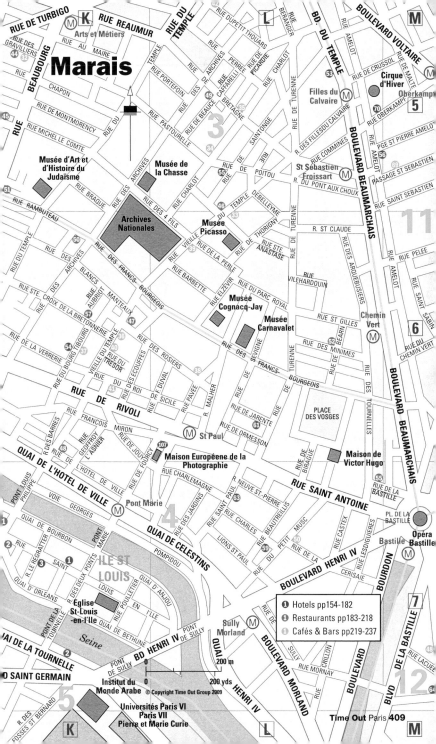

Street Index

STREET INDEX

Street Index

STREET INDEX

STREET INDEX

Paris RER

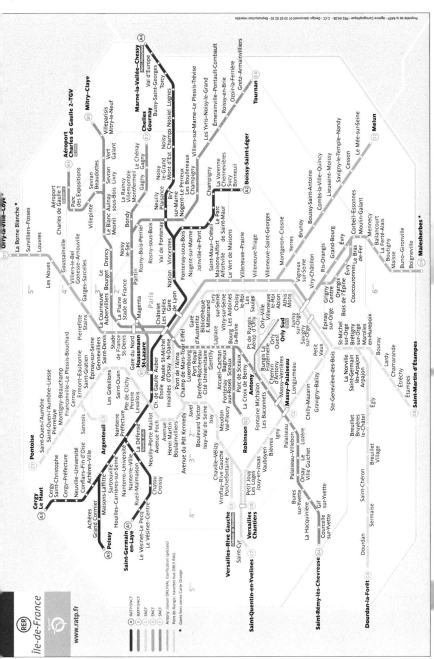

île-de-France

www.ratp.fr

Paris Métro

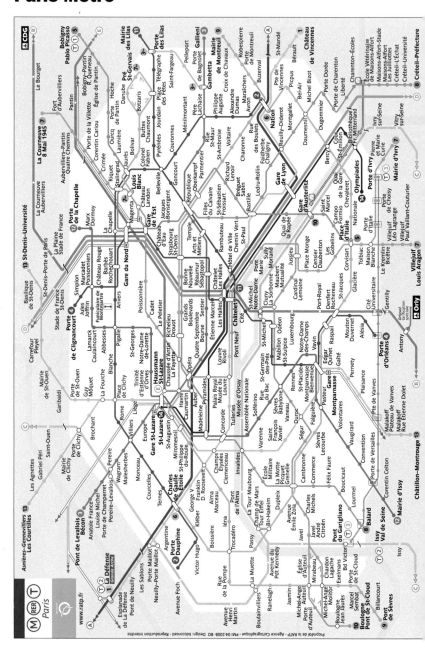

www.ratp.fr

Propriété de la RATP - Agence Cartographique - PMI CA-2008- BO Design : bdconseil - Reproduction interdite